REPRESENTATION

REPRESENTATION

SECOND EDITION

EDITED BY

STUART HALL
JESSICA EVANS AND SEAN NIXON

The Open University

$SAGE

Los Angeles | London | New Delhi
Singapore | Washington DC

Los Angeles | London | New Delhi
Singapore | Washington DC

SAGE Publications Ltd
1 Oliver's Yard
55 City Road
London EC1Y 1SP

SAGE Publications Inc.
2455 Teller Road
Thousand Oaks, California 91320

SAGE Publications India Pvt Ltd
B 1/I 1 Mohan Cooperative Industrial Area
Mathura Road
New Delhi 110 044

SAGE Publications Asia-Pacific Pte Ltd
3 Church Street
#10-04 Samsung Hub
Singapore 049483

Editor: Mila Steele
Editorial assistant: James Piper
Production editor: Imogen Roome
Copyeditor: Sarah Bury
Proofreader: Sharika Sharma
Indexer: Avril Ehrlich
Marketing manager: Michael Ainsley
Cover design: Wendy Scott
Typeset by: C&M Digitals (P) Ltd, Chennai, India
Printed in Great Britain by Ashford Colour Press Ltd.

The Open University
Walton Hall
Milton Keynes
MK7 6AA
United Kingdom
www.open.ac.uk

Library of Congress Control Number: 2012950346

British Library Cataloguing in Publication data

A catalogue record for this book is available from
the British Library

MIX
Paper from
responsible sources
FSC® C011748

ISBN 978-1-84920-547-4
ISBN 978-1-84920-563-4 (pbk)

CONTENTS

Contents

Contents

Contents

ACKNOWLEDGEMENTS

Grateful acknowledgement is made to the following sources for permission to reproduce material in this book:

CHAPTER 1

Text

Reading A: *Looking at the Overlooked: Four Essays on Still Life Painting* first published in English by Reaktion Books 1990 © Reaktion Books 1990

Readings B and C: Barthes, R. (1972) *Mythologies*, Random House (UK) Ltd. Reprinted by permission of Hill and Wang, a division of Farrar, Straus & Giraux, Inc.: Excerpts from 'The world of wrestling' and 'Myth today' from *Mythologies* by Roland Barthes, translated by Annette Lavers. Translation copyright © 1972 by Jonathan Cape Ltd

Reading D: Barthes, R. (1977) *Image-Music-Text*, HarperCollins Publishers Ltd

Reading E: Laclau, E. And Mouffe, C. (1990) *New Reflections on the Revolution of Time*, Verso

Reading F: *From The Female Malady* by Elaine Showalter, Copyright © 1985 by Elaine Showalter. Reprinted by permission of Pantheon Books, a division of Random House, Inc. Also by permission of Little Brown and Company (UK)

Table 1.1:   courtesy of the library, Scott Polar Research Institute, Cambridge.

Figures

Figure 1.1:   Copyright Tate Gallery, London

Figure 1.2:   © Damien Hirst and Science Ltd. All rights reserved, DACS 2013/Photographed by Prudence Cuming Associates Ltd.

Figure 1.3:   San Diego Museum of Art (Gift of Anne R. and Amy Putnam)

Figure 1.4:   Colorsport

Figure 1.5:   Courtesy of Gucci/Mario Testino

Figure 1.6:   Panzani Frères

Figure 1.7:   Jaguar Cars Ltd/J. Walter Thompson, London

Figure 1.8:   Photo: Jean Loup Charmet

Figure 1.9:   Madrid, Prado/Photo: Giraudon

Figure 1.10: Photo: P. Regnard, from *Iconographie photographique de la Salpêtrière*, 1878

CHAPTER 2

Text

Reading A: Nichols, Bill (2010) 'The Qualities of Voice' in *Introduction to Documentary*, pp 42–9, by permission of Indiana University Press

Reading B: Corner, J. (2002) 'Performing the real: documentary diversions', *Television and New Media*, vol. 3, no. 3, pp 262–7, SAGE Publications Ltd.

Reading C: Bousé, Derek (2000) 'Historia Fabulosus' in *Wildlife Films*, pp 91–106, by permission of University of Pennsylvania Press

Figures

Figure 2.1:   © Ramin Talaie/Corbis

CHAPTER 3

Text

Reading B: Lawrence, E.A. (1991) 'His very silence speaks: the horse who survived Custer's Last Stand', in Browne, R.B. and Browne, P. (eds) *Digging into Popular Culture, Theories and Methodologies in Archaeology, Anthropology and Other Fields*, Copyright © 1991 by Bowling Green State University Popular Press

Reading C: O'Hanlon, M. (1993) *Paradise Portraying the New Guinea Highlands*, British Museum Press

Reading D: Clifford, J. (1995) 'Paradise', *Visual Anthropology Review*, 11 (1), American Anthropology Association

Reading E: Coombes, A. (1994) *Reinventing Africa*, Yale University Press. Copyright © 1994 by Annie E.S. Coombes

Reading F: Picton, John, 'To see or Not To See! That is the Question', *African Arts*, Winter 2010, Vol. 43(4), pp. 1, 4–6 (MIT), by permission of John Picton, Emeritus Professor of African Art, SOAS (School of Oriental and African Studies), University of London

Figures

CHAPTER 4

Text

Reading A: McClintock, A. (1995) *Imperial Leather*, Routledge

Reading B: Dyer, R. (1986) *Heavenly Bodies*, Macmillan Press Ltd, also by permission of St Martin's Press, Inc.

Reading C: Gilman, S. (1985) *Difference and Pathology*, used by permission of the publisher, Cornell University Press

Reading D: Mercer, K. (1994) *Welcome to the Jungle*, Routledge

Figures

Figure 4.9:	Courtesy of the Print Collection, Lewis Walpole Library, Yale University
Figures 4.10, 4.11, 4.12, 4.14:	Copyright pictures: Felix de Rooy, Negrophilia Foundation Amsterdam. Photographer: Pierre Verhoeff
Figure 4.13:	Mary Evans Picture Library
Figures 4.15, 4.16, 4.17, 4.18:	Ronald Grant Archive
Figure 4.19:	Culver Pictures
Figure 4.20:	Source unknown
Figure 4.21:	Courtesy of George Eastman House
Figure 4.22:	Edwin Long (1829–91) *The Marriage Market, Babylon*. Royal Holloway and Bedford New College, Surrey. The Bridgeman Art Library, London
Figure 4.23:	Reproduced from: S. Gilman (1985) *Difference and Pathology*, Cornell University Press
Figure 4.24:	Reproduced from Cesare Lombroso and Guillaume Ferraro (1893) *La donna delinquente: la prostituta e la donna normale*, L. Roux
Figure 4.25:	George Rodger/Magnum
Figure 4.26:	Reproduced from: John Grand-Carteret (1909) *Die Erotik in der französchen Karikatur*, Vienna, C.W. Stern
Figures 4.27, 4.28:	Copyright David Bailey/Autograph
Figure 4.29:	Photo from *Looking for Langston*. Copyright Sunil Gupta, *Looking for Langston*, Director: Isaac Julien/Sankofa
Figure 4.30:	Jimmy Freeman, 1981. Copyright © 1981 The Estate of Robert Mapplethorpe
Figure 4.31:	Copyright 1987 (The Estate of) Rotimi Fani-Kayode/Courtesy: Autograph
Figure 4.32:	© Howard C. Smith/isiphotos.com/Corbis

CHAPTER 5

Text

Reading A: Neale, S. (1983) 'Masculinity as spectacle', *Screen*, 24, (6), Oxford University Press
Reading B: Nixon, S. (1996) *Hard Looks*, Routledge

Figures

Figure 5.1:	Copyright © Giorgio Armani/accessed at www.footluxe.com
Figure 5.2:	First image courtesy of Nick Kamen. Photo: Shilland and Co. Second image courtesy of Select Men. Photo: Bartle Bogle Hegarty
Figure 5.3:	Reproduced from *The Face*, August 1986/Tony Hodges and Partners Advertising Agency

CHAPTER 6

Text

Figures

Every effort has been made to trace all copyright owners, but if any have been inadvertently overlooked, the publishers will be pleased to make the necessary arrangements at the first opportunity.

INTRODUCTION

Stuart Hall

The chapters in this volume all deal, in different ways, with the question of representation. This is one of the central practices that produces culture and a key 'moment' in what has been called the 'circuit of culture' (see Du Gay et al., 1997). But what does representation have to do with 'culture'? What is the connection between them? To put it simply, culture is about 'shared meanings'. Now, language is the privileged medium in which we 'make sense' of things, in which meaning is produced and exchanged. Meanings can only be shared through our common access to language. So language is central to meaning and culture and has always been regarded as the key repository of cultural values and meanings.

But how does language construct meanings? How does it sustain the dialogue between participants which enables them to build up a culture of shared understandings and so interpret the world in roughly the same ways? Language is able to do this because it operates as a *representational system*. In language, we use signs and symbols – whether they are sounds, written words, electronically produced images, musical notes, even objects – to stand for or represent to other people our concepts, ideas and feelings. Language is one of the 'media' through which thoughts, ideas and feelings are represented in a culture. Representation through language is therefore central to the processes by which meaning is produced. This is the basic, underlying idea which underpins all six chapters in this book. Each chapter examines 'the production and circulation of meaning through language' in different ways, in relation to different examples, different areas of social practice. Together, these chapters push forward and develop our understanding of how representation actually *works*.

'Culture' is one of the most difficult concepts in the human and social sciences and there are many different ways of defining it. In more traditional definitions of the term, 'culture' is said to embody the 'best that has been thought and said' in a society. It is the sum of the great ideas, as represented in the classic works of literature, painting, music and philosophy – the 'high culture' of an age. Belonging to the same frame of reference, but more 'modern' in its associations, is the use of 'culture' to refer to the widely distributed forms of popular music, publishing, art, design and

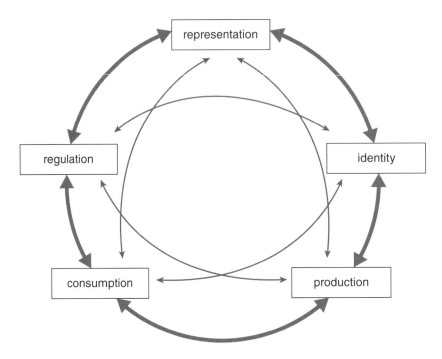

The circuit of culture

literature, or the activities of leisure-time and entertainment, which make up the everyday lives of the majority of 'ordinary people' – what is called the 'mass culture' or the 'popular culture' of an age. High culture versus popular culture was, for many years, the classic way of framing the debate about culture – the terms carrying a powerfully evaluative charge (roughly, high = good; popular = debased). In recent years, and in a more 'social science' context, the word 'culture' is used to refer to whatever is distinctive about the 'way of life' of a people, community, nation or social group. This has come to be known as the 'anthropological' definition. Alternatively, the word can be used to describe the 'shared values' of a group or of society – which is like the anthropological definition, only with a more sociological emphasis. You will find traces of all these meanings somewhere in this book. However, as its title suggests, 'culture' is usually being used in these chapters in a some-what different, more specialized way.

What has come to be called the 'cultural turn' in the social and human sciences, especially in cultural studies and the sociology of culture, has tended to emphasize the importance of *meaning* to the definition of culture. Culture, it is argued, is not so much a set of *things* – novels and paintings or TV programmes and comics – as a process, a set of *practices*. Primarily, culture is concerned with the production and the exchange of meanings – the 'giving and taking of meaning' – between the members of a society or group. To say that two people belong to the same culture is to say that they interpret the world in roughly the same ways and can express themselves, their thoughts and feelings about the world, in ways which will be understood by each other. Thus, culture depends on its participants interpreting meaningfully what is happening around them, and 'making sense' of the world, in broadly similar ways.

This focus on 'shared meanings' may sometimes make culture sound too unitary and too cognitive. In any culture, there is always a great diversity of meanings about any topic, and more than one way of interpreting or representing it. Also, culture is about feelings, attachments and emotions as well as concepts and ideas. The expression on my face 'says something' about who I am (identity) and what I am feeling (emotions) and what group I feel I belong to (attachment), which can be 'read' and understood by other people, even if I didn't intend deliberately to communicate anything as formal as 'a message', and even if the other person couldn't give a very logical account of how s/he came to understand what I was 'saying'. Above all, cultural meanings are not only 'in the head'. They organize and regulate social practices, influence our conduct and consequently have real, practical effects.

The emphasis on cultural practices is important. It is participants in a culture who give meaning to people, objects and events. Things 'in themselves' rarely, if ever, have any one, single, fixed and unchanging meaning. Even something as obvious as a stone can be a stone, a boundary marker or a piece of sculpture, depending on *what it means* – that is, within a certain context of use, within what the philosophers call different 'language games' (i.e. the language of boundaries, the language of sculpture, and so on). It is by our use of things, and what we say, think and feel about them – how we represent them – that we *give them a meaning*. In part, we give objects, people and events meaning by the frameworks of interpretation which we bring to them. In part, we give things meaning by how we use them, or integrate them into our everyday practices. It is our use of a pile of bricks and mortar which makes it a 'house'; and what we feel, think or say about it that makes a 'house' a 'home'. In part, we give things meaning by how we *represent* them – the words we use about them, the stories we tell about them, the images of them we produce, the emotions we associate with them, the ways we classify and conceptualize them, the values we place on them. Culture, we may say, is involved in all those practices which are not simply genetically programmed into us – like the jerk of the knee when tapped – but which carry meaning and value for us, which need to be *meaningfully interpreted by* others, or which *depend on meaning* for their effective operation. Culture, in this sense, permeates all of society. It is what distinguishes the 'human' element in social life from what is simply biologically driven. Its study underlines the crucial role of the *symbolic* domain at the very heart of social life.

Where is meaning produced? Our 'circuit of culture' suggests that, in fact, meanings are produced at several different sites and circulated through several different processes or practices (the cultural circuit). Meaning is what gives us a sense of our own identity, of who we are and with whom we 'belong' – so it is tied up with questions of how culture is used to mark out and maintain identity within and difference between groups (which is the main focus of **Woodward**, ed., 1997). Meaning is constantly being produced and exchanged in every personal and social interaction in which we take part. In a sense, this is the most privileged, though often the most neglected, site of culture and meaning. It is also produced in a variety of different *media*; especially, these days, in the modern mass media, the means of global communication, by complex technologies, which circulate meanings between different cultures on a scale and with a speed hitherto unknown in history. (This is the focus of **Du Gay**, ed., 1997.) Meaning is also produced whenever we express ourselves in, make use of, consume or appropriate cultural 'things'; that is, when we incorporate them in different ways into the everyday rituals and practices of daily life and in this way give them value or significance. Or when we weave narratives, stories – and fantasies – around them. (This is the focus of **Mackay**, ed., 1997.) Meanings also regulate and organize our conduct and practices – they help to set the rules, norms and conventions by which social life is ordered and governed. They are also, therefore, what those who wish to govern and regulate the conduct and ideas of others seek to structure and shape. (This is the focus of **Thompson**, ed., 1997.) In other words, the question of meaning arises in relation to *all* the different moments or practices in our 'cultural circuit' – in the construction of identity and the marking of difference, in production and consumption, as well as in the regulation of social conduct. However, in all these instances, and at all these different institutional sites, one of the privileged 'media' through which meaning is produced and circulated is *language*.

So, in this book, where we take up in depth the first element in our 'circuit of culture', we start with this question of meaning, language and representation. Members of the same culture must share sets of concepts, images and ideas which enable them to think and feel about the world, and thus to interpret the world, in roughly similar ways. They must share, broadly speaking, the same 'cultural codes'. In this sense, thinking and feeling are themselves 'systems of representation', in which our concepts, images and emotions 'stand for' or represent, in our mental life, things which are or may be 'out there' in the world. Similarly, in order to *communicate* these meanings to other people, the participants to any meaningful exchange must also be able to use the same linguistic codes – they must, in a very broad sense, 'speak the same language'. This does not mean that they must all, literally, speak German or French or Chinese. Nor does it mean that they understand perfectly what anyone who speaks the same language is saying. We mean 'language' here in a much wider sense. Our partners must speak enough of the same language to be able to 'translate' what 'you' say into what 'they' understand, and vice versa. They must also be able to read visual images in roughly similar ways. They must be familiar with broadly the same ways of producing sounds to make what they would both recognize as 'music'. They must all interpret body language and facial expressions in broadly similar ways. And they must know how to translate their feelings and ideas into these various languages. Meaning is a dialogue – always only partially understood, always an unequal exchange.

Why do we refer to all these different ways of producing and communicating meaning as 'languages' or as 'working like languages'? How do languages work? The simple answer is that languages work *through representation*. They are 'systems of representation'. Essentially, we can say that all these practices 'work like languages', *not* because they are all written or spoken (they are not), but because they all use some element to stand for or represent what we want to say, to express or communicate a thought, concept, idea or feeling. Spoken language uses sounds, written language uses words, musical language uses notes on a scale, the 'language of the body' uses physical gesture, the fashion industry uses items of clothing, the language of facial expression uses ways of arranging one's features, television uses digitally or electronically produced dots on a screen, traffic lights use red, green and amber – to 'say something'. These elements – sounds, words, notes, gestures, expressions, clothes – are part of our natural and material world; but their importance for language is not what they *are* but what they *do*, their function. They construct meaning and transmit it. They signify. They don't have any clear meaning *in themselves*. Rather, they are the vehicles or media which *carry meaning* because they operate as *symbols*, which stand for or represent (i.e. symbolize) the meanings we wish to communicate. To use another metaphor, they function as *signs*. Signs stand for or *represent* our concepts, ideas and feelings in such a way as to enable others to 'read', decode or interpret their meaning in roughly the same way that we do.

Language, in this sense, is a signifying practice. Any representational system which functions in this way can be thought of as working, broadly speaking, according to the principles of representation through language. Thus, photography is a representational system, using images on light-sensitive paper to communicate photographic meaning about a particular person, event or scene. Exhibition or display in a museum or gallery can also be thought of as 'like a language', since it uses objects on display to produce certain meanings about the subject matter of the exhibition. Music is 'like a language' in so far as it uses musical notes to communicate feelings and ideas, even if these are very abstract, and do not refer in any obvious way to the 'real world'. (Music has been called 'the most noise conveying the least information'.) But turning up at football matches with banners and slogans, with faces and bodies painted in certain colours or inscribed with certain symbols, can also be thought of as 'like a language' – in so far as it is a symbolic practice which gives meaning or expression to the idea of belonging to a national culture, or identification with one's local community. It is part of the language of national identity, a discourse of national belongingness. Representation, here, is closely tied up with both identity and knowledge. Indeed, it is difficult to know what 'being English', or indeed French, German, South African or Japanese, *means* outside all the ways in which our ideas and images of national identity or national cultures have been represented. Without these 'signifying' systems, we could not take on such identities (or indeed reject them) and consequently could not build up or sustain that common 'life-world' which we call a culture.

So it is through culture and language *in this sense* that the production and circulation of meaning takes place. The conventional view used to be that 'things' exist in the material and natural world; that their material or natural characteristics are what determines or constitutes them; and that they have a perfectly clear meaning, *outside* how they are represented. Representation, in this view, is a process of secondary importance, which enters into the field only after things have been fully formed and their meaning constituted. But since the 'cultural turn' in the human and social sciences, meaning is thought to be *produced* – constructed – rather than simply 'found'. Consequently, in what has come to be called a 'social constructionist approach', representation is conceived as entering into the very constitution of things; and thus culture is conceptualized as a primary or 'constitutive' process, as important as the economic or material 'base' in shaping social subjects and historical events – not merely a reflection of the world after the event.

'Language' therefore provides one general model of how culture and representation work, especially in what has come to be known as the *semiotic* approach – *semiotics* being the study or 'science of signs' and their general role as vehicles of meaning in culture. In more recent years, this preoccupation with meaning has taken a different turn, being more concerned not with the detail of how 'language' works, but with the broader role of *discourse* in culture. Discourses are ways of referring to or constructing knowledge about a particular topic of practice: a cluster (or *formation*) of ideas, images and practices, which provide ways of talking about, forms of knowledge and conduct associated with, a particular topic, social activity or institutional site in society. These *discursive formations*, as they are known, define what is and is not appropriate in our formulation of, and our practices in relation to, a particular subject or site of social activity; what knowledge is considered useful, relevant and 'true' in that context; and what sorts of persons or 'subjects' embody its characteristics. 'Discursive' has become the general term used to refer to any approach in which meaning, representation and culture are considered to be constitutive.

There are some similarities, but also some major differences, between the *semiotic* and the *discursive* approaches, which are developed in the chapters that follow. One important difference is that the *semiotic* approach is concerned with the *how* of representation, with how language produces meaning – what has been called its 'poetics'; whereas the *discursive* approach is more concerned with the *effects and consequences* of representation – its 'polities'. It examines not only how language and representation produce meaning, but how the knowledge which a particular discourse produces connects with power, regulates conduct, makes up or constructs identities and subjectivities, and defines the way certain things are represented, thought about, practised and studied. The emphasis in the *discursive* approach is always on the historical specificity of a particular form or 'regime' of representation: not on 'language' as a general concern, but on specific *languages* or meanings, and how they are deployed at particular times, in particular places. It points us towards greater historical specificity – the way representational practices operate in concrete historical situations, in actual practice.

The general use of language and discourse as models of how culture, meaning and representation work, and the 'discursive turn' in the social and cultural sciences which has followed, is one of the most significant shifts of direction in our knowledge of society which has occurred in recent years. The discussion around these two versions of 'constructionism' – the semiotic and discursive approaches – is threaded through and developed in the six chapters that follow. The 'discursive turn' has not, of course, gone uncontested. You will find questions raised about this approach and critiques offered, as well as different variants of the position explored, by the different authors in this volume. Elsewhere in this series (in **Mackay**, ed., 1997, for example) alternative approaches are explored, which adopt a more 'creative', expressive or performative approach to meaning, questioning, for example, whether it makes sense to think of music as 'working like a language'. However, by and large, with some variations, the chapters in this book adopt a broadly 'constructionist' approach to representation and meaning.

In Chapter 1 on 'The work of representation', Stuart Hall fills out in greater depth the theoretical argument about meaning, language and representation briefly summarized here. What do we mean by saying that 'meaning is produced through language'? Using a range of examples – which it is important to work through for yourself – the chapter takes us through the argument of exactly what this entails. Do things – objects, people, events in the world – carry their own, one, true meaning, fixed like number plates on their backs, which it is the task of language to reflect accurately? Or are meanings constantly shifting as we move from one culture to another, one language to another, one historical context, one community, group or subculture to another? Is it through our systems of representation, rather than 'in the world', that meaning is fixed? It is clear that representation is neither as simple nor transparent a practice as it first appears and that, in order to unpack the idea, we need to do some work on a range of examples, and bring to bear certain concepts and theories, in order to explore and clarify its complexities.

The question – 'Does visual language reflect a truth about the world which is already there or does it produce meanings about the world through representing it?' – forms the basis of Chapter 2, 'Recording reality: documentary film and television' by Frances Bonner. Bonner explores the historical development of documentary filmmaking and its emergence as an increasingly important television genre. Documentary film, like earlier forms of documentary photography, was often claimed by its producers to offer a privileged, truthful account of the world. 'Recording reality' on to film brought the realities of the social or natural environment to audiences. For Bonner, such a conception of documentary film (and TV) fails to grasp the complex ways in which 'reality' is represented within very specific representational practices by documentary filmmakers. Bonner details the development of distinctive ways of representing reality within documentary film and TV, showing how these changed overtime. What is evident from her chapter is the great diversity of approaches to the making of documentary and the range of sub-genres within this field of cultural production. Of particular note are her comments on two of the most popular genres of documentary on television – the natural history documentary and the more recent genre of the docusoap. Bonner asks why these forms of television are so popular and how they are able to produce not just compelling representations of the natural and social world respectively, but what might be at stake in how they represent and record reality. What are the consequences of these ways of representing the world and how do they shape how we, as viewers, subsequently act within it?

Chapter 3, 'The poetics and the politics of exhibiting other cultures' by Henrietta Lidchi, takes up some of the same questions about representation, but in relation to a different subject matter and a different set of signifying practices. Whereas Chapter 2 deals with the practices of film and television – the production of meaning through images – Chapter 3 deals with exhibition – the production of meaning through the display of objects and artefacts from 'other cultures' within the context of the modern museum. Here, the elements exhibited are often 'things' rather than 'words or images' and the signifying practice involved is that of arrangement and display within a physical space, rather than layout on the page of an illustrated magazine or journal. Nevertheless, as this chapter argues, exhibition too is a 'system' or 'practice of representation' – and therefore works 'like a language'. Every choice – to show this rather than that, to show this in relation to that, to say this about that – is a choice about how to represent 'other cultures'; and each choice has consequences both for *what* meanings are produced and for *how* meaning is produced. Henrietta Lidchi shows how those meanings are inevitably implicated in relations of *power* – especially between those who are doing the exhibiting and those who are being exhibited.

The introduction of questions of power into the argument about representation is one of the ways in which the book consistently seeks to probe, expand and complexify our understanding of the process of representation. In Chapter 4, 'The spectacle of the "Other"', Stuart Hall takes up this theme of 'representing difference' from Chapter 3, but now in the context of more contemporary popular cultural forms (news photos, advertising, film and popular illustration). It looks at how 'racial', ethnic and sexual difference has been 'represented' in a range of visual examples across a number of historical archives. Central questions about how 'difference' is represented as 'Other', and the essentializing of 'difference' through stereotyping, are addressed. However, as the argument develops, the chapter takes up the wider question of how signifying practices actually structure the way we 'look'; how different modes of 'looking' are being inscribed by these representational practices; and how violence, fantasy and 'desire' also play into representational practices, making them much more complex and their meanings more ambivalent. The chapter ends by considering some counter-strategies in the 'politics of representation' – the way meaning can be struggled over, and whether a particular regime of representation can be challenged, contested and transformed.

The question of how the spectator or the consumer is drawn into and implicated by certain practices of representation returns in Sean Nixon's Chapter 5, 'Exhibiting masculinity', on the construction of new gendered identities in contemporary advertising, magazines and consumer industries addressed especially towards men. Nixon asks whether representational practices in the media in recent years have been constructing new 'masculine identities'. Are the different languages of consumer culture, retailing and display developing new 'subject-positions', with which young men are increasingly invited to identify? And, if so, what do these images tell us about how the meanings of masculinity are shifting in late-modern visual culture? 'Masculinity', Nixon argues, far from being fixed and given biologically, accretes a variety of different meanings – different ways of 'being' or 'becoming masculine' – in different historical contexts. To address these questions, Nixon not only expands and applies some of the theoretical perspectives from earlier chapters, but adds new ones, including a psychoanalytically informed cultural analysis and film theory.

In the final Chapter 6, 'Genre and gender: the case of soap opera', Christine Gledhill and Vicky Ball take us into the rich, narrative world of popular culture and its genres, with an examination of how representation is working in television soap opera. These are enormously popular sources of fictional narrative in modern life, circulating meanings throughout popular culture – and increasingly worldwide – which have been traditionally defined as 'feminine' in their appeal, reference and mode of operation. Gledhill and Ball unpack the way this gendered identification of a TV genre has been constructed. They consider how and why such a 'space of representation' should have opened up within popular culture; how genre and gender elements interact in the narrative structures and representational forms; and how these popular forms have been ideologically shaped and inflected. They examine how the meanings circulated in soap operas – so frequently dismissed as stereotypical and manufactured – nevertheless enter into the discursive arena where the meaning of masculine and feminine identifications are being contested and transformed.

The book uses a wide range of examples from different cultural media and discourses, mainly concentrating on *visual* language. These examples are a key part of your work on the book – they are not simply 'illustrative'. Representation can only be properly analysed in relation to the actual concrete forms which meaning assumes, in the concrete practices of signifying, 'reading' and interpretation; and these require analysis of the actual signs, symbols, figures, images, narratives, words and sounds – the material forms – in which symbolic meaning is circulated. The examples provide an opportunity to practise these skills of analysis and to apply them to many other similar instances which surround us in daily cultural life.

It is worth emphasizing that there is no single or 'correct' answer to the question, 'What does this image mean?' or 'What is this ad saying?' Since there is no law which can guarantee that things will have one, true meaning, or that meanings won't change over time, work in this area is bound to be interpretative – a debate between not who is 'right' and who is 'wrong', but between equally plausible, though sometimes competing and contested, meanings and interpretations. The best way to 'settle' such contested readings is to look again at the concrete example and to try to justify one's 'reading' in detail in relation to the actual practices and forms of signification used, and what meanings they seem to you to be producing.

One soon discovers that meaning is not straightforward or transparent, and does not survive intact the passage through representation. It is a slippery customer, changing and shifting with context, usage and historical circumstances. It is therefore never finally fixed. It is always putting off or 'deferring' its rendezvous with Absolute Truth. It is always being negotiated and inflected, to resonate with new situations. It is often contested, and sometimes bitterly fought over. There are always different circuits of meaning circulating in any culture at the same time, overlapping discursive formations, from which we draw to create meaning or to express what we think.

Moreover, we do not have a straightforward, rational or instrumental relationship to meanings. They mobilize powerful feelings and emotions, of both a positive and negative kind. We feel their contradictory pull, their ambivalence. They sometimes call our very identities into question. We struggle over them because they matter – and these are contests from which serious consequences can flow. They define what is 'normal', who belongs – and therefore, who is excluded. They are deeply inscribed in relations of power. Think of how profoundly our lives are shaped, depending on which meanings of male/female, black/white, rich/poor, gay/straight, young/old, citizen/alien are in play in which circumstances. Meanings are often organized into sharply opposed binaries or opposites. However, these binaries are constantly being undermined, as representations interact with one another, substituting for each other, displacing one another along an unending chain. Our material interests and our bodies can be called to account, and differently implicated, depending on how meaning is given and taken, constructed and interpreted in different situations. But equally engaged are our fears and fantasies, the sentiments of desire and revulsion, of ambivalence and aggression. The more we look into this process of representation, the more complex it becomes to describe adequately or explain – which is why the various chapters enlist a variety of theories and concepts, to help us unlock its secrets.

The embodying of concepts, ideas and emotions in a symbolic form which can be transmitted and meaningfully interpreted is what we mean by 'the practices of representation'. Meaning must enter the domain of these practices, if it is to circulate effectively within a culture. And it cannot be considered to have completed its 'passage' around the cultural circuit until it has been 'decoded' or intelligibly received at another point in the chain. Language, then, is the property of neither the sender nor the receiver of meanings. It is the shared cultural 'space' in which the production of meaning through language – that is, representation – takes place. The receiver of messages and meanings is not a passive screen on which the original meaning is accurately and transparently projected. The 'taking of meaning' is as much a signifying practice as the 'putting into meaning'. Speaker and hearer or writer and reader are active participants in a process which – since they often exchange roles – is always double-sided, always interactive. Representation functions less like the model of a one-way transmitter and more like the model of a dialogue – it is, as they say, *dialogic*. What sustains this 'dialogue' is the presence of shared cultural codes, which cannot guarantee that meanings will remain stable forever – though attempting to fix meaning is exactly why *power* intervenes in *discourse*. But, even when power *is* circulating through meaning and knowledge, the codes only work if they are to some degree shared, at least to the extent that they make effective 'translation' between 'speakers' possible. We should perhaps learn to think of meaning less in terms of 'accuracy' and 'truth' and more in terms of effective exchange – a process of *translation*, which facilitates cultural communication while always recognizing the persistence of difference and power between different 'speakers' within the same cultural circuit.

REFERENCES

DU GAY, P. (ed.) (1997) *Production of Culture/Cultures of Production*, London, Sage/The Open University (Book 4 in this series).

DU GAY, P., HALL, S., JANES, L., MACKAY, H. and NEGUS, K. (1997) *Doing Cultural Studies: The Story of the Sony Walkman*, London, Sage/The Open University (Book 1 in this series).

HALL, S. (ed.) (1977) *Representation: Cultural Representations and Signifying Practices*, London, Sage/The Open University (Book 2 in this series).

MACKAY, H. (ed.) (1997) *Consumption and Everyday Life*, London, Sage/The Open University (Book 5 in this series).

THOMPSON, K. (ed.) (1997) *Media and Cultural Regulation*, London, Sage/The Open University (Book 6 in this series).

WOODWARD, K. (ed.) (1997) *Identity and Difference*, London, Sage/The Open University (Book 3 in this series).

CHAPTER ONE

THE WORK OF REPRESENTATION

Stuart Hall

1 REPRESENTATION, MEANING AND LANGUAGE

In this chapter we will be concentrating on one of the key processes in the 'cultural circuit' (see Du Gay et al., 1997, and the Introduction to this volume) – the practices of *representation*. The aim of this chapter is to introduce you to this topic, and to explain what it is about and why we give it such importance in cultural studies.

The concept of representation has come to occupy a new and important place in the study of culture. Representation connects meaning and language to culture. But what exactly do people mean by it? What does representation have to do with culture and meaning? One common-sense usage of the term is as follows: 'Representation means using language to say something meaningful about, or to represent, the world meaningfully, to other people.' You may well ask, 'Is that all?' Well, yes and no. Representation *is* an essential part of the process by which meaning is produced and exchanged between members of a culture. It *does* involve the use of language, of signs and images which stand for or represent things. But this is a far from simple or straightforward process, as you will soon discover.

How does the concept of representation connect meaning and language to culture? In order to explore this connection further, we will look at a number of different theories about how language is used to represent the world. Here we will be drawing a distinction between three different accounts or theories: the *reflective*, the *intentional* and the *constructionist* approaches to representation. Does language simply reflect a meaning which already exists out there in the world of objects, people and events (*reflective*)? Does language express only what the speaker or writer or painter wants to say, his or her personally intended meaning (*intentional*)? Or is meaning constructed in and through language (*constructionist*)? You will learn more in a moment about these three approaches.

Most of the chapter will be spent exploring the *constructionist* approach, because it is this perspective which has had the most significant impact on cultural studies in recent years. This chapter chooses to examine two major variants or models of the constructionist approach – the *semiotic* approach, greatly influenced by the Swiss linguist, Ferdinand de Saussure, and the *discursive* approach, associated with the French philosopher and historian, Michel Foucault. Later chapters in this book will take up these two theories again, among others, so you will have an opportunity to consolidate your understanding of them, and to apply them to different areas of analysis. Other chapters will introduce theoretical paradigms which apply constructionist approaches in different ways to that of semiotics and Foucault. All, however, put in question the very nature of representation. We turn to this question first.

1.1 Making meaning, representing things

What does the word **representation** really mean, in this context? What does the process of representation involve? How does representation work?

To put it briefly, representation is the production of meaning through language. The *Shorter Oxford English Dictionary* suggests two relevant meanings for the word:

1 To represent something is to describe or depict it, to call it up in the mind by description or portrayal or imagination; to place a likeness of it before us in our mind or in the senses; as, for example, in the sentence, 'This picture represents the murder of Abel by Cain.'

2 To represent also means to symbolize, stand for, to be a specimen of, or to substitute for; as in the sentence, 'In Christianity, the cross represents the suffering and crucifixion of Christ.'

The figures in the painting *stand in the place of*, and at the same time, *stand for* the story of Cain and Abel. Likewise, the cross simply consists of two wooden planks nailed together; but in the context of Christian belief and teaching, it takes on, symbolizes or comes to stand for a wider set of meanings about the crucifixion of the Son of God, and this is a concept we can put into words and pictures.

ACTIVITY 1

Here is a simple exercise about representation. Look at any familiar object in the room. You will immediately recognize what it is. But how do you *know* what the object is? What does 'recognize' mean?

Now try to make yourself conscious of what you are doing – observe what is going on as you do it. You recognize what it is because your thought processes decode your visual perception of the object in terms of a concept of it which you have in your head. This must be so because, if you look away from the object, you can still *think* about it by conjuring it up, as we say, 'in your mind's eye'. Go on – try to follow the process as it happens: there is the object ... and there is the concept in your head which tells you what it is, what your visual image of it *means*.

Now, tell me what it is. Say it aloud: 'It's a lamp' – or a table or a book or the phone or whatever. The concept of the object has passed through your mental representation of it to me *via* the word for it which you have just used. The word stands for or represents the concept, and can be used to reference or designate either a 'real' object in the world or indeed even some imaginary object, like angels dancing on the head of a pin, which no one has ever actually seen.

This is how you give meaning to things through language. This is how you 'make sense of' the world of people, objects and events, and how you are able to express a complex thought about those things to other people, or communicate about them through language in ways which other people are able to understand.

Why do we have to go through this complex process to represent our thoughts? If you put down a glass you are holding and walk out of the room, you can still *think* about the glass, even though it is no longer physically there. Actually, you can't think with a glass. You can only think with *the concept of* the glass. As the linguists are fond of saying, 'Dogs bark. But the concept of "dog" cannot bark or bite.' You can't speak with the actual glass, either. You can only speak with the *word* for glass – GLASS – which is the linguistic sign which we use in English to refer to objects out of which you drink water. This is where *representation* comes in. Representation is the production of the meaning of the concepts in our minds through language. It is the link between concepts and language which enables us to *refer to* either the 'real' world of objects, people or events, or indeed to imaginary worlds of fictional objects, people and events.

So there are *two* processes, two **systems of representation**, involved. First, there is the 'system' by which all sorts of objects, people and events are correlated with a set of concepts or *mental representations* which we carry around in our heads. Without them, we could not interpret the world meaningfully at all. In the first place, then, meaning depends on the system of concepts and images formed in our thoughts which can stand for or 'represent' the world, enabling us to refer to things both inside and outside our heads.

Before we move on to look at the second 'system of representation', we should observe that what we have just said is a very simple version of a rather complex process. It is simple enough to see how we might form concepts for things we can perceive – people or material objects, like chairs, tables and desks. But we also form concepts of rather obscure and abstract things, which we can't in any simple way see, feel or touch. Think, for example, of our concepts of war, or death, or friendship or love. And, as we have remarked, we also form concepts about things we have never seen, and possibly can't or won't ever see, and about people and places we have plainly made up. We may have a clear concept of, say, angels, mermaids, God, the Devil, or of Heaven and Hell, or of Middlemarch (the fictional provincial town in George Eliot's novel), or Elizabeth (the heroine of Jane Austen's *Pride and Prejudice*).

We have called this a '*system* of representation'. That is because it consists not of individual concepts, but of different ways of organizing, clustering, arranging and classifying concepts, and of establishing complex relations between them. For example, we use the principles of similarity and difference to establish relationships between concepts or to distinguish them from one another. Thus, I have an idea that in some respects birds are like planes in the sky, based on the fact that they are similar because they both fly – but I also have an idea that in other respects they are different, because one is part of nature while the other is man-made. This mixing and matching of relations between concepts to form complex ideas and thoughts is possible because our concepts are arranged into different classifying systems. In this example, the first is based on a distinction between flying/not flying and the second is based on the distinction between natural/man-made. There are other principles of organization like this at work in all conceptual systems: for example, classifying according to sequence – which concept follows which – or causality – what causes what – and so on. The point here is that we are talking about not just a random collection of concepts, but concepts organized, arranged and classified into complex relations with one another. That is what our conceptual system actually is like. However, this does not undermine the basic point. Meaning depends on the relationship between things in the world – people, objects and events, real or fictional – and the conceptual system, which can operate as *mental representations* of them.

Now it could be the case that the conceptual map which I carry around in my head is totally different from yours, in which case you and I would interpret or make sense of the world in totally different ways. We would be incapable of sharing our thoughts or expressing ideas about the world to each other. In fact, each of us probably does understand and interpret the world in a unique and individual way. However, we are able to communicate because we share broadly the same conceptual maps and thus make sense of or interpret the world in roughly similar ways. That is indeed what it means when we say we 'belong to the same culture'. Because we interpret the world in roughly similar ways, we are able to build up a shared culture of meanings and thus construct a social world which we inhabit together. That is why 'culture' is sometimes defined in terms of 'shared meanings or shared conceptual maps' (see **Du Gay et al.**, 1997).

However, a shared conceptual map is not enough. We must also be able to represent or exchange meanings and concepts, and we can only do that when we also have access to a shared language. Language is therefore the second system of representation involved in the overall process of constructing meaning. Our shared conceptual map must be translated into a common language, so that we can correlate our concepts and ideas with certain written words, spoken sounds or visual images. The general term we use for words, sounds or images which carry meaning is *signs*. These signs stand for or represent the concepts and the conceptual relations between them which we carry around in our heads and together they make up the meaning-systems of our culture.

Signs are organized into languages and it is the existence of common languages which enable us to translate our thoughts (concepts) into words, sounds or images, and then to use these, operating as a language, to express meanings and communicate thoughts to other people. Remember that the term 'language' is being used here in a very broad and inclusive way. The writing system or the spoken system of a particular language are both obviously 'languages'. But so are visual images, whether produced by hand, mechanically, electronically, digitally or some other means, when they are used to express meaning. And so are other things which aren't 'linguistic' in any ordinary sense: the 'language' of facial expressions or of gesture, for example, or the 'language' of fashion, of clothes, or of traffic lights. Even music is a 'language', with complex relations between different sounds and chords, though it is a very special case since it can't easily be used to reference actual things or objects in the world (a point further elaborated in **Du Gay**, ed., 1997, and **Mackay**, ed., 1997). Any sound, word, image or object which functions as a sign, and is organized with other signs into a system which is capable of carrying and expressing meaning is, from this point of view, 'a language'. It is in this sense that the model of meaning which I have been analysing here is often described as a 'linguistic' one; and that all the theories of meaning which follow this basic model are described as belonging to 'the linguistic turn' in the social sciences and cultural studies.

At the heart of the meaning process in culture, then, are two related 'systems of representation'. The first enables us to give meaning to the world by constructing a set of correspondences or a chain of equivalences between things – people, objects, events, abstract ideas, etc. – and our system of concepts, our conceptual maps. The second depends on constructing a set of correspondences between our conceptual map and a set of signs, arranged or organized into various languages which stand for or represent those concepts. The relation between 'things', concepts and signs lies at the heart of the production of meaning in language. The process which links these three elements together is what we call 'representation'.

1.2 Language and representation

Just as people who belong to the same culture must share a broadly similar conceptual map, so they must also share the same way of interpreting the signs of a language, for only in this way can meanings be effectively exchanged between people. But how do we know which concept stands for which thing? Or which word effectively represents which concept? How do I know which sounds or images will carry, through language, the meaning of my concepts and what I want to say with them to you? This may seem relatively simple in the case of visual signs, because the drawing, painting, camera or TV image of a sheep bears a resemblance to the animal with a woolly coat grazing in a field to which I want to refer. Even so, we need to remind ourselves that a drawn or painted or digital version of a sheep is not exactly like a 'real' sheep. For one thing, most images are in two dimensions whereas the 'real' sheep exists in three dimensions.

Visual signs and images, even when they bear a close resemblance to the things to which they refer, are still signs: they carry meaning and thus have to be interpreted. In order to interpret them, we must have access to the two systems of representation discussed earlier: to a conceptual map which correlates the sheep in the field with the concept of a 'sheep'; and a language system which in visual language, bears some resemblance to the real thing or 'looks like it' in some way. This argument is clearest if we think of a cartoon drawing or an abstract painting of a 'sheep', where we need a very sophisticated conceptual and shared linguistic system to be certain that we are all 'reading' the sign in the same way. Even then we may find ourselves wondering whether it really is a picture of a sheep at all. As the relationship between the sign and its referent becomes less clear-cut, the meaning begins to slip and slide away from us into uncertainty. Meaning is no longer transparently passing from one person to another ...

FIGURE 1.1   William Holman Hunt, *Our English Coasts ('Strayed Sheep')*, 1852

FIGURE 1.2
Q: When is a sheep not a sheep?
A: When it's a work of art. (Damien Hirst, *Away from the Flock*, 1994)

So, even in the case of visual language, where the relationship between the concept and the sign seems fairly straightforward, the matter is far from simple. It is even more difficult with written or spoken language, where words don't look or sound anything like the things to which they refer. In part, this is because there are different kinds of signs. Visual signs are what are called *iconic* signs. That is, they bear, in their form, a certain resemblance to the object, person or event to which they refer. A photograph of a tree reproduces some of the actual conditions of our visual perception in the visual sign. Written or spoken signs, on the other hand, are what is called *indexical*.

They bear no obvious relationship at all to the things to which they refer. The letters T, R, E, E do not look anything like trees in nature, nor does the word 'tree' in English sound like 'real' trees (if indeed they make any sound at all!). The relationship in these systems of representation between the sign, the concept and the object to which they might be used to refer is entirely *arbitrary*. By 'arbitrary' we mean that in principle any collection of letters or any sound in any order would do the trick equally well. Trees would not mind if we used the word SEERT – 'trees' written backwards – to represent the concept of them. This is clear from the fact that, in French, quite different letters and a quite different sound is used to refer to what, to all appearances, is the same thing – a 'real' tree – and, as far as we can tell, to the same concept a large plant that grows in nature. The French and English seem to be using the same concept. But the concept which in English is represented by the word TREE is represented in French by the word ARBRE.

1.3 Sharing the codes

The question, then, is: how do people who belong to the same culture, who share the same conceptual map and who speak or write the same language (English) know that the arbitrary combination of letters and sounds that makes up the word TREE will stand for or represent the concept 'a large plant that grows in nature'? One possibility would be that the objects in the world themselves embody and fix in some way their 'true' meaning. But it is not at all clear that real trees *know* that they are trees, and even less clear that they know that the word in English which represents the concept of themselves is written TREE whereas in French it is written ARBRE! As far as they are concerned, it could just as well be written COW or VACHE or indeed XYZ. The meaning is *not* in the object or person or thing, nor is it *in* the word. It is we who fix the meaning so firmly that, after a while, it comes to seem natural and inevitable. The meaning is *constructed by the system of representation*. It is constructed and fixed by the *code*, which sets up the correlation between our conceptual system and our language system in such a way that, every time we think of a tree, the code tells us to use the English word TREE, or the French word ARBRE. The code tells us that, in our culture – that is, in our conceptual and language codes – the concept 'tree' is represented by the letters T, R, E, E, arranged in a certain sequence, just as in Morse code, the sign for V (which in the Second World War Churchill made 'stand for' or represent 'Victory') is Dot, Dot, Dot, Dash, and in the 'language of traffic lights', Green = Go! and Red = Stop!

One way of thinking about 'culture', then, is in terms of these shared conceptual maps, shared language systems and the *codes which govern the relationships of translation between them*. Codes fix the relationships between concepts and signs. They stabilize meaning within different languages and cultures. They tell us which language to use to convey which idea. The reverse is also true. Codes tell us which concepts are being referred to when we hear or read which signs. By arbitrarily fixing the relationships between our conceptual system and our linguistic systems (remember, 'linguistic' in a broad sense), codes make it possible for us to speak and to hear intelligibly, and establish the translat-ability between our concepts and our languages which enables meaning to pass from speaker to hearer and be effectively communicated within a culture. This translatability is not given by nature or fixed by the gods. It is the result of a set of social conventions. It is fixed socially, fixed in culture. English or French or Hindi speakers have, over time, and without conscious decision or choice, come to an unwritten agreement, a sort of unwritten cultural covenant that, in their various languages, certain signs will stand for or represent certain concepts. This is what children learn, and how they become not simply biological individuals but cultural subjects. They learn the system and conventions of representation, the codes of their language and culture, which equip them with cultural 'know-how', enabling them to function as culturally competent subjects. Not because such knowledge is imprinted in their genes, but because they learn its conventions and so gradually *become* 'cultured persons' – i.e. members of their culture. They unconsciously internalize the codes which allow them to express certain concepts and ideas through their systems of representation – writing, speech, gesture, visuali-zation, and so on – and to interpret ideas which are communicated to them using the same systems.

You may find it easier to understand, now, why meaning, language and representation are such critical elements in the study of culture. To belong to a culture is to belong to roughly the same con-ceptual and linguistic universe, to know how concepts and ideas translate into different languages, and how language can be interpreted to refer to or *reference* the world. To share these things is to see the world from within the same conceptual map and to make sense of it through the same language sys-tems. Early anthropologists of language, like Sapir and Whorf, took this insight to its logical extreme when they argued that we are all, as it were, locked into our cultural perspectives or 'mind-sets', and that language is the best clue we have to that conceptual universe. This observation, when applied to all human cultures, lies at the root of what, today, we may think of as cultural or linguistic *relativism*.

ACTIVITY 2

You might like to think further about this question of how different cultures conceptually classify the world and what implications this has for meaning and representation.

The English make a rather simple distinction between sleet and snow. The Inuit (Eskimos) who have to survive in a very different, more extreme and hostile climate, apparently have many more words for snow and snowy weather. Consider the list of Inuit terms for snow from the Scott Polar Research Institute in Table 1.1. There are many more than in English, making much finer and more complex distinctions. The Inuit have a complex classificatory conceptual system for the weather compared with the English. The novelist Peter Hoeg, for example, writing about Greenland in his novel, *Miss Smilla's Feeling For Snow* (1994, pp. 5–6), graphically describes 'frazzil ice' which is 'kneaded together into a soapy mash called porridge ice, which gradually forms free-floating plates, pancake ice, which one, cold, noonday hour, on a Sunday, freezes into a single solid sheet'. Such distinctions are too fine and elaborate even for the English who are always talking about the weather! The question, however, is – do the Inuit actually experience snow differently from the English? Their language system suggests they conceptualize the weather differently. But how far is our experience actually bounded by our linguistic and conceptual universe?

TABLE 1.1 Inuit terms for snow and ice

snow		ice	siku
blowing —	piqtuluk	— pan, broken —	siqumniq
is snowstorming	piqtuluktuq	— water	immiugaq
falling —	qanik	melts — to make water	immiuqtuaq
— is falling; — is snowing	qaniktuq	candle —	illauyiniq
light falling —	qaniaraq	flat —	qaimiq
light — is falling	qaniaraqtuq	glare —	quasaq
first layer of — in fall	apilraun	piled —	ivunrit
deep soft —	mauya	rough —	iwuit
packed — to make water	aniu	shore —	tugiu
light soft —	aquluraq	shorefast —	tuvaq
sugar—	pukak	slush —	quna
waterlogged, mushy —	masak	young —	sikuliaq
— is turning into *masak*	masaguqtuaq		
watery —	maqayak		
wet —	misak		
wet falling —	qanikkuk		
wet — is falling	qanikkuktuq		
— drifting along a surface	natiruvik		
— is drifting along a surface	natiruviktuaq		
— lying on a surface	apun		
snowflake	qanik		
is being drifted over with —	apiyuaq		

One implication of this argument about cultural codes is that, if meaning is the result, not of something fixed out there, in nature, but of our social, cultural and linguistic conventions, then meaning can never be *finally* fixed. We can all 'agree' to allow words to carry somewhat different meanings – as we have, for example, with the word 'gay', or the use, by young people, of the word 'wicked' as a term of approval. Of course, there must be *some* fixing of meaning in language or we would never be able to understand one another. We can't get up one morning and suddenly decide to represent the concept of a 'tree' with the letters or the word VYXZ, and expect people to follow what we are saying. On the other hand, there is no absolute or final fixing of meaning. Social and linguistic conventions do change over time. In the language of modern managerialism, what we used to call 'students', 'clients', 'patients' and 'passengers' have all become 'customers'. Linguistic codes vary significantly between one language and another. Many cultures do not have words for concepts which are normal and widely acceptable to us. Words constantly go out of common usage, and new phrases are coined: think, for example, of the use of 'down-sizing' to represent the process of firms laying people off work. Even when the actual words remain stable, their connotations shift or they acquire a different nuance. The problem is especially acute in translation. For example, does the difference in English between *know* and *understand* correspond exactly to and capture exactly the same conceptual distinction as the French make between *savoir* and *connaître*? Perhaps; but can we be sure?

The main point is that meaning does not inhere *in* things, in the world. It is constructed, produced. It is the result of a signifying practice – a practice that *produces* meaning, that *makes things mean*.

1.4 Theories of representation

There are, broadly speaking, three approaches to explaining how representation of meaning through language works. We may call these the reflective, the intentional and the constructionist or constructivist approaches. You might think of each as an attempt to answer the questions, 'Where do meanings come from?' and 'How can we tell the "true" meaning of a word or image?'

In the **reflective approach**, meaning is thought to lie in the object, person, idea or event in the real world, and language functions like a mirror, to *reflect* the true meaning as it already exists in the world. As the poet Gertrude Stein once said, 'A rose is a rose is a rose'. In the fourth century BC, the Greeks used the notion of *mimesis* to explain how language, even drawing and painting, mirrored or imitated nature; they thought of Homer's great poem, *The Iliad*, as 'imitating' a heroic series of events. So the theory which says that language works by simply reflecting or imitating the truth that is already there and fixed in the world is sometimes called 'mimetic'.

Of course there is a certain obvious truth to mimetic theories of representation and language. As we've pointed out, visual signs do bear some relationship to the shape and texture of the objects which they represent. But, as was also pointed out earlier, a two-dimensional visual image of a *rose* is a sign – it should not be confused with the real plant with thorns and blooms growing in the garden. Remember also that there are many words, sounds and images which we fully well understand but which are entirely fictional or fantasy and refer to worlds which are wholly imaginary – including, many people now think, most of *The Iliad*! Of course, I can use the word 'rose' to *refer* to real, actual plants growing in a garden, as we have said before. But this is because I know the code which links the concept with a particular word or image. I cannot *think* or *speak* or *draw* with an actual rose. And if someone says to me that there is no such word as 'rose' for a plant in her culture, the actual plant in the garden cannot resolve the failure of communication between us. Within the conventions of the different language codes we are using, we are both right – and for us to understand each other, one of us must learn the code linking the flower with the word for it in the other's culture.

The second approach to meaning in representation argues the opposite case. It holds that it is the speaker, the author, who imposes his or her unique meaning on the world through language. Words mean what the author intends they should mean. This is the **intentional approach**. Again, there is some point to this argument since we all, as individuals, do use language to convey or communicate things which are special or unique to us, to our way of seeing the world. However, as a general theory of representation through language, the intentional approach is also flawed. We cannot be the sole or unique source of meanings in language, since that would mean that we could express ourselves in entirely private languages. But the essence of language is communication and that, in turn, depends on shared linguistic conventions and shared codes. Language can never be wholly a private game. Our private intended meanings, however personal to us, have to *enter into the rules, codes and conventions of language* to be shared and understood. Language is a social system through and through. This means that our private thoughts have to negotiate with all the other meanings for words or images which have been stored in language which our use of the language system will inevitably trigger into action.

The third approach recognizes this public, social character of language. It acknowledges that neither things in themselves nor the individual users of language can fix meaning in language. Things don't *mean*: we *construct* meaning, using representational systems – concepts and signs. Hence it is called the constructivist or **constructionist approach** to meaning in language. According to this approach, we must not confuse the *material* world, where things and people exist, and the *symbolic* practices and processes through which representation, meaning and language operate. Constructivists do not deny the existence of the material world. However, it is not the material world which conveys meaning: it is the language system or whatever system we are using to represent our concepts. It is social actors who use the conceptual systems of their culture and the linguistic and other representational systems to construct meaning, to make the world meaningful and to communicate about that world meaningfully to others.

Of course, signs may also have a material dimension. Representational systems consist of the actual *sounds* we make with our vocal chords, the *images* we make on light-sensitive paper with cameras, the *marks* we make with paint on canvas, the digital *impulses* we transmit electronically. Representation is a practice, a kind of 'work', which uses material objects and effects. But the *meaning* depends not on the material quality of the sign, but on its *symbolic function*. It is because a particular sound or word *stands for, symbolizes or represents* a concept that it can function, in language, as a sign and convey meaning – or, as the constructionists say, signify (sign-i-fy).

1.5 The language of traffic lights

The simplest example of this point, which is critical for an understanding of how languages function as representational systems, is the famous traffic lights example. A traffic light is a machine which produces different coloured lights in sequence. The effect of light of different wavelengths on the eye – which is a natural and material phenomenon – produces the sensation of different colours. Now these things certainly do exist in the material world. But it is our culture which breaks the spectrum of light into different colours, distinguishes them from one another and attaches names – Red, Green, Yellow, Blue – to them. We use a way of *classifying* the colour spectrum to create colours which are different from one another. We *represent* or symbolize the different colours and classify them according to different colour-concepts. This is the conceptual colour system of our culture. We say 'our culture' because, of course, other cultures may divide the colour spectrum differently. What's more, they certainly use different actual *words* or *letters* to identify different colours: what we call 'red', the French call 'rouge', and so on. This is the linguistic code – the one which correlates certain words (signs) with certain colours (concepts), and thus enables us to communicate about colours to other people, using 'the language of colours'.

But how do we use this representational or symbolic system to regulate the traffic? Colours do not have any 'true' or fixed meaning in that sense. Red does not mean 'Stop' in nature, any more than Green means 'Go'. In other settings, Red may stand for, symbolize or represent 'Blood' or 'Danger' or 'Communism'; and Green may represent 'Ireland' or 'The Countryside' or 'Environmentalism'. Even these meanings can change. In the 'language of electric plugs', Red used to mean 'the connection with the positive charge' but this was arbitrarily and without explanation changed to Brown! But then for many years the producers of plugs had to attach a slip of paper telling people that the code or convention had changed, otherwise how would they know? Red and Green work in the language of traffic lights because 'Stop' and 'Go' are the meanings which have been assigned to them in our culture by the code or conventions governing this language, and this code is widely known and almost universally obeyed in our culture and cultures like ours – though we can well imagine other cultures which did not possess the code, in which this language would be a complete mystery.

Let us stay with the example for a moment, to explore a little further how, according to the constructionist approach to representation, colours and the 'language of traffic lights' work as a signifying or representational system. Recall the *two* representational systems we spoke of earlier. First, there is the conceptual map of colours in our culture – the way colours are distinguished from one another, classified and arranged in our mental universe. Secondly, there are the ways words or images are correlated with colours in our language – our linguistic colour codes. Actually, of course, a *language* of colours consists of more than just the individual words for different points on the colour spectrum. It also depends on how they function in relation to one another – the sorts of things which are governed by grammar and syntax in written or spoken languages, which allow us to express rather complex ideas. In the language of traffic lights, it is the sequence and position of the colours, as well as the colours themselves, which enable them to carry meaning and thus function as signs.

Does it matter which colours we use? No, the constructionists argue. This is because what signifies is not the colours themselves but (a) the fact that they are different and can be distinguished from one another; and (b) the fact that they are organized into a particular sequence – Red followed by Green, with sometimes a warning Amber in between which says, in effect, 'Get ready! Lights about to change.' Constructionists put this point in the following way. What signifies, what carries meaning – they argue – is not each colour in itself nor even the concept or word for it. It is *the difference between Red and Green* which signifies. This is a very important principle, in general, about representation and meaning, and we shall return to it on more than one occasion in the chapters that follow. Think about it in these terms. If you couldn't differentiate between Red and Green, you couldn't use one to mean 'Stop' and the other to mean 'Go'. In the same way, it is only the difference between the letters P and T which enable the word SHEEP to be linked, in the English language code, to the concept of 'the animal with four legs and a woolly coat', and the word SHEET to 'the material we use to cover ourselves in bed at night'.

In principle, any combination of colours – like any collection of letters in written language or of sounds in spoken language – would do, provided they are sufficiently different not to be confused. Constructionists express this idea by saying that all signs are arbitrary. 'Arbitrary' means that there is no natural relationship between the sign and its meaning or concept. Since Red only means 'Stop' because that is how the code works, in principle any colour would do, including Green. It is the code that fixes the meaning, not the colour itself. This also has wider implications for the theory of representation and meaning in language. It means that signs themselves cannot fix meaning. Instead, meaning depends on *the relation between* a sign and a concept which is fixed by a code. Meaning, the constructionists would say, is 'relational'.

ACTIVITY 3

Why not test this point about the arbitrary nature of the sign and the importance of the code for yourself? Construct a code to govern the movement of traffic using two different colours – Yellow and Blue – as in the following:

When the yellow light is showing ...

Now add an instruction allowing pedestrians and cyclists only to cross, using Pink.

Provided the code tells us clearly how to read or interpret each colour, and everyone agrees to interpret them in this way, any colour will do. These are just colours, just as the word SHEEP is simply a jumble of letters. In French the same animal is referred to using the very different linguistic sign, MOUTON. Signs are arbitrary. Their meanings are fixed by codes.

As we said earlier, traffic lights are machines, and colours are the material effect of light waves on the retina of the eye. But objects – things – can also function as signs, provided they have been assigned a concept and meaning within our cultural and linguistic codes. As signs, they work symbolically – they represent concepts, and signify. Their effects, however, are felt in the material and social world. Red and Green function in the language of traffic lights as signs, but they have real material and social effects. They regulate the social behaviour of drivers and, without them, there would be many more traffic accidents at road intersections.

1.6 Summary

We have come a long way in exploring the nature of representation. It is time to summarize what we have learned about the constructionist approach to representation through language.

Representation is the production of meaning through language. In representation, construction-ists argue, we use signs, organized into languages of different kinds, to communicate meaning-fully with others. Languages can use signs to symbolize, stand for or reference objects, people and events in the so-called 'real' world. But they can also reference imaginary things and fantasy worlds or abstract ideas which are not in any obvious sense part of our material world. There is no simple relationship of reflection, imitation or one-to-one correspondence between language and the real world. The world is not accurately or otherwise reflected in the mirror of language. Language does not work like a mirror. Meaning is produced within language, in and through vari-ous representational systems which, for convenience, we call 'languages'. Meaning is produced by the practice, the 'work', of representation. It is constructed through signifying – i.e. meaning-producing – practices.

How does this take place? In fact, it depends on two different but related systems of rep-resentation. First, the concepts which are formed in the mind function as a system of mental representation which classifies and organizes the world into meaningful categories. If we have a concept for something, we can say we know its 'meaning'. But we cannot communicate this mean-ing without a second system of representation, a language. Language consists of signs organized into various relationships. But signs can only convey meaning if we possess codes which allow us to translate our concept into language – and vice versa. These codes are crucial for meaning and representation. They do not exist in nature but are the result of social conventions. They are a crucial part of our culture – our shared 'maps of meaning' – which we learn and unconsciously internalize as we become members of our culture. This constructionist approach to language thus introduces the symbolic domain of life, where words and things function as signs, into the very heart of social life itself.

ACTIVITY 4

All this may seem rather abstract. But we can quickly demonstrate its relevance by an example from painting.

Look at the painting of a still life by the Spanish painter, Juan Sanchez Cotán (1521–1627), entitled *Quince, Cabbage, Melon and Cucumber* (Figure 1.3). It seems as if the painter has made every effort to use the 'language of painting' accurately to reflect these four objects, to capture or 'imitate nature'. Is this, then, an example of a *reflective* or *mimetic* form of representation – a painting reflecting the 'true meaning' of what already exists in Cotán's kitchen? Or can we find the operation of certain codes, the language of painting used to produce a certain meaning? Start with the question, what does the painting mean to you? What is it 'saying'? Then go on to ask, how is it saying it – how does representation work in this painting?

Write down any thoughts at all that come to you on looking at the painting. What do these objects say to you? What meanings do they trigger off?

FIGURE 1.3 Juan Cotán, *Quince, Cabbage, Melon and Cucumber*, c. 1602

Now read the edited extract from an analysis of the still life by the art critic and theorist, Norman Bryson, included as Reading A at the end of this chapter. Don't be concerned, at this stage, if the language seems a little difficult and you don't understand all the terms. Pick out the main points about the way *representation* works in the painting, according to Bryson.

Bryson is by no means the only critic of Cotán's painting, and certainly doesn't provide the only 'correct' reading of it. That's not the point. The point of the example is that he helps us to see how, even in a still life, the 'language of painting' does *not* function simply to reflect or imitate a meaning which is already there in nature, but to *produce meanings*. The act of painting is a *signifying practice*. Take note, in particular, of what Bryson says about the following points:

1 The way the painting invites you, the viewer, to look – what he calls its 'mode of seeing'; in part, the function of the language is to position you, the viewer, in a certain relation to meaning.
2 The relationship to food which is posed by the painting.
3 How, according to Bryson, 'mathematical form' is used by Cotán to distort the painting so as to bring out a particular meaning. Can a distorted meaning in painting be 'true'?
4 The meaning of the difference between 'creatural' and 'geometric' space: the language of painting creates its own kind of space.

If necessary, work through the extract again, picking up these specific points.

2 SAUSSURE'S LEGACY

The social constructionist view of language and representation which we have been discussing owes a great deal to the work and influence of the Swiss linguist, Saussure, who was born in Geneva in 1857, did much of his work in Paris, and died in 1913. He is known as the 'father of modern linguistics'. For our purposes, his importance lies not in his detailed work in linguistics, but in his general view of representation and the way his model of language shaped the *semiotic* approach to the problem of representation in a wide variety of cultural fields. You will recognize much about Saussure's thinking from what we have already said about the *constructionist* approach.

For Saussure, according to Jonathan Culler (1976, p. 19), the production of meaning depends on language: 'Language is a system of signs.' Sounds, images, written words, paintings, photographs, etc. function as signs within language 'only when they serve to express or communicate ideas. ... [To] communicate ideas, they must be part of a system of conventions ...' (ibid.). Material objects can function as signs and communicate meaning too, as we saw from the 'language of traffic lights' example. In an important move, Saussure analysed the **sign** into two further elements. There was, he argued, the *form* (the actual word, image, photo, etc.), and there was the *idea or concept* in your head with which the form was associated. Saussure called the first element, the **signifier**, and the second element – the corresponding concept it triggered off in your head – the **signified**. Every time you hear or read or see the *signifier* (e.g. the word or image of a *Walkman*, for example), it correlates with the *signified* (the concept of a portable cassette-player in your head). Both are required to produce meaning but it is the relation between them, fixed by our cultural and linguistic codes, which sustains representation. Thus, 'the sign is the union of a form which signifies (*signifier*) ... and an idea signified (*signified*). Though we may speak ... as if they are separate entities, they exist only as components of the sign ... [which is] the central fact of language' (Culler, 1976, p. 19).

Saussure also insisted on what in section 1 we called the arbitrary nature of the sign: 'There is no natural or inevitable link between the signifier and the signified' (ibid.). Signs do not possess a fixed or essential meaning. What signifies, according to Saussure, is not RED or the essence of 'red-ness', but *the difference between RED and GREEN*. Signs, Saussure argued, 'are members of a system and are defined in relation to the other members of that system'. For example, it is hard to define the meaning of FATHER except in relation to, and in terms of its difference from, other kinship terms, like MOTHER, DAUGHTER, SON, and so on.

This marking of difference within language is fundamental to the production of meaning, according to Saussure. Even at a simple level (to repeat an earlier example), we must be able to distinguish, within language, between SHEEP and SHEET, before we can link one of those words to the concept of an animal that produces wool, and the other to the concept of a cloth that covers a bed. The simplest way of marking difference is, of course, by means of a binary opposition – in this example, all the letters are the same except P and T. Similarly, the meaning of a concept or word is often defined in relation to its direct opposite – as in night/day. Later critics of Saussure were to observe that binaries (e.g. *black/white*) are only one, rather simplistic, way of establishing difference. As well as the stark difference between *black* and *white*, there are also the many other, subtler differences between *black* and *dark grey*, *dark grey* and *light grey*, *grey* and *cream* and *off-white*, *off-white* and *brilliant white*, just as there are between *night, dawn, daylight, noon, dusk*, and so on. However, his attention to binary oppositions brought Saussure to the revolutionary proposition that a language consists of signifiers, but in order to produce meaning, the signifiers have to be organized into 'a system of differences'. It is the differences between signifiers which signify.

Furthermore, the relation between the *signifier* and the *signified*, which is fixed by our cultural codes, is not – Saussure argued – permanently fixed. Words shift their meanings. The concepts (signifieds) to which they refer also change, historically, and every shift alters the conceptual map of the culture, leading different cultures, at different historical moments, to classify and think about the world differently. For many centuries, western societies have associated the word BLACK with everything that is dark, evil, forbidding, devilish, dangerous and sinful. And yet, think of how the perception of black people in America in the 1960s changed after the phrase 'Black is Beautiful' became a popular slogan – where the *signifier*, BLACK, was made to signify the exact opposite meaning (*signified*) to its previous associations. In Saussure's terms, 'Language sets up an arbitrary relation between signifiers of its own choosing on the one hand, and signifieds of its own choosing on the other. Not only does each language produce a different set of signifiers, articulating and dividing the continuum of sound (or writing or drawing or photography) in a distinctive way; each language produces a different set of signifieds; it has a distinctive and thus arbitrary way of organizing the world into concepts and categories' (Culler, 1976, p. 23).

The implications of this argument are very far-reaching for a theory of representation and for our understanding of culture. If the relationship between a signifier and its signified is the result of a system of social conventions specific to each society and to specific historical moments, then all meanings are produced within history and culture. They can never be finally fixed but are always subject to change, both from one cultural context and from one period to another. There is thus no single, unchanging, universal 'true meaning'. 'Because it is arbitrary, the sign is totally subject to history and the combination at the particular moment of a given signifier and signified is a contingent result of the historical process' (Culler, 1976, p. 36). This opens up meaning and representation, in a radical way, to history and change. It is true that Saussure himself focused exclusively on the state of the language system at one moment of time rather than looking at linguistic change over time. However, for our purposes, the important point is the way this approach to language *unfixes* meaning, breaking any natural and inevitable tie between signifier and signified. This opens representation to the constant 'play' or slippage of meaning, to the constant production of new meanings, new interpretations.

However, if meaning changes, historically, and is never finally fixed, then it follows that 'taking the meaning' must involve an active process of **interpretation**. Meaning has to be actively 'read' or 'interpreted'. Consequently, there is a necessary and inevitable imprecision about language. The meaning we take, as viewers, readers or audiences, is never exactly the meaning which has been given by the speaker or writer or by other viewers. And since, in order to say something meaningful, we have to 'enter language', where all sorts of older meanings which pre-date us, are already stored from previous eras, we can never cleanse language completely, screening out all the other, hidden meanings which might modify or distort what we want to say. For example, we can't entirely prevent some of the negative connotations of the word BLACK from returning to mind when we read a headline like, 'WEDNESDAY – A BLACK DAY ON THE STOCK EXCHANGE', even if this was not intended. There is a constant *sliding of meaning* in all interpretation, a margin – something in excess of what we intend to say – in which other meanings overshadow the statement or the text, where other associations are awakened to life, giving what we say a different twist. So interpretation becomes an essential aspect of the process by which meaning is given and taken. The *reader* is as important as the *writer* in the production of meaning. Every signifier given or encoded with meaning has to be meaningfully interpreted or decoded by the receiver (Hall, 1980). Signs which have not been intelligibly received and interpreted are not, in any useful sense, 'meaningful'.

2.1 The social part of language

Saussure divided language into two parts. The first consisted of the general rules and codes of the linguistic system, which all its users must share, if it is to be of use as a means of communication. The rules are the principles which we learn when we learn a language and they enable us to use language to say whatever we want. For example, in English, the preferred word order is subject–verb–object ('the cat sat on the mat'), whereas in Latin, the verb usually comes at the end. Saussure called this underlying rule-governed structure of language, which enables us to produce well-formed sentences, the **langue** (the language system). The second part consisted of the particular acts of speaking or writing or drawing, which – using the structure and rules of the *langue* – are produced by an actual speaker or writer. He called this **parole**. '*La langue* is the system of language, the language as a system of forms, whereas *parole* is actual speech [or writing], the speech acts which are made possible by the language' (Culler, 1976, p. 29).

For Saussure, the underlying structure of rules and codes (*langue*) was the social part of language, the part which could be studied with the law-like precision of a science because of its closed, limited nature. It was his preference for studying language at this level of its 'deep structure' which made people call Saussure and his model of language, **structuralist**. The second part of language, the individual speech-act or utterance (*parole*), he regarded as the 'surface' of language. There were an infinite number of such possible utterances. Hence, *parole* inevitably lacked those structural properties – forming a closed and limited set – which would have enabled us to study it 'scientifically'. What made Saussure's model appeal to many later scholars was the fact that the closed, structured character of language at the level of its rules and laws, which, according to Saussure, enabled it to be studied scientifically, was combined with the capacity to be free and unpredictably creative in our actual speech acts. They believed he had offered them, at last, a scientific approach to that least scientific object of inquiry – culture.

In separating the social part of language (*langue*) from the individual act of communication (*parole*), Saussure broke with our common-sense notion of how language works. Our common-sense intuition is that language comes from within us – from the individual speaker or writer; that it is this speaking or writing subject who is the author or originator of meaning. This is what we called, earlier, the *intentional* model of representation. But according to Saussure's schema, each authored statement only becomes possible because the 'author' shares with other language-users the common rules and codes of the language system – the *langue* – which allows them to communicate with each other meaningfully. The author decides what she wants to say. But she cannot 'decide' whether or not to use the rules of language, if she wants to be understood. We are born into a language, its codes and its meanings. Language is therefore, for Saussure, a social phenomenon. It cannot be an individual matter because we cannot make up the rules of language individually, for ourselves. Their source lies in society, in the culture, in our shared cultural codes, in the language system – not in nature or in the individual subject.

We will move on in section 3 to consider how the constructionist approach to representation, and in particular Saussure's linguistic model, was applied to a wider set of cultural objects and practices, and evolved into the *semiotic* method which so influenced the field. First, we ought to take account of some of the criticisms levelled at his position.

2.2 Critique of Saussure's model

Saussure's great achievement was to force us to focus on language itself, as a social fact; on the process of representation itself; on how language actually works and the role it plays in the production of meaning. In doing so, he saved language from the status of a mere transparent medium between *things* and *meaning*. He showed, instead, that representation was a practice. However, in his own work, he tended to focus almost exclusively on the two aspects of the sign – *signifier* and *signified*. He gave little or no attention to how this relation between *signifier/signified* could serve the purpose of what earlier we called *reference* – i.e. referring us to the world of things, people and events outside language in the 'real' world. Later linguists made a distinction between, say, the meaning of the word BOOK and the use of the word to refer to a *specific* book lying before us on the table. The linguist, Charles Sanders Pierce, while adopting a similar approach to Saussure, paid greater attention to the relationship between signifiers/signifieds and what he called their *referents*. What Saussure called signification really involves *both* meaning and reference, but he focused mainly on the former.

Another problem is that Saussure tended to focus on the *formal* aspects of language – how language actually works. This has the great advantage of making us examine representation as a practice worthy of detailed study in its own right. It forces us to look at language for itself, and not just as an empty, transparent, 'window on the world'. However, Saussure's focus on language may have been too exclusive. The attention to its formal aspects did divert attention away from the more interactive and dialogic features of language – language as it is actually used, as it functions in actual situations, in dialogue between different kinds of speakers. It is thus not surprising that, for Saussure, questions of *power* in language – for example, between speakers of different status and positions – did not arise.

As has often been the case, the 'scientific' dream which lay behind the structuralist impulse of his work, though influential in alerting us to certain aspects of how language works, proved to be illusory. Language is *not* an object which can be studied with the law-like precision of a science. Later cultural theorists learned from Saussure's 'structuralism' but abandoned its scientific premise. Language remains rule-governed. But it is not a 'closed' system which can be reduced to its formal elements. Since it is constantly changing, it is by definition *open-ended*. Meaning continues to be produced through language in forms which can never be predicted beforehand and its 'sliding', as we described it above, cannot be halted. Saussure may have been tempted to the former view because, like a good structuralist, he tended to study the state of the language system at one moment, as if it had stood still, and he could halt the flow of language-change. Nevertheless it is the case that many of those who have been most influenced by Saussure's radical break with all reflective and intentional models of representation, have built on his work not by imitating his scientific and 'structuralist' approach, but by applying his model in a much looser, more open-ended – i.e. 'post-structuralist' – way.

2.3 Summary

How far, then, have we come in our discussion of theories of *representation*? We began by contrasting three different approaches. The *reflective* or *mimetic* approach proposed a direct and transparent relationship of imitation or reflection between words (signs) and things. The *intentional* theory reduced representation to the intentions of its author or subject. The *constructionist* theory proposed a complex and mediated relationship between things in the world, our concepts in thought and language. We have focused at greatest length on this approach. The correlations between these levels – the material, the conceptual and the signifying – are governed by our cultural and linguistic codes and it is this set of interconnections which produces meaning. We then showed how much this general model of how systems of representation work in the production of meaning owed to the work of Ferdinand de Saussure. Here, the key point was the link provided by the codes between the forms of expression used by language (whether speech, writing, drawing, or other types of representation) – which Saussure called the *signifiers* – and the mental concepts associated with them – the *signifieds*. The connection between these two systems of representation produced *signs*; and signs, organized into languages, produced meanings, and could be used to reference objects, people and events in the 'real' world.

3 FROM LANGUAGE TO CULTURE: LINGUISTICS TO SEMIOTICS

Saussure's main contribution was to the study of linguistics in a narrow sense. However, since his death, his theories have been widely deployed, as a foundation for a general approach to language and meaning, providing a model of representation which has been applied to a wide range of cultural objects and practices. Saussure himself foresaw this possibility in his famous lecture notes, collected posthumously by his students as the *Course in General Linguistics* (1960), where he looked forward to 'A science that studies the life of signs within society ... I shall call it semiology, from the Greek *semeion* "signs"' (p. 16). This general approach to the study of signs in culture, and of culture as a sort of 'language', which Saussure foreshadowed, is now generally known by the term **semiotics**.

FIGURE 1.4 Wrestling as a language of 'excess'

The underlying argument behind the semiotic approach is that, since all cultural objects convey meaning, and all cultural practices depend on meaning, they must make use of signs; and in so far as they do, they must work like language works, and be amenable to an analysis which basically makes use of Saussure's linguistic concepts (e.g. the *signifier/signified* and *langue/parole* distinctions, his idea of underlying codes and structures, and the arbitrary nature of the sign). Thus, when in his collection of essays, *Mythologies* (1972), the French critic, Roland Barthes, studied 'The world of wrestling', 'Soap powders and detergents', 'The face of Greta Garbo' or The *Blue Guides* to Europe', he brought a *semiotic* approach to bear on 'reading' popular culture, treating these activities and objects as signs, as a language through which meaning is communicated. For example, most of us would think of a wrestling match as a competitive game or sport designed for one wrestler to gain victory over an opponent. Barthes, however, asks, not 'Who won?' but 'What is the meaning of this event?' He treats it as a *text* to be *read*. He 'reads' the exaggerated gestures of wrestlers as a grandiloquent language of what he calls the pure spectacle of excess.

READING B

You should now read the brief extract from Barthes's 'reading' of 'The world of wrestling', provided as Reading B at the end of this chapter.

In much the same way, the French anthropologist, Claude Lévi-Strauss, studied the customs, rituals, totemic objects, designs, myths and folk-tales of so-called 'primitive' peoples in Brazil, not by analysing how these things were produced and used in the context of daily life among the Amazonian peoples, but in terms of what they were trying to 'say', what messages about the culture they communicated. He analysed their meaning, not by interpreting their content, but by looking at the underlying rules and codes through which such objects or practices produced meaning and, in doing so, he was making a classic Saussurean or structuralist 'move', from the *paroles* of a culture to the underlying structure, its *langue*. To undertake this kind of work, in studying the meaning of a television programme like *EastEnders*, for example, we would have to treat the pictures on the screen as signifiers, and use the code of the television soap opera as a *genre*, to discover how each image on the screen made use of these rules to 'say something' (signifieds) which the viewer could 'read' or interpret within the formal framework of a particular kind of television narrative (see the discussion and analysis of TV soap operas in Chapter 6).

In the semiotic approach, not only words and images but objects themselves can function as signifiers in the production of meaning. Clothes, for example, may have a simple physical function – to cover the body and protect it from the weather. But clothes also double up as signs. They construct a meaning and carry a message. An evening dress may signify 'elegance'; a bow tie and tails, 'formality'; jeans and trainers, 'casual dress'; a certain kind of sweater in the right setting, 'a long, romantic, autumn walk in the wood' (Barthes, 1967). These signs enable clothes to convey meaning and to function like a language – 'the language of fashion'. How do they do this?

ACTIVITY 5

Look at the example of clothes in a magazine fashion spread (Figure 1.5). Apply Saussure's model to analyse what the clothes are 'saying'? How would you decode their message? In particular, which elements are operating as signifiers and what concepts – signifieds – are you applying to them? Don't just get an overall impression – work it out in detail. How is the 'language of fashion' working in this example?

The clothes themselves are the *signifiers*. The fashion code in western consumer cultures like ours correlates particular kinds or combinations of clothing with certain concepts ('elegance', 'formality', 'casualness', 'romance'). These are the *signifieds*. This coding converts the clothes into *signs*, which can then be read as a language. In the language of fashion, the signifiers are arranged in a certain sequence, in certain relations to one another. Relations may be of similarity – certain items 'go together' (e.g. casual shoes with jeans). Differences are also marked – no leather belts with evening wear. Some signs actually create meaning by exploiting 'difference': e.g. Doc Marten boots with a flowing long skirt. These bits of clothing 'say something' – they convey meaning. Of course, not everybody reads fashion in the same way. There are differences of gender, age, class, race. But all those who share the same fashion code will interpret the signs in roughly the same ways. 'Oh, jeans don't look right for that event. It's a formal occasion – it demands something more elegant.'

You may have noticed that, in this example, we have moved from the very narrow linguistic level from which we drew examples in the first section, to a wider, cultural level. Note, also, that

FIGURE 1.5 Advertisement for Gucci, in *Vogue*, September 1995

two linked operations are required to complete the representation process by which meaning is produced. First, we need a basic *code* which links a particular piece of material which is cut and sewn in a particular way (*signifier*) to our mental concept of it (*signified*) – say a particular cut of material to our concept of 'a dress' or 'jeans'. (Remember that only some cultures would 'read' the signifier in this way, or indeed possess the concept of (i.e. have classified clothes into) 'a dress', as different from 'jeans'.) The combination of signifier and signified is what Saussure called a *sign*. Then, having recognized the material as a dress, or as jeans, and produced a sign, we can progress to a second, wider level, which links these signs to broader, cultural themes, concepts or meanings – for example, an evening dress to 'formality' or 'elegance', jeans to 'casualness'. Barthes called the first, descriptive level, the level of **denotation**; the second level, that of **connotation**. Both, of course, require the use of codes.

Denotation is the simple, basic, descriptive level, where consensus is wide and most people would agree on the meaning ('dress', 'jeans'). At the second level – *connotation* – these signi-fiers, which we have been able to 'decode' at a simple level by using our conventional conceptual classifications of dress to read their meaning, enter a wider, second kind of code – 'the language of fashion' – which connects them to broader themes and meanings, linking them with what we may call the wider *semantic fields* of our culture: ideas of 'elegance', 'formality', 'casualness' and 'romance'. This second, wider meaning is no longer a descriptive level of obvious interpretation. Here we are beginning to interpret the completed signs in terms of the wider realms of social ideology – the general beliefs, conceptual frameworks and value systems of society. This second level of signification, Barthes suggests, is more 'general, global and diffuse. … It deals with "fragments of an ideology...". These signifieds have a very close communication with culture, knowledge, history and it is through them, so to speak, that the environmental world [of the culture] invades the system [of representation]' (Barthes, 1967, pp. 91–2).

3.1 Myth today

In his essay 'Myth today', in *Mythologies*, Barthes gives another example which helps us to see exactly how representation is working at this second, broader cultural level. Visiting the barbers' one day, Barthes is shown a copy of the French magazine *Paris Match*, which has on its cover a picture of 'a young Negro in a French uniform saluting with his eyes uplifted, probably fixed on the fold of the tricolour' (the French flag) (1972, p. 116). At the first level, to get any meaning at all, we need to decode each of the signifiers in the image into their appropriate concepts: e.g. a soldier, a uniform, an arm raised, eyes lifted, a French flag. This yields a set of signs with a simple, literal message or meaning: *a black soldier is giving the French flag a salute* (denotation). However, Barthes argues that this image also has a wider, cultural meaning. If we ask, 'What is *Paris Match* telling us by using this picture of a black soldier saluting a French flag?', Barthes suggests that we may come up with the message: '*that France is a great Empire, and that all her sons, without any colour discrimination, faithfully serve under her flag, and that there is no better answer to the detractors of an alleged colonialism than the zeal shown by this Negro in serving his so-called oppressors*' (connotation) (ibid.).

Whatever you think of the actual 'message' which Barthes finds, for a proper semiotic analysis you must be able to outline precisely the different steps by which this broader meaning has been produced. Barthes argues that here representation takes place through two separate but linked processes. In the first, the signifiers (the elements of the image) and the signifieds (the concepts – soldier, flag and so on) unite to form a sign with a simple denoted message: *a black soldier is giving the French flag a salute*. At the second stage, this completed message or sign is linked to a second set of signifieds – a broad, ideological theme about French colonialism. The first completed meaning functions as the signifier in the second stage of the representation process and, when linked with a wider theme by a reader, yields a second, more elaborate and ideologically framed message or meaning. Barthes gives this second concept or theme a name – he calls it 'a purposeful mixture of "French imperiality" and "militariness"'. This, he says, adds up to a 'message' about French colonialism and her faithful Negro soldier-sons. Barthes calls this second level of signification the level of *myth*. In this reading, he adds, 'French imperiality is the very drive behind the myth. The concept reconstitutes a chain of causes and effects, motives and intentions. ... Through the concept ... a whole new history ... is implanted in the myth ... the concept of French imperiality ... is again tied to the totality of the world: to the general history of France, to its colonial adventures, to its present difficulties' (Barthes, 1972, p. 119).

READING C

Turn to the short extract from 'Myth today' (Reading C at the end of this chapter), and read Barthes's account of how myth functions as a system of representation. Make sure you understand what Barthes means by 'two staggered systems' and by the idea that myth is a 'meta-language' (a second-order language).

For another example of this two-stage process of signification, we can turn now to another of Barthes's famous essays.

ACTIVITY 6

Now, look carefully at the advertisement for Panzani products (Figure 1.6) and, with Barthes's analysis in mind, do the following exercise:

1. What *signifiers* can you identify in the ad?
2. What do they mean? What are their *signifieds?*
3. Now, look at the ad as a whole, at the level of 'myth'. What is its wider, cultural message or theme? Can you construct one?

FIGURE 1.6 'Italian-ness' and the Panzani ad

READING D

Now read the second extract from Barthes, in which he offers an interpretation of the *Panzani* ad for spaghetti and vegetables in a string bag as a 'myth' about Italian national culture. The extract from 'Rhetoric of the image', in *Image-Music-Text* (1977), is included as Reading D at the end of this chapter.

Barthes suggests that we can read the Panzani ad as a 'myth' by linking its completed message (this is a picture of some packets of pasta, a tin, a sachet, some tomatoes, onions, peppers, a mushroom, all emerging from a half-open string bag) with the cultural theme or concept of Italianicity' (or as we would say, 'Italian-ness'). Then, at the level of the myth or meta-language, the Panzani ad becomes a message about the essential meaning of Italian-ness as a national culture. Can commodities really become the signifiers for myths of nationality? Can you think of ads, in magazines or on television, which work in the same way, drawing on the myth of 'Englishness'? Or 'Frenchness'? Or 'American-ness'? Or 'Indian-ness'? Try to apply the idea of 'Englishness' to the ad reproduced as Figure 1.7.

FIGURE 1.7   An image of 'Englishness' – advertisement for Jaguar

4 DISCOURSE, POWER AND THE SUBJECT

What the examples above show is that the semiotic approach provides a method for analysing how visual representations convey meaning. Already, in Roland Barthes's work in the 1960s, as we have seen, Saussure's 'linguistic' model is developed through its application to a much wider field of signs and representations (advertising, photography, popular culture, travel, fashion, etc.). Also, there is less concern with how individual words function as signs in language, and more about the application of the language model to a much broader set of cultural practices. Saussure held out the promise that the whole domain of meaning could, at last, be systematically mapped. Barthes, too, had a 'method', but his semiotic approach is much more loosely and interpretively applied; and, in his later work (for example, *The Pleasure of the Text*, 1975), he is more concerned with the 'play' of meaning and desire across texts than he is with the attempt to fix meaning by a scientific analysis of language's rules and laws.

Subsequently, as we observed, the project of a 'science of meaning' has appeared increasingly untenable. Meaning and representation seem to belong irrevocably to the interpretative side of the human and cultural sciences, whose subject matter – society, culture, the human subject – is not amenable to a positivistic approach (i.e. one which seeks to discover scientific laws about society). Later developments have recognized the necessarily interpretative nature of culture and the fact that interpretations never produce a final moment of absolute truth. Instead, interpretations are always followed by other interpretations, in an endless chain. As the French philosopher, Jacques Derrida, put it, writing always leads to more writing. Difference, he argued, can never be wholly captured within any binary system (Derrida, 1981). So any notion of a *final* meaning is always endlessly put off, deferred. Cultural studies of this interpretative kind, like other qualitative forms of sociological inquiry, are inevitably caught up in this 'circle of meaning'.

In the semiotic approach, representation was understood on the basis of the way words functioned as signs within language. But, for a start, in a culture, meaning often depends on larger units of analysis – narratives, statements, groups of images, whole discourses which operate across a variety of texts, areas of knowledge about a subject which have acquired widespread authority. Semiotics seemed to confine the process of representation to language, and to treat it as a closed, rather static, system. Subsequent developments became more concerned with representation as a source for the production of social *knowledge* – a more open system, connected in more intimate ways with social practices and questions of power. In the semiotic approach, the subject was displaced from the centre of language. Later theorists returned to the question of the subject, or at least to the empty space which Saussure's theory had left; without, of course, putting him/her back in the centre, as the author or source of meaning. Even if language, in some sense, 'spoke us' (as Saussure tended to argue), it was also important that in certain historical moments, some people had more power to speak about some subjects than others (male doctors about mad female patients in the late nineteenth century, for example, to take one of the key examples developed in the work of Michel Foucault). Models of representation, these critics argued, ought to focus on these broader issues of knowledge and power.

Foucault used the word 'representation' in a narrower sense than we are using it here, but he is considered to have contributed to a novel and significant general approach to the problem of representation. What concerned him was the production of knowledge (rather than just meaning) through what he called **discourse** (rather than just language). His project, he said, was to analyse 'how human beings understand themselves in our culture' and how our knowledge about 'the social, the embodied individual and shared meanings' comes to be produced in different periods. With its emphasis on cultural understanding and shared meanings, you can see that Foucault's project was still to some degree indebted to Saussure and Barthes (see Dreyfus and Rabinow, 1982, p. 17) while in other ways departing radically from them. Foucault's work was much more historically grounded, more attentive to historical specificities, than the semiotic approach. As he said, 'relations of power, not relations of meaning' were his main concern. The particular objects of Foucault's attention were the various disciplines of knowledge in the human and social sciences – what he called 'the subjectifying social sciences'. These had acquired an increasingly prominent and influential role in modern culture and were, in many instances, considered to be the discourses which, like religion in earlier times, could give us the 'truth' about knowledge.

We will return to Foucault's work in some of the subsequent chapters in this book (for example, Chapter 5). Here, we want to introduce Foucault and the *discursive* approach to representation by outlining three of his major ideas: his concept of *discourse*; the issue of *power and knowledge*; and the question of *the subject*. It might be useful, however, to start by giving you a general flavour, in Foucault's graphic (and somewhat over-stated) terms, of how he saw his project differing from that of the semiotic approach to representation. He moved away from an approach like that of Saussure and Barthes, based on 'the domain of signifying structure', towards one based on analysing what he called 'relations of force, strategic developments and tactics':

> Here I believe one's point of reference should not be to the great model of language (*langue*) and signs, but to that of war and battle. The history which bears and determines us has the form of a war rather than that of a language: relations of power not relations of meaning ...

(Foucault, 1980, pp. 114–15)

Rejecting both Hegelian Marxism (what he calls 'the dialectic') and semiotics, Foucault argued that:

> Neither the dialectic, as logic of contradictions, nor semiotics, as the structure of communication, can account for the intrinsic intelligibility of conflicts. 'Dialectic' is a way of evading the always open and hazardous reality of conflict by reducing it to a Hegelian skeleton, and 'semiology' is a way of avoiding its violent, bloody and lethal character by reducing it to the calm Platonic form of language and dialogue.

(ibid.)

4.1 From language to discourse

The first point to note, then, is the shift of attention in Foucault from 'language' to 'discourse'. He studied not language, but *discourse* as a system of representation. Normally, the term 'discourse' is used as a linguistic concept. It simply means passages of connected writing or speech. Michel Foucault, however, gave it a different meaning. What interested him were the rules and practices that produced meaningful statements and regulated discourse in different historical periods. By 'discourse', Foucault meant 'a group of statements which provide a language for talking about – a way of representing the knowledge about – a particular topic at a particular historical moment. ... Discourse is about the production of knowledge through language. But ... since all social practices entail *meaning*, and meanings shape and influence what we do – our conduct – all practices have a discursive aspect' (Hall, 1992, p. 291). It is important to note that the concept of *discourse* in this usage is not purely a 'linguistic' concept. It is about language *and* practice. It attempts to overcome the traditional distinction between what one *says* (language) and what one *does* (practice). Discourse, Foucault argues, constructs the topic. It defines and produces the objects of our knowledge. It governs the way that a topic can be meaningfully talked about and reasoned about. It also influences how ideas are put into practice and used to regulate the conduct of others. Just as a discourse 'rules in' certain ways of talking about a topic, defining an acceptable and intelligible way to talk, write, or conduct oneself, so also, by definition, it 'rules out', limits and restricts other ways of talking, of conducting ourselves in relation to the topic or constructing knowledge about it. Discourse, Foucault argued, never consists of one statement, one text, one action or one source. The same discourse, characteristic of the way of thinking or the state of knowledge at any one time (what Foucault called the *episteme*), will appear across a range of texts, and as forms of conduct, at a number of different institutional sites within society. However, whenever these discursive events 'refer to the same object, share the same style and ... support a strategy ... a common institutional, administrative or political drift and pattern' (Cousins and Hussain, 1984, pp. 84–5), then they are said by Foucault to belong to the same **discursive formation**.

Meaning and meaningful practice is therefore constructed within discourse. Like the semioticians, Foucault was a 'constructionist'. However, unlike them, he was concerned with the production of knowledge and meaning, not through language but through discourse. There were therefore similarities, but also substantive differences between these two versions.

The idea that 'discourse produces the objects of knowledge' and that nothing which is meaningful exists *outside discourse*, is at first sight a disconcerting proposition, which seems to run right against the grain of common-sense thinking. It is worth spending a moment to explore this idea further. Is Foucault saying – as some of his critics have charged – that *nothing exists outside discourse*? In fact, Foucault does *not* deny that things can have a real, material existence in the world. What he does argue is that '*nothing has any meaning outside discourse*' (Foucault, 1972). As Laclau and Mouffe put it, 'we use [the term discourse] to emphasize the fact that every social configuration is *meaningful*' (1990, p. 100). The concept of discourse is not about whether things exist, but about where meaning comes from.

⊢READING E

Turn now to Reading E, by Ernesto Laclau and Chantal Mouffe, a short extract from *New Reflections on the Revolution of Our Time* (1990), from which we have just quoted, and read it carefully. What they argue is that physical objects *do* exist, but they have no fixed meaning; they only take on meaning and become objects of knowledge *within discourse*. Make sure you follow their argument before reading further.

1 In terms of the discourse about 'building a wall', the distinction between the linguistic part (asking for a brick) and the physical act (putting the brick in place) does not matter. The first is linguistic, the second is physical, but both are 'discursive' – meaningful within discourse.

2 The round leather object which you kick is a physical object – a ball. But it only becomes 'a football' within the context of the rules of the game, which are socially constructed.

3 It is impossible to determine the meaning of an object outside its context of use. A stone thrown in a fight is a different thing ('a projectile') from a stone displayed in a museum ('a piece of sculpture').

This idea that physical things and actions exist, but they only take on meaning and become objects of knowledge within discourse, is at the heart of the *constructionist* theory of meaning and representation. Foucault argues that since we can only have a knowledge of things if they have a meaning, it is discourse – not the things-in-themselves – which produces knowledge. Subjects like 'madness', 'punishment' and 'sexuality' only exist meaningfully *within* the discourses about them. Thus, the study of the discourses of madness, punishment or sexuality would have to include the following elements:

1 statements about 'madness', 'punishment' or 'sexuality' which give us a certain kind of knowledge about these things;

2 the rules which prescribe certain ways of talking about these topics and exclude other ways – which govern what is 'sayable' or 'thinkable' about insanity, punishment or sexuality, at a particular historical moment;

3 'subjects' who in some ways personify the discourse – the madman, the hysterical woman, the criminal, the deviant, the sexually perverse person – with the attributes we would expect these subjects to have, given the way knowledge about the topic was constructed at that time;

4 how this knowledge about the topic acquires authority, a sense of embodying the 'truth' about it, constituting the 'truth of the matter', at a historical moment;

5 the practices within institutions for dealing with the subjects – medical treatment for the insane, punishment regimes for the guilty, moral discipline for the sexually deviant – whose conduct is being regulated and organized according to those ideas;

6 acknowledgement that a different discourse or *episteme* will arise at a later historical moment, supplanting the existing one, opening up a new *discursive formation*, and producing, in its turn, new conceptions of 'madness' or 'punishment' or 'sexuality', new discourses with the power and authority, the 'truth', to regulate social practices in new ways.

4.2 Historicizing discourse: discursive practices

The main point to get hold of here is the way discourse, representation, knowledge and 'truth' are radically *historicized* by Foucault, in contrast to the rather ahistorical tendency in semiotics. Things meant something and were 'true', he argued, *only within a specific historical context*. Foucault did not believe that the same phenomena would be found across different historical periods. He thought that, in each period, discourse produced forms of knowledge, objects, subjects and practices of knowledge, which differed radically from period to period, with no necessary continuity between them.

Thus, for Foucault, for example, mental illness was not an objective fact, which remained the same in all historical periods, and meant the same thing in all cultures. It was only *within* a definite discursive formation that the object, 'madness', could appear at all as a meaningful or intelligible construct. It was 'constituted by all that was said, in all the statements that named it, divided it up, described it, explained it, traced its development, indicated its various correlations, judged it, and possibly gave it speech by articulating, in its name, discourses that were to be taken as its own' (1972, p. 32). And it was only after a certain definition of 'madness' was put into practice, that the appropriate subject – 'the madman' as current medical and psychiatric knowledge defined 'him' – could appear.

Or, take some other examples of discursive practices from his work. There have always been sexual relations. But 'sexuality', as a specific way of talking about, studying and regulating sexual desire, its secrets and its fantasies, Foucault argued, only appeared in western societies at a particular historical moment (Foucault, 1978). There may always have been what we now call homosexual forms of behaviour. But 'the homosexual' as a specific kind of social subject, was *produced*, and could only make its appearance, within the moral, legal, medical and psychiatric discourses, practices and institutional apparatuses of the late nineteenth century, with their particular theories of sexual perversity (Weeks, 1981, 1985). Similarly, it makes nonsense to talk of the 'hysterical woman' outside the nineteenth-century view of hysteria as a very widespread female malady. In *The Birth of the Clinic* (1973), Foucault charted how 'in less than half a century, the medical understanding of disease was transformed' from a classical notion that disease existed separate from the body, to the modern idea that disease arose within and could be mapped directly by its course through the human body (McNay, 1994). This discursive shift changed medical practice. It gave greater importance to the doctor's 'gaze' which could now 'read' the course of disease simply by a powerful look at what Foucault called 'the visible body' of the patient – following the 'routes ... laid down in accordance with a now familiar geometry ... the anatomical atlas' (Foucault, 1973, pp. 3–4). This greater knowledge increased the doctor's power of surveillance vis-à-vis the patient.

Knowledge about and practices around *all* these subjects, Foucault argued, were historically and culturally specific. They did not and could not meaningfully exist outside specific discourses, i.e. outside the ways they were represented in discourse, produced in knowledge and regulated by the discursive practices and disciplinary techniques of a particular society and time. Far from accepting the trans-historical continuities of which historians are so fond, Foucault believed that more significant were the radical breaks, ruptures and discontinuities between one period and another, between one discursive formation and another.

4.3 From discourse to power/knowledge

In his later work Foucault became even more concerned with how knowledge was put to work through discursive practices in specific institutional settings to regulate the conduct of others. He focused on the relationship between knowledge and power, and how power operated within what he called an institutional *apparatus* and its *technologies* (techniques). Foucault's conception of the *apparatus* of punishment, for example, included a variety of diverse elements, linguistic and non-linguistic:

> discourses, institutions, architectural arrangements, regulations, laws, administrative measures, scientific statements, philosophic propositions, morality, philanthropy, etc. ... The apparatus is thus always inscribed in a play of power, but it is also always linked to certain co-ordinates of knowledge. ... This is what the apparatus consists in: strategies of relations of forces supporting and supported by types of knowledge (Foucault, 1980, pp. 194, 196).

This approach took as one of its key subjects of investigation the relations between knowledge, power and the body in modern society. It saw knowledge as always inextricably enmeshed in relations of power because it was always being applied to the regulation of social conduct in practice (i.e. to particular 'bodies'). This foregrounding of the relation between discourse, knowledge and power marked a significant development in the *constructionist* approach to representation which we have been outlining. It rescued representation from the clutches of a purely formal theory and gave it a historical, practical and 'worldly' context of operation.

You may wonder to what extent this concern with discourse, knowledge and power brought Foucault's interests closer to those of the classical sociological theories of ideology, especially Marxism with its concern to identify the class positions and class interests concealed within particular forms of knowledge. Foucault, indeed, does come closer to addressing some of these questions about ideology than, perhaps, formal semiotics did (though Roland Barthes was also concerned with questions of ideology and myth, as we saw earlier). But Foucault had quite specific and cogent reasons why he rejected the classical Marxist problematic of 'ideology'. Marx had argued that, in every epoch, ideas reflect the economic basis of society, and thus the 'ruling ideas' are those of the ruling class which governs a capitalist economy, and correspond to its dominant interests. Foucault's main argument against the classical Marxist theory of ideology was that it tended to reduce all the relations between knowledge and power to a question of *class* power and *class* interests. Foucault did not deny the existence of classes, but he was strongly opposed to this powerful element of economic or class *reductionism* in the Marxist theory of ideology. Secondly, he argued that Marxism tended to contrast the 'distortions' of bourgeois knowledge against its own claims to 'truth' – Marxist science. But Foucault did not believe that *any* form of thought could claim an absolute 'truth' of this kind, outside the play of discourse. *All* political and social forms of thought, he believed, were inevitably caught up in the interplay of knowledge and power. So, his work rejects the traditional Marxist question, 'in whose class interest does language, representation and power operate?'

Later theorists, like the Italian, Antonio Gramsci, who was influenced by Marx but rejected class reductionism, advanced a definition of 'ideology' which is considerably closer to Foucault's position, though still too preoccupied with class questions to be acceptable to him. Gramsci's notion was that particular social groups struggle in many different ways, including ideologically, to win the consent of other groups and achieve a kind of ascendancy in both thought and practice over them. This form of power Gramsci called **hegemony**. Hegemony is never permanent, and is not reducible to economic interests or to a simple class model of society. This has some similarities to Foucault's position, though on some key issues they differ radically. (The question of hegemony is briefly addressed again in Chapter 4.)

What distinguished Foucault's position on discourse, knowledge and power from the Marxist theory of class interests and ideological 'distortion'? Foucault advanced at least two, radically novel, propositions.

1 Knowledge, power and truth

The first concerns the way Foucault conceived the linkage between knowledge and power. Hitherto, we have tended to think that power operates in a direct and brutally repressive fashion, dispensing with polite things like culture and knowledge, though Gramsci certainly broke with that model of power. Foucault argued that not only is knowledge always a form of power, but power is implicated in the questions of whether and in what circumstances knowledge is to be applied or not. This question of the application and *effectiveness* of **power/knowledge** was more important, he thought, than the question of its 'truth'.

Knowledge linked to power not only assumes the authority of 'the truth', but has the power to *make itself true*. All knowledge, once applied in the real world, has real effects and, in that sense at least, 'becomes true'. Knowledge, once used to regulate the conduct of others, entails constraint, regulation and the disciplining of practices. Thus, 'There is no power relation without the correlative constitution of a field of knowledge, nor any knowledge that does not presuppose and constitute at the same time, power relations' (Foucault, 1977, p. 27).

According to Foucault, what we think we 'know' in a particular period about, say, crime, has a bearing on how we regulate, control and punish criminals. Knowledge does not operate in a void. It is put to work, through certain technologies and strategies of application, in specific situations, historical contexts and institutional regimes. To study punishment, you must study how the combination of discourse and power – power/knowledge – has produced a certain conception of crime and the criminal, has had certain real effects both for criminal and for the punisher, and how these have been set into practice in certain historically specific prison regimes.

This led Foucault to speak, not of the 'truth' of knowledge in the absolute sense – a truth which remained so, whatever the period, setting, context – but of a discursive formation sustaining a **regime of truth**. Thus, it may or may not be true that single parenting inevitably leads to delinquency and crime. But if everyone believes it to be so, and punishes single parents accordingly, this will have real consequences for both parents and children and will become 'true' in terms of its real effects, even if in some absolute sense it has never been conclusively proven. In the human and social sciences, Foucault argued:

> Truth isn't outside power. ... Truth is a thing of this world; it is produced only by virtue of multiple forms of constraint. And it induces regular effects of power. Each society has its regime of truth, its 'general politics' of truth; that is, the types of discourse which it accepts and makes function as true, the mechanisms and instances which enable one to distinguish true and false statements, the means by which each is sanctioned ... the status of those who are charged with saying what counts as true.

(Foucault, 1980, p. 131)

2 New conceptions of power

Secondly, Foucault advanced an altogether novel conception of power. We tend to think of power as always radiating in a single direction – from top to bottom – and coming from a specific source – the sovereign, the state, the ruling class and so on. For Foucault, however, power does not 'function in the form of a chain' – it circulates. It is never monopolized by one centre. It 'is deployed and exercised through a net-like organization' (Foucault, 1980, p. 98). This suggests that we are all, to some degree, caught up in its circulation – oppressors and oppressed. It does not radiate downwards, either from one source or from one place. Power relations permeate all levels of social existence and are therefore to be found operating at every site of social life – in the private spheres of the family and sexuality as much as in the public spheres of politics, the economy and the law. What's more, power is not only negative, repressing what it seeks to control. It is also *productive*. It 'doesn't only weigh on us as a force that says no, but ... it traverses and produces things, it induces pleasure, forms of knowledge, produces discourse. It needs to be thought of as a productive network which runs through the whole social body' (Foucault, 1980, p. 119).

The punishment system, for example, produces books, treatises, regulations, new strategies of control and resistance, debates in Parliament, conversations, confessions, legal briefs and appeals, training regimes for prison officers, and so on. The efforts to control sexuality produce a veritable explosion of discourse – talk about sex, television and radio programmes, sermons and legislation, novels, stories and magazine features, medical and counselling advice, essays and articles, learned theses and research programmes, as well as new sexual practices (e.g. 'safe' sex) and the pornography industry. Without denying that the state, the law, the sovereign or the dominant class may have positions of dominance, Foucault shifts our attention away from the grand, overall strategies of power, towards the many, localized circuits, tactics, mechanisms and effects through which power circulates – what Foucault calls the 'meticulous rituals' or the 'micro-physics' of power. These power relations 'go right down to the depth of society' (Foucault, 1977, p. 27). They connect the way power is actually working on the ground to the great pyramids of power by what he calls a capillary movement (capillaries being the thin-walled vessels that aid the exchange of oxygen between the blood in our bodies and the surrounding tissues). Not because power at these lower levels merely reflects or 'reproduces, at the level of individuals, bodies, gestures and behaviour, the general form of the law or government' (Foucault, 1977, p. 27) but, on the contrary, because such an approach 'roots [power] in forms of behaviour, bodies and local relations of power which should not at all be seen as a simple projection of the central power' (Foucault, 1980, p. 201).

To what object are the micro-physics of power primarily applied, in Foucault's model? To the body. He places the body at the centre of the struggles between different formations of power/knowledge. The techniques of regulation are applied to the body. Different discursive formations and apparatuses divide, classify and inscribe the body differently in their respective regimes of power and 'truth'. In *Discipline and Punish*, for example, Foucault analyses the very different ways in which the body of the criminal is 'produced' and disciplined in different punishment regimes in France. In earlier periods, punishment was haphazard, prisons were places into which the public could wander and the ultimate punishment was inscribed violently on the body by means of instruments of torture and execution, etc. – a practice the essence of which is that it should be public, visible to everyone. The modern form of disciplinary regulation and power, by contrast, is private, individualized; prisoners are shut away from the public and often from one another, though continually under surveillance from the authorities; and punishment is individualized. Here, the body has become the site of a new kind of disciplinary regime.

Of course this 'body' is not simply the natural body which all human beings possess at all times. This body is *produced* within discourse, according to the different discursive formations – the state of knowledge about crime and the criminal, what counts as 'true' about how to change or deter criminal behaviour, the specific apparatus and technologies of punishment prevailing at the time. This is a radically historicized conception of the body – a sort of surface on which different regimes of power/knowledge write their meanings and effects. It thinks of the body as 'totally imprinted by history and the processes of history's deconstruction of the body' (Foucault, 1977, p. 63).

4.4 Summary: Foucault and representation

Foucault's approach to representation is not easy to summarize. He is concerned with the production of knowledge and meaning through discourse. Foucault does indeed analyse particular texts and representations, as the semioticians did. But he is more inclined to analyse the whole *discursive formation* to which a text or a practice belongs. His concern is with knowledge provided by the human and social sciences, which organizes conduct, understanding, practice and belief, the regulation of bodies as well as whole populations. Although his work is clearly done in the wake of, and is profoundly influenced by, the 'turn to language' which marked the *constructionist* approach to representation, his definition of *discourse* is much broader than language, and includes many other elements of practice and institutional regulation which Saussure's approach, with its linguistic focus, excluded. Foucault is always much more historically specific, seeing forms of power/ knowledge as always rooted in particular contexts and histories. Above all, for Foucault, the production of knowledge is always crossed with questions of power and the body; and this greatly expands the scope of what is involved in representation.

The major critique levelled against his work is that he tends to absorb too much into 'discourse', and this has the effect of encouraging his followers to neglect the influence of the material, economic and structural factors in the operation of power/knowledge. Some critics also find his rejection of any criterion of 'truth' in the human sciences in favour of the idea of a 'regime of truth' and the will-to-power (the will to make things 'true') vulnerable to the charge of relativism. Nevertheless, there is little doubt about the major impact which his work has had on contemporary theories of representation and meaning.

4.5 Charcot and the performance of hysteria

In the following example, we will try to apply Foucault's method to a particular example. Figure 1.8 shows a painting by André Brouillet of the famous French psychiatrist and neurologist, Jean-Martin Charcot (1825–93), lecturing on the subject of female hysteria to students in the lecture theatre of his famous Paris clinic at La Salpêtriére.

ACTIVITY 7

Look at Brouillet's painting (Figure 1.8). What does it reveal as a representation of the study of hysteria?

Brouillet shows a hysterical patient being supported by an assistant and attended by two women. For many years, hysteria had been traditionally identified as a female malady and although Charcot demonstrated conclusively that many hysterical symptoms were to be found in men, and a significant proportion of his patients were diagnosed male hysterics, Elaine Showalter observes that 'for Charcot, too, hysteria remains symbolically, if not medically, a female malady' (1987, p. 148). Charcot was a very humane man who took his patients' suffering seriously and treated them with dignity. He diagnosed hysteria as a genuine ailment rather than a malingerer's excuse (much as has happened, in our time, after many struggles, with other illnesses, like anorexia and ME). This painting represents a regular feature of Charcot's treatment regime, where hysterical female patients displayed before an audience of medical staff and students the symptoms of their malady, ending often with a full hysterical seizure.

The painting could be said to capture and represent, visually, a discursive 'event' – the emergence of a new regime of knowledge. Charcot's great distinction, which drew students from far and wide to study with him (including, in 1885, the young Sigmund Freud from Vienna), was his demonstration 'that hysterical symptoms such as paralysis could be produced and relieved

FIGURE 1.8   André Brouillet, *A Clinical Lesson at La Salpêtriére* (given by Charcot), 1887

by hypnotic suggestion' (Showalter, 1987, p. 148). Here we see the practice of hypnosis being applied in practice.

Indeed, the image seems to capture *two* such moments of knowledge production. Charcot did not pay much attention to what the patients said (though he observed their actions and gestures meticulously). But Freud and his friend Breuer did. At first, in their work when they returned home, they used Charcot's hypnosis method, which had attracted such wide attention as a novel approach to treatment of hysteria at La Salpêtriére. But some years later they treated a young woman called Bertha Pappenheim for hysteria, and she, under the pseudonym 'Anna O', became the first case study written up in Freud and Breuer's path-breaking *Studies in Hysteria* (1974/1895). It was the 'loss of words', her failing grasp of the syntax of her own language (German), the silences and meaningless babble of this brilliantly intellectual, poetic and imaginative but rebellious young woman, which gave Breuer and Freud the first clue that her linguistic disturbance was related to her resentment at her 'place' as dutiful daughter of a decidedly patriarchal father, and thus deeply connected with her illness. After hypnosis, her capacity to speak coherently returned, and she spoke fluently in three other languages, though not in her native German. Through her dialogue with Breuer, and her ability to 'work through' her difficult relationship in relation to language, 'Anna O' gave the first example of the 'talking cure' which, of course, then provided the whole basis for Freud's subsequent development of the psycho-analytic method. So we are looking, in this image, at the 'birth' of two new psychiatric *epistemes*: Charcot's method of hypnosis and the conditions which later produced psychoanalysis.

The example also has many connections with the question of *representation*. In the picture, the patient is performing or 'representing' with her body the hysterical symptoms from which she is 'suffering'. But these symptoms are also being 're-presented' – in the very different medical language of diagnosis and analysis – to her (his?) audience by the professor: a relationship which involves *power*. Showalter notes that, in general, 'the representation of female hysteria was a central aspect of Charcot's work' (1987, p. 148). Indeed, the clinic was filled with lithographs and paintings. He had his assistants assemble a photographic album of nervous patients, a sort of visual inventory of the various 'types' of hysterical patient. He later employed a professional photographer to take charge of the service. His analysis of the displayed symptoms, which seems to be what is happening in the painting, accompanied the hysterical 'performance'. He did not flinch from the spectacular and theatrical aspects associated with his demonstrations of hypnosis as a treatment regime. Freud thought that 'Every one of his "fascinating lectures"' was 'a little work of art in construction and composition'. Indeed, Freud noted, 'he never appeared greater to his listeners than after he had made the effort, by giving the most detailed account of his train of thought, by the greatest frankness about his doubts and hesitations, to reduce the gulf between teacher and pupil' (Gay, 1988, p. 49).

ACTIVITY 8

Now look carefully at the picture again and, bearing in mind what we have said about Foucault's method of and approach to representation, answer the following questions:

1 Who commands the centre of the picture?

2 Who or what is its 'subject'? Are (1) and (2) the same?

3 Can you tell that knowledge is being produced here? How?

4 What do you notice about relations of power in the picture? How are they represented? How does the *form* and *spatial relationships* of the picture represent this?

5 Describe the 'gaze' of the people in the image: who is looking at whom? What does *that* tell us?

6 What does the age and gender of the participants tell us?

7 What message does the patient's body convey?

8 Is there a *sexual* meaning in the image? If so, what?

9 What is the relationship of you, the viewer, to the image?

10 Do you notice anything else about the image which we have missed?

READING F

Now read the account of Charcot and La Salpêtriére offered by Elaine Showalter in 'The performance of hysteria' from *The Female Malady*, reproduced as Reading F at the end of this chapter. Look carefully at the two photographs of Charcot's hysterical women patients. What do you make of their captions?

5 WHERE IS 'THE SUBJECT'?

We have traced the shift in Foucault's work from language to discourse and knowledge, and their relation to questions of power. But where in all this, you might ask, is the subject? Saussure tended to abolish the subject from the question of representation. Language, he argued, speaks us. The subject appears in Saussure's schema as the author of individual speech-acts (*paroles*). But, as we have seen, Saussure did not think that the level of the *paroles* was one at which a 'scientific' analysis of language could be conducted. In one sense, Foucault shares this position. For him, it is *discourse*, not the subject, which produces knowledge. Discourse is enmeshed with power, but it is not necessary to find 'a subject' – the king, the ruling class, the bourgeoisie, the state, etc. – for *power/knowledge* to operate.

On the other hand, Foucault *did* include the subject in his theorizing, though he did not restore the subject to its position as the centre and author of representation. Indeed, as his work developed, he became more and more concerned with questions about 'the subject', and in his very late and unfinished work, he even went so far as to give the subject a certain reflexive awareness of his or her own conduct, though this still stopped short of restoring the subject to his/her full sovereignty.

Foucault was certainly deeply critical of what we might call the traditional conception of the subject. The conventional notion thinks of 'the subject' as an individual who is fully endowed with consciousness; an autonomous and stable entity, the 'core' of the self, and the independent, authentic source of action and meaning. According to this conception, when we hear ourselves speak, we feel we are identical with what has been said. And this identity of the subject with what is said gives him/her a privileged position in relation to meaning. It suggests that, although other people may misunderstand us, *we* always understand ourselves because *we were the source of meaning in the first place*.

However, as we have seen, the shift towards a constructionist conception of language and representation did a great deal to displace the subject from a privileged position in relation to knowledge and meaning. The same is true of Foucault's discursive approach. It is discourse, not the subjects who speak it, which produces knowledge. Subjects may produce particular texts, but they are operating within the limits of the *episteme*, the *discursive formation*, the *regime of truth*, of a particular period and culture. Indeed, this is one of Foucault's most radical propositions: the 'subject' is *produced within discourse*. This subject *of* discourse cannot be outside discourse because it must be *subjected to* discourse. It must submit to its rules and conventions, to its dispositions of power/knowledge. The subject can become the bearer of the kind of knowledge which discourse produces. It can become the object through which power is relayed. But it cannot stand outside power/knowledge as its source and author. In 'The subject and power' (1982), Foucault writes that:

> My objective ... has been to create a history of the different modes by which, in our culture, human beings are made subjects. ... It is a form of power which makes individuals subjects. There are two meanings of the word *subject*: subject to someone else's control and dependence, and tied to his

39

[*sic*] own identity by a conscience and self-knowledge. Both meanings suggest a form of power which subjugates and makes subject to.

(Foucault, 1982, pp. 208, 212)

Making discourse and representation more historical has therefore been matched, in Foucault, by an equally radical historicization of *the subject*. 'One has to dispense with the constituent subject, to get rid of the subject itself, that's to say, to arrive at an analysis which can account for the constitution of the subject within a historical framework' (Foucault, 1980, p. 115).

Where, then, is 'the subject' in this more discursive approach to meaning, representation and power?

Foucault's 'subject' seems to be produced through discourse in *two* different senses or places. First, the discourse itself produces 'subjects' – figures who personify the particular forms of knowledge which the discourse produces. These subjects have the attributes we would expect as these are defined by the discourse: the madman, the hysterical woman, the homosexual, the individualized criminal, and so on. These figures are specific to specific discursive regimes and historical periods. But the discourse also produces a *place for the subject* (i.e. the reader or viewer, who is also 'subjected to' discourse) from which its particular knowledge and meaning most makes sense. It is not inevitable that all individuals in a particular period will become the subjects of a particular discourse in this sense, and thus the bearers of its power/knowledge. But for them – us – to do so, they – we – must locate themselves/ourselves in the *position* from which the discourse makes most sense, and thus become its 'subjects' by 'subjecting' ourselves to its meanings, power and regulation. All discourses, then, construct **subject-positions**, from which alone they make sense.

This approach has radical implications for a theory of representation. For it suggests that discourses themselves construct the subject-positions from which they become meaningful and have effects. Individuals may differ as to their social class, gender, 'racial' and ethnic characteristics (among other factors), but they will not be able to take meaning until they have identified with those positions which the discourse constructs, *subjected* themselves to its rules, and hence become the *subjects of its power/knowledge*. For example, pornography produced for men will only 'work' for women, according to this theory, if in some sense women put themselves in the position of the 'desiring male voyeur' – which is the ideal subject-position which the discourse of male pornography constructs – and look at the models from this 'masculine' discursive position. This may seem, and is, a highly contestable proposition. But let us consider an example which illustrates the argument.

5.1 How to make sense of Velasquez' *Las Meninas*

Foucault's *The Order of Things* (1970) opens with a discussion of a painting by the famous Spanish painter, Velasquez, called *Las Meninas*. It has been a topic of considerable scholarly debate and controversy. The reason I am using it here is because, as all the critics agree, the painting itself does raise certain questions about the nature of *representation*, and Foucault himself uses it to talk about these wider issues of the subject. It is these arguments which interest us here, not the question of whether

Foucault's is the 'true', correct or even the definitive reading of the painting's meaning. That the painting has no one, fixed or final meaning is, indeed, one of Foucault's most powerful arguments.

The painting is unique in Velasquez' work. It was part of the Spanish court's royal collection and hung in the palace in a room which was subsequently destroyed by fire. It was dated '1656' by Velasquez' successor as court painter. It was originally called 'The Empress with her Ladies and a Dwarf', but by the inventory of 1666, it had acquired the title of 'A Portrait of the Infanta of Spain with her Ladies in Waiting and Servants, by the Court Painter and Palace Chamberlain Diego Velasquez'. It was subsequently called *Las Meninas* – 'The Maids of Honour'. Some argue that the painting shows Velasquez working on *Las Meninas* itself and was painted with the aid of a mirror – but this now seems unlikely. The most widely held and convincing explanation is that Velasquez was working on a full-length portrait of the King and Queen, and that it is the royal couple who are reflected in the mirror on the back wall. It is at the couple that the princess and her attendants are looking and on them that the artist's gaze appears to rest as he steps back from his canvas. The reflection artfully includes the royal couple in the picture. This is essentially the account which Foucault accepts.

ACTIVITY 9
Look at the picture carefully, while we summarize Foucault's argument.

FIGURE 1.9 Diego Velasquez, *Las Meninas*, 1656

Las Meninas shows the interior of a room – perhaps the painter's studio or some other room in the Spanish Royal Palace, the Escorial. The scene, though in its deeper recesses rather dark, is bathed in light from a window on the right. 'We are looking at a picture in which the painter is in turn looking out at us,' says Foucault (1970, p. 4). To the left, looking forwards, is the painter himself, Velasquez. He is in the act of painting and his brush is raised, 'perhaps ... considering whether to add some finishing touch to the canvas' (p. 3). He is looking at his model, who is sitting in the place from which we are looking, but we cannot see who the model is because the canvas on which Velasquez is painting has its back to us, its face resolutely turned away from our gaze. In the centre of the painting stands what tradition recognizes as the little princess, the Infanta Maragarita, who has come to watch the proceedings. She is the centre of the picture we are looking at, but she is not the 'subject' of Velasquez' canvas. The Infanta has with her an 'entourage of duennas, maids of honour, courtiers and dwarfs' and her dog (p. 9). The courtiers stand behind, towards the back on the right. Her maids of honour stand on either side of her, framing her. To the right at the front are two dwarfs, one a famous court jester. The eyes of many of these figures, like that of the painter himself, are looking out towards the front of the picture at the sitters.

Who are they – the figures at whom everyone is looking but whom we cannot look at and whose portraits on the canvas we are forbidden to see? In fact, though at first we think we cannot see them, the picture tells us who they are because, behind the Infanta's head and a little to the left of the centre of the picture, surrounded by a heavy wooden frame, is a mirror; and in the mirror – at last – are reflected the sitters, who are in fact seated *in the position from which we are looking*: 'a reflection that shows us quite simply what is lacking in everyone's gaze' (p. 15). The figures reflected in the mirror are, in fact, the King, Philip IV, and his wife, Mariana. Beside the mirror, to the right of it, in the back wall, is another 'frame', but this is not a mirror reflecting forwards; it is a doorway leading *backwards* out of the room. On the stair, his feet placed on different steps, 'a man stands out in full-length silhouette'. He has just entered or is just leaving the scene and is looking at it from behind, observing what is going on in it but 'content to surprise those within without being seen himself' (p. 10).

5.2 The subject of/in representation

Who or what is *the subject* of this painting? In his comments, Foucault uses *Las Meninas* to make some general points about his theory of representation and specifically about the role of the subject:

1 'Foucault reads the painting in terms of representation and the subject' (Dreyfus and Rabinow, 1982, p. 20). As well as being a painting which shows us (represents) a scene in which a portrait of the King and Queen of Spain is being painted, it is also a painting which *tells us something about how representation and the subject work*. It produces its own kind of knowledge. Representation and the subject are the painting's underlying message – what it is about, its sub-text.

2   Clearly, representation here is *not* about a 'true' reflection or imitation of reality. Of course, the people in the painting 'may look like' the actual people in the Spanish court. But the discourse of painting in the picture is doing a great deal more than simply trying to mirror accurately what exists.

3   Everything in a sense is *visible* in the painting. And yet, what it is 'about' – its meaning – depends on how we 'read' it. *It is as much constructed around what you can't see as what you can.* You can't see what is being painted on the canvas, though this seems to be the point of the whole exercise. You can't see what everyone is looking at, which is the sitters, unless we assume it is a reflection of them in the mirror. They are both in and not in the picture. Or rather, they are present through a kind of substitution. We cannot see them because they are not directly represented: but their 'absence' is represented – *mirrored* through their reflection in the mirror at the back. The meaning of the picture is produced, Foucault argues, through this complex inter-play between *presence* (what you see, the visible) and *absence* (what you can't see, what has displaced it within the frame). Representation works as much through what is *not* shown, as through what is.

4   In fact, a number of substitutions or displacements seem to be going on here. For example, the 'subject' and centre of the painting we are looking at seems to be the Infanta. But the 'subject' or centre is also, of course, the sitters – the King and Queen – whom we can't see but whom the others are looking at. You can tell this from the fact that the mirror on the wall in which the King and Queen are reflected is also almost exactly at the centre of the field of vision of the picture. So the Infanta and the royal couple, in a sense, share the place of the centre as the principal 'subjects' of the painting. It all depends on where you are looking from – in towards the scene from where you, the spectator, is sitting or outwards from the scene, from the position of the people in the picture. If you accept Foucault's argument, then there are *two* subjects to the painting and *two* centres. And the composition of the picture – its discourse – forces us to oscillate between these two 'subjects' without ever finally deciding with which one to identify. Representation in the painting seems firm and clear – everything in place. But our vision, the way we *look* at the picture, oscillates between two centres, two subjects, two positions of looking, two meanings. Far from being finally resolved into some absolute truth which is *the* meaning of the picture, the discourse of the painting quite deliberately keeps us in this state of suspended attention, in this oscillating process of looking. Its meaning is always in the process of emerging, yet any final meaning is constantly deferred.

5   You can tell a great deal about how the picture works as a discourse, and what it means, by following the orchestration of *looking* – who is looking at what or whom. *Our* look – the eyes of the person looking at the picture, the spectator – follows the relationships of looking as represented in the picture. We know the figure of the Infanta is important because her attendants are looking at her. But we know that someone even more important is sitting in front of the scene, whom we can't see, because many figures – the Infanta, the jester, the painter himself – are looking at them! So the spectator (who is also 'subjected' to the discourse of the painting) is doing two kinds of looking. Looking at the scene from the position outside, in front of, the picture. And at the same time, looking out of the scene, by *identifying with* the looking being done by the figures in the painting.

Projecting ourselves into the subjects of the painting help us as spectators to see, to 'make sense' of it. We take up the positions indicated by the discourse, identify with them, subject ourselves to its meanings, and become its 'subjects'.

6   It is critical for Foucault's argument that the painting does not have a completed meaning. It only means something in relation to the spectator who is looking at it. The spectator completes the meaning of the picture. Meaning is therefore constructed in the dialogue between the painting and the spectator. Velasquez, of course, could not know who would subsequently occupy the position of the spectator. Nevertheless, the whole 'scene' of the painting had to be laid out in relation to that ideal point in front of the painting from which *any* spectator must look if the painting is to make sense. The spectator, we might say, is painted into position in front of the picture. In this sense, the discourse produces a *subject-position* for the spectator-subject. For the painting to work, the spectator, whoever he or she may be, must first 'subject' himself/herself to the painting's discourse and, in this way, become the painting's ideal viewer, the producer of its meanings – its 'subject'. This is what is meant by saying that the discourse constructs the spectator as a subject – by which we mean that it constructs a place for the subject-spectator who is looking at and making sense of it.

7   Representation therefore occurs from at least three positions in the painting. First of all there is us, the spectator, whose 'look' puts together and unifies the different elements and relationships in the picture into an overall meaning. This subject must be there for the painting to make sense, but he/she is not represented in the painting. Then there is the painter who painted the scene. He is 'present' in two places at once, since he must at one time have been standing where we are now sitting, in order to paint the scene, but he has then put himself into (represented himself in) the picture, looking back towards that point of view where we, the spectator, have taken his place. We may also say that the scene makes sense and is pulled together in relation to the court figure standing on the stair at the back, since he too surveys it all but – like us and like the painter – from somewhat outside it.

8   Finally, consider the mirror on the back wall. If it were a 'real' mirror, it should now be representing or reflecting *us*, since we are standing in that position in front of the scene to which everyone is looking and from which everything makes sense. But it does not mirror us, it shows *in our place* the King and Queen of Spain. Somehow the discourse of the painting positions us in the place of the Sovereign! You can imagine what fun Foucault had with this substitution.

Foucault argues that it is clear from the way the discourse of representation works in the painting that it *must* be looked at and made sense of from that one subject-position in front of it from which we, the spectators, are looking. This is also the point-of-view from which a camera would have to be positioned in order to film the scene. And, lo and behold, the person whom Velasquez chooses to 'represent' sitting in this position is the Sovereign – 'master of all he surveys' – who is both the 'subject of' the painting (what it is about) and the 'subject in' the painting – the one whom the discourse sets in place, but who, simultaneously, makes sense of it and understands it all by a look of supreme mastery.

6 CONCLUSION: REPRESENTATION, MEANING AND LANGUAGE RECONSIDERED

We started with a fairly simple definition of representation. Representation is the process by which members of a culture use language (broadly defined as any system which deploys signs, any signifying system) to produce meaning. Already, this definition carries the important premise that things – objects, people, events in the world – do not have in themselves any fixed, final or true meaning. It is us – in society, within human cultures – who make things mean, who signify. Meanings, consequently, will always change, from one culture or period to another. There is no guarantee that every object in one culture will have an equivalent meaning in another, precisely because cultures differ, sometimes radically, from one another in their codes – the ways they carve up, classify and assign meaning to the world. So one important idea about representation is the acceptance of a degree of *cultural relativism* between one culture and another, a certain lack of equivalence, and hence the need for *translation* as we move from the mind-set or conceptual universe of one culture or another.

We call this the *constructionist* approach to representation, contrasting it with both the *reflective* and the *intentional* approaches. Now, if culture is a process, a practice, how does it work? In the *constructionist perspective*, representation involves making meaning by forging links between three different orders of things: what we might broadly call the world of things, people, events and experiences; the conceptual world – the mental concepts we carry around in our heads; and the signs, arranged into languages, which 'stand for' or communicate these concepts. Now, if you have to make a link between systems which are not the same, and fix these at least for a time so that other people know what, in one system, corresponds to what in another system, then there must be something which allows us to translate between them – telling us what word to use for what concept, and so on. Hence the notion of *codes*.

Producing meaning depends on the practice of interpretation, and interpretation is sustained by us actively using the code – *encoding*, putting things into the code – and by the person at the other end interpreting or *decoding* the meaning (Hall, 1980). But note that, because meanings are always changing and slipping, codes operate more like social conventions than like fixed laws or unbreakable rules. As meanings shift and slide, so inevitably the codes of a culture imperceptibly change. The great advantage of the concepts and classifications of the culture which we carry around with us in our heads is that they enable us to *think* about things, whether they are there, present, or not; indeed, whether they ever existed or not. There are concepts for our fantasies, desires and imaginings as well as for so-called 'real' objects in the material world. And the advantage of language is that our thoughts about the world need not remain exclusive to us, and silent. We can translate them into language, make them 'speak', through the use of signs which stand for them – and thus talk, write, communicate about them to others.

Gradually, then, we complexified what we meant by representation. It came to be less and less the straightforward thing we assumed it to be at first – which is why we need *theories* to explain it. We looked at two versions of constructionism – that which concentrated on how *language* and *signification* (the use of signs in language) works to produce *meanings*, which after Saussure and Barthes we called *semiotics*; and that, following Foucault, which concentrated on how *discourse* and *discursive practices* produce knowledge. I won't run through the finer points in these two approaches again, since you can go back to them in the main body of the chapter and refresh your memory. In semiotics, you will recall the importance of *signifier/signified*, *langue/parole* and 'myth', and how the marking of difference and binary oppositions are crucial for meaning. In the *discursive* approach, you will recall discursive formations, power/knowledge, the idea of a 'regime of truth', the way discourse also produces the subject and defines the *subject-positions* from which knowledge proceeds and, indeed, the return of questions about 'the subject' to the field of representation. In several examples, we tried to get you to work with these theories and to apply them. There will be further debate about them in subsequent chapters.

Notice that the chapter does *not* argue that the *discursive* approach overturned everything in the *semiotic* approach. Theoretical development does not usually proceed in this linear way. There was much to learn from Saussure and Barthes, and we are still discovering ways of fruitfully applying their insights – without necessarily swallowing everything they said. We offered you some critical thoughts on the subject. There is a great deal to learn from Foucault and the *discursive* approach, but by no means everything it claims is correct and the theory is open to, and has attracted, many criticisms. Again, in later chapters, as we encounter further developments in the theory of representation, and see the strengths and weaknesses of these positions applied in practice, we will come to appreciate more fully that we are only at the beginning of the exciting task of exploring this process of meaning construction, which is at the heart of culture, to its full depths. What we have offered here is, we hope, a relatively clear account of a set of complex, and as yet tentative, ideas in an unfinished project.

REFERENCES

BARTHES, R. (1967) *The Elements of Semiology*, London, Cape.

BARTHES, R. (1972) *Mythologies*, London, Cape.

BARTHES, R. (1975) *The Pleasure of the Text*, New York, Hall & Wang.

BARTHES, R. (1977) *Image-Music-Text*, Glasgow, Fontana.

BRYSON, N. (1990) *Looking at the Overlooked: Four Essays on Still Life Painting*, London, Reaktion Books.

COUSINS, M. AND HUSSAIN, A. (1984) *Michel Foucault*, Basingstoke, Macmillan.

CULLER, J. (1976) *Saussure*, London, Fontana.

DERRIDA, J. (1981) *Positions*, Chicago, IL, University of Chicago Press.

DREYFUS, H. AND RABINOW, P. (eds) (1982) *Beyond Structuralism and Hermeneutics*, Brighton, Harvester.

DU GAY, P. (ed.) (1997) *Production of Culture/Cultures of Production*, London, Sage/The Open University (Book 4 in this series).

DU GAY, P., HALL, S., JANES, L., MACKAY, H. AND NEGUS, K. (1997) *Doing Cultural Studies: The Story of the Sony Walkman*, London, Sage/The Open University (Book 1 in this series).

FOUCAULT, M. (1970) *The Order of Things*, London, Tavistock.

FOUCAULT, M. (1972) *The Archaeology of Knowledge*, London, Tavistock.

FOUCAULT, M. (1973) *The Birth of the Clinic*, London, Tavistock.

FOUCAULT, M. (1977) *Discipline and Punish*, London, Tavistock.

FOUCAULT, M. (1978) *The History of Sexuality*, Harmondsworth, Allen Lane/Penguin.

FOUCAULT, M. (1980) *Power/Knowledge*, Brighton, Harvester.

FOUCAULT, M. (1982) 'The subject and power', in Dreyfus and Rabinow (eds), *Beyond Structuralism and Hermeneutics*, Brighton, Harvester.

FREUD, S. AND BREUER, J. (1974) *Studies on Hysteria*, Harmondsworth, Pelican. First published 1895.

GAY, P. (1988) *Freud: A Life for Our Time*, London, Macmillan.

HALL, S. (1980) 'Encoding and decoding', in Hall, S., Hobson, D., Lowe, A. and Willis, P. (eds), *Culture, Media, Language*, London, Hutchinson.

HALL, S. (1992) 'The West and the Rest', in Hall, S. and Gieben, B. (eds), *Formations of Modernity*, Cambridge, Polity Press/The Open University.

HOEG, P. (1994) *Miss Smilla's Feeling For Snow*, London, Flamingo.

LACLAU, E. AND MOUFFE, C. (1990) 'Post-Marxism without apologies', in Laclau, E (ed.), *New Reflections on the Revolution of Our Time*, London, Verso.

MACKAY, H. (ed.) (1997) *Consumption and Everyday Life*, London, Sage/The Open University (Book 5 in this series).

MCNAY, L. (1994) *Foucault: A Critical Introduction*, Cambridge, Polity Press.

SAUSSURE, F. DE (1960) *Course in General Linguistics*, London, Peter Owen.

SHOWALTER, E. (1987) *The Female Malady*, London, Virago.

WEEKS, J. (1981) *Sex, Politics and Society*, London, Longman.

WEEKS, J. (1985) *Sexuality and its Discontents*, London, Routledge.

READING A: Norman Bryson, 'Language, reflection and still life'

With Cotán, too, the images have as their immediate function the separation of the viewer from the previous mode of seeing [...]: they decondition the habitual and abolish the endless eclipsing and fatigue of worldly vision, replacing these with brilliance. The enemy is a mode of seeing which thinks it knows in advance what is worth looking at and what is not: against that, the image presents the constant surprise of things seen for the first time. Sight is taken back to a [primal] stage before it learned how to scotomise [break up/divide] the visual field, how to screen out the unimportant and not see, but scan. In place of the abbreviated forms for which the world scans, Cotán supplies forms that are articulated at immense length, forms so copious or prolix that one cannot see where or how to begin to simplify them. They offer no inroads for reduction because they omit nothing. Just at the point where the eye thinks it knows the form and can afford to skip, the image proves that in fact the eye had not understood at all what it was about to discard.

The relation proposed in Cotán between the viewer and the foodstuffs so meticulously displayed seems to involve, paradoxically, no reference to appetite or to the function of sustenance which becomes coincidental; it might be described as anorexic, taking this word in its literal and Greek sense as meaning 'without desire'. All Cotán's still lifes are rooted in the outlook of monasticism, specifically the monasticism of the Carthusians [monks], whose order Cotán joined as a lay brother in Toledo in 1603. What distinguishes the Carthusian rule is its stress on solitude over communal life: the monks live in individual cells, where they pray, study – and eat – alone, meeting only for the night office, morning mass and afternoon vespers. There is total abstention from meat, and on Fridays and other fast days the diet is bread and water. Absent from Cotán's work is any conception of nourishment as involving the conviviality of the meal – the sharing of hospitality [...]. The unvarying stage of his paintings is never the kitchen but always the *cantarero*, a cooling-space where for preservation the foods are often hung on strings (piled together, or in contact with a surface, they would decay more quickly). Placed in a kitchen, next to plates and knives, bowls and pitchers, the objects would inevitably point towards their consumption at table, but the *cantarero* maintains the idea of the objects as separable from, dissociated horn, their function as food. In *Quince, Cabbage, Melon and Cucumber* [Figure 1.3] no-one can touch the suspended quince or cabbage without disturbing them and setting them rocking in space: their motionlessness is the mark of human absence, distance from the hand that reaches to eat; and it renders them immaculate. Hanging on strings, the quince and the cabbage lack the weight known to the hand. Their weightlessness disowns such intimate knowledge. Having none of the familiarity that comes from touch, and divorced from the idea of consumption, the objects take on a value that is nothing to do with their role as nourishment.

What replaces their interest as sustenance is their interest as mathematical form. Like many painters of his period in Spain, Cotán has a highly developed sense of geometrical order;

but whereas the ideas of sphere, ellipse and cone are used for example in El Greco to assist in organising pictorial composition, here they are explored almost for their own sake. One can think of *Quince, Cabbage, Melon and Cucumber* as an experiment in the kind of transformations that are explored in the branch of mathematics know as topology. We begin on the left with the quince, a pure sphere revolving on its axis. Moving to the right, the sphere seems to peel off its boundary and disintegrate into a ball of concentric shells revolving around the same vertical axis. Moving to the melon the sphere becomes an ellipse, from which a segment has been cut; a part of the segment is independently shown. At the right the segmented shapes recover their continuous boundary in the corrugated form of the cucumber. The curve described by all these objects taken together is not at all informal but precisely logarithmic; it follows a series of harmonic or musical proportions with the vertical co-ordinates of the curve exactly marked by the strings. And it is a complex curve, not just the arc of a graph on a two-dimensional surface. In relation to the quince, the cabbage appears to come forward slightly; the melon is further forward than the quince, the melon slice projects out beyond the ledge, and the cucumber overhangs it still further. The arc is therefore not on the same plane as its co-ordinates, it curves in three dimensions: it is a true hyperbola [...].

The mathematical engagement of these forms shows every sign of exact calculation, as though the scene were being viewed with scientific, but not with creaturely, interest. Geometric space replaces creatural space, the space around the body that is known by touch and is created by familiar movements of the hands and arms. Cotán's play with geometric and volumetric ideas replaces this cocoon-like space, defined by habitual gestures, with an abstracted and homogeneous space which has broken with the matrix of the body. This is the point: to suppress the body as a source of space. That bodily or tactile space is profoundly unvisual: the things we find there are things we reach for – a knife, a plate, a bit of food – instinctively and almost without looking. It is this space, the true home of blurred and hazy vision, that Cotán's rigours aim to abolish. And the tendency to geometrise fulfils another aim, no less severe: to disavow the painter's work as the source of the composition and to re-assign responsibility for its forms elsewhere – to mathematics, not creativity. In much of still life, the painter first arrays the objects into a satisfactory configuration, and then uses that arrangement as the basis for the composition. But to organise the world pictorially in this fashion is to impose upon it an order that is infinitely inferior to the order already revealed to the soul through the contemplation of geometric form: Cotán's renunciation of composition is a further, private act of self-negation. He approaches painting in terms of a discipline, or ritual: always the same *cantarero*, which one must assume has been painted in first, as a blank template; always the same recurring elements, the light raking at forty-five degrees, the same alternation of bright greens and yellows against the grey ground, the same scale, the same size of frame. To alter any of these would be to allow too much room for personal self-assertion, and the pride of creativity; down to its last details the painting must be presented as the result of discovery, not invention, a picture of the work of God that completely effaces the hand of man (in Cotán visible brushwork would be like blasphemy).

Source: Bryson, 1990, pp. 65–70.

READING B: Roland Barthes, 'The world of wrestling'

[T]he function of the wrestler is not to win; it is to go exactly through the motions which are expected of him. It is said that judo contains a hidden symbolic aspect; even in the midst of efficiency, its gestures are measured, precise but restricted, drawn accurately but by a stroke without volume. Wrestling, on the contrary, offers excessive gestures, exploited to the limit of their meaning. In judo, a man who is down is hardly down at all, he rolls over, he draws back, he eludes defeat, or, if the latter is obvious, he immediately disappears; in wrestling, a man who is down is exaggeratedly so, and completely fills the eyes of the spectators with the intolerable spectacle of his powerlessness.

This function of grandiloquence is indeed the same as that of ancient theatre, whose principle, language and props (masks and buskins) concurred in the exaggeratedly visible [...]. The gesture of the vanquished wrestler [signifies] to the world a defeat which, far from disguising, he emphasizes and holds like a pause in music [...]. [This is] meant to signify the tragic mode of the spectacle. In wrestling, as on the stage in antiquity, one is not ashamed of one's suffering, one knows how to cry, one has a liking for tears.

Each sign in wrestling is therefore endowed with an absolute clarity, since one must always understand everything on the spot. As soon as the adversaries are in the ring, the public is overwhelmed with the obviousness of the roles. As in the theatre, each physical type expresses to excess the part which has been assigned to the contestant. Thauvin, a fifty-year-old with an obese and sagging body, whose type of asexual hideousness always inspires feminine nicknames, displays in his flesh the characters of baseness ... [H]is part is to represent what, in the classical concept of the *salaud*, the 'bastard' (the key-concept of any wrestling-match), appears as organically repugnant. The nausea voluntarily provoked by Thauvin shows therefore a very extended use of signs: not only is ugliness used here in order to signify baseness, but in addition ugliness is wholly gathered into a particularly repulsive quality of matter: the pallid collapse of dead flesh (the public calls Thauvin la barbeque, 'stinking meat'), so that the passionate condemnation of the crowd no longer stems from its judgement, but instead from the very depth of its humours. It will thereafter let itself be frenetically embroiled in an idea of Thauvin which will conform entirely with this physical origin: his actions will perfectly correspond to the essential viscosity of his personage.

It is therefore in the body of the wrestler that we find the first key to the contest. I know from the start that all of Thauvin's actions, his treacheries, cruelties and acts of cowardice, will not fail to measure up to the first image of ignobility he gave me; I can trust him to carry out intelligently and to the last detail all the gestures of a kind of amorphous baseness, and thus fill to the brim the image of the most repugnant bastard there is: the bastard-octopus. Wrestlers therefore have a physique as peremptory as those of the characters of the *Commedia dell'Arte*, who display in advance, in their costumes and attitudes, the future contents of their parts: just as Pantaloon can never be anything but a ridiculous cuckold, Harlequin an astute servant and the Doctor a stupid pedant, in the same way Thauvin will never be anything but an ignoble traitor, Reinères (a tall blond fellow with a limp body and unkempt hair) the moving image of passivity, Mazaud (short and arrogant like a cock) that of grotesque conceit, and Orsano (an effeminate teddy-boy first seen in a blue-and-pink dressing-gown) that, doubly humorous, of a vindictive *salope*, of bitch (for I do not think that the public of the Elysée-Montmartre, like Littré, believes the word *salope* to be a masculine).

The physique of the wrestlers therefore constitutes a basic sign, which like a seed contains the whole fight. But this seed proliferates, for it is at every turn during the fight, in each new situation, that the body of the wrestler casts to the public the magical entertainment of a temperament which finds its natural expression in a gesture. The different strata of meaning throw light on each other, and form the most intelligible of spectacles. Wrestling is like a diacritic writing: above the fundamental meaning of his body, the wrestler arranges comments which are episodic but always opportune, and constantly help the reading of the fight by means of gestures, attitudes and mimicry which make the intention utterly obvious. Sometimes the wrestler triumphs with a repulsive sneer while kneeling on the good sportsman; sometimes he gives the crowd a conceited smile which forebodes an early revenge; sometimes, pinned to the ground, he hits the floor ostentatiously to make evident to all the intolerable nature of his situation; and sometimes he erects a complicated set of signs meant to make the public understand that he legitimately personifies the ever-entertaining image of the grumbler, endlessly confabulating about his displeasure.

We are therefore dealing with a real Human Comedy, where the most socially-inspired nuances of passion (conceit, rightfulness, refined cruelty, a sense of 'paying one's debts') always felicitously find the clearest sign which can receive them, express them and triumphantly carry them to the confines of the hall. It is obvious that at such a pitch, it no longer matters whether the passion is genuine or not. What the public wants is the image of passion, not passion itself. There is no more a problem of truth in wrestling than in the theatre. In both, what is expected is the intelligible representation of moral situations which are usually private. This emptying out of interiority to the benefit of its exterior signs, this exhaustion of the content by the form, is the very principle of triumphant classical art. [...]

Source: Barthes, 1972, pp. 16–18.

READING C: Roland Barthes, 'Myth today'

In myth, we find again the tri-dimensional pattern which I have just described: the signifier, the signified and the sign. But myth is a peculiar system, in that it is constructed from a semiological chain which existed before it: it *is a second-order semiological system*. That which is a sign (namely the associative total of a concept and an image) in the first system, becomes a mere signifier in the second. We must here recall that the materials of mythical speech (the language itself, photography, painting, posters, rituals, objects, etc.), however different at the start, are reduced to a pure signifying function as soon as they are caught by myth. Myth sees in them only the same raw material; their unity is that they all come down to the status of a mere language. Whether it deals with alphabetical or pictorial writing, myth wants to see in them only a sum of signs, a global sign, the final term of a first semiological chain. And it is precisely this final term which will become the first term of the greater system which it builds and of which it is only a part. Everything happens as if myth shifted the formal system of the first significations sideways. As this lateral shift is essential for the analysis of myth, I shall represent it in the following way, it being understood, of course, that the spatialization of the pattern is here only a metaphor:

It can be seen that in myth there are two semiological systems, one of which is staggered in relation to the other: a linguistic system, the language (or the modes of representation which are assimilated to it), which I shall call the *language-object*, because it is the language which myth gets hold of in order to build its own system; and myth itself, which I shall call *metalanguage*, because it is a second language, *in which* one speaks about the first. When he reflects on a metalanguage, the semiologist no longer needs to ask himself questions about the composition of the language-object, he no longer has to take into account the details of the linguistic schema; he will only need to know its total term, or global sign, and only inasmuch as this term lends itself to myth. This is why the semiologist is entitled to treat in the same way writing and pictures: what he retains from them is the fact that they are both *signs*, that they both reach the threshold of myth endowed with the same signifying function, that they constitute one just as much as the other, a language-object.

Source: Barthes, 1972, pp. 114–15.

READING D: Roland Barthes, 'Rhetoric of the image'

Here we have a Panzani advertisement: some packets of pasta, a tin, a sachet, some tomatoes, onions, peppers, a mushroom, all emerging from a half-open string bag, in yellows and greens on a red background. Let us try to 'skim off' the different messages it contains.

The image immediately yields a first message whose substance is linguistic; its supports are the caption, which is marginal, and the labels, these being inserted into the natural disposition of the scene [...]. The code from which this message has been taken is none other than that of the French language; the only knowledge required to decipher it is a knowledge of writing and French. In fact, this message can itself be further broken down, for the sign *Panzani* gives not simply the name of the firm but also, by its assonance, an additional signified, that of 'Italianicity'. The linguistic message is thus twofold (at least in this particular image): denotational and connotational. Since, however, we have here only a single typical sign, namely that of articulated (written) language, it will be counted as one message.

Putting aside the linguistic message, we are left with the pure image (even if the labels are part of it, anecdotally). This image straightaway provides a series of discontinuous signs. First (the order is unimportant as these signs are not linear), the idea that what we have in the scene represented is a return from the market. A signified which itself implies two euphoric values: that of the freshness of the products and that of the essentially domestic preparation for which

they are destined. Its signifier is the half-open bag which lets the provisions spill out over the table, 'unpacked'. To read this first sign requires only a knowledge which is in some sort implanted as part of the habits of a very widespread culture where 'shopping around for oneself is opposed to the hasty stocking up (preserves, refrigerators) of a more 'mechanical' civilization. A second sign is more or less equally evident; its signifier is the bringing together of the tomato, the pepper and the tri-coloured hues (yellow, green, red) of the poster; its signified is Italy or rather *Italianicity.* This sign stands in a relation of redundancy with the connoted sign of the linguistic message (the Italian assonance of the name *Panzani*) and the knowledge it draws upon is already more particular; it is a specifically 'French' knowledge (an Italian would barely perceive the connotation of the name, no more probably than he would the Italianicity of tomato and pepper), based on a familiarity with certain tourist stereotypes. Continuing to explore the image (which is not to say that it is not entirely clear at the first glance), there is no difficulty in discovering at least two other signs: in the first, the serried collection of different objects transmits the idea of a total culinary service, on the one hand as though Panzani furnished everything necessary for a carefully balanced dish and on the other as though the concentrate in the tin were equivalent to the natural produce surrounding it; in the other sign, the composition of the image, evoking the memory of innumerable alimentary paintings, sends us to an aesthetic signified: the '*nature morte*' or, as it is better expressed in other languages, the 'still life'; the knowledge on which this sign depends is heavily cultural. [...]

Source: Barthes, 1977, pp. 33–5.

READING E: Ernesto Laclau and Chantal Mouffe, *New Reflections on the Revolution of Our Time*

DISCOURSE

Let us suppose that I am building a wall with another bricklayer. At a certain moment I ask my workmate to pass me a brick and then I add it to the wall. The first act – asking for the brick – is linguistic; the second – adding the brick to the wall – is extralinguistic. Do I exhaust the reality of both acts by drawing the distinction between them in terms of the linguistic/extra-linguistic opposition? Evidently not, because, despite their differentiation in those terms, the two actions share something that allows them to be compared, namely the fact that they are both part of a total operation which is the building of the wall. So, then, how could we characterize this totality of which asking for a brick and positioning it are, both, partial moments? Obviously, if this totality includes both linguistic and non-linguistic elements, it cannot itself be either linguistic or extralinguistic; it has to be prior to this distinction. This totality which includes within itself the linguistic and the non-linguistic, is what we call discourse. In a moment we will justify this denomination; but what must be clear from the start is that by discourse we do not mean a combination of speech and writing, but rather that speech and writing are themselves but internal components of discursive totalities.

Now, turning to the term discourse itself, we use it to emphasize the fact that every social configuration is *meaningful.* If I kick a spherical object in the street or if I kick a ball in a football match, the *physical* fact is the same, but *its meaning* is different. The object is a football only to the extent that it establishes a system of relations with other objects, and these relations are not given by the mere referential materiality of the objects, but are, rather, socially constructed. This systematic set of relations is what we call discourse. The reader will no doubt see that, as we showed in our book, the discursive character of an object does not, by any means, imply putting its *existence* into question. The fact that a football is only a football as long as it is integrated within a system of socially constructed rules does not mean that it thereby ceases to be a physical object. A stone exists independently of any system of social relations, but it is, for instance, either a projectile or an object of aesthetic contemplation only within a specific discursive configuration. A diamond in the market or at the bottom of a mine is the same physical object; but, again, it is only a commodity within a determinate system of social relations. For that same reason it is the discourse which constitutes the subject position of the social agent, and not, therefore, the social agent which is the origin of discourse – the same system of rules that makes that spherical object into a football, makes me a player. The existence of objects is independent of their discursive articulation […].

[...] This, however, leaves two problems unsolved. The first is this: is it not necessary to establish here a distinction between meaning and action? Even if we accept that the meaning of an action depends on a discursive configuration, is not the action itself something different from that meaning? Let us consider the problem from two angles. Firstly, from the angle of meaning. Here the classical distinction is between semantics – dealing with the meaning of words; syntactics – dealing with word order and its consequences for meaning; and pragmatics – dealing with the way a word is actually used in certain speech contexts. The key point is to what extent a rigid separation can be established between semantics and pragmatics – that is, between meaning and use. From Wittgenstein onwards it is precisely this separation which has grown ever more blurred. It has become increasingly accepted that the meaning of a word is entirely context-dependent. As Hanna Fenichel Pitkin points out:

> Wittgenstein argues that meaning and use are intimately, inextricably related, because use helps to determine meaning. Meaning is learned from, and shaped in, instances of use; so both its learning and its configuration depend on pragmatics. ... Semantic meaning is compounded out of cases of a word's use, including all the many and varied language games that are played with it; so meaning is very much the product of pragmatics.
>
> (Pitkin, 1972)

[...] That is to say, in our terminology, every identity or discursive object is constituted in the context of an action. [...]

The other problem to be considered is the following: even if we assume that there is a strict equation between the social and the discursive, what can we say about the natural world, about the facts of physics, biology or astronomy that are not apparently integrated in meaningful totalities constructed by men? The answer is that natural facts are also discursive facts. And they are so for the simple reason that the idea of nature is not something that is already there, to be read from the appearances of things, but is itself the result of a slow and complex historical and social construction. To call something a natural object is a way of conceiving it that depends upon a classificatory system. Again, this does not put into question the fact that this entity which we call a stone exists, in the sense of being present here and now, independently of my will; nevertheless the fact of its being a stone depends on a way of classifying objects that is historical and contingent. If there were no human beings on earth, those objects that we call stones would be there nonetheless; but they would not be 'stones', because there would be neither mineralogy nor a language capable of classifying them and distinguishing them from other objects. We need not stop for long on this point. The entire development of contemporary epistemology has established that there is no fact that allows its meaning to be read transparently.

REFERENCE

PITKIN, H.F. (1972) *Wittgenstein and Justice*, Berkeley, CA, University of California Press.

Source: Laclau and Mouffe, 1990, pp. 100–3.

Ernesto Laclau and Chantal Mouffe

READING F: Elaine Showalter, 'The performance of hysteria'

The first of the great European theorists of hysteria was Jean-Martin Charcot (1825–1893), who carried out his work in the Paris clinic at the Salpêtrière. Charcot had begun his work on hysteria in 1870. While he believed that hysterics suffered from a hereditary taint that weakened their nervous system, he also developed a theory that hysteria had psychological origins. Experimenting with hypnosis, Charcot demonstrated that hysterical symptoms such as paralysis could be produced and relieved by hypnotic suggestion. Through careful observation, physical examination, and the use of hypnosis, Charcot was able to prove that hysterical symptoms, while produced by emotions rather than by physical injury, were genuine, and not under the conscious control of the patient. Freud, who studied at the Salpêtrière from October 1885 to February 1886, gave Charcot the credit for establishing the legitimacy of hysteria as a disorder. According to Freud, 'Charcot's work restored dignity to the subject; gradually the sneering attitude which the hysteric could reckon meeting with when she told her story, was given up; she was no longer a malingerer, since Charcot had thrown the whole weight of his authority on the side of the reality and objectivity of hysterical phenomena.' Furthermore, Charcot demonstrated that hysterical symptoms also occurred in men, and were not simply related to the vagaries of the female reproductive system. At the Salpêtrière there was even a special wing for male hysterics, who were frequently the victims of trauma from railway accidents. In restoring the credibility of the hysteric, Freud believed, Charcot had joined other psychiatric saviors of women and had 'repeated on a small scale the act of liberation commemorated in the picture of Pinel which adorned the lecture hall of the Salpêtrière' (Freud, 1948, p. 18).

Yet for Charcot, too, hysteria remained symbolically, if not medically, a female malady. By far the majority of his hysterical patients were women, and several, such as Blanche Wittmann, known as the 'Queen of the Hysterics,' became celebrities who were regularly featured in his books, the main attractions at the Salpêtrière's Bal des Folles, and hypnotized and exhibited at his popular public lectures. Axel Munthe, a doctor practicing in Paris, wrote a vivid description of Charcot's Tuesday lectures at the Salpêtrière: 'The huge amphitheatre was filled to the last place with a multicoloured audience drawn from tout Paris, authors, journalists, leading actors and actresses, fashionable demimondaines.' The hypnotized women patients put on a spectacular show before this crowd of curiosity seekers.

Some of them smelt with delight a bottle of ammonia when told it was rose water, others would eat a piece of charcoal when presented to them as chocolate. Another would crawl on all fours on the floor, barking furiously when told she was a dog, flap her arms as if trying to fly when turned into a pigeon, lift her skirts with a shriek of terror when a glove was thrown at her feet with a suggestion of being a snake. Another would walk with a top hat in her arms rocking it to and fro and kissing it tenderly when she was told it was her baby.

(Munthe, 1930, pp. 296, 302–3)

The grand finale would be the performance of a full hysterical seizure.

Furthermore, the representation of female hysteria was a central aspect of Charcot's work. His hysterical women patients were surrounded by images of female hysteria. In the lecture hall, as Freud noted, was Robert-Fleury's painting of Pinel freeing the madwomen. On the opposite wall was a famous lithograph of Charcot, holding and lecturing about a swooning and half-undressed young woman before a room of sober and attentive men, yet another representation that seemed to be instructing the hysterical woman in her act [Figure 1.8].

Finally, Charcot's use of photography was the most extensive in nineteenth-century psychiatric practice. As one of his admirers remarked, 'The camera was as crucial to the study of hysteria as the microscope was to histology' (quoted in Goldstein, 1982, p. 215). In 1875 one of his assistants, Paul Regnard, had assembled an album of photographs of female nervous patients. The pictures of women exhibiting various phases of hysterical attacks were deemed so interesting that a photographic workshop or atelier was installed within the hospital. By the 1880s a professional photographer.

Albert Londe, had been brought in to take charge of a full-fledged photographic service. Its methods included not only the most advanced technology and apparatus, such as laboratories, a studio with platforms, a bed, screens, black, dark-gray, and light-gray background curtains, headrests, and an iron support for feeble patients, but also elaborate administrative techniques of observation, selection of models, and record-keeping. The photographs of women were published in three volumes called *Iconographie photographique de la Salpêtriére.* Thus Charcot's hospital became an environment in which female hysteria was perpetually presented, represented, and reproduced.

Such techniques appealed to Charcot because his approach to psychiatric analysis was strongly visual and imagistic. As Freud has explained, Charcot 'had an artistically gifted temperament – as he said himself, he was a "*visuel*", a seer, ... He was accustomed to look again and again at things that were incomprehensible to him, to deepen his impression of them day by day until suddenly understanding of them dawned upon him' (Freud, 1948, pp. 10–11). Charcot's public lectures were among the first to use visual aids – pictures, graphs, statues, models, and illustrations that he drew on the blackboard in colored chalk – as well as the presence of the patients as models.

The specialty of the house at the Salpêtriére was *grande hystérie*, or 'hystero-epilepsy,' a prolonged and elaborate convulsive seizure that occurred in women. A complete seizure involved three phases: the epileptoid phase, in which the woman lost consciousness and foamed at the mouth; the phase of clownism, involving eccentric physical contortions; and the phase of *attitudes passionnelles*, a miming of incidents and emotions from the patient's life. In the *iconographies*, photographs of this last phase were given subtitles that suggested Charcot's interpretation of hysterical gestures as linked to female sexuality, despite his disclaimers: 'amorous supplication', 'ecstasy', 'eroticism' [Figure 1.10]. This interpretation of hysterical gestures as sexual was reinforced by Charcot's efforts to pinpoint areas of the body that might induce convulsions when pressed. The ovarian region, he concluded, was a particularly sensitive hysterogenic zone.

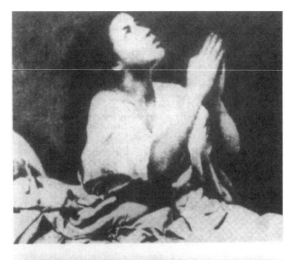

FIGURE 1.10 Two portraits of Augustine: amorous supplication (top), ecstasy (bottom)

Because the behavior of Charcot's hysterical stars was so theatrical, and because it was rarely observed outside of the Parisian clinical setting, many of his contemporaries, as well as subsequent medical historians, have suspected that the women's performances were the result of suggestion, imitation, or even fraud. In Charcot's own lifetime, one of his assistants admitted that some of the women had been coached in order to produce attacks that would please the *maître* (discussed in Drinker, 1984, pp. 144–8). Furthermore, there was a dramatic increase in the incidence of hysteria during Charcot's tenure at the Salpêtriére. From only 1 percent in 1845, it rose to 17.3 percent of all diagnoses in 1883, at the height of his experimentation with hysterical patients (see Goldstein, 1982, pp. 209–10).

When challenged about the legitimacy of hystero-epilepsy, however, Charcot vigorously defended the objectivity of his vision. 'It seems that hystero-epilepsy only exists in France,' he declared in a lecture of 1887, 'and I could even say, as it has sometimes been said, that it only exists at the Salpêtriére, as if I had created it by the force of my will. It would be truly marvellous if I were thus able to create illnesses at the pleasure of my whim and my caprice. But as for the truth, I am absolutely only the photographer; I register what I see' (quoted in Didi-Huberman, 1982, p. 32). Like Hugh Diamond at the Surrey Asylum, Charcot and his followers had absolute faith in the scientific neutrality of the photographic image; Londe boasted: 'La plaque photographique est la vraie retine du savant' ('The photographic plate is the true retina of the scientist') (ibid., p. 35).

But Charcot's photographs were even more elaborately framed and staged than Diamond's Victorian asylum pictures. Women were not simply photographed once, but again and again, so that they became used to the camera and to the special status they received as photogenic subjects. Some made a sort of career out of modeling for the *iconographies*. Among the most frequently photographed was a fifteen-year-old girl named Augustine, who had entered the hospital in 1875. Her hysterical attacks had begun at the age of thirteen when, according to her testimony, she had been raped by her employer, a man who was also her mother's lover. Intelligent, coquettish, and eager to please, Augustine was an apt pupil of the atelier. All of her poses suggest the exaggerated gestures of the French classical acting style, or stills from silent movies. Some photographs of Augustine with flowing locks and white hospital gown also seem to imitate poses in nineteenth-century paintings, as Stephen Heath points out: 'a young girl composed on her bed, something of the Pre-Raphaelite Millais's painting *Ophelia*' (Heath, 1982, pp. 36–7). Among her gifts was her ability to time and divide her hysterical performances into scenes, acts, tableaux, and intermissions, to perform on cue and on schedule with the click of the camera.

But Augustine's cheerful willingness to assume whatever poses her audience desired took its toll on her psyche. During the period when she was being repeatedly photographed, she developed a curious hysterical symptom: she began to see everything in black and white. In 1880, she began to rebel against the hospital regime; she had periods of violence in which she tore her clothes and broke windows. During these angry outbreaks she was anaesthetized with ether or chloroform. In June of that year, the doctors gave up their efforts with her case, and she was put in a locked cell. But Augustine was able to use in her own behalf the histrionic abilities that for a time had made her a star of the asylum. Disguising herself as a man, she managed to escape from the Salpêtrière. Nothing further was ever discovered about her whereabouts.

REFERENCES

DIDI-HUBERMAN, G. (1982) *Invention de 'Hystérie: Charcot et l'Iconographie Photographique de La Salpêtriére*, Paris, Macula.

DRINKER, G.F. (1984) *The Birth of Neurosis: Myth, Malady and the Victorians*, New York, Simon & Schuster.

FREUD, S. (1948) 'Charcot', in Jones, E. (ed.), *Collected Papers, Vol. 1*, London, Hogarth Press.

GOLDSTEIN, J. (1982) 'The hysteria diagnosis and the politics of anticlericalism in late nineteenth-century France', *Journal of Modern History*, No. 54.

HEATH, S. (1982) *The Sexual Fix*, London, Macmillan.

MUNTHE, A. (1930) *The Story of San Michele*, London, John Murray.

Source: Showalter, 1987, pp. 147–54.

CHAPTER TWO

RECORDING REALITY: DOCUMENTARY FILM AND TELEVISION

Frances Bonner

1 INTRODUCTION

This chapter takes up the approaches to and questions about representation already introduced and uses them to talk about a particular *genre* of film and television programmes: documentaries.

We are looking at the documentary genre because it makes – initially through the use of its name with its origins in the word 'document' – truth claims, assertions that it is telling us honestly about the real world. You have learnt in the first chapter that Foucault was willing only to talk about 'regimes of truth', and that we can only make meanings through representations. We are not suddenly reversing position here. This chapter will look at the different ways in which documentary film and television make representations, but that these are representations that claim a privileged relationship with the truth about the material with which they concern themselves.

The chapter will start by considering documentaries as non-fiction texts, since this is the most basic way to conceive them. The distinction between fiction and non-fiction is based on the assumption that one is 'made-up' and one is 'real'. Both produce representations and both are the concern of this book. Non-fictional representations tell us about the world in which we live in a very direct way, but they are still very carefully crafted by the filmmakers. Before moving into this consideration, let us briefly look at a substantial example of the documentary endeavour, the growing body of work known initially as *Seven Up*.

Seven Up is a famous and influential documentary, so influential that the title of the initial film now describes a form of documentary following a group of individuals at intervals over the course of their lives. The initial text was a 1964 television programme directed by Paul

Almond in Granada's investigative current affairs series, *World in Action*. It is now associated with Michael Apted, who was a researcher on the first documentary but has directed all the subsequent ones, which now get cinematic as well as television releases. It was designed to present a picture of British society at that time through an examination of fourteen seven-year-old children. The children were chosen from a variety of backgrounds; they were of different classes and from the country and the city. Perhaps inadvertently indicating what was seen as more representative at the time, there were ten boys and only four girls and, except for one mixed-race boy, all were white. There was only a short preparation period, so the children were rather hastily chosen and less representative of the nation than might have been the case had the future of the programme been known. Apted has since regretted that it shows rather 'the extremes of the social system' and lacks much of a middle ground (quoted in Moran, 2002, p. 390). It was initially intended to be a one-off programme in which Almond set out explicitly to test the Jesuit maxim: 'Give me the child until he is seven, and I will give you the man'. Both Almond and Apted thought the seven-year-olds would already demonstrate that their future was determined by the class they were born into. The children were interviewed about their attitudes to money, rich and poor people and education, and were asked about what they thought they would do when they were grown up. We hear the questions they were asked but do not see the interviewer. Their speaking to the camera is interspersed with shots of them at play.

The great success of the documentary meant that a follow-up programme was made seven years later to see what had become of the children, and this has continued every seven years after since then. There have now been eight series, with the latest appearing in 2012. Each subsequent episode includes clips from earlier years and has a varying number of participants as some of the original fourteen decide that they no longer wish to be involved, or that they would like to return after an absence. Several other countries, including the USA and Russia, have their own versions.

It is difficult now to realise how novel this approach was at the time; subsequent documentaries and the major developments of reality television have rendered the intimate, personal approach to telling larger truths about a society commonplace. The first episode now seems curiously formal with its authoritative voice-over narration and naïve subjects unaware how much their appearance on camera would mean for their later lives. The children were chosen to indicate the life chances of those from their own particular segment of society, but they were also individuals whose progress could be traced, whose stories could subsequently be caught up on. The political or sociological approach of the first examination of the determining character of class shifted as shared family events, like marriages and children, now organize the episodes. It may have been intended to represent the difficulties for social mobility in the early 1960s, but over the years it became a domestically focused document about social change, even though many of the individuals did follow very similar paths to those they had described when young. Here, it provides a useful example to start our consideration of the genre because of its longevity and because it demonstrates both political and personal representations.

2 WHAT DO WE MEAN BY 'DOCUMENTARY'?

2.1 Non-fiction texts

Documentaries, whether film or television, are non-fiction texts. This is the most basic way in which a documentary is seen to differ from a fictional feature film. At some level a documentary makes a claim on the truth, asserting that what it talks about and shows is 'real', not a made-up story like the typical Hollywood thriller or romantic comedy. In Chapter 1 you read how one of the criticisms of Saussure's semiotic system was that it did not pay enough attention to the relationship between signs and their referents. The referents for the signs in non-fictional texts are objects and practices that exist in the world, they are referenced directly rather than indirectly as is the case for fiction, where they are (mostly) made to be like actual objects and practices.

Yet while all documentaries are non-fiction, not all non-fiction texts are documentaries, not even those which have extremely strong relationships with the real world.

The very first films were just such texts. At the end of the nineteenth century, the Lumière brothers filmed French workers leaving a factory and a train arriving at a station, among many other situations, just by positioning a camera and exposing the few minutes of film available on a roll at the time. They called these films 'actualities' and audiences marvelled at the filmed record because it showed a moving image of what had happened in the past and usually at another place from where the film was being screened. Photographs had done something of that in they could represent a past event, but the novelty of temporal displacement was greater when what was shown was movement and the duration of that past event. Actualities showed what had actually been happening in front of the camera as the audience member would have seen it if positioned similarly at that place at that time.

They documented what was happening, in the same way that films we take on holiday, whether in a local park or on safari in Kenya, can do, but neither these nor the Lumières' films are considered documentaries. In John Grierson's well-known phrase, documentaries involve the 'creative treatment of actuality' (Hardy, 1979, p. 11). Grierson is one of the most important figures in the early days of documentary. He led documentary production organizations in Britain and Canada and is usually credited with coining the word 'documentary' to describe Robert Flaherty's *Moana* (1927). Flaherty also directed other key films, such as *Nanook of the North* (1922) and *Man of Aran* (1934). All of these are ethnographic documentaries, that is, they depict the lives of people in other cultures in ways discussed by Henrietta Lidchi in Chapter 3.

We usually think of 'creative' as being associated with fictional work, not with that claiming to represent actuality. What could Grierson have been thinking of? Brian Winston glosses Grierson's definition as 'image-making of pre-existing reality' (2008, p. 9). Does this help clarify the apparent contradiction or take it back to Lumière-type record-footage?

I think Grierson is more helpful in stressing the importance of the act of creation, since the Lumières certainly produced images. If we think of this as a three-step process – the first step is the event in the real word, then the record of it on film, and finally the incorporation of this film into a documentary – then we can see the shift more clearly. The record of the real event may be holiday footage in its raw state, not after it has been passed through an editing programme. The camera may have been pointed at a scene – of, say, children feeding ducks, or lions eating a gazelle. What we have is a record of what happened in front of the camera lens without it being staged for it or 'treated' afterwards.

Such holiday footage is not a documentary, rather it is like the kind of material that is used in newsreels or kept in archives as raw footage. All can subsequently appear in documentaries. We can edit our holiday footage into a story about the virtues of holidaying close to home and post it as an amateur documentary on YouTube, for example. A few seconds of silent newsreel footage showing Archduke Ferdinand going into a building in Sarajevo shortly before his assassination triggered the First World War, or an only slightly longer segment where the very last Tasmanian Tiger paces in its Hobart zoo cage, are both used again and again in documentaries on the origins of the War or the extinction of species, respectively. *Senna*, Asif Kapadia's 2010 feature-length documentary about the Formula 1 driver, Ayrton Senna, is composed entirely of archival footage of various kinds: home movies, old TV footage and the rather primitive in-car camera material of the 1980s and early 1990s. It is the creative work of selection, editing and developing a narrative that transforms this raw footage into a documentary film.

Major American theorist Bill Nichols believes that one of the characteristics of a documentary is that it seeks to make an argument about the historical (that is, the 'real') world (1991, p. 111). The Sarajevo footage is incorporated into documentaries arguing that it was key to the declaration of the First World War as well as arguments that it was incidental. As a biographical film, *Senna* is primarily concerned with depicting the racing driver's life and yet it still advances arguments about him: that he was more charismatic and more reckless than current drivers; and that he was far more interested in racing than in the money or the politics associated with it.

In being shot for a newsreel or for family memories, the archival footage or Senna's home movies have reasons for coming into existence, but occasionally this kind of material is overwhelmed by what it records accidentally. The most famous of these is almost certainly the footage Abraham Zapruder shot, intending to get just a home movie of the American President's visit to his city, which recorded the moment when John F. Kennedy was assassinated. Stella Bruzzi examines this at great length to demonstrate the difference between what the footage is able to show and what has been made of it subsequently. This is an argument about how filmed material is made to *mean* various things. She notes its similarity to George Holliday's footage of the LAPD (Los Angeles Police Department) beating of Rodney King, or the film of the second aeroplane flying into the Twin Towers on 9/11, saying 'the text is simple, its meaning is not' for 'indeterminacy is the overriding characteristic of accidental footage' (Bruzzi, 2006, pp. 22–3). Subsequent use of the footage in trials, official inquiries and many investigative films and television programmes employ it persuasively to make an argument, but the cases made can be very different, indeed completely contradictory.

ACTIVITY 1

This chapter will conclude with a consideration of natural history documentaries. To precede this, consider the holiday footage posited above of ducks or lion. I have already suggested that it could be made into an amateur documentary on taking local holidays, but imagine how it could be incorporated into two natural history programmes with very different arguments about the world, perhaps about the role of human intervention in wild animals' lives. The same footage would then be part of different representations. Sketch out how different arguments could shape the story illustrated by the footage.

Raw footage has to be made into an argument, or, to paraphrase Grierson, filmed actuality has to be treated creatively for it to become documentary film or television. The film of Ayrton Senna is not Senna himself; it is a representation of Senna, and he is sadly no less dead because we can see an apparently living representation. The gap between sign and referent is obvious. Documentaries are particular kinds of attempts to represent the world and their claims for superior abilities to do so, as well as the techniques they engage in to enhance their claims, are what this chapter concentrates on. They may start with film no more conclusive than that just mentioned, but by incorporating it with other material and shaping the whole into a meaningful argument or picture, whether by editing, narration or some other technical device, produce a film or television programme which can be named and promoted as 'a documentary'.

2.2 Defining documentary

We have already noted Grierson's coining of the term and the definition ascribed to him, 'the creative treatment of actuality', because this is where discussion of documentary usually begins, but we need a more precise starting point now. Grierson said of *Moana* in 1926 that it had 'documentary value' and here he was picking up the French term 'documentaire' which was used at that time 'to distinguish serious travel and expedition films from travelogues' (Aitken, 1990, p. 80). By the 1930s in the UK 'documentary' was being used 'to describe socially purposive actuality films' (p. 80). Creativity was in the service of a social purpose. This perception, including the need to separate it from related material of different character, was still evident in 1995 when the influential British television documentary theorist John Corner considered the large amount of non-fictional material on television, naming travel shows, sports footage and current affairs film as 'documentarianism'. 'Core' documentary though 'however entertaining it is also required to be, almost always works with a "serious" expositional (or frequently journalistic) purpose and, in Britain at least, this purpose has often been that of social inquiry set against a recognised (and visualised) context of economic inequality, social class difference and social change, together with the consequent "problems" thus produced' (Corner, 1995, p. 77). We shall see below in section 5 that Corner later revised this view for a changed situation, but the description provides continuity, usefully naming a still recognizable body of documentary work and introduces the key word 'serious' which will recur.

More recent definitions of documentary that try to refine this are usually declared unsatisfactory because they fail to allow for the great range of films and television programmes that they need to encompass. It is more common for contemporary critics to leave the matter of definition unresolved, even Nichols's declaring documentary a 'fuzzy concept' (2001, p. 23). He talks of their being the output of institutions known for producing documentaries, such as the Discovery Channel, but admits that this is a circular argument. More usefully, he notes how documentary directors share 'a common self-chosen mandate to represent the historical world rather than to imaginatively invent alternative ones' while viewers know that documentaries assert an indexical relationship to the historical world (2001, pp 25, 22–41). 'Historical' here as before means the world in which we live, the 'real' world as opposed to a fictional one. The observations about the people making the texts, the institutions showing them and the viewers watching them indicate a shared semiotic situation where there is a consensus about how a sign operates within a given culture: documentaries are those texts which are made and received as documentaries. The most important thing is that their referent is non-fictional.

Other writers find themselves in this same definitional quandary, saying 'a documentary itself is the crucial point at which the factual event, the difficulties of representation and the act of watching a documentary are confronted – if not resolved' (Bruzzi, 2006, p. 7) or '[w]hat makes a documentary a documentary resides … in the complex interaction between text, context, producer and spectator' (Ward, 2005, p. 11). Like Nichols, both these valuably include the person watching and making sense of the text, *as a documentary*, though there needs to be more than just the belief of a viewer that what they are viewing is a documentary. There is a whole group of films and television programmes which are made to take advantage of viewers' beliefs about documentary practices and mislead for comic effect. These, like *This is Spinal Tap* or Chris Morris's *Brass Eye* series, are called mockumentaries.

You have already learnt of Foucault's argument about discourses and discursive formations. Nichols refers to discourse similarly, although he advances a grouping of discourses under a term that Foucault would not have recognized. In investigating the status of the knowledge produced by documentary film, he claims that documentary asserts its presence in relation to 'discourses of sobriety', alongside, but not equal to them. He names these discourses as: '[s]cience, economics, politics, foreign policy, education, religion, welfare' (1991, p. 3). Like Foucault, he links discourses to power, saying 'Through them power exerts itself. Through them things are made to happen' (p. 4). He argues that documentary's membership of this grouping is compromised by its desire to tell stories and by its desire to do so in aesthetically innovative ways. More recently, he has commented that documentary 'may not be accepted as an equal partner in scientific inquiry or foreign policy initiatives … [but] this genre still upholds a tradition of sobriety' (2001, p. 39). Is he talking about more than seriousness here?

Some documentaries are amusing, some have comic sections and as we shall see below (in section 5) some are made just to be diverting, but Nichols's discussion assumes the same elements as Grierson's and Corner's, that documentary has serious intent and that the arguments it advances have the hope of revealing unknown aspects of the world or bringing about social change.

READING A

Now read the excerpt from Nichols (2001, pp. 42–9) about documentary 'voice'. This extends his discussion of how documentary makes an argument and introduces some terms related to 'modes' that will be discussed further in the next section. Do not worry about them at this stage. His discussion of narration is important. Make sure you understand what he means by 'voice of God/authority' narration and the filmmaker's perspective.

Take a moment to think about the following questions:

- What do you think is the difference in the effect on viewers between seen and unseen narrators?
- How can documentaries have a voice when they use no commentary on or off screen?

3 TYPES OF DOCUMENTARY

3.1 Categorizing documentary

To extend our knowledge of documentary representation beyond its being a shared understanding between producers and consumers about films and television programmes which claim to be talking about actuality not fiction, it is necessary to consider how some texts are organized. Nichols's documentary modes provide a widely shared approach to categorization, even if many texts do not fit neatly into any single category. He argues that there are six modes: expository, observational, participatory, reflexive, performative and poetic (Nichols, 2001). He also asserts that, if the reasonably rare poetic mode is placed first with the expository, this represents a genealogy, i.e. the modes come into existence successively (Nichols, 2010). Bruzzi (2006) criticized him on the basis that the modes co-exist and that the performative mode is much more apparent throughout the period discussed and across the other modes. We will consider her argument about performativity below.

If we dispense with the idea of a succession of modes and of their rigid separation, Nichols's categorization is valuable and understanding it helps advance our knowledge of documentary representation since the terms are widely used by filmmakers and analysts.

Expository documentaries are ones that address the viewer directly, often using 'voice-of-God' narration, which means, as you will recall from the first reading, that there is voice-over narration making claims and assertions and telling viewers how to understand what is being shown. This is why Nichols claims that the expository mode is didactic – such films want to teach their viewers about a situation by telling them how to think about it. This is a very common televisual form used, for example, by most of the war documentaries on the History Channel. The voice does not have to be unseen and unacknowledged; it may be identified or even anchored to an on-screen presenter. Nature documentaries commonly use the expository form, and we can recognize examples, whether, say, Sir David Attenborough is on screen as a presenter of material he has helped shape, or providing a voice-over for someone else's film. Most English-speaking viewers familiar with natural history documentaries would recognize Attenborough's voice, but this only increases its authoritativeness. His commentary tells us what animal behaviour means; it does not invite us to make up our own mind about it.

The observational mode is what is meant when people talk of 'fly-on-the-wall' camerawork and documentaries. The metaphor clearly expresses the filmmaker's wish to observe without being noticed and to record what is happening without intervening in what is happening or being said. Obviously, even with lightweight digital equipment, the presence of someone recording people's activities and speech is hard to overlook and the subjects being filmed need to be instructed to ignore the camera and crew (and need to obey those instructions). There are various legal frameworks and industrial codes of practice forbidding concealed camera use, so the equipment and its operators must be visible to the film's subjects. Observational documentarists work on the assumption that over time subjects come to forget that they are being filmed and revert to acting naturally. Where narration is of the essence for the expository mode, it is alien to the observational, being regarded as an intrusion. Viewers are shown what occurred in front of the lens and the editing process is used to shape the material into a coherent picture, but the only other guidance a viewer is given in pure observational film is an occasional title on the screen, perhaps giving a person's name or a location.

The Direct Cinema movement, which started in the USA during the 1960s, argued for the virtues of the observational mode and for the impropriety of intervention, even of editing out of chronological order, believing that only in this way could the real world be represented. Mark Cousins and Kevin Macdonald explain the rigidity exponents required:

> [T]he advocates of Direct Cinema were always quick to codify exactly what they thought was the 'right' way to make a documentary and what was the 'wrong' way, drawing up a kind of filmic ten commandments: thou shalt not rehearse; thou shalt not interview; thou shalt not use commentary; thou shalt not use film lights; thou shalt not stage events; thou shalt not dissolve.

(Cousins and Macdonald, 1996, p. 250)

Famous exponents include D.A. Pennebaker (maker of *Don't Look Back*, the 1967 film of Bob Dylan's first tour of the UK) and the Maysles brothers, Albert and David. Bruzzi demonstrates how the latter's *Salesman* (1968), which follows the activities of a group of Bible salesmen in the early 1960s, breaks the claims to purity of direct cinema, especially through a chronological editing, although in doing so they made a more satisfying and arguably more moving film (Bruzzi, 2006, pp. 76–9).

Even though the observational mode in general does not really require abiding by the stringencies of Direct Cinema, too great a transgression can still cause debate. A chronological editing is usually accepted, as generally are interviews, but the discovery that the subjects have been directed to perform certain actions or to engage in what in a fiction film would simply be a normal 're-take' can lead to producers being rebuked by critics, broadcasters and knowledgeable viewers. As was the case with the expository mode, the observational is also a common mode for television documentaries.

The interactive or participatory mode (both terms are still used, though Nichols had clearly come to prefer the latter by his 2001 book) can be seen as the opposite of the observational. This is the mode in which the interactions of filmmaker and subject are shown, or at the very least heard. It assumes that a relationship has built up between the two parties, that viewers are aware of this and that it is honest for this to become part of the eventual film or programme. Again, beliefs about the right way to represent the real world are in operation, but this world is seen as one in which it is admitted that a documentary is being made.

Although the Maysles were still adherents of Direct Cinema when they made *Grey Gardens* (1975), about two relatives of Jackie Kennedy Onassis living in apparent penury, neither the mother nor the daughter who were the principal subjects were willing to abide by the protocols that they not address the camera or speak to the directors. Regardless of the Maysles's initial wishes, the film that eventuated was participatory, as both Big and Little Edie perform for the camera and talk to the Maysles, who are heard replying. The filmmakers even leave in a scene where they can be seen reflected in a mirror. This has become such a famous film that it remains readily available on DVD, as well as having been given fictional treatment under the same name, *Grey Gardens* (dir. Michael Sucsy, 2009) with Jessica Lange and Drew Barrymore playing the mother and daughter.

Another primarily observational film that became inadvertently participatory is Bob Connolly and Robin Anderson's *Black Harvest* (1992). This was the last film of their Highland Trilogy, which is particularly relevant here because of its links with the Wahgi tribe whose culture is discussed in Henrietta Lidchi's analysis of the Paradise exhibition in Chapter 3. The first film, *First Contact* (1982), is centred on archival film shot by Mick Leahy who is pictured in Plate 3.IX. He and two brothers trekked into the Papua New Guinea Highlands prospecting for gold and became the first white men the tribal people there had seen, hence the title. The filmmakers combine the archival material with interviews, both with some Wahgi people who recall that occasion and with the surviving brother as well as other contemporary location footage. They use quite a bit of voice-over narration and the film sits most easily in the expository category. It was nominated for a documentary Oscar, and with the other two films usefully demonstrates some of the problems that arise from trying to apply a categorization. Despite the voice-over, the argument it produces comes principally from the juxtaposition of the interviews, especially when a suddenly stammering Dan Leahy explains the circumstances in which he and his brother killed tribal people, rather than the didacticism in the narration.

Observational documentary puts more responsibility for the creation of meaning with the viewer, who may or may not make the same interpretation of the text's provision of information and its juxtapositions as other viewers or indeed as the filmmaker may have hoped. The central figure of the second and third films is Joe Leahy, a mixed race coffee plantation owner who is the son of Mick Leahy. They focus on his interactions with the Ganiga, a neighbouring tribe and continue the theme of the problematic interactions between a tribal people and the modern world.

The second film, *Joe Leahy's Neighbours* (1989), concerns the coffee industry. *Black Harvest*, however, is mainly about the problems caused by a slump in global coffee prices, but also includes an outbreak of tribal warfare in which the filmmakers get caught up. Although they have to this point been invisible, unheard and unaddressed in the films, viewers suddenly hear a Ganiga voice telling 'Bob', the co-director and cameraman, to run because the rival tribe are attacking. Connolly keeps the camera running as he and his companions flee, and the jerky view given provides heightened realism as we see his wife, co-director and sound operator, Robin Anderson, running in front of him. This representation of what it is like to be caught in a skirmish in which the weapons are arrows and spears, is certainly a participatory one, but it is a single instance and does not transform the film as *Grey Gardens* was transformed.

Without in any way wanting to detract from the quality of the multi-award winning trilogy, the films are quite conventional in their composition. The first primarily expository and the other two primarily observational, they are exemplary ethnographic filmmaking in terms of the time spent living with the people being filmed (eighteen months for the final film) and the editing skills displayed in the selection and compilation are of the highest order, but none are technically radical. Many documentaries are similarly hybrid and perhaps we should think of the categorization as talking about dominant rather than exclusive modes. The Highlands Trilogy films certainly use the observational mode as their dominant one overall, but all three exhibit blurred boundaries. Nichols himself addressed some of these problems, using precisely this term for his 1994 book *Blurred Boundaries*.

It is perhaps more common for participatory filmmakers to be heard on the soundtrack than seen on screen. We hear the filmmaker's occasional questions of her homeless subjects in Penny Woolcock's BBC4 film *On the Streets* (2010), though when one of them threatens to cut himself with a penknife, her hand appears in frame and she prevents it happening as well as telling him not to do it. More characteristically, when her focus character, Jean, becomes engaged, Woolcock says, off screen, 'Aren't you supposed to kiss him now?' and Jean complies. This kind of thing is more usual than the assertive showing off of the subjects in *Grey Gardens*, which is so blatant that it could also be seen as of the performative mode.

In the next mode, the reflexive one, documentaries reveal themselves as constructed texts, not just by showing the filmmaker or the camera, but by making their construction a key part of the story. Mike Rubbo's *Waiting for Fidel* (1974), Michael Moore's *Roger and Me* (1989) and Nick Broomfield's *The Leader, his Driver and the Driver's Wife* (1991) all show the process of waiting for the ostensible subject of the film to appear. They can be seen to have made a virtue of limited access, or indeed no access at all, and to have created a film out of something that presumably happens regularly in documentary filmmaking but which is not usually regarded as of sufficient moment to be included in a finished product. They are about the process of filmmaking as much as they are about politics or the consequences of free market capitalism.

Nichols's discussion of the performative is principally concerned with the way that the mode operates to convey the subjective and affective dimensions of our knowledge of the world (Nichols, 2001, p. 131). He notes how frequently they have autobiographical components, but also how often they concern 'the social subjectivity … of the underrepresented or the misrepresented, of women and ethnic minorities, gays and lesbians' (p. 133). Ngozi Onwurah's deeply moving film *The Body Beautiful* (1991) dramatizes the relationship between the filmmaker and her white mother, casting non-speaking actors alongside her own, equally non-speaking, mother, as well as using the filmmaker's own voice to tell the events of her mother's life and the emotions they both feel.

The problems of categorization are probably most evident with the overlaps between the reflexive and performative modes. The three 'waiting' films mentioned above could also be seen as performative, since neither mode is clearly dominant. Broomfield and Moore both foreground their performance and affective response to the situation in most of their films (you may be familiar with Broomfield's *Kurt and Courtney* or Moore's *Fahrenheit 9/11*). Morgan Spurlock's *Supersize Me* (2004) is less mixed in modes. Spurlock performs an action, eating nothing but McDonald's food for a month, on camera. It is not an action required in filmmaking; he needs to perform it to make his particular film and he talks to camera about what he is doing, but his film is far more clearly a performative than a reflexive one.

Whether the performance is by the subjects, the filmmaker, or, as in Onwurah's film, both, this mode quite clearly is not presenting an actuality that would have occurred had the cameras not been there. It is staged especially to be filmed, by documentarists who believe that in doing so they will be able both to represent an experience that they wish to draw attention to and draw a larger audience to their argument. Grierson's 'creative treatment of actuality' is fully in operation here.

The previous five modes can be seen as reacting to perceived tendencies and weaknesses of one another, even if Nichols's argument that each is a reaction to the preceding one creates far too linear and clear-cut a picture. Ward suggests rather that they are 'dialectically inter-related' (2005, p. 22). Given that you should be able to find examples of each mode being screened in any week, and that these will have been made by filmmakers convinced that their chosen approach uses the most appropriate mode, Ward's assertion seems a good one.

ACTIVITY 2

'Dialectically inter-related' implies a particular relationship between the modes. In talking of the 'waiting' films, I indicated that they might be regarded as 'hybrids' of reflexive and performative. What differences do you think are being signalled by these two terms and how could they relate dialectically? How might this differ from suggesting that films or television programmes often show a dominant mode?

The final mode is the poetic one and it can readily be seen as quite distinctive. Nichols did not include it in his initial categorization, but when he later introduced it, he placed it first in his chronological listing (2001, pp. 102–5). All of the other modes construct narratives. They represent the historical world through stories that assert that they are telling us how it is. The poetic mode is concerned rather to *evoke* how the world, or the section of it under consideration, is. One characteristic type is the 'city symphony', which builds a picture of a city from a long sequence of shots of it arranged on aesthetic bases rather than narrative or analytical ones. An early example is Walther Ruttman's *Berlin: Symphony of a City* (1927).

It is not just an old-fashioned mode. The nature films produced by Jacques Perrin, like *Microcosmos* (Claude Nuridsany and Marie Perennou, 2001) and *Travelling Birds* (Jacques Clozard and Michel Debats, 2002, also known as *Winged Migration*) can be regarded as poetic evocations of what it might be like down among the grass stalks in the insect world, or high up in the air on the wing. The *Variety* review of the latter noted that viewers came out knowing no more than when they went in – that birds migrate south in the (northern hemisphere) winter – but also refers to the 'sustained bout of cinematic euphoria' from watching the extended spectacle (Nesselson, 2002, p. 50). The poetic documentary provides an experience rather than advancing an argument or disseminating knowledge. The experience, though, is not gained through testimony, as is the case with the performative mode.

3.2 Alternative categories

Bruzzi's discussion of documentary contests Nichols's approach, not just by arguing against its genealogical character, but also by seeing the performative mode as far more widespread than he did. She emphasizes how much the genre is brought into being by the actions of the filmmaker, how much therefore it is performative in the terms first outlined by J.L. Austin and then taken up by Judith Butler. Austin was concerned with performative language, how certain speech acts were capable of changing the world when performed by appropriate people – a declaration of war, the sentencing of a prisoner, or for a somewhat more pleasant example, 'I now pronounce you man and wife' when said by a licensed person to a heterosexual couple actually brings about the state of marriage. The process of making a documentary brings the situation it shows (and the ways it shows it) into existence.

Bruzzi does not see all film as performative, but she does see the mode as more honest about the relationship between the real and its documentary representation (2006, p. 187). She asserts that 'the performative documentary uses performance within a non-fiction context to draw attention to the impossibilities of authentic documentary representation' (p. 185). The presence of cameras and of filmmakers alters the situation being recorded, so that those films which acknowledge that they are films rather than slices of 'authentic' life are admitting what she sees as the fundamental quality of documentary: 'that documentaries are a negotiation between the filmmaker and reality, and, at heart, a performance' (p. 186). She chooses as two of her chief examples filmmakers whose work has been previously described here as hybrids of the reflexive and the performative: Nick Broomfield and Michael Moore.

The performance need not be that of the filmmaker, as Brian Hill's musical documentaries demonstrate. These British films are idiosyncratic attempts to provide new perspectives on common documentary topics. Hill has made four films in this style where his producer audio-records his subjects talking about their lives, before passing the recordings to the poet Simon Armitage. Armitage writes lyrics based on the recordings that are then taken back to the initial speakers who sing them to camera in appropriate locations. It may sound tortuous, but *Feltham Sings* (2002), for example, provides new insights into the experience of incarcerated young offenders as well as possibly attracting a new audience jaded by the predictability of television films about juvenile prisons and prisoners. Both the offenders and the prison officers sing their parts in a way that certainly would not be found in 'real life'. They perform for the camera in a far from naturalistic way, but Channel 4, which commissioned the film, the filmmaker and the documentary establishment all accept that the resulting film and three others by Hill, *Drinking for England* (1998), *Pornography: The Musical* (2003) and *Songbirds* (2005) about female offenders, are documentaries. To revert to Nichols's modes, these are performative works. They include poetic elements in the way the musical styles (ballad or rap, for instance) intensify the experience of the offenders/singers for the viewer.

Many of the films that Bruzzi discusses insightfully as performative ones and that Nichols's categorizations, which she does call on, would make reflexive as well as performative are discussed by Jon Dovey under the title 'klutz films' (2000, pp. 27–50). Considering them in this way not only allows us another way of looking at some well-known films, but also helps raise an issue of representation that involves the names chosen for categories. All those chosen by Nichols have very calm, neutral names suitable for a discourse calling on the tradition of sobriety. Dovey introduced his term in a book on television called *Freakshow: First Person Media and Factual Television*, signalling by this his interest in self-portrayal which he quite rightly saw as becoming more evident in contemporary television. Calling something reflexive or performative rather than a 'klutz film' is more distanced and probably respectful, but the lively slang word 'klutz' draws attention to a distinctive common feature that enables people investigating documentary style to talk about why this approach might work and why it has proved successful.

The term 'klutz' refers to an inept, not very bright and perhaps clumsy person. Dovey glosses the klutz as 'a failure who makes mistakes and denies any mastery of the communicative process' (2000, p. 27). Dovey clearly does not believe that Nick Broomfield, Michael Moore and Ross McElwee, three of his chief examples, are really like that; he calls the klutz a constructed autobiographical persona. On camera all three filmmakers seem to bumble around, asking obvious questions and even getting in the way of their subjects, when they are able to engage with them at all. Dovey mentions all three of the 'waiting' films, but does not name Rubbo's a klutz film, since it is too early for his study and Rubbo does not develop a klutz persona elsewhere.

Ross McElwee made the ambitiously titled *Sherman's March: A meditation on the possibility of romantic love in the South during an era of nuclear proliferation* in 1985. McElwee is his own camera and sound operator and had made four films before this. He had been given a grant to make the film and, furthermore, *Sherman's March* was awarded the prize for best documentary at the Sundance Film Festival in 1986. Despite all this evidence of his competence and experience as a documentary filmmaker, McElwee presents himself as technically incompetent, leaving in a sequence with sound problems and explaining that a scene is incomplete because he forgot to remove the lens cap. His professional 'klutziness' is in harmony with the social ineptitude he asserts and shows in his interactions with women – the principal concern of the film. Dovey distinguishes McElwee from Broomfield and Moore on the basis of his revelation of his private self. His films are more truly autobiographical (Dovey, 2000, pp. 40–1).

A prominent part of the 'klutz' persona as used to generate documentary is a striking naïvety and it is easy to understand how useful this is as a starting point for the investigation of a situation. Broomfield's investigation of *Heidi Fleiss: Hollywood Madam* (1995) is made not only easier, as he has to ask for information about almost everything with the result that viewers learn as he does, but also more palatable to watch by his apparent open-eyed innocence. Consider how different a knowing, experienced brothel-visiting guide would be and how difficult it would be to avoid sleaziness. The very same naïvety can be seen in Louis Theroux's visit to a Nevada brothel in his television series. Theroux had been a reporter on Moore's *TV Nation* series and learnt the virtues of the klutz approach there, which he has since adopted.

ACTIVITY 3

If you are familiar with Michael Moore's work, like *Bowling for Columbine*, *Fahrenheit 9/11* or *Sicko*, think of how his large shambling presence in the films enables certain information to be conveyed. His persona is a representation of a particular kind of information seeker. List some words to describe it that contrast it both with the anonymous voice of God/authority narration and with an opinionated presenter of a prestige television series such as Andrew Marr or David Starkey.

FIGURE 2.1 Michael Moore speaking during a press conference, near the New York Stock Exchange on Wall Street, in New York City © Ramin Talaie/Corbis

Documentarists regularly discuss their work, introducing it at special screenings and film festivals, defending their practices and allowing those audience members privileged to hear them to register the differences between the on-screen persona and the off-screen one. There are many opportunities in print and online for a much wider group of people interested in documentary to encounter the filmmakers' self-presentations. In discussing their work, documentarists regularly explain their methods and advocate the superiority of the style or mode they have chosen, as well as elaborating on the situation explored and defending the ethical character of their interactions with their subjects. It is very much worthwhile seeking out such events, websites or publications. A collection of interviews with Broomfield, for instance, is very informative (see Wood, 2005). I have hardly ever heard or read a filmmaker's comments which did not enrich my understanding of the film. People who appear all-ego in a film are frequently disarming and modest about their achievements when appearing live. Similarly, klutzes reveal themselves as much sharper and far more self-aware than in their on-screen performance.

The video diary is another form that can be produced from within a klutz persona, though most are not. One of the oddities of klutz films is that they seem only to be made by men. Indeed, Dovey's outline of the category names it as a male one and explores the ways it talks about contemporary masculinity (2000, p. 41).

ACTIVITY 4

Take a moment to consider why the klutz might be a useful figure for male but not female filmmakers. Women can easily be klutzes in ordinary life and the persona is used by some female comics – think of Miranda Hart – but even when female documentarists do appear on camera, this is not a persona they adopt (nor, to be fair, do most men).

There seems no absolute reason why the category is masculine. Perhaps it is that women are less likely to be indulged (or funded to make films) if they reveal themselves as apparently incompetent. There is something rather childlike about the klutz filmmaker persona which can appear almost appealing at times, which is why the word 'indulge' seems appropriate. Viewers seem willing to believe that Moore cannot really be as dim as he sometimes appears, but a woman is unlikely to be given that latitude.

These alternative ways of categorizing documentaries are by no means as influential as Nichols's. No one other than Dovey talks of 'klutz' films, despite the insights the term encourages. It is important, though, that you realize that even when there are highly influential categories organizing the ways in which we can analyse representations, they are not the only way to do so, nor do they provide the last word on them.

3.3 Ethical documentary filmmaking

I referred above to the regularity with which documentarists speak publicly about their work, mentioning their 'defending' it and the ethical practices involved in its production. This may seem odd, but could be because of the residues of their operation within the discourses of sobriety and their claims to be showing some part of the world as it 'really is' as well as advancing an argument about that. Their public appearances then involve their continuing the interaction with actuality and explaining the character of their representational practice. The kind of public appearance, which for a feature film director is primarily about promoting the film, for a documentary director is often far more pointed and before a live audience at documentary film festivals, such as that regularly held in Sheffield, UK.

Like many writers on the field, Nichols too considered the ethics of a documentarian. There are two main aspects of documentary ethics that need particular attention: honesty in representing the situation fairly; and propriety in the relations with the people depicted. Nichols's comments in Reading A about Silver's use of the long take rather than an edit to show how he negotiated the presence of his camera inside the meeting hall is a comment about a good ethical practice (an edit could have covered events happening at two different times). We shall see below how filmmakers need to inform viewers of the status of certain kinds of representation that might be misunderstood, for example, by superimposing the word 'reconstruction' on a scene if it had not been filmed as it happened initially.

One aspect of proper dealing with subjects that frequently arises is the matter of 'informed consent'. Subjects agree to being filmed within particular situations and usually have to sign 'waivers' giving permission for the filmmaker to film them and to the use of the footage taken. What such a form 'waives' is usually the right to sue for misrepresentation. It is not at all uncommon for documentary subjects to dislike the way a film shows them to be, or to become unhappy when they see commentary about the film and the way they appear. We shall see an instance of this in the discussion of *Sylvania Waters* below (in section 5.2). The tendency for documentarists to concern themselves with social issues, as noted by Corner (see section 2.2 above), means that there are many documentaries about people with various forms of disability. Ethical filmmakers working with intellectually disabled people try to include footage of them acknowledging their willingness to be filmed as part of demonstrating that consent has been sought and given, because of quite reasonable concerns with previous instances of exploitation.

4 DRAMATIZATION AND THE DOCUMENTARY

4.1 Scripting and re-enactment in the documentary

Because documentaries represent the real world and make truth claims about their representations, the use of actors and scripts for anything other than the voice-over or the on-screen narration is regarded unfavourably in some quarters. Both professionally and academically, such practices can be condemned as dramatization unsuited to the documentary purpose. Despite this, a very substantial proportion of documentaries use scripts and actors. I will use the term 're-enactment' to cover the considerable number of terms used when what is shown has been created for the filming rather than happening regardless of the camera's presence, but where there are still truth claims being made. Re-enactments, whether by the actual people involved or by actors, are regarded as compromising the relationship between documentary material and the real event. For some critics, even the original subjects (re-)speaking their own words is just another form of dramatization.

Scripting and re-enactment were common in the early days of documentary, especially in the Griersonian corpus (Ward, 2005, p. 39). In part this was because of technical limitations. When the absence of lightweight cameras and recording facilities made location filming difficult, it was not possible to shoot a lot of film of what was happening and make a story and argument from it in the editing suite. The film had to be scripted in advance after conducting research into the topic and the subjects were often asked to perform those parts of their daily lives that were required. This was part of a different conception of acceptable ways of representing actuality. The credits of Robert Flaherty's ethnographic documentary *Man of Aran* (1934) reveal a cast list comprising the Man of Aran, his wife and his son, and gives the names of those enacting these key roles, revealing thereby that this is a family constructed for the film. The film is notorious for its revival of a dangerous mode of shark fishing that had not been used for several decades before the film was made, but which Flaherty wanted to show. That criticism of the film still centres on the atemporal inclusion (the fishing shown did not represent the fishing engaged in at the time of filming) rather than on the casting of the principal roles and Flaherty's direction of their actions. This indicates where the emphasis on actuality was, and to an extent still is, being placed.

It is valuable to start a general examination of more recent practices of dramatization from the extremes of feature films which make no claim to be documentaries but which do assert a relationship with real events. 'Biopic' names the genre of biographical film following some part of the life of one or more real persons, such as *Walk the Line* (2005), Johnny Cash and June Carter, *A Beautiful Mind* (2001), mathematician John Forbes Nash Jnr, or, for an extreme example, *I'm Not There* (2007) (the film in which Bob Dylan was played by five different actors, none of whose characters was named as Dylan). These are acted throughout, often with stars, like Joaquin Phoenix, Reese Witherspoon, Russell Crowe or Richard Gere, playing the lead roles. 'Biopic' is not a popular genre term and is not used to talk about shorter episodes in people's lives, so *Frost/Nixon* (2008) based on the very brief period when David Frost interviewed ex-US president, Richard Nixon for a television show, is not referred to as a biopic, but rather as 'based on a true story', a rubric which is applied to many feature films, biopics or not.

ACTIVITY 5

Feature films promoted as being 'based on a true story' or as telling the life story of a famous person are frequent and popular releases. Think about the films currently screening or recently released on DVD. How many fit this category? List some reasons why you think they may not have been made as documentaries. What aspects do you think would have had to be changed?

Even though there has been a revival in the popularity of documentaries made for cinema release, they are still much less popular than fiction features, so none of these, or similar films, was promoted as being a documentary. Being 'based on a true story' is (apparently) less off-putting at the box office as well as allowing greater latitude for constructing an appealing narrative, in which, even if outright invention of sections is avoided, certain events are emphasized and others downplayed. The use of star actors makes promoting the films much easier than would trying to get media interested in a real person. Of course the real people involved may not still be alive anyway. When we watch a star (or even a lesser but still recognizable) actor in a role, we watch both the actor and the performance of character; when a star is cast as another famous person they are usually chosen because they can approximate a physical as well as a behavioural recreation of that individual. The representation is a complex one: in *Walk the Line* Reese Witherspoon needs to remain recognizably herself (why else pay the salary she commands?) as well as embody a convincing June Carter.

The television equivalent of the biopic, and equally unwilling to name itself documentary, can most often be found under the extremely unhelpful names 'movie of the week', 'telemovie' or the dismissive 'trauma drama'. Most commonly made for American networks and targeted at female audiences, these often tell the story of a female victim of crime or other disaster (*Death of an American Cheerleader* – 1994), if possible with a heartrending story of eventual redemption or triumph over tragedy. These too are acted and scripted throughout, but are less likely to use stars and more likely to concern ordinary people who have become newsworthy through misadventure rather than individuals who are themselves famous.

It is more usual for dramatization to be simply part of the mix of a television documentary, together with on-screen narration or with expert commentary, for example. When actuality footage is unavailable, rather than use a talking head telling the audience about an event, or allow a camera to focus on a document while a voice-over reads it, actors may be employed to 'bring the event to life'.

After the invention of lightweight cameras and synchronous sound capabilities in the 1960s made location shooting easier, practices which had until then been regarded as acceptable fell from favour. The influential manifestos of the American Direct Cinema practitioners, mentioned above, were predicated on this technology being available. In their wake, re-enactment and dramatization became rarer. In the last twenty years they have returned very noticeably. Dramatization did not disappear in the interim, although it required the development of a specialized form. A considerable number of 'dramatized documentaries' or 'documentary dramas' were produced. This practice will be considered below (in section 4.2).

Re-enactment is to be found in many historical documentaries whether about famous people, like Casanova, or famous events, as in *Virtual History: The Secret Plot to Kill Hitler* (2004) where not only actors were used to play the various roles, but, as Craig Hight points out, CGI masks over their faces were used to make them look more like the actual people involved. Hight calls this the 'graphic verité' mode of digital documentary production, noting also the superimposition of wear and tear marks on the film to make it appear archival rather than newly produced (Hight, 2008, p. 17). This is an extreme example of a representation involving dramatic and technical recreation, and the use of the word 'virtual' in the title served to signal to viewers that high levels of fictionalization were present. Work like this is quite rare and it is still more common for re-enactment to be interspersed with presenters, actual documents, such as photographs or birth certificates, and location film.

Subtitles announcing that a scene is a 'reconstruction' cover instances where actors are used, where the original people repeat previous actions and where non-actors perform roles. They have become more common following sustained criticism and regulatory sanctioning of Carlton TV's *The Connection* (1996), in which acted scenes of drug dealing were presented as if they were real ones. At about the same time, the same accusation was levelled at a Channel 4 documentary on rent boys in Glasgow, *Too Much Too Young: Chickens* (1997). Both were required to pay substantial fines for misrepresentation. Although the filmmakers involved defended the ethical character of their work, arguing that to have filmed the real people involved would have placed them in danger, they were judged to have been remiss in letting viewers assume they were watching 'the real thing'. It was not the use of actors that was being condemned; rather it was the failure to inform the audience of the status of the representation that was at fault.

Rather than a fine, instances of 're-staging' in the docusoap *Driving School* led to the release of BBC guidelines on 'Staging and re-staging in factual programmes' to ensure, as Bruzzi points out, that audiences were made aware of the status of material screened (2006, p. 44). 'Re-staging' indicates that the subject was asked to repeat certain actions and will be examined further below when the matter of docusoaps and the guidelines will be engaged with (section 5.2). It is not incidental that the instances declared to be malpractice concern texts set in the present day; historical re-enactment, especially of periods prior to the development of film technologies, can more readily be recognized by audiences as necessarily created specifically for the film. There are various other conventions, such as allowing actors to be seen but not heard (clearly), or placing them in an obviously fake setting, that are used to signal re-enactment without the need for on-screen warnings.

Michael Wood's Story of England was a historical documentary series screened on the BBC in 2010. It traced events in the Leicestershire village of Kibworth over the last thousand or so years, using archaeological evidence, archival records, location shooting, interviews with experts and residents and direct narration from the on-screen presenter, who also wrote the series, Michael Wood. It took a novel approach to re-enactment that provided clear signs of the status of the representation. At various stages, for example when wanting to talk about the relationship between ordinary parishioners and the 'mother church', rather than just read out the record of bequests or employ actors to perform a scripted version of this, the filmmaker had present-day inhabitants of the village, in their ordinary twenty-first-century clothing, read the words of people who may well have been their forebears. It enlivened the script, supported an argument the series was advancing about continuity in English village history, and was a very obviously marked instance of 'dramatization'. The last episode of the series included villagers dressed up in Victorian costume performing sentimental music hall songs, but this was presented as a real concert staged for the people themselves as part of the celebration of their history which surrounded the documentary's production. Elsewhere the episode continued the practice of having modern-dress locals reading documents from the past.

The impression may have been given in the comment on biopics above that documentary films made for cinema release and following a documentary style (whether or not they call themselves explicitly documentaries) do not use re-enactment. This is not the case. *Touching the Void* was a very successful 2003 documentary about a mountaineering accident in the Peruvian Andes some twenty years earlier. The director, Kevin Macdonald, who makes both fictional and documentary films as well as writing on documentary, decided against making this a fictional feature starring Tom Cruise (Corner, 2006, p. 93). Instead he combined location footage, interviews on location and elsewhere with the three men involved, the climbers (Joe Simpson and Simon Yates) and the chance-met acquaintance asked to guard their base camp, Richard Hawking, with re-enactment of the event by climbing actors of the same age that the principals had been when the accident occurred. Their part of the film was shot, presumably for safety, in the European Alps. The first section of the film showed the Siula Grande, which had not been climbed by anyone prior to Simpson and Yates, with voice-over from the climbers about their pleasure in climbing. It also introduced the accident, where Simpson fell during the descent and Yates found himself having to cut the rope joining them. Believing Simpson dead, Yates descended the mountain, but Simpson had fallen into a crevasse and arduously made his way back to the base camp. Questions about the morality of Yates's action were endemic in the mountaineering world thereafter and the film was based on Simpson's book explaining the event. Ethical debates about the film centred on Macdonald's decision to make the two principal figures revisit for the first time the scene of their prior trauma. Some of this is explored in the 'Making of ...' extra on the DVD.

Another mountaineering accident film based on a true story was made in 2010, *127 Hours*, but in this case, the director, Danny Boyle, did take the fictional route and the film was not conceived or presented as a documentary. The mountaineer Aaron Ralston was played by Hollywood star James Franco and the film was promoted on two bases: its 'true story' foundation and the extreme reactions of viewers (fainting, running out of the cinema) to the extended scene, over four minutes long, where the lead character, trapped under a fallen rock, has to amputate his own arm with a penknife. *Touching the Void* had caused viewers to flinch or exclaim at the verbal description of precisely how Simpson's kneecap and leg had broken and at his pain on dragging it over bare rocks in his climb down the latter part of the mountain, but this was not on the same scale of viewer engagement as *127 Hours* at all.

ACTIVITY 6

Take a few minutes to consider the differences between a fully fictional representation of a man cutting off his own arm and what might have been acceptable in something labelled documentary. Viewers can know that however graphic the representation of amputation in the fictional feature, special effects will have been used to achieve it. Documentaries obviously use special effects too. *Virtual History: The Secret Plot to Kill Hitler* has already been mentioned and *Walking with Dinosaurs* will be discussed in section 6 below, but do you think a filmmaker constructing a documentary representation of Ralston's ordeal would have taken the same decision? What do you imagine critics' responses would have been? Is the fact that the sequence is 'based on a real story' relevant to people's emotional reactions, i.e. do you think that people would have been less likely to faint had the story been presented as entirely fictional?

Censors might have deemed the sequence excessive and ordered it cut had the representation not had a factual basis. This example also provides an opportunity for you to think of both the visual and the aural representation. Many viewers looked away from the fictionalized version, but it is much less easy to stop hearing (and those of us who look away from visual sequences often rely on the soundtrack to tell us when it is safe to look again).

In a BBC *The Culture Show* interview, Boyle drew attention to the importance of James Franco's acting, in particular his face. He points out that we see far more gruesome sights in *Jackass 3* or any of the *Saw* films than he presented, but that good actors can take viewers places unavailable otherwise. This does not point to the 'true story' status at all, but I think we should consider it as very significant that Franco was playing a role based on an actual person and what he had really had to do.

4.2 Docudrama

For the most part, in talking of re-enactment, we have been looking at examples that clearly mix different practices, but still assert (in programme descriptions and promotional material) that they are documentaries. It is now time to consider the separate category of fully dramatized works which still assert a relationship to documentary. Again, there are nomenclature problems. Derek Paget, the leading writer on the form, subtitles his 1998 book on the topic *Dramadoc/Docudrama on Television*, acknowledging both the slippages in the term and the televisual location of the form. He suggested then that whichever term came last revealed the dominant tendency in the text (1998, p. 93), but in later work seems to have opted for the slightly more respectful sounding 'docudrama' for all instances (e.g. Paget, 2002).

This has been quite an important type of programme in the UK, where it is often used to address social or legal problems. Material that would in the USA be made into a 'movie of the week', in the UK becomes a docudrama, though usually only if it has a broader, more political ambit. *Cathy Come Home* (Ken Loach, 1966), which is often spoken of as the first docudrama, dramatized post-war housing problems through constructing a compound story from real case histories of homeless people and people at risk of the fictional life of 'Cathy', her husband and children. The resulting drama was interspersed with voice-overs providing statistics about the situation and vox pop style comments from unidentified ordinary people. Social and political change eventuated after the screening, including the establishment of the charity Shelter. *Who Bombed Birmingham?* (Michael Beckham, 1990) about the circumstances following a 1974 IRA bombing, led eventually to the release of the wrongfully imprisoned Birmingham Six, when it both demonstrated errors in the forensic tests for explosives and named the actual bombers. Most docudramas, though, bring about much less, if any, change in the real state of affairs, but the term still signifies a serious piece of work with the intent of exposing a social or political wrong and hence their claimed membership of the category of serious or 'core' documentary.

5 DOCUMENTARY – AN HISTORIC GENRE?

5.1 'Postdocumentary'?

At the beginning of this century, the leading British documentary theorist and critic, John Corner, started to address the changed landscape for factual television, including documentary. He suggested that it might be regarded as a postdocumentary culture (Corner, 2000, 2002). He did not mean by this that the genre of documentary television was over, but that the climate was distinctively different from how it had been when he and others first started writing on it in the 1980s. His particular provocation was trying to establish how *Big Brother* might be incorporated into the field of documentary, although he clearly says he has no wish to claim it as 'documentary proper' (2002, p. 257). While the term 'postdocumentary' has not caught on, and Corner himself more recently relegates it to a footnote (2006, p. 96, note 10), the way he expanded the field of documentary has been very influential.

He first considers the traditional functions of documentaries, none of which applies to *Big Brother*, or indeed to many other new factual television forms. Early Griersonian documentaries in particular played a part in the project of democratic civics, aiming to teach and promote certain types of citizenship. Documentaries also worked as journalistic inquiry and exposition, using commentary and interviews as forms of reportage and witnessing. Both of these are very conventional, but some documentaries function as radical interrogation, aiming to provide an alternative perspective on events or activities (Corner, 2002, pp. 259–60). Corner admits that this is very much a broad-brush picture and that there are many more variants, but says that all of the documentaries gathered under this group of functions have low commodity character, that their use value is higher than their exchange value (2002, p. 260). This relates to their seriousness of purpose, to their makers' desire to educate or to inform their audience about aspects of the world with which they may be unfamiliar, or possibly contribute to social change.

This does not apply to the new forms, for which Corner claims the new function of diversion. Here the desire to entertain is foremost, which means that their commodity character is high. They are thoroughly embedded in the market economy with spin-offs, celebrity versions and the ability to produce (usually short-term) media careers for some of the non-professionals taking part. Such programmes are 'lighter' than traditional documentary and focus on high-intensity incident, anecdotal knowledge and 'snoopy sociability' (2002, p. 260). These characteristics are an important part of Corner's desire not to be seen to be asserting that prior to the postdocumentary period, documentaries failed to entertain (p. 261). Most documentarists recognized that providing some entertainment was a vital part of attracting an audience (or funding to be made in the first place), but this was not their primary concern, and while they may have had 'snoopy' tendencies, they were masked by an investigatory intent. Popular factual entertainment, which is a term that scholars such as Annette Hill (2005) are much happier applying to *Big Brother* or other reality game shows, aims to be entertaining above all. These scholars accept that programmes such as *Animal Hospital* (2005), might be seen as documentary if its function was expanded to include diverting an audience.

In suggesting that documentaries could have a primary aim of entertainment and that they could function to divert viewers, Corner was making a decisive shift away from Nichols's view that documentaries aimed to be part of the discourse of sobriety. It probably also meant that the qualities of argument became much less prominent.

⌐READING B

Now read the extract from Corner 2002 (some of pp. 262–7) which continues his analysis of postdocumentary television.

Corner was writing in 2001, while only the second British series of *Big Brother* was airing. (It has now concluded following nine outings.) Some of his comments are quite clearly speculative about possible developments in factual television programming. To what extent do you think he was accurate about tendencies in British or European television? Do you think it reasonable to have described *Big Brother* as a form of documentary, even if a diverting one? Why (not)?

Like most early reality television, *Big Brother* was a different undertaking for those participating and viewing after the first series. Because there had been no similar programme, the participants did not know what kind of behaviour would be rewarded – either by Big Brother himself or by the viewers voting contestants off. The producers' 'casting' of contestants was similarly more naïve. The extent to which viewers may have been able to learn something about real-world behaviour (if in an artificial set-up) in the first series, about which Corner was writing, was almost certainly greater than would have been the case for subsequent series. People came to be chosen for the show to provide set roles in an anticipated 'mix' and started to behave in ways they thought appropriate to succeed in the artificial situation; the producers introduced stranger and stranger 'twists' into the situation as time went on. Later series continued to be popular factual television in that the programme was never scripted, but its claims to be part of the documentary field diminished, for most analysts, to zero.

The developments which Corner names postdocumentary and which referred to far more than *Big Brother*, followed in part from the expansion of the number of television channels and the need to fill a greatly increased amount of airtime without a concomitant increase in the amount of advertising (or government grant) to fund it. Cheap production was required, and another aspect of the commodity character of the resultant programmes could be seen in those that relied on a revenue stream from public voting. Discussing some of the same situation as Corner, but starting from a study of the Discovery Channel, which provides one or more dedicated channels in 155 countries, Elfriede Fürsich argues that entertainment had become more important than it previously was in non-fiction programming. She says that this led to the commissioning and programming of shows that were non-critical and non-political and that focused on 'celebratory worldwide understanding' (Fürsich, 2003, p. 133). These qualities maximize sales as well as the longevity of the product. She is not here talking of the new forms addressed by Corner, but of programmes which aimed to inform rather than divert. Her perception that such shows carefully operate between credibility and commercialization, reducing the extent of the latter to avoid harming the former too much, is a precursor of Corner's view of the high commodity character of the new forms.

5.2 Docusoaps

Docusoaps are one of the additions to the televisual landscape that led Corner to argue for the consideration of documentaries functioning to entertain. They draw heavily on the practices of observational documentary, presenting themselves as having been shot from a fly-on-the-wall perspective with minimal intervention, although they do use a voice-over, which Direct Cinema advocates would have disapproved of, but which is still at times employed by conventional observational documentaries. In contrast, though, the voice-over in docusoaps tends to operate from a cynical or even snide perspective. Docusoaps take viewers into particular workplaces and show what happens there week after week, interweaving several narrative threads, as soap operas do. Such intercutting implies a simultaneity of event underlined by the frequent use of the term 'meanwhile' in the docusoap's voice-over. The 'soap' part of their name developed not just from this, but more because they were made as serials with continuing subjects and themes, rather than just in series. Despite the name, docusoaps do not operate fully like soap operas. Perhaps most importantly, they focus on one or more 'larger than life' characters, acting up for the camera and even at times addressing viewers directly.

What is now generally regarded as the first example, *Sylvania Waters*, Paul Watson's 1993 study of a dysfunctional upwardly mobile Australian family, was presented as a standard documentary series. In this, it was in the mode of his previous works, such as *Family*, his 1974 British investigation of an ordinary Reading family that a few regard as itself a precursor of docusoap, or *The Fishing Party* (1985), which exposed the leisure activities and crassness of wealthy Englishmen. Watson's work regularly caused controversy because of questions about how informed his subjects were about how he intended to represent them. *Sylvania Waters* continued this, with the central character, Noelene, complaining widely, including at a 1994 Edinburgh Television Festival event to which she had been flown as a guest, that Watson had cross-cut between events that had not happened at the same time (Baker, 2006, p.155). *Sylvania Waters* was also criticized for being shot in a glossy manner with music more suited to a travelogue. Most of all, it was criticized for the voice-over provided by the youngest son of the family. This was scripted to include echoes of the concluding moments of a soap, as in the first episode's conclusion: 'Watch next week to see if Mum really will keep her promise to take me out of school.' The series thus explicitly signalled its melodramatic serial quality. It also confused the matter of 'voice' discussed in the first reading. In handing the voice-over to the fifteen-year-old son of the family being investigated, some critics thought that the filmmaker's own voice had been muted or displaced.

It was an expensive production, shot on film, with a prestige producer, directors (Brian Hill and Kate Woods) and time slot. Subsequent programmes, now named docusoaps, have been much less costly, shot digitally and screened in the early evening for a family audience. BBC1's *Airport*, starting in 1996, was one of the highly popular early examples and demonstrates clearly the way the sub-genre operated to entertain rather than to advance an argument about the work of airport personnel. Gail Coles stresses the incorporation of elements of sitcom and reality TV (2000, p. 28). Docusoaps took the concern with ordinary people, carefully cast for dramatic potential, their embodiment of stereotypical qualities, making them easily recognizable as 'types' from reality TV, while the ability to be comically entertaining, intentionally or not, echoed sitcoms. Concern with the subjects' personal lives came both from reality shows and soaps.

Docusoaps were set in workplaces, initially service industry ones like cruise liners, shopping centres and airports, but while they frequently showed the stress of the working conditions and the interaction with customers, the stories that were the focus and flagged in the continuity lines were of health, romance and personal triumph. Work was represented as a site for personal display and interaction, not as an industrial setting where labour was more or less exploited. Coles suggests that viewers are not watching to find more about the locations, though the workplace usually provides the title, but to follow the characters' lives (2000, p. 36). She comments several times on the characteristic 'hamminess' of the performance of the key docusoap characters, like *Airport*'s Jeremy Spake, with his camp asides to the camera (p. 36). She later discusses the frequency of camp characters in docusoaps generally, ascribing it to the usefulness of exhibitionism and performance, themselves part of the spectacle of camp, to the genre. She notes of the characters how 'the seriousness of their observations of ordinary life are deflated by the playful, ironic style in which they are presented', part of which, as already noted, is directed by the voice-over (p. 38).

Dovey says docusoaps dominated network factual programming from 1996 to 1999, displacing most serious documentary during that time (2000, p. 133). They were much criticized: '[I]t has almost become a generic feature of docu-soaps that they resist any temptation to adopt an overtly critical stance on their subjects' (Kilborn, 2000, p. 116). This was part of their failure to adhere to the documentary function of producing an argument, Dovey finding none evident at all, just a 'narrativization' of the everyday world in which not even character development happens since the subjects are cast for their 'set of two-dimensional qualities which they continue to act out over and over' (Dovey, 2000, pp. 152–3). The topics of docusoaps 'suggest a portrait of the operators of the new service economy, a new ethnography of consumerism, leisure and aspirational desire' (2000, p. 140). The intercutting between different storylines was so metronomic that it suggested they were all equally significant, even if, in a powerful example from *Airport* provided by Dovey, one concerned 500 escaped budgerigars, another a policewoman's ill-fitting shoes and the third the fate of a family of refugees (p. 144).

Bruzzi's (2006) discussion of the development of docusoaps contrasts the naval study *HMS Brilliant* (1995) with *The House* (1995), an examination of the Royal Opera House, as two expensive observational documentary series, only the second of which leads to docusoap. There have been many observational documentaries set aboard navy vessels (e.g. *Ark Royal* (2002) and *Warship* (2008)), which require substantial cooperation between the Navy and the filmmakers. All have public relations aspects, as have almost all documentaries about the forces requiring cooperation to gain access, but it is still possible for such documentaries to be revealing. As Bruzzi points out, *HMS*

Brilliant was distinctive in being the first instance when a camera crew had been allowed on board during active deployment in a war zone and also was able to follow the first British navy crew to take Wrens on board (Bruzzi, 2006, pp. 124–5). The resultant series was not a docusoap; it had no voice-over and made its argument about the two main features observed through the juxtaposition of narrative threads or masked interviews. ('Masked' refers to interviews where the person asking the questions is neither heard nor seen. They are a common and easily recognizable feature of news, current affairs and documentary. Viewers do not need to see an interviewer to know that a minister speaking about a topical item on a news broadcast is responding to a question. 'Noddies', cutaways which show an interviewer acknowledging an answer by smiling or nodding, may be necessary to cover edits in longer interviews, but are wasted space when there is only time for a sound bite.)

The relevance of *The House* for docusoap development rests both in the ironic, opinionated voice-over scripted for Jancis Robinson to deliver and in the particular 'crisis structure' pursued (Bruzzi, 2006, p. 126). The production crew were alerted to developing situations in advance so that they could be present to film crises, like the sacking of the box office manager, around which episodes could then be structured. Bruzzi argues that this also led to a focus on personalities and so the features of docusoap – ironic voice-over, the pursuit of characters and a crisis structure, as well as fast editing between several narratives – were all established (pp. 126–7).

Driving School (1997) was an important and popular docusoap exhibiting all of these characteristics. Its story of Maureen, a middle-aged woman repeatedly failing her driving test, and her hapless instructors attracted a peak audience of 12.45 million to its early evening time slot (Bruzzi, 2006, p. 129). Revelations that certain events, such as Maureen waking her husband during the night to help her revise before a test, were re-staged to be filmed, and that a meeting between two instructors was completely set up to provide a continuity segment, led to the BBC drafting guidelines on 'Staging and re-staging in factual programmes' that identified acceptable and unacceptable practices. The general thrust was to ensure that footage should depict what had happened and that if it proved necessary to stage or re-stage anything, it should clearly be identified as such. There was also a requirement not to intercut scenes in ways which proved misleading about the chronology of events. Bruzzi points out that *Driving School* would have been in breech of several of these (p. 131).

In the early days of docusoaps some of the characters focused on, like Maureen, or indeed Noelene from *Sylvania Waters* who released a single, became minor celebrities, engaging in shopping centre appearances and the like. That has faded with the decline in the popularity of the form. There are some suggestions that it peaked around 2002 and has all but disappeared, but there are still docusoaps to be found, even if, as in the nature of television programmes, they have modulated quite a bit and changed their place in the schedule. *White Van Men* is a 2010 docusoap which retains most of the older features, but now screens on Five a little later in the evening. *Emergency Bikers* (also on Five) and *Traffic Cops* are two more characteristic 2010 instances and indicate a major modulation to the form: the reduction of cynicism with the move to slightly greater seriousness in the choice of workplace. The slang titles might appear to counteract this, but the ironic voice-over, the fondness for larger than life characters, especially camp ones, and the emphasis on personal relationships have all disappeared, as has the strong serial character. The situations are now quite banal, following police or other emergency personnel on their regular beats, usually looking at three instances, leading, in the case of *Traffic Cops*, to arrests and giving the results of charges in voice-over at the end of each episode. Most contemporary docusoaps are self-contained within the episode.

To examine what has happened and how there has been an incorporation of some of Corner's older function of education for citizenship along with the entertainment, we shall start by looking at one site that has proved very productive for more recent docusoaps – customs, immigration and quarantine. The long-running series *Border Security* started in New Zealand as *Border Patrol*, before being formatted for Australia in 2004, and then in 2009 for the USA (where it is called *Homeland Security USA*). The Australian series is widely exported, screening under the title *Nothing to Declare* on Channel One as well as on a couple of pay channels in the UK, in various European countries and across Asia. Peter Hughes has discussed the public relations role of the Australian series, which started during a period when the conservative government was engaged in a scare campaign about the threat refugees and other foreigners posed to the country. He stresses the importance of the access the filmmakers were given, allowing them to produce substantial amounts of footage at little cost. In return, the docusoap showed the good job the officials were doing in halting illegal immigrants, impeding drug smugglers and stopping people knowingly or unknowingly bringing suspect plant and animal products into Australia (Hughes, 2010). He talks of the programme's popularity being partly explained by its demonstrating that action is being taken to reduce the extent of risk in contemporary risk society (p. 444). The programme does this by showing ordinary working people calmly and professionally conducting successful operations in defence of the nation's borders each week, at the same time that its serial character indicates that the risk continues.

The voice-over positions viewers to judge the travellers and tourists by pointing out tell-tale signs of nervousness that may betray smugglers or those wanting to work illegally, as well as expressing astonishment at the quantities of forbidden foodstuffs some people carry in their luggage. While there may be some jokiness about those moving through the airports, there is no making fun of the workers or their senior staff, as was standard in the early docusoaps.

Much of this series is as banal as the recent British ones; neither very often encounters serious offences (and if they do, it is likely that legal requirements would prohibit their broadcast). Both, however, can be seen as educating citizens, negatively through the revelation of bad behaviour and positively through showing how our safety and well-being is being looked after. Corner indicates that Grierson regarded 'national advertising' as a legitimate concern for documentaries (2002, p. 259). Jacqui L'Etang observes that Grierson often used the terms documentary and propaganda interchangeably and saw nothing wrong with producing such material (1999). Hughes's argument that *Border Security* serves a public relations function is obviously related. His analysis of the programme showing action being taken against risk that is constantly present in contemporary society is, however, worth considering further.

Television programmes about the emergency services were the very first type of programmes to be called reality TV, when instances like *Cops* and *Rescue 911* were screened in the USA in the late

1980s and early 1990s. The term shifted to the challenge game shows and revamped talent quests where it remains, but the appeal of the original topic has remained. The BBC's *999* and ITV's *Blues and Twos* were emergency services programmes of the early 1990s which mixed dramatic reconstruction with actuality footage and advised viewers on what to do if they found themselves in similar situations (Corner, 1996, p. 184). Corner notes of these programmes that 'the psychodynamics of anxiety and insecurity become principal terms of the viewing relationship' (p. 184). This can be seen as continuing the focus on risk that Hughes detected in *Border Security/Nothing to Declare* that is also part of the way in which emergency services docusoaps represent the modern world.

ACTIVITY 7

Think for a moment about how programme titles prepare us for a particular kind of viewing experience. How does the change of title from *Border Security* to *Nothing to Declare* position British viewers differently from Australian ones?

Watch at least some of an episode of an emergency services docusoap, whether law and order or medical. Pay particular attention to the narration. Does it suggest that viewers might be advised to be, as Corner notes, anxious and insecure? Are there any ways in which concerns about the riskiness of the societies we live in are allayed by the end of the programme?

Many of these programmes make use of surveillance camera footage. Perhaps because we are most accustomed to the use of this in news reports of criminal behaviour, this kind of material operates to signal our existence in a risk society. It is incorporated into docusoaps, usually as enabling a pursuit to be continued or danger to be intensified, but is rare during the concluding segments of reassurance.

Law and order stories are staples of fiction films and programmes and this popularity leaks into non-fiction sites also. There is still space for serious documentaries and docudramas exposing injustice and looking into legal problems, but the modulation of docusoaps into ones focused on the activities of the law and other emergency services that are designed to entertain and reassure indicates two things. One is the persistent social usefulness of a light documentary style programme on the work of emergency services, and the other that, for the most part, docusoaps featuring excessive characters in service industry settings were a feature of the televisual past.

A few docusoaps with veterinary settings, like *Animal Madhouse* (2010), retain the more extreme elements though still with an element of emergency services and with enough teaching about how to be a good pet owner to fit in the contemporary mainstream televisual environment. Docusoaps located in medical or veterinary sites most commonly lack the facetious commentary and resemble the risk and reassurance structure, although they are marked by a greater concern with the eliciting of viewer empathy. Nonetheless Hughes's observations about risk are valuable when considering contemporary docusoaps. There is a significant difference in screening amusing representations of the life of driving instructors or cruise ship singers which focus on their relationships with their clients and fellow workers, and showing a night's activity of a couple of traffic police as they arrest drunken drivers and car thieves. The hospitals and police workplaces are sites where the threats to personal well-being are handled, if not contained. This is even more the case than with customs and quarantine, which required politicization of border issues to be seen readily as threats to individual citizens' well-being. The very representation of this as a site of continual vigilance against would-be transgressors was part of this politicization, this inclusion of an additional kind of risk. A conventional observational documentary about British customs, *The Duty Men*, broadcast in 1987, did not represent the customs officers or police involved in this way, being more focused on catching drug smugglers.

The borderline between the new docusoaps and observational documentaries is far less clear than was the case when docusoaps were first identified. *Helicopter Heroes* (2007) resembles the risk reassurance instances in its promotional presentation of emergency service workers. The ordinary accident victims helped by the flying paramedics are not presented as violent or criminal. Their activities may have been ill-judged, but they exemplify the dangers of everyday life, whether at work, driving along the road or engaged in recreational activities. This BBC series appears to be a more expensive production, incorporating no surveillance footage, as the police instances so often do, but equally advancing no argument more demanding than that the men and women depicted are doing a valuable job (which no doubt they are).

Observational documentaries did not disappear entirely into docusoaps; they continue to be a popular televisual form, which may exhibit, in Fürsich's (2003) term, the useful 'celebratory world-wide understanding' to encourage international sales. *One Born Every Minute*, following several couples' experiences in a maternity hospital, could be seen as an example here, more serious than a docusoap, but commissioned for subsequent series after its successful 2009 screening. While *One Born Every Minute* did not, to my knowledge, use actual surveillance footage from the hospital's regular security tapes, the documentary crew established a similar battery of cameras to monitor the activities of the expectant parents.

One difference between docusoaps and documentaries is that only the former can be seen as part of what John Ellis calls 'consolatory entertainment' (2007). Ellis uses the term for the undemanding programmes that are watched by large numbers of people even though they acknowledge that there are better programmes available. It would include the kind of television that is watched because it is the least objectionable of the available offerings when a person wishes to watch television but is not strongly drawn to any particular programme. Ellis instances the type of programmes presented by Cilla Black and Bruce Forsythe (2007, p. 14), but I believe docusoaps could also be included, especially in contrast to more formal documentaries which could be precisely the 'better programmes available' that Ellis uses as contrast. His description outlines the conservatism of consolatory entertainment, and the uncritical approach of docusoaps would fit well here, but he also notes its 'welcoming and inclusive' character, as well as its suitability for family viewing. Most of the programming to be found on contemporary expanded television services could be regarded as consolatory entertainment and Corner's observation about popular factual programming's function as diversion is very much in tune with this.

5.3 Reality TV

Although Corner wrote of the postdocumentary culture to try to examine *Big Brother*, few people since have regarded this or similar reality game shows, like *Survivor* (2000–) or even *I'm a Celebrity ... Get Me Out of Here* (2002–) as part of the field. They remain more likely to be called 'popular factual entertainment', or of course 'reality TV'. The extent of the casting of the ordinary or celebrity participants, the way they perform for the cameras and the voting viewers, the complete artificiality of the settings and the various tasks set by the producers all seem to remove the programmes too far from a concern with actuality, however much they may divert.

Wife Swap (2003–) or *Faking It* (2000–6) provide more possible examples for exploration of whether the ambit of the term 'documentary' has expanded. You may not have had an opportunity to see the latter since there have not been recent episodes, though *Wife Swap* was still being made at the time of writing and old episodes were screening on pay and some of the additional digital channels. The programme is also briefly considered in Chapter 6. Both programmes started with an artificial situation – typical of the way 'reality TV' immediately disregards reality. The wives of two very different families were required to exchange places for two weeks and live one week according to the rules of their own family and one by those of their 'pretend' one. There was no voting, no special house, no additional tasks and the families were encouraged to behave 'normally'. In *Faking It*, a person unskilled in one particular practice, like conducting an orchestra, was coached for a month before trying to convince experts that they had the skill in question. Again, the artificiality was (supposedly) limited to the initial set-up. However, this meant that the entire situation could be regarded as staged and therefore not in any way a representation of any actuality. Both programmes came from Channel 4, so the BBC guidelines on staging did not apply, but viewers were left in no doubt about the artificiality of the frame of the activity screened.

The matter of whether this type of programme is included in the field of documentary is not yet settled. Recent books on documentary usually discuss whether they should be incorporated, but while the majority do include docusoaps, it is most common for those likely to be termed 'reality TV' to be left in limbo. Bruzzi concludes her chapter, taking up Corner's documentaries of diversion, by observing the continuing impact of their legacy to documentary – a greater emphasis on entertainment and drama, but referring to them as 'popular factual entertainment' (Bruzzi, 2006, p. 151).

ACTIVITY 8

As you can see, there is no definite decision on the extent of the field of documentary television. Most critics see the desirability of including some of the newer lighter programmes, but just how many of them varies from critic to critic. Think about how far you would extend the field. Reflect on which programmes you thought were documentaries at the beginning of this week. Is your opinion still the same? Would you admit the initial docusoaps or only the later risk and reassurance ones? Is that because you still want a concern with social issues from programmes claiming to be documentaries? Where do you stand on *Wife Swap*? Or *The World's Strictest Parents*? Why are they in (or out)?

6 NATURAL HISTORY DOCUMENTARIES

6.1 Documenting animal life

There have already been several references to films about the natural world, but it is now time to examine this distinctive and highly popular form of documentary more extensively. Natural history programmes are a common part of television schedules and the main content of dedicated pay channels like Discovery and Animal Planet (co-owned by Discovery and the BBC) as well as National Geographic. Only a small number of nature documentaries are made for cinema release, but they are likely to be among the most popular documentaries at the box office. *March of the Penguins* (2005) not only received an Oscar for best documentary in 2006, but is the highest grossing (animal) documentary of all time, having grossed US$127 million worldwide by 2007 (Rodier, 2007, p. 16).

A good starting point is John Berger's essay 'Why look at animals?', from his collection *About Looking* (1980). He begins with an assertion that the relationship between humans and animals changed in the nineteenth century. Prior to that, animals helped to define who we were, they acted metaphorically to represent qualities and, domesticated and wild, they were very present in our surrounds. As useful animals, such as mousers, watchdogs and plough horses, disappeared from our lives to be marginalized in special places, there was a massive growth in the keeping of pets rather than animals who provided services (Berger, 1980, pp. 12–13).

Public zoos came into existence as animals began to disappear from everyday life. London Zoo opened in 1828. In the same period, the use of animal figures as children's toys increased. Zoos, pets, stuffed animal toys and wildlife photography all represent for Berger the marginalization of animals (pp. 20–24). The zoos Berger discusses have changed – the essay was written in 1977 – but it is worth noting that zoo attendance has dropped while the prevalence of the other items has increased, along with the number of television programmes about animals. One reason suggested elsewhere for the decline in zoo attendance is that visitors are dissatisfied by the stasis of the animals for the majority of the time, or their meaningless movement. Accustomed to wildlife television, they want animals always to be engaged in activities like hunting and mating.

Berger notes that the most important aspect of wildlife photography is its ability to make visible the invisible, that the frozen thousandth of a second provides a view of animals otherwise utterly unavailable (p. 14). A similar phenomenon is to be found with moving images where we are shown views which would not normally be at all possible. Such access is not only made part of the promotion of films like *Travelling Birds*, but also is a major focus of the 'Making of…' documentaries that appear as DVD extras or are screened separately on television. The still photograph and the moving television show both present selected moments of greater and more meaningful drama and remove from our knowledge of animals the duration of their rest, their inactivity – or perhaps their digestive processes. Watching ungulates browse for the hours of the day it is necessary for them to survive on such minimally nutritious food as grass is not good televisual spectacle, so it is edited out.

'Anthropomorphism' is the term used to refer to the attributing of human qualities to animals (or even plants and technological devices). Berger argues that anthropomorphism was inevitable until the end of the eighteenth century as 'an expression of their [animals'] proximity'. In his view of anthropomorphism as characterizing a pre-industrial and better way of interrelating with animals, Berger differs from most other writers using the term. For scientists, anthropomorphism is an undesirable way of thinking and a customary charge brought against the understandings advanced by natural history television. It is regarded as a misrepresentation of animal behaviour.

READING C⊢

Now read the extract from Derek Bousé's *'Historia Fabulosus'* in *Wildlife Films* (2000), which discusses the link between the anthropomorphism of films about animals and the long tradition of animal fables. Bousé suggests a different trajectory for anthropomorphism, relates it specifically to film and television, and values it differently. Outline the main differences between Berger and Bousé. How easy do you think it is to regard animal behaviour without being anthropomorphic?

Lindahl Elliot quotes Neil Evernden to talk of physical, emotional and cultural anthropomorphism whereby as well as 'attributing a human form, emotion or sensation to something, we can attribute a human *explanation* to the non-human world' (2001, p. 290, his emphasis) as when we talk of 'competition'. He does not approve of this, yet as a semiotician he wants to dispute the possibility of ever being able to escape anthropomorphism since the words and images we use are always signs which we understand culturally. We cannot understand, represent and talk about animals other than through specific kinds of human understandings. He takes issue, though, with the production of images presented as from the animal's viewpoint, often even named 'eagle cam' or 'shark cam', arguing that the images gained from cameras attached to the animal are still framed and presented from a human point of view (POV), still bounded by the capabilities of human visioning technologies, our generic conventions and the ways we have learnt to read (and disregard) editing practices (Lindahl Elliot, 2001, p. 300).

He argues in particular about the techniques used in the BBC documentary series presented by Sir David Attenborough, *The Private Life of Plants*, which was able to produce a high-rating series about the televisually unpromising static objects by treating them as animals through the use of time-lapse photography, computer controlled to capture moments of movement. This then made possible the anthropomorphism of apparently unmoving subjects (pp. 300–1). The series begins by showing a bramble 'invading' its surroundings, compressing a week or more's growth into a matter of seconds. It is not Lindahl Elliot's point, but similar technological provision of the 'invisible' is also provided by the infra-red or heat-sensitive imaging which gives us night-views of animals unavailable otherwise.

Nature documentaries, he argues, are put together from segments captured by photographers but compiled in the studio by editors and directors to tell narratives which will not only entertain viewers but lead them to call in other members of the household to view the astonishing sequences, for example, to see a puma eating a rabbit (though probably not the precise rabbit we had just previously been shown).

A 2010 episode of the BBC programme *Autumnwatch Unsprung* introduced viewers to Smudge, a trained pigeon who had 'starred' in many films and television programmes showing how editing and digital post-production had made him appear far more threatened, by predators and planes, than had ever really been the case. It was not long after another of the occasional exposés of improper practices in natural history still and moving photography. The major focus of this exposé had been the use of trained rather than wild animals, yet the *Autumnwatch Unsprung* personnel, all television naturalists, greeted the bird and showed footage of him at work as entirely unproblematic. There had certainly been 'staging' of the event, but natural history programmes are replete with instances where the 'authenticity' of the images is compromised: not just the 'making visible the invisible' already mentioned, but the construction of sites like beehives or ant nests where a side has been cut away to allow cameras to film or the insertion of tiny cameras into nest boxes especially erected in areas where filming is possible.

I think there is little doubt that anthropomorphism organizes much of the way we take pleasure from natural history programmes. Think of any of the many, many programmes on meerkats from *Meerkats United* in 1987 to the various series of *Meerkats Manor* screened since 2003 or even the 2007 film *The Meerkats*, the script of which was written by crime writer Alexander McCall Smith, creator of *The No. 1 Ladies Detective Agency*. Here not only can we see how individual animals are named to make long-running series about similar-looking animals comprehensible, but also how the voice-over that identifies them also describes their activities as analogues of human ones. We can also see quite high levels of sentimentality operating here. Virtually any screening of their 'antics' will evoke viewer exclamations of 'how cute' and probably we have all at some stage 'played meerkat', holding up our hands in imitation of their paws when on alert. It is perhaps because they are so easy to anthropomorphize that meerkats have been able to get the stranglehold they have on the lighter type of natural history television. In general terms, insects are less amenable to anthropomorphism despite the sociability of bees, the aggression and humanizable shape of praying mantises, or the prevalence of ant farms in schools and children's bedrooms. With due respect to *Microcosmos*, the comparative rarity of insect documentaries may be more the result of the perceived riskiness of devoting filming time to creatures about which a segment of the population may have phobias.

We can move more closely into a consideration of anthropomorphizing by focusing on the 'anthro' part of the term. What kind of human is it that provides the model through which animal behaviour is to be read?

Lindahl Elliot suggests that the viewers of natural history are predominantly male (2001, p. 302), but this needs some unpacking because the appeal is far more evenly spread. It may be that it appears male because it is against a range of programmes like dramas and reality TV where the viewers are more likely to be female. Documentary television as a whole may in general be more watched by men if the considerable number of military history programmes are considered. Barbara Crowther provides British data to suggest that while male and female viewers both watch natural history programmes, men include them high in their top ten favourite programme types, while women do not have them in the top ten at all. In other words, this is not a matter of viewing but favouring, though nonetheless informative for that (Crowther, 1997, p. 295).

Crowther's primary argument is that the POV of natural history documentaries, and in particular the voice-over, is not only a male but a masculinist one. She argues that the form is conservative and concentrates her argument on the way it supports patriarchal views of the world and of the way things 'naturally' are. She notes how animals are presented as having a gender (i.e. cultural qualities) rather than a sex (biological ones), in part by the language used, so there is talk of male 'territorial aggression' and female 'mothering instincts'. Thus it is not only anthropomorphic, but (gender) stereotypically so.

It is more common for programmes to focus on male animals than female ones and to consider the behaviour followed from the point of view of the males. Crowther notes the use of the term 'harem' to describe groups of female animals as a very major instance of masculine anthropomorphism (1997, p. 291). It is perfectly possible to describe the behaviour of animals from a female POV, while continuing the anthropomorphism which is almost certainly important to drawing a broad audience, especially if Lindahl Elliot is right about the difficulty of avoiding it.

ACTIVITY 9

Think of a group of ungulates, like deer, or cetaceans, like seals. Recall how conventional descriptions talk about dominant males gathering groups of females and defending their territory from competing males. Try to recast a voice-over that described the same behaviour from the viewpoint of a female or a group of them.

Might it be equally probable and no more anthropomorphic to suggest that the females gather in groups and accept the most aggressive of the available males on the basis that he will keep off the less successful males and ensure that their offspring have the best available genetic material? Have you ever heard anything in a natural history film or programme suggesting this?

In the time since Crowther wrote, there has been something of a diminution of explicitly masculinist language, but no major refocusing of POV. Survival of the fittest is, as Crowther noted, still survival of the fittest male (1997, p. 292).

Crowther outlines the three principal narratives by which natural history television represents animals as: the life-cycle story, the quest narrative and the triumph of science over nature (unravelling nature's secrets). She notes how frequently an animal's life-cycle is only the reproductive cycle, with no concern with post-reproductive life or with those animals who do not engage in the reproductive cycle (p. 292). This has changed somewhat and the meerkats remain a good example and not just because they do appear to live in groups led by a dominant female. (The working title of *The Meerkats* film was *Queen of the Kalahari*.) Although the focus is on the reproductive cycle, the role of 'non-productive' females in looking after the young is discussed. Elsewhere, there may be very occasional reference to 'bachelor' groups, though this may be with a view to identifying the ones that will challenge to take over as the new alpha male.

The quest narrative is the story of the human male seeking out information. Corner notes the frequency of documentaries structured like detective stories where presenters 'find things out' (2006, p. 92). Not all presenters or quests are like this, since Crowther was writing before the programmes of Steve Irwin, who with his followers has made the quest very different. Crowther stays with scientists rather than adventurers and argues that actual female biologists like Dian Fossey become subjects of feature films not television documentaries. Perhaps in response to Crowther's quite justifiable and widely accepted criticism, there have been shifts in British natural history presentation with female presenters, such as Charlotte Oehlenbroek, who is a biologist and worked with Jane Goodall, or Kate Humble, venturing around the globe or into the sea to report on animal behaviour. Also redressing the over-representation of male presenters is the pay-TV type of nature documentary that uses a celebrity to talk about a particular animal, for example *In the Wild: Orang-utans with Julia Roberts* (1998), calling on a woman as readily as a man.

Crowther claims that the dominant discourse for natural history programmes is sociobiology, a much contested determinist approach that is presented as unproblematic by nature television producers and that tends to be a particularly patriarchal form. Another consideration of the relationship between science and natural history documentaries is discussed by Meryl Aldridge and Robert Dingwall, who claim that expensive, prestige productions in particular tend to present comments on evolution as a sequence that is purposive, heading towards a particular outcome, or even following a particular design, rather than the random arrival at combinations that work better than others in certain contingencies, e.g. including those suited to surviving particular predators (Aldridge and Dingwall, 2003, pp. 447–8).

Much of the material discussed in this section was written about 'blue-chip' documentaries. This refers to expensive, serious work which takes several years to produce and has high production values and an underpinning in scholarly work, whether this is brought to the forefront of the programme or not. Although the term is most often used of the kind of natural history documentaries presented by Sir David Attenborough, it can also be applied to ones on other topics, such as Simon Schama's 2006 series *Power of Art*. *The Blue Planet* (2002), very much a blue-chip natural history series, cost £850,000 an episode in 2002, meaning a £7 million outlay for the series co-produced by the BBC and National Geographic (Cottle, 2004, p. 88). As is frequently the case with material which may be regarded as commercial confidential, available data is patchy and it is not possible to know how profitable this series was for the BBC, but in June 2007, a similarly blue-chip series, *Planet Earth*, became one of the biggest international hits, grossing more than £22 million on sales to 95 countries and territories.

But these slow, expensive monsters are exceptions. Frequently, as Simon Cottle points out, commissioning editors have no more than £30,000 per hour to spend to fill 50 hours of television time. He instances *Vets in the Sun* (2001), set in Abu Dhabi, as one response to this tiny production budget. This brings us back to the changed televisual landscape that led Corner to talk of the new documentary function of diversion. To docusoaps and reality TV should be added animal adventures. Fürisch suggests that the structure of the great Discovery success, *The Crocodile Hunter* (1997–2004), lay in its combination of cheap production with entertainment and adventure. Steve Irwin's international success led to a growth in the production of animal adventurer programmes with presenters like Steve Leonard. Here the appeal is at least as much about the danger in which the presenter places himself (yes, again it is a male activity), as it is with what we are shown about the natural world.

Where once producers regarded audiences as squeamish and cut away before, for instance, the leopard made its kill, they and audiences have changed and the shot of the kill is now the treasured one towards which the show is structured. This can apply to blue chip as well as the cheaper programmes, but there are also the compilation shows of nothing but kill shots, e.g. *Predators* (2010). Cottle quotes a producer noting the difference between shark treatment on different channels, with Animal Planet being gentler since it targets more women and children than Discovery (2004, pp. 93–4). Sharks have been especially favoured in programming representing the world as a dangerous place, since the great success of the fiction film *Jaws* (1975).

We noted above something of the influence of CGI (computer-generated imagery) on documentary. The most substantial example of this is in natural history, most especially in the various *Walking with* programmes, starting with *Walking with Dinosaurs* (1999). Though Grierson would not have been able to foresee such a thing, there is no doubt that his 'creative treatment of actuality' applies here. This series was entirely produced by special effects, both old-fashioned, like puppetry and matte paintings, and newer, like computer imaging. There was therefore no immediate way in which the producers could claim to be representing any actuality. Work had to be engaged in to produce the understanding among viewers that this was a documentary and that its representations were based in reality. This was done through stressing the scientific basis for the creations of the extinct animals, their behaviour and their surroundings. Pre-release publicity, discussions in the media while the series was first screening and, very importantly, again, a 'Making of…' programme/DVD extra all stressed the way in which each decision about how to 'bring dinosaurs to life' was based on fossil evidence. Palaeontologists who had been consulted by the producers spoke of how they arrived at their suggestions. Rival palaeontologists disputed some of the detail, but still helped in creating a receptive climate for this being seen not as fiction, but as a documentary representation based on factual evidence.

Karen Scott and Anne White draw attention to a rival source influencing the representation, one which did not help the construction of the work as a documentary. This was the importance of *Jurassic Park* (1993), a fiction film, the huge success of which had established certain viewer expectations of dinosaur appearance and behaviour (Scott and White, 2003, p. 320). Like the earlier instance of the role of *Jaws* in popularizing sharks as documentary subjects, *Jurassic Park* was part of the *climate of reception* into which *Walking with Dinosaurs* appeared. The documentary was aimed at informing viewers about dinosaurs and their lives (and did so), but it was equally aimed at entertaining them. As such it was clearly suited to the new televisual environment, even if it was not cheap to make. It was in fact very expensive to produce, but able to recoup costs through international sales and many spin-off products, some of which stressed its factuality and other its usefulness for play. It also had considerable longevity. *Jurassic Park* was important in underpinning the entertainment component, and fortunately, although fictional, it had called on palaeontological advice for its realization of the extinct reptiles. When there was dispute among the scientists about some aspects, it was more likely that the *Walking with Dinosaurs* producers would follow the same line as *Jurassic Park* so that viewers would more readily accept the later representation as convincing.

7 CONCLUSION

In looking at documentaries about animals we have seen both the continuity of 'core' documentary in the serious blue-chip series, expository in mode whether using on- or off-screen narration, but also the growth of new styles designed to increase the proportions of entertainment and diversion. The use of computer imaging represents a form of dramatization and we see the management of this in the calling on palaeontologists to assert that the representations are based in scientific evidence and thus are able to claim the status of the real, so that the series can be named a documentary one.

Animal documentaries also demonstrate the great importance to documentary generally of narration. Very few natural history documentaries are able to operate without someone, either in voice-over or interacting on location, telling us what is happening and interpreting it for us. Except in Direct Cinema, all of Nichols's modes use some form of spoken or written words to direct our attention and try to anchor a particular preferred meaning, though the extent to which they actually do so varies considerably. Some of the newer types of animal programme, like the adventurer ones or the pets and vets shows, if we decided to locate them here, even use ironic though still anthropomorphic commentary.

Anthropomorphism is probably the most important aspect of the previous section. In considering it, we have been able to see a very specific and thoroughgoing representational practice that is contrary to the discourse of sobriety most common in core documentary. Nonetheless, anthropomorphism is very important to the way in which animals and our relationship with them are represented in documentaries and beyond.

Moving now away from how natural history documentaries employ characteristic practices of representation, this chapter more generally has demonstrated the way in which documentaries represent the historical world. At the heart of documentary representation is the claim to be telling the truth, to be representing what is real. Now it may well be that what is represented is more 'a' truth. Inevitably, and necessarily, directors select material and arrange it to make the argument they are advancing; without that selection and arrangement what we have is raw footage.

I said at the beginning that it was easiest to think of documentary as dealing with non-fiction, and this is still true. It is why dramatization is such a troublesome area. For some critics, there should be no acting in a documentary, but Bruzzi's arguments about how strongly documentaries are performative caution us about requiring this by noting *inter alia* that non-actors perform themselves and that directors require enactment even just by instructing their subjects to walk from one place to another and then stop moving. The Direct Cinema advocates and those who still talk of fly-on-the-wall documentaries believe that it is possible to capture a 'slice of life' without intervention, but we know that this rarely happens, and we should not anyway set the bar so high. Instead we should be alert for the ways particular kinds of documentary go about constructing their view of their topic.

Documentaries inform us about the world we live in, the world around us that we are unfamiliar with, and the lives of people like and unlike us. The proliferation of television channels, in conjunction with other modes of distribution, means that there are documentaries available to more people than has ever been the case before. There are still documentaries screened initially in cinemas, and public broadcasters still see documentary programmes as a key part of their remit. Pay television provides dedicated documentary channels, though they are usually dominated by programmes on popular history (i.e. war) or animals. But this is only the conventional, rather old-fashioned view. If we include documentaries made primarily to divert or entertain, like docusoaps, a much larger section of television programming comes under consideration.

This does not though mean that it has become any easier to see some of the more experimental or avant-garde documentaries. Works that can be classified in Nichols's terms in the poetic mode or, using his conception, the performative, are more rarely encountered. Occasionally they may be seen at an art-house cinema or in the late-night schedule of a public broadcaster. The main place, however, to encounter new developments and challenging styles of documentary is still at film festivals, both the wide-ranging ones named after the hosting city (London, Edinburgh) and the dedicated documentary festivals like that held annually in Sheffield. In addition to all this conventional and less conventional dissemination, and especially for those not living in the larger cities, the growth of professional and self-published online documentaries, available through specialized portals, further expands the ways in which the historical world is represented.

REFERENCES

AITKEN, I. (1990) *Film and Reform: John Grierson and the Documentary Film Movement*, London, Routledge.

ALDRIDGE, M. AND DINGWALL, R. (2003) 'Teleology on television? Implicit models in broadcast wildlife and nature programmes', *European Journal of Communication*, 18(4), 435–53.

BAKER, M. (2006) *Documentary in the Digital Age*, Oxford, Focal Press.

BERGER, J. (1980) 'Why look at animals?', in *About Looking*, London, Writers and Readers, pp. 1–26.

BOUSÉ, D. (2000) *Wildlife Films*, Philadelphia, PA, University of Pennsylvania Press.

BRUZZI, S. (2006) *New Documentary* (2nd edition), London, Routledge.

COLES, G. (2000) 'Docusoap: actuality and the serial format', in Carson, B. and Llewellyn-Jones, M. (eds), *Frames and Fictions on Television: The Politics of Identity within Drama*, Exeter, UK, Intellect, pp. 27–39.

CORNER, J. (1995) *Television Form and Public Address*, London, Edward Arnold.

CORNER, J. (1996) *The Art of the Record: A Critical Introduction to Documentary*, Manchester, Manchester University Press.

CORNER, J. (2000) 'Documentary in a post-documentary culture? A note on forms and their functions', Unpublished paper presented at the European Science Forum seminar 'Changing media – changing Europe'. Available at: www.lboro.ac.uk/research/changing.media/John%20Corner%20paper.htm (accessed 20 November 2010).

CORNER, J. (2002) 'Performing the real: documentary diversions', *Television and New Media,* 3(3), 255–69.

CORNER, J. (2006) 'A fiction (un)like any other', *Critical Studies in Television*, 1(1), 89–96.

COTTLE, S. (2004) 'Producing nature(s): on the changing production ecology of natural history TV', *Media Culture and Society*, 26(1), 81–101.

COUSINS, M. AND MACDONALD, K. (1996) *Imagining Reality*, London, Faber & Faber.

CROWTHER, B. (1997) 'Viewing what comes naturally: a feminist approach to television natural history', *Women's Studies International Forum*, 20(2), 289–300.

DOVEY, J. (2000) *Freakshow: First Person Media and Factual Television*, London, Pluto Press.

ELLIS, J. (2007) *TV FAQ: Uncommon Answers to Common Questions about TV*, London, I. B. Tauris.

FÜRSICH, E. (2003) 'Between credibility and commodification: nonfiction entertainment as a global media genre', *International Journal of Cultural Studies*, 6(2), 131–53.

HARDY, F. (ed.) (1979) *Grierson on Documentary* (revised edition), London, Faber & Faber.

HIGHT, C. (2008) 'Primetime digital documentary animation: the photographic and graphic within play', *Studies in Documentary Film*, 2(1), 9–31.

HILL, A. (2005) *Reality TV: Audiences and Popular Factual Television*, London, Routledge.

HUGHES, P. (2010) 'Governmentality, blurred boundaries, and pleasure in the docusoap *Border Security', Continuum: Journal of Media and Culture*, 24(3), 439–49.

KILBORN, R. (2000) 'The docu-soap: A critical assessment' in Izod, J and Kilborn, R. with Hibberd, M. (eds), *From Grierson to the Docu-soap: Breaking the Boundaries,* Luton, University of Luton Press, pp. 111–119.

L'ETANG, J. (1999) 'John Grierson and the public relations industry in Britain', *Screening the Past*, 7. Available at: www.latrobe.edu.au/screeningthepast/firstrelease/fr0799/jlfr7d.htm (accessed 20 November 2010).

LINDAHL ELLIOT, N. (2001) 'Signs of anthropomorphism: the case of natural history television documentaries', *Social Semiotics*, 11(3), 289–305.

MORAN, J. (2002) 'Childhood, class and memory in the *Seven Up* films', *Screen,* 43(4), 387–402.

NESSELSON, L. (2002) 'Pic has bird's eye view', *Variety*, 7 January, 45–50.

NICHOLS, B. (1991) *Representing Reality: Issues and Concepts in Documentary*, Bloomington, IN, Indiana University Press.

NICHOLS, B. (1994) *Blurred Boundaries: Questions of Meaning in Contemporary Culture*. Bloomington, IN, Indiana University Press.

NICHOLS, B. (2001) *Introduction to Documentary*, Bloomington, IN, Indiana University Press.

NICHOLS, B. (2010) *Introduction to Documentary* (2nd edition), Bloomington, IN, Indiana University Press.

PAGET, D. (1998) *No Other Way to Tell It: Dramadoc/Docudrama on Television*, Manchester, Manchester University Press.

PAGET, D. (2002) 'Seven theses about border genres: five modest proposals about docudrama' *Screening the Past*, 14. Available at: www.latrobe.edu.au/screeningthepast/firstrelease/fr0902/paget/dpfr14b.htm (accessed 31 December 2012).

RODIER, M. (2007) 'Nature calls', *Screen International*, 1599, 8 June, 16–17.

SCOTT, K.D. AND WHITE, A.M. (2003) 'Unnatural history? Deconstructing the *Walking with Dinosaurs* phenomenon', *Media Culture and Society*, 25(3), 315–32.

WARD, P. (2005) *Documentary: The Margins of Reality*, London, Wallflower.

WINSTON, B. (2008) *Claiming the Real II: Documentary: Grierson and Beyond,* (2nd edition), London, BFI.

WOOD, J. (2005) *Nick Broomfield: Documenting Icons*, London, Faber & Faber.

READING A: Bill Nichols, 'The qualities of voice'

If documentaries represent issues and aspects, qualities and problems found in the historical world, they can be said to speak about this world through both sounds and images. The question of speech raises the question of 'voice'. Since documentaries are not lectures, questions of speech and voice are not meant entirely literally.

The spoken word, of course does play a vital role in most documentary film and video: some films, like [...] *Shoah* (1985), seem, at first glance, to be nothing but speech. And yet, when documentaries speak about the historical world, they do so with all the means at their disposal, especially with sounds and images in relation to each other, or, in silent films, with images alone.

When [...] the various interviewees in *Shoah* speak to us about their past, a key aspect of understanding the force and severity of that past lies in registering its effect on their way of speaking and acting in the present. Even the most speech-oriented of documentaries – often referred to as 'talking head' films – convey meanings, hint at symptoms, and express values on a multitude of levels apart from what is literally said. What does it mean, then, to raise the question of 'voice' in documentary?

In Chapter 2 we said that documentaries represent the historical world by shaping its photographic record of some aspect of the world from a distinct perspective or point of view. As such they become one voice among the many voices in an arena of social debate and contestation. The fact that documentaries are not a reproduction of reality gives them a voice of their own. They are a representation of the world, the voice of documentary, then, is the means by which this particular point of view or perspective becomes known to us.

The voice of documentary can make a case or present an argument as well as convey a point of view. Documentaries seek to persuade or convince us: by the strength of their argument or point of view and the appeal, or power, of their voice. The voice of documentary is the specific way in which an argument or perspective is expressed. Like a plot, an argument can be presented in many ways. 'Freedom of choice is vital for women who must decide whether to have an abortion.' This is an argument, or point of view, but one documentary might work performatively to convey what women in such a position feel or experience, as *Speak Body* (1987) does, with its array of women's voices heard off screen as we see fragments of female bodies on screen, while another work might rely on interviews with women in different countries to underscore the social impact that access or impediments to abortion procedures create, as *Abortion Stories: North and South* (1984) does, with its array of women who testify on camera to their experience in various North and South American countries. *Speak Body* and *Abortion Stories* make basically the same argument, but they do so from distinctly different perspectives and hence with distinctly different voices.

The idea of voice is also tied to the idea of an informing logic overseeing the organization of a documentary compared to the idea of a compelling story organizing a fiction. Not mutually exclusive, there is nonetheless the sense that an informing logic, conveyed by a distinct voice, has dominance in documentary compared to the compelling story, conveyed by a distinct style, that has dominance in narrative fiction. Voice, then, is a question of *how* the logic, argument, or viewpoint of a film gets conveyed to us.

Voice is clearly akin to style, the way in which a film, fiction or non-fiction, inflects its subject matter and the flow of its plot or argument in distinct ways, but style operates differently in documentary than in fiction. The idea of the voice of documentary stands for something like '*style plus.*' Style in fiction derives primarily from the director's translation of a story into visual form; it gives the visual manifestation of a plot, a style distinct from its written counterpart as script, novel, play, or biography. Style in documentary derives partly from the director's attempt to translate her perspective on the historical world into visual terms, but it also stems from her direct involvement with the film's actual subject. That is, fictional style conveys a distinct, imaginary world, whereas documentary style or voice reveals a distinct form of engagement with the historical world.

[...]

Jon silver uses a long take at the opening of *Watsonville on Strike* (1989) (about a farmworker strike in the California coastal town of Watsonville) while we hear him arguing with the union director about whether he can continue to film inside the union hall. This stylistic choice (long take over editing) also bears witness to an existential necessity: Silver must actually negotiate his own right to be there, his own right to film, in this specific moment. Everything is at risk at a precise instant of historical time that anything other than a long take could represent but not authenticate in quite so direct a manner. The long take is a record of that moment seen from Silver's literal, and political, point of view as it gradually but dramatically reveals itself to us.

When the director threatens to have Silver thrown out of the hall, he responds by panning his camera to the on-looking Chicano/Chicana workers and asks them, in Spanish rather than in the English he uses with the Anglo director, – What do you say? Is it all right for me to film? The record of his question and their enthusiastic response, all within the same shot as the director's intransigent refusal to grant permission, testifies to Silver's desire to represent himself as a straight-forward, above-board activist whose spontaneous loyalty lies with the workers rather than union representatives. We *see* him display this spontaneous loyalty when he pans the camera away from the director and toward the workers rather than cutting to another discussion at another time or place. He does not cut until the director has wagged his finger at him and warned, 'If you put my picture on television, I'll sue you.'

The voice of the film reveals Silver's willingness to acknowledge the reality of the moment rather than slip into the illusion that people act as if the camera, and filmmaker, were not there. His voice, represented in the long take and camera movement, as much as in what he actually says, reveals *how* he makes his argument on behalf of the worker's [sic] cause. Like style, but with an added sense of ethical and political accountability, voice serves to give concrete embodiment to a filmmaker's engagement with the world.

The voice of documentary testifies to the character of the filmmaker like [...] Jon Silver, to *how* he acquits himself in the face of social reality, as much as to his creative vision. Style takes on an ethical dimension. The voice of documentary conveys a sense of what the filmmaker's social point of view is and of how this point of view becomes manifest in the act of making the film.

Bill Nichols

The voice of documentary is not restricted to what is verbally said, either by voices of unseen 'gods' and plainly visible 'authorities' who represent the filmmaker's point of view – who speak *for* the film, or by social actors who represent their own points of view – who speak *in* the film. The voice of documentary speaks with all the means available to its maker. These means can be summarized as the selection and arrangement of sound and image, that is, the working out of an organizing logic for the film. This entails, at least, the following decisions: (1) when to cut, or edit, and what to juxtapose and how to frame or compose a shot (close-up or long shot, low or high angle, artificial or natural lighting, colour or black and white, whether to pan, zoom in or out, track or remain stationary, and so on), (2) whether to record synchronous sound at the time of shooting, and whether to add additional sound, such as voice-over translations, dubbed dialogue, music, sound effects, or commentary, at a later point, (3) whether to adhere to an accurate chronology or rearrange events to support a point, (4) whether to use archival or other people's footage and photographs or only those images shot by the filmmaker on the spot, and (5) which mode of representation to rely on to organize the film (expository, poetic, observational, participatory, reflexive, or performative).

When we represent the world from a particular point of view we do so with a voice that shares qualities with other voices. Genre conventions are one way to cluster such qualities.

[...]

Other conventions, such as the ones that characterize the various modes of documentary – expository and observational documentary, for example – are specific to the medium.

Together, generic forms and modes establish some of the constraints that identify a given voice, but they do not wholly determine that voice. Each voice retains a uniqueness. This uniqueness stems from the specific utilization of forms and modes, of techniques and style in a given film, and from the specific pattern of encounter that takes place between filmmaker and subject. The voice of a documentary serves as evidence of a perspective, an argument, or an encounter. Our recognition that such a voice addresses us in a distinct way is a key part of our recognition of a given film as a documentary.

The fact that the voice of a documentary relies on all the means available to it, not just spoken words, means that the argument or point of view carried by a documentary can be more or less explicit. The most explicit form of voice is no doubt the one conveyed by spoken, or written, words. These are words that stand for the point of view of the film directly and are what we typically refer to as 'voice-of-God' or 'voice-of-authority' commentary.

Commentary is a voice that addresses us directly; it lays out its point of view explicitly. The comments can be passionately partisan, as it is in bold graphic intertitles of *Salt for Svanetia*, made in the Soviet Union in 1930 as Stalin was implementing a Five Year Plan to accelerate industrialization and agricultural production. These titles proclaim the arrival of the road that will bring much-needed salt to this remote region as a massive triumph of the highest order. In other cases, comments can be seemingly impartial, as in the reportorial style of most television journalists. In both cases, this voice of direct address to the viewer argues for a position that says, in effect, 'See it this way.' This can be a galvanizing voice or a reassuring one, but its tone provides us with a ready-made point of view to which we will, it is hoped, subscribe.

Source: Nichols, 2001, pp. 42–9.

READING B: John Corner, 'Performing the real: documentary diversions'

This article places *Big Brother* in the context of shifts in factual television's forms and functions. Having identified some of the distinctive features of *Big Brother*'s construction of telereality, it reviews the category of 'documentary' across some of its dominant modes. The current emphasis on formats that divert as much as they inform or question is given particular attention, and the wider social and cultural coordinates of this trend are noted. The possibility that we are moving into a 'postdocumentary' culture is posed. This is a culture in which many conventional elements of documentary will continue to develop, but in a radically changed setting – economic and cultural – for all audio-visual documentation.

Where do we locate Big Brother, and the shift in the relationship between television and everyday life that it signals, within the generic system of the medium? This generic system is not, as we know, a neat and stable set of discrete categories of work. It is a changing and increasingly hybridized set of practices, forms, and functions, one in which both cultural and commodity value lie most often in the right blend of the familiar and the new, of fulfilled expectation and shock.

We might place *Big Brother* within the history of the game show – this would certainly be true to some of its ingredients and part of its appeal. Location with the history of the talk show, particularly in its newer variants of revelation and confrontation, would be instructive too. At times, the tones and values of a 'Jerry Springer experience' are closely shadowed. We might see it as an experiment in a kind of drama – a less direct connection perhaps, but questions of theatricality and the performance aesthetic nevertheless hold the possibility of illuminating some of its shape and impact.

Author's Note: Some of the material in this article was first used in a web paper for the European Science Foundation project, 'Changing Media/ Changing Europe.' I am grateful to the ESF project for allowing my ideas an initial airing.

However, 'documentary' is the category that seems most obvious to start with and work from. This, despite the clear disjunction between the terms of the series and those even of most other types of 'reality TV' variant on the observational documentary model, let alone those of the more established, mainstream formats. For it is clear that right at the heart of the series is the idea of observing what is a mode of 'real' behavior. Such observation finds its grounding reference, and a large part of its interest and pleasure, in the real characteristics of real people, even if the material and temporal conditions for that behavior have been entirely constructed by television itself.

Big Brother comprehensively and openly gives up on the kinds of 'field naturalism' that have driven the documentary tradition into so many contradictions and conundrums for near on eighty years, most especially in its various modes of observational filming (e.g., cinema vérité, direct cinema, and the various bastardized 'fly-on-the-wall' recipes of television). Instead, *Big Brother* operates its claims to the real within a fully managed artificiality, in which almost everything that might be deemed to be true about what people do and say is necessarily and obviously predicated on the larger contrivance of them being there in front of the camera in the first place. Documentary has a lengthy and various history of concern for the historical and social world, the imaging of which in terms of followable and significant action (even for the duration of a scene) continues to pose considerable problems of accessibility and scopic coherence, despite new technology. Alongside this concern with the outer world, an interest in inner stories has developed too, particularly in the last decade of work on television. The development of inner stories often requires extensive use of interview and sometimes of part-dramatization to get the personal and the microsocial fully realized on the screen. The inner story (for example, about the road accident, about the crime, about the illness) has tended in some treatments to be pulled rather sharply away from its broader social conditions and contingencies. The documentary foreground has frequently become a highly defined narrative of localized feelings and experiences presented against what is often a merely sketchy if not entirely token background of social setting. Clearly, both the changing formats of the talk show and the soap opera have mapped out in advance some elements of the 'structure of feeling' (Raymond Williams's phrase is entirely appropriate to the affective emphasis) toward which a new documentary energy has been drawn. An adjustment in, as it were, the 'focal length' of documentary has been required, together with a changed tonality of the documentary voice (quite literally, in the case of the registers required of commentary in routing us through inner stories with optimum satisfaction). The viewing invitation slides from the dynamics of understanding to the involving, but at the same time more passive, transaction of vicarious witness and empathy.

Big Brother in a sense takes the next logical step in this process and dispenses with the difficulties of extracting the personal from the social (e.g., all those problems about authenticity in docusoap, all that debate about 'directorial intervention') by building its own social precisely for the purpose of revealing the personal. This social is *comprehensively available* to television, it has indeed been built for the daily delivery of behavior to camera. Strictly speaking, then, the circumstances are not so much those of observation as those of *display*; living space is also performance space. The availability is both tightly spatial and urgently temporal, clearly. But it is also, in its scopic comprehensiveness, emotional. 'Outside' and 'inside,' objectification and subjectification, empathy and detachment, fondness and dislike – these are positional variables on a spectatorial grid across which rapid switching can occur. The interplay between observed action, the 'cameos' of to-camera participant testimony, and the framing of voiced-over commentary is the required communicational mix for delivering this form of viewing experience. The use of the internet to extend further the public existence and availability of the event, to create optional and selective viewing opportunities 'beyond the edges' of the television text itself, enhances the sense of a concurrent, live, and open narrative (perhaps previously most marked in sports coverage). It also provides another resource in exercising spectator control (voting participants off the show). Whereas Orwell's Big Brother used surveillance to inhibit the terms of normal living in private space, *Big Brother* promotes abnormal terms of living within surveillance space. Whatever the more serious justifications for this that may be advanced in self-justification (for a popular 'experiment' in modern human interaction, a few hired psychologists always need to be on hand), the clear purpose of the whole microsocial event is to deliver fun.

Yet to say this does not amount to claiming that *Big Brother* is trying (and failing) to be a 'proper documentary.' That would be a wildly inaccurate misreading of its design and success as well as begging big questions about what precisely constitutes the 'proper.' It is simply to suggest that in coming to terms with how the series works, we need among things to see how its practices, forms, and functions are placed within what I am calling the 'postdocumentary' culture of television. We also need to note how, within that culture, the legacy of documentary is still at work, albeit in partial and revised form.

In this article, I want to develop some points about postdocumentary television as one way among others of approaching the new and entertaining forms of tele-factuality that will directly concern most other contributors. I will, at stages, want to review and reconsider some of the elements of documentarism in its more established forms in order to plot more clearly the nature of current shifts.

We can start by reviewing the idea of 'documentary' itself. As I suggested above, this might now be an unhelpful category with which to assess the changes occurring in factual television and particularly unhelpful in thinking about the new links between popular knowledge and audio-visual experience. The problem is that too many assumptions and, I think, too many idealizations have now gathered around the notions of the 'social' and the 'public,' which the term mobilizes. Paradoxically, for us to understand much of the current change in television's factual output, the term needs pressing back toward the broader category of 'documentation' from which it initially sprang (most explicitly, for Britain, in John Grierson's written advocacy of a documentary cinema during the early 1930s – see

Hardy, 1979). In doing this, we are not only going from narrowness to breadth, we are being descriptive rather than evaluative. We are trying to re-locate the rich, generically ambitious (in some versions, rather preposterous) idea of documentary within the bewildering range of practices now available for depicting the real on screen, including the screen of the computer. *Big Brother* is just one particular, highly successful, formula within this range.

I have noted in recent writing (Corner, 2000) that the term *documentary* is always much safer when used as an adjective rather than a noun, although its noun usage is, of course, a form of abbreviation, championed by the cinema pioneers and established through sheer familiarity. To ask 'is this a documentary project?' is more useful than to ask 'is this film a documentary?' with its inflection toward firm definitional criteria and the sense of something being more object than practice. This is particularly true of documentary work within television, and my feeling is that in the next few years it will become more obviously so. Documentary within cinema (in many countries now a marginal form where it exists at all) still has the strong contrast with its dominant Other – feature film – against which it can be simply defined as 'nonfiction.' Television nonfiction describes half the schedule, and so the question of generic identifiers becomes immediately more troublesome. Before I address directly the question of change, and the sorts of change, like that indicated by *Big Brother*, which seem to warrant my postdocumentary label, I want to say a few things about documentary functions.

DOCUMENTARY FUNCTIONS

The functions of documentary work have been at least as important in its history and generic identity as its forms. Both function and form have an unstable, historically contingent character, but there has been enough broad continuity across national histories of media development for us to talk about a documentary tradition. One might introduce a third element here – production practices. Specific production practices, forms, and functions all work to hold together (or not) the documentary identity at different times and places. Briefly put, they concern how a film or program was made (according to what recipes, methods, and ethics), how it looks and sounds, and what job it was designed to do, what kind of impact and use-value it was to have for audiences. Only in relation to at least one of these features, and probably by reference to more than one, we will identify something as documentary work, thus placing it at the intersection point of a number of lines upon which can be plotted matters of degree rather than of categoric kind. These lines lead to and from other things, including news, advertising, and drama as well as a whole range of presenter-led television (e.g., cooking, travel, motoring, sport) and, of course more recently, the various possible formats and settings for location 'games,' tests, and challenges.

It seems to me that there are three classic functions to which documentary exposition, testimony, and observation have variously been harnessed.

1 *The Project of Democratic Civics.* Documentary is regarded here as providing publicity and propaganda for dominant versions of citizenship. This is documentary cinema in its classic, modernist-realist phase, funded (directly or indirectly) by official bodies. In Britain, it is certainly this function that

Grierson saw the documentary as primarily fulfilling in the 1920s and 1930s. Not surprisingly, extensive and 'heavy' use of commentary is a defining feature. It should also be noted that a directly affective, as well as a cognitive, impact is often sought, an intention for which the use of music and a range of rhetorical tropes, visual and verbal, gives support. The protocols of informational rationalism that frequently govern broadcast journalism do not hold sway across documentary discourse in this mode, given its function as a form of promotionalism, indeed often a form of national advertising.

2 *Documentary as Journalistic Inquiry and Exposition.* This is essentially the documentary as reporting, possibly the most extensive use of documentary methods on television (at least, until very recently). Through in-camera presentation, or commentary voice-over, and perhaps with interviews interspersing either or both, the documentary work grounds itself not in an idea of 'publicity' (see above) but an idea of 'reportage,' which importantly includes an experience of looking at kinds of visual evidence, an experience of witness (see Ellis, 1999 on the importance of this notion).

3 *Documentary as Radical Interrogation and Alternative Perspective.* This is documentary as developed initially within the independent cinema movements that have maintained a presence in some national audio-visual cultures (the work of Bill Nichols – see Nichols, 1991 – is the major text for US developments and an essential reference for all writing on this topic). The authorial position is not 'official' nor does it claim journalistic warrant. Implicitly, sometimes explicitly, the documentary discourse attempts a criticism and a correction of other accounts in circulation. Some public broadcast systems have tried to develop work of a parallel kind (Channel 4

in Britain would be a good example). A wide range of styles has been deployed, including techniques of disruption and distancing taking their cue from nonrealist cinema but also including direct-cinema styles of observationalism, modes of dramatization, and kinds of personal testimony extending well beyond both the duration and format of the conventional interview. The anthropological levels of scrutiny offered by some projects in observational and oral history television could be included here.

This typology leaves out many important variants that have flourished within different national television systems, but I believe it has a certain rough adequacy (in Corner, 1996, I explore examples across all three categories over a sixty-year period). It is worth noting that all of the above functions tend to produce, by design, work quite low in commodity character. Use value is stronger than exchange value (leaving aside for the moment the question of how the audience realizes this use value).

To these three functions, there has been added, by a process of steady development (involving one or two periods of faster change), a fourth function to which I have already alluded in my opening comments. This started within the established documentary parameters but is now evolving beyond them by a process both of 'longitudinal' subgeneric developments and intensive cross-fertilization with other formats.

4 *Documentary as Diversion.* At one time, this was most often manifest in the occasional 'lightness' (of topic and/or treatment) shown by many television documentary series as part of their mix. In many countries, it has become a new documentary imperative for the production of 'popular factual entertainment.' Performing this function, documentary is a vehicle variously for the high-intensity incident (the reconstructed accident, the police raid), for anecdotal knowledge (gossipy first-person accounts), and for snoopy sociability (as an amused bystander to the mixture of mess and routine in other people's working lives). Propagandist, expositional, or analytic goals are exchanged for modes of intensive or relaxed diversion – the primary viewing activity is onlooking and overhearing, perhaps aligned to events by intermittent commentary.

In seeking its new pact with the popular, documentary-as-diversion has tended to shadow previously established fictional formats. So the early reality TV shows, focusing on the work of police and emergency services, learned a lot from the style of dramatic action narratives (Bondebjerg, 1996 and Kilborn, 1994 remain suggestive accounts). 'Docusoaps' have clearly learned a lot from the more relaxed rhythms of the soap opera and a good bit, too, from the newer styles of talk show (Dovey, 2000 offers a critical review in the context of broader intergeneric shifts). We are, of course, presently seeing a whole range of documentary-style projects emerge that have made strong and successful connections with the idea of the 'game' (one often also cast as an 'experiment,' with location spaces – interior or exterior – as 'laboratory').

Clearly, *Big Brother*'s preplanned group surveillance within a 'game frame,' that permits a measure of viewer intervention through the regular voting-off of participants, is the outstanding example of this. Other instances would include the BBC's rather more ambitiously anthropological *Castaways*, with an entire small community assembled on a remote Scottish island for the purposes of a social and psychological scrutiny by television, a scrutiny at once both informative and entertaining. Channel 4's *The 1900 House* and now the *The 1940s House*, worked with the idea of taking a family back to the conditions of previous periods for a sustained experiment in domestic living. They combined observationalism, participant direct address, and commentary to develop family narrative, historical exposition, and elements of the game-show challenge with great success.

Within the basic framework of taking a number of people to a comprehensively tele-available location for some form of 'experiment in living,' clearly quite a wide range of options present themselves. Most examples use a constrained time-frame to provide a structure and an urgency of plot to the narrative. The more obvious titles (e.g., *Shipwrecked, Survivor*) have been quite quickly gone through. Social cohesion, personality, and capacity to perform tasks can variously be emphasized within combinations of the instructive and the entertaining. The 'self' can be put on display in various modes of affection, solidarity, insincerity, confrontation, and downright aggression (two, phased onscreen captions before an advertising break in one episode of *Big Brother* are more generally revealing of its dynamics – 'ALLIANCES ... and ALLEGATIONS'). Participant self-reflection and commentary can deepen the plots thrown up by interaction. Self-knowledge can strengthen viewer empathy, while 'self-ignorance' (along with its partner, overconfidence) holds, as ever, its classic potential for comic effect. A good deal of embarrassment and humiliation is assured, with the 'outrageous' always there as an engaging possibility within the pressures and play of *relationships* – a moment of personal confrontation or the transgression of group or game

'rules.' The mutually modifying interplay of relationships and identities delivers the crucial open plot of the program's narrative. One might use the term 'selving' to describe the central process whereby 'true selves' are seen to emerge (and develop) from underneath and, indeed, through, the 'performed selves' projected for us, as a consequence of the applied pressures of objective circumstance and group dynamics. A certain amount of the humdrum and the routine may be a necessary element in giving this selving process, this *unwitting* disclosure of personal core, its measure of plausibility, aligning it with the mundane rhythms and naturalistic portrayals of docusoap, soap opera itself, and, at times, the registers of game-show participation. Karen Lury (1996) gives a very useful account of some of the paradoxes and tensions of 'ordinary performance' that this type of portrayal encourages from its participants. She also emphasizes how crucial these are in regulating the viewing experience as a kind of para-social encounter in which, as it were, the risks of 'being and seeming' taken by others are part of the pleasure.

Here, the relative failure on British television of *Survivors* (ITV 2001) is interesting. This format replaced an enforced domesticity with the exoticism of group life on a desert island setting. Its viewing figures were only half those expected, and the show had to be radically rescheduled within a week or so of opening. One of its problems may well have followed from the way in which its emphatic, indeed almost camp, exoticism (a sub-Malinowski stress on tribes, gods, and the mythic force of the natural elements) pulled away from viewer fascination with the more familiar dimensions of 'living together' that characterize *Big Brother*.

I would not want to underestimate the real degree of innovative adaptation and creativity that has gone into these developments. Questions of scopic appeal, forms of talk, and narrative system have been vigorously readdressed in all but the most dull and imitative of formats. The organization of an observed spectacle that is both personal (sustained by forms of personal talk as well as by personal depiction) and social (sustained by interaction, at least some of which needs to be confrontational enough to provide the appropriate intensity) requires a high level of prior stage management. This is such as to defy most previous protocols of documentarism, with their various anxious (and sometimes concealed) playoffs between authenticity and artifice.

In documentary as diversion, by contrast with the previous three functions, we have forms that are very high in exchange value, strategically designed for their competitive strength in the television marketplace. They are far less clear in their use value (although this cannot be dismissed merely because it does not seem to conform to traditional knowledge criteria). It is important to see the newer forms of documentary as having an identity quite distinct from that provided by the longstanding requirement for documentary to do some entertaining to gain and keep a popular audience. Their identity is also different from those many other forms of presenter-based factual formats (including importantly travel programs and the more adventurous types of cooking and motoring series), which, as I noted earlier, have an established link with selected elements of documentary portrayal. Television documentary producers have often produced work that entertains, sometimes in surprising and subversive ways, sometimes with populist

calculation. However, when a piece of work in documentary format is entirely designed in relation to its capacity to deliver entertainment, quite radical changes occur both to the forms of representation and to viewing relations.

ELEMENTS OF A POSTDOCUMENTARY CONTEXT?

There has, then, been a decisive shift toward diversion. This has not had the effect of completely displacing 'serious' output but it has certainly had the effect of reworking the identity of this output both within television's generic system and within the pattern of viewing habits and expectations. In what ways might this constitute a postdocumentary setting?

First of all, and most obviously, because audiovisual documentation, under the drive of diversion, has become too extensive and varied to allow documentary what one might see as its minimum sufficient level of generic identity. There has been a quite radical dispersal of documentary energies across the schedules. As a category of work, documentary has required certain things to be assumed, taken as given (it is, indeed, a question-begging category and always has been). Looking and sounding different from other kinds of program helped this process along, supporting what we might call 'documentary authority.' Extensive borrowing of the 'documentary look' by other kinds of program, and extensive borrowing of nondocumentary kinds of look (the dramatic look, the look of advertising, the look of the pop video) by documentary, have complicated the rules for recognizing a documentary. They have thereby contributed to a weakening of documentary status.

John Corner

Second, as I noted earlier, a performative, playful element has developed strongly within new kinds of factual production. This is evident not only in documentary styling (including the much wider scope given to musical accompaniment) but also in such features as the degree of self-consciousness now often displayed by the participants in observational sequences. This self-display is no longer viewable as an attempt to feign natural behavior but is taken as a performative opportunity in its own right. As such, it constitutes a staple element of docusoap in contrast with the self-restrained naturalism of demeanor, speech, and behavior in classic observationalism. Such naturalism, often highly implausible when subject to close analysis, was nevertheless considered as one founding marker of documentary integrity. Within the calculatedly nonnatural setting of *Big Brother*, performance is freed from even the minimal requirement made of 'lead players' in docusoap to project their personality outward to the viewer from a context of circumstantial clutter and action. The 'house' is a predefined stage precisely for personality to be *competitively* displayed (the intimate to-camera testimony of the video room being one privileged moment) and for its 'ordinary' participants to enter the celebrity system of popular culture with minimal transitional difficulty (we know them as performers already), if only for a brief period. As so often in contemporary circuits of fame, intensity is in inverse proportion to duration! Gossip pleasures abound as surmise and rumor join the data generated by the spectacle itself to provide a thick judgmental and speculative discourse around participants' motives, actions, and likely future behavior. In the first British series, the activities of 'Naughty Nick' in covertly attempting to manipulate voting,

his subsequent admonishment by the rest of the group after the discovery of his tactics, and then his ousting from the house by the program managers constitute a paradigm case. Even the most optimistic producer could not have imagined such a wonderful enhancement to the developing story. In the second British series (2001), the central portrayal of house events is set within a thick and extensive context of chat show interview and speculation together with phone-in assessments – a self-generating gossip machine.

I noted earlier how the new levels of representational play and reflexivity will undoubtedly have an impact on the conventional rhetorics of documentary seriousness, requiring in some cases quite radical adjustments and accommodations to be made. Documentary is no longer classifiable as a 'discourse of sobriety' to use Bill Nichols's much-cited phrase (see Nichols, 1991). It has become suffused with a new 'lightness of being,' and it will need care and creativity to get the mix right in specific projects for specific audiences. This aesthetic instability, and the reorientations around tone and content, also bears witness to a degree of instability in the factual programming *market*, an uncertainty and a risk about who wants to watch what and why.

As yet, it is hard to gauge the implications of the new playfulness for documentary credibility. Newspaper stories about the forms of representational fraud in the newer formats have combined with the brazenly performative nature of much on-screen action in a way that must have raised popular audience awareness of just how constructed audio-visual documentation can be. But this also appears to have gone along with, if anything, an increased viewing enthusiasm. In the 'diverting' mode, it is clear, belief in the veracity of what you are watching is not a prerequisite to engagement and pleasure. Indeed, quite the reverse rule would seem to apply. What also seems clear is that the generous license accorded to the more diverting modes cannot, as yet, be simply transferred across to more serious kinds of documentary claims-making. In the notable British case of Carlton Television's *The Connection*, a documentary purporting to show the activities of a Colombian drug cartel, there was widespread and deep public disquiet when revelations of 'staging' and falsification appeared in newspapers (see Winston, 2000 for details of this instance). Only research on viewing groups will enable us to understand what new blurrings, and what new differentiations, now inform the interpretative frameworks used by different segments of the audience. However, it is hard to see how *any* form of television documentary program can remain completely unaffected by the new ecology of the factual.

Third, and related to these questions about style and performance, the broader range of cognitive and affective investments that people make in audio-visual documentation is likely to have undergone a shift, even if, again, only audience research (now very much required in this area) can establish its scale. The 'back story' to this shift involves changes in the nature of public and private life over the last two decades and the complex ways in which both the contours of social knowledge and emotional experience have been reconfigured. Such processes have strongly national dimensions, of course, but at their broadest, they involve the way in which selfhood is set within culture and culture set within a particular political and economic order. The terms of 'seeing others' and 'seeing things' on the screen today are very different from those of the defining moments of documentary history, those moments when an expository realism seemed to resonate at least partially with a public, democratic rhetoric of reform and progress. These stealthier and more long-term changes are ones to which the newer forms of factual programming, with their emphasis on microsocial narrative and their forms of play around the self observed and the self-in-performance, seem to have brought an accelerated momentum.

'Documentary' is a category that has very largely been defined and applied in relation to a sense of public values, and, of course, there has been considerable variety in just how such values have been thought about and positioned in national life. Ideas have been framed by a range of authoritarian, liberal, and radical perspectives. In many countries, however, I think there is a quiet but deepening crisis over the very idea of 'the public.' This is something to do with changing terms of citizenship and a move away from the once-established (whether coercive or voluntary) forms of solidarity. It is very much to do with the changing character of the national and international economy and the increasing emphasis on market systems, market values, and the dynamics of consumption. These have generated a version of 'the popular,' grounded in consumption, which is often in direct tension with notions of 'the public.' Throughout the twentieth century, these two terms have displayed a developing history of tension, often overlaid by an assumed synonymity. They now offer increasingly disconnected versions of the self in society and present to many social democratic projects profound challenges of reconfiguration and reframing within different areas of social and economic policy. Television's role as agency both of public knowledge and of

John Corner

111

popular entertainment has in a number of countries led to an awkward straddling across a dual value system, and a dual set of criteria, often for many years. Indeed, several debates in television studies have their origins in this duality, sometimes unrecognized, with the one side frequently perceived only in the terms of the other, either in advocacy or in critique. Within the contemporary crisis around public values, broadcast documentary is, in fact, more vulnerable than news programming, since it is premised upon a deeper and a broader engagement with perceptions of social community – its varieties, rhythms, problems, and tensions, the interplay of the specific with the general. Documentary has assumed and fostered rhetorics of belonging and involvement, albeit with elements of the manipulative, the socially exclusive, or the sentimental, that are now increasingly difficult to sustain, even in revised form. A mood at once both more cynical and more comic, a mood in which versions of performance cut through questions of sincerity and authenticity, has started to change television's terms of secondary seeing. Within this new affective order, this emerging 'structure of feeling,' a busy dialectic of attraction and dislike, provides the mainspring of the entertainment. The very volatility of the feelings here allows for a viewing combination in which what are, for nonfictional formats, quite unparalleled modes of 'getting close' become mixed with a remarkably cold, objectifying distance.

POPULAR FACTUAL ENTERTAINMENT AND THE SURVIVAL OF DOCUMENTARY

I have described a situation in which subjective factors to do with audience expectations,

social affiliation, and modes of cognition and affect combine with the objective factors of a multichannel and intensively commercialized television industry. Only a more systematic attempt to measure what is going on in the schedules under different program categories, as well as sustained inquiry into viewer choice, expectation, and judgment, can allow us to be confident about the scale and direction of change. The combination of factors presents a challenge to the documentary project both at infrastructural and cultural levels. Its funding base is threatened by the intensified commodity status of all programs in the television marketplace. Meanwhile, the aesthetic, political, and cultural coordinates that helped hold it together have both reduced in strength and shifted apart.

I would not expect the production of serious documentary simply to disappear in these circumstances. As I indicated at the start of this article, my use of the idea of 'postdocumentary culture' is not meant to signal that documentary is now finished but to signal the scale of its relocation as a set of practices, forms, and functions. Some established strands of practice will undoubtedly continue across the disjunctions I have discussed. They will win viewers and deserve critical support. But they will do this in what, for many national television systems, will be a radically changed setting for audio-visual production and consumption. To the extent it wishes to enjoy a popular reach, the future documentary project in television will need strategically to reconfigure itself within the new economic and cultural contexts.

I am aware that much discussion of the threat to documentary carries the ring, if not the explicit claim, of a protectionism, one that is finally aesthetically and socially conservative. The contrary option, welcoming the brave new populist-realisms for their decentering, postmodern energies and thereby downplaying the consequences of their market rationale and their commodity cynicism, looks as crass as ever, although doubtless some commentators will continue to sound that note. It is not surprising that, in this situation, a degree of ambivalence is often a defining feature of academic commentary, as the diverse commercial and sociocultural dimensions of the 'popular' seem to resist neat separation. Brants (1998) and Blumler (1999) provide together a useful exchange on the broader but related question of evaluating 'infotainment.' Moreover, the question of precisely *how far*, and at *what rate*, new forms of programming are driving out the more established modes of practice and function is not yet properly answered. In a recent survey, Brian Winston (2000) suggested that the success of popular factual entertainment in the schedules, far from exerting a directly displacing effect, may have been, for the time being at least, 'the price of survival' of other, more serious fare. Whatever the pattern finally to emerge, producers with a commitment to the popular audience that goes beyond profitability but that can nevertheless also generate profits will clearly be an important factor in documentary's survival.

Documentary, in all its complexity as an indicator, points essentially to a project of political and cultural modernism, predicated on quite specific contexts of mediation and of public and private experience. Its characteristic modes have shown an expositional and analytic dynamic together with a real ethnographic zeal in the portrayal of different forms of living. At the same time, authoritarian and patrician tones have frequently become woven into its textures. It has in many countries bestowed a mixed representational legacy – of investigative, exploratory energy and of epistemic and aesthetic containment. It has served to open up and also to close down. Neither postmodern skepticism nor the techniques of digital manipulation present documentary with its biggest future challenge. This will undoubtedly come from the requirement to reorient and refashion itself in an audio-visual culture where the dynamics of diversion and the aesthetics of performance dominate a greatly expanded range of popular images of the real.

Big Brother's distinctive mixture of surveillance and display, placing the viewing audience both as voyeurs and as talent-show judges, has certainly been an important moment in the emergence of reality television from its documentary origins. It has worked cleverly with its ingredients, some of which have been drawn from other formats while others have been quite new. In taking a popular audience beyond the confines of the broadcast text into the continuity of an online narrative, it will also prove to have been significant. In assessing it, we should neither simplify nor forget the relationship between its representational system and its commodity functions. By 'performing the real' with such strategic zeal, framing its participants both as game players and as television 'actors,' it has helped mark a shift in the nature of television as a medium for documentation. Perhaps it marks a shift, too, in the nature of that broader sphere, a sphere where vectors both of structure and agency combine to produce experience, that John Hartley (1996) has suggestively dubbed 'popular reality.'

John Corner

REFERENCES

BLUMLER, J. (1999) 'Political communication systems all change: a response to Kees Brants', *European Journal of Communication*, 14(2), 241–9.

BONDEBJERG, I.B. (1996) 'Public discourse/private fascination: hybridization in "True Life Story" genres', *Media, Culture and Society*, 18(1), 27–45.

BRANTS, K. (1998) 'Whose afraid of infotainment?', *European Journal of Communication*, 13(3), 315–35.

CORNER, J. (1996) *The Art of Record*, Manchester, Manchester University Press.

CORNER, J. (2000) 'What can we say about documentary?', *Media, Culture and Society*, 22(5), 681–8.

DOVEY, J. (2000) *Freakshow: First Person Media and Factual Television*, London, Pluto Press.

ELLIS, J. (1999) *Seeing Things: Television in the Age of Uncertainty*, London, I. B. Tauris.

HARDY, F. (ed.) (1979) *Grierson on Documentary*, London, Faber & Faber.

HARTLEY, J. (1996) *Popular Reality*, London, Arnold.

KILBORN, R. (1994) 'How real can you get? Recent developments in reality television', *European Journal of Communication*, 9(4), 421–39.

LURY, K. (1996) 'Television performance: being, acting and "corpsing"', *New Formations*, 27(Winter), 114–27.

NICHOLS, B. (1991) *Representing Reality*, Bloomington, IN, Indiana University Press.

WINSTON, B. (2000) *Lies, Damned Lies and Documentary*, London, British Film Institute.

Source: Corner, 2002, pp. 262–7.

READING C: Derek Bousé, 'Historia Fabulosus'

Given the irresistible power of narrative, it should come as no surprise that there were written works that dealt with wildlife and the natural world in story form well before Aristotle and Pliny. The inhabitants of earlier ages knew several types of animal stories (typically about animals who talked) that had grown out of mythic and folkloric traditions around the world. Today, however, the best known type of these ancient animal stories is the animal fable, or *beast fable*. The form itself was already established by the time it became linked to the name of Aesop in the fifth century B.C.

[…]

The fables had undergone many revisions, however, and by the time of the European Renaissance there were several efforts to reassemble and retranslate complete collections, some of which are still read today.

Yet there may be a darker side to the tradition of using the fables to educate; as part of so many people's childhood reading the fables are at 'the very roots of that kind of humanisation which turns animals into facets of human character.'(Blount 1975, p. 26)

[…]

The use of humanized animals to teach moral lessons, or in some other way to confront fundamental human conflicts, shows up in many other types of stories, from myths to fairy tales.

[…]

Yet the animals in the Aesopic fables are still recognizable *as animals* rather than as people in animal garb. As such, they can be seen as among the earliest written attempts to fathom the behavior of animals, if only by casting it in human terms that made it easier to grasp. Although humanizing animals may actually do little to help us understand their behavior, it is nevertheless an almost automatic human response to try to understand others by way of analogy to ourselves. This involves the application of *self-knowledge* and *role-taking*, which social psychologists have identified as normal parts of our everyday attempts to make sense of the actions of others, and to divine their motivations.

[…]

The humanized characterization of animals in the fables were often consistent with what was known, or at least believed, at the time about various animal species and their behavioral patterns. This can be seen in their use of common species stereotypes. Barry Lopez has observed, for example, that the wolf in the Aesopic fables is stereotyped as a 'base, not very intelligent creature, of ravenous appetite, gullible, impudent, and morally corrupt.' (1978, p. 251) […]

Yet the fables' frequent combination of animal stereotypes and human attributes in a single character was more subtle and suggestive. The line between anthropomorphism as a literary device and reigning belief about animal behavior was often blurred, so that the human qualities attributed to a given animal species, even where comically portrayed, could be interpreted by readers as among the real attributes of that species.

While it is almost always the case that seeing elements of humanity reflected in the natural world comes from having projected them there in the first place, in the fables this was clearly

115

intentional. Since then, as animal stories have become more closely linked to natural history study, their creators have attempted to present them more realistically and have tended to disavow any humanizing intentions. As a result, such stories have increasingly been presented in the guise of fact. Thus, human attributes, where discernible, appear not so much to have been projected onto the animals as *found* there. At least, it has been a profitable illusion.

FROM FABLE TO COMMODITY

It might be tempting at this point to conclude that we had uncovered an essential truth about wildlife films by putting them in the oldest possible historical contexts, particularly that of the fable. For if they are part of an ancient tradition of animal storytelling, and if the leading type of animal story in that tradition is the fable, then we might conclude, as many have, that wildlife films are merely latter-day fables. We might go on to reason that they must also stem from the same urges, and serve essentially the same purposes as earlier fables did for their audiences. [...]

Even Disney once wrote that we 'can learn a lot from nature,' especially about 'the thing ... we call moral behavior.' Writer-producer Barry Clark has offered a more comprehensive analysis: 'whether by design or by default, most of our nature films, in my view, are intended to serve as fables or moral tales, in which animals are employed as surrogate humans, manipulated by the filmmakers to enact contemporary culture myths, which serve the primary purpose of defining and reinforcing social values.' (Personal correspondence with author, December 1997)

It might be surprising to those outside the industry to learn just how many inside it regard wildlife films as primarily a storytelling form, and as part of a cultural tradition of storytelling. Cultural historians would no doubt also find it satisfying to be able to connect wildlife films by way of an unbroken line to a source two thousand or more years in the cultural past. This, of course, would greatly simplify the task of coming to terms with these hybrids of natural history and storytelling that have long evaded both categorization and adequate definition.

Although a degree of *fableizing* can in fact be found in wildlife films, as the basis for an overview or 'theory' of the genre, a strictly fableist view slights the rich history of the subject and betrays a kind of historicist fallacy in which genealogy overshadows social context. Such a view might well cause us to overlook the fact that, whatever their cultural origins, there is a considerable variety of wildlife film models, storylines, and types. More importantly, we might also overlook the fact that all of them are products of a vastly complex, heavily mediated global culture. As such, they can give rise to a number of different 'readings', and serve a number of different social functions: scientific research and documentation, education, wildlife conservation advocacy, animal rights advocacy, artistic expression, as well as mass entertainment, advertising, tourism promotion, and other, more overt forms of commerce. Some of these do in fact reinforce dominant social values; others, like advocacy for animals, may challenge dominant values or at least give rise to 'oppositional readings.'

Either way, the fact that wildlife films are industrialized commodities produced for sale in a competitive global marketplace makes their existence and value *as messages* fundamentally different from that of fables, tales, and myths in earlier social orders, even when their plotlines are similar to traditional narratives and resonate with the familiar mythic elements to which people have responded for centuries. Moreover, it is important to bear in mind that wildlife films are primarily a visual rather than a verbal form (voice-over narration notwithstanding), and that they are seen by most viewers on television. It is worth considering, therefore, some of the ways the experience of television-viewing differs fundamentally from that of reading or of listening to a storyteller.

[…]

However compelling, intimate, and natural they may seem, or however much they may resemble traditional fables, tales, and myths, the stories told by wildlife films are now as subject as all other forms of television to the influence of competition for ratings and sales. As such, they may be a better reflection of the values and perspectives of global media industries and international finance than of human communities – at least in the sense in which 'community' has traditionally been understood. It is true that the 'community' of wildlife filmmakers, despite its international makeup, exerts some collegial influence on the shape of wildlife films, and on the types of stories that are told. This *secondary audience*, however, is often far removed from the *primary audience* of the viewing public, and may be unlikely to mirror its interests and values. Moreover, as more wildlife films are co-produced by firms from several different countries, and as international presales become necessary to secure financing, there is a move away from the expression of clearly identifiable regional or national difference. Although at the narrative level wildlife films transcend cultural boundaries, recently the tendency has been even more

strongly in the direction of international themes and styles suitable for multiple markets. To earn back their investments, wildlife films must have stories that are easily exportable and able to travel well across cultural borders. The need for such financially safe stories, as Rosenberg argues, 'demands a formulaic response. As filmmakers we are all caught up in a ratings game which … inevitably leads to producers churning out the same old tried and tested formulas which have proved so popular. … How can anyone be brave and original when programme ideas have to be pre-sold with the bottom line of assured, high ratings?!' (1996, p. 29) The safest formula may well be one that derives from traditional narratives. This need not be incompatible with ratings-driven television, which has often thrived on some of our most enduring myths and stories. Because wildlife films are produced for a global market that is increasingly insensitive to regional differences, there may even be more pressure than in mainstream programming to seek common denominators – in this case, patterns and formulas shared by many cultures. Nevertheless, despite their similarities to folk tales and myths, wildlife films inescapably remain industrial commodities.

In attempting, therefore, to uncover some of the primary historical influences that shaped wildlife film as a distinct film genre defined largely by its narrative codes, the place to begin may not, after all, be at the beginning – that is, with the Greeks. Instead, it may be more useful to start with the era in the late nineteenth and early twentieth centuries when mass-produced, mass-mediated culture began to assume its modern role in society. It was during this time that a number of cultural, social scientific, technological, and literary currents began to converge and gain momentum, leading to a reemergence of anthropomorphic animal storytelling. The Darwinian paradigm shift had already altered the psychological and symbolic significance of wild animals in relation to humans. This had led to greater sympathy for animals (at least in some quarters), and to a new interest in 'animal psychology' – a broad term encompassing observation of animal behavior (later to become the modern study of *ethology*) as well as theories of animal cognition and reasoning. As speculations increased about what animals think and how they experience the world, it was perhaps inevitable that animal stories reflecting the animal point-of-view should begin appearing. With increasing interest in natural science generally, and the accompanying demand for natural history literature for a popular audience, the animal story thus emerged as one of the most popular literary genres in the United States in the late nineteenth century. Wild animals became the protagonists in a series of 'realistic' novels and short stories, written and mass-produced for a modern, literate, largely urban audience. It was under such industrial conditions that narrative formulas and techniques of character development were tested, refined, and perfected. This in turn gave rise to models of narrative and character that would endure into the twentieth century and be easily adapted to filmic storytelling, where an animal's point-of-view could be communicated even more dramatically and convincingly.

The packaging and selling of commodified nature thus became as much a growth industry in the late nineteenth century as it would in the late twentieth. Those who entered the field, whatever their background or qualifications, became important as intermediaries between the public and the natural world.

However fit or unfit they were to play the part, their role was to define, explain, and justify the ways of nature to humans. That some of them saw this as a solemn responsibility did not mean that they necessarily understood nature themselves. Still, their interpretations and characterizations of it were thought to have great influence on the perceptions of the public in the late nineteenth century, and this led to growing concern among some critics and nature advocates.

As the twentieth century dawned, questions began to be raised about the representation of nature in popular media, some of which have never been adequately answered. Among them was that of the efficacy of attempting to impose narrative structure on nature (or, worse, presuming to have found it there). For with narrative came dramatic protagonists, and questions as to whether animal *protagonism* was even appropriate as a form of nature discourse. Were there really 'heroes' in nature? Was there tragedy? Questions such as these led, of course, to debates over anthropomorphism, and ultimately to charges of fakery and deception similar to those leveled at wildlife films in the 1990s. There were also other concerns that were less literary, yet still more pressing, several of which still have contemporary relevance. Should animal storytelling be the basis for natural history education? That is, should animal stories whether in books or on film, be used as natural history texts in schools? What, exactly, did they teach? Did they reinforce social values? Did they accurately convey 'natural values'? Or did they pervert both? Was the mass-production of engaging, sympathetic animal stories an effective means of enlisting public support for the cause of wildlife protection? If disappearing species, such as the wolf, became ubiquitous in mass-produced stories and images, could it undermine public perceptions of the reality of their dwindling numbers, or of the threats to their existence? In a word, the rise of animal storytelling at the end of the nineteenth century can be seen as a dress rehearsal for the controversies of the 1980s and 1990s, when many of the same sorts of problems, questions, and issues were confronted, but where few, if any, were resolved.

REFERENCES

BLOUNT, M. (1975) *Animal Land: The Creatures of Children's Fiction*, New York, William Morrow.

LOPEZ, B. (1978) *Of Wolves and Men,* New York, Charles Scribner's Sons.

ROSENBERG, M. (1996) 'Evolution theory', *Broadcast*, October 11, p. 29.

Source: Bousé, 2000, pp. 91–106.

CHAPTER THREE

THE POETICS AND THE POLITICS OF EXHIBITING OTHER CULTURES

Henrietta Lidchi

1 INTRODUCTION

As the title suggests this chapter develops the central theme of the book, representation. It is about objects, or more specifically *systems of representation* that produce meaning through the display of objects. Like the two previous chapters it is concerned with the process of representation – the manner in which meaning is constructed and conveyed through language and objects. It will consider *representation* in the singular – the activity or process – as well as *representations* – the resultant entities or products. Where this chapter differs is in its focus: it examines not so much language, as how meaning is created through classification and display. Moreover, it contemplates this process in the particular context of objects said to be 'ethnographic'. So the chapter is concerned with ethnographic museums; in other words institutions whose representational strategies feature the ethnographic objects or artefacts of 'other cultures'. It will not, however, seek to answer fully the question of how these representational systems are received. The question of consumption is too large to be tackled in any great detail here (though see there is some discussion in section 5.4); for a fuller discussion, see Du Gay, ed. (1997).

Why investigate ethnographic exhibitions and displays? Because ethnographic museums have had to address issues of representation in a concerted fashion. Museum curators are no longer perceived as the unassailable keepers of knowledge about their collections; museums are no longer simply revered as spaces promoting knowledge and enlightenment, the automatic resting place for historic and culturally important ethnographic objects. How the West classifies, categorizes and represents other cultures has emerged as a topic of legitimate debate (see Macdonald, 2006, p. 3).

This chapter addresses two significant critiques of museums. These take a *constructionist* view of representation. The first uses the insights from *semiotics* and the manner in which language constructs and conveys meaning to analyse the diversity of ways in which exhibitions create representations of other cultures. By considering how meanings are constructed and produced, this critique concerns itself primarily with the semiotics or *poetics* of exhibiting. The second critique forefronts questions of discourse and power to interrogate the historical nature of museums and collecting. It argues that there is a link between the rise of ethnographic museums and the expansion of western nations. By exploring the link between knowledge of other cultures and the imperial nations, this critique considers representation in the light of the *politics* of exhibiting.

This chapter therefore considers both the *poetics* and the *politics* of exhibiting. It builds on the twofold structure delineated in Chapter 1, contrasting the approach that concentrates on *language* and *signification*, with another that prioritizes *discourse* and *discursive* practices. The differences at the heart of these critiques will be brought out by the case studies deployed. In these, the insights gained will be used in specific contexts to discuss how objects, exhibitions and museums function to represent other cultures.

The chapter is divided into four main sections. Section 2 presents some preliminary working definitions. First, it will review what is meant by a 'museum' and 'ethnography'. Then it will reflect on how objects acquire meaning as a prelude to considering how meaning is produced within the context of an exhibition or museum.

Section 3 attends to one of the principal ways in which museums represent other cultures – the exhibition. Using a case study, it will highlight the manner in which ethnographic displays are vehicles of meaning, how objects, texts and photographs work to create a representation of a particular people, at a precise historical moment. The focus of this section will be an exhibition which opened in 1993 at the Museum of Mankind – the then location of the Department of Ethnography of the British Museum (the Museum of Mankind closed in 1997 and moved back to the British Museum becoming Department of Africa, Oceania and the Americas) – entitled *Paradise: Change and Continuity in the New Guinea Highlands*. The theme of section 3 is the *poetics* of exhibiting.

Section 4 explores the critiques that go beyond the issue of construction and the exhibition context to question the politics of museums. The main thrust of this critique concerns the relationship between knowledge and power. The focus here is on the institution whose activities of collecting and curating cease to be neutral or innocent activities but emerge as an instrumental means of knowing and possessing the 'culture' of others. This section will consider in detail the collection and interpretation of the artefacts known as the Benin Bronzes.

Finally, section 5 is a coda to the chapter. In this revised edition, this is the section which differs most significantly from the first edition. Section 5 reviews the impact of the representational critique of ethnographic museums reflected in the earlier sections. It highlights the extent to which museums have become the subject of academic discourse since the 1980s and the ever-widening series of concerns that have emerged from this. Section 5 suggests that this has resulted in a paradigmatic shift and discusses a few of the most compelling models for analysing collections and museums that have emerged.

2 ESTABLISHING DEFINITIONS, NEGOTIATING MEANINGS, DISCERNING OBJECTS

2.1 Introduction

Section 2 begins by considering the key terms: 'museum', 'ethnography', 'object', 'text' and 'context'. Reflecting on the meaning and function of a museum through the analysis of contrasting definitions will provide a basis on which to question contemporary usage and assumptions underlying these terms in later sections. Section 2 argues that a museum is a historically constituted space, and uses this to highlight contemporary definitions of an ethnographic museum. It then moves on to consider the status of 'objects' in order to investigate the manner in which their meaning is constructed. Using the unusual case of a horse called Comanche, it shows how even seemingly mundane objects can be endowed with value and thus be transformed into a vehicle of contested meaning.

2.2 What is a 'museum'?

If you look up 'museum' in a dictionary, it is likely that you will find a definition *approximating* to the functional one chosen here: 'Museums exist in order to acquire, safeguard, conserve, and display objects, artefacts and works of arts of various kinds' (Vergo, 1993, p. 41). But we must also ask: is this definition essential or historical? Does its interpretation vary over time?

To answer this, let us seek an older, alternative definition of the museum. If we explore the classical etymology of the word museum (*musaeum*), we find that it could encompass two meanings. On the one hand, it signified 'a mythological setting inhabited by the nine goddesses of poetry, music, and the liberal arts', namely 'places where the Muses dwell' (Findlen, 1989, p. 60). Nature as the 'primary haunt of the Muses' was a museum in its most literal sense. On the other hand, the term also referred to the library at Alexandria, to a public site devoted to scholarship and research. So this early classical etymology allows for the museum's potential for expansiveness. It does not specify spatial parameters: the open spaces of gardens and the closed confines of the study were equally appropriate spaces for museums. Museums could therefore reconcile curiosity and scholarship, private and public domains, the whimsical and the ordered (Findlen, 1989, pp. 60–2).

In the sixteenth and seventeenth centuries an alternative and varied terminology was accorded to contemporary 'museums', depending partly on the social and geographical location of the collectors. The *Wunderkammer* and *Kunstkammer* (the cabinets of 'wonder' and 'arts') of European aristocrats and princes were contemporaneous with the personal 'theatres of nature', 'cabinets of curiosities' and *studiolo* of the erudite and scholarly collector. British collecting occurred 'lower down' the social scale: the British scholar collected 'the curiosities of art and nature', establishing cabinets with less ordered and hierarchical collections than their continental counterparts (MacGregor, 1985, p. 147). Let us examine the constitution of a British 'cabinet of curiosities' or 'closet of rarities' (the name given to diverse assemblages of rare and striking artefacts), to pry deeper into its systems of classification and the representation of the world that it generated and disclosed.

John Tradescant the elder, a botanist and gardener, built a 'collection of rarities' from his early visits to the European mainland and the Barbary coast, where he collected plants and natural specimens. Later, partly owing to the enthusiasm of his patron, the powerful (subsequently assassinated) Duke of Buckingham, others were commissioned to undertake collecting to augment the Tradescant 'cabinet', though this was always an adjunct to Tradescant's botanical interests. In 1628, upon settling in Lambeth, Tradescant transformed his cabinet of curiosities into an ever-expanding *musaeum*. After his appointment in 1630 as Keeper of His Majesty's Gardens, the collection was bequeathed in its entirety to his son, John Tradescant the younger.

What did it contain?

The collection was composed of an extraordinary rich amalgam of miscellaneous objects, harvested 'with less than critical discrimination', according to MacGregor (1985, p. 152). In his catalogue of 1656, '*Musaeum Tradescantianum; Or, A Collection of Rarities Preserved at South Lambeth neer London*', Tradescant the younger described the content of the museum in some detail.

READING A

Reading A at the end of this chapter contains four extracts from the 1656 catalogue *Musaeum Tradescantianum; Or, A Collection of Rarities Preserved at South Lambeth neer London*, prepared by Tradescant the younger. Read them in the light of the following questions.

1 Extracts 1 and 2 detail the categories used by Tradescant the younger. What are they?

2 Consider Extracts 3 and 4 to discern what type of material is included in these categories.

3 How does such a classification differ from one you might expect to find today?

In Extracts 1 and 2 Tradescant the younger divides his 'materialls' into two types – natural and artificial – and within these types, he further subdivides into categories. He also classifies the materials into two separate spaces – the closed internal space of the *Musaeum Tradescantianum* and the open external space of his garden.

The difference between natural and artificial 'materialls' – or *naturalia* and *artificialia* – is ostensibly between that which is naturally occurring and that which is derived from nature but transformed by human endeavour. The 'materialls' included under both categories are, however, exceedingly diverse.

In Extracts 3 and 4 we find that the category of *naturalia* includes naturally occurring specimens ('Egges' of 'Estridges', 'Pellican'); mythical creatures ('Phoenix', 'Griffin'); or objects which qualify by virtue of provenance ('Kings-fisher from the *West India's*'), an unusual association ('Cassaway or Emeu that dyed at *S. James's, Westminster*') or the 'curious' and colourful nature of the specimen ('two feathers of the Phoenix tayle'). The categories are tolerant of a variety of materials and provenances. Natural specimens

(Continued)

(Continued)

from Continental Europe are juxtaposed with those of the West Indies or Brazil, parts of natural specimens are classified with wholes, the identified is listed with the unidentifiable, common birds are classed with the Mauritian 'Dodar'. The manner in which Tradescant and his collaborators divided and subdivided the natural world seems by today's standards fairly idiosyncratic: birds (which they dismember), four-footed beasts, fishes, shell-creatures, insects, minerals, outlandish fruit (see Extract 2).

The divisions implemented in the more qualitative category of *artificialia* seem even more eccentric. This medley of curious items produces an equivalence between 'ethnographic' objects ('*Pohatan*, King of *Virginia's* habit', see Figure 3.1); artefacts with mythological references ('Stone of *Sarrigs*-Castle where *Hellen* of *Greece* was born'); objects that are the product of feats of human ingenuity ('Divers sorts of Ivory-balls'); fantastical objects ('blood that rained in the *Isle of Wight*') or merely fanciful ones ('*Edward the Confessors* knit-gloves'). The category of 'rarities' appears particularly discretionary, since most of the objects in the collection could be classified as 'rare, or supposedly rare, objects' (Pomian, 1990, p. 46) – '*Anne of Bullens* Night-vayle embroidered with silver', for instance.

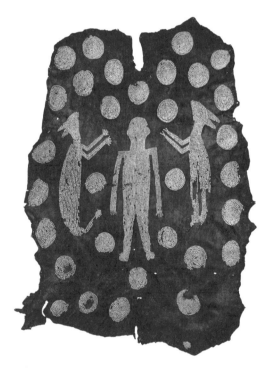

FIGURE 3.1 Powhatan's Mantle, from Tradescant's collection of rarities, now in the Ashmolean Museum, Oxford. Originally described as '*Pohatan*, King of *Virginia's* habit ...'

The information or *interpretation* contained in the catalogue indicates certain priorities. The descriptions of the natural 'materialls' are frequently objective and economic, except in those circumstances where the curiosity of the item or the particularity of its association is being recorded (outlandish fruit). This kaleidoscopic view of nature predates the introduction of the hierarchical Linnaean system of classification (named after the Swedish botanist, Linne), so typical of contemporary natural history collections (and the one adapted for ethnographical collections in the Pitt Rivers Museum – see section 4). The description of the artificial 'materialls' is often fuller, although this depends on their categorization. Those objects featured for their technical virtuosity are described in this light, whereas other items are recorded in terms of their surprising nature ('Match-coat from *Greenland* of the Intrails of Fishes'). Some *artificialia* are remarkable for their association with well-known historical characters or their exotic origins, or both, in the case of '*Pohatan*, King of *Virginia's* habit', for instance.

The descriptions are, nevertheless, very different from those one might find today. There is little of what one might call 'hard information', or 'objective description'. Garments are not described in terms of their shape, their dimensions, their colour, their age, their maker or their owner, unless the latter was a renowned personage. The constituting materials are noted if they are remarkable, in the same way that the properties of *naturalia* are only noted if they are extraordinary. There are no references to how these 'materialls' were collected, when, or by whom. These 'facts' or insights, inconsequential to the Tradescants, would nowadays be considered indispensable elements to the proper cataloguing of collections ('materialls').

What does Tradescant's museum represent?

What is being *represented* here is the puzzling quality of the natural and artificial world. In the early sixteenth century, a conspicuously extraordinary object with puzzling and exotic associations was worthy of inclusion in a cabinet by virtue of its 'curiosity' – its unusualness as perceived by the collector. To the contemporary observer, the internal arrangement appears arbitrary, and the terminology – 'closet of rarities' or 'cabinet of curiosities' – further corroborates the view that these cabinets were the specious products of personal preference, non-scientific and whimsical. To dismiss these cabinets on the basis of their exuberance, the plethora and diversity of items included, and the singularity of the classificatory system would, however, be a mistake. It would deny the methods – those 'rational' principles – that underpinned these stunning constructions:

> These were collections with encyclopaedic ambition, intended as a miniature version of the universe, containing specimens of every category of things and helping to render visible the totality of the universe, which otherwise would remain hidden from human eyes.
>
> (Pomian, 1990, p. 69)

To collect curiosities or rarities indicated a particular kind of inquisitiveness: 'curiosity' emerged, momentarily, as a legitimate intellectual pursuit, signifying an open, searching mind. The collector's interest in spectacular and curious objects was born of an attitude which saw Nature, of which man was part, not as 'repetitive, or shackled to a coherent set of laws' but as a phenomenon which 'was subject to unlimited variability and novelty' (Shelton, 1994, p. 184). For the curious, collecting was quest. Its purpose? To go beyond the obvious and the ordinary, to uncover the hidden knowledge which would permit him (for it was always him) a more complete grasp of the workings of the world in all its dimensions (Pomian, 1990, p. 57). This alternative definition of science tolerated diversity and miscellany because they were 'essential elements in a programme whose aim was nothing less than universality' (Impey and MacGregor, 1985, p. 1). So Tradescant's 'closet of rarities', unique though it undoubtedly was, was also part of a larger socio-cultural movement adhering to a broadly unified perception of the world and the purpose of collecting which reached its apogee in the sixteenth and seventeenth centuries.

The Tradescants' collection was exceptional for another reason. The collection was personal, expansive and varied, but not exclusive. Interesting specimens were placed at the disposal of serious scholars and the general public:

> More significant ... than these distinguished visitors were the ordinary people who flocked to see the collection for a fee – seemingly sixpence – for the Tradescants differed ... from every collector then known of in England – in the general accessibility of their collections. Most of these visitors no doubt saw the rarities in much the same light as had the founder of the collection – 'the Biggest that Can be Gotten ... Any thing that Is Strang'.

(MacGregor, 1985, p. 150)

This aspect was to come into its own once the collection had been acquired by deed of gift by Elias Ashmole, who in turn gave it to the University of Oxford, thereby ensuring its transformation into the twentieth-century public museum that bears his name – the Ashmolean.

This exploration of the *Musaeum Tradescantianum* brings several important points to light about the nature of museums.

1 *Representation.* Collecting and uniting these extraordinary and varied articles – be they naturally or artificially produced – into one cabinet served to create a staggering encapsulation of the world's curiosities. This account was, in turn, an attempt at a complete *representation* of the diversity of existence in miniature – a 'microcosm'.

2 *Classification.* In describing the world, the *Musaeum Tradescantianum* worked within a classificatory system which made a distinction between two types of objects: *artificialia* and *naturalia*. Other contemporary cabinets included the categories of *antiqua* (mementoes from the past) and *scientifica* (implements, etc.). The Tradescant classificatory system did not articulate the divisions we might use today between the real and the mystical, the antique and the contemporary, the New World and the Old. The representation of the world generated by the museum applied rules of classification and collection which were, for the original collectors and cataloguers, logical and consistent with a historically specific form of knowledge and scholarship, however inappropriate they may seem to us today.

3 *Motivation.* The *Musaeum* is a *motivated* representation of the world in the sense that it sought to encapsulate the world in order to teach others about it and to convert others to the salience of this approach. Moreover, quite exceptionally for its time, this representation was aimed at a larger audience than scholars.

4 *Interpretation.* If we reflect back to the definition which began this section, namely that 'museums exist to acquire, safeguard, conserve and display objects, artefacts or works of arts of various kinds', we find that the *Musaeum Tradescantianum* fits this description as easily as a contemporary museum might. Yet the manner and spirit in which the *Musaeum Tradescantianum* undertook these activities was clearly quite different. This is particularly evident in its mode of classification. The

way in which the *Musaeum Tradescantianum* acquired, safeguarded, conserved, and displayed was in accordance with a distinct world-view which saw sense in what might be termed a hodge-podge of marvellous objects, a logical vision which had abandoned theological principles of classification, but had yet to adopt scientific ones (Pomian, 1990, p. 64).

So, unexpectedly perhaps, we find that our preliminary definition still holds; but, more importantly, we have established that a museum does not deal solely with *objects* but, more importantly, with what we could call, for the moment, *ideas* – notions of what the world is, or should be. Museums do not simply issue objective descriptions or form logical assemblages; they generate representations and attribute value and meaning in line with certain perspectives or classificatory schemas which are historically specific. They do not so much reflect the world through objects as use them to mobilize representations of the world past and present.

If this is true of all museums, what kind of classificatory schema might an 'ethnographic' museum employ and what kinds of representations might it mobilize?

2.3 What is an 'ethnographic museum'?

To answer this we must know what the word 'ethnography' means.

Ethnography comes from *ethnos*, meaning 'people/race/nation', and *graphein*, meaning 'writing/description'. So a common definition might state that ethnography seeks 'to describe nations of people with their customs, habits and points of difference'. We are confronted by the knowledge that a definition of ethnography seeks to include notions of science and difference. As a word, 'ethnography' has acquired a range of meanings. Contemporary usage frequently invokes 'ethnography' to describe in-depth, empirical research and a variety of data collection techniques which rely on prolonged and intensive interaction between the researcher and her/his subjects of research, which usually results in the production of an 'ethnographic text'. But, historically, the definition has been far more specific. In the British context, 'ethnography' refers to the research methods and texts that were linked with the human sciences of *anthropology* (the science of man or mankind, in the widest sense) and *ethnology* (the science which considers races and people and their relationship to one another, their distinctive physical and other characteristics). So when one refers to ethnographic museums today, one is placing them within a discrete discipline and theoretical framework of anthropology, which is itself allied to a research technique – ethnographic fieldwork – and the specific ethnographic texts which report on these studies. Today the whole arena of academic practice, text and collections is sometimes encompassed under the catch-all term 'museum anthropology'.

Until the nineteenth century, most of what we would now label as 'ethnographic' objects were collected in a sporadic and fortuitous way, acquisitions whose value lay in their novelty or 'curiosity'. For these objects to be labelled as ethnographic and be lodged within an 'ethnographic' museum or department necessitated the development of a human science which would identify them as such, set in train a different system of classification and generate other motives for collecting them. In the context of museums, ethnographic and ethnological collections predated the establishment of anthropology, which emerged as a human science in the late nineteenth century but more properly in the early twentieth century. But the rise of anthropology as an academic discipline was significantly linked to the rise of ethnographic departments in museums (see section 4). What this new human science (anthropology), but also the older sciences of cultures (ethnography and ethnology), sought to study was the way of life, primarily but not exclusively, of non-European peoples or nations. The classificatory system devised in ethnographic museums is, therefore, predominantly a geographical or social one. The objects which ethnographic museums hold in their collections were mostly made or used by those who at one time or another were believed to be 'exotic', 'pre-literate', 'primitive', 'simple', 'savage' or 'vanishing races', and who are now described as, among other things, 'aboriginal', 'indigenous', 'first nations', or 'autochthonous': those peoples or nations whose cultural forms were historically contrasted with complex civilizations beyond Europe, such as China or the Islamic World or Ancient Egypt, and who, at various moments in their history, encountered explorers, traders, missionaries, colonizers and, most latterly but inevitably, western anthropologists.

So in referring to 'ethnographic museums' or 'ethnographic exhibitions', one is identifying institutions or exhibitions which feature objects as the 'material culture' of peoples who have been considered, since the mid-nineteenth century, to have been the appropriate target for anthropological research. Ethnographic museums produce certain kinds of representations and mobilize distinct classificatory systems which are framed by anthropological theory and ethnographic research. As such, what needs to be noted about ethnographic museums is that they do not simply reflect *natural* distinctions, but serve to create *cultural* ones, which acquire their cogency when viewed through the filtering lens of a particular discipline. The geographical and social distinctions deployed are constructed, but equally they are located historically: in the struggle for power between what has been called 'the West and the Rest' (Hall, 1992). Contrary to popular assumptions, we can assert that the science of anthropology, like all sciences 'hard' or otherwise, is not primarily a *science of discovery*, but a *science of invention*. In other words, it is not *reflective* of the essential nature of cultural difference, but classifies and *constitutes* this difference systematically and coherently, in accordance with a particular view of the world that emerges in a specific place, at a distinct historical moment and within a specific body of knowledge. So, at any historical juncture, the specific definitions of 'museum' and 'ethnography' function as floating signifiers, naming devices which attach themselves to and serve to signify certain kinds of cultural practices (see Shelton, 2006; Durrans, 2012). They are contingent, not essential.

2.4 Objects and meanings

Do the artefacts which form the core of a museum's collections provide it with stability amid all this flux and contingency? Not necessarily. Any such stability would rest on the conflation between two notable characteristics of museum objects (and objects in general) – their **physical presence** and their **meaning**. In the next section, we shall consider the dialectic between the two, and look at how their meanings fare as classification systems change.

Collected objects (and written records and photographs – themselves objects) are sometimes identified as the most persistent and indissoluble connections museums have between the past and present. 'Other peoples' artefacts are amongst the most "objective" data we can expect from them, and provide an intelligible baseline from which to begin the more difficult task of interpreting cultural meanings' (Durrans, 1992, p. 146).

Objects are often described as documents or evidence from the past, and are regarded as pristine material embodiments of cultural essences which transcend the vicissitudes of time, place and historical contingency. Their *physicality* delivers a promise of stability and objectivity; it suggests a stable and unambiguous world.

But this is a simplification and we can see this once we turn to the question of *meaning*. To treat these physical manifestations of the social world as permanent objective evidence is to fail to make a distinction between their undisputed *physical presence* and their ever-changing *meaning*:

> All the problems that we have with metaphors raise their head in a new guise when we identify objects. We do not escape from the predicaments that language prepares for us by turning away from the semiotics of words to the semiotics of objects. It would be illusory to hope that objects present us with a more solid, unambiguous world.
>
> (Douglas, 1992, pp. 6–7)

The fixity of an object's physical presence cannot deliver guarantees at the level of meaning. In the museum context, a conflation may be encouraged between the stability of presence and that of meaning. The status of the object as invariant in presence and meaning is underpinned by the popular representation of museums as grand institutions safeguarding, collecting, exhibiting and engaging in a scholarly fashion with the nation's material wealth. The traditional perception of curatorial practice as a descriptive rather than an interpretative activity lends further support to this elision. But it is clear that artefacts do not 'spirit' themselves into museum collections: they are collected, interpreted and exhibited – all purposeful and motivated activities (as we shall see in sections 3 and 4). If, unlike other historical events, artefacts can survive relatively intact as 'authentic' and 'primary' material from the past, it *does not* follow that they have kept their primary or 'original' meanings intact, since the specifics of these can rarely be recaptured or replayed. The distinction between physical presence and meaning must, therefore, be maintained.

It may be useful to illustrate this point by using an example. Through the following reading we will consider how a fairly mundane object might change its meaning over time.

READING B

Turn to Reading B (at the end of this chapter) and make notes on the edited extracts of 'His very silence speaks: the horse who survived Custer's Last Stand' by Elizabeth A. Lawrence, paying particular attention

(Continued)

(Continued)

to the reasons behind the horse's value as an object. How might the semiotic tools you were introduced to in Chapter 1 equip you to understand the changing meaning of the horse as object?

Lawrence's article features the life of an unusual horse – Comanche (Figure 3.2) – and its extraordinary afterlife as an artefact, in order to catalogue its changing meaning. The article is useful since common expectation would be that a stuffed horse would, in all probability, have a relatively unambiguous meaning.

FIGURE 3.2 Comanche: 'the horse who survived Custer's Last Stand'

Lawrence shows that the value bestowed on Comanche as an object was not due to his intrinsic worth: as a natural specimen of the equine species, he was only as good as any other. His distinction was his intimate connection with a significant historical encounter, the Battle of the Little Big Horn, which came to be known as 'Custer's Last Stand'. This is signalled by Comanche's changing fate as a museum exhibit. Initially displayed as an oddity among zoological specimens at the World's Columbian Exposition in Chicago in 1893, Comanche was subsequently transformed into a valued exhibit at the University of Kansas. In this second incarnation, Comanche became the site of struggle, initially revolving around his proper niche, but subsequently around his symbolic meaning.

In her article, Lawrence draws out the distinctions between Comanche's physical presence as a live and stuffed horse, in addition to giving an account of his shifting meaning. Here I propose to extend her analysis by disaggregating the different levels of meaning, using the tools provided by Roland Barthes in, *Elements of Semiology* (1967) and *Image–Music–Text* (1977) (previously introduced in Chapter 1).

As a lone exhibit and a stuffed horse, very little recommends Comanche, apart from his function as a *sign*. As you may recall from Chapter 1, the *sign* is defined by its components, the *signifier* and the *signified*. The difference between these two components, as defined by Barthes, is as follows: the 'substance of the *signifier* is always material (sounds, objects, images)' (1967, p.47), whereas the *signified* 'is not "a thing" but a *mental representation of "the thing"*' (1967, p.42) (my emphasis). So Comanche, both as a living horse, but more importantly as stuffed object, is the *signifier*; what is repeatedly *signified* is 'Custer's Last Stand' or, more precisely, the *mental representation* of a defeat and a military tragedy. However, such a brief semiotic 'reading' does not provide a comprehensive explanation of Comanche's endurance as a powerful and changeable sign in the century since his death. It might be productive to investigate the different levels at which *signification* takes place.

As you know, for Barthes, signs operate within systems, but these systems function to create different orders of meaning. In the following analysis, Barthes's concepts of **connotation** and **denotation** will be used to explore the articulation of signification around Comanche. In his usage of these terms, Barthes courted some controversy, but I shall bypass this debate and use these terms to invoke two levels of meaning creation. Here, *denotation* will refer to the first level, or order, of meaning which derives from a *descriptive* relationship, between signifier and signified, corresponding to the most obvious and consensual level at which objects mean something. In this case, Comanche most obviously and consistently denotes a horse, and on this most people would agree. *Connotation* refers to a second level, or order, of meaning which guides one to look at the way in which the *image (object) is understood*, at a broader, more associative, level of meaning. It therefore makes reference to more changeable and ephemeral structures, such as the rules of social life, of history, of social practices, ideologies and usage. At this level, Comanche's meaning undergoes great variation. For obvious reasons: its connotations cannot weather, intact, the changes in society's perception of itself.

Let us apply the concepts of *denotation* and *connotation* – to see how they can further extend our understanding of Comanche's enduring popularity. Comanche, initially as a living animal and subsequently as an object or sign, *denotes* immediately, repeatedly and mechanically *a horse*, and the historic event and traumatic defeat of which he, as a horse, was a silent witness namely 'Custer's Last Stand'. As a horse, he also denotes the valued bond between a man and his mount. At these two levels his meaning never changes.

Comanche's *connotations*, however, change over time. Initially he is the link between the living and the dead, connoting the 'anger of defeat', the 'sorrow for the dead cavalrymen' and the 'vengeance towards the Indians'. Later, as an incongruous feature in the Columbian Exposition in Chicago in 1893, he connotes conquest and the victory of the civilized over the 'murderous savage'. In the twentieth century, he ceases to have an objective value, connoting alternatively late nineteenth-century sentimentalism, good professional taxidermy, or a lucky charm. For some communities, his significance increases. For the Native American students at the University of Kansas he becomes a politicized artefact (not least because of his name). Comanche, as a mascot, emphatically signifies the bias of Euro-American ('white') historical narratives and the denial of the circumstances leading up to 'Custer's Last Stand'. Consequently, Comanche comes to represent mainstream America's amnesia and its denial of Native American experience and perspectives. These connotations deny Comanche his role as an objective witness. They transform him into a subjective and invalid symbol of white oppression. At the time of Lawrence's essay (1991), Comanche's legitimacy had been re-established by means of a text which navigates the reader towards a newer and, from today's perspective, more balanced and comprehensive interpretation of the events of 'Custer's Last Stand'.

Thus, Comanche's popularity derives from the shifting relationship between his connotations and denotations. His descriptive power maintains a greater stability (denotation) than his relevance and meaning, which are both questioned and re-negotiated (connotation). It is, after all, the perception of 'Custer's Last Stand' that changes – not Comanche's link with it. Over time, this allows his meaning to be 'read' in different ways. Comanche continues to denote the historic battle. What the battle signifies for Americans, Native or non-Native, is subject to change – as is Comanche's function as he metamorphoses from oddity, to lucky symbol, to suspect mascot, to educational tool.

So, to summarize, Lawrence's article argues that the value of objects resides in the meaning that they are given – the way they are *encoded*. By charting the trajectory of a once living and potentially banal object – a stuffed horse – and demonstrating how even steadfast categories like 'horse' can acquire extraordinary and controversial meanings, Lawrence demonstrates how the physical presence of an object cannot stabilize its meaning. Comanche's relevance derives from the fact that, as a symbol, he remains powerful, in part because his presence is differently interpreted in different periods and in different contexts.

But Lawrence's article offers other valuable insights: the first relating to *text*, the second concerning the *context*. Let us survey each of these briefly as they build on some of the work of Chapter 1.

2.5 The uses of text

If we consider the object of Lawrence's article, we find no difficulty in identifying it. It is, after all, a horse. With ethnographic objects, taken from geographically distant and culturally unfamiliar peoples, such convenient points of reference may be difficult to establish because they are not so immediately recognizable. For these objects, the function of any accompanying text is crucial. As we have seen, the defining feature of ethnographic objects is that they are products of the practice of ethnography. To read and understand them, therefore, we need *texts* that can interpret and translate their meaning for us. 'Texts' here refer not only to the written word, but to fabrics of knowledge that can be used as reference, including oral texts, social texts and academic texts. These perform the same function – they facilitate interpretation. In the ethnographic context, the primary, though not exclusive, source of this background knowledge is the ethnographic text.

As Chapter 1 argued, language is not a transparent 'window on the world'; it produces meaning and understanding. The purpose of ethnographic texts is ostensibly that of **decoding** – to render comprehensible that which is initially unfamiliar, to establish a 'reading' of an event or an object. In ethnographic texts, such a 'reading' is frequently accomplished by a translation, the transposition of alien concepts or ways of viewing the world, from one language to another or from one conceptual universe to another. This is a far from simple process. Ethnographic texts adopt an objective and descriptive mode, but their production necessitates a substantial degree of translation, transposition and construction. Ethnographic texts can only successfully *decode* – unravel the meaning of that which is unfamiliar, distant, incomprehensible – if they simultaneously *encode* – translate, de-exoticize, and transform that which is alien into that which is comprehensible.

All texts involve an economy of meaning: foregrounding certain interpretations and excluding others, seeking to plot a relatively unambiguous route through meaning. Ethnographic texts, more consciously than others perhaps, direct the reader towards a *preferred reading* since they must navigate the reader on a directed route through potentially complex and unfamiliar terrain. This preferred reading involves the dual process of unravelling certain meanings – *decoding* – but equally of selection and creativity which allows certain meanings to surface – **encoding**. A basket, for instance, might be decoded in many ways (the work of a particular artist; a fine exemplar; an ancient, unique specimen, etc.) but the accompanying text will encode it towards one or other of these, thereby guiding its interpretation and circumscribing its meaning. It will render intelligible the nature, history and cultural particularity of ethnographic objects. In so doing it will provide a compelling and convincing reading – it will 'quicken' and solidify the meaning. Recalling Lawrence's article, we may remember that it was the label – the *text* – which fixed Comanche's meaning in the most direct way and it was the text, therefore, which became the focus of dispute, negotiation and subsequent re-interpretation.

2.6 Questions of context

Reading Lawrence's article, the point that emerges most forcefully is the manner in which new layers of meaning are appended to Comanche over time, but in such a way that no new layer completely eclipses the previous one. Whatever Comanche's re-contextualization, he never completely loses his original meaning; it is re-articulated or added to. The palimpsest provides a useful metaphor for this process, where new layers of meaning are superimposed over older ones, or re-articulated, once the object is placed in a different context. This process, illustrated by Comanche's trajectory, is true for all objects. It is a particularly relevant way of perceiving the overlapping meanings of ethnographic collections, since they are most frequently the result of cultural, spatial and temporal displacement. 'Almost nothing displayed in museums was made to be seen in them. Museums provide an experience of most of the world's art and artefacts that does not bear even the remotest resemblance to what their makers intended' (Vogel, 1991, p. 191).

Ethnographic objects in historically important collections accumulate a palimpsest of meanings. So we can think of objects as elements which participate in a 'continuous history' (Ames, 1992, p. 141), where the makers, collectors and curators are simply points of origination, congregation and dispersal (Douglas, 1992, p. 15): a history that extends 'from origin to current destination, including the changing meanings as the object is continually redefined along the way' (Ames, 1992, p. 141).

Viewing objects as palimpsests of meaning allows one to incorporate a rich and complex social history into the contemporary analysis of the object. Contemporary curatorial practice does attempt to chart the flow by attempting to establish when objects were collected, by whom, from where, for what purpose, what the originating culture was, who the maker was, what the maker intended, how and when it was used (was it strictly functional or did it have other purposes?) and what other objects were used in conjunction with it. However, as we shall see in section 3, this does not sufficiently problematize the manner in which objects acquire meanings. Those who critique museums from the standpoint of the *politics* of collecting argue that such an analysis fails to address the fact that ethnographic objects have entered into western collections largely as the result of unequal relationships of power. As we progress through this chapter we will see that questions of context and collecting are more complex and can become more vexed than the above framework suggests.

2.7 Summary

> Museums not only collect and store fragments of culture: they themselves are part of culture …; a special zone where living culture dies and dead culture springs to life.

> (Durrans, 1993, p. 125)

This section started by arguing that at different points in history museums have had distinct ways of viewing objects and conferring meaning, value and validity. Using the example of the *Museaum Tradescantianum*, we saw that museums endow objects with importance because they are seen as representing some form of cultural value, perhaps an unusual association, a geographical location, or a distinct type of society. This initial example allowed us to argue that the meaning of objects is neither natural nor fixed: it is culturally constructed and changes from one historical context to another, depending on what system of classification is used. This theme was elaborated in relation to 'ethnographic' objects. It was argued that the category of 'ethnography' emerged as a particular academic discipline. It followed that objects were not intrinsically 'ethnographic', but that they had to be collected and described in terms that rendered them so. This analysis was taken further when we considered the ways in which objects acquire meaning. It was argued that to understand the levels at which objects acquire meaning, we have to investigate the texts that are used to interpret them in addition to the nature of their historical trajectory. An object offers no guarantees at the level of signification; the stability which derives from its *physical presence* must be conceptually divorced from the shifting nature of its *meaning*.

In the next section we will consider how objects may acquire meaning in the distinct context of an exhibition.

3 FASHIONING CULTURES: THE POETICS OF EXHIBITING

3.1 Introduction

In this section, we move from discussion of the object to the practices of exhibiting. It is the exhibition context which seems to provide us with the best forum for an examination of the creation of meaning. Exhibitions are discrete events which articulate objects, texts, visual representations, reconstructions and sounds to create an intricate and bounded representational system. It is an especially appropriate context for exploring the **poetics of exhibiting**: the practice of producing meaning through the internal ordering and conjugation of the separate but related components of an exhibition.

In order to provide a 'reading' of some depth I have chosen a case study format. The exhibition – *Paradise: Change and Continuity in the New Guinea Highlands* – was unusual. It sought to examine the contemporary moment among the Wahgi people of the Highlands of Papua New Guinea, while integrating a record of its own creation. It was the subject of two extended commentaries: one by Michael O'Hanlon, the anthropologist/curator of the exhibition (*Paradise: Portraying the New Guinea Highlands*, 1993), the other by James Clifford (*Paradise*, 1995, reprinted in 1997), an anthropologist and cultural critic. The following section will use the exhibition as a jumping off point to investigate what it can teach us about the general principles of meaning construction in the exhibition context. As we will see, *Paradise: Change and Continuity in the New Guinea Highlands* utilized a variety of exhibiting techniques which were combined to provide a rich and complex display, including some, such as reconstructions, scene painting and mimicry, that are today much less common (see Shelton, 2006, pp. 73–4). Consequently, the 'reading' presented here articulates a particular view of the exhibition. It is not, nor can it be, a comprehensive assessment of the diversity of issues involved; it is selective. Those who want other 'readings' should refer to the texts cited above in their original, full state, rather than the extracts included here.

3.2 Introducing *Paradise*

The exhibition *Paradise: Change and Continuity in the New Guinea Highlands* (hereafter *Paradise*) opened at the Museum of Mankind, formely the home of the Department of Ethnography (now the Department of Africa, Oceania and the Americas) of the British Museum, on 16 July 1993 and closed on 2 July 1995. During the two years of its life *Paradise* could be found on the second floor of the Museum of Mankind. As part of a programme of rolling temporary exhibitions, its ostensible purpose was to bring the culture and history of the Wahgi people of the Highlands of Papua New Guinea to the attention of the public in London and beyond. A wheelchair ramp, a narrow corridor and two glass doors separated *Paradise* from the rest of the museum. Walking through them one entered the introductory space, with a large full-colour picture (Plate 3.I in the colour plate section) of:

… a genial-looking man stand[ing] casually in front of a corrugated iron wall and frame window; he wears a striped apron of some commercial material, exotic accoutrements and gigantic headdress of red and black feathers. His face is painted black and red; a bright white substance is smeared across his chest. He looks straight at you, with a kind of smile.

(Clifford, 1995, p. 93)

The introductory panel, 'Paradise', on the left of the photograph, disclosed the aim of the exhibition: to show 'something of the history and culture of the Wahgi people of the New Guinea Highlands'. It then introduced the structuring themes of the exhibition – change and continuity.

ACTIVITY 1

Read as much as you can of the panel text from Plate 3.I and consider how the exhibition is being introduced – what does the text tell you about the significance of the term 'Paradise'?

How might this establish a *preferred reading* of the exhibition?

This introductory text tells us a number of things: primarily, that 'Paradise' symbolizes both *change* – the transforming effect of coffee wealth – and *continuity* – the capacity for cultural forms to adapt to transforming circumstances. This tension is symbolized by the elements of the photograph: the birds of paradise feathers versus the corrugated iron for example, both integral to the picture and, by implication, Wahgi life. But this introduction also foregrounds the issues of *representation*: *Paradise*, the exhibition – the reconstruction of reality – is a subversion of Paradise, the 'myth' – the stereotype of the South Pacific. In contrast to a false image, it implies, this exhibition proposes a corrective, more authentic description of a particular South Pacific community. It is closer to the truth but not all-inclusive – we are only shown 'something' of the history and culture of the Wahgi. So the introduction alerts us to the veracity of the reconstruction or representation. Although it makes claims of objectivity and representativeness, it disavows claims to comprehensiveness.

So even at the moment of entry we are drawn into the practice of signification and construction. The introductory panel contains within itself the structure of the whole exhibition, providing us with a mental map. We learn of the rationale of the exhibition and are alerted to its possible future content. So this initial panel sets the parameters of the representation and establishes a distinct narrative and sequencing.

What is the exhibition about? Wahgi history and culture.

What does this mean? It means recent contact, change and continuity reflected through material culture, including adornment, as transformed and preserved through the income from cash-cropping coffee.

The introductory narrative helps to guide the unfamiliar visitor through difficult and potentially dazzling terrain – the complexities of Wahgi culture could not, pragmatically, be fully explicated in this restricted exhibition space. To generate a meaningful path through the exhibition, the curator, the designers and technicians must choose which objects to display and which display methods might achieve the greatest impact, as well as what kinds of information might be included in the panels, label text or captions. These choices are in part 'repressive', in the sense that they direct the visitor towards certain interpretations and understandings, opening certain doors to meaning but inevitably closing off others.

But let us consider the importance and use of the photographic image (Plate 3.I). We might first remark that the persuasiveness of the text is significantly enhanced by the photograph that accompanies it. Photographs can ease the work of representation within the exhibition context by virtue of their verisimilitude. As we shall see later, photographs in this exhibition were also used more actively in the practice of *signification*.

PLATES 3.I – 3.XV VIEWS OF THE *PARADISE* EXHIBITION, MUSEUM OF MANKIND, LONDON

PLATE 3.I   The introductory section of the exhibition

The personal image which initiates the exhibition declares that this is not the South Pacific as we all know it from the Rogers and Hammerstein film – a stereotype – this is an *authentic* Waghi. The image *denotes* Wahgi reality; it is one of a collection of photographs that objectively records an event – the opening of the store. It purports to be an adequate and truthful reflection of the event. But this denotation of 'Wahgi reality' has meaningful effects.

PLATE 3.II   Foreground: (right) the bridewealth banners and First Contact display; (left) the compensation payment poles. Background: wall cases and free-standing glass cases containing Wahgi wigs and other items of adornment

PLATE 3.III   Sequential parts of the exhibition: (left to right) coffee production, the trade-store and shield displays

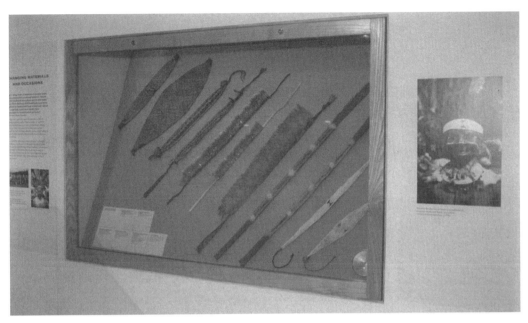

PLATE 3.IV Wall case containing Wahgi items of adornment, old and new. Note the headband made of flame-coloured Big Boy bubble gum wrappers

PLATE 3.V *Bolyim* house (right). Note the simulated pig jaws strung around the middle, and upturned beer bottles around the base

PLATE 3.VI *Bolyim* house showing accompanying panel text and photographs

PLATE 3.VII Coffee production display. Note the artificial coffee bush, the coffee beans drying on the plastic sheeting, the hand-powered coffee pulper, and weighing scales

PLATE 3.VIII Coffee production display, panel text and photographs. Note the similarity between the display and the photographs featured on the panel

PLATE 3.IX First Contact display, showing 'First Contact' panel with black-and-white photographs displayed against enlargement of black-and-white photograph taken by Mick Leahy

First, it 'naturalizes' the text: the photograph makes it appear less as a *construction* of Wahgi reality than a *reflection* of it, since both the 'reality' and the effects of the processes being described in the exhibition (those of change and continuity) are represented in the photograph. *Naturalization* is an important concept that will be taken up through this analysis and later on in this section in the discussion of 'myth'.

But the photograph relays a complex message. It includes *connotations* of the hybrid nature of adornment (the bamboo frame is covered with imported fabric, the paints are commercially produced); the ambivalence of coffee wealth and its effect on taste (the adoption of black plumes for adornment); the nature of a typical Papua New Guinea trade-store (reconstructed in the main gallery). These only become clear once the visitor has completed the full circuit of the exhibition: on passing this photograph on the way out s/he may 'read' it more fully, being less startled by its exuberance and more aware of its encapsulation of the exhibition themes.

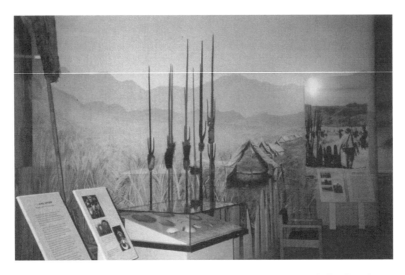

PLATE 3.X First Contact display, showing *kulia jimben* spears against scene painting (reflecting photograph in Plate 3.IX)

PLATE 3.XI First Contact display, showing bridewealth banners, and the '… and after' panel text and photographs. Note the similarity between the blow-up of the middle photograph and the reconstructed bridewealth banner

PLATE 3.XII Trade-store display. Note the warning on the door (and weighing scales from neighbouring coffee production display)

PLATE 3.XIII Interior of trade-store display, showing the variety of products on sale

PLATE 3.XIV The side of the trade-store display, showing how a connection was created with the neighbouring shield display

Second, it tends to legitimate the photographer/curator voice since the image denotes and guarantees O'Hanlon's having been there in the Highlands. It connotes *authentic* anthropological knowledge: this means being appropriately familiar with the Wahgi. By association, it authenticates the objects: they were collected while *he-was-there*.

But this brilliant photograph has an additional 'ethnographic' purpose. It connotes 'difference' in all its exotic resplendence (a connotation incorporated into the exhibition poster) while simultaneously domesticating and transcending it. As one's eyes move from photograph to text, what is at first stunning and

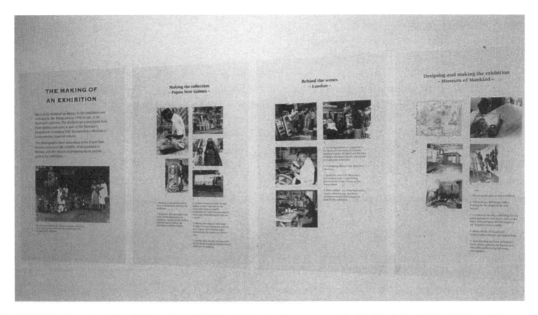

PLATE 3.XV Panels on 'The Making of an Exhibition', showing the process of collecting in the field with the assistance of the Wahgi, and the process of exhibiting in London

vibrant but indecipherable – except for the smile – is subsequently *translated*. This is recognizably a wealthy man in the midst of a celebration. He quickly becomes *known* and *familiar* to us. He is not simply 'a Wahgi', he is Kauwiye (Andrew) Aipe, a genial entrepreneur. Moreover, he is welcoming us to the exhibition space, to the Wahgi way of life and the context in which Wahgi artefacts acquire meaning. Once the exotic is translated and proves hospitable, we can proceed into the remainder of the exhibition space.

This brief introduction alerts us to the type of construction and representation attempted in ethnographic exhibitions. Ethnographic exhibitions often adopt the format of contextualizing and reconstructing. Curators/designers work with objects and contextualize them so that these assume a purposive role; objects are commonly selected as representative, rather than unique, examples. As both cultural expressions and physical proof, these provide insights into cultural phenomena of which they are taken to be the physical manifestation ('representation'). The visitor is therefore drawn into a new and different world in which unfamiliar objects might be made intelligible, where the design encourages a reduction in distance between the visitor and the 'originating culture' (the culture from which the objects were appropriated). Since the primary purpose of such exhibitions is the translation of difference – to acquaint the viewer with unfamiliar concepts, values and ideas – their key motive is communication through understanding and interpretation. Ethnographic exhibitions are typically syncretic (pulling together things from different sources). Nevertheless, though their ostensible form is that of *mimesis*, the invocation and imitation of a unfamiliar 'reality', their effectiveness depends on a high degree of selectivity and construction. It is this – the *poetics* of exhibiting – that the rest of this section will address.

145

3.3 *Paradise* regained

[T]he next, larger, space [of the exhibition] draws you in. It contains striking things: a reconstructed highland trade-store, rows of oddly decorated shields, wicked-looking ... spears, and bamboo poles covered with leaves which, on closer inspection, turn out to be paper money.

(Clifford, 1995, p. 93)

The themes of the next large space are those of contact and coffee, war, shields and peacemaking. It is here that we notice the full effect of the design of the exhibition, the cacophony of colour and objects promised by the initial photograph of Kauwiye Aipe.

ACTIVITY 2

Look at a selection of photographs of the exhibition spaces following the introductory space (Plates 3.II–3.V). These will give you a flavour of the exhibition. When looking at these, consider how the objects are exhibited. How might different methods of display affect your perception of the objects?

In the exhibition we discover that there are several methods of display. I have disaggregated them as follows:

- on open display – shields (Plate 3.III)
- table cases – shells, items of adornment (Plate 3.II)
- wall cases – items of adornment (Plate 3.IV)
- reconstructions – bridewealth banners, trade-store, *bolyim* house (Plates 3.II, 3.III, 3.V)
- simulacra – compensation payment poles (Plate 3.II).

We could think of these methods of display as different but equivalent techniques, but this interpretation is not wholly adequate. In the *Paradise* example, the selection of these different contexts was influenced by lack of funds, which meant that the curator was obliged to use a display structure inherited from the previous exhibition (O'Hanlon, 1993, pp. 82–5).

Here we are concerned with the *effects* of these different display techniques. *Paradise* utilized a diversity of display techniques, so its richness allows us to address the different levels in which methods of display create contexts for the production of meaning.

All these forms of display incorporate Wahgi material culture, but the different techniques affect our perception and reaction to the objects. This can be illustrated by taking a simple example. A straightforward reconstruction, such as the coffee production display (Plates 3.VII, 3.VIII), includes artefacts known as Wahgi because of their context of use. They are included because of their role in Wahgi life. These are not ostentatious objects but mechanical and mundane items which appear to need very little interpretation. They exemplify the literal reality of Wahgi life, in which they feature quite heavily. The combination of the artefacts is not ambiguous, it is 'obvious': they belong together. The accompanying photographs show just such a combination of artefacts being used by the Wahgi. So the visitor is encouraged to trust – by virtue of the presence and combination of artefacts – that this is a 'reflection' of Wahgi reality. Such representations work to *denote* 'Wahgi reality' and *connote* the 'naturalness' of the display technique.

The glass cases, in contrast, establish distance by placing the object in a more sterile and ordered environment (Plates 3.II, 3.IV). This more conventional museum approach connotes the artificiality of display technique. Ethnographic objects are rarely made for glass cases, nor are they habitually selected and disaggregated from other associated objects while in use. Putting material artefacts in glass cases therefore underlines the dislocation and re-contextualization that is at the root of collecting and exhibiting. So whereas reconstruction may establish a context which evokes and recreates the 'actual' environment of production or use of an object, glass cases render the objects more distant; they do not merge into their context in the same way as they might if they were placed in a reconstructed site (Plates 3.II, 3.III).

These distinctions are amplified by the use of text. In the reconstructions, numerous objects are displayed in combination and assigned communal labels; but in the glass cases the objects are given individual identities. Each object, then, is accorded a particular value, interpreted and explained. So in open displays the presence of the object and its context or *presentation* eclipses the fact that it is being *represented*. The fact of representation is obscured. We perceive here the process of *naturalization*, as the objects appear *naturally* suited to this context, seeming to speak for or represent themselves. In glass cases, however, the work involved in representation is made more overt by virtue of the artificial separation and presentation of the object.

But there is one last type of display that remains unmentioned – the simulacra. The differences between reconstructions and simulacra are subtle. The reconstructions are partially 'authentic' artefacts – made by the museum technicians according to Wahgi design and incorporating Wahgi materials, be it shells, fibre or trade goods. The simulacra are *imitations* of real Wahgi objects such as the compensation payment poles (Plate 3.II). These are neither genuine Wahgi objects, nor do they incorporate them, but as objects they draw from Wahgi reality in their design. We can designate them, after Barthes, as 'trick effects': since their purpose is to make what is heavily *connoted* pass as *denoted* (Barthes, 1977, pp. 21–2). Their presence is initially unquestioned – they appear to denote 'Wahgi reality' – until we see the 'real thing' in the photographs on the curving adjacent wall (Plate 3.II). At first these banners appear authentic, it is the accompanying text and photographs that intentionally alert us to their subterfuge:

The ... banners made of banknotes only really make sense when one sees the nearby color photograph of men holding them aloft in a procession. The 'Ah ha' response comes when looking at the picture, not the object. The banners are strange and beautiful in their way, but clearly simulacra ... They become secondary, not 'the real thing' seen so clearly in the image.

(Clifford, 1995, p. 99)

But their presence is nevertheless important, since these tangibly simulated objects smooth the representational work: if the text interprets and directs the reading of the object, then the object draws the reader to the text. The 'trick' is to validate the text. The presence of these simulacra in conjunction with the 'real thing' in the form of the photograph anchors the representation of Wahgi peace-making and compensation written about in the accompanying text.

3.4 Structuring *Paradise*

This part of section 3 will examine how images and texts can be used to create meaning in the exhibition context, by analysing a specific display in *Paradise*.

Clearly, texts and images can have a number of functions. In order to disaggregate these I shall use the terms presentation, representation and presence. I will use the terms **presentation** to refer to the overall arrangement and the techniques employed; **presence** to imply the type of object and the power it exerts; and **representation** to consider the manner in which the objects work in conjunction with contexts and texts to produce meaning (Dubé, 1995, p. 4).

ACTIVITY 3

Looking at the photographs of the First Contact display carefully (Plates 3.IX, 3.X, 3.XI), examine how the texts and the images are used in the context of this discrete space. You do not need to dwell at length on this. Simply reflect on the different types of texts used in this display. What might their roles be? What roles are the photographs given: do they illustrate, amplify, authenticate the text? How might these photographs denote a changing historical period?

Let us consider the 'texts' and what narrative techniques are used, before moving on to consider the function and significance of photographs in *Paradise*. As in most exhibitions, *Paradise* used several types of texts:

1 *Panels*. These contain thematic information or delineate a particular arena of human activity.
2 *Labels*. These are assigned to particular objects, offering explanations of how the object is articulated in its social contexts.
3 *Photographic captions*. These exemplify or subvert certain concepts or descriptions contained in other texts.

The difference between these texts is quite subtle. Panel texts connote authority but are, conversely, more interpretative. Labels and captions, on the other hand, are more 'literal'; they claim to describe what is there. This is partly determined by space. Nevertheless these texts work together and separately, each *encoding* through the semblance of *decoding*. The difference between these texts, but also their contribution to signification, can be exemplified at the level of translation.

Ethnographic exhibitions frequently make use of indigenous terms within the substance of their texts. This is done for many reasons, partly to acknowledge the insufficiency of translation, but equally because in an ethnographic exhibition it accords a 'voice' to the people featured. Such concessions to indigenous language have, furthermore, proved popular and acceptable to the audiences who visit ethnographic exhibitions. But utilizing indigenous languages has certain effects. On labels, they are often entered as descriptions to signify the object – the *bolyim* house, a *mond* post – and a connection is created between object and description which appears transparent, definitive and transcendent. This is a *bolyim* house – no need for translation (Plate 3.VI). Panels frequently have sayings, asides or proverbs, in unfamiliar languages encouraging the reader to enter, momentarily at least, into the conceptual universe – the way of seeing – of the people concerned. In the 'First Contact' panel, for instance, Kekanem Goi's remark recounting his first reaction to the patrol's arrival ('*Alamb kipe gonzip alamb ende worn mo*?') is translated ('Is it ghosts, the dead who have come?') to denote the shock of the encounter between the 'whites' and the Wahgi (Plate 3.IX). However, the process of inclusion is a complex one, involving selection, translation and interpretation. Meaning must be altered so that an allegory or metaphor deriving from one culture is made comprehensible in the language of another.

So here we see that, though texts impart information, they are also economies of meaning, selecting what they would ideally like the visitor to know – what is important. They also reinforce certain aspects of design. In the First Contact display the spears are not given labels, but one can easily 'read' them since their arrangement (Plate 3.X) overtly reflects the content of one of the large photographs (Plate 3.IX). No overt guidance (text) is needed since they can be interpreted against the photograph.

This is one of the functions of the photographs in the First Contact display. At one level, the type of reconstruction attempted seeks simply to mimic the content of the photographs. The scene painting reflects the image of Mick Leahy's encampment (Plate 3.X), the reconstructed fence and the group of *kula jimben* spears – some collected in the 1930s, others in the 1990s – recreate the situation in the black-and-white photograph of the Leahy patrol camp (Plate 3.IX). The bridewealth banner reflects the colour picture, itself a blow-up of one of the pictures in the panel (Plate 3.XI). This is not all. The images, in addition to authenticating the (re)construction and the objects, serve to connote the passage of time. This is related by the quality of the reproduction (grainy/clear) and its type (colour/black and white) – a message easily understood. The 'faded' colour of the bridewealth banner picture (taken in the 1950s) contrasts with the 'true' colour of the other, more recent, pictures (taken in the 1980s) and the black-and-white grainy reproductions of those taken in the 1930s (Clifford, 1995, pp. 99–100). The interplay and proximity of these images of changing quality and type reinforces the theme of the text and locates the objects to create a very rich representation of change and continuity.

But some photographs have a function which extends beyond *presentation* and *representation*. In the *Paradise* exhibition they are fully a substitute for *presence*. In the case of the bridewealth banners, most especially, the large photographic panel *substitutes* for the object (Plates 3.II and 3.XI). In addition, the photograph – the representation of the real banner – overshadows the adjacent reconstruction – the partially authentic artefact which incorporates *real* Wahgi shells and fibre – by being far more vibrant and arresting:

> It is no longer a question of a photo providing 'context' for an object. We confront an object that cannot be present physically, a 1950s bridewealth banner – long disassembled, as is its proper fate. This banner has been 'collected' in the photographs. Given its prominence, the color image seems somehow more real, in a sense more 'authentic' than ... the less impressive older banner propped beside it ...

(Clifford, 1995, p. 100)

For Clifford, this is a preferable state of affairs. Collecting would decisively remove the object from its original context and store it in a museum, bestowing on it false immortality, but collecting the object-as-photograph provides a legitimate alternative. It records the existence of the object but does not disrupt its proper cultural disposal. So photographs, in the exhibition context, potentially furnish solutions to tricky questions. They accord a *presence* to ephemeral artefacts – artefacts that would be destroyed in their original social context: the bridewealth banners and *bolyim* house, for instance. They also give presence to those that cannot be exported legally – such as the Bird of Paradise feathers (Plate 3.I) – or practically – the Wahgi themselves (Plate 3.XV).

In the *Paradise* exhibition, therefore, photographs have three effects: they enhance the *presentation* of the exhibition; they substitute for the physical *presence* of ethnographic 'objects' or 'subjects'; and they ease the work of representation by providing a 'real' context which either contextualizes the object or allows a blueprint for the display design.

3.5 *Paradise*: the exhibit as artefact

In the preceding sections we have considered how objects, texts and contexts have worked in conjunction to produce meaning. Let us bring these to bear on the trade-store exhibit to examine how the context of display, and by extension the exhibition, can be considered as a fiction and an artefact. The word fiction is not used here in a derogatory way, but rather in its *neutral* sense: the Latin verb *fingere*, from which fiction derives, means that something has been fashioned and made through human endeavour. O'Hanlon candidly acknowledges his role as author (1993, see the Introduction and Chapter 3). As an articulated but bounded representational system, the trade-store will be used here as a metaphor for the *Paradise* exhibition as a whole (Plate 3.III).

The trade-store clearly operates on the level of *presentation*. It mimics a 'real' Highlands store with a corrugated iron roof. The reconstruction is 'authentic', even down to its incorporation of the usual notice on its door – '*No ken askim long dinau*' ('Don't ask for credit') – and the floor – sandy and littered with beer bottle tops (Plates 3.XII, 3.XIV). The hodge-podge of goods, all imported, purposefully attempts to 'capture something of the raw colours of such enterprises' (O'Hanlon,

1993, p. 89) (Plate 3.XIII). And is their function purely presentation? No. The presence of these goods clearly heightens our power of imagination; the combination is fascinating; each item draws our attention. One stops to read the different brand names – Cambridge cigarettes, *LikLik Wopa* ('little whopper' biscuits), Paradise *Kokonas* (coconut biscuits), Big Sister pudding, the ubiquitous Coca-Cola – and to take in the exuberance of the display.

On the level of *presence*, the items denote 'the expanding range of goods on sale' (O'Hanlon, 1993, p. 89), most particularly what can be bought with coffee wealth. The store was intended as 'a reconstruction, stocked with the goods which would be on sale during the Wahgi coffee season' (panel text). So these objects are genuine and representative samples of the totality of artefacts that could be found in a store (they were brought over from Papua New Guinea). The store *enlivens* the representation of Wahgi life. Its presence – as an artefact in its own right – *anchors* the narrative in the panel text, which conversely interprets the meaning of the whole and the miscellany of goods which it contains.

Considering the context of display – the trade-store – the arrangements of these objects seems appropriate, 'natural' even. Imagine these trade goods ordered in a glass case: the isolation would affect our perception, drawing us to the object rather than the combination. It is the contrived miscellany of objects in the trade-store that makes it compelling and produces meaning; the whole is bigger than the sum of its parts. The trade-store is itself a system of representation, externally and internally narrated. Each object is interpreted through its label, which cross-refers to others, the advertising slogans and to the panel text. Furthermore, the store goods are interpreted in two different languages – *tok pisin* (the local *lingua franca*), and English. These trade labels reaffirm difference but also transcend it.

The trade-store is an enabling context which 'quickens' our understanding of the ambivalent impact of coffee wealth, transforming exchange relations, encouraging warfare. But this representation is articulated with the adjacent displays (Plate 3.III), coffee production – the source of money – and the shields, which connote in their design and form 'South Pacific' beer cans (Plate 3.III, 3.XIV). Indeed, the trade-store, though denotative of a 'typical' Highlands store, has another level of artifice – two 'trick effects'. O'Hanlon tells us that he has had to cut away the front to permit visibility and surreptitiously included 'South Pacific' empties along the far wall, not because this is representative of reality, but because a reference to beer must be included in a depiction of New Guinea life (1993, pp. 89–90). Their inclusion here enables us to make an effortless move to the next display (Plate 3.III, 3.XIV).

The display takes us back to the initial image and functions covertly as a focal point for our other senses. It is the first time one can remark the change in the scene painting and it is from the trade-store that we become aware that the sounds can be heard. What effects might these have?

Let us first take the case of the scene painting. In the introductory space, scene painting is restricted to the depiction of two mountain ranges and the sky. In the main exhibition space it is varied to denote the physical and social environment of the Highlands of New Guinea, alternatively dense Highlands vegetation (behind the trade-store and the hand-coffee mill) and an enclosed camp identical to the one in the photographs of the Leahy expedition or a Wahgi village (behind the *bolyim* house and *mond* post). The scene painting works with the photographs and the reconstructions to innocently denote the

Wahgi world, to reflect the physical environment of the Highlands of New Guinea 'as-it-really-is'. This denotation of 'Wahgi reality' is affirmed aurally, by the continuous looped three-minute tape featuring New Guinea early morning sounds, cicadas, singing, Jew's harp, but also bingo calls, issuing from the trade-store. These sounds locate the visitor in the Highlands. Providing a contrast with the busy London streets, but equally with the quiet reverence of the other galleries, these aural representations deepen the impression of entering the Wahgi physical and social world because they work on an affective, emotional level. Amplifying the themes of the exhibition, these sounds 'collected in the field' denote the Highlands but connote tradition (through sounds of Jew's harp, singing) and change (through the recognizable sound of bingo). So what at first seemed different is, with repetition, made familiar and the visitor is encouraged to imagine they are in the New Guinea Highlands. But this representation 'as-it-really-is' necessarily supports a distinct thematic narrative about the way in which change and continuity shape contemporary Wahgi life.

Thus we can think of *Paradise*, the exhibition, as a complex representational system featuring objects (made and used by the Wahgi), reconstructions (of Wahgi material, of Wahgi design, but made by museum staff) and simulacra whose cogency derives from the articulation of these different elements into a narrative with texts, images and sounds. At one level the *Paradise* exhibition is 'typically' ethnographic: its focus is the socio-cultural whole that is Wahgi life, and it uses objects as exemplars, each a sample of a representative type whose presence guarantees the veracity of the representation. It is typical in the sense that it is necessarily selective: what is displayed is a representation of Wahgi life, constructed, authored and partial.

3.6 The myths of *Paradise*

In the preceding analysis two things were learned:

1 the extent to which exhibitions are constructions, and
2 that the end of this construction is to persuade, to render 'natural' or 'innocent' what is profoundly 'constructed' and 'motivated'.

The first aspect has been extensively investigated; it is the second that concerns us now. The point of departure (the argument to follow) is simply that *all* cultural producers – advertisers, designers, curators, authors (including this one) – are involved in the creation of 'myths' in the manner in which Barthes defines this. As a consequence, these producers are inevitably the holders of symbolic power.

We shall look at 'myth' by critically assessing the contrasting accounts of exhibition production by Clifford (1995) and O'Hanlon (1993). The *Paradise* exhibition, unusually, included panels and text which highlighted the conditions of production of the exhibition, the role of the author and curator, and his relationship with the community he chose to represent. Such a candid account is placed at the end of the exhibition, and so one can 'read' the exhibition as a partial truth, retrospectively. *Paradise* was a resourceful, considered and complex exhibition which addressed the problematic aspects of its own production and political accountability. This self-reflexivity and knowingness opens it up for valuable and critical comment, of a kind that can push the student and cultural critic beyond a stereotypical characterization of the process of exhibiting.

READINGS C and D

Let us consider certain extracts from O'Hanlon's (1993) book and Clifford's (1995) commentary; see Readings C and D at the end of this chapter.

These two texts have alternative purposes and voices. O'Hanlon writes as a curator/anthropologist. He recounts the process of collecting and exhibiting as he sees it, to strip it of its aura or 'magic'. Clifford's text offers a different perspective, from the point of view of the cultural critic and the visitor; someone who is enthusiastic about *Paradise*, but who uses it to push the analysis on to questions of power. *These are both partial views – texts about texts – and must be read as such.* They constitute part of an ongoing dialogue.

You should take notes on these two extracts, particularly the differing views on *collecting* and *exhibiting*. How does each seek to qualify their point of view? How do their interpretations contrast?

Let us first consider O'Hanlon's perspective.

O'Hanlon's account of collecting adopts a reflexive tone which acknowledges the contingencies of collecting as well as the potential inapplicability of an anthropologist's categories. He represents collecting as a valuable educational experience. He argues that collecting does not involve a 'rupture' of artefacts from their local context, but requires complex negotiations between the Wahgi and himself, dictated by existing – Wahgi – categories of social relations and local political agendas. He is directed by and drawn into a complex series of relationships in which he is attributed the status of an agent by his Wahgi friends. His departure places him at one remove from the expectations of a continuing relationship of indebtedness.

Collecting Wahgi material culture, and prompting its production, pushes O'Hanlon to recognize the limits of knowledge. It alerts him to cultural complexities and the convoluted meanings of certain artefacts. It creates an artificial social situation, bringing the subtleties of Wahgi classification and definitions to his attention, which he might otherwise have missed. For instance, although the Wahgi are prepared to make certain ritually significant items for O'Hanlon (*geru* boards), they are not prepared to make others (*bolyim* house).

So collecting emerges from O'Hanlon's account as a complex, negotiated process, where the anthropologist does *not* have the power one might otherwise expect. It necessitates, instead, local knowledge, resources and resourcefulness.

In relationship to exhibiting, O'Hanlon stresses that the exhibition is an authored text and assemblage – an *artefact*. He avows his desire that the Wahgi should have a degree of *presence* in the exhibition and writes that he would like to honour the Wahgi's request for stones and posts to be put in the first antechamber of the exhibition (an antechamber that was subsequently changed by the designers). He notes, furthermore, that his exhibition should accord the Wahgi a 'voice' by using

Wahgi or *tok pisin* text. Secondly, he overtly signals the constructed nature of the exhibition within the exhibition itself: the last panels foreground the different stages of its production (Plate 3.XV).

Clifford (1995), on the other hand, reviews the display, because it tackles issues and provides information which, in most exhibitions remain obscured. He nevertheless subjects the materials provided to further scrutiny. For Clifford, like O'Hanlon, *Paradise* is an artefact fashioned by the interplay between curators, designers and the museum as institution, but not necessarily the Wahgi. He critically questions the extent to which the Wahgi could be considered partners or co-authors and cites the following evidence. First, he signals the lack of a significant Wahgi 'voice'. Secondly, he views the self-reflexivity incorporated into the exhibition (Plate 3.XV) as being less provocative than it might be. Thirdly, he examines the exact nature of the 'continuing relationship of indebtedness' between O'Hanlon and the Wahgi. Using the example of the 'taboo stones', he argues that the Wahgi had little effective power. Finally, he asks to what extent specific interpersonal relationships struck up between the anthropologist and his colleagues or friends within the community ('in the field') can be mapped on to the institutional setting.

ACTIVITY 4

We now have two different views of the process of collecting and exhibiting. What do you think of these views? Which strikes you as the more compelling, and why?

We can add to these two commentaries on the practices of collecting and exhibiting another critical dimension, using Barthes's theory of 'myth', or mythical speech, which was discussed in Chapter 1. Two aspects of his exposition may be useful here, to push the dialogue, and the analysis of exhibiting above, further.

First, Barthes calls 'myth' a second-order semiological language. This means that, in contrast to ordinary language, it does not work on the basis of an arbitrary, unmotivated relationship between the signifier and signified. With 'myth', there is always some form of 'motivation', namely some purpose, intent or rationale underlying its use. Furthermore, the persuasiveness of 'myths' derives from their 'natural justification' of their purpose:

> What the world supplies to myth is an historical reality, defined, even if this goes back quite a while, by the way in which men have produced or used it; what myth gives back in return is a *natural* image of this reality.

> (Barthes, 1989, p. 155)

So myth 'naturalizes' speech, transmuting what is essentially *cultural* (historical, constructed and motivated) into something which it materializes as *natural* (transhistorical, innocent and factual). Myth's duplicity is therefore located in its ability to 'naturalize' and make 'innocent' what is profoundly motivated.

The second point follows from this and concerns the ability of myth to 'de-politicize' speech:

> Myth does not deny things, on the contrary, its function is to talk about them; simply, it *purifies* them, it makes them *innocent*, it gives them a *natural* and *eternal* justification, it gives them a clarity which is not that of an explanation but that of a statement of fact.

(Barthes, 1989, p. 156, my emphasis)

So by asserting that myth de-politicizes speech, Barthes argues that myth does not hide or conceal its motivation. Instead, by giving it a universal, transhistorical basis and by stressing objectivity, and its origins in nature, myth **purifies** its motivation.

How might these insights provide an additional 'reading' of the texts to the ones we have just explored?

In this section we have treated the *Paradise* exhibition as a fashioned event and a complex system of signification. Both these aspects can be addressed by Barthes's analysis of 'myth'.

Let us first consider 'motivation'. *Paradise*, like all exhibitions or any other cultural products, was clearly the result of a series of deliberate actions: the collection was purchased, the exhibition planned, written and constructed. The objects were removed from Wahgi cultural life and re-presented in cases, restored in the quasi-'natural' setting of a reconstruction or represented in scene paintings and photographs. *Paradise* was not a rambling narrative with a number of disconnected objects thrown together; it was a highly structured event in which *even* the apparent miscellanies were designed to seem 'real'.

Moreover, the overwhelming purpose of the exhibition was that of representing Wahgi *reality*: the artefacts, once part of the Wahgi social universe, visibly correspond to 'Wahgi reality' as captured in the photographs or mimicked in the reconstructions. So the phenomenon of Wahgi cultural life is domesticated and transformed – it is 'naturalized'. The exhibition adopts a factual, easy tone where selected representative objects are described in objective terms and where sounds, scene-painting reconstructions, photographs and quotations all accord a *presence* to the Wahgi.

So *Paradise*, like all exhibitions, is a descriptive and motivated event. But doesn't O'Hanlon go some way to recognizing this?

O'Hanlon does not deny his agency as an anthropologist; he incorporates it into his narratives (the exhibition and the book). Aware as he is of the complexities of collecting and exhibiting, he sets out to explore the contingencies and conditions of possibility of both. O'Hanlon's motivations are clearly 'natural' and acceptable, given his professional status, as is his desire to show a recent collection. Being the first major display of material culture from the Highlands of Papua New Guinea in Britain, the exhibition was both appropriate and timely. Collecting, furthermore, affords O'Hanlon the opportunity of speculating on the blurred category of Wahgi material culture that he has to work within. He argues that, in the New Guinea context, collecting is not necessarily rupture, but exchange (his methods have differed quite considerably from the exploitative collecting trips of others) conceived and effected in synchrony with the Wahgi view of the world. O'Hanlon therefore questions whether the Wahgi would necessarily view collecting as *appropriation*, belonging, as they do, to an elaborate culture of exchange.

O'Hanlon explores his motivations as a collector/curator. Barthes might interpret this as an act of *purification*. The intense attention to the intricacies of the various practices leading up to the exhibition encourages a reading of collecting and exhibiting as exchanges in which the collector and the Wahgi are partners. The panel at the end of the exhibition particularly hints at the **symbolic power** of the exhibition, namely the way in which it constructs and persuades through delineating a path through meaning. The presentation of the Waghi as knowing agents and cultural producers, and of O'Hanlon as author and curator, *purifies* the *symbolic power* of the exhibition and the curator.

Clifford, on the other hand, implicitly draws a distinction between the *symbolic* power of the exhibition and the institutional power of the British Museum. He agrees that O'Hanlon has acknowledged his relatively powerful role as author and circumscriber of meaning through his last panel, and through his book. But Clifford remains unconvinced that the relationship between the Wahgi and the institution – the British Museum – is sufficiently examined. Clifford argues that the two – *symbolic power* and *institutional power* – are interdependent, and that while O'Hanlon fully acknowledges his symbolic power, he does not tackle the institutional relationship.

What might the implications be of prioritizing a reading of exhibition as *mythical structure* rather than simply as *artefact*? There are implications concerning authorship and power. If the exhibition is a form of mythical speech, then the anthropologist is a kind of mythologist: out of the oddments of the present and the debris of the past s/he puts together new constructions and meanings that are persuasive and necessarily disguised because they are interpretations which are received as facts and truths. But it must be remarked that if one opts to perceive an exhibition as a mythical structure, then the *symbolic power* of the anthropologist is not a choice but an *inevitability*. Collecting and authorship necessitate the production of 'partial truths' and 'persuasive fictions'.

Clifford in his analysis, hints at an important distinction. We can differentiate between *symbolic power* – which is inevitable and located around the author (and therefore under individual control: for example, the relationship between O'Hanlon and the Wahgi) – and *institutional power* – which is more exclusionary and situated round the institution (the direct relationship between the British Museum and the Wahgi, and the latter's relative power of sanction). As we shall see (in section 4) the question of *institutional power* is an influential critique when exercised in relation to museums, since it reaches beyond the internal articulation of meaning to the broader issue of the role of the museum in society at large and its relationship to knowledge.

ACTIVITY 5

So, to the two different views of the process of collecting and exhibiting, we have added another dimension. Has this discussion of 'myth' altered your view of exhibiting? Why?

3.7 Summary

This section subjected ethnographic displays to a particular type of analysis. Drawing on semiotic theory – the work of Barthes – in relation to a case study – the *Paradise* exhibition – we showed how exhibitions trace a particular path through meaning and motivation. Initially treating the exhibition as an artefact, the analysis explored the various ways in which objects, contexts, texts and visual representations were deployed to construct meaning. It explored the internal ordering of the various elements and their articulation, but disaggregated the display into several levels – presence, presentation and representation – allowing us to examine the *poetics* of exhibiting. Treating an ethnographic display as an artefact provided a means of detecting the complex web of signification and how it was produced. We then considered the different views offered in the commentaries on *Paradise* relating to the practices of collecting and exhibiting. We found that these commentaries gave distinct interpretations, and we added to this a theoretical alternative which pushed us towards a more 'political' interpretation of exhibiting, by proposing that an exhibition is a mythical structure. This, in turn, permitted us to question exhibitions and museums in line with two different analyses of power: *symbolic* and *institutional*.

4 CAPTIVATING CULTURES: THE POLITICS OF EXHIBITING

4.1 Introduction

The last section considered exhibiting in terms of its *poetics* – the internal articulation and production of meaning. This section will invoke a theoretical model and texts to explore the *politics* of exhibiting – the role of exhibitions/museums in the production of social *knowledge*. Whereas section 3 used the work of Roland Barthes, this section will refer to the work of Michel Foucault, whose writings were also discussed in Chapter 1. So the model of representation used in this section will focus on broader issues of knowledge and power. Examining the **politics of exhibiting** will cause the question of *institutional power*, raised in section 3, to be specifically addressed. As noted in previous sections, museum collections do not simply 'happen': artefacts have to be made to be collected, and collected to be exhibited. Collections and exhibitions are historical, social and political events. This section will present yet another 'reading' of the practices of exhibiting: a critique which argues that the practices of collecting and exhibiting are powerful activities, and that an analysis of the relationship between power and knowledge should be incorporated into any investigation into exhibiting/museums. Examples from a specific historical, political moment – the late nineteenth century – will be used in this section for reasons that will become apparent.

4.2 Knowledge and power

The aspects of Michel Foucault's work that we shall investigate here concern the specific definition he gives to *discourse* and the axis he defines between *power/knowledge*. In establishing these definitions, we are adopting a new interpretation of anthropological knowledge.

Discourse, as you may recall from Chapter 1 (section 4), is a group of statements which provides a language for talking about a particular topic, one that constructs that topic in a particular way. It is a way of formulating a topic and a field of inquiry which answers specific 'governing statements' (questions) and produces 'strategic knowledge': *savoir*. For Foucault, in contrast to Barthes, knowledge cannot be reduced to the realm of pure 'meaning' or 'language' because all knowledge operates as a historically situated social practice: all knowledge is **power/knowledge**. So 'strategic knowledge' is knowledge inseparable from relationships of power (Foucault, 1980, p. 145). Discourses, according to this definition, do not reflect 'reality' or innocently designate objects. Rather, they *constitute them in specific contexts according to particular relations of power*. So if the subject of anthropological inquiry is discursively constituted, this implies that this knowledge does not simply operate at the level of 'meaning' or 'ideas', nor does it innocently mirror 'reality'. On the contrary:

> [anthropology] itself is possible only on the basis of a certain situation, of an absolutely singular event ... [anthropology] has its roots, in fact, in a possibility that properly belongs to the history of our culture. ... [Anthropology] can assume its proper dimensions only within the historical sovereignty – always restrained, but always present – of European thought and the relation that can bring it face to face with all other cultures as well as with itself.
>
> (Foucault, 1989, pp. 376–7)

So if we take the emergent social science of anthropology or ethnology in the latter part of the nineteenth century, we could characterize it as a rather diffuse body of knowledge constituted by scholars that acquired a hesitant disciplinary status by virtue of its placement in small institutional bases, most particularly museums. Alternatively, one can see it as more complicit, a discipline which, despite its aspiration to general human relevance and enlightenment, was primarily a discourse about the culturally or racially despised, developed by the members of a dominant culture in the imperial context (Stocking, 1985, p. 112). Stocking, for example, argues that as a discipline it codified knowledge in such a manner that it could be called upon as 'a moral as well as a scientific justification for the often bloody process' of imperial expansion (1987, p. 273). It can be argued that it provided a classificatory schema for the 'races' of humankind, thereby encouraging and aiding their regulation.

Foucault's meditation on the subject of discourse reflected his more general preoccupation with the genesis of the human sciences. For Foucault, studying the genesis of the human sciences revealed that these are not 'enlightened' sciences – progressive views of the human condition – but particular forms of knowledge which emerged at a distinct historical moment. While they constituted themselves as enlightened, they were more properly united in their desire to regulate human subjects. For Foucault, the new human 'sciences', of which anthropology is one, sought to codify and regulate certain sections of society: women, 'natives', the insane, the infirm and the criminal classes, which, as sciences, they discursively constituted as real subjects of knowledge on the basis of material evidence (see Chapter 1). These sciences were allied to techniques of regulation (the prison, the mental asylum, the hospital, the university) and the rise of the nation-state. Discourses systematically formed the objects of which they spoke (Barrett, 1991, p. 130) in accordance with newly emerging relationships of power which sought not to control violently but to discipline in institutional settings, most usually through the emphasis on the body.

Using a Foucauldian perspective suggests that anthropology emerged as a distinctive type of knowledge at a defined historical moment (the mid- to late nineteenth century) and was inscribed with particular relationships of power (Empire and colonial expansion) and therefore largely depended in some measure on the unequal encounter of what has elsewhere been called 'the West and the Rest' (Hall, 1992).

One may ask to what extent does this new critical dimension contribute to an analysis of ethnographic display?

Employing a Foucauldian framework necessitates recasting the field of anthropology as a discursive formation: one constituted through the operation of several discourses which does not reflect 'real' distinctions between peoples, but creates them. Furthermore, as a science that mobilizes a classificatory system, it manufactures these distinctions on the basis of a certain *representation* of this difference, and subsequently uses this typology to determine whom it seeks to study and what the best research methods might be. Correspondingly, as anthropological discourses change, so do representations and the kinds of evidence needed to support these types of knowledge. These factors clearly have implications in terms of material culture and methods of display.

Let us now see how using a Foucauldian argument concerning the relationship between discourse and representation might present a different perspective on the museum context from that of section 3.

4.3 Displaying others

Ethnographic artefacts were constituent items of the oldest collections, but in many cases the delineation of artefacts as specifically 'ethnographic', whether by virtue of circumscribed displays, specific departments, or museums, only took on a scientific status late in the nineteenth century (see Shelton 2006). Indeed, anthropology was to find its first institutional home in museums, rather than universities. 'In a period when not only anthropology, but science generally was much more "object" – or specimen – orientated than today' (Stocking, 1987, p. 263), the existence of collections propelled anthropology towards institutionalization, as curators started to define themselves professionally as anthropologists. One of the most notable museums to emerge in the nineteenth century was the Pitt Rivers Museum in Oxford (Gosden and Larson, 2007).

We will examine the relationship between discourse and exhibiting in the context of the Pitt Rivers Museum. Older displays seem to furnish us with particularly good examples of the processes at work, perhaps because we recognize their artifice more readily (Lavine and Karp, 1991, p. 1).

Augustus Henry Lane Fox (later Pitt Rivers, after inheriting a substantial fortune), the founder and patron of the Pitt Rivers Museum, developed a particular interest in collecting objects after visiting the Great Exhibition at Crystal Palace in 1851. Initially a collector of arms, he soon broadened his interest to encompass archaeological and ethnographic items (Chapman, 1985, p. 16). He was interested in theories of evolution and human antiquity as well as 'racial' theories. By the comparison of artefacts from different periods and places, in particular the 'commoner class of objects', he sought to establish historical sequences which visibly mapped technological development and small alterations in form over time. He believed that only through the 'persistence of forms' could one 'show that disparate peoples possessed common traits, and thus re-established their past connection' (Chapman, 1985, p. 23). By arranging sequences of artefacts, one could reflect on 'the sequence of ideas by which mankind has advanced from the condition of lower animals' (Lane Fox, quoted in Chapman, 1985, p. 33) because the technological sophistication of objects stood for, or *represented*, the intangible aspects of culture. For Lane Fox, continuities in the form of artefacts provided decisive evidence for ethnological and evolutionary connections (Figure 3.3).

Lane Fox was dedicated to the idea of displaying these connections in a museum. In the early 1860s he sought a wider audience for his collection and eventually, in 1884, signed the Deed of Gift donating his collection of ethnographic and archaeological material to the University of Oxford on condition that it was exhibited in the manner he determined (Gosden and Larson 2007, p.16–17).

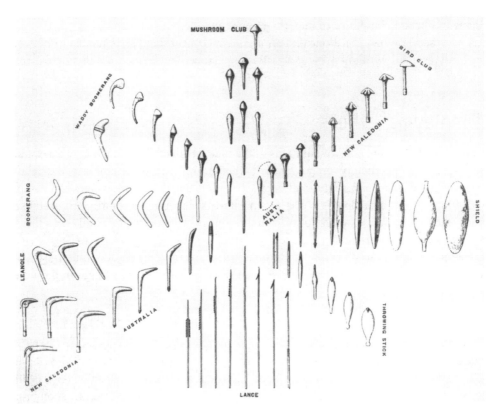

FIGURE 3.3 'Clubs, Boomerangs, Shields and Lances': an illustration from Henry Lane Fox's *The Evolution of Culture* (Oxford, Pitt Rivers Museum, 1875b)

The Pitt Rivers collection thus distinguished itself by virtue of its arrangement. The systematic approach owed more to a Linnean natural historical classification (of groups, genera and species) than the more common geographical classification typical of other contemporary ethnographic displays (Figure 3.4) (Chapman, 1985, pp. 25–6; Coombes 1994a, pp. 117–19; Lane Fox, 1875a). Pitt Rivers arranged his artefacts primarily in a *typological* manner, namely one that privileged form and function but was cross-cut by geographical principles of regional groupings. Artefacts were arranged sequentially to permit comparative analysis. Archaeological artefacts from ancient peoples and contemporary ethnographical materials – from 'survivals' – were arranged side by side to form a complex representation whose purpose was the illustration of human evolution and history. In this manner, the Pitt Rivers Museum and collection provided a predominant and compelling *typological* representation, which spoke volumes about the determination of its founder to promote a particular strand of anthropological inquiry, and therefore of knowledge and discourse (Figure 3.5, see Gosden and Larson, 2007). The representation of other cultures that it gave rise to was determined by Pitt Rivers' preferred view of functional *evolutionary discourse*. In presenting this focused view, the Pitt Rivers Museum did not reflect the 'complex and comprehensive' debates taking place in the emerging discipline of anthropology or among the Museums Association concerning the classification of ethnographic material, but accorded with more popular views of the relationship between the 'races' which it legitimated by virtue of its position as a scientific discourse (Coombes, 1994a, p. 117).

FIGURE 3.4 An ethnographic gallery of the British Museum, c. 1900

FIGURE 3.5   The main exhibition hall of the Pitt Rivers Museum, Oxford, c. 1970

What issues are raised by examining the Pitt Rivers display and in what manner is this form of representation different from that of the *Musaeum Tradescantianum*?

First, one has to consider how the inclusion of the artefacts was determined by the type of knowledge that was brought to bear on them and how these legitimated certain discourses. As 'curiosities', ethnographic artefacts occupied an equivalent place to other decontextualized objects – artefacts to prompt the imagination and philosophical reflection. The Tradescant display now appears whimsical and disorderly in its arrangement, reflective of a particular world-view which applied classificatory criteria (artificial versus natural curiosities) but also a hierarchy of value (in terms of curiosities and rarities) very different from the evolutionary ones. Collecting was seemingly an idiosyncratic process, even though undeniably already the product of exploration, conquest and colonization.

Ethnographic artefacts in the Pitt Rivers collection, by contrast, were subjected to the ostensibly more rigorous discourse of science. Utilized as 'evidence' and 'proof', they were the material embodiments of the socio-cultural complexities of other cultures. These ethnographic artefacts were systematically collected, selected and arranged according to a classificatory schema whose function was to illustrate the progress of human history by according different cultures different places on the evolutionary ladder (Coombes, 1994a, p. 118). Pitt Rivers himself was keen to contrast the science and comprehensive reach of his approach with the incompleteness of earlier cabinets of curiosities. '[T]hese ethnological *curiosities*, as they have been termed, have been chosen without any regard to their history or psychology ... they have not been obtained in sufficient number or variety to render classification possible' (Lane Fox, 1875a, p. 294).

What distinguishes Pitt Rivers' approach is the fact that the classification scheme and assessment criteria invoked are deemed 'scientific', where this refers to a positivistic framework of knowledge, and where the representation (the method of display) reinforces and derives from the evolutionary discourse that frames it.

Secondly, the Pitt Rivers Museum, as a nineteenth-century museum, had a more instrumental vision of its role in public education and the specific benefits for its audience. Its typically congested display was less a collection for the edification of the contemplative scholar or the interested visitor, than a detached, objective, positivist tool promoting the 'diffusion of instruction' and 'rational amusement' of the mass of the British population, who were judged as improperly ignorant of the nature of human development and 'history' (Coombes, 1994a, pp. 121, 123). So the Pitt Rivers Museum mobilized an evaluative discourse concerning the civilizing effect of culture on the mass of the population. The museum was expected to bring social benefit by shaping the intellect and transforming social behaviour (Bennett, 1994, p. 26).

In the late nineteenth century, bids for anthropology to be recognized as a science of humanity coincided with the rapid expansion of the 'museum idea'. The 'museum idea', simply put, was the belief that museums were an ideal vehicle for public instruction: by contemplating cultural artefacts on display, the common man/woman could become receptive to 'their improving influence' (Bennett, 1994, p. 23). The belief in the 'multiplication of culture's utility' was not restricted to museums but extended to art galleries and libraries (ibid.). The rise of anthropology as a discipline coincided with, and was supported by, the ferment in exhibiting activity, either in the shape of the great exhibitions or in the shape of museums which arose in great numbers all over Britain between 1890 and 1920 (Greenhalgh, 1993, p. 88). It can therefore be argued that the Pitt Rivers Museum was implicated in other discourses of 'self' and 'other' which produced a division between geographically distanced cultures, but also between the cultures of the different classes of British society.

To conclude, it has been shown that both the Tradescant and the Pitt Rivers collections/museums are historical products. What distinguishes the Pitt Rivers collection is the particular articulation between the evolutionary discourse and the method of display which it implemented. The Pitt Rivers Museum, at this historical juncture (the late nineteenth century) promoted and legitimized the reduction of cultures to objects, so that they could be judged and ranked in a hierarchical relationship with each other. This anthropological – or more properly, ethnographic – discourse did not reflect the 'real' state of the cultures it exhibited so much as the power relationship between those *subjected* to such classification and those *promoting* it.

4.4 Museums and the construction of culture

As we have shown in the previous section, a Foucauldian interpretation of exhibiting states that ethnographic objects are defined and classified according to the frameworks of knowledge that allow them to be understood. We have considered the representations that museums produced and how these are linked to discourse. But, as was hinted in the last section, and as you saw in Chapter 1, Foucault also argues that discourses do not operate in isolation they occur in formations – **discursive formations**. The term *discursive formation* refers to the systematic operation of *several* discourses or statements constituting a 'body of knowledge', which work together to construct a specific object/topic of analysis in a particular way, and to limit the other ways in which that object/topic may be constituted. In the case of museum displays, such a formation might include anthropological, aesthetic and educational discourses. The internal cohesion of a *discursive formation*, for Foucault, does not depend on putative 'agreement' between statements. There may seem to be fierce internal debates, and different statements within the field of knowledge may appear antagonistic or even irreconcilable. But this does not undermine the cohesion or the creation of a 'body of knowledge' or a 'body of truth' around a particular object in a systematic and ordered fashion (Hall, 1992, p. 291).

In the following activity, we will consider how several competing discourses served to construct particular objects as desirable and valuable ethnographic artefacts. The case under consideration is that of the Benin Bronzes.

⌐IREADING E

The extracts in Reading E are drawn from the work of Annie E. Coombes (1994a). Although these extracts may seem a little fragmented, it is important to understand the argument that Coombes makes concerning the articulation of discourses around the artworks from the Royal Court of Benin, Nigeria, known as the Benin Bronzes (Figure 3.6 (a) and (b)). Some background context may be of use here. These artefacts were the subject of controversy both because of the manner in which they were appropriated (in a punitive expedition that was mounted in 1897 as a reprisal for the killing of a British party by Benin forces), and because of the objects' technical expertise and aesthetic qualities. Coombes has selected her case well: the appropriation and display of the Benin Bronzes are particularly well documented. Coombes can, therefore, examine how these objects were discursively produced through the articulation of a number of discourses, but equally how power/knowledge worked within the institutional context.

Read the Coombes' extracts (Reading E at the end of this chapter) and make notes in the light of the following questions:

1 How were the Bronzes discussed? How did commentators rationalize their origins? How were these objects discursively produced?
2 How were they displayed?
3 What institutional factors determined the Bronzes' prestige among curators?

Coombes suggests the Benin Bronzes are an important case for two reasons.

First, they are counter-suggestive. She argues that the artistry of the Benin Bronzes should have challenged prevailing scientific and aesthetic discourses which held that African cultures were incapable of complex artistic achievement. The Benin Bronzes were first discursively produced as survivals of the impact of the foreign forces – the Portuguese – but most particularly of 'recognized' civilizations such as ancient Egypt, since, it was argued, the people of Benin were not capable of such artistic expression. Those scholarly publications which questioned these assumptions were initially ignored, whereas those which integrated these atypical artefacts into pre-existing discourses, most particularly the discourse on 'degeneration', gained ground. Coombes recounts how the Benin Bronzes were incorporated into a discourse in which degeneration and artistic ability were proved to be compatible. So the Bronzes' uniqueness did not challenge prevailing discourse; rather the discourse domesticated the problem of the Bronzes. Coombes deploys a Foucauldian framework to understand how the Benin artefacts were discursively constructed, making reference to the various 'scientific' – notably anthropological – and aesthetic discourses that competed to incorporate the Benin artefacts. She alludes to a discursive formation that is particularly rigid.

FIGURE 3.6 (a) A commemorative head of an *oba* (king), Benin bronze (cast brass) sixteenth-seventeenth century

FIGURE 3.6 (b) Figure of armed Portuguese soldier, Benin bronze (cast brass) sixteenth-seventeenth century

Coombes asserts that these scientific discourses derived a significant measure of their persuasiveness from their agreement with other popular discourses on 'race'. She explores, in this connection, the images of Benin produced by the popular press. She shows that these *acknowledged* the artistic quality of the artefacts but always in the context of reports illustrating *the degeneracy* of Benin civilization and amid frequent mentions of the massacre of the English prior to the punitive raid.

Secondly, Coombes delineates the relationship between the Benin Bronzes, anthropological discourses and museums in a manner which casts museums as the seat of institutional power. She investigates the relationship between power/knowledge in three separate museum contexts: the Horniman Museum, the British Museum and the Pitt Rivers. Coombes shows the distinctions in their discursive constructions of the Benin Bronzes but connects these differences to struggles for power within and between these institutions. At the Horniman, Quirk alters his opinion of the Benin Bronzes once these are displayed at the British Museum, to gain prestige. For Read and Dalton, at the British Museum, the transformation in their discursive construction of the Benin artefacts is linked to bids for power and recognition within the British Museum (and to their being thwarted in their desires to purchase the totality of the Bronzes). The Pitt Rivers, predictably perhaps, manages to incorporate the Benin Bronzes into a typological display of casting technology and therefore a display on ironwork, paying particular attention to the *cire perdue* method.

Coombes develops her thesis to address the link between the Benin Bronzes and colonial power. She argues that these artworks from the Royal Court of Benin did not come to occupy the status of 'artefacts' by accident, but by virtue of colonial **appropriation** (Figure 3.7). She deepens this connection between appropriation, colonialism and collecting by observing that the artefacts were sold to pay for the Protectorate.

FIGURE 3.7 British officers of the Benin punitive expedition with bronzes and ivories taken from the royal compound, Benin City, 1897

In summary, by considering the historical articulation of several sets of discourses, Coombes shows how a body of knowledge can be created not only around a particular region of the world, but also around the material culture that it produces. She demonstrates how there is consistency despite disagreement. Discourses, she argues, work in formations which frame the manner in which one can think and talk of these objects and the subjects that produce them. She incorporates a discussion of power, concluding that collecting and exhibiting are the by-products of colonial power. So in relationship to a particular category of objects – the Benin Bronzes – she argues that knowledge is undeniably yoked to power, and in this case *institutional power* since it is the museum and its internal struggles that shape how the Bronzes are ultimately perceived.

Let us push this analysis further by considering the link between exhibiting and looking.

4.5 Colonial spectacles

The interconnection between power and exhibiting outlined by Coombes (1994a, 1994b) seems most persuasive when one explores the issue of 'living exhibits': the peoples that were brought over to feature in the colonial, national and international exhibitions staged in Europe and America in the nineteenth and twentieth centuries (see the discussion of 'the Hottentot Venus' in Chapter 4, section 4.3). Let us review the work of Foucault to discern how power and visibility are joined in the exhibitionary form of the 'spectacle'.

Foucault's analysis of power/knowledge incorporates a theory of *visibility*. Foucault can be thought of as a 'visual historian' because he examined the manner in which objects and subjects were 'shown'. He argued the phenomenon of 'being seen' was neither an automatic nor a natural process, but linked to what power/knowledge guides one to see – it relied on one's being 'given to be seen' (Rajchman, 1988). Furthermore, in the human sciences, what is seen and counts as 'evidence' is most usually linked to corrective action. The human sciences therefore differ from the hard sciences: perceiving electrons does not elicit questions of what to *do* with them, but 'seeing' the poor, the infirm, the mad or 'savages', unleashes precisely these questions (Rajchman, 1988, p. 102). So being made visible is an ambiguous privilege, connected to the operation of power. Applying this to the instance of ethnographic objects: in the Pitt Rivers Museum, the subtlety and significance of differences in material culture can only be 'seen' if one is already implicated in a discourse that applies an evolutionary schema in which these objects can be used as 'proof' of the discourse and thus differentiated, ordered and classified in that way.

The link between visibility and power is rendered most compelling when one considers human subjects and in particular the great spectacles of the colonial period – the national and international exhibitions that were mounted in Great Britain, and elsewhere, between 1850 and 1925. These exhibitions were notable for a great many things: their promotion of exploration, trade, business interests, commerce; their dependence on adequate rail links, colonial trading networks, and advertising; their launching of now familiar products such as Colman's mustard, Goodyear India rubber and ice cream; their notable effect on the institutionalization of collecting and internalization of commerce (Beckenbridge, 1989). Among these notable distractions, they provided another type of spectacle:

the display of peoples. In this section we will look, very briefly, at ethnographic displays which showed peoples, not objects.

The Exposition Universelle (Paris) in 1867 was the first to include colonial subjects as service workers, while the first exhibition to inaugurate displays of people simply *as spectacle* – as objects of the gaze – was the Exposition Universelle (Paris) of 1889. These 'authentic' manifestations of 'primitive culture' became a popular feature of most exhibitions into the early decades of this century. The last exhibition to feature dependent peoples in this manner in Britain took place at the British Empire Exhibition (1924–25) at Wembley (though some might argue it continues today in other forms) (Benedict et al., 1983, p. 52). Dependent peoples were brought over as displays to provide viewers with the experience of being in other worlds. Situated in 'authentic' villages, they were asked to re-enact their everyday lives for the viewing public. These peoples were classified in terms of the geography of the exhibition, but equally, sometimes, according to putative notions of their 'relationship' to each other in evolutionary terms. At the St Louis Louisiana Purchase Exposition of 1904, where people from the Philippines were accorded a significant place in the Hall of Anthropology, the various villages and their tribes were helpfully ordered in a fashion which 'faithfully' portrayed the evolution of human development, from the lowest to the highest level (Greenhalgh, 1988, p. 101).

In the era where the primary data used for the comparison of cultures was often provided by colonial administrators and not anthropologists, such displays provided remarkable opportunities. The 'armchair anthropologists' of the period were initially keen to derive benefit from the presence of these authentic living 'specimens' or scientifically significant objects. These human exhibits provided valuable evidence for an emerging discipline. They were real, authentic exemplars of 'primitive' people, 'survivals' of other histories, 'vanishing races' or genuine 'degenerates' (depending on the particular anthropological discourse one held). On their bodies were written the traces of earlier cultures. This physical evidence provided 'proof that could not otherwise be obtained but which could tangibly substantiate contemporary physical anthropological discourses. In 1900, W. H. Rivers, who was to become an influential figure in British anthropology, suggested that 'the Anthropological Institute should seek special permission from the exhibition proprietors in order to "inspect" these people prior to the exhibits opening to the general public' so that evidence could be collected (Coombes, 1994a, p. 88).

They could be and were measured, classified and photographed. Photographic representations in the shape of photographs of anthropometric measurements or colour postcards fuelled scientific speculation and popular understanding. The popularity of these exhibitions – many millions of visitors from all walks of life trooped past native villages – helped to support the dominant popular discourse that other cultures were 'survivals' or 'savages'. This was particularly so when 'primitive' or 'savage' customs came into view: the Igorots at the St Louis Fair purchasing, roasting and eating dog meat (Figure 3.8) or the Ainu at the Japan British Exhibition of 1910 photographed with a bear skull.

So one can argue that the blurring of 'scientific' and 'popular' anthropological discourses served in more or less subtle ways to legitimize and substantiate a discourse of European imperial superiority (Greenhalgh, 1988, p. 109). To understand these displays the visitor had to bring certain kinds of knowledge with him/her, reinforced by other representations – photographs, postcards, museum displays,

FIGURE 3.8 Igorots eating dog meat in the Philippine exhibit at the St Louis Louisiana Purchase Exposition, 1904

paintings – and had to be implicated within a particular geography of power. The display of people was a display of a power asymmetry, which these displays, in a circular fashion, served to legitimize (Benedict et al., 1983, p. 45; Coombes, 1994a and 1994b, p. 88). The exhibitions and displays can equally be thought of as 'symbolic wishful thinking' which sought to construct a spurious unity (a 'one world' framed in evolutionary terms) in which colonizer and colonized could be reunited and where those of 'vastly different cultural tradition and aspirations are made to appear one' (Benedict et al., 1983, p. 52).

Thus, a Foucauldian model allows one to argue that being able to 'see' these native villages and their constituent populations was clearly neither a 'natural' process, nor an accidental one, but a socio-historical one, which was allied to and reinforced standard museological representations of peoples through ethnographic artefacts. The argument which connects museological representations with spectacular ones is supported when it becomes clear that some of the ethnographic collections featured in the colonial, national or international exhibitions, or the photographs of these visiting peoples, were often incorporated into the ethnographical collections or archives of established museums.

So here the relationship between scientific knowledge (anthropology), popular culture, the geography of power (colonialism) and visibility (photograph, display) is rendered particularly overt. But a note of caution must also be registered. The Foucauldian model is a totalizing one: it produces a vision of museums and exhibiting which is primarily based on social control. If Coombes's (1994a) analysis is taken to its logical end point, that even the Benin Bronzes failed to pierce the solid structure of pre-existing ethnographic discourse, then one is left with the question of how intellectual paradigms change. What are the points of fracture? How have we come to the point where the Benin Bronzes can be 'seen' as 'art' when previously they could not? And how are we to understand this new state of knowledge? Although Coombes's longer text (1994a) provides a much more comprehensive account of the tensions in the process of exhibiting, than the short extract presented here, it is nevertheless the case that a Foucauldian-based analysis argues convincingly that collections are always excisions, they are not extracted willingly from originating cultures, but removed, often painfully, from the body of other, less powerful, cultures. These collections, it further argues, assume the rationale of education to lend future purpose but also to justify the original act. So collecting is perceived as a pursuit inevitably dogged by its own history, always betrayed by hidden intent. Collecting is, in short, a discredited and ignoble occupation. This Foucauldian critique links collecting and exhibiting to such an extent that it puts into question whether the ends can ever justify the means. Provocative though this critique undoubtedly is, it produces neither a convincing evocation of the historically fraught and paradoxical relationship (Shelton, 2006; Durrans, 2012) between ethnography and museums, nor an acknowledgement of the pragmatic decision making at the heart of the process of exhibiting.

4.6 Summary

This section has specifically addressed the *politics of exhibiting*. It has advanced a significantly different view from the one proposed by Mary Douglas (see section 2.4 above), namely that objects circulate in continuous history where makers, collectors and curators are simply points of origination, congregation and dispersal, in a circular system (Douglas, 1992, p. 15). According to this view, the activities of collecting and exhibiting are not neutral, but powerful. Indeed, it has been argued using a Foucauldian model that it is impossible to dissociate the supposedly neutral and enlightened world of scholarship on one hand from the world of politics and power on the other. So this section does not focus on the production of meaning, but the linkages between representation and museums as seats of institutional power. The examples used substantiate the proposition that significant linkages existed in the nineteenth century between desires for institutional power, the rise of anthropology as an academic discipline, and the popularity of colonial discourses.

Thus, an argument that considers the *politics of exhibiting* advances the view that museums *appropriate* and *display* objects for certain ends. Objects are incorporated and constructed by the articulation of pre-existing discourses. The museum becomes an arbiter of meaning since its institutional position allows it to articulate and reinforce the scientific credibility of frameworks of knowledge or *discursive formations* through its methods of display.

Moreover, we have found that an argument about power/knowledge can be articulated around exhibiting and displays, particularly in terms of *visibility*. The *politics of exhibiting* means museums make certain cultures *visible*; in other words, they allow them to be subjected to the scrutiny of power. This derives from a historically unequal relationship between western powers and non-western peoples.

We have seen that, at one moment, what allowed a *human subject* to be transformed into an *ethnographic object* was a particular relationship of knowledge to power in association with wider social changes whereby, in the exhibition context, the colonizer/seer/knower was made separate and distinct from the colonized/seen/known. In this section, it has been argued that, just as power reduced cultures to objects (in the Pitt Rivers collection), it also allowed the objectification of human subjects (in displays). In this manner, the ability to display ethnographic objects or subjects required certain types of knowledge (for interpretation and narrative) allied with a particular relationship of power.

5 DEVISING NEW MODELS: MUSEUMS AND THEIR FUTURES

5.1 Introduction

The very nature of exhibiting ... makes it a contested terrain.

(Lavine and Karp, 1991, p. 1)

The purpose of the last three sections has been to contextualize and analyse the practices of exhibiting, using theoretical models which forefront the *poetics* and *politics of representation*. So now if we re-evaluate our original definition of the museum, namely that it is an institution which exists 'in order to acquire, safeguard, conserve, and display objects, artefacts and works of arts of various kinds' (Vergo, 1993, p. 41), we find that these terms have acquired far from objective or neutral meanings. Although analyses undertaken in the previous sections are influential they can be criticized for obscuring particular issues. An analysis that forefronts the *poetics of exhibiting*, by examining the product – the exhibit – rather than the process of exhibiting, may exclude the 'hidden histories' of production. An analysis that investigates the *politics of exhibiting* may be fruitfully used for nineteenth-century examples, which rely so heavily on evolutionary paradigms. Nevertheless, it may produce an over-deterministic account revolving around social control. Both analyses have potential for providing renewed insights, neither presents a complete picture.

At this point in the first edition (1997), I argued that the 1990s were a tipping point. Issues of representation were ever more to the fore, as the mass and variety of critique was creating changes in practice and new ways of thinking about ethnographic collections. This view still holds true. In this revised edition, I will reprise some of the important debates reviewed in the first edition and consider their lasting impact in representational terms. These debates have been situated in the midst of changes in anthropology as a discipline, but equally among wider transformations in museums, culturally and politically, including a more active debate, nationally and internationally, as to the moral and legal ownership of cultural property. This links back to previous sections. Over the course of the last decade new models for the proper conduct of ethnography in museums (museum anthropology) have clarified themselves and become embedded. This demonstrates why analysing ethnographic displays in terms of their *poetics* and *politics* continues to prove so fruitful. This brings the chapter to a close and closer to current thinking.

5.2 Anthropology and colonial knowledge

In 1997, I noted that the assumptions underlying anthropology as a discipline were necessarily disrupted by the political experience and academic impact of decolonization. In the wake of this, anthropology was forced to review the pernicious influence of colonialism on knowledge construction and re-evaluate the complicity and the validity of its primary research and collecting method: fieldwork. The effectiveness of this critique has meant a shift in anthropological focus towards new subjects and perspectives, away from a localized view of authenticity and culture towards broader theoretical issues as well as questions of decolonization, globalization and cultural revivalism, and their impact on indigenous peoples (see Clifford, 1997a; Marcus, 2002). This refashioning and enlarging of the anthropological project has necessarily had an impact on the field of exhibiting (Shelton, 2006; Durrans, 2012). A common response has been to advocate that curators, in their role as cultural producers and intermediaries, be more accountable to the cultures they represent, and to interpret them in the light of transnational power structures and cultural influences. A more radical approach has been promoted by some museums allied to university anthropology departments. This proposes a role for the curator as cultural mediator – a self-proclaimed *agent provocateur* who intervenes through experimental forms of installation rather than display (Porto, 2007; see also Figure 3.11 below).

5.3 The writing of anthropological knowledge

If one critique of anthropology repositions it as a science of invention not discovery, then this has had literary effects. In the 1980s there was a density of writing which considered ethnographic monographs as texts and analysed them in terms of their rhetorical strategies (Clifford and Marcus, 2010). Clifford Geertz (1988), for example, having classified the work of key anthropological figures as a series of literary genres, concluded that the task of writing ethnographies has become 'morally, politically, even epistemologically delicate' (1988, p. 130). It is now generally accepted that ethnographic texts are not accurate descriptions of one culture by another, but the writing of one culture by another. This perspectival shift transforms what was once taken as *truth* into *representation* and forefronts issues of authority and authorship. In the field of anthropology, this has yielded a greater circumspection as to its claims to knowledge, and a disciplinary emphasis on accountability towards the subjects and communities among whom anthropologists undertake research (Simpson, 1996, see Chapter 3). In museum anthropology, these moves are at the heart of a number of research and presentational strategies which seek to integrate 'voice', either literally through language, speech or recordings (audio and audio-visual), or tacitly through new strategies for interpretation and incorporation of contemporary culture.

If we cast our mind back to the *Paradise* exhibition, we can see the influence of these and other shifts (see section 3.3). *Paradise* features hybrid cultural products that denote the perpetuation and re-creation of tradition through the appropriation of new forms or consumer goods. In *Paradise* the later panels as well as the chapters on exhibiting and collecting in the accompanying publication, acknowledge the partiality of anthropological knowledge and the ambiguous role of the anthropologist. The theme of the exhibition – change and continuity – specifically allows for the inclusion of hybrid Wahgi artefacts: headbands sewn from Big Boy bubble gum wrappers (Plate 3.IV) reflecting the colour of older headbands, or the shields used for warfare but appropriating new derivative ornamentation. The contexts of display are not classical: reconstructions include modern consumer items (Coca-Cola in the trade-store, South Pacific beer surrounding the *bolyim* house), simulacra mimic the hybrid nature of the peacemaking banners (incorporating money). The objects, the reconstructions, the simulacra and the photographs frustrate the categories of 'authenticity' and 'tradition'. Wahgi material culture includes artefacts that are hybrid and syncretic. O'Hanlon (1993) indicates through this strategy that he recognizes that objects are not *innately* 'ethnographic', but must be *designated* as such, and that collecting accords of a level of permanence in terms of meaning and value.

5.4 Collections as partial truths

Since the 1980s, anthropology has come to view the history of its own knowledge production as 'partial'. This uses 'partial' for its double meaning: (1) 'partial' in the sense that anthropological knowledge (as constructed and produced through ethnography) can only ever comprise a part of the whole; and (2) 'partial' in the sense of subjective. This has informed many currents in anthropology and is expressed in a variety of ways. In the museum context, it is evident through the curatorial and academic interest since the 1990s in the activity of collecting. Writings about collections and collecting have been subject to a number of trends, although most share the view that collections are *representations* – fragmentary and subjective constructions (as discussed in section 2.2). These collections reflect the intents of their collectors, and the motivations of the institutions that house them, who may be alternatively celebrated for their connoisseurial eye or criticized for their methods of extraction.

Writing on New Guinea, Gosden states '[c]olonial culture was a profoundly material culture' (2000, p. 232). It is no surprise, then, that in scrutinizing the context of collecting, museum anthropology has recently focused on *colonial collecting*. This addresses the activities of those military, political agents, administrators, traders and missionaries with formal and informal links to power as well as anthropologists working under the oversight of colonial powers who are sometimes typecast as 'double-agents' (Marcus, 2002, p. 193). The colonial collecting model departs from the perspective that collections '"say" more about the contacts … cultures had with the European collectors, than about the cultures in which the objects were made or used' (ter Keurs, 2007a, p. 3). It seeks to historicize ethnographic collections, looking at visual and material culture to assess how colonialism created persuasive representations of other cultures.

ACTIVITY 6

Consider how this links back to issues of *power* and *visibility* explored in section 4.5?

It might seem fairly clear that a Foucauldian perspective on colonial collecting would argue for a cyclical metonymic entrapment allied to unilateral power; collectors create, through objects, the images of 'others' they themselves already have.

At times the emphasis on the colonial collector has had the ambiguous effect of privileging his/her subjective motivations to the detriment of all other perspectives, including the analysis of the collections themselves and an account of local agency. However, what is frequently revealed through research is the difference between theory and practice in colonial collecting. Collection records are uneven, there are distinctions between what individuals wished to do and what they were actually doing on the ground, and there are variations between professional and private approaches to collecting. All of these factors have representational effects, both in the past and in the present (ter Keurs, 2007b; O'Hanlon, 2000). The gradual realization of these complexities has prompted a more ethnographic treatment of colonial collecting typified by the case study approach. This treats colonial situations as politically dynamic and the collections that result as the product of a series of negotiations between parties, the argument being made is that there is greater inter-cultural texture to local encounters and objects collected than has often been credited in the more restrictive colonial model (Gosden and Knowles, 2001; O'Hanlon and Welsh, 2000).

How can the products of colonial collecting be reconciled to the present? How can selective memories be counteracted? These are the key representational questions. In answering them, authors and commentators grapple with material and institutional legacies formed all over the world as a consequence of Empire and colonialism. This includes those institutions created during the colonial period which have now been transformed into national museums, post-independence. For those writing about colonial collecting, the choice sometimes boils down to whether they believe that partial truths told and retold in museums are simply a means of recycling of objects which cannot shirk the vestiges of colonial pasts (see section 4.5) or the means to address a post-colonial future (ter Keurs, 2007b).

Susan Legêne (2007) looks at the Dutch/Indonesian case to address these questions, considering the roots of the current politico-cultural declaration of a 'shared cultural heritage' between the Netherlands and Indonesia. Legêne describes a complex history linking collections in Amsterdam, Leiden and Jakarta and shows them to be products of the Ethical Policy (*Ethische politiek*), introduced and promoted by the Dutch government in Indonesia after 1901. For Legêne, the collecting that took place under this twentieth-century policy was marked by empathy *and* cultural distance in a manner that distinguished it from nineteenth-century colonial collecting. Collecting under the Ethical Policy was individually practised but highly codified and the results were rapidly transformed into museum collections. For Legêne, this marked a new moment in the politics of display because of the dissemination of a shared, or 'common', knowledge of Indonesian cultural forms. Consequently, Indonesian culture was institutionalized through the acquisition of recognized 'collective objects' (Legêne, 2007, p. 222) more effectively than before. Dutch consumption of such representations thrived because national self-identification under the Ethical Policy was that of 'enlightened' colonialists. Furthermore, it persisted with relatively little challenge after the formal end of Dutch colonial rule (1949) due to the lengthy cultural estrangement between the Netherlands and Indonesia following Indonesian independence (see Figure 3.9).

FIGURE 3.9 The end of colonial collecting? Removal of portraits of Dutch governor generals of the Dutch East Indies, December 1949 (here of J. B. van Hueutsz). For Legêne (2007), the removal of such symbolic objects from Indonesia marked the beginning of a cultural estrangement that denied colonial culture in the newly independent nation. Magnum Photos/Henri-Cartier-Bresson

> The notion of sharing cultural heritage between Indonesia and the Netherlands refers to collections which […] used to be approached as one cultural body of objects. It is important […] that we promote an historical approach to this very notion of sharing. Such an historical approach implies the need for an identification of the various episodes in (post) colonial history, which each time have inscribed *new* layers of meaning to existing collections.

(Legêne, 2007, p. 239)

Legêne argues strongly for a re-evaluation of the idea of 'shared cultural heritage'. 'Sharing' denotes a benign interpretation of the material culture dispersed between the Netherlands and Indonesia, but there are a number of connotations. These differ nationally and internationally depending on what is viewed as being shared, on what basis and by whom (Legêne, 2007, pp. 220 and 239). Legêne's larger argument is that the post-colonial project within museums – either politically or intellectually – must be sensitive to the fact that collections cannot be reclaimed as 'pure products' through expunging tainted colonial veneers, on either side of the national (or cultural) equation. Collections can be at one and the same time *colonial* and *transcultural* (a product of the interchange and hybridization of cultures through the colonial encounter). They are embedded in and generated by the multiple and intersecting histories of colonialism (and post-colonialism) though, equally, this neither determines nor exhausts collections' potential for meaning and relevance (Clifford, 1997b, p. 193). Addressing the complex linkages between the Netherlands and Indonesia in the twentieth century, Legêne issues a tacit qualification to the museological literature which enthusiastically advocates shared and collaborative work as a moral means for redressing the colonial histories of objects, by giving the very meaning of 'sharing' a colonial history .

Legêne's closing observations concerning layers of meanings point to the influence of another ethnographic model in thinking about collections, that of *biography*. Unlike the colonial model, this advocates a more active interpretation of objects and individuals, placing emphasis on the entangled contexts of meaning-making. In this model, making, acquiring, depositing and displaying of collections are a series of meaningful activities subject to a number of negotiations (echoing Douglas's semiotic approach on p. 133 in section 2.6). At the more stringent end of the colonial collecting model, collecting is dispossession (of the people) or death (of the object) and the museum an end point, both literally and metaphorically. In the biographical model, an object on entering the museum retains its potential and power as a material thing, and accumulates new and important 'life histories' (Appadurai, 1986, p. 17).

The biographical model draws on the work of Appadurai (1986) and Kopytoff (1986), who launched a reappraisal of the anthropological project by refocusing it on the circulation and exchange of objects in order to unravel how 'things' acquire meanings and value once made and integrated into human activity. In identifying their ethnographic objects, Appadurai and Kopytoff cast the net beyond 'authentic' and 'ritual' objects and pinpoint syncretic and commodified items as holders and bestowers of meaning (something O'Hanlon (1993) was obviously cognizant of in *Paradise*). The logic is straightforward: if anthropology is a discipline that no longer believes in the pure category of 'traditional societies' (or 'primitive cultures'), then it can no longer reasonably obsess about 'traditional objects' as its primary form of data.

The biographical model is appealing for two principal reasons: (1) it proposes a wider arena of relevant anthropological objects, and (2) it restores agency to individuals and collections. Arguing that objects have 'lives' and 'afterlives' gives them agency, because they are capable of continuously re-insinuating themselves in different political and individual circumstances and at each point can have meaningful effects. Furthermore, the biographical model extends this agency to the (usually) anonymous makers. Those who engaged in these transactions – made, traded or sold objects – are understood to have had their own purposes for doing this and some clear consequences in mind. It is further argued that certain objects have retained these meanings into the present, as outstanding debts or extended relationships (this is reflected in O'Hanlon's discussion of Wahgi intent on pp. 153–4 in section 3.6; see Clifford, 1997b). New research, therefore, may involve taking collections 'back' as objects or photographs to original/historical field sites as a means of initiating contemporary research into the collection's continuing significance for different constituencies (see the following section and Figure 3.10). In the biographical model, neither objects nor makers are automatically enslaved to colonial power relations, because relationships to power are understood as fraught with contingency, subjectivity and subversive potential.

The biographical model has influenced museological thinking and practice and is beneficial for the reasons mentioned above. Casting our mind back to Lawrence's article in section 2 on Custer's horse Comanche, we can see it is biographical in the broadest sense. It describes Comanche as a palimpsest of meanings, meanings which accumulate and change as he travels through time. The distinction between Douglas's semiotic model (p. 133 in section 2.6) and the biographical one is the interpretation of agency and subjectivity. The biographical model incorporates the view that there is intent, not simply contingency.

The language of 'biographies' is now increasingly popular when writing about collections but it is not neutral in effect. MacGregor, for example, treads the same ground as Vogel (p. 133 in section 2.6), when he argues that 'things […] so often change – or are changed – long after they have been created, taking on meaning that could never have been imagined at the outset' (2010, p. xxi). However, MacGregor sees potential where Vogel sees problems. He argues that there is wonder and promise in the fact that meanings are accretions that change over time, and (somewhat more controversially) that objects gain lasting significance in institutional and international settings far from their contexts of origin. Consequently, the biographical model can be employed in the context of asserting a 'universal' value to collections. Recalling the discussion of 'myth' (see section 3.6), this could be seen as a neat way of purifying motivation in favour of meaning, thus avoiding knotty questions of institutional power (see section 5.6).

5.5 Museums and contact zones

An influential element in the discussion of museums in the 1990s and 2000s was the emphasis on museums' educational mandate and public accountability. This occurred within a vigorous public policy discussion as to the role of museums in society and their need to address visitors beyond their traditional constituencies. Ivan Karp and Stephen D. Lavine state in their volume *Exhibiting Cultures* (1991) that the public's agenda is increasingly influenced by 'multicultural and intercultural issues' so that 'the inherent contestability of museum exhibitions is bound to open the choices made in those exhibitions to heated debate' (Lavine and Karp, 1991, p. 1). Stephen E. Weil (2002, p. 31), writing from a North American perspective, links the rise in the discourse of public access to an increasing need for private funding. He argues that the surge in museum numbers all over the world after the Second World War created a different kind of equilibrium nationally and internationally, away from the hegemony of western public institutions (Kreps, 2003, p. 1; Weil, 2002, p. 31). For Weil, this means that the need to court public opinion and understand public preferences has superseded more traditional museum concerns for academic transcendence and prestige. For Weil, it is indicative that this shift has happened at the very moment when western museums and their historical ideologies are under attack (Weil, 2002, pp. 201–3). He concludes that the degree of control which the public can exert over museums through attendance, protest or, the most powerful of all, publicity has grown (see also Ames, 1992). For western museums, success is now measured in terms of good management, public approval, financial rigour within an overarching moral structure (Weil, 2005). So museums, in addition to doing 'things right', need to 'do the right things' (Weil, 2005).

This emphasis on participation, public accountability and moral probity is at the core of the new conceptualization of museums as 'contact zones'. The *museum-as-contact-zone* paradigm came to prominence through the work of Clifford (1997b) and emerges from an anthropologically motivated critique. Clifford uses the term to describe the new possibilities inherent in conceptualizing museums as spaces of encounter: 'When museums are seen as contact zones, their organizing structure as a *collection* becomes an ongoing historical, political and moral *relationship* – a power-charged set of exchanges, of push and pull' (Clifford, 1997b, p. 192).

For Clifford, presenting museums as part of a network of ongoing relationships introduces new kinds of politics and possibilities (with positive benefits, but not without tensions) in terms of participation, consultation, active collaboration and sharing of authority. In museum anthropology, this paradigm specifies that ethnographic collections and museum projects should be used for 'contact work' (Clifford, 1997b; Nicks, 2003). 'Contact work' describes a range of museological practices that invite members of indigenous communities to whom the collections are especially connected ('source' or 'originating' communities), or diasporic communities who are linked by ancestry, to comment and critically appraise collections. The invitation is based on the desire to incorporate traditional knowledge and personal memory into existing curatorial understanding with the expectation that these distinct points of view will correct any errors, be integrated into the management of collections, and be acknowledged in future interpretation (Peers and Brown, 2003). It includes the promotion of loans and taking museum work away from the body of the institution, in order to re-situate collections closer to their communities of origin (Figure 3.10), and in different public settings. Within the last decade, this model has been especially pioneered in the 'settler countries' – Canada, the United States, Australia and New Zealand – as a means to address the historical exclusion of local aboriginal and indigenous cultures in museums and in wider society. Its influence, however, is much more pervasive. In its broadest interpretation, it is used to describe community participation of varied types in all museums, and to represent museums as spaces where different cultural forms can be enacted and where divergent cultural opinions can be voiced, embraced and resolved. This re-presentation tacitly confronts the previous representation of museums as dusty, aloof and imperious, if not imperial. Both the narrow and wider interpretation of *museum-as-contact-zone* aligns with the 'new museology', a critique that emerged during the 1980s, which put forward a mandate of democratization and participation for museums (Kreps, 2003, p. 10). In both paradigms, the responsibility of museums shifts away from collections and towards people (or citizens), in the belief that it is the duty of museums to reflect the views of a wider range of constituencies because 'important social benefits can flow to the general public from access to diverse cultural heritages' (Phillips 2011, p. 135).

In the first edition, I exemplified the changing power of the public opinion through the well-known boycott of the ethnographic display *The Spirit Sings: Artistic Traditions of Canada's First People* in Canada in 1988. The boycott of the Glenbow Museum, in Calgary, Alberta, grew out

FIGURE 3.10 Chantal Knowles, curator at National Museums Scotland, Edinburgh, showing items from the Hudson's Bay Company collection (acquired in the Northwest Territories (NWT), Canada, in the 1860s) to students at Elizabeth Mackenzie Elementary School, Behchoko, NWT, in March 2007. This was part of a touring exhibition and outreach programme bringing historic collections to the Tlicho community, whose ancestors traded with the Hudson's Bay Company factors (PWNHC, 2006). (© T. Andrews/GNWT)

of the larger action organized by Lubicon Lake Indian Band of Cree of Northern Alberta to draw attention to their unresolved land claim during the Winter Olympics. It explicitly challenged the cultural authority of curatorial experts and institutions, and their 'entitlement' to interpret Canadian aboriginal material culture, given that the exhibition's chief financial support was from Shell Oil, drilling, at the time, on traditional lands (Ames, 1991, p. 9).

> The irony of using a display of North American Indian artefacts to attract people to the Winter Olympics being organized by interests who are still actively seeking to destroy Indian people seems painfully obvious.
>
> (Chief Bernard Ominayak, 1988, quoted in Harrison, 1988, p. 7)

The protest gained public support and prominent media attention nationally and internationally. The direct result was the creation of a task force which issued the report *Turning the Page: Forging New Partnerships Between Museums and First Peoples* (1992). This contained a number of recommendations, the essence of which was increased 'dialogue' between curators and aboriginal/indigenous peoples and 'partnership': a sharing of responsibility for the management of cultural patrimony. It remains a museological watershed in Canada – the moment when the relationship between aboriginal Canadians and the museum community was decisively re-conceptualized (Phillips, 2011, pp 11–5). The national controversy surrounding *The Spirit Sings* has to be read against the specific history of conquest, local indigenous politics, contemporary popular opinion and Canada's distinctive national definition of multiculturalism (points fully discussed in Phillips, 2011, pp. 48–70). However, Herle (1994, p. 47) and others (Peers and Brown, 2003; Phillips, 2011) have documented how its recommendations have normalized a series of collaborative museum practices ('contact work') whose underlying principles are those of balancing institutional, legal and scientific imperatives against indigenous ethical concerns and spiritual care. While one cannot read directly from culture to politics and vice versa, it is clear that a number of presentational strategies – the use of self-reflexivity, dialogue or polyvocality, and the right for those represented to have a say in exhibit development – are the recognizable signifiers of 'contact work'. Phillips (2011, pp. 3–22) asserts that the research and representational strategies adopted in the wake of the Canadian Task Force and the North American Graves and Repatriation Act of 1991 (NAGPRA 1991) has resulted in the 'indigenization' of museum practices in North America. In the United States the most publicly symbolic and politically conspicuous institutional example is the National Museum of the American Indian (NMAI), which opened in 2004 as part of the Smithsonian Institution on the Mall in Washington, DC. NMAI's mandate of decolonization of museum display, community collaboration and participation in the representation of indigenous Americans, North and South, has been nationally ambitious and consistently implemented (see West, 2000) and its emergence has occurred in the context of a growth of the number of tribal museums and cultural centres throughout North America (Lonetree, 2009). These new national dynamics in North America refer us back to Weil's comments (2002, 2005) as to the factors influencing the politics of representation: the changing dynamics of power between museums (nationally and internationally) and visitor agency.

5.6 Art, artefact and ownership

The last context in which museum representations will be considered in this chapter is an international one. In the international museum context, no issue denotes 'doing things right'/'doing the right thing' more than that of cultural property.

The term 'cultural property' is generally used to identify archaeological, ethnographic and historical objects that 'embody or express or evoke [a] culture' (Merryman, 1990, p. 513), where culture and nation may be seen as synonymous. Debates about cultural property in the ethnographic arena revolve around two significant issues. The first is the question of ownership, namely the legal, moral and cultural title to any given item. The second is that classification. While the legal title to museums' collections is usually clear, the cultural and moral title is frequently less straightforward, since acquiring items in politically heightened or unequal circumstances at the very least begs questions as to free will and adequate recompense. The issue of classification relates to recognition and the attribution of quality, rarity and value. Whether an ethnographic object is treated as 'art' or 'artefact' highlights whether it is generally seen as having universal value as an outstanding piece of craftsmanship (art) as distinct from local significance of a functional or spiritual item (artefact). Ethnographic collections have struggled long and hard with this dialectic, and the ambiguities and contestations that inevitably arise from decisively placing any object in either category. However, in international market conditions and in declarations of universal relevance to humankind, the shift of an object from the 'artefact' category into the acceptable canon of non-western 'art' is undoubtedly a promotion in value.

Using the terms 'cultural property'/'cultural objects' in relation to museum collections acknowledges that there are ownership debates active for collections circulating in the international context on legal and illegal grounds (Glass, 2004). Since the middle of the nineteenth century, cultural property has been the subject to international regulation. The Hague Convention, passed in 1954, in the aftermath of the Second World War, was the 'first universal convention to deal solely with the protection of cultural property', providing an internationalist rationale for its protection (Merryman, 1986, p. 836). Subsequently, the United Nations, UNESCO and Unidroit have created a number of legal instruments to regulate the international movement of cultural property, most notably the 1970 UNESCO and the 1995 Unidroit Conventions addressing illicit trade and export. These aim to stop free trade in cultural objects and argue for the return, restitution or repatriation of all works of art that have been illegally taken from their country of origin. They exist in addition to national laws that regulate the export of cultural property. Collections in museums, especially national museums, have often been treated as 'cultural patrimony' – a form of shared cultural wealth and inheritance. The crucial question arising out of the discussion of cultural objects in terms of patrimony is whether they should be deemed part of a global (or universal) inheritance or a national one. Needless to say views on this differ: they are influenced by the status of the works in question, guiding arguments for retention or return. A small illustration: the word 'repatriation', which has become popular in response to the UNESCO and Unidroit conventions, refers to *patria* – homeland/nation. By virtue of use, it implies that there exists a nation of origin to which all objects must culturally belong (Merryman, 1986, pp. 844–5, 1990, p. 521).

The issues surrounding cultural property are complex and thorny, so a tangible example is helpful. The final reading in this chapter, by John Picton (2010), is an opinion piece which debates cultural property and illicit trade in the context of a display of African art. It was written in response to a vigorous discussion as to the morality and legality of the exhibition *African Terra Cotta: A Millenary Heritage*, which opened at the Barbier-Mueller Museum in Geneva in 2009. The controversy was sparked by a press article in a Swiss daily newspaper, *Le Temps* (Huysecom, 2009), which reported that the featured works were most likely acquired after the looting of an archaeological site in Mali in the 1970s, a claim supported by scholars and not unilaterally rejected by the museum. It was noted that while Switzerland had signed the relevant UNESCO and Unidroit treaties against illegal export, it only ratified the UNESCO treaty in 2003, potentially allowing illicitly traded collections to enter Switzerland legally beforehand.

READING F

Read and make notes on this edited extract (Reading F at the end of this chapter) by John Picton (2010) featured in the journal *African Arts*. Pay particular attention to the arguments given by Picton as to the importance of display and the distinctions he outlines between the display of collections made in the distant past (Benin) and more recent past (Terra Cottas).

Picton focuses on archaeological material, since this is an object of particular concern, but his article reviews a number of arguments regarding the public display of potentially illegally exported works of art. He does this in order to counter standard responses to their display and to advance his view that public understanding and display fosters international accountability and enhances knowledge. Picton states unambiguously that illegal excavation and illicit trade are reprehensible when proven, but he issues a note of caution against those who are quick to judge the likely source of works featured in western museums. Here he highlights the distinction between individual actions, national policies and international legislation, and the fact that these rarely align straightforwardly. He argues that African art has had many means of coming into collections, not all of which have been wrongful. For Picton, proven ritual function or former integration into local life do not necessarily conclude that objects are illegally bought or sold.

In considering legal issues, Picton recognizes that the looting of African art operates in an economic system of supply and demand, where the financial rewards are impressive. The financial disparity between 'source countries' (providing artworks) and 'market countries' (buying artworks) is often cited as the generating force for illicit trade, and the reasons why international legislation can be effective in stemming the tide. Picton upholds moves to impose laws, but is sceptical whether these can eradicate illicit trade and plunder given the full range of twentieth-century history. However, he does perceive a difference in the traffic today and the conditions for seizure in the past, and therefore proposes different solutions. Looking at Benin, he explores four cases for return and the need to recognize cultural and ritual continuity in use, though he argues, echoing Legêne's (2007) point, that these works can never be put back into their original context. For Picton, the greatest protection from looting is public knowledge and research. Consequently, exhibitions and publications, which admit the histories of their collections, generate public accountability and protect cultural property by making collections known all over the world.

Picton treads a careful path, sidestepping the pitfalls of the two views characterized by Merryman (1986) as 'nationalist' and 'internationalist'. The nationalist view asserts that all cultural property should remain in its country of origin and be protected from sale and export. For its critics, this view is the blinkered perspective of source countries because it conflates culture and nation and argues for a transhistorical (and somewhat unproblematic definition of) cultural identity. It ignores the arbitrariness of the modern nation-state and sidesteps issues of infrastructure (Appiah, 2006). The internationalist view believes in the preservation of cultural objects (art) on the basis of their universal value and a lack of nationality. It favours cosmopolitan cultural institutions as resting places for all forms of art so they can be best appreciated alongside similar work and be of greatest value to humankind. For its critics, this is a predictably self-serving posture adopted by powerful interests (dealers, museums, collectors) in market nations to legitimize institutionalized covetousness and historic inequalities (Opoku, 2009). Merryman, writing in the 1980s (1986, pp. 849–50), argues that the discourse of repatriation and retentive nationalism is holding sway; nearly thirty years later this seems less the case with a discourse of universalism featuring prominently on the international stage. As Durrans (2012) notes, ethnographic collections have different institutional homes and those which exist within large metropolitan and culture-history focused institutions are most often spoken of, and dealt with, as art: a universal human entitlement.

ACTIVITY 7

It may be interesting to reflect how these positions might align with the models of collecting reviewed in section 5.4.

A nationalist position would be substantiated by a colonial collecting argument whereas biographical evidence could provide support for an internationalist position. Given the discussions throughout this chapter what are your views?

There is much commentary on these issues, and this suggests that there is no simple way to answer these questions. Another view is expressed by Appiah (2006) who, like Picton (2010), offers a similarly measured response though a more internationalist solution. Appiah draws on an analogous case: the illegal export of the Djenné-jéno terra cottas from Mali in the 1980s and the moves to restitute items sold on the international art market. He remarks:

> The problem for Mali is not that it doesn't have enough Malian art. The problem is that it doesn't have enough money. In the short run, allowing Mali to stop the export of much of the art in its territory has the positive effect of making sure that there is some world-class art in Mali for Malians to experience. But an experience limited to Malian art – or, anyway, art made in the territory that is now Mali – makes no more sense for a Malian than it does for anyone else. […] If UNESCO had spent as much effort to make it possible for great art to get into Mali as it has done to stop great art getting out, it would have been serving better the interests that Malians, like all people, have in a cosmopolitan aesthetic experience.

(Appiah, 2006, p. 39)

Like Picton, Appiah is distrustful of international instruments and agendas, and believes that the nation-state is not always the best, or the most disinterested, advocate for culture. He bemoans the lack of systematic funding of education and research in 'source countries'. Like Picton, he believes that African art should be allowed to circulate and be seen internationally, though for Appiah this is argued on the basis of its universal benefit: the best art is flagrantly international in source and impact (2006, p. 40). He proposes that while there is a rationale for keeping or returning artworks to their country of origin, there are equally compelling reasons for allowing them to remain and be seen elsewhere, to build up critical appreciation (and protection) worldwide. Citing the 'punitive expedition' to the Kingdom of Asante's capital in Kumasi, he suggests a need for pragmatism: it is unlikely that all of the works disseminated throughout the world will be returned (though some have). For Appiah, the more astute strategy for Ghana would be to negotiate a collection of important European artworks to be shown in Kumasi (2006, p. 41). This would truly provide a corrective to the 'punitive expedition'. He notes that one of the ironies of the plunder of Kumasi in 1874 was that the British looted an exceptional treasury of art and artefacts from around the world, some likely looted as the products of war (Appiah, 2006, pp. 38 and 41).

6 CONCLUSION

[A]rtifacts can uniquely serve as trans-temporal and trans-spatial witnesses […] testifying both to the worst and the best of historical human achievement and experience, they can expand our horizons and can help us to imagine ways out of contemporary quandaries.

(Phillips, 2011, p.135, p. 250)

Museums have proved to be adaptable mechanisms for post-colonial purposes.

(Nicks, 2003, p. 24)

Section 5 considered how ethnographic museums have been affected by critiques highlighting the *poetics* and *politics* of representation. It suggested that these critiques generated new models for unpacking the histories of collections, focusing on their colonial origins and unfolding biographies. It examined how changes in museum practice have mirrored the changing perceptions of the discipline of anthropology: its subject matter, its wider accountability and the impact of international legislation. As the discipline of anthropology has 'de-colonized' so ethnographic museums have begun to perceive themselves as 'contact zones'. This paradigmatic shift (which has taken decisive hold since the publication of the first edition of this chapter) advocates the inclusion of different perspectives and opinions voiced by 'originating' or 'source' communities, local diasporas and visitors more generally. This incorporation of non-curatorial values at structural levels suggests a widespread acceptance that ethnographic collecting and exhibiting are symbolically and institutionally powerful activities. The beginning of this chapter set up a relatively uncontroversial definition of museums which has been progressively reassessed. Over the course of the chapter, museums have emerged as dynamic but potentially controversial entities; cultural producers that continuously construct representations through objects. The chapter advocated the use of several strategies for understanding the *systems of representation* utilized in museums, especially ethnographic ones.

Section 2 set out definitions and identified issues of construction and context. It looked at the historical location of the *Musaeum Tradescantianum* and critically examined its 'world-view' through both catalogue and displays. Section 3 addressed the *poetics* of exhibiting. Here exhibitions were seen as a relatively precise process of selection, interpretation and meaning construction. A case study, the *Paradise* exhibition, was analysed using semiotic tools. The elements of exhibitions – objects, texts, contexts of display, visual representation – were investigated separately and in combination to ascertain how they produced particular types of meaning. They were shown to be skilfully deployed to *present* and *represent* other cultures and this led to a further consideration of mythical structures and *symbolic power*. Section 4 explored the *politics* of exhibiting, focusing on the link between power and knowledge. Here selectivity was given a more ambivalent gloss by contending that it was a product of *institutional power* allied to discursive formations. The link between power, knowledge and visibility was demonstrated in relation to the reception of 'artefacts' – the Benin Bronzes – and human subjects, describing the manner in which anthropological knowledge had legitimized ways of seeing in the context of colonial, national and international exhibitions. Section 5 brought things to a close, by briefly surveying contemporary interpretations of the social, professional and moral functions of museums.

FIGURE 3.11 *Au bon vivant*, a large installation that was part of *Le musée cannibale*, a temporary exhibition about the practice of ethnography in museums at the Musée d'Ethnographie, Neuchâtel, 2002–3. The banqueting hall used the metaphor of feasting and consumption. Each table was a display case which, through the judicious choice of objects and texts, reflected a well-known genre of ethnographic display (see Lidchi, 2006). (Photography by Alain Germond © Musée d'ethnographie Neuchâtel)

The critiques of museums that have arisen over the past thirty years have been cogent and influential, and have shifted the practice of ethnographic exhibitions and museums in important ways, towards more collaborative, accountable and, ultimately more international, approaches. This has been typified either as 'the crisis in representation' (Marcus, 2002) or the 'post-narrative' context (Shelton, 2006, pp. 77–8; see Durrans, 2012, for critique of 'post-narrative'). What this means is a profound, and possibly unchartable, diversification of the ethnographic project in museums at a boom period in museum growth more generally. So what conclusion can one reach? Museums are systems of representation: they are arbiters of meaning and confer validity upon objects in line with specific or articulated discourses. Moreover, the processes of acquiring objects, researching collections and mounting displays can be understood as requiring both symbolic and institutional power. Today, neither the meanings attributed nor the values conferred are above contestation; indeed, the value of collections and the value of museums are topics extensively debated and sometimes expressed in displays playfully structured around critique (see Figure 3.11). Ironically, or happily, these academic and professional critiques, and the new models arising as a consequence, far from diminishing the importance of ethnographic collections have reaffirmed their value. Those objects formerly described as merely 'ethnographic' are now equally perceived as 'art' and, more importantly, as agents or material witnesses which can generate new possibilities for the understanding of specific and intertwined colonial and post-colonial histories and aid in the future management of national or international relations.

REFERENCES

AMES, M.M. (1991) 'Biculturalism in exhibitions', *Museum Anthropology*, 15(2), 7–15.

AMES, M.M. (1992) *Cannibal Tours and Glass Boxes: The Anthropology of Museums*, Vancouver, BC, University of British Columbia Press.

APPADURAI, A. (1986) 'Introduction: commodities and the politics of value', in Appadurai, A. (ed.), *The Social Life of Things: Commodities in Cultural Perspective*, Cambridge, Cambridge University Press.

APPIAH, K.A. (2006) 'Whose culture is it?', *The New York Review of Books*, LIII(2), pp. 38–41.

BARRETT, M. (1991) *The Politics of Truth: From Marx to Foucault*, Cambridge, Polity Press.

BARTHES, R. (1967) *Elements of Semiology* (tr. A. Lavers and C. Smith), London, Jonathan Cape.

BARTHES, R. (1977) *Image–Music–Text* (tr. S. Heath), New York, Hill & Wang.

BARTHES, R. (1989) *Mythologies* (tr. A. Lavers), London, Paladin.

BECKENBRIDGE, C.A. (1989) 'The aesthetics and politics of colonial collecting: India at World Fairs', *Comparative Studies in Society and History*, 31(2), 195–216.

BENEDICT, B. ET AL. (1983) *The Anthropology of World Fairs: San Francisco's Panama Pacific International Exposition of 1915*, London, Lowie Museum/Scolar Press.

BENNETT, T. (1994) 'The multiplication of culture's utility: the art gallery versus the alehouse', Inaugural lecture, Griffith University, Brisbane.

CHAPMAN, W.R. (1985) 'Arranging ethnology: A. H. L. F. Pitt Rivers and the typological tradition', in Stocking, G. W. Jr (ed.), *Objects and Others*, London and Madison, WI, University of Wisconsin Press.

CLIFFORD, J. (1995) 'Paradise', *Visual Anthropology Review*, 11(1), 92–117.

CLIFFORD, J. (1997a) 'Traveling cultures', in Clifford, J., *Routes: Travel and Translation in the Late 20th Century*, Cambridge, MA, Harvard University Press.

CLIFFORD, J. (1997b) 'Museums as contact zones', in Clifford, J., *Routes: Travel and Translation in the Late 20th Century*, Cambridge, MA, Harvard University Press.

CLIFFORD, J. AND MARCUS, G.E. (2010) *Writing Culture: The Poetics and Politics of Ethnography* (25th anniversary edition), Los Angeles, CA, University of California Press.

COOMBES, A.E. (1994a) *Reinventing Africa: Museums, Material Culture and Popular Imagination in Late Victorian and Edwardian England*, London and New Haven, CT, Yale University Press.

COOMBES, A.E. (1994b) 'The recalcitrant object: culture contact and question of hybridity', in Barker, F. et al. (eds), *Colonial Discourse/Postcolonial Theory*, Manchester, Manchester University Press.

DOUGLAS, M. (1992) *Objects and Objections*, Toronto Semiotic Circle, Monograph Series of TSC No. 9, Toronto, University of Toronto.

DUBÈ, P. (1995) 'Exhibiting to see, exhibiting to know', *Museum International*, 47(1), 4–5.

DU GAY, P. (ed.) (1997) *Production of Culture/Cultures of Production*, London, Sage/The Open University (Book 4 in this series).

DURRANS, B. (1992) 'The future of the other', in Lumley, R. (ed.), *The Museum Time Machine*, London, Comedia.

DURRANS, B. (1993) 'The future of ethnographic exhibitions', *Zeitschrift für Ethnology*, 118, 125–39.

DURRANS, B. (2012) 'Anthropology and museums', in Farndon, R., Harris, O., Marchand, T., Shore, C., Strang, V. ,Wilson, R. and Nuttall, M. (eds) *The SAGE Handbook of Social Anthropology*, London/ New York, Sage.

FINDLEN, P. (1989) 'The museum: its Classical etymology and Renaissance genealogy', *Journal of the History of Collections*, 1(1), 59–78.

FOUCAULT, M. (ed.) (1980) *Power/Knowledge* (tr. C. Gordon, L. Marshall, J. Mepham and K. Soper), Hemel Hempstead, Harvester Wheatsheaf.

FOUCAULT, M. (1989) *The Order of Things*, London, Tavistock/Routledge.

GEERTZ, C. (1988) *Works and Lives: The Anthropologist as Author*, Cambridge, Polity Press.

GLASS, A. (2004) 'Return to sender: on the politics of cultural property and the proper address of art', *Journal of Material Culture*, 9 (2), 115-139.

GOSDEN, C. (2000) 'On his todd: material culture and colonialism', in O'Hanlon, M. and Welsh, R. L. (eds), *Hunting the Gatherers*: *Ethnographic Collectors*, *Agents and Agency in Melanesia*, *1870s–1930s*, Methodology and History in Anthropology Series (Vol. 6), Oxford, Berghahn Books.

GOSDEN, C. AND KNOWLES, C. (2001) *Collecting Colonialism: material culture and colonial change*, Oxford, Berg.

GOSDEN, C. AND LARSON, F. (2007) *Knowing Things: exploring the collections at the Pitt Rivers Museum 1884–1945*, Oxford, Oxford University Press.

GREENHALGH, P. (1988) *Ephemeral Vistas: the Expositions Universelles, Great Exhibitions and World Fairs, 1851–1939*, Manchester, Manchester University Press.

GREENHALGH, P. (1993) 'Education, entertainment and politics: lessons from the Great International Exhibitions', in Vergo, P. (ed.), *The New Museology*, London, Reaktion Books.

HALL, S. (1992) 'The West and the Rest: discourse and power', in Hall, S. and Gieben, B. (eds), *Formations of Modernity*, Cambridge, Open University Press/Polity Press.

HARRISON, J.D. (1988) 'The Spirit Sings and the future of anthropology', *Anthropology Today*, 4(6), 6–9.

HERLE, A. (1994) 'Museums and First Peoples in Canada', *Journal of Museum Ethnography*, 6, 39–66.

HUYSECOM, E. (2009) 'Le pillage de l'histoire Africaine', *Le Temps*, 27 April. Available at: http//:www/ letemps.ch (accessed 9 March 2011).

IMPEY, O. AND MACGREGOR, A. (1985) 'Introduction', in Impey, O. and MacGregor, A. (eds), *The Origins of Museums: The Cabinet of Curiosities in Sixteenth- and Seventeenth-Century Europe*, Oxford, Clarendon Press.

KARP, I. AND LAVINE, S.D. (eds) (1991) *Exhibiting Cultures: The Poetics and Politics of Museum Display*, Washington, DC, Smithsonian Institution Press.

TER KEURS, P.J. (2007a) 'Introduction: theory and practice of colonial collecting', in ter Keurs, P. J. (ed.), *Colonial Collecting Revisited*, Leiden, CNWS Publications.

TER KEURS, P.J. (ed.) (2007b) *Colonial Collecting Revisited*, Leiden, CNWS Publications.

KOPYTOFF, I. (1986) 'The cultural biography of things: commoditization as process', in Appadurai, A. (ed.), *The Social Life of Things: Commodities in Cultural Perspective*, Cambridge, Cambridge University Press.

KREPS, C.F. (2003) *Liberating Culture: Cross-Cultural Perspectives on Museums, Curation and Heritage Preservation*, London, Routledge.

LANE FOX, A.H. (1875a) 'On principles of classification adopted in the arrangement of his anthropological collection, now exhibiting in the Bethnal Green Museum', *Journal of the Royal Anthropological Institute*, 4, 293–308.

LANE FOX, A.H. (1875b) *The Evolution of Culture*, Oxford, Pitt Rivers Museum.

LAVINE, S.D. AND KARP, I. (1991) 'Introduction: museums and multiculturalism', in Karp, I. and Lavine, S. D. (eds), *Exhibiting Cultures: The Poetics and Politics of Museum Display*, Washington, DC, Smithsonian Institution Press.

LAWRENCE, E.A. (1991) 'His very silence speaks: the horse who survived Custer's Last Stand', in Browne, R. B. and Browne, P. (eds), *Digging into Popular Culture: Theories and Methodologies in Archaeology, Anthropology and Other Fields*, Bowling Green, OH, Bowling Green State University Popular Press.

LEGÊNE, S. (2007) 'Enlightenment, empathy, retreat: the cultural heritage of the *Ethische Politiek*', in ter Keurs, P. J. (ed.), *Colonial Collecting Revisited*, Leiden, CNWS Publications.

LIDCHI, H. (2006) 'Culture and constraints: further thoughts on ethnography and exhibiting', *International Journal of Heritage Studies*, 12(1), 93–114.

LONETREE, A. (2009) 'Museums as sites of decolonization: truth telling in national and tribal museums', in Sleeper-Smith, S. (ed.), *Contesting Knowledge: Museum and Indigenous Perspectives*, Lincoln, NB, University of Nebraska Press.

MACDONALD, S. (2006) 'Introduction', in MacDonald, S. (ed.), *A Companion to Museum Studies*, Chichester, Wiley-Blackwell.

MACGREGOR, A. (1985) 'The cabinet of curiosities in seventeenth-century Britain', in Impey, O. and MacGregor, A. (eds), *The Origins of Museums: The Cabinet of Curiosities in Sixteenth- and Seventeenth-Century Europe*, Oxford, Clarendon Press.

MACGREGOR, N. (2010) *A History of the World in a Hundred Objects*, London, Allen Lane.

MARCUS, G.E. (2002) 'Problems in the reception of ethnography and the challenge of a new pedagogy', in Gonseth, M.-O., Hainard, J. and Kaehr, R. (eds), *Le Musée Cannibale*, Neuchâtel, MEN.

MERRYMAN, J.H. (1986) 'Two ways of thinking about cultural property', *American Journal of International Law*, 80(4), 831–53.

MERRYMAN, J.H. (1990) '"Protection" of the "cultural heritage"', *American Journal of Comparative Law*, Supplement US Law in an Era of Democratization, 38, 513–22.

NICKS, T. (2003) 'Museums and contact zones: introduction', in Peers, L. and Brown, A. J. (eds), *Museums and Source Communities*, London, Routledge.

O'HANLON, M. (1993) *Paradise: Portraying the New Guinea Highlands*, London, British Museum Press.

O'HANLON, M. (2000) 'Introduction: the ethnographic collection from obscurity to obliquy', in O'Hanlon, M. and Welsh, R.L. (eds), *Hunting the Gatherers: Ethnographic Collectors, Agents and Agency in Melanesia, 1870s–1930s*, Methodology and History in Anthropology Series (Vol. 6), Oxford, Berghahn Books.

O'HANLON, M. AND WELSH, R.L. (eds) (2000) *Hunting the Gatherers: Ethnographic Collectors, Agents and Agency in Melanesia, 1870s–1930s*, Methodology and History in Anthropology Series (Vol. 6), Oxford, Berghahn Books.

OPOKU, K. (2009) 'Looting of African artefacts for western museum', 23 May. Available at: http://www.afrikanet.info/menu/kultur/datum/2009/05/23/looting-of-african-artefacts-for-western-museum/?type=98&cHash=03eee38766 (accessed 9 March 2011).

PEERS, L. AND BROWN, A.J. (eds) (2003) *Museums and Source Communities*, London, Routledge.

PHILLIPS, R.B. (2011) *Museum Pieces: Towards the Indigenization of Canadian Museums*, Montreal, McGill Queen's University Press

PICTON, J. (2010) 'To see or not to see! That is the question', *African Arts*, Winter, 1, 4–6.

POMIAN, K. (1990) *Collectors and Curiosities: Paris and Venice, 1500–1800* (tr. E. Wills-Portier), Cambridge, Polity Press.

PORTO, N. (2007) 'From exhibition to installing ethnography: experiments at the Museum of Anthropology of the University of Coimbra, Portugal, 1999–2005', in MacDonald, S. and Basu, P. (eds), *Exhibition Experiments*, Oxford, Blackwell.

PWNHC (PRINCE OF WALES NORTHERN HERITAGE CENTER) (2006) *Dè T'a Hoti T'seeda: We Live Securely by the Land*. An exhibition of Dene material selection from the collections of National Museums Scotland, Yellowknife, Government of the Northwest Territories.

RAJCHMAN, J. (1988) 'Foucault's art of seeing', *October*, 44(Spring), 89–117.

SHELTON, A.A. (1994) 'Cabinets of transgression: Renaissance collections and the incorporation of the New World', in Eisner, J. and Cardinal, R. (eds), *The Cultures of Collecting*, London, Reaktion Books.

SHELTON, A.A. (2006) 'Museums and anthropologies', in MacDonald, S. (ed.), *A Companion to Museum Studies*, Chichester, Wiley-Blackwell.

SIMPSON, M.G. (1996) *Making Representations: Museums in the Post-Colonial Era*, London, Routledge.

STOCKING, G.W. JR (ed.) (1985) *Objects and Others*, London and Madison, WI, University of Wisconsin Press.

STOCKING, G.W. JR. (1987) *Victorian Anthropology*, London, Collier Macmillan.

TASK FORCE ON MUSEMS AND FIRST PEOPLES (1992) *Turning the Page: Forging New Partnerships between Museums and First Peoples*, Ottawa, Assembly of First Nations and Canadian Association of Museums

TRADESCANT, J. (1656) *Museum Tradescantianum; Or, A collection of Rarities Preserved at South Lambeth neer London*, London, John Grismond.

VERGO, P. (1993) 'The reticent object', in Vergo, P. (ed.), *The New Museology*, London, Reaktion Books.

VOGEL, S. (1991) 'Always true to the object, in our fashion', in Karp, I. and Lavine, S. D. (eds), *Exhibiting Cultures: The Poetics and Politics of Museum Display*, Washington, DC, Smithsonian Institution Press.

WEIL, S. E. (2002) *Why Museums Matter*, London and Washington, DC, Smithsonian Institution Press.

WEIL, S. E. (2005) 'A success/failure matrix for museum', *Museum News*, January/February, 36–40.

WEST, R. JR (2000) *The Changing Presentation of the American Indian*, Washington, DC, National Museum of the American Indian, Smithsonian Institution/University of Washington Press.

ACKNOWLEDGEMENTS

I would like to thank Brian Durrans and Michael O'Hanlon for their critical insights into the first edition as well as Alison Deeprose and Saul Peckham who ensured that the excellent photographs were taken. Julie Adams was a critical reader for the second edition, Ruth Phillips and Brian Durrans very generously provided advance copies of new texts to assist with the development of the chapter. Marc Olivier-Gonseth and Tom Andrews generously gave permission for the use of new photographs.

READING A: John Tradescant the younger, extracts from *Musaeum Tradescantianum*

The following four extracts are all from the 1656 catalogue *Musaeum Tradescantianum; Or, A Collection of Rarities Preserved at South Lambeth neer London*, prepared by John Tradescant the younger.

EXTRACT 1

The first extract is contained in the preface addressed *To The Ingenious Reader*.

Now for the materialls themselves I reduce them unto two sorts; one *Naturall*, of which some are more familiarly known & named amongst us, as divers sorts of Birds, fourefooted Beasts and Fishes to whom I have given usual *English* names. Other are lesse familiar ... as the shell Creatures, Insects, Mineralls, Outlandish-Fruits and the like, which are part of the *Materia Medica* ... The other sort is *Artificialls* such as Utensills, Householdstuffe, Habits, Instruments of Warre used by severall Nations, rare curiosities of Art &c. These are also expressed in *English* (saving the Coynes, which would vary but little if Translated) for the ready satisfying whomsoever may desire a view thereof. The *Catalogue* of my *Garden* I have also added in the Conclusion (and given the names of the *Plants* both in *Latine* and *English*) that nothing may be wanting which at present comes within view, and might be expected from

Your ready friend

John Tradescant.

EXTRACT 2: THE INDEX

A view of the whole.

1 Birds with their eggs, beaks, feathers, clawes, spurres. (page 1)

2 Fourfooted beasts with some of their hides, homes, and hoofs. (5)

3 Divers sorts of strange fishes. (8)

4 Shell-creatures, whereof some are called *Mollia*, some *Crustacea*, others *Testacea*, of these are both *univalvia*, and *bivalvia*. (10)

5 Severall sorts of Insects, terrestrial – *anelytra*, *coleoptera*, *aptera*, *apoda*. (14)

6 Mineralls, and those of neare nature with them, as Earths, Coralls, Salts, Bitumens, Petrified things, choicer Stones, Gemmes. (17)

7 Outlandish Fruits from both the *Indies*, with Seeds, Gummes, Roots, Woods, and divers Ingredients Medicinall, and for the Arts of Dying. (26)

8 Mechanicks, choice pieces in Carvings, Turnings, Paintings. (36)

9 Other variety of Rarities. (42)

10 Warlike Instruments, European, Indian, & c. (44)

11 Garments, Habits, Vests, Ornaments, (47)

12 Utensils, and Householdstuffe. (52)

13 *Numismata*, Coynes ancient and modern, both gold, silver, and copper, Hebrew, Greeke, Roman both Imperial and Consular. (55)

14 Medalls, gold, silver, copper and lead. (66)

Hortus Tradescantianus

15 An enumeration of his Plants, Shrubs, and Trees both in English and Latine. (73)

16 A *Catalogue* of his Benefactors. (179)

EXTRACT 3

The third and fourth extracts contain some examples of the entries featured in the catalogue into two of the sections listed above.

Under the subdivided section: T. Some kindes of *Birds* their Egges, Beaks, Feathers, Clawes, and Spurres' the following items are featured:

1. *EGGES*

[…]

Crocodiles,

Estridges,

[…]

Divers sorts of Egges from *Turkie*: one given for a Dragons egge.

Easter Egges of the Patriarchs of *Jerusalem*

2. *BEAKS, or HEADS*

Cassaway, or Emeu,

Griffin,

[...]

Aracari of *Brasil*, his beak four inches long, almost two thick, like a Turkes sword.

[…]

Guarya of *Marahoon Brasil*: his beak like a *Poland* sword.

Jabira, Brasil, [...]

3. *FEATHERS*

Divers curious and beautifully coloured feathers of Birds from the West India's.

The breast of a Peacock from the West India's.

[...]

Two feathers of the Phoenix tayle.

[...]

4. *CLAWES*

The claw of the bird Rock; who, as Authors report, is able to trusse an Elephant. Eagles clawes.

Cock spurs three inches long.

A legge and claw of the Cassawary or Emeu that dyed at *S. James's, Westminster*.

Twenty several sorts of clawes of other strange birds, not found described by Authors.

5. *Whole BIRDS*

Kings-fisher from the *West India's*.

[…]

A black bird with red shoulders and pinions, from *Virginia*.

Matuitui, the bigness of a Thrush, short neck and legges.

[...]

Penguin, which never flies for want of wings.

[…]

Pellican. [...]

Dodar, from the Island *Mauritius*; it is not able to file being so big. [...]

The Bustard as big as a Turky, usually taken by Greyhounds on *Newmarket-heath*.

Divers sorts of Birds-nests of various forms.

EXTRACT 4

Under the sections 'VII Mechanick artficiall Works in Carvings, Turnings, Sowings and

Paintings', 'VIII. Variety of Rarities' and 'X. Garments, Vestures, Habits, Ornaments', the following items are featured:

VII. Mechanick artificiall Works in Carvings, Turnings, Sowings and Paintings Several curious painting in little forms, very ancient.

[...]

The Indian lip-stone which they wear the in lip. [...]

Halfe a Hasle-nut with 70 pieces of household-stuffe in it.

A Cherry-stone holding 10 dozen of Tortois-shell combs, made by *Edward Gibbons*.

[...]

Divers sorts of Ivory-balls turned one within another, some 6, some 12 folds; very excellent work.

[...]

VIII. Variety of Rarities

Indian morris-bells of shells and fruits. [...]

Indian Conjurers rattle, wherewith he calls up Spirits.

[...]

A Circumcision Knife of stone, and the instrument to take up the *praeputium* of silver.

[...]

A piece of the Stone of *Sarrigs*-Castle where *Hellen* of *Greece* was born.

A piece of the Stone of the Oracle of *Apollo*.

[...]

Ancient Iron-Money in crosse-plates, like Anchors, preserved in *Pontefract*-Castle, *Yorke-shire*.

[...]

A Brazen-ball to warm the Nunnes hands,

[...]

Blood that rained in the *Isle of Wight*, attested by Sir *Jo: Oglander.*

[...]

X. Garments, Vestures, Habits, Ornaments. An Arabian vest. [...]

A Portugall habit,

[...]

A Greinland-habit.

[...]

Match-coat from *Greenland* of the Intrails of Fishes.

Pohatan, King of *Virginia's* habit all embroidered with shells, or Roanoke.

[...]

Nunnes penitentiall Girdles of Haire.

[...]

Handkerchiffs of severall sorts of excellent needle-work.

Edward the Confessors knit-gloves.

Anne of Bullens Night-vayle embroidered with silver.

[...]

Henry 8. hawking glove, hawks-hood, dogs-coller.

Source: Tradescant, 1656.

READING B: Elizabeth A. Lawrence, 'His very silence speaks: the horse who survived Custer's Last Stand'

No man of the immediate command of Lieutenant Colonel (Brevet Major General) George A. Custer survived to describe the dramatic clash between Seventh U.S. Cavalrymen and Sioux and Cheyenne warriors which became known as 'Custer's Last Stand'. Fought on a Montana hillside on June 25, 1876, the conflict in which approximately 210 cavalrymen lost their lives has evoked extraordinary interest. [...] Although the Custer Battle was part of a larger two-day military engagement, the Battle of the Little Big Horn, it is the 'Last Stand' that has exerted such a profound influence on people's imagination. The image of Custer's men, outnumbered and surrounded, fighting to the death against overwhelming odds is a perennially fascinating image. [...]

Much of the appeal of Custer's Last Stand is rooted in the mystery that surrounds the event [...]. [The sole being] who became famous as a survivor was mute [...]. [T]wo days following the battle a cavalry horse from Custer's command was found alive – Comanche, the mount [... of] Captain Myles W. Keogh of Troop I. Seldom in history have people wished so fervently that an animal could speak and illuminate the unknown elements of the battle, and the actions and motivations of its controversial leader. Although other Seventh Cavalry horses survived [... and] great numbers of victorious Indians lived through the battle, Comanche became widely known as the 'sole survivor' of Custer's Last Stand. This designation has been an inextricable part of his fame. [...]

Following his discovery, the badly wounded horse was rescued from the battlefield, nursed back to health, and maintained as an honored member of the Seventh Cavalry. [...]

From the cavalrymen he represented, Comanche took on the mantle of heroism. The horse [...] became a link between the living and the dead. His endurance and invincibility were symbols for survival in the face of overwhelming odds. The wounded horse became the focus for various emotions – the bitter anger of defeat, sorrow for the dead cavalrymen and vengeance toward the Indian Nations.

Comanche lived for fifteen-and-a-half years following the Little Big Horn Battle. [...] As the 'lone survivor', he earned his own place in history through fortitude, and conferred fame upon his rider. The strong bond between Captain Keogh and his horse [...] took on legendary proportions and was purported to be the reason for the animal's unlikely survival. [...] Comanche became known not only as a paragon of endurance, but of faithfulness as well [...] a symbolic expression of humankind's ancient dream of unity with the animal world.

[...]

During his retirement, Comanche was not only an honored soldier referred to as the 'second commanding officer' of his regiment, but a pampered pet as well. [...]

Throughout his life, Comanche stood for the honor of the defeated men who had died for their country and for the shame and anger the nation felt at the Indians' victory. As the years unfolded, the horse was also embued with broader meanings, for the United States was undergoing an era of dramatic change, Comanche's life as an Indian fighter came full circle, spanning the time from the great Indian victory at the Little Big Horn through the Indians' total defeat at Wounded Knee in 1890 (an engagement often referred to as 'the Seventh's revenge'). [...]

When Comanche died at Fort Riley in 1891, [...] his remains were preserved and mounted by Lewis L. Dyche of the Natural History Museum at the University of Kansas, where he is still displayed. One of [Dyche's] conditions [...] was that he could exhibit the stuffed horse along with his other zoological specimens at the World's Columbian Exposition at Chicago in 1893. Thus Comanche's posthumous role began as an oddity – a domestic animal standing among wild species – an incongruous attraction for throngs of people who attended the fair. [...] The purpose of the Exposition was to [...] celebrate American progress. [...] 1893 was a time to take pride in the accomplishments of expansion and the final conquest of a once wild continent, which many people construed as the victory of 'civilization over savagery'. [...]

America was entering the machine age, and the end of the horse era [...] was fast approaching. Comanche was an extremely popular attraction at the Chicago Fair. [...] In describing Dyche's display of wild fauna among which the horse stood, anthropomorphism and racism were often combined. For example, two wolverines were said to be 'meditating upon some kind of meanness' and so were referred to as 'Indian devils'. [...] Comanche, 'the old war horse', was designated as 'the only surviving horse of the Custer massacre' [...] Custer's Last Stand, became inextricably identified with the term 'massacre,'

an inappropriate word since the battle involved armed fighting forces on both sides. [...]

Little information has come to light regarding Comanche's first few decades as a museum specimen, which [...] began in 1902 when he was placed in the newly constructed Dyche Hall at the University of Kansas. [...] From 1934 until 1941, the building which housed him was closed and Comanche was stored in the basement of a university auditorium. [...]

Comanche's significance [...] is reflected by the numerous requests to obtain him – either as a loan or permanent possession – that have been and still are received by the University of Kansas. [...]

Beginning in about 1938, and continuing sporadically [...] into the present, the greatest number of requests have involved relocating Comanche at the Custer Battlefield National Monument Museum. [...] In general, National Park officials and Custer Battlefield personnel have opposed transferring Comanche to the battle site. [...] One regional director, for example, considered the horse 'not essential to the proper interpretation of the battle,' stating that 'if we retrieved the horse, it would be entirely on sentimental grounds.' He added that though the horse would exert 'a potent spell' upon students [...] it would [...] make the visitor 'goggle and exclaim' rather than understand. One official even asserted that Comanche's main value was as 'an interesting example of the techniques of taxidermy in transition' [...]

[...] Whereas for those who want him at Fort Riley Comanche epitomizes the glory of cavalry life, and for those who would move him to Montana he is an inseparable part of the battle that made him immortal, for the University of Kansas he represents cherished tradition. [...]

To insure Comanche's retention [...] graduates wrote letters insisting that their alma mater 'hold that line' against any attempt to remove him, for they remembered 'battle-scarred old "Faithful"' who 'was "our silent partner" and in our hearts became a real part of the University.' Because of Comanche's courage and endurance, students would rub Comanche's nose or steal a strand of his tail hair to bring luck in exams (before he was encased in glass). [...]

And so Comanche has stayed, secure in his special humidified glass 'stall' at the University of Kansas. Prior to 1970, there was a brief label outlining the horse's history. [...] The first sentence stated: 'Comanche was the sole survivor of the Custer massacre at the Battle of the Little Big Horn on June 25, 1876' [...] In 1970, the idea of Comanche as 'sole survivor' and the inaccuracy of 'massacre' for what was in reality a battle took on new significance. [...] American Indian students at the university took up the challenge that, for them, was embodied by the display and interpretation of the cavalry horse in the museum. As a result of this different kind of onslaught, Comanche's image would be transformed to accommodate new meanings. [...]

Calling the Comanche exhibit a 'racist symbol', a group of native American university students protested that the horse perpetuated the stereotype of Custer and his troops being 'massacred' by 'savage' Indians who were in the wrong. And since in reality large numbers of Indians lived through the battle, the students were distressed over the designation of the horse as the sole survivor of the Little Big Horn. [...]

A committee representing the native American students met with the museum director and asked that the Comanche exhibit be closed until a more accurate label was written. The director and other officials complied. [...] Recalling those events, the museum director told me, 'Comanche was one of the greatest learning experiences of my life.' In November 1971, a celebration sponsored by both Indians and whites accompanied the reopening of the Comanche exhibit. There was now a long text that began by explaining that the horse stands 'as a symbol of the conflict between the United States Army and the Indian tribes of the Great Plains that resulted from the government's policy of confinement of Indians on reservations and extermination of those Indians who refused to be confined,' and detailed the Indians' struggle to retain their land and way of life. The Battle of the Little Big Horn was designated as an Indian victory, and the 1890 engagement was accurately termed 'the Massacre of Wounded Knee Creek'.

Although the Indians had first wanted the horse permanently removed from the museum, they compromised [...] Comanche could be a 'learning tool' for both sides. Thus he was transformed from an object representing a federal defeat to a subject articulating the Indian peoples' way of life and struggle for existence.

[...]

Now, the horse was not just 'a symbol of the Indians' past victories, but 'what modern Indians can accomplish' ('Comanche Once Angered Indians', *Olathe Daily News*, January 10, 1978).

[...] Comanche, in his new role, led the way for further beneficial changes within the museum. [...] Indian exhibits were disassociated from those dealing with 'primitive man'. Native American religious objects, previously appearing as 'curios', were labelled in a more respectful manner or removed. The whole idea of how best to exhibit cultural relics and artifacts was […] re-examined and addressed. [...]

[...] Comanche has continued to be a highlight for the 120,000 annual visitors to the Dyche Museum [...]

Although artifacts such as guns and arrows whose provenance can be traced to the Little Big Horn are highly valued [...] Comanche still surpasses all battle relics. As a once-living creature whose posthumous existence is even more meaningful than his cavalry career, [...] he has an image of courage and endurance with which people continue to identify, adapting it to their own ethos and times. Beyond [Comanche's] capacity to lend a sense of immediacy to Custer's Last Stand [... and] more than a battle relic from a bygone era, 'his very silence speaks in terms more eloquent than words', articulating a timeless message protesting human kind's aggressive domination of nature, the oppression of the weak by the strong, and even the universal barbarity of war.

Source: Lawrence, 1991, pp. 84–94.

READING C: Michael O'Hanlon, *Paradise: Portraying the New Guinea Highlands*

COLLECTING IN CONTEXT

[M]aking a collection itself proved to be more interesting than I had naively expected. It confronted me with my own taken-for-granted assumptions as to the nature of the transactions I was engaged in, the definition of 'material culture', and what actually constituted a 'Wahgi artefact'. [...] I did not find myself a free agent [...] My collecting was constrained by local processes and rules, with the upshot that the collection I made partly mirrored in its own structure local social organisation. And while many comments on collecting have focused upon the 'rupture' involved in removing artefacts from their local context to install them in the rather different one of a museum or gallery, this was not necessarily the way in which the Wahgi themselves chose to view the matter.

[...]

[W]hat I had in mind was the full repertoire of portable Wahgi goods, including personal adornment of all kinds, clothing, netbags, household goods, weaponry. Possibly I could also commission a *bolyim* house and *mond* post. The emphasis was to be on completeness, with contemporary material, such as the contents of a trade-store, represented equally with traditional items. [...]

[T]he money which I had available to purchase artefacts and assistance still represented a substantial local asset. I worried that it might prove difficult to manage the tension between the demands of the immediate community, who would be likely to want me to buy exclusively from them, and my own wish to purchase a wider range of artefacts than they would be likely to possess [...].

My concern was largely misplaced: Kinden proved to have quite clear ideas as to how to proceed. There should, he declared, be a specific order in which people should be entitled to offer artefacts for sale, particularly in the case of the most valuable category, netbags. [...]

[...] While at one level [the collection] certainly reflected my own conception of what 'a collection of Wahgi material culture' should include, at another level the collection necessarily embodied local conditions and processes. The fact that it was constituted predominantly of Komblo artefacts reflected the *realpolitik* of field collection, and the order in which the artefacts were acquired partially reproduced local social structure, including its characteristic tensions [...] I suspect that most ethnographic collections contain much more of an indigenous ordering than their contemporary reputation – as having been assembled according to alien whim and 'torn' from a local context – often allows. A final arena of cultural negotiation related to what should be given in return for artefacts acquired [...].

[R]eluctance to specify a price stemmed from the fact that the transactions were rarely purchases in any simple sense. They had as much the character of local exchanges, in which precise amounts are not necessarily worked out in advance [...]

As people became clearer as to what I wanted to collect (once they had internalised my stereotype of their material culture), they began to become interested in the collection's contents and representativeness. Some speculated that it would not be possible to obtain such discontinued items as aprons ornamented with pigs tails [...] Men began on their own initiative to make examples of abandoned categories of artefact [...]

Other artefacts, for example the *geru* boards believed to promote pig growth and to alleviate sickness, I knew I would have to commission. [...]

I also found that the practicalities entailed in making a collection of artefacts revealed complexities which I had not previously appreciated. Sometimes, these were minor social and technical details which I had observed before but never really seen [...] At other times, collecting highlighted variations among Wahgi themselves in their approach to artefacts. [...]

On occasion, collecting artefacts threw up points entirely new to me. While I did know that Wahgi men, like many other Highlanders, consider women to be polluting in certain respects, I had not realised that skirts were potentially defiling, or that washing rid them of their polluting qualities (worried women told me that my 'skin' would become 'ashy' if I handled unwashed skirts).

[...]

The way in which people react to the making of a collection tells us, in fact, something about their historical experience. In such areas as the Southern Highlands, which were subjected to colonial pressure that was even more sudden and overwhelming than was the case in the Western Highlands, making a collection may precipitate an emotional rediscovery of what was lost or suppressed in local culture. [...]

The Wahgi instance was rather different. Certain items, such as the *bolyim* house which I thought I might commission, most men were simply not prepared to make. Equally, after reflection, people abandoned their initial enthusiasm for staging a mock battle to mark my first departure from the field. Both *bolyim* houses and warfare remain sufficiently integral to ongoing culture for it to be dangerous to invoke them without due cause. But the many cultural practices which *were* re-enacted in the context of making the collection did not seem to me to be done in any mood of emotional rediscovery. Rather, demonstrations of how stone axes used to be made, or of how highly pearl shells were formerly valued, tended to be carried out with a caricatured seriousness which collapsed into laughter. There was sometimes a sense that people felt they had been absurd to esteem shells in the way they had, to have laboured as long as they did to grind hard stones down to make axes. Now they knew better. Making items for the collection and demonstrating their use was, for the Wahgi, less a rediscovery of culture from which they had been estranged than a marker of how far they had come. Indeed, it was in the context of my collecting that some younger people encountered such items as wooden pandanus bowls and *geru* boards for the first time; such artefacts were becoming museum pieces in a double sense.

The notion that such older material cultural forms are becoming 'museumified' is supported by the recent establishment of the remarkable Onga Cultural Centre at Romonga, just to the west of the Wahgi culture area (Burton, 1991). [...]

Its focus is entirely upon traditional material culture, narrowly conceived. [...]

As my period in the Highlands drew to a close, I felt a growing sense of interpenetration between Wahgi frames of reference and my collecting. [...]

[...] The crates which Michael Du had made for the collection had to be painted with the Museum of Mankind's address, and labelled as 'fragile'. It was important that this should be done legibly to minimise the risk of damage, or of the crates going astray. The only practised painter I knew was Kaipel, who had decorated many of the shields which the crates now contained, and he spent an afternoon meticulously labelling them. [...]

The extent to which my collecting activities had been partly assimilated to local frames of reference, emerged when the first of the collections I made in the Wahgi was being packed. On the one hand, the collection was a project which, in being exported, would be launched on a wider stage. It would 'be revealed', as Wahgi say of items like *geru* boards and ceremonial wigs. Before such objects are publicly revealed, those launching them solicit ghostly support through consuming a private sacrificial meal. As he outlined the arrangements for the meal he organised for the collection's departure, Kinden commented that he did not know who *my* ancestors were: the unspoken implication was that it would be *his* ancestors whose ghostly help would be sought.

On the other hand, the completion of the collection was also a leave-taking. If there is a single model for leave-taking in Wahgi society it is that of marriage, when a girl departs her natal kin to live among her husband's clanspeople. [...]

[Anamb] proposed that the collection should undergo the ceremony of beautification which is performed for a bride the evening before her departure. This was a suggestion with considerable political spin on it, a point I also noted when the same idiom of kinship was invoked in negotiating what was to be paid for artefacts. For if the collection was like a bride, then what I had paid for it was like bridewealth; and the point about bridewealth is that it is only the *first* of the payments which are owed to a bride's kin. [...] Anamb's comparison was his way of highlighting my continuing relationship of indebtedness to those who had helped me, as well as a specific attempt to constitute himself as the 'source person' of any benefit which might flow to me from the collection.

EXHIBITING IN PRACTICE

Exhibition outline

The gallery in which the exhibition is to take place lies at the end of a corridor. [...] the antechamber should include the only component of the exhibition specifically suggested by those Wahgi with whom I discussed the exhibition. Their main wish, as earlier noted, was that a contingent of performers should visit the museum to dance and to demonstrate traditional cultural practices. [...] In the absence of the sponsorship which might make such a visit possible, the only specific proposal they made was that the exhibition should have at its start the large stones, painted posts and cordyline plants which mark the entrance to an area that is in some way special or restricted (as Kinden had marked off my fieldbase). Kulka Nekinz even painted and presented me with two such posts. In part, I think it was felt that since Wahgi themselves traditionally mark special territory in this way, it was appropriate so to mark the entrance to a Wahgi exhibition. This was reinforced in Kinden's mind by a visit he and I had made a decade earlier to the ethnography exhibitions at the National Museum in the capital, Port Moresby. Kinden had observed near the museum entrance a row of posts or bollards which he had interpreted as similarly delimiting the exhibitions there.

[...]

Visitors to the earlier *Living Arctic* exhibition, which had also used such quotations from Native Americans, repeatedly recorded their approval at the provision of such an 'indigenous voice' – even though the selection of that voice is, of course, the curator's.

[...]

My argument in fact has been that the exhibition is itself a large artefact, whose manufacture merits a measure of the interest usually confined to the component objects included within it. [...]

[A]t the end of the exhibition, there is [...] vacant wall space [...] where an acknowledgement of the fabricated nature of the exhibition might be made.

This could best be done by including a miscellany of photographs to illustrate the artefacts' passage from field to museum display. The photographs [...] would [...] acknowledge the exhibition's own

'sources' [and include] a picture of the crates leaving Mt. Hagen; an illustration of the artefacts being unpacked upon arrival in London; photographs of the gallery [...] showing its refitting for the present exhibition.

No photographic record remains, however, of the moment which for me illustrated an unavoidable contingency attached to collecting and preserving some artefacts but not others. In the museum's repository, the process of unpacking the crates in which the collection had travelled was complete. The crates' contents, now safely swaddled in tissue paper, awaited fumigation, conservation, registration and careful storage as Wahgi artefacts. Meanwhile, other Wahgi artefacts – the crates themselves, no less carefully made by Michael Du, painted by Zacharias and labelled by Kaipel the sign-writer – awaited disposal.

REFERENCE

BURTON, J. (1991) 'The Romunga Haus Tumbuna, Western Highlands Province, PNG', in Eoe, S. M. and Swadling, P. (eds), *Museums and Cultural Centres in the Pacific*, Port Moresby, Papua New Guinea National Museum.

Source: O'Hanlon, 1993, pp. 55–93.

READING D: James Clifford, 'Paradise'

The only consistently non-contemporaneous times signalled by the *Paradise* photographs are explorer Mick Leahy's black and white records of the 1933 'first contact' and the final 'Making of an Exhibition' panels. The former are appropriate [...] the latter seem more problematic. Why should a Wahgi man crafting objects for the exhibition be in small black and white, while other Wahgi performing at the pig festival ten years earlier are in full colour? Why should the work of the museum staff appear to be taking place in some different time from the complex, contemporary, real, historical times presented elsewhere in the show? Given the limited size of the exhibit, and its somewhat minimalist touch, 'The Making of an Exhibition' panels register the appropriate people and activities. But given the lack of color and size in the photos they risk appearing as an afterthought. Even at its current scale, the section might have included a large color image of the women who made many of the adjacent netbags, instead of a modest black and white. And I, at least, would have found a way to show Michael O'Hanlon in the highlands – an image missing from both exhibition *and* catalogue. How are modesty and authority complicit in this absence? [...]

O'Hanlon's original plan called for the prominent use of Wahgi quotations in the 'first contact' section. Arguing for this strategy, he noted that an earlier exhibit at the Museum of Mankind, *Living Arctic*, made extensive use of quotations from Native Americans, and that these had been much appreciated by visitors. In the current exhibit, Wahgi are very little 'heard'. Very brief quotations, often with allegorical resonances, are placed at the head of each long interpretive plaque, but these have no independent presence. Nor do we read, in the catalogue, any extended Wahgi intepretations of exhibit topics or process. Wahgi agency, stressed throughout, has no translated voice. As the *Living Arctic* experiment showed, this could be a powerful means of communication, albeit always under curatorial orchestration. Why was the tactic dropped? So as not to overcomplicate the message? So as not to privilege certain Wahgi? In order to avoid the awkwardness, even bad faith, that comes with 'giving voice' to others on terms not their own?

The staging of translated, edited 'Voices' to produce a 'polyphonic' ethnographic authority has never been an unproblematic exercise. But represented voices can be powerful indices of a living people: more so than even photographs which, however realistic and contemporary, always evoke a certain irreducible past tense (Barthes, 1981). And to the extent that quotations are attributed to discrete individuals, they can communicate a sense of indigenous *diversity*. One of the exhibit's scattered Wahgi statements chastises young women for their new, unrespectable, netbag styles. We immediately 'hear' a man of a certain generation. What if longer, more frequent, and sometimes conflicting personal statements had been included? My point is not to second-guess O'Hanlon and his collaborators at the Museum. There were tradeoffs, and one cannot do everything in a small, or even in a large, exhibit. I wish, simply, to underline significant choices constituting both object and authority in *Paradise*, choices revealed but not analysed in the catalogue. [...]

[A] poignant scene ends the catalogue. Museum basements are revealing places, and here collecting is seen to be an act of both retrieval and disposal. The scene illustrates, for O'Hanlon, 'an unavoidable contingency attached to collecting and preserving some artefacts but not others.' But the phrase 'unavoidable contingency' may not quite do justice to the specific institutional constraints and (not-inevitable) choices at work. The custom-made crates could have made striking additions to a show differently conceived. Space considerations, conventions of proper collection and display, a concern not to overcomplicate the message – all these no doubt conspired to make their disposal seem inevitable. [...]

Paradise is directed at a certain London museum public and at a sophisticated (in places specialist) catalogue readership. That it is not addressed to the Wahgi is obvious and, given who is likely to see and read the productions, appropriate. This fact does not, however, close the personal and institutional question of responsibility to the Wahgi. It may be worth pushing the issue a bit farther than O'Hanlon does, for it is of general importance for contemporary practices of cross-cultural collecting and display. What are the relational politics, poetics and pragmatics of representation here? In what senses do the *Paradise* exhibition and book reflect Wahgi perspectives and desires? Should they? [...]

O'Hanlon offers a sensitive account of all this, portraying himself yielding to, and working within, local protocols. He tends, overall, to present a potentially fraught process as a steady convergence of interests – a fable, if not of rapport, at least of complicity. He also gives glimpses of the relationship's more problematic aspects. As the collection is about to depart for London, it is ritually treated like a bride, departing to live with her husband's people (marriage being the primary model of leave-taking for the Wahgi). [...]

O'Hanlon closes his second chapter with Anamb's power play, an incident that reveals how dialogical relations of collecting both include and exclude people. Moreover, Anamb raises, Melanesian style, a far-reaching political question. What do O'Hanlon, the Museum of Mankind, and indeed the visitors and readers who 'consume' these artefacts owe the Wahgi who have sent them? Payment does not end the connection with 'source people'. Quite the opposite: in collecting relations money, objects, knowledge, and cultural value are exchanged and appropriated in continuing local/global circuits. How should the benefits of these relationships be shared? If collecting is conceived as exchanging, what ongoing constraints are imposed on exhibition practices? The catalogue chapter on 'Exhibiting in Practice' drops these political issues.

According to O'Hanlon, those who helped him in the Highlands made few specific requests about the nature of the exhibit. They did, however, want the personal and political relationships involved to proceed properly. Anamb's attempt to ensure a 'continuing relationship of endebtedness' doubtless had more to do with keeping the exchange going and sharing the wealth than with faithfully representing his viewpoint or giving him voice. Independent of exhibit content, the issue of reciprocity remains. Does the Museum officially recognize any ongoing exchange connection with Wahgi tribes or individuals? [...] What is the nature of the responsibility incurred in the making of this exhibit? Do Wahgi understand it primarily as a personal, kin-like relation with O'Hanlon? Or is there an institutional, even geo-political dimension? These questions, opened up by the catalogue, encourage more concreteness in our discussions of the politics of collecting and representation. [...]

The most specific Wahgi request concerning the exhibition was, in fact, passed over. In the highlands, special or restricted places are marked off by small clusters of 'taboo stones' and painted posts. O'Hanlon's sponsor Kinden marked his highland collecting camp in this way, to keep the acquisitions safe. He and others asked that the exhibit be identified as a Wahgi area by placing similar stones and posts at the entry. Indeed, two posts were specially painted for the purpose and given to O'Hanlon. But no stones or posts appear at the entrance to *Paradise*. Apparently the museum design staff thought they might obstruct the flow of visitors (large school groups, for example) at a place where it was important that people move along. In this instance, practical concerns that were surely soluble (the stones are only a foot or two high) were here able to override a clearly expressed Wahgi desire for the exhibition.

London is distant from the New Guinea Highlands. There is no Wahgi community nearby that could constrain the exhibit organizers' freedom. It is worth noting this obvious fact because in many places, today, it is no longer obvious. An exhibition of First Nations artefacts in Canada will be under fairly direct scrutiny, often coupled with demands for consultation or curatorial participation (Clifford, 1991). [...] O'Hanlon's rather scrupulous reciprocity in collecting did not have to be reproduced in exhibiting. A general intent to do something that would not offend the (distant) Wahgi was enough. Thus if the Taboo Stones were 'impractical' they could go.

How far must an exhibition go in reflecting indigenous viewpoints? Some Wahgi urged O'Hanlon not to emphasize warfare in the exhibition. The exhibit does feature war (dramatic shields and spears) but compensates by following with peacemaking. Would this satisfy the Wahgi who asked that fighting be played down? And would we want to satisfy them on this score?

[A]ssuming requests come from individuals of wide local authority should they be followed without question? Is the decision by a more powerful institution to override or supplement indigenous views always 'imperialist?' Yes *and* no. In a structural sense, large metropolitan museums stand in a relation of historical privilege and financial power with respect to the small populations whose works they acquire and recontextualize. This geopolitical position is determining, at certain levels.

[...] O'Hanlon's pointed corrective, in its focus on collecting and exhibiting in practice, risks overreacting, omitting more structural, or geopolitical levels of differential power. Thus his lack of attention to the disappearance of Wahgi agency when discussing the work in London, [...]

REFERENCES

BARTHES, R. (1981) *Camera Lucida*, New York, Hill & Wang.

CLIFFORD, J. (1991) 'Tour Northwest Coast museums: travel reflections', in Karp, I. and Lavine, S. D. (eds), *Exhibiting Cultures: The Poetics and Politics of Museum Display*, Washington, DC, Smithsonian Institution Press.

Source: Clifford, 1995, pp. 92–117.

James Clifford

READING E: Annie E. Coombes, 'Material culture at the crossroads of knowledge: the case of the Benin "bronzes"'

In 1897, a series of events took place in Benin City, in what was then the Niger Coast Protectorate, which ended in the wholesale looting of royal insignia from the court of Benin. These incidents, and the resulting loot, gained instant notoriety across a range of British journals and newspapers which serviced both a mass popular readership and a professional middle class. They also received coverage in the more specialist journals serving the emergent 'anthropological' professionals. Such a spread of coverage provides the basis for mapping the configurations of interests in Africa [...] and the possibility of understanding the interrelation of knowledges produced in what were often presented as discreet spheres [...]

If the valourisation of cultural production has any impact on a reassessment of the general culture and society of the producer, then the influx of sixteenth-century carved ivories and lost wax castings from Benin City onto the European art and antiquities market, together with the subsequent proliferation of popular and 'scientific' treatises which their 'discovery' generated, should have fundamentally shaken the bedrock of the derogatory Victorian assumptions about Africa, and more specifically, the African's place in history. Yet [...] this was certainly not the case.

[...]

Those museums whose collections were enriched as a result of the punitive raid on Benin received their share of public attention in both the 'scientific' press and in the local, national and illustrated press. The Benin collections acquired by Liverpool's Mayer Museum, the Pitt Rivers Museum in Oxford, and London's Horniman Free Museum and the British Museum, all featured prominently in the press over this period. [...]

The objects [from Benin] acquired by the Horniman Free Museum in London were among some of the earliest examples of artifacts from the expedition which claimed any attention in the general, as opposed to the scientific, press. Almost immediately after acquiring the Benin artifacts, Richard Quick, the curator of the Museum, began to expose them to a variety of publics, developing what was to become a very efficient publicity machine for the Horniman collection. Photographs of items in the Horniman collection appeared in the *Illustrated London News*, and other illustrated journals in both the local and national press. These were not the carved ivory tusks or bronze plaques which had already received so much acclaim, but consisted of a carved wooden 'mirror-frame' with two European figures in a boat, a hide and goatskin fan, and two ivory armlets rather poorly reproduced. Described by the *Illustrated London News* reporter as 'relics of a less savage side of the native life', and noted for their 'fine carving' and 'antiquity', they were none the less accompanied by the inevitable descriptions of 'hideous sacrificial rites'. [...] Such sentiments, and the expression of regret concerning what was perceived at this early date as a dearth of relics from a lost 'civilisation which dates back far beyond the Portuguese colonisation of three centuries ago, and probably owes much to the Egyptian influence', are common in the early coverage of material culture from Benin. Quick's own publications on the collection favour the argument concerning Egyptian influence, which he goes to some lengths to substantiate. Significantly, at this early date of 1897, there is less astonishment or curiosity over the origin of the objects than emerges in later writings from the 'scientific' or museums establishment. [...]

One of the factors which transformed the terms of discussion of Benin material amongst emergent museum professionals, and which fired the interest in the origin of the bronzes, was the exhibition in September 1897, at the British Museum, of over three hundred bronze plaques from Benin City. By 1899, it is clear that the British Museum exhibition, together with the publications of Charles Hercules Read and O. M. Dalton (those curators at the Museum responsible for ethnographic material) and of H. Ling Roth, had extended the significance of the Benin artifacts beyond their original association with the bloody events leading up to their acquisition. Ironically, one of the results of this was to open up the possibility of an African origin for the bronzes.

To corroborate this, we have only to compare some of Quick's earlier statements with the radical changes of opinion and increased significance concerning the Benin material that appear in his writings published *after* the British Museum exhibition and publications. By 1899, he felt confidently able to describe the objects in the Horniman collection as valuable works of art' (Quick, 1899, p. 248) [...]

[...] Quick hoped that by demonstrating any similarities between some of the iconographic details of the objects in the Horniman collection, and those in the possession of the British Museum, he would register their importance and consequently increase the public profile of his own museum. This instance should signal the institutional allegiances and strategic negotiations that were partly responsible for the shift in terms used to describe and categorise Benin material, and, more specifically, its transformation from the status of 'relic' to 'work of art' in museum circles, with repercussions in other less specialised spheres.

[...]

In 1898 [...] H. Ling Roth, director of the Bankfield Museum in Halifax, and an individual who figured prominently in the history of interpretations of Benin culture, published his 'Notes on Benin Art' in the *Reliquary*. [...] Ling Roth's chief contention was that it was possible to define two phases or periods of Benin casting. [...] Ling Roth was not interested in setting up a hierarchy, since both phases were credited with equal workmanship and skill. [... He] makes clear his admiration for the work of both proposed periods, on the grounds of technical skill, elegant and thorough detailing, clarity and sharpness of design, and variety of illustration and ornamentation, together with what he perceived as an artistic sense of the balance between foreground relief and decoration, and background ornamentation. [...] Ling Roth also established a long history, from an early date, of iron smelting and gold casting amongst different African societies. Furthermore, while emphasising that there was a world of difference 'between the crude castings of the average native African and the beautiful results' from Benin, he emphasised that there was no evidence extant to suggest that there was any such 'high-class art' in the Iberian Peninsula at the end of the fifteenth century, and certainly not elsewhere in Europe. This, therefore, called into question the argument of a Portuguese origin for the bronzes.

[H]e advanced a hypothesis completely at odds with the ethnographic curators at the British Museum, Read and Dalton. [...] Ling Roth suggested that, because the Portuguese figures were later additions attached to the surface of many of the bronze plaques, this method of casting must have pre-dated the Portuguese colonisation of Benin (Ling Roth, 1898, p. 171). [...] The unsettled conclusion he arrived at, in 1898, was that this sophisticated art existed in Benin prior to the advent of the Portuguese, and was therefore entirely of African origin.

Lieutenant-General Pitt Rivers, whose substantial collection Ling Roth used to illustrate much of his article [...], supported Ling Roth's hypothesis in private. In a letter to the eminent Oxford anthropologist, Edward Burnett Tylor, in August 1898, Pitt Rivers suggested that, 'It does not follow that because European figures are represented that it all came from Europe. Most of the forms are indigenous, the features are nearly all negro, the weapons are negro' (Pitt Rivers Museum, 1898).

[...]

In September 1900, Charles Kingsley transferred Mary Kingsley's collection of objects from Benin and other parts of West Africa to the Pitt Rivers Museum. [...] The Benin material was highly prized by the Museum, the donation being praised as an example of 'the now extinct artistic bronze work of Benin, which has created so much stir of recent years, since the punitive expedition first brought these forgotten treasures to light' (Pitt Rivers Museum, 1900, p. 3). [...]

In 1903, this material was the subject of a special display in the lower gallery to demonstrate ironwork processes with particular reference to the *cire perdue* method associated with Benin, and illustrated in this instance with examples from both Benin and Ashanti. The display seems to have been a fairly permanent feature in the Museum. [...] The entry in the annual reports for [1910] testifies to the consistent interest in Benin material from the point of view of the technological processes involved.

[...]

By 1898, Read and Dalton had already lectured at the Anthropological Institute exhibiting some [...] carved ivory tusks and also photographs of the brass plaques in the British Museum's collection. [...]

[Read and Dalton (1898, p. 371) acknowledged] that these complex and detailed figures, cast with such skill and expertise, 'were produced by a people long acquainted with the art of casting metals'. The authors go so far as to compare their mastery of the *cire perdue* process to the best work of the Italian Renaissance, not only in relation to the plaques but because of the demonstrated facility for casting in the round. [...] Any question of the bronzes actually being contemporary, however, was immediately dismissed with reference to the inferior quality of contemporary casting. There was no danger here of transgressing the image of Benin as a degenerate culture.

Significantly, the point at which ethnologists decided to intervene in the debate over the origin of the Benin bronzes was precisely the moment when the paradox of technical sophistication versus social savagery threatened a break with the evolutionary paradigm, which up to that time had also supplied the classificatory principles under which most collections of material culture from the colonies were organised. Consequently, the concept of degeneration was summoned up as an aesthetic principle, to appease anxiety over these recalcitrant objects which refused to conform to comfortably familiar taxonomic solutions.

[...]

In 1899, Read and Dalton published a special presentation book entitled *Antiques from the City of Benin and other Parts of West Africa in the British Museum*. This contained several significant shifts from their earlier 1898 argument regarding the origin of the bronzes. [...] Read and Dalton [...]

had initially rested their case on a Portuguese or Egyptian origin for the bronzes. However, by 1899, Read felt obliged to warn the reader that one of the dangers of this hypothesis was that, since Europeans were better acquainted with Egyptian material, there would inevitably be a tendency to compare other lesser known cultures with Egyptian civilisation. More importantly, Read and Dalton were now both prepared to concede what Ling Roth had suggested in 1898, that although certain aspects of the ornamentation might still be attributable to the Egyptians, the Benin castings may well have preceded, or at any rate come into being independently of, Egyptian predecessors! [...] Why were the two spokespeople from the national collection prepared to concede such a thing, when by this date there was effectively very little additional empirical data available than the previous year?

I would argue that the degree to which the Benin aesthetic is assigned an African origin corresponds partly to the stepping up of pressure from ethnologists and anthropologists in the museum for government recognition and financial support. Furthermore, the course of Read and Dalton's argument for an African origin is inextricably linked to the fortunes of the Ethnographic Department within the British Museum itself. Unlike the already thriving department of Egyptology (the other tentative 'home' for the bronzes if an Egyptian origin were proven, and an autonomous department within the museum by 1886), ethnography was only granted the status of an autonomous department in 1941. The fact that so many commentaries could so confidently claim an Egyptian source for the Benin bronzes was not at all surprising, given the extent to which Ancient Egypt had made something of a comeback in the popular imagination of nineteenth-century Europe.

[...]

In September 1897, a series of some three hundred brass plaques from Benin were put on public exhibition in the British Museum. The provincial and national press almost unanimously described the exhibits as remarkable and extraordinary examples of skilled workmanship, often repeating the opinion that such work would not discredit European craftsmen. [...] In the British Press, coverage of the exhibition positions the significance of the Benin bronzes as primarily relics of the punitive expedition. [...] The same obsession with the origin of the exhibits and their alleged antiquity repeats itself here, although the most frequently posited solution is an Egyptian origin.

There is, however, another set of discourses running through both popular and scientific reports which suggest controversy of a different order. [...] Initially, it was assumed that the vast hoard of brass plaques, temporarily on loan to the British Museum, would eventually become the property of the Museum through the Trustees' acquisition of the artifacts. The Foreign Office had agreed to the loan after official representation had been made to the government on behalf of the British Museum to secure some specimens [...]. In fact, over a third of the bronze plaques had already been sold off as revenue for the Protectorate. The ensuing public auction of items from Benin aroused much bitterness amongst those museum staff with an interest in the affairs of the Ethnographic department.

[...]

[T]he influx of Benin material culture into nineteenth-century Britain made an important impact in several ways. It generated debate amongst different communities of interest in Africa, which had the potential to shift certain popular pre-conceptions regarding the

209

Annie E. Coombes

African's lack of competence to produce complex, technically sophisticated, art work. The attempts by those who saw themselves as part of the scientific community to provide an alternative context in which to interpret these finds, other than as 'curio' or 'relic' of past misdemeanours, drew public attention to a hidden history of long-established and affluent African societies. [...] Crucially, though, despite the promise of a revisionist history that such initiatives presented, whenever Benin material is discussed over the period 1897 to 1913, the writer invariably exhibits complete incredulity that such work could possibly be produced by Africans. While certain aspects of the anthropological knowledge on Benin suggested definitions and values which contradicted some of those stereotypes promulgated in the popular middle-class illustrated press, the fact that Benin was consistently treated as an anomaly of African culture by anthropologists ensured that the more racialised sense of the term 'degenerate', popularised by the press accounts, was always inherent in descriptions of Benin culture. This incredulity at the African's skill should also alert us to the fact that the degree to which the European credited a society with making 'works of art' (technically, conceptually and in terms of design) was not necessarily commensurate with any reassessment of their position on the evolutionary ladder. Indeed, the value of the brasses and ivories was considerably enhanced by actually reinforcing their origins as African and by stressing their status as an anomaly in terms of other examples of African carving and casting. Through such a procedure their notoriety was assured. Their value as 'freak' productions in turn enhanced the status of the museum in which they were held.

[...] The ethnographic curators' decision to assign an African, as opposed to Egyptian, origin to the bronzes placed these contested and now highly desirable objects squarely in the domain of the Ethnographic department, rather than ambiguously positioned between Egyptology and European Antiquities. This highlighted the importance of ethnography as opposed to the already well-endowed Egyptology department in the Museum. How far such a hypothesis was a deliberate strategy for more recognition on the part of the ethnographers remains a matter of conjecture. Yet one thing is certain: this history is instructive of the kinds of negotiative processes by which 'scientific' knowledge of the culture of the colonies was produced, and gives the lie to a simplistic empirical account which takes such narratives at face value, without acknowledging the institutional and other political factors at play.

REFERENCES

LING ROTH, H. (1898) 'Notes on Benin art', *Reliquary*, V, 167.

PITT RIVERS MUSEUM (1898) E. B. Tylor Papers, Box 6 (1) and (2). Pitt Rivers to E. B. Tylor, 7 August 1898.

PITT RIVERS MUSEUM (1900) *Annual Report of the Pitt Rivers Museum 1900*, Oxford, Pitt Rivers Museum.

QUICK, R. (1899) 'Notes on Benin carvings', *Reliquary*, V, 248–55.

READ, C. H. AND DALTON, O. M. (1898) 'Works of art from Benin City', *Journal of the Anthropological Institute*, XXVII, 362–82.

Source: Coombes, 1994a, pp. 7, 23, 26, 27, 44–8, 57–9, 61–2, 146–7.

READING F: John Picton, 'To see or not to see! That is the question'

This brief essay is a response to "African Terra Cottas: A Millenary Heritage,", the recent exhibition at the Barbier-Mueller Museum, Geneva. We know […] that some people will say this material is all illegal and that, for that reason alone, it should not be shown. […] [T]here are others who will say: But this is great art, it belongs to the world, and we should not be prevented from seeing it by a misplaced act of political correctness. What are we to think? […] After all the antiquities of Mali, Nigeria, and elsewhere in Africa are indeed great art, and yet illegal excavation inevitably entails the destruction of knowledge and largely unknown civilizations.

This is not a new problem, nor is it a specifically African problem. […]

All works of art have histories, not because of anything inherent in the artefacts themselves, but because of the often very complex relationships between people and the things they make, and the things they see others making. There are bound to be aspects of this narrative that make us feel uncomfortable. None of us want knowledge of the African past effaced through ignorance and illegality. […] In our assessment of the problems concerning the movement of things from one part of the world to another, we must accept, whether we like it or not, that illegal excavation, theft, tomb robbing, appropriation by one means or another, as well as legitimate sale, have as great antiquity as the very things we wish to preserve, study, and rejoice in.

I have already cited some African examples: ancient Egypt, Axum, Asante; so, what about the art of Benin City? This material is located not just in the British Museum: The largest collection is in Berlin, while every major museum from St Petersburg to Los Angeles has something. If we are to engage in a process of restitution, at what point do our claims cease? […] We can do nothing about the ancestral sculpture from Oron in southeastern Nigeria which were chopped up for firewood in a hungry Biafra, but what are we to make of the looting of Igbo sculptures by Nigerian soldiers during the civil war in the late 1960s, which ended up as trophies fixed to the fronts of military vehicles, while much else found its way into the international market. Once the war was over, Igbo sculptors carved new masks, just as in Benin City brass casters made new works of art for ongoing cult and ceremonial needs in the reinvention of the kingdom under the leadership of Eweka II. […]

When we consider the presence of African art in 'the West' it is obvious that there always were several means whereby these things arrived here. Military plunder, as in Benin City […], is one; and while we would no longer find this morally acceptable, the Nigerian civil war example suggests the plunder still happens. Other means of acquisition include legitimate gift, exchange or purchase […] I would include, here, the acquisition of material in the former Belgian Congo by Emil Torday for the British Museum a century ago. […] [T]he presence of this material in 'the West' cannot possibly be regarded as contentious. Theft is another route; and […] many of us know well is that in the 1990s both the museum and the university in Ife [Nigeria] were subjected to armed robbery. One would hope that no-one in 'the West' would knowingly purchase such material unless the purpose was to give it all back to the Ife museums it was stolen from. On the other hand, there is the complication of legal sale but illicit export. […] What are we to do? In the end, rhetorical questions and stereotypical attitudes will get us nowhere, so here are a few suggestions.

First, we must continue, for what it's worth, to condemn illegal excavation. […] [S]ites in Nigeria, ancient Jenne, and elsewhere […] have been plundered and the possibilities of our knowing these civilizations very considerably disabled. […] Tragically, there is no getting away from the fact that Nigerians, Malians, and others in West Africa have […] been instrumental in destroying their own cultural heritage in order to feed those of 'the West', the collectors and connoisseurs who are unlucky enough to possess more money than sense. […]

Nevertheless legitimate archaeological excavation could succeed in countering illegal work, but only if funding and trained personnel were expanded […]. The trouble is that most of the funding would have to come from 'the West', and it is hard to imagine such an eventuality. […] Can […] the governments of the countries concerned find ways of legitimizing the activities currently deemed illegal? I would accept that this is highly problematic. […] In West Africa there is just too much money still to be made through illegality and it won't be stopped by right-minded people […] Unless or until governments – in Africa and the 'West' – can do more to fund and otherwise encourage legitimate excavation by trained personnel, this will remain a lost cause.

Secondly, for all existing collections, their best protection is publication and photography. Then at least no-one can legitimately claim ignorance. […] Nevertheless, publication stands as a second line of offence, following expanded excavation and research programs. The trouble is, this too costs money. […] Moreover, it is so often the case that in the museums in West Africa I am most familiar with, photography is forbidden. This is a huge mistake. Most photographers are neither thieves nor gunmen, but merely innocent bystanders who want a record of their journey and the things they saw; there could be times when it is only the photographs snapped by a tourist that could provide the evidence needed to prove a theft. […]

A third line of defence against the present situation is the publicity that comes from exhibition and display; this brings us right back to the ceramic sculptures, presumed by some to be the results of illegal plunder, on display at the Barbier-Mueller Museum in Geneva. Should material that might in whole or in part entail illegal activity be placed on display for people to see and admire? Of course it should, provided there is no attempt to cover up or otherwise deny the facts or possibilities of illegality. […] [I]t remains appropriate to know (most of) the truth about a work or a collection. At least we get to know where things are; and it's not as if museums and universities in Africa already have all the facilities needed for the proper care and display of antiquities and works of art. […] For the moment […] even if something might come from an illegal excavation, even if it might have been removed from its country of origin by illicit means, it is better for it to be on display in the public domain because at least then the facts of the matter have a chance of being assembled and the situation assessed. Moreover, it cannot be forgotten that as religious affiliations change in Africa and objects are no longer needed for the ritual affairs of a community, they inevitably will either rot away or pass into some other framework of ownership. Theft is always reprehensible [...] but people do have the right to sell or otherwise dispose of things they no longer need. The fact that a work of art, once in a shrine or temple, is now in a museum, wherever that museum might be, cannot automatically imply that the process of its disposal was necessarily illegal. More research is the only answer. [...]

As for the several thousand works of art taken by British Military personnel from Benin City in 1897, we have to remember four significant facts. First, the context from which this material came no longer exists. When Benin was reinvented in the years following the accession of Eweka II in 1914, the pre-1897 palace had been destroyed. There was no record of its layout, and no records kept as to where things were taken from. We cannot, in other words, put anything back where it once was. Second, Benin art is now scattered though the museums of the world. The three most comprehensive collections are Berlin, the British Museum and Lagos (purchased back by colonial government in the 1940s–1950s), but many museums may have just a few [...] pieces. The very idea of coordinated repatriation is hard to imagine. Third, many of the works of art cast in the years since 1914 have been stolen from the shrines of the royal palace, suggesting that Nigeria is not yet a safe place for its works of art. Fourth, if material were repatriated, where would it go? There is no facility currently in Nigeria [...]. However, suppose there were? Just suppose that in Benin City a secure display and conservation facility with appropriate climatic control had been built; it would be very hard to resist the proposal that material not required for display should be returned to Benin City where it could be seen in a city in the context of its ongoing circumstances of ritual and ceremonial. This is a vision worth holding on to, yet it would not be repatriation to an original context, but the inception of an entirely new context in which to view the art of Benin City.

There is, of course, a great difference between the plunder of the present and booty looted by military personnel in a past age. Most countries in West Africa, indeed throughout the continent, have museums, archaeologists, and some form of legal protection for antiquities. A century ago this was not the case; and while this does not excuse military plunder, it does place the depredations of our present age in a context in which the institutions of a modern nation state have been violated and its laws broken. [...] Illegal excavation violates an archaeological context, for the material removed cannot be put back: the context of discovery no longer exists. Nevertheless when an archaeological site has been looted or a museum robbed, there is a clear-cut framework for the restitution of the works of art concerned [...]

[...] I [...] think it is better for works of art and antiquities to be placed in the public domain through exhibition and publication than hidden away for the private delight of a few. Then at least we can know the material for what it is, and there is the hope that, sooner or later, an appropriate program of research and publication will ensue. The plunder will not stop just because museums and galleries refuse to show the things that come out of these illegal activities. [...] Museums and galleries should not be condemned for showing

John Picton

illegally excavated material but they should be criticized for any failure to acknowledge the illicit status of the material that they exhibit.

If collectors and museums feel uncomfortable about this, the remedy is simple: Stop collecting dodgy material. If […] they wish to acquire works of art that have been removed from their previous circumstances by (possibly) illegitimate means, they should be able to do so provided they have first sought the permission of the relevant African government […] [T]hey must also be prepared to take a proactive role in assisting the processes of legitimate research and its publication and display, and there must be an unambiguous acceptance of the principle of repatriating stolen museum material. To this end, the Barbier-Mueller Museum in Geneva should be congratulated for letting us see the art and consider the problems it raises.

Source: Picton, 2010, pp. 1, 4–6.

CHAPTER FOUR

THE SPECTACLE OF THE 'OTHER'

Stuart Hall

1 INTRODUCTION

How do we represent people and places which are significantly different from us? Why is 'difference' so compelling a theme, so contested an area of representation? What is the secret fascination of 'otherness', and why is popular representation so frequently drawn to it? What are the typical forms and representational practices which are used to represent 'difference' in popular culture today, and where did these popular figures and stereotypes come from? These are some of the questions about representation which we set out to address in this chapter. We will pay particular attention to those representational practices which we call 'stereotyping'. By the end we hope you will understand better how what we call 'the spectacle of the "Other"' works, and be able to apply the ideas discussed and the sorts of analysis undertaken here to the mass of related materials in contemporary popular culture – for example, advertising which uses black models, newspaper reports about immigration, racial attacks or urban crime, and films and magazines which deal with 'race' and ethnicity as significant themes.

The theme of 'representing difference' is picked up directly from the previous chapter, where Henrietta Lidchi looked at how 'other cultures' are given meaning by the discourses and practices of exhibition in ethnographic museums of 'the West'. Chapter 3 focused on the 'poetics' and the 'politics' of exhibiting – both how other cultures are made to signify through the discourses of exhibition (poetics) and how these practices are inscribed by relations of power (politics) – especially those which prevail between the people who are represented and the cultures and institutions doing the representing. Many of the same concerns arise again in this chapter. However, here, *racial and ethnic* difference is foregrounded. You should bear in mind, however, that what is said about racial difference could equally be applied in many instances to other dimensions of difference, such as gender, sexuality, class and disability.

Our focus here is the variety of images which are on display in popular culture and the mass media. Some are commercial advertising images and magazine illustrations which use racial stereotypes, dating from the period of slavery or from the popular imperialism of the late nine-teenth century. However, Chapter 4 brings the story up to the present. Indeed, it begins with images from the competitive world of modern athletics. The question which this comparison across time poses is: have the repertoires of representation around 'difference' and 'otherness' changed or do earlier traces remain intact in contemporary society?

The chapter looks in depth at theories about the representational practice known as 'stereotyp-ing'. However, the theoretical discussion is threaded through the examples, rather than being intro-duced for its own sake. The chapter ends by considering a number of different strategies designed to intervene in the field of representation, to contest 'negative' images and transform representational practices around 'race' in a more 'positive' direction. It poses the question of whether there can be an effective 'politics of representation'.

Once again, then, *visual* representation takes centre stage. The chapter sustains the overall theme by continuing our exploration of *representation* as a concept and a practice – the key first 'moment' in the cultural circuit. Our aim is to deepen our understanding of what representation is and how it works. Representation is a complex business and, especially when dealing with 'dif-ference', it engages feelings, attitudes and emotions and it mobilizes fears and anxieties in the viewer, at deeper levels than we can explain in a simple, common-sense way. This is why we need theories – to deepen our analysis. The chapter, then, builds on what we have already learned about representation as a signifying practice, and continues to develop critical concepts to explain its operations.

1.1 Heroes or villains?

Look, first, at Figure 4.1. It is a picture of the men's 100 metres final at the 1988 Olympics which appeared on the cover of the Olympics Special of the *Sunday Times* colour magazine (9 October 1988). It shows the black Canadian sprinter, Ben Johnson, winning in record time from Carl Lewis and Linford Christie: five superb athletes in action, at the peak of their physical prowess. All of them men and – perhaps, now, you will notice consciously for the first time – all of them black!

ACTIVITY 1

How do you 'read' the picture – what is it saying? In Barthes's terms, what is its 'myth' – its underlying message?

One possible message relates to their racial identity. These athletes are all from a racially defined group – one often discriminated against precisely on the grounds of their 'race' and colour, whom we are more accustomed to see depicted in the news as the victims or 'losers' in terms of achievement. Yet here they are, winning!

In terms of difference, then, a positive message: a triumphant moment, a cause for celebration. Why, then, does the caption say, 'Heroes and villains'? Who do you think is the hero, who the villain?

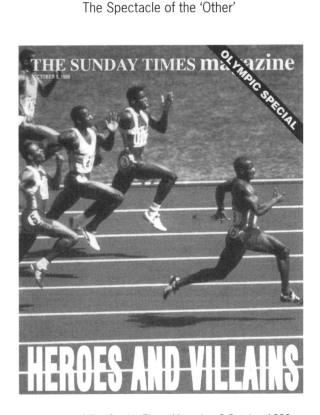

FIGURE 4.1 'Heroes and villains', cover of *The Sunday Times Magazine,* 9 October 1988

Even if you don't follow athletics, the answer isn't difficult to discover. Ostensibly about the Olympics, the photo is in fact a trailer for the magazine's lead story about the growing menace of drug-taking in international athletics – what inside is called 'The Chemical Olympics'. Ben Johnson, you may recall, was found to have taken drugs to enhance his performance. He was disqualified, the gold medal being awarded to Carl Lewis, and Johnson was expelled from world athletics in disgrace. The story suggests that *all* athletes – black or white – are potentially 'heroes' and 'villains'. But in this image, Ben Johnson personifies this split in a particular way. He is *both* 'hero' and 'villain'. He encapsulates the extreme alternatives of heroism and villainy in world athletics in one black body.

There are several points to make about the way the representation of 'race' and 'otherness' is working in this photo. First, if you think back to Chapters 1 and 3, you will remember the work of Barthes on the idea of 'myth'. This photo, too, functions at the level of 'myth'. There is a literal, denotative level of meaning – this *is* a picture of the 100 metres final and the figure in front *is* Ben Johnson. Then there is the more connotative or thematic meaning – the drug story. And within that, there is the sub-theme of 'race' and 'difference'. Already, this tells us something important about how 'myth' works. The image is a very powerful one, as visual images often are. But its *meaning* is highly ambiguous. It can carry more than one meaning. If you didn't know the context, you might be tempted to read this as a moment of unqualified triumph. And you wouldn't be 'wrong' since this, too, is a perfectly acceptable meaning to take from the image. But, as the caption suggests, it is *not* produced here as an image of 'unqualified triumph'. So, the same photo can carry several, quite different, sometimes diametrically opposite meanings. It can be a picture of disgrace or of triumph, or both. Many meanings, we might say, are potential within the photo. But there is no one, true meaning. Meaning 'floats'. It cannot be finally fixed. However, attempting to 'fix' it is the work of a representational practice, which intervenes in the many potential meanings of an image in an attempt to privilege one.

So, rather than a 'right' or 'wrong' meaning, what we need to ask is, 'Which of the many meanings in this image does the magazine mean to privilege?' Which is the **preferred meaning**? Ben Johnson is the key element here because he is both an amazing athlete, winner and record-breaker, *and* the athlete who was publicly disgraced because of drug-taking. So, as it turns out, the preferred meaning is *both* 'heroism' and 'villainy'. It wants to say something paradoxical like, 'In the moment of the hero's triumph, there is also villainy and moral defeat.' In part, we know this is the preferred meaning which the magazine wants the photo to convey because this is the meaning which is singled out in the caption: 'Heroes and villains'. Roland Barthes (1977) argues that, frequently, it is the caption which selects one out of the many possible meanings from the image, and *anchors* it with words. The 'meaning' of the photograph, then, does not lie exclusively in the image, but in the conjunction of image *and* text. Two discourses – the discourse of written language and the discourse of photography – are required to produce and 'fix' the meaning (see Hall, 1972).

FIGURE 4.2 Linford Christie, holding a Union Jack, having won the men's 100 metres Olympic gold medal, Barcelona, 1992

As we have suggested, this photo can also be 'read', connotatively, in terms of what it has to 'say' about 'race'. Here, the message could be – black people shown being good at something, winning *at last*! But in the light of the 'preferred meaning', hasn't the meaning with respect to 'race' and 'otherness' changed as well? Isn't it more something like, 'even when black people are shown at the summit of their achievement, they often fail to carry it off'? This having-it-both-ways is important because, as I hope to show you, people who are in any way significantly different from the majority – 'them' rather than 'us' – are frequently exposed to this *binary* form of representation. They seem to be represented through sharply opposed, polarized, binary extremes – good/bad, civilized/primitive, ugly/excessively attractive, repelling-because-different/ compelling-because-strange-and-exotic. And they are often required to be *both things at the same time*! We will return to these split figures or 'tropes' of representation in a moment.

But first, let us look at another, similar news photo, this time from another record-breaking 100 metres final. Linford Christie, subsequently captain of the British Olympics squad, at the peak of his career, having just won the race of a lifetime. The picture captures his elation, at the moment of his lap of honour. He is holding the Union Jack. In the light of the earlier discussion, how do you 'read' *this* photograph (Figure 4.2)? What is it 'saying' about 'race' and cultural identity?

ACTIVITY 2

Which of the following statements, in your view, comes closest to expressing the 'message' of the image?

a 'This is the greatest moment of my life! A triumph for me, Linford Christie.'

b 'This is a moment of triumph for me and a celebration for black people everywhere!'

c 'This is a moment of triumph and celebration for the British Olympic team and the British people!'

d 'This is a moment of triumph and celebration for black people and the British Olympic team. It shows that you can be "Black" and "British"!'

There is, of course, no 'right' or 'wrong' answer to the question. The image carries many meanings, all equally plausible. What is important is the fact that this image both shows an event (denotation) and carries a 'message' or meaning (connotation) – Barthes would call it a 'meta-message' or *myth* – about 'race', colour and 'otherness'. We can't help reading images of this kind as 'saying something', not just about the people or the occasion, but about their 'otherness', their 'difference'. *'Difference' has been marked.* How it is then interpreted is a constant and recurring preoccupation in the representation of people who are racially and ethnically different from the majority population. Difference signifies. It 'speaks'.

In a later interview, discussing his forthcoming retirement from international sport, Christie commented on the question of his cultural identity – where he feels he 'belongs' (*The Sunday Independent*, 11 November 1995). He has very fond memories of Jamaica, he said, where he was born and lived until the age of seven. But 'I've lived here [in the UK] for 28 [years]. I can't be anything other than British' (p. 18). Of course, it isn't as simple as that. Christie is perfectly well aware that most definitions of 'Britishness' assume that the person who belongs is 'white'. It is much harder for black people, wherever they were born, to be accepted as 'British'. In 1995, the cricket magazine, *Wisden*, had to pay libel damages to black athletes for saying that they couldn't be expected to display the same loyalty and commitment to winning for England because they are black. So Christie knows that every image is *also* being 'read' in terms of this broader question of cultural belongingness and difference.

Indeed, he made his remarks in the context of the negative publicity to which he has been exposed in some sections of the British tabloid press, a good deal of which hinges on a vulgar, unstated but widely recognized 'joke' at his expense: namely that the tight-fitting Lycra shorts which he wears are said to reveal the size and shape of his genitals. This was the detail on which the *Sun* focused on the morning after he won an Olympic gold medal. Christie has been subject to continuous teasing in the tabloid press about the prominence and size of his 'lunchbox' – a euphemism which some have taken so literally that, he revealed, he has been approached by a firm wanting to market its lunchboxes around his image! Linford Christie has observed about these innuendoes: 'I felt humiliated ... My first instinct was that it was racist. There we are, stereotyping a black man. I can take a good joke. But it happened the day after I won the greatest accolade an athlete can win ... I don't want to go through life being known for what I've got in my shorts. I'm a serious person' (p. 15).

ACTIVITY 3

What is going on here? Is this just a joke in bad taste, or does it have a deeper meaning? What do sexuality and gender have to do with images of black men and women? Why did the black French writer from Martinique, Frantz Fanon, say that white people seem to be obsessed with the sexuality of black people?

It is the subject of a widespread fantasy, Fanon says, which fixates the black man at the level of the genitals. 'One is no longer aware of the Negro, but only of a penis; the Negro is eclipsed. He is turned into a penis' (Fanon, 1986 [1952], p. 170).

What, for example, did the French writer, Michael Cournot, whom Fanon quotes, mean when he wrote that 'Four Negroes with their penises exposed would fill a cathedral'? (Fanon, 1986 [1952], p. 169). What is the relationship of these fantasies of sexuality to 'race' and ethnicity in the representation of 'otherness' and 'difference'?

We have now introduced another dimension into the representation of 'difference' – adding sexuality and gender to 'race', ethnicity and colour. Of course, it is well established that sport is one of the few areas where black people have had outstanding success. It seems natural that images of black people drawn from sport should emphasize the body, which is the instrument of

FIGURE 4.3 Florence Griffith-Joyner in the *Sunday Times*, 1988

athletic skill and achievement. It is difficult, however, to have images of bodies in action, at the peak of their physical perfection, without those images also, in some way, carrying 'messages' about *gender* and about *sexuality*. Where black athletes are concerned, what are these messages about?

ACTIVITY 4

Look, for example, at the picture from the *Sunday Times* 1988 Olympic Special, of the black American sprinter, Florence Griffith-Joyner, who won three gold medals at Seoul (Figure 4.3). Can you 'read' this photo without getting some 'messages' about 'race', gender and sexuality – even if what the meanings are remain ambiguous? Is there any doubt that the photo is 'signifying' along all three dimensions? In representation, one sort of difference seems to attract others – adding up to a 'spectacle' of otherness. If you're not convinced, you might think of this in the context of the remark by 'Flo-Jo's' husband, Al Joyner, quoted in the text next to the photo: 'Someone Says My Wife Looked Like A Man'. Or consider the photo (which was reproduced on the following page of the article) of Al Joyner's sister, Jackie Joyner-Kersee, who also won a gold medal and broke world records at Seoul in the heptathlon, preparing to throw a javelin, accompanied by text quoting another observation by Al Joyner: 'Somebody Says My Sister Looked Like A Gorilla' (Figure 4.4).

FIGURE 4.4 Jackie Joyner-Kersee in the *Sunday Times,* 1988

There is an additional point to be made about these photographs of black athletes in the press. They gain in meaning when they are read in context, against or in connection with one another. This is another way of saying that images do not carry meaning or 'signify' on their own. They accumulate meanings, or play off their meanings against one another, across a variety of texts and media. Each image carries its own, specific meaning. But at the broader level of how 'difference' and 'otherness' is being represented in a particular culture at any one moment, we can see similar representational practices and figures being repeated, with variations, from one text or site of representation to another. This accumulation of meanings across different texts, where one image refers to another, or has its meaning altered by being 'read' in the context of other images, is called **inter-textuality**. We may describe the whole repertoire of imagery and visual effects through which 'difference' is represented at any one historical moment as a *regime of representation*.

An interesting example of *inter-textuality*, where the image depends for its meaning on being 'read' in relation to a number of other, similar images, can be found in Figure 4.5. This is Carl Lewis, one of the sprinters you saw in Figure 4.1, taken from a Pirelli advertisement. At first glance, the image summons up echoes of all the previous images we have been looking at – superbly honed athletic bodies, tensed in action, super-men and super-women. But here the meaning is differently

FIGURE 4.5 Carl Lewis, photographed for a Pirelli advertisement

inflected. Pirelli is a tyre firm with a reputation for producing calendars with pictures of beautiful women, scantily clad, in provocative poses – the prototypical 'pin-up'. In which of these two contexts should we 'read' the Carl Lewis image? One clue lies in the fact that, though Lewis is male, in the ad he is wearing elegant, high-heeled red shoes!

ACTIVITY 5

What is *this* image saying? What is *its* message? How does it 'say' it?

This image works by the marking of 'difference'. The conventional identification of Lewis with black male athletes and with a sort of 'super-masculinity' is disturbed and undercut by the invocation of his 'femininity' – and what marks this is the signifier of the red shoes. The sexual and racial 'message' is rendered ambiguous. The super-male black athlete may not be all he seems. The ambiguity is amplified when we compare this image with all the other images – the stereotypes we are accustomed to see – of black athletes in the press. Its meaning is inter-textual – i.e. it requires to be read 'against the grain'.

ACTIVITY 6

Does this photo reinforce or subvert the stereotype? Some people say it's just an advertiser's joke. Some argue that Carl Lewis has allowed himself to be exploited by a big corporate advertiser. Others argue that he deliberately set out to challenge and contest the traditional image of black masculinity. What do you think?

In the light of these examples, we can rephrase our original questions more precisely. Why is 'otherness' so compelling an object of representation? What does the marking of racial difference tell us about representation as a practice? Through which representational practices are racial and ethnic difference and 'otherness' signified? What are the 'discursive formations', the repertoires or regimes of representation, on which the media are drawing when they represent 'difference'? Why is one dimension of difference – e.g. 'race' – crossed by other dimensions, such as sexuality, gender and class? And how is the representation of 'difference' linked with questions of power?

1.2 Why does 'difference' matter?

Before we analyse any more examples, let us examine some of the underlying issues posed by our first question. Why does 'difference' matter? How can we explain this fascination with 'otherness'? What theoretical arguments can we draw on to help us unpack this question?

Questions of 'difference' have come to the fore in cultural studies in recent decades and been addressed in different ways by different disciplines. In this section, we briefly consider *four* such theoretical accounts. As we discuss them, think back to the examples we have just analysed. In each, we start by showing how important 'difference' is – by considering what is said to be its positive aspect. But we follow this by some of the more negative aspects of 'difference'. Putting these two together suggests why 'difference' is both necessary and dangerous.

1   The first account comes from linguistics – from the sort of approach associated with Saussure and the use of language as a model of how culture works, which was discussed in Chapter 1. The main argument advanced here is that *'difference' matters because it is essential to meaning; without it, meaning could not exist.* You may remember from Chapter 1 the example of *white/black.* We know what *black* means, Saussure argued, not because there is some essence of 'blackness' but because we can contrast it with its opposite – *white.* Meaning, he argued, is relational. It is the *'difference'* between *white* and *black* which signifies, which carries meaning. Carl Lewis in that photo can represent 'femininity' or the 'feminine' side of masculinity because he can *mark his 'difference'* from the traditional stereotypes of black masculinity by using the *red shoes* as a signifier. This principle holds for broader concepts too. We know what it is to be 'British', not only because of certain national characteristics, but also because we can mark its 'difference' from its 'others' – 'Britishness' is not-French, not-American, not-German, not-Pakistani, not-Jamaican,

and so on. This enables Linford Christie to signify his 'Britishness' (by the flag) while contesting (by his black skin) that 'Britishness' must always mean 'whiteness'. Again, 'difference' signifies. It carries a message.

So meaning depends on the difference between opposites. However, when we discussed this argument in Chapter 1, we recognized that, though binary oppositions – *white/black, day/night, masculine/feminine, British/alien* – have the great value of capturing the diversity of the world within their either/or extremes, they are also a rather crude and reductionist way of establishing meaning. For example, in so-called black-and-white photography, there is actually no pure 'black' or 'white', only varying shades of grey. 'Black' shades imperceptibly into 'white', just as men have *both* 'masculine' and 'feminine' sides to their nature; and Linford Christie certainly wants to affirm the possibility of being both 'black' *and* 'British' though the normal definition of 'Britishness' assumes that it is white.

Thus, while we do not seem able to do without them, binary oppositions are also open to the charge of being reductionist and over-simplified – swallowing up all distinctions in their rather rigid two-part structure. What is more, as the philosopher Jacques Derrida has argued, there are very few neutral binary oppositions. One pole of the binary, he argues, is usually the dominant one, the one which includes the other within its field of operations. There is always a relation of power between the poles of a binary opposition (Derrida, 1972). We should really write, **white**/*black*, **men**/*women*, **masculine**/*feminine*, **upper class**/*lower class*, **British**/*alien* to capture this power dimension in discourse.

2 The second explanation also comes from theories of language, but from a somewhat different school from that represented by Saussure. *The argument here is that we need 'difference' because we can only construct meaning through a dialogue with the 'Other'.* The great Russian linguist and critic, Mikhail Bakhtin, who fell foul of the Stalinist regime in the 1940s, studied language, not (as the Saussureans did) as an objective system, but in terms of how meaning is sustained in the *dialogue* between two or more speakers. Meaning, Bakhtin argued, does not belong to any one speaker. It arises in the give-and-take between different speakers. 'The word in language is half someone else's. It becomes "one's own" only when ... the speaker appropriates the word, adapting it to his own semantic expressive intention. Prior to this ... the word does not exist in a neutral or impersonal language ... rather it exists in other people's mouths, serving other people's intentions: it is from there that one must take the word and make it one's own' (Bakhtin, 1981 [1935], pp. 293–4). Bakhtin and his collaborator, Volosinov, believed that this enabled us to enter into a struggle over meaning, breaking one set of associations and giving words a new inflection. Meaning, Bakhtin argued, is established through dialogue – it is fundamentally *dialogic*. Everything we say and mean is modified by the interaction and interplay with another person. Meaning arises through the 'difference' between the participants in any dialogue. *The 'Other', in short, is essential to meaning.*

This is the positive side of Bakhtin's theory. The negative side is, of course, that therefore meaning cannot be fixed and that one group can never be completely in charge of meaning. What it means to be 'British' or 'Russian' or 'Jamaican' cannot be entirely controlled by the British, Russians or Jamaicans, but is always up for grabs, always being negotiated, in the dialogue between these national cultures and their 'others'. Thus it has been argued that you cannot know what it meant to be 'British' in the nineteenth century until you know what the British thought of Jamaica, their prize colony in the Caribbean, or Ireland, and more disconcertingly, *what the Jamaicans or the Irish thought of them* ... (Hall, 1994).

3 The third kind of explanation is anthropological, and you have already met it in **Du Gay et al**. (1997). The argument here is that culture depends on giving things meaning by assigning them to different positions within a classificatory system. The marking of 'difference' is thus the basis of that symbolic order which we call culture. Mary Douglas, following the classic work on symbolic systems by the French sociologist, Emile Durkheim, and the later studies of mythology by the French anthropologist, Claude Lévi-Strauss, argues that social groups impose meaning on their world by ordering and organizing things into classificatory systems (Douglas, 1966). Binary oppositions are crucial for all classification, because one must establish a clear difference between things in order to classify them. Faced with different kinds of food, Lévi-Strauss argued (1970), one way of giving them meaning is to start by dividing them into two groups – those which are eaten 'raw' and those eaten 'cooked'. Of course, you can also classify food into 'vegetables' and 'fruit'; or into those which are eaten as 'starters' and those which are eaten as 'desserts'; or those which are served up at dinner and those which are eaten at a sacred feast or the communion table. Here, again, 'difference' is fundamental to cultural meaning.

However, it can also give rise to negative feelings and practices. Mary Douglas argues that what really disturbs cultural order is when things turn up in the wrong category; or when things fail to fit any category – such as a substance like mercury, which is a metal but also a liquid, or a social group like mixed-race *mulattoes*, who are neither 'white' nor 'black' but float ambiguously in some unstable, dangerous, hybrid zone of indeterminacy in-between (Stallybrass and White, 1986). Stable cultures require things to stay in their appointed place. Symbolic boundaries keep the categories 'pure', giving cultures their unique meaning and identity. What unsettles culture is 'matter out of place' – the breaking of our unwritten rules and codes. Dirt in the garden is fine, but dirt in one's bedroom is 'matter out of place' – a sign of pollution, of symbolic boundaries being transgressed, of taboos broken. What we do with 'matter out of place' is to sweep it up, throw it out, restore the place to order, bring back the normal state of affairs. The retreat of many cultures towards 'closure' against foreigners, intruders, aliens and 'others' is part of the same process of purification (Kristeva, 1982).

According to this argument, then, symbolic boundaries are central to all culture. Marking 'difference' leads us, symbolically, to close ranks, shore up culture and to stigmatize and expel anything which is defined as impure, abnormal. However, paradoxically, it also makes 'difference' powerful, strangely attractive precisely because it is forbidden, taboo, threatening to cultural order. Thus, 'what is socially peripheral is often symbolically centred' (Babcock, 1978, p. 32).

4   The fourth kind of explanation is psychoanalytic and relates to the role of 'difference' in our psychic life. *The argument here is that the 'Other' is fundamental to the constitution of the self to us as subjects, and to sexual identity.* According to Freud, the consolidation of our definitions of 'self' and of our sexual identities depends on the way we are formed as subjects, especially in relation to that stage of early development which he called the Oedipus complex (after the Oedipus story in Greek mythology). A unified sense of oneself as a subject and one's sexual identity – Freud argued – are not fixed in the very young child. However, according to Freud's version of the Oedipus myth, at a certain point the boy develops an unconscious erotic attraction to the Mother, but finds the Father barring his way to 'satisfaction'. However, when he discovers that women do not have a penis, he assumes that his Mother was punished by castration, and that he might be punished in the same way if he persists with his unconscious desire. In fear, he switches his identification to his old 'rival', the Father, thereby taking on the beginnings of an identification with a masculine identity. The girl child identifies the opposite way – with the Father. But she cannot 'be' him, since she lacks the penis. She can only 'win' him by being willing, unconsciously, to bear a man's child – thereby taking up and identifying with the Mother's role, and 'becoming feminine'.

This model of how *sexual 'difference'* begins to be assumed in very young children has been strongly contested. Many people have questioned its speculative character. On the other hand, it has been very influential, as well as extensively amended by later analysts. The French psychoanalyst, Jacques Lacan (1977), for example, went further than Freud, arguing that the child has no sense of itself as a subject separate from its mother until it sees itself in a mirror, or as if mirrored in the way it is looked at by the Mother. Through identification, 'it desires the object of her desire, thus focusing its libido on itself (see Segal, 1997). It is this reflection from outside oneself, or what Lacan calls the 'look from the place of the other', during 'the mirror stage', which allows the child for the first time to recognize itself as a unified subject, relate to the outside world, to the 'Other', develop language and take on a sexual identity. (Lacan actually says, 'mis-recognize itself, since he believes the subject can never be fully unified.) Melanie Klein (1957), on the other hand, argued that the young child copes with this problem of a lack of a stable self by splitting its unconscious image of and identification with the Mother into its 'good' and 'bad' parts, internalizing some aspects, and projecting others on to the outside world. The common element in all these different versions of Freud is the role which is given by these different theorists to the 'Other' in subjective development. Subjectivity can only arise and a sense of 'self' be formed through the symbolic and unconscious relations which the young child forges with a significant 'Other' which is outside – i.e. different from – itself.

At first sight, these psychoanalytic accounts seem to be positive in their implications for 'difference'. Our subjectivities, they argue, depend on our unconscious relations with significant others. However, there are also negative implications. The psychoanalytic perspective assumes that there is no such thing as a given, stable inner core to 'the self' or to identity. Psychically, we are never fully unified as subjects. Our subjectivities are formed through this troubled, never-completed, unconscious dialogue with – this internalization of – the 'Other'. It is formed in relation to something which completes us but which – since it lies outside us – we in some way always lack.

What's more, they say, this troubling split or division within subjectivity can never be fully healed. Some indeed see this as one of the main sources of neurosis in adults. Others see psychic problems arising from the splitting between the 'good' and 'bad' parts of the self – being pursued internally by the 'bad' aspects one has taken into oneself, or alternatively, projecting on to others the 'bad' feelings one cannot deal with. Frantz Fanon (referred to earlier), who used psychoanalytic theory in his explanation of racism, argued (1986 [1952]) that much racial stereotyping and violence arose from the refusal of the white 'Other' to give recognition 'from the place of the other', to the black person (see Bhabha, 1986b; Hall, 1996).

These debates about 'difference' and the 'Other' have been introduced because this chapter draws selectively on all of them in the course of analysing racial representation. It is not necessary at this stage for you to prefer one explanation of 'difference' over others, or to choose between them. They are not mutually exclusive since they refer to very different levels of analysis – the linguistic, the social, the cultural and the psychic levels respectively. However, there are two general points to note at this stage. First, from many different directions, and within many different disciplines, this question of 'difference' and 'otherness' has come to play an increasingly significant role. Secondly, 'difference' is **ambivalent**. It can be both positive and negative. It is both necessary for the production of meaning, the formation of language and culture, for social identities and a subjective sense of the self as a sexed subject – and at the same time, it is threatening, a site of danger, of negative feelings, of splitting, hostility and aggression towards the 'Other'. In what follows, you should always bear in mind this ambivalent character of 'difference', its divided legacy.

2 RACIALIZING THE 'OTHER'

Holding these theoretical 'tools' of analysis in reserve for a moment, let us now explore further some examples of the repertoires of representation and representational practices which have been used to mark racial difference and signify the racialized 'Other' in western popular culture. How was this archive formed and what were its typical figures and practices?

There are three major moments when the 'West' encountered black people, giving rise to an avalanche of popular representations based on the marking of racial difference. The first began with the sixteenth-century contact between European traders and the West African kingdoms, which provided a source of black slaves for three centuries. Its effects were to be found in slavery and in the post-slave societies of the New World (discussed in section 2.2). The second was the European colonization of Africa and the 'scramble' between the European powers for the control of colonial territory, markets and raw materials in the period of 'high Imperialism' (see below, section 2.1). The third was the post-Second World War migrations from the 'Third World' into Europe and North America (examples from this period are discussed in section 2.3). Western ideas about 'race' and images of racial difference were profoundly shaped by those three fateful encounters.

2.1 Commodity racism: Empire and the domestic world

We start with how images of racial difference drawn from the imperial encounter flooded British popular culture at the end of the nineteenth century. In the middle ages, the European image of Africa was ambiguous – a mysterious place, but often viewed positively: after all, the Coptic Church was one of the oldest 'overseas' Christian communities; black saints appeared in medieval Christian iconography; and Ethiopia's legendary 'Prester John', was reputed to be one of Christianity's most loyal supporters. Gradually, however, this image changed. Africans were declared to be the descendants of Ham, cursed in *The Bible* to be in perpetuity 'a servant of servants unto his brethren'. Identified with Nature, they symbolized 'the primitive' in contrast with 'the civilized world'. The Enlightenment, which ranked societies along an evolutionary scale from 'barbarism' to 'civilization', thought Africa 'the parent of everything that is monstrous in Nature' (Edward Long, 1774, quoted in McClintock, 1995, p. 22). Curvier dubbed the Negro race a 'monkey tribe'. The philosopher Hegel declared that Africa was 'no historical part of the world ... it has no movement or development to exhibit'. By the nineteenth century, when the European exploration and colonization of the African interior began in earnest, Africa was regarded as 'marooned and historically abandoned ... a fetish land, inhabited by cannibals, dervishes and witch doctors ...' (McClintock, 1995, p. 41).

The exploration and colonization of Africa produced an explosion of popular representations (Mackenzie, 1986). Our example here is the spread of imperial images and themes in Britain through commodity advertising in the closing decades of the nineteenth century.

The progress of the great white explorer-adventurers and the encounters with the black African exotic was charted, recorded and depicted in maps and drawings, etchings and (especially) the new photography, in newspaper illustrations and accounts, diaries, travel writing, learned treatises, official reports and 'boy's-own' adventure novels. Advertising was one means by which the imperial project was given visual form in a popular medium, forging the link between Empire and the domestic imagination. Anne McClintock argues that, through the racializing of advertisements (commodity racism), 'the Victorian middle-class home became a space for the display of imperial spectacle and the reinvention of race, while the colonies – in particular Africa – became a theatre for exhibiting the Victorian cult of domesticity and the reinvention of gender' (1995, p. 34).

Advertising for the objects, gadgets, gee-gaws and bric-a-brac with which the Victorian middle classes filled their homes provided an 'imaginary way of relating to the real world' of commodity production and, after 1890, with the rise of the popular press, from the *Illustrated London News* to the Harmsworth *Daily Mail*, the imagery of mass commodity production entered the world of the working classes via the spectacle of advertising (Richards, 1990). Richards calls it a 'spectacle' because advertising translated *things* into a fantasy visual display of *signs and symbols*. The production of commodities became linked to Empire – the search for markets and raw materials abroad supplanting other motives for imperial expansion.

This two-way traffic forged connections between imperialism and the domestic sphere, public and private. Commodities (and images of English domestic life) flowed outwards to the colonies;

raw materials (and images of 'the civilizing mission' in progress) were brought into the home. Henry Stanley, the imperial adventurer, who famously traced Livingstone ('Dr Livingstone, I presume?') in Central Africa in 1871, and was a founder of the infamous Congo Free State, tried to annex Uganda and open up the interior for the East Africa Company. He believed that the spread of commodities would make 'civilization' in Africa inevitable and named his native bearers after the branded goods they carried – Bryant and May, Remington, and so on. His exploits became

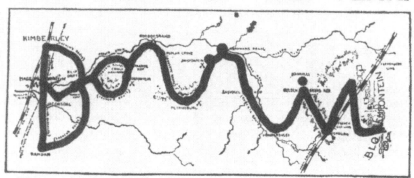

FIGURE 4.6 Bovril advertisement claiming to depict Lord Roberts' historical march from Kimberley to Bloemfontein during the South African (Boer) War, 1900

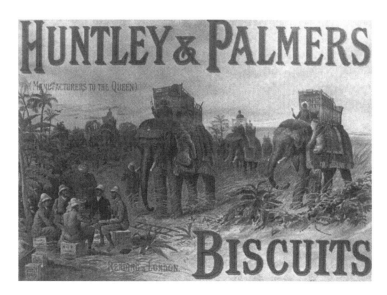

FIGURE 4.7 Huntley and Palmers' biscuit advertisement

 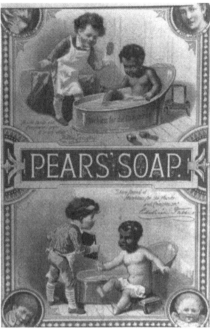

FIGURE 4.8   Nineteenth-century advertisements for Pears' Soap

associated with Pears' Soap, Bovril and various brands of tea. The gallery of imperial heroes and their masculine exploits in 'Darkest Africa' were immortalized on matchboxes, needle cases, toothpaste pots, pencil boxes, cigarette packets, board games, paperweights, sheet music. 'Images of colonial conquest were stamped on soap boxes ... biscuit tins, whisky bottles, tea tins and chocolate bars. ... No pre-existing form of organized racism had ever before been able to reach so large and so differentiated a mass of the populace' (McClintock, 1995, p. 209) (see Figures 4.6, 4.7 and 4.8).

Soap symbolized this 'racializing' of the domestic world and 'domestication' of the colonial world. In its capacity to cleanse and purify, soap acquired, in the fantasy world of imperial advertising, the quality of a fetish object. It apparently had the power to wash black skin white as well as being capable of washing off the soot, grime and dirt of the industrial slums and their inhabitants – the unwashed poor – at home, while at the same time keeping the imperial body clean and pure in the racially polluted contact zones 'out there' in the Empire. In the process, however, the domestic labour of women was often silently erased.

ACTIVITY 7

Look, now, at the two advertisements for Pears' Soap (Figure 4.8). Before reading further, write down briefly what you think these ads are 'saying'.

◄READING A

Now read Anne McClintock's analysis of Pears' advertising campaigns in Reading A: 'Soap and commodity spectacle' at the end of this chapter.

2.2 Meanwhile, down on the plantation ...

Our second example is from the period of plantation slavery and its aftermath. It has been argued that, in the USA, a fully-fledged racialized ideology did not appear among the slave-holding classes (and their supporters in Europe) until slavery was seriously challenged by the Abolitionists in the nineteenth century. Frederickson (1987) sums up the complex and sometimes contradictory set of beliefs about racial difference which took hold in this period:

> Heavily emphasized was the historical case against the black man based on his supposed failure to develop a civilized way of life in Africa. As portrayed in pro-slavery writing, Africa was and always had been the scene of unmitigated savagery, cannibalism, devil worship, and licentiousness. Also advanced was an early form of biological argument, based on real or imagined physiological and anatomical differences – especially in cranial characteristics and facial angles – which allegedly explained mental and physical inferiority. Finally there was the appeal to deep-seated white fears of widespread miscegenation [sexual relations and interbreeding between the races], as pro-slavery theorists sought to deepen white anxieties by claiming that the abolition of slavery would lead to inter-marriage and the degeneracy of the race. Although all these arguments had appeared earlier in fugitive or embryonic form, there is something startling about the rapidity with which they were brought together and organized in a rigid polemical pattern, once the defenders of slavery found themselves in a propaganda war with the abolitionists.

(Frederickson, 1987, p. 49)

This racialized discourse is structured by a set of **binary oppositions**. There is the powerful opposition between 'civilization' (white) and 'savagery' (black). There is the opposition between the biological or bodily characteristics of the 'black' and 'white' 'races', polarized into their extreme opposites – each the signifiers of an absolute difference between human 'types' or species. There are the rich distinctions which cluster around the supposed link, on the one hand, between the white 'races' and intellectual development – refinement, learning and knowledge, a belief in reason, the presence of developed institutions, formal government and law, and a 'civilized restraint' in their emotional, sexual and civil life, all of which are associated with 'Culture'; and on the other hand, the link between the black 'races' and whatever is instinctual – the open expression of emotion and feeling rather than intellect, a lack of 'civilized refinement' in sexual and social life, a reliance on custom and ritual, and the lack of developed civil institutions, all of which are linked to 'Nature'. Finally, there is the polarized opposition between racial 'purity' on the one hand, and the 'pollution' which comes from intermarriage, racial hybridity and interbreeding.

The Negro, it was argued, found happiness only when under the tutelage of a white master. His/her essential characteristics were fixed forever – 'eternally' – in Nature. Evidence from slave insurrections and the slave revolt in Haiti (1791) had persuaded whites of the instability of the Negro character. A degree of civilization, they thought, had rubbed off on the 'domesticated' slave, but underneath slaves remained by nature savage brutes; and long buried passions, once loosed, would result in 'the wild frenzy of revenge, and the savage lust for blood' (Frederickson, 1987, p. 54). This view was justified with reference to so-called scientific and ethnological 'evidence', the basis of a new kind of 'scientific racism'. Contrary to biblical evidence, it was asserted, blacks/whites had been created at different times – according to the theory of 'polygenesis' (many creations).

Racial theory applied the **Culture/Nature** distinction differently to the two racialized groups. Among whites, 'Culture' *was opposed to* 'Nature'. Among blacks, it was assumed, 'Culture' *coincided with* 'Nature'. Whereas whites developed 'Culture' to subdue and overcome 'Nature', for blacks, 'Culture' and 'Nature' were interchangeable. David Green discussed this view in relation to anthropology and ethnology, the disciplines which (see Chapter 3) provided much of the 'scientific evidence' for it.

> Though not immune to the 'white man's burden' [approach], anthropology was drawn through the course of the nineteenth century, even more towards causal connections between race and culture. As the position and status of the 'inferior' races became increasingly to be regarded as fixed, so socio-cultural differences came to be regarded as dependent upon hereditary characteristics. Since these were inaccessible to direct observation they had to be inferred from physical and behavioural traits which, in turn, they were intended to explain. Socio-cultural differences among human populations became subsumed within the identity of the individual human body. In the attempt to trace the line of determination between the biological and the social, the body became the totemic object, and its very visibility the evident articulation of nature and culture.

(Green, 1984, pp. 31–2)

Green's argument explains why the racialized body and its meanings came to have such resonance in popular representations of difference and 'otherness'. It also highlights the connection between *visual discourse* and *the production of (racialized) knowledge*. The body itself and its differences were visible for all to see, and thus provided 'the incontrovertible evidence' for a naturalization of racial difference. The representation of 'difference' through the body became the discursive site through which much of this 'racialized knowledge' was produced and circulated.

2.3 Signifying racial 'difference'

Popular representations of racial 'difference' during slavery tended to cluster around two main themes. First was the subordinate status and 'innate laziness' of blacks – 'naturally' born to, and fitted only for, servitude but, at the same time, stubbornly unwilling to labour in ways appropriate to their nature and profitable for their masters. Second was their innate 'primitivism', simplicity and lack of culture, which made them genetically incapable of 'civilized' refinements. Whites took inordinate amusement from the slaves' efforts to imitate the manners and customs of so-called 'civilized' white folks. (In fact, slaves often deliberately parodied their masters' behaviour by their exaggerated imitations, laughing at white folks behind their backs and 'sending them up'. The practice – called *signifying* – is now recognized as a well-established part of the black vernacular literary tradition. See, for example, Figure 4.9, reprinted in Gates, 1988).

Typical of this racialized regime of representation was the practice of reducing the cultures of black people to Nature, or **naturalizing** 'difference'. The logic behind naturalization is simple. If the differences between black and white people are 'cultural', then they are open to modification and change. But if they are 'natural' – as the slave-holders believed – then they are beyond history, permanent and fixed. 'Naturalization' is therefore a representational strategy designed to *fix* 'difference', and thus *secure it forever*. It is an attempt to halt the inevitable 'slide' of meaning, to secure discursive or ideological 'closure'.

In the eighteenth and nineteenth centuries popular representations of daily life under slavery, ownership and servitude are shown as so 'natural' that they require *no comment*. It was part of the natural order of things that white men should sit and slaves should stand; that white women rode and slave men ran after them shading them from the Louisiana sun with an umbrella; that white overseers should inspect slave women like prize animals, or punish runaway slaves with casual forms of torture (like branding them or urinating in their mouths), and that fugitives should kneel to receive their punishment (see Figures 4.10, 4.11, 4.12). These images are a form of ritualized degradation. On the other hand, some representations are idealized and sentimentalized rather than degraded, while remaining stereotypical. These are the 'noble savages' to the 'debased servants' of the previous type. For example, the endless representations of the 'good' Christian black slave, like Uncle Tom, in Harriet Beecher Stowe's pro-abolitionist novel, *Uncle Tom's Cabin,* or the ever-faithful and devoted domestic slave, Mammy. A third group occupy an ambiguous middle-ground – tolerated though not admired. These include the 'happy natives' – black entertainers, minstrels and banjo-players who seemed not to have a brain in their head but sang, danced and cracked jokes all day long, to entertain white folks; or the 'tricksters' who were admired for their crafty ways of avoiding hard work, and their tall tales, like Uncle Remus.

For blacks, 'primitivism' (Culture) and 'blackness' (Nature) became interchangeable. This was their 'true nature' and they could not escape it. As has so often happened in the representation of women, their biology *was* their 'destiny'. Not only were blacks represented in terms of their essential characteristics. They were *reduced to their essence.* Laziness, simple fidelity, mindless 'cooning', trickery, childishness belonged to blacks *as a race, as a species.* There was nothing else to the kneeling slave *but* his servitude; nothing to Uncle Tom *except* his Christian forbearing; nothing to Mammy *but* her fidelity to the white household – and what Fanon called her 'sho' nuff good cooking'.

FIGURE 4.9 'A Black Lecture on Phrenology'

FIGURE 4.10   Slavery: a scene from a planter's life in the West Indies

FIGURE 4.11   Slavery: a slave auction in the West Indies, c. 1830

FIGURE 4.12   Slavery: drawing of a Creole lady and black slave in the West Indies

FIGURE 4.13   A girl and her golliwog: an illustration by Lawson Wood, 1927

In short, these are *stereotypes*. We will return, in section 4, to examine this concept of *stereotyping* more fully. But for the moment, we note that 'stereotyped' means 'reduced to a few essentials, fixed in Nature by a few, simplified characteristics'. Stereotyping of blacks in popular representation was so common that cartoonists, illustrators and caricaturists could summon up a whole gallery of 'black types' with a few, simple, essentialized strokes of the pen. Black people were reduced to the signifiers of their physical difference – thick lips, fuzzy hair, broad face and nose, and so on. For example, that figure of fun who, as doll and marmalade emblem, has amused little children down the ages: the Golliwog (Figure 4.13). This is only one of the many popular figures which reduces black people to a few simplified, reductive and essentialized features. Every adorable little 'piccaninny' was immortalized for years by his grinning innocence on the covers of the *Little Black Sambo* books. Black waiters served a thousand cocktails on stage, screen and in magazine ads. Black Mammy's chubby countenance smiled away, a century after the abolition of slavery, on every packet of Aunt Jemima's Pancakes.

3 STAGING RACIAL 'DIFFERENCE': 'AND THE MELODY LINGERED ON …'

The traces of these racial stereotypes – what we may call a 'racialized regime of representation' – have persisted into the late twentieth century (Hall, 1981). Of course, they have always been contested. In the early decades of the nineteenth century, the anti-slavery movement (which led to the abolition of

British slavery in 1834) did put into early circulation an alternative imagery of black–white relations and this was taken up by the American abolitionists in the USA in the period leading up to the Civil War. In opposition to the stereotypical representations of racialized difference, abolitionists adopted a different slogan about the black slave – 'Are you not a man and brother? Are you not a woman and a sister?' – emphasizing not difference, but a common humanity. The anniversary coins minted by the anti-slavery societies represented this shift, though not without the marking of 'difference'. Black people are still seen as childish, simple and dependent, though capable of, and on their way to (after a paternalist apprenticeship), something more like equality with whites. They were represented as either supplicants for freedom or full of gratitude for being freed – and consequently still shown kneeling to their white benefactors (Figure 4.14).

This image reminds us that the Uncle Tom of Harriet Beecher Stowe's novel was not only written to appeal to anti-slavery opinion but in the conviction that, 'with their gentleness, their lowly docility of heart – their childlike simplicity of affection and facility of forgiveness', blacks were, if anything, *more* fitted than their white counterparts to 'the highest form of the peculiarly Christian life' (Stowe, quoted in Frederickson, 1987, p. 111). This sentiment counters one set of stereotypes (their savagery) by substituting another (their eternal goodness). The extreme racialization of the imagery has been modified; but a sentimentalized version of the stereotyping remained active in the discourse of anti-slavery.

FIGURE 4.14 Two images of slaves kneeling: (left) from the sheet music of a French song, and (right) the female version of the well-known emblem of the English Abolition Society

After the Civil War, some of the grosser forms of social and economic exploitation, physical and mental degradation associated with plantation slavery were replaced by a different system of racial segregation – legalized in the South, more informally maintained in the North. Did the old, stereotypical 'regime of representation', which had helped to construct the image of black people in the white imaginary, gradually disappear?

That would seem too optimistic. A good test case is the American cinema, *the* popular art form of the first half of the twentieth century, where one would expect to find a very different representational repertoire. However, in critical studies like Leab's *From Sambo to Superspade* (1976), Cripps' *Black Film as Genre* (1978), Patricia Morton's *Disfigured Images* (1991), and Donald Bogle's *Toms, Coons, Mulattoes, Mammies and Bucks: An Interpretative History of Blacks in American Films* (1973), the astonishing persistence of the basic racial 'grammar of representation' is documented – of course with many variations and modifications, allowing for differences in time, medium and context.

Bogle's study identifies the five main *stereotypes* which, he argues, made the cross-over: *Toms* – the Good Negroes, always 'chased, harassed, hounded, flogged, enslaved and insulted, they keep the faith, ne'er turn against their white massas, and remain hearty, submissive, stoic, generous, selfless and oh-so-kind' (p. 6). *Coons* – the eye-popping piccanninies, the slapstick entertainers, the spinners of tall tales, the 'no-account "niggers", those unreliable, crazy, lazy, subhuman creatures, good for nothing more than eating watermelons, stealing chickens, shooting crap, or butchering the English language' (pp. 7–8). *The Tragic Mulatto* – the mixed-race woman, cruelly caught between 'a divided racial inheritance' (p. 9), beautiful, sexually attractive and often exotic, the prototype of the smouldering, sexy heroine, whose partly white blood makes her 'acceptable', even attractive, to white men, but whose indelible 'stain' of black blood condemns her to a tragic conclusion. *Mammies* – the prototypical house-servants, usually big, fat, bossy and cantankerous, with their good-for-nothing husbands sleeping it off at home, their utter devotion to the white household and their unquestioned subservience in their workplaces (p. 9). Finally, the *Bad Bucks* – physically big, strong, no-good, violent, renegades, 'on a rampage and full of black rage', 'over-sexed and savage, violent and frenzied as they lust for white flesh' (p. 10). There are many traces of this in contemporary images of black youth – for example, the 'mugger', the 'drug-baron', the 'yardie', the gansta-rap singer, the 'niggas with attitude' bands and more generally black urban youth 'on the rampage'.

The film which introduced these black 'types' to the cinema was one of the most extraordinary and influential movies of all times, D.W. Griffiths' *The Birth of a Nation* (1915), based on a popular novel, *The Clansman*, which had already put some of these racialized images into circulation. Griffiths, a 'founding father' of the cinema, introduced many technical and cinematic innovations and virtually single-handedly constructed the 'grammar' of silent feature-film-making. Up to then,

American movies had been two- or three-reel affairs, shots running no longer than ten or fifteen minutes, crudely and casually filmed. But *Birth of a Nation* was rehearsed for six weeks, filmed in nine, later edited in three months, and finally released as a hundred-thousand dollar spectacle, twelve reels in length and over three hours in running time. It altered the entire course and concept of American movie-making, developing the close-up, cross-cutting, rapid-fire editing, the iris, the split-screen shot and realistic and impressionistic lighting. Creating sequences and images yet to be seen, the film's magnitude and epic grandeur swept audiences off their feet.

(Bogle, 1973, p. 10)

More astonishingly, it not only marked the 'birth of the cinema', but it told the story of 'the birth of the American nation' – identifying the nation's salvation with the 'birth of the Ku Klux Klan', that secret band of white brothers with their white hoods and burning crosses, 'defenders of white womanhood, white honour and white glory', shown in the film putting the blacks to rout in a magnificent charge, who 'restore(d) to the South everything it has lost including its white supremacy' (1973, p. 12), and who were subsequently responsible for defending white racism in the South by torching black homes, beating up black people and lynching black men.

There have been many twists and turns in the ways in which the black experience was represented in mainstream American cinema. But the repertoire of stereotypical figures drawn from 'slavery days' has never entirely disappeared – a fact you can appreciate even if you are not familiar with many of the examples quoted. For a time, film-makers like Oscar Mischeaux produced a 'segregated' cinema – black films exclusively for black audiences (see Gaines, 1993). In the 1930s black actors principally appeared in mainstream films in the subordinate roles of jesters, simpletons, faithful retainers and servants. Bill 'Bojangles' Robinson faithfully butlered and danced for the child star, Shirley Temple; Louise Beavers steadfastly and cheerfully cooked in a hundred white family-kitchens; while Hattie McDaniel (fat) and Butterfly McQueen (thin) 'mammied' to Scarlet O'Hara's every trick and infidelity in *Gone With The Wind* – a film all about 'race' which failed to mention it (Wallace, 1993). Stepin Fetchit (*step in and fetch it*) was made to roll his eyes, spread his dim-witted grin, shuffle his enormous feet and stammer his confused way through twenty-six films – the archetypal 'coon'; and when he retired, many followed in his footsteps. The 1940s was the era of the black musicals – *Cabin in the Sky*, *Stormy Weather*, *Porgy and Bess*, *Carmen Jones* – and black entertainers like Cab Calloway, Fats Waller, Ethel Waters, Pearl Bailey, including two famous, type-cast 'mulatto *femmes fatales*', Lena Home and Dorothy Dandridge. They didn't make me into a maid but they didn't make me anything else either. I became a butterfly pinned to a column singing away in Movieland', was Lena Home's definitive judgement (quoted in Wallace, 1993, p. 265).

Not until the 1950s did films begin cautiously to broach the subject of 'race' as problem (*Home of the Brave*, *Lost Boundaries*, *Pinky*, to mention a few titles) – though largely from a white liberal perspective. A key figure in these films was Sidney Poitier – an extremely talented black actor, whose roles cast him as a 'hero for an integrationist age'. Bogle argues that Poitier, the first black actor to be allowed 'star billing' in mainstream Hollywood films, 'fitted' *because* he was cast so rigorously 'against the grain'. He was made to play on screen everything that the stereotyped black figure was *not*: 'educated and intelligent, he spoke proper English, dressed conservatively, and had the best of table manners. For the mass white audience, Sidney Poitier was a black man who met their standards. His characters were tame; never did they act impulsively; nor were they threats to the system. They were amenable and pliant. And finally they were non-funky, almost sexless and sterile. In short, they were the perfect dream for white liberals anxious to have a coloured man in for lunch or dinner' (Bogle, 1973, pp. 175–6). Accordingly, in 1967, he actually starred in a film entitled *Guess Who's Coming To Dinner*. Despite outstanding film performances (*The Defiant Ones*, *To Sir With Love*, *In the Heat of the Night*), 'there was nothing there', as one critic kindly put it, 'to feed the old but potent fear of the over-endowed Negro' (Cripps, 1978, p. 223).

FIGURE 4.15   Still from *Charlie McCarthy, Detective*

FIGURE 4.16   Ann Sheridan and Hattie McDaniel in *George Washington Slept Here*, 1942

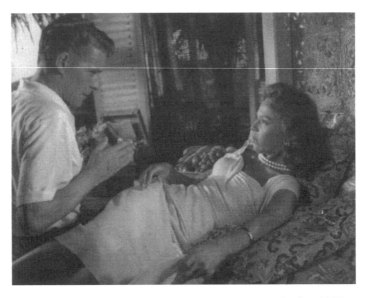

FIGURE 4.17 Dorothy Dandridge, the 1950s definitive tragic mulatto, in *Island in the Sun*, 1957

FIGURE 4.18 Sidney Poitier and Tony Curtis, in *The Defiant Ones*, 1958

3.1 Heavenly bodies

Did nobody transcend this regime of racialized representation in the American cinema in its heyday up to the 1960s? If anyone could have, that person was Paul Robeson, who was a major black star and performer in the arts between 1924 and 1945, achieving enormous popularity with audiences on both sides of the Atlantic. Richard Dyer, in his full-length study of Robeson in *Heavenly Bodies* (1986), observes that, 'His image insisted on his blackness – musically, in his primary association with Negro folk music, especially spirituals; in the theatre and films, in the recurrence of Africa as a motif; and in general in the way his image is so bound up with the notions of racial character, the nature of black folks, the Negro essence, and so on. Yet he was a star equally popular with black and white audiences.' Dyer asks, 'How did the period permit black stardom? What were the qualities this black person could be taken to embody, that could catch on in a society where there had never been a black star of this magnitude?' (pp. 67, 69). One answer is that in his performances on stage, theatre and screen, Robeson was 'read' differently by black and white audiences. 'Black and white discourses on blackness seem to be valuing the same things – spontaneity, emotion, naturalness – yet giving them a different implication' (p. 79).

Robeson's is a complex case, shot through with ambivalences. Dyer identifies a number of themes through which Robeson came to embody 'the epitome of what black people are like' (p. 71). His musical talent, sonorous voice, his intellect, physical presence and stature, coupled with his simplicity, sincerity, charm and authority allowed him to portray the 'male heroes of black culture' in plays like *Toussaint Ouverture* and films like *The Emperor Jones*, but also 'the stereotypes of the white imagination' in *Show Boat*, *Shuffle Along*, *Voodoo* and *Sanders of the Biver* (p. 73) (Figure 4.19). Robeson himself said that 'The white man has made a fetish of intellect and worships the God of thought; the Negro feels rather than thinks, experiences emotions directly rather than interprets them by roundabout and devious abstractions, and apprehends the outside world by means of intuitive perceptions' (quoted in Dyer, 1986, p. 76). This sentiment, embodied in several of his films, gave his performances a vibrant emotional intensity. But it also played directly into the black/white, emotion/intellect, nature/culture binary oppositions of racial stereotyping.

Something of the same ambivalence can be detected in relation to other themes, Dyer argues, such as the representation of blackness as 'folk' and what he calls 'atavism' (for a definition, see below). The emotional intensity and 'authenticity' of black performers was supposed to give them a genuine feel for the 'folk' traditions of black people – 'folk', here, signifying spontaneity and naturalness as opposed to the 'artificiality' of high art. Robeson's singing epitomized this quality, capturing what was thought to be the essence of the Negro spirituals in, for example, the universally popular and acclaimed song, *Old Man River*. He sang it in a deep, sonorous voice which, to blacks, expressed their long travail and their hope of freedom, but, also, to whites, what they had always heard in spirituals and Robeson's voice – 'sorrowing, melancholy, suffering' (Dyer, 1986, p. 87). Robeson gradually altered the words of this song to make it more political – 'to bring out and extend its reference to oppression and to alter its meaning from resignation to struggle' (p. 105). The line which, in the stage performance of *Show Boat*, went 'Ah'm tired of livin' an' scared of dyin'' was altered in the film to the much more assertive 'I must keep fightin' until I'm dyin'' (p. 107). On the other hand, Robeson sang black folk songs and spirituals in a 'pure' voice and 'educated' diction, without any of jazz's use of syncopation or delay in phrasing, without any of the 'dirty' notes of black blues, gospel and soul music or the nasal delivery characteristic of 'folk' or the call-and-response structure of African and slave chants.

FIGURE 4.19   Paul Robeson in *Sanders of the River*, 1935

FIGURE 4.20   Paul Robeson with Wallace Ford and Henry Wilcoxon, at the Giza pyramids in Egypt, during the filming of *Jericho*, 1937

By 'atavism', Dyer means a return to or 'recovery of qualities that have been carried in the blood from generation to generation. ... It suggests raw, violent, chaotic and "primitive" emotions' and in the Robeson context, it was closely associated with Africa and the 'return' to 'what black people were supposed to be like deep down' and 'a guarantee of the authentic wildness within of the people who had come from there' (1986, p. 89). Robeson's 'African' plays and films (*Sanders of the River*, *Song of Freedom*, *King Solomon's Mines*, *Jericho*) were full of 'authentic' African touches, and he researched a great deal into the background of African culture. 'In practice, however', Dyer observes, 'these are genuine notes inserted into works produced decidedly within American and British discourses on Africa' (p. 90).

ACTIVITY 8

Look, now, at the photograph of Robeson in a version of African dress (Figure 4.19), taken on the set of *Sanders of the River* (1935). Now, look at the second photograph (Figure 4.20), Robeson with Wallace Ford and Henry Wilcoxon at the Giza pyramids. What strikes you about these photographs? Write down briefly anything which strikes you about the 'meaning' of these images.

READING B⊢

Now read Richard Dyer's brief analysis of the second of these images (Reading B at the end of this chapter).

Undoubtedly, part of Robeson's immense impact lay in his commanding physical presence. 'His sheer size is emphasized time and again, as is the strength presumed to go with it' (Dyer, 1986, p. 134). One can perhaps judge the relevance of this to his representation of blackness from the nude study of Robeson taken by the photographer, Nicholas Muray, which, in Dyer's terms, combines beauty and strength with passivity and pathos (see Figure 4.21).

ACTIVITY 9

What do you think?

Even so outstanding a performer as Paul Robeson, then, could inflect, but could not entirely escape, the representational regime of racial difference which had passed into the mainstream cinema from an earlier era. A more independent representation of black people and black culture in the cinema would have to await the enormous shifts which accompanied the upheavals of the Civil Rights movement in the 1960s and the ending of legal segregation in the South, as well as the huge migration of blacks into the cities and urban centres of the North, which profoundly challenged the 'relations of representation' between racially defined groups in American society.

A second, more ambiguous, 'revolution' followed in the 1980s and 1990s, with the collapse of the 'integrationist' dream of the Civil Rights movement, the expansion of the black ghettos,

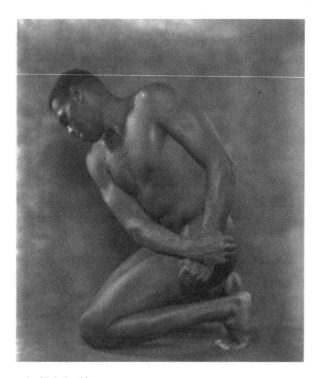

FIGURE 4.21   Paul Robeson, by Nicholas Muray

the growth of the black 'underclass', with its endemic poverty, ill-health and criminalization, and the slide of some black communities into a culture of guns, drugs and intra-black violence. This has, however, been accompanied by the growth of an affirmative self-confidence in, and an insistence on 'respect' for, black cultural identity, as well as a growing 'black separatism', which features nowhere so visibly as in the massive impact of black music (including 'black rap') on popular music and the visual presence of the music-affiliated 'street-style' scene. These developments have transformed the practices of racial representation, in part because the question of representation itself has become a critical arena of contestation and struggle. Black actors agitated for and got a wider variety of roles in film and television. 'Race' came to be acknowledged as one of the most significant themes of American life and times. In the 1980s and 1990s, blacks themselves entered the American cinema mainstream as independent film-makers – like Spike Lee (*Do the Right Thing*), Julie Dash (*Daughters of the Dust*) or John Singleton (*Boys 'n' the Hood*) – able to put their own interpretations on the way blacks figure within 'the American experience'. This has broadened the regime of racial representation – the result of a historic 'struggle around the image' – a politics of representation – whose strategies we need to examine more carefully.

4 STEREOTYPING AS A SIGNIFYING PRACTICE

Before we pursue this argument, however, we need to reflect further on how this racialized regime of representation actually works. Essentially, this involves examining more deeply the set of representational practices known as **stereotyping**. So far, we have considered the essentializing, reductionist and naturalizing effects of stereotyping. Stereotyping reduces people to a few, simple, essential characteristics, which are represented as fixed by Nature. Here, we examine four further aspects: (a) the construction of 'otherness' and exclusion; (b) stereotyping and power; (c) the role of fantasy; and (d) fetishism.

Stereotyping as a signifying practice is central to the representation of racial difference. But what is a stereotype? How does it actually work? In his essay on 'Stereotyping', Richard Dyer (1977) makes an important distinction between *typing* and *stereotyping*. He argues that, without the use of *types*, it would be difficult, if not impossible, to make sense of the world. We understand the world by referring individual objects, people or events in our heads to the general classificatory schemes into which – according to our culture – they fit. Thus we 'decode' a flat object on legs on which we place things as a 'table'. We may never have seen that kind of 'table' before, but we have a general concept or category of 'table' in our heads, into which we 'fit' the particular objects we perceive or encounter. In other words, we understand 'the particular' in terms of its 'type'. We deploy what Alfred Schutz called *typifications*. In this sense, 'typing' is essential to the production of meaning (an argument we made earlier in Chapter 1).

Richard Dyer argues that we are always 'making sense' of things in terms of some wider categories. Thus, for example, we come to 'know' something about a person by thinking of the *roles* which he or she performs: is he/she a parent, a child, a worker, a lover, boss, or an old age pensioner? We assign him/her to the *membership* of different groups, according to class, gender, age group, nationality, 'race', linguistic group, sexual preference, and so on. We order him/her in terms of *personality type* – is he/she a happy, serious, depressed, scatter-brained, over-active kind of person? Our picture of who the person 'is' is built up out of the information we accumulate from positioning him/her within these different orders of typification. In broad terms, then, 'a *type* is any simple, vivid, memorable, easily grasped and widely recognized characterization in which a few traits are foregrounded and change or "development" is kept to a minimum' (Dyer, 1977, p. 28).

What, then, is the difference between a *stereotype*? Stereotypes get *hold of* the few 'simple, vivid, memorable, easily grasped and widely recognized' characteristics about a person, *reduce* everything about the person to those traits, *exaggerate* and *simplify* them. This is the process we described earlier. So the first point is – *stereotyping reduces, essentializes, naturalizes and fixes 'difference'*.

Secondly, stereotyping deploys a strategy *of 'splitting'*. It divides the normal and the acceptable from the abnormal and the unacceptable. It then excludes or *expels* everything which does not fit, which is different. Dyer argues that:

a system of social- and stereo-types refers to what is, as it were, within and beyond the pale of normalcy [i.e. behaviour which is accepted as 'normal' in any culture]. Types are instances which indicate those who live by the rules of society (social types) and those who the rules are designed to exclude (stereotypes). For this reason, stereotypes are also more rigid than social types. ... [B] oundaries ... must be clearly delineated and so stereotypes, one of the mechanisms of boundary maintenance, are characteristically fixed, clear-cut, unalterable.

(Dyer, 1977, p. 29)

So, another feature of stereotyping is its practice of *closure* and *exclusion*. It symbolically *fixes* boundaries, and excludes everything which does not belong.

Stereotyping, in other words, is part of the maintenance of social and symbolic order. It sets up a symbolic frontier between the 'normal' and the 'deviant', the 'normal' and the 'pathological', the 'acceptable' and the 'unacceptable', what 'belongs' and what does not or is 'Other', between 'insiders' and 'outsiders', Us and Them. It facilitates the 'binding' or bonding together of all of Us who are 'normal' into one 'imagined community'; and it sends into symbolic exile all of Them – 'the Others' – who are in some way different – 'beyond the pale'. Mary Douglas (1966), for example, argued that whatever is 'out of place' is considered as polluted, dangerous, taboo. Negative feelings cluster around it. It must be symbolically excluded if the 'purity' of the culture is to be restored. The feminist theorist, Julia Kristeva, calls such expelled or excluded groups 'abjected' (from the Latin meaning, literally, 'thrown out') (Kristeva, 1982).

The third point is that *stereotyping tends to occur where there are gross inequalities of power*. Power is usually directed against the subordinate or excluded group. One aspect of this power, according to Dyer, is *ethnocentrism* – 'the application of the norms of one's own culture to that of others' (Brown, 1965, p. 183). Again, remember Derrida's argument that, between binary oppositions like Us/Them, 'we are not dealing with ... peaceful coexistence ... but rather with a violent hierarchy. One of the two terms governs ... the other or has the upper hand' (1972, p. 41).

In short, stereotyping is what Foucault called a 'power/knowledge' sort of game. It classifies people according to a norm and constructs the excluded as 'other'. Interestingly, it is also what Gramsci would have called an aspect of the struggle for hegemony. As Dyer observes:

The establishment of normalcy (i.e. what is accepted as 'normal') through social- and stereo-types is one aspect of the habit of ruling groups ... to attempt to fashion the whole of society according to their own world view, value system, sensibility and ideology. So right is this world view for the ruling groups that they make it appear (as it *does* appear to them) as 'natural' and 'inevitable' – and for everyone – and, in so far as they succeed, they establish their hegemony.

(Dyer, 1977, p. 30)

Hegemony is a form of power based on leadership by a group in many fields of activity at once, so that its ascendancy commands widespread consent and appears natural and inevitable.

4.1 Representation, difference and power

Within stereotyping, then, we have established a connection between representation, difference and power. However, we need to probe the nature of this *power* more fully. We often think of power in terms of direct physical coercion or constraint. However, we have also spoken, for example, of power *in representation*; power to mark, assign and classify; of *symbolic* power; of *ritualized* expulsion. Power, it seems, has to be understood here not only in terms of economic exploitation and physical coercion, but also in broader cultural or symbolic terms, including the power to represent someone or something in a certain way – within a certain 'regime of representation'. It includes the exercise of *symbolic power* through representational practices. Stereotyping is a key element in this exercise of symbolic violence.

In his study of how Europe constructed a stereotypical image of 'the Orient', Edward Said (1978) argues that, far from simply reflecting what the countries of the Near East were actually like, 'Orientalism' was the *discourse* 'by which European culture was able to manage – and even produce – the Orient politically, sociologically, militarily, ideologically, scientifically and imaginatively during the post-Enlightenment period'. Within the framework of western hegemony over the Orient, he says, there emerged a new object of knowledge – 'a complex Orient suitable for study in the academy, for display in the museum, for reconstruction in the colonial office, for theoretical illustration in anthropological, biological, linguistic, racial and historical theses about mankind and the universe, for instances of economic and sociological theories of development, revolution, cultural personalities, national or religious character' (pp. 7–8). This form of power is closely connected with knowledge, or with the practices of what Foucault called 'power/knowledge'.

FIGURE 4.22   Edwin Long, *The Babylonian Marriage Market,* 1882

249

ACTIVITY 10

For an example of Orientalism in visual representation, look at the reproduction of a very popular painting, *The Babylonian Marriage Market* by Edwin Long (Figure 4.22). Not only does the image produce a certain way of knowing the Orient – as 'the mysterious, exotic and eroticized Orient', but also the women who are being 'sold' into marriage are arranged, right to left, in ascending order of 'whiteness'. The final figure approximates most closely to the western ideal, the norm; her clear complexion accentuated by the light reflected on her face from a mirror.

Said's discussion of Orientalism closely parallels Foucault's power/knowledge argument: a *discourse* produces, through different practices of *representation* (scholarship, exhibition, literature, painting, etc.), a form of *racialized knowledge of the Other* (Orientalism) deeply implicated in the operations of *power* (imperialism).

Interestingly, however, Said goes on to define 'power' in ways which emphasize the similarities between Foucault and Gramsci's idea of *hegemony*:

In any society not totalitarian, then, certain cultural forms predominate over others; the form of this cultural leadership is what Gramsci has identified as *hegemony*, an indispensable concept for any understanding of cultural life in the industrial West. It is hegemony, or rather the result of cultural hegemony at work, that gives Orientalism its durability and its strength. ... Orientalism is never far from ... the idea of Europe, a collective notion identifying 'us' Europeans as against all 'those' non-Europeans, and indeed it can be argued that the major component in European culture is precisely what made that culture hegemonic both in and outside Europe: the idea of European identity as a superior one in comparison with all the non-European peoples and cultures. There is, in addition, the hegemony of European ideas about the Orient, themselves reiterating European superiority over Oriental backwardness, usually overriding the possibility that a more independent thinker ... may have had different views on the matter.

(Said, 1978, p. 7)

You should also recall here our earlier discussion in Chapter 1, about introducing *power* into questions of representation. Power, we recognized there, always operates in conditions of unequal relations. Gramsci, of course, would have stressed 'between classes', whereas Foucault always refused to identify *any* specific subject or subject-group as the source of power, which, he said, operates at a local, tactical level. These are important differences between these two theorists of power.

However, there are also some important similarities. For Gramsci, as for Foucault, power also involves knowledge, representation, ideas, cultural leadership and authority, as well as economic constraint and physical coercion. Both would have agreed that power cannot be captured by thinking exclusively in terms of force or coercion: power also seduces, solicits, induces, wins consent.

It cannot be thought of in terms of one group having a monopoly of power, simply radiating power *downwards* on a subordinate group by an exercise of simple domination from above. It includes the dominant *and* the dominated within its circuits. As Homi Bhabha has remarked, apropos Said, 'it is difficult to conceive ... subjectification as a placing *within* Orientalist or colonial discourse for the dominated subject without the dominant being strategically placed within it too' (Bhabha, 1986a, p. 158). Power not only constrains and prevents: it is also productive. It produces new discourses, new kinds of knowledge (i.e. Orientalism), new objects of knowledge (the Orient), it shapes new practices (colonization) and institutions (colonial government). It operates at a micro-level – Foucault's 'micro-physics of power' – as well as in terms of wider strategies. And, for both theorists, power is to be found everywhere. As Foucault insists, power circulates.

The circularity of power is especially important in the context of representation. The argument is that everyone – the powerful and the powerless – is caught up, *though not on equal terms*, in power's circulation. No one – neither its apparent victims nor its agents – can stand wholly outside its field of operation (think, here, of the Paul Robeson example).

4.2 Power and fantasy

A good example of this 'circularity' of power relates to how black masculinity is represented within a racialized regime of representation. Kobena Mercer and Isaac Julien (1994) argue that the representation of black masculinity 'has been forged in and through the histories of slavery, colonialism and imperialism'.

As sociologists like Robert Staples (1982) have argued, a central strand of the 'racial' power exercised by the white male slave master was the denial of certain masculine attributes to black male slaves, such as authority, familial responsibility and the ownership of property. Through such collective, historical experiences black men have adopted certain patriarchal values such as physical strength, sexual prowess and being in control as a means of survival against the repressive and violent system of subordination to which they have been subjected.

The incorporation of a code of 'macho' behaviour is thus intelligible as a means of recuperating some degree of power over the condition of powerlessness and dependency in relation to the white master subject. ... The prevailing stereotype (in contemporary Britain) projects an image of black male youth as 'mugger' or 'rioter'. ... But this regime of representation is reproduced and maintained in hegemony because black men have had to resort to 'toughness' as a defensive response to the prior aggression and violence that characterizes the way black communities are policed. ... This cycle between reality and representation makes the ideological fictions of racism empirically 'true' – or rather, there is a struggle over the definition, understanding and construction of meanings around black masculinity within the dominant regime of truth.

(Mercer and Julien, 1994, pp. 137–8)

During slavery, the white slave master often exercised his authority over the black male slave, by depriving him of all the attributes of responsibility, paternal and familial authority, treating him as a child. This 'infantilization' of difference is a common representational strategy for both men and women. (Women athletes are still widely referred to as 'girls'. And it is only recently that many Southern US whites have ceased referring to grown black men as 'Boy!', while the practice still lingers in South Africa.) Infantilization can also be understood as a way of symbolically 'castrating' the black man (i.e. depriving him of his 'masculinity'); and, as we have seen, whites often fantasized about the excessive sexual appetites and prowess of black men – as they did about the lascivious, over-sexed character of black women – *which they both feared and secretly envied*. Alleged rape was the principal 'justification' advanced for the lynching of black men in the Southern states until the Civil Rights movement (Jordan, 1968). As Mercer observes, 'The primal fantasy of the big black penis projects the fear of a threat not only to white womanhood, but to civilization itself, as the anxiety of miscegenation, eugenic pollution and racial degeneration is acted out through white male rituals of racial aggression – the historical lynching of black men in the United States routinely involved the literal castration of the Other's "strange fruit"' (1994a, p. 185).

The outcomes were often violent. Yet the example also brings out the circularity of power and the *ambivalence* – the double-sided nature – of representation and stereotyping. For, as Staples, Mercer and Julien remind us, black men sometimes responded to this infantilization by adopting a sort of caricature-in-reverse of the hyper-masculinity and super-sexuality with which they had been stereotyped. Treated as 'childish', some blacks in reaction adopted a 'macho', aggressive – masculine style. But this only served to confirm the fantasy among whites of their ungovernable and excessive sexual nature (see Wallace, 1979). Thus, 'victims' can be trapped by the stereotype, unconsciously confirming it by the very terms in which they try to oppose and resist it.

This may seem paradoxical, but it does have its own 'logic'. This logic depends on representation working at two different levels at the same time: a conscious and overt level, and an unconscious or suppressed level. The former often serves as a displaced 'cover' for the latter. The conscious attitude among whites – that 'Blacks are not proper men, they are just simple children' – may be a 'cover', or a cover-up, for a deeper, more troubling fantasy – that 'Blacks are really super-men, better endowed than whites, and sexually insatiable'. It would be improper and 'racist' to express the latter sentiment openly, but the fantasy is present, and secretly subscribed to by many, all the same. Thus when blacks act 'macho', they seem to challenge the stereotype (that they are only children) – but in the process, they confirm the fantasy which lies behind or is the 'deep structure' of the stereotype (that they are aggressive, over-sexed and over-endowed). The problem is that blacks are trapped by the *binary structure* of the stereotype, which is split between two extreme opposites – and are obliged to *shuttle endlessly between them*, sometimes being represented as *both of them at the same time*. Thus blacks are both 'childlike' *and* 'over-sexed', just as black youth are 'Sambo simpletons' and/or 'wily, dangerous savages', and older men both 'barbarians' and/or 'noble savages' – Uncle Toms.

The important point is that stereotypes refer as much to what is imagined in fantasy as to what is perceived as 'real'. And, what is visually produced, by the practices of representation, is only half the story. The other half – the deeper meaning – lies in *what is not being said, but is being fantasized, what is implied but cannot be shown.*

So far, we have been arguing that 'stereotyping' has its own *poetics* – its own ways of working – and its *politics* – the ways in which it is invested with power. We have also argued that this is a particular type of power – a *hegemonic* and *discursive* form of power, which operates as much through culture, the production of knowledge, imagery and representation, as through other means. Moreover, it is *circular*: it implicates the 'subjects' of power as well as those who are 'subjected to it'. But the introduction of the sexual dimension takes us to another aspect of 'stereotyping': namely, its basis in *fantasy* and *projection* – and its effects of *splitting* and *ambivalence*.

In *Orientalism*, Said remarked that the 'general idea about who or what was an "Oriental"' emerged according to 'a detailed logic governed' – he insisted – 'not simply by empirical reality but by a battery of desires, repressions, investments and projections' (1978, p. 8). But where does this battery of 'desires, repressions, investments and projections' come from? What role does *fantasy* play in the practices and strategies of racialized representation? If the fantasies which lie behind racialized representations cannot be shown or allowed to 'speak', how do they find expression? How are they 'represented'? This points us in the direction of the representational practice known as *fetishism*.

4.3 Fetishism and disavowal

Let us explore these questions of fantasy and fetishism, summing up the argument about representation and stereotyping, through a concrete example.

READING C

Read first the short edited extract on 'The deep structure of stereotypes' from *Difference and Pathology* by Sander Gilman (1985), Reading C at the end of this chapter.

Make sure you understand why, according to Gilman, stereotyping always involves what he calls (a) the splitting of the 'good' and 'bad' object; and (b) the projection of anxiety on to the Other.

In a later essay, Gilman refers to the 'case' of the African woman, Saartje (or Sarah) Baartman, known as 'The Hottentot Venus', who was brought to England in 1819 by a Boer farmer from the Cape region of South Africa and a doctor on an African ship, and regularly exhibited over five years in London and Paris (Figure 4.23). In her early 'performances', she was produced on a raised stage like a wild beast, came and went from her cage when ordered, 'more like a bear in a chain than a human being' (quoted from *The Times*, 26 November 1810, in Lindfors, unpublished paper). She created a considerable public stir. She was subsequently baptized in Manchester, married an African and had two children, spoke Dutch and learned some English, and, during a court case in Chancery, taken out to protect her from exploitation, declared herself 'under no restraint' and 'happy to be in England'. She then reappeared in Paris where she had an amazing public impact, until her fatal illness from smallpox in 1815.

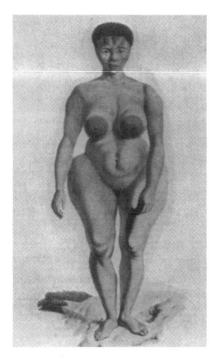

FIGURE 4.23 'The Hottentot Venus' – Saartje Baartman

Both in London and Paris, she became famous in two quite different circles: among the general public as a popular 'spectacle', commemorated in ballads, cartoons, illustrations, in melodramas and newspaper reports; and among the naturalists and ethnologists, who measured, observed, drew, wrote learned treatises about, modelled, made waxen moulds and plaster casts, and scrutinized every detail, of her anatomy, dead and alive (Figure 4.24). What attracted both audiences to her was not only her size (she was a diminutive four feet six inches tall) but her *steatopygia* – her protruding buttocks, a feature of Hottentot anatomy – and what was described as her 'Hottentot apron', an enlargement of the labia 'caused by the manipulation of the genitalia and considered beautiful by the Hottentots and Bushmen' (Gilman, 1985, p. 85). As someone crudely remarked, 'she could be said to carry her fortune behind her, for London may never before have seen such a "heavy-arsed heathen"' (quoted in Lindfors, p. 2).

I want to pick out several points from 'The Hottentot Venus' example in relation to questions of stereotyping, fantasy and fetishism.

First, note the preoccupation – one could say the obsession – with *marking 'difference'*. Saartje Baartman became the embodiment of 'difference'. What's more, her difference was 'pathologized': represented as a pathological form of 'otherness'. Symbolically, she did not fit the ethnocentric norm which was applied to European women and, falling outside a western classificatory system of what 'women' are like, she had to be constructed as 'Other'.

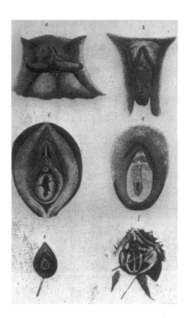

FIGURE 4.24 '[E]very detail of her anatomy': Sexual anomalies in women, from Cesare Lombroso and Guillaume Ferrero, *La donna deliquente: la prostituta e la donna normale* (Turin, L. Roux, 1893)

Next, observe her reduction to Nature, the signifier of which was her *body*. Her body was 'read', like a text, for the living evidence – the proof, the Truth – which it provided of her absolute 'otherness' and therefore of an irreversible difference between the 'races'.

Further, she became 'known', represented and observed through a series of polarized, binary oppositions. 'Primitive', not 'civilized', she was assimilated to the Natural order – and therefore compared with wild beasts, like the ape or the orangutan – rather than to the Human Culture. This naturalization of difference was signified, above all, by her sexuality. She was reduced to her body and her body in turn was reduced to her sexual organs. They stood as the essential signifiers of her place in the universal scheme of things. In her, Nature and Culture coincided, and could therefore be substituted for one another, read off against one another. What was seen as her 'primitive' sexual genitalia signified her 'primitive' sexual appetite, and vice versa.

Next, she was subjected to an extreme form of reductionism – a strategy often applied to the representation of women's bodies, of whatever 'race', especially in pornography. The 'bits' of her that were preserved served, in an essentializing and reductionist manner, as 'a pathological summary of the entire individual' (Gilman, 1985, p. 88). In the models and casts of them which were preserved in the Museé de L'Homme, she was literally turned into a set of separate objects, into a thing – 'a collection of sexual parts'. She underwent a kind of symbolic dismantling or *fragmentation* – another technique familiar from both male and female pornography. We are reminded here of Frantz Fanon's description in *Black Skin, White Masks* of the way he felt disintegrated, as a black man, by the look of the white person: 'the glances of the other fixed me there, in the sense in which a chemical solution is fixed by a dye. I was indignant; I demanded an explanation. Nothing happened. I burst

FIGURE 4.25 Nuba Wrestlers, by George Rodger

apart. Now the fragments have been put together again by another self (Fanon, 1986 [1952], p. 109). Saartje Baartman did not exist as 'a person'. She had been disassembled into her relevant parts. She was 'fetishized' – turned into an object. This substitution of a *part* for the *whole*, of a *thing* – an object, an organ, a portion of the body – for a *subject*, is the effect of a very important representational practice – *fetishism*.

Fetishism takes us into the realm where fantasy intervenes in representation; to the level where what is shown or seen, in representation, can only be understood in relation to what cannot be seen, what cannot be shown. *Fetishism* involves the substitution of an 'object' for some dangerous and powerful but forbidden force. In anthropology, it refers to the way the powerful and dangerous spirit of a god can be displaced on to an object – a feather, a piece of stick, even a communion wafer – which then becomes charged with the spiritual power of that for which it is a substitute. In Marx's notion of 'commodity fetishism', the living labour of the worker has been displaced and disappears into things – the commodities which workers produce but have to buy back as though they belonged to someone else. In psychoanalysis, 'fetishism' is described as the substitute for the 'absent' phallus – as when the sexual drive becomes displaced to some other part of the body. The substitute then becomes eroticized, invested with the sexual energy, power and desire which cannot find expression in the object to which it is really directed. *Fetishism* in representation borrows from all these meanings. It also involves *displacement*. The phallus cannot be represented because it is forbidden, taboo. The sexual energy, desire and danger, all of which are emotions powerfully associated with the phallus, are transferred to another part of the body or another object, which substitutes for it.

256

An excellent example of this trope is the photograph of the two Nubian wrestlers from a book of photographs by the English documentarist, George Rodger (Figure 4.25). This image was appended in homage to the back cover of her book, *The Last of the Nuba* (1976) by Leni Riefenstahl, the former Nazi filmmaker whose reputation was built upon the films she made of Hitler's 1934 Nuremberg rally (*Triumph of the Will*) and the 1936 Berlin Olympics (*Olympiad*).

Gilman (1985) describes a similar example of racial fetishism in the 'The Hottentot Venus'. Here the sexual object of the onlookers' gaze was *displaced* from her genitalia, which is what really obsessed them, to her buttocks. 'Female sexuality is tied to the image of the buttocks and the quintessential buttocks are those of the Hottentot' (1985, p. 91).

Fetishism, as we have said, involves **disavowal**. Disavowal is the strategy by means of which a powerful fascination or desire is both *indulged* and at the same time *denied*. It is where what has been tabooed nevertheless manages to find a displaced form of representation. As Homi Bhabha observes, 'It is a non-repressive form of knowledge that allows for the possibility of simultaneously embracing two contradictory beliefs, one official and one secret, one archaic and one progressive, one that allows the myth of origins, the other that articulates difference and division' (1986a, p. 168). Freud, in his remarkable essay on 'Fetishism', wrote:

the fetish is the substitute for the woman's (the mother's) penis that the little boy once believed in and – for reasons familiar to us – does not want to give up. ... It is not true that the [male] child ... has preserved unaltered his belief that women have a phallus. He has retained the belief, but he has also given it up. In the conflict between the weight of the unwelcome perception and the force of his counter-wish, a compromise has been reached. ... Yes, in his mind the woman *has* got a penis, in spite of everything; but the penis is no longer the same as it was before. Something else has taken its place, has been appointed its substitute ...

(Freud, 1977 [1927], p. 353)

(We should note, incidentally, that Freud's tracing of the origin of fetishism back to the castration anxiety of the male child gives this trope the indelible stamp of a male-centred fantasy. The failure of Freud and much of later psychoanalysis to theorize female fetishism has been the subject of extended recent critique (see *inter alia* McClintock, 1995).)

So, following the general logic of fetishism as a representational strategy, we could say of the Nubian wrestler, 'Though it is forbidden, I *can* look at the wrestler's genitals because they are no longer as they were. Their place has been taken by the head of his wrestling companion.' Thus, of Leni Riefenstahl's use of the Rodger photograph of the Nuba wrestlers, Kobena Mercer observes that 'Riefenstahl admits that her fascination with this East African people did not originate from an interest in their "culture" but from a photograph of two Nubian wrestlers by ... George Rodger. ... In this sense her anthropological alibi for an ethnographic voyeurism is nothing more than the secondary elaboration, and rationalization, of the primal wish to see this lost image again and again' (Mercer, 1994, p. 187).

Fetishism, then, is a strategy for having-it-both-ways: for both representing and not-representing the tabooed, dangerous or forbidden object of pleasure and desire. It provides us with what Mercer calls an 'alibi', what earlier we called a 'cover' or a 'cover-story'. We have seen how, in the case of 'The Hottentot Venus', not only is the gaze displaced from the genitalia to the buttocks, but also, this allows the observers to *go on looking* while disavowing the sexual nature of their gaze. Ethnology, science, the search for anatomical evidence, here play the role as the 'cover', the disavowal, which allows the illicit desire to operate. It allows a double focus to be maintained – looking and not looking – an ambivalent desire to be satisfied. What is declared to be different, hideous, 'primitive', deformed is at the same time being obsessively enjoyed and lingered over *because* it is strange, 'different', exotic. The scientists can look at, examine and observe Saartje Baartman naked and in public, classify and dissect every detail of her anatomy, on the perfectly acceptable alibi that it is all being done in the name of Science, of objective knowledge, ethnological evidence, in the pursuit of Truth. This is what Foucault meant by knowledge and power creating a 'regime of truth'.

So, finally, fetishism licenses an unregulated *voyeurism*. Few could argue that the 'gaze' of the (largely male) onlookers who observed 'The Hottentot Venus' was disinterested. As Freud (1977 [1927]) argued, there is often a sexual element in 'looking', an eroticization of the gaze (an argument developed in Chapter 5). Looking is often driven by an unacknowledged search for illicit

FIGURE 4.26 German caricature of man viewing 'The Hottentot Venus' through a telescope, early nineteenth century

pleasure and a desire which cannot be fulfilled. 'Visual impressions remain the most frequent pathway along which libidinal excitation is aroused' (Freud, 1977 [1927], p. 96). We go on looking, even if there is nothing more to see. He called the obsessive force of this pleasure in looking 'scopophilia'. It becomes perverse, Freud argued, only 'if restricted exclusively to the genitals, connected with the over-riding of disgust ... or if, instead of being preparatory to the normal sexual aim, it supplants it' (p. 80).

Thus voyeurism is perfectly captured in the German caricature of the white gentleman observing 'The Hottentot Venus' through his telescope (Figure 4.26). He can look forever without being seen. But, as Gilman observes, look forever as he may, he 'can see nothing but her buttocks' (1985, p. 91).

5 CONTESTING A RACIALIZED REGIME OF REPRESENTATION

So far we have analysed some examples from the archive of racialized representation in western popular culture of different periods (sections 1, 2 and 3), and explored the representational practices of difference and 'otherness' (especially section 4). It is time to turn to the final set of questions posed in our opening pages. Can a dominant regime of representation be challenged, contested or changed? What are the counter-strategies which can begin to subvert the representation process? Can 'negative' ways of representing racial difference, which abound in our examples, be reversed by a 'positive' strategy? What effective strategies are there? And what are their theoretical underpinnings?

Let me remind you that, theoretically, the argument which enables us to pose this question at all is the proposition (which we have discussed in several places and in many different ways) that *meaning can never be finally fixed*. If meaning could be fixed by representation, then there would be no change – and so no counter-strategies or interventions. Of course, we *do* make strenuous efforts to fix meaning – that is precisely what the strategies of stereotyping are aspiring to do, often with considerable success, for a time. But ultimately, meaning begins to slip and slide; it begins to drift, or be wrenched, or inflected into new directions. New meanings are grafted on to old ones. Words and images carry connotations over which no one has complete control, and these marginal or submerged meanings come to the surface, allowing different meanings to be constructed, different things to be shown and said. That is why we referred you to the work of Bakhtin and Volosinov in section 1.2. For they have given a powerful impetus to the practice of what has come to be known as **trans-coding**: taking an existing meaning and reappropriating it for new meanings (e.g. 'Black is Beautiful').

A number of different *trans-coding* strategies have been adopted since the 1960s, when questions of representation and power acquired a centrality in the politics of anti-racist and other social movements. We only have space here to consider three of them.

5.1 Reversing the stereotypes

In the discussion of racial stereotyping in the American cinema, we discussed the ambiguous position of Sidney Poitier and talked about an *integrationist* strategy in US filmmaking in the 1950s. This strategy, as we said, carried heavy costs. Blacks could gain entry to the mainstream – but only at the cost of adapting to the white image of them and assimilating white norms of style, looks and behaviour. Following the Civil Rights movement, in the 1960s and 1970s, there was a much more aggressive affirmation of black cultural identity, a positive attitude towards difference and a struggle over representation.

The first fruit of this counter-revolution was a series of films, beginning with *Sweet Sweetback's Baadasss Song* (Martin Van Peebles, 1971), and Gordon Parks' box-office success, *Shaft*. In *Sweet Sweetback*, Van Peebles values positively all the characteristics which would normally have been negative stereotypes. He made his black hero a professional stud, who successfully evades the police with the help of a succession of black ghetto low-lifers, sets fire to a police car, shafts another with a pool cue, lights out for the Mexican border, making full use of his sexual prowess at every opportunity, and ultimately gets away with it all, to a message scrawled across the screen: 'A BAADASSS NIGGER IS COMING BACK TO COLLECT SOME DUES'. *Shaft* was about a black detective, close to the streets but struggling with the black underworld and a band of black militants as well as the Mafia, who rescues a black racketeer's daughter. What marked *Shaft* out, however, was the detective's absolute lack of deference towards whites. Living in a smart apartment, beautifully turned out in casual but expensive clothes, he was presented in the advertising publicity as a 'lone black Super-spade – a man of flair and flamboyance who has fun at the expense of the white establishment'. He was 'a violent man who lived a violent life, in pursuit of black women, white sex, quick money, easy success, cheap "pot" and other pleasures' (Cripps, 1978, pp. 251–4). When asked by a policeman where he is going, Shaft replies, 'I'm going to get laid. Where are you going?' The instant success of *Shaft* was followed by a succession of films in the same mould, including *Superfly*, also by Parks, in which Priest, a young black cocaine dealer, succeeds in making one last big deal before retirement, survives both a series of violent episodes and vivid sexual encounters to drive off at the end in his Rolls Royce, a rich and happy man. There have been many later films in the same mould (e.g. *New Jack City*) with, at their centre (as the rap singers would say), 'bad-ass black men, with attitude'.

We can see at once the appeal of these films, especially, though not exclusively, to black audiences. In the ways their heroes deal with whites, there is a remarkable absence, indeed a conscious reversal of, the old deference or childlike dependency. In many ways, these are 'revenge' films – audiences relishing the black heroes' triumphs over 'Whitey', loving the fact that they're getting away with it! What we may call the moral playing-field is levelled. Blacks are neither always worse nor always better than whites. They come in the usual human shapes – good, bad and indifferent. They are no different from the ordinary (white) average American in their tastes, styles, behaviour, morals, motivations. In class terms, they can be as 'cool', affluent and well groomed as their white counterparts. And their 'locations' are the familiar real-life settings of ghetto, street, police station and drug-bust.

At a more complex level, they placed blacks for the first time at the centre of the popular cinematic genres – crime and action films – and thus made them essential to what we may call the 'mythic' life and culture of the American cinema – more important, perhaps, in the end, than their 'realism'. For this is where the collective fantasies of popular life are worked out, and the exclusion of blacks from its confines made them precisely, peculiar, different, placed them 'outside the picture'. It deprived them of the celebrity status, heroic charisma, the glamour and pleasure of identification accorded to the white heroes *of film noir*, the old private eye, crime and police thrillers, the 'romances' of urban low-life and the ghetto. With these films, blacks had arrived in the cultural mainstream – with a vengeance!

These films carried through one counter-strategy with considerable single-mindedness – reversing the evaluation of popular stereotypes. And they proved that this strategy could secure box-office success and audience identification. Black audiences loved them because they cast black actors in glamorous and 'heroic' as well as 'bad' roles; white audiences took to them because they contained all the elements of the popular cinematic genres. Nevertheless, among some critics, the judgement on their success as a representational counter-strategy has become more mixed. They have come to be seen by many as 'blaxploitation' films.

ACTIVITY 11

Can you hazard a guess as to why they have come to be seen in this way?

To reverse the stereotype is not necessarily to overturn or subvert it. Escaping the grip of one stereotypical extreme (blacks are poor, childish, subservient, always shown as servants, everlastingly 'good', in menial positions, deferential to whites, never the heroes, cut out of the glamour, the pleasure, and the rewards, sexual and financial) may simply mean being trapped in its stereotypical 'other' (blacks are motivated by money, love bossing white people around, perpetrate violence and crime as effectively as the next person, are 'bad', walk off with the goodies, indulge in drugs, crime and promiscuous sex, come on like 'Super-spades' and *always get away with it!*). This may be an advance on the former list, and is certainly a welcome change, but it has not escaped the contradictions of the binary structure of racial stereotyping and it has not unlocked what Mercer and Julien call 'the complex dialectics of power and subordination' through which 'black male identities have been historically and culturally constructed' (1994, p. 137). The black critic, Lerone Bennett acknowledged that 'after it [*Sweet Sweetback* ...] we can never again see black people in films (noble, suffering, losing) in the same way'. But he also thought it 'neither revolutionary nor black', indeed, a revival of certain 'antiquated white stereotypes', even 'mischievous and reactionary'. As he remarked, 'nobody ever fucked his way to freedom' (quoted in Cripps, 1978, p. 248). This is a critique which has, in retrospect, been delivered about the whole foregrounding of black masculinity during the Civil Rights movement, of which these films were undoubtedly a by-product. Black feminist critics have pointed out how the black resistance to white patriarchal power during the 1960s was often accompanied by the adoption of an exaggerated 'black male macho' style and sexual aggressiveness by black leaders towards black women (Davis, 1983; hooks, 1992; Wallace, 1979).

5.2 Positive and negative images

The second strategy for contesting the racialized regime of representation is the attempt to substitute a range of 'positive' images of black people, black life and culture for the 'negative' imagery which continues to dominate popular representation. This approach has the advantage of righting the balance. It is underpinned by an acceptance – indeed, a celebration – of difference. It inverts the binary opposition, privileging the subordinate term, sometimes reading the negative positively: 'Black is Beautiful'. It tries to construct a positive identification with what has been abjected. It greatly expands the *range* of racial representations and the *complexity* of what it means to 'be black', thus challenging the reductionism of earlier stereotypes. Much of the work of contemporary black artists and visual practitioners fall into this category. In the photographs specially taken to illustrate David Bailey's critique of 'positive images' in 'Rethinking black representation' (1988), we see black men looking after children and black women politically organizing in public – giving the conventional meaning of these images a different inflection (Figures 4.27 and 4.28).

Underlying this approach is an acknowledgement and celebration of diversity and difference in the world. Another kind of example is the United Colours of Benetton advertising series, which uses ethnic models, especially children, from many cultures and celebrates images of racial and ethnic hybridity. But here, again, critical reception has been mixed (Bailey, 1988). Do these images

FIGURE 4.27 Photograph by David A. Bailey

FIGURE 4.28 Photograph by David A. Bailey

evade the difficult questions, dissolving the harsh realities of racism into a liberal mishmash of 'difference'? Do these images *appropriate* 'difference' into a spectacle in order to sell a product? Or are they genuinely a political statement about the necessity for everyone to accept and 'live with' difference, in an increasingly diverse, culturally pluralist world? Sonali Fernando (1992) suggests that this imagery 'cuts both ways: on the one hand suggesting a problematizing of racial identity as a complex dialectic of similarities as well as differences, but on the other ... homogenizing all non-white cultures as other' (p. 65).

The problem with the positive/negative strategy is that adding positive images to the largely negative repertoire of the dominant regime of representation increases the diversity of the ways in which 'being black' is represented, but does not *necessarily* displace the negative. Since the binaries remain in place, meaning continues to be framed by them. The strategy challenges the binaries – but it does not undermine them. The peace-loving, child-caring Rastafarian can still appear, in the following day's newspaper, as an exotic and violent black stereotype ...

5.3 Through the eye of representation

The third counter-strategy locates itself *within* the complexities and ambivalences of representation itself, and tries to *contest it from within*. It is more concerned with the *forms* of racial representation than with introducing a new *content*. It accepts and works with the shifting, unstable character of meaning, and enters, as it were, into a struggle over representation, while acknowledging that, since meaning can never be finally fixed, there can never be any final victories.

Thus, instead of avoiding the black body, because it has been so caught up in the complexities of power and subordination within representation, this strategy positively takes the body as the principal site of its representational strategies, attempting to make the stereotypes work against themselves. Instead of avoiding the dangerous terrain opened up by the interweaving of 'race', gender and sexuality, it deliberately contests the dominant gendered and sexual definitions of racial difference by *working on* black sexuality. Since black people have so often been fixed, stereotypically, by the racialized gaze, it may have been tempting to refuse the complex emotions associated with 'looking'. However, this strategy makes elaborate play with 'looking', hoping by its very attention, to 'make it strange' – that is, to de-familiarize it, and so make explicit what is often hidden – its erotic dimensions (Figure 4.29). It is not afraid to deploy humour – for example, the comedian, Lenny Henry, forces us by the witty exaggerations of his Afro-Caribbean caricatures, to laugh *with* rather than at his characters. Finally, instead of refusing the displaced power and danger of 'fetishism', this strategy attempts to use the desires and ambivalences which tropes of fetishism inevitably awaken.

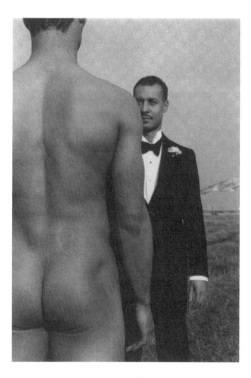

FIGURE 4.29   Still from Isaac Julien's *Looking for Langston*, 1989

ACTIVITY 12

Look first at Figure 4.30.

It is by Robert Mapplethorpe, a famous gay, white, American photographer, whose technically brilliant studies of black nude male models have sometimes been accused of fetishism and of fragmenting the black body, in order to appropriate it symbolically for his personal pleasure and desire.

Now look at Figure 4.31. It is by the gay, black, Yoruba photographer, Rotimi Fani-Kayode, who trained in the USA and practised in London until his premature death, and whose images consciously deploy the tropes of fetishism, as well as using African and modernist motifs.

How far do these images, in your view, bear out the above comments about each photographer?

Do they use the tropes of representation in the same way?

Is their effect on the viewer – on the way you 'read' the images – the same? If not, what is the difference?

FIGURE 4.30   Jimmy Freeman by Robert Mappelthorpe (Copyright © 1981 The Estate of Robert Mappelthorpe)

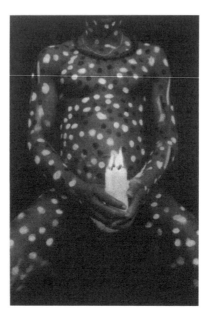

FIGURE 4.31   Sonponnol, 1987, by Rotimi Fani-Kayode

⌐READING D

Now read the brief extract from Kobena Mercer's essay 'Reading racial fetishism' (1994), in which he advances the argument against Mapplethorpe summarized above (see Reading D at the end of this chapter).

At a later point, in a second part to the same essay, Mercer changed his mind. He argued that Mapplethorpe's aesthetic strategy exploits the ambivalent structure of fetishism (which affirms difference while at the same time denying it). It unsettles the fixity of the stereotypical 'white' gaze at the black body and reverses it:

> Blacks are looked down upon and despised as worthless, ugly and ultimately unhuman. But in the blink of an eye, whites look up to and revere black bodies, lost in awe and envy as the black subject is idealized as the embodiment of its aesthetic ideal.

> (Mercer, 1994, p. 201)

Mercer concludes:

> it becomes necessary to reverse the reading of racial fetishism, not as a repetition of racist fantasies but as a deconstructive strategy, which begins to lay bare the psychic and social relations of ambivalence at play in cultural representations of race and sexuality.

> (p. 199)

ACTIVITY 13

Which of Mercer's two readings of fetishism in Mapplethorpe's work do you find most persuasive?

You won't expect 'correct' answers to my questions, for there are none. They are a matter of interpretation and judgement. I pose them to drive home the point about the complexity and ambivalences of representation as a practice, and to suggest how and why attempting to dismantle or subvert a racialized regime of representation is an extremely difficult exercise, about which – like so much else in representation – there can be no absolute guarantees.

6 CONCLUSION

In this chapter, we have pushed our analysis of representation as a signifying practice a good deal further, opening up some difficult and complex areas of debate. What we have said about 'race' can in many instances be applied to other dimensions of 'difference'. We have analysed many examples, drawn from different periods of popular culture, of how a racialized regime of representation emerged, and identified some of its characteristic strategies and tropes. In activities, we have tried to get you to apply some of these techniques. We have considered several theoretical arguments as to why 'difference' and 'otherness' are of such central importance in cultural studies. We have thoroughly unpacked stereotyping as a representational practice, looking at how it works (essentializing, reductionism, naturalization, binary oppositions), at the ways it is caught up in the play of power (hegemony, power/knowledge), and at some of its deeper, more unconscious effects (fantasy, fetishism, disavowal). Finally, we have considered some of the counter-strategies which have attempted to intervene in representation, *trans-coding* negative images with new meanings.

The field of representation, however, is not static. In the period from the late 1980s to the present, the ways in which racial and ethnic difference have been coded within popular representation has continued to shift, with new patterns emerging. These are patterns which work with and upon some of the underlying, deeper structures which this chapter has explored. It is appropriate to very briefly reflect on these changes in this conclusion.

The most striking feature of the representation of 'racial' difference in the media has been the increase in the volume, range and normalization of racialized representation. By this I mean that there are many more blacks in the popular media than was the case in the late 1980s, they occur across a range of categories of cultural life and alongside this there has been an acceptance of the fact that black people are an integral part of the fabric of British life, especially in its urban centres. One manifestation of this is evident in the vox pops or impromptu street interviews used by television news. In these vox pops it has become accepted that if you interview ordinary people in order to elicit their views on a topic of the day, then you ought to have one or two of them who are black, but not necessarily because they are black. In this regard it has become more accepted – normalized – that they are a constituent part of contemporary British society.

The same could be said of areas of public life like advertising where more black people figure in the everyday situations depicted. This includes being shown as part of racially mixed couples. Black actors or characters can even become stars of commercials, such as the former customer services rep Howard Brown, who became the face of Halifax Building Society's long-running television campaign. In popular television drama, from soap opera to science fiction, black family life and storylines in which black characters are central protagonists have also increased. In the field of sport, whose history of racialized representation this chapter has already explored, black sportsmen and women are widely and positively represented. The case of Premier League football is especially striking. Even a cursory glance at the coverage given of the 'national game' reveals that black players are among the most high-profile stars who receive praise for their skill and prowess. Who could not miss the impact of footballers like the former Arsenal striker Thierry Henry or Chelsea's Didier Drogba in the era of the Premier League and the star status they acquired. In the case of Henry, this recognition fed into the world of advertising where his reputation as a wonderful footballer with electric pace and grace was used to sell cars in the celebrated 'Va Va Voom' campaign for Renault Clio. As the example of Thierry Henry shows – and as other examples from the field of popular music and entertainment would also reveal – the normalization of black stars has been nurtured by the growing influence of celebrity culture. Whatever else one might say about this phenomenon, it has proved an important agent in the growing visibility and status of black people in the popular media.

FIGURE 4.32 Thierry Henry being interviewed on Media Day at Red Bull Arena in Harrison, New Jersey © Howard C. Smith/isiphotos.com/Corbis

The increased volume, range and normalization of racialized representation which we have described prompt an important question. Why have these processes occurred? Is the normalization of representations of racial difference the result of a specific set of cultural policies? Has there been a conversion among the administrators of sport, advertising, the entertainment and music industry to the cause of racial equality and the politics of representation? It is true that partly as a result of campaigns against racism in the media in the 1970s and 1980s, and the wider political struggles around equal opportunities in employment, that there has been recognition of the need to address institutional racism and explicit racial discrimination. The leverage generated by these reforms should not be underestimated. But cultural change does not happen in quite such a programmatic way. It is more that there has been a kind of 'multi-cultural drift' in which people now accept, whether they like it or not, that Britain, especially urban Britain, has a diverse population. What Britain looks like, whom the British are, has been irrevocably transformed by the legacy of post-war migration.

The process of what I have called 'multi-cultural drift' alerts us to the fact that change has taken place alongside the persistence of older patterns of racialized representation. Thus, while blacks can be celebrated within popular culture, the older forms of splitting and denigration remain at work. In the popular press and celebrity magazines, for example, the splitting of black subjects remains evident. Ashley Cole, the Chelsea footballer, can go from being a football star and celebrity one minute to being denigrated as a money-grabbing, sexually promiscuous bad boy the next. Made a hero one day and pulled down the next. The splitting of good and bad black subjects is also apparent across the coverage given to black folk across the popular press. Black stars can figure in the celebrity coverage, but these depictions sit alongside the continuing demonization of black youth in the 'hard news' coverage of crime and disorder. Despite the campaigns against institutional racism, there remains the lingering suspicion in the popular press that street crime is almost exclusively a black crime. The fixing of the idea of black criminality in the 1970s and the suspicion that hangs over black youth continues to exert an influence. This is not just a problem of representation within the tabloids. It is a perception of black pathology which informs the high numbers of young black men who are stopped by the police under current 'stop and search' laws. This is despite the fact that the numbers of black people actually charged and subsequently convicted of crime is negligible. This is what I mean by the persistence of deeper structures of racialized representation.

There is a final point to make about the contemporary patterns of racialized representation. If black people have acquired a great visibility and legitimacy within popular culture in areas like music, fashion, entertainment, they are much less visible or present within the world of corporate power. They are not part of Britain's global rich, or marginally so. They are not well represented among company directors and chief executives of big corporations. While black figures and celebrities may have exploded across the field of popular representation, there remains marked limits to their representation and participation in the centres of cultural and economic power.

REFERENCES

BABCOCK, B. (1978) *The Reversible World: Symbolic Inversion in Art and Society*, Ithaca, NY, Cornell University Press.

BAILEY, D. (1988) 'Rethinking black representation', in *Ten/8*, No. 31, Birmingham.

BAKHTIN, M. (1981) *The Dialogic Imagination*, Austin, TX, University of Texas. First published 1935.

BARTHES, R. (1977) 'Rhetoric of the image', in *Image–Music–Text,* Glasgow, Fontana.

BHABHA, H. (1986a) 'The Other question', in *Literature, Politics and Theory,* London, Methuen.

BHABHA, H. (1986b) 'Foreword' to Fanon, F., *Black Skin, White Masks*, London, Pluto Press.

BOGLE, D. (1973) *Toms, Coons, Mulattoes, Mammies and Bucks: An Interpretative History of Blacks in American Films*, New York, Viking Press.

BROWN, R. (1965) *Social Psychology*, London and New York, Macmillan.

CRIPPS , T. (1978) *Black Film as Genre*, Bloomington, IN, Indiana University Press.

DAVIS, A. (1983) *Women, Race and Class,* New York, Random House.

DERRIDA, J. (1972) *Positions*, Chicago, IL, University of Chicago Press.

DOUGLAS, M. (1966) *Purity and Danger*, London, Routledge and Kegan Paul.

DU GAY, P., HALL, S., JANES, L., MACKAY, H. AND NEGUS, K. (1997) *Doing Cultural Studies: The Story of the Sony Walkman,* London, Sage/The Open University (Book 1 in this series).

DYER, R. (ed.) (1977) *Gays and Film*, London, British Film Institute.

DYER, R. (1986) *Heavenly Bodies,* Basingstoke, Macmillan/British Film Institute.

FANON, F. (1986) *Black Skin, White Masks*, London, Pluto Press. First published 1952.

FERNANDO, S. (1992) 'Blackened images', in Bailey, D. A. and Hall, S. (eds), *Critical Decade, Ten/8,* No. 2(2), Birmingham.

FREDERICKSON, G. (1987) *The Black Image in the White Mind*, Hanover, NH, Wesleyan University Press.

FREUD, S. (1977) 'Fetishism', in *On Sexualities*, Pelican Freud Library, Vol. 7, Harmondsworth, Penguin. First published 1927.

GAINES, J. (1993) 'Fire and desire: race, melodrama and Oscar Mischeaux', in Diawara, M. (ed.), *Black American Cinema*, New York, Routledge.

GATES, H.L. (1988) *The Signifying Monkey*, Oxford, Oxford University Press.

GILMAN, S. (1985) *Difference and Pathology*, Ithaca, NY, Cornell University Press.

GREEN, D. (1984) 'Classified subjects: photography and anthropology – the technology of power', *Ten/8*, No. 14, Birmingham.

HALL, C. (1994) *White, Male and Middle Class*, Cambridge, Polity Press.

HALL, S. (1972) 'Determinations of news photographs', in *Working Papers in Cultural Studies No. 3*, Birmingham, University of Birmingham.

HALL, S. (1981) 'The whites of their eyes', in Brunt, R. (ed.), *Silver Linings*, London, Lawrence & Wishart.

HALL, S. (1996) 'The after-life of Frantz Fanon', in Read, A. (ed.), *The Fact of Blackness: Frantz Fanon and Visual Representation*, Seattle, WA, Bay Press.

HOOKS, B. (1992) *Black Looks: Race and Representation*, Boston, MA, South End Press.

JORDAN, W. (1968) *White over Black*, Chapel Hill, NC, University of North Carolina Press.

KLEIN, M. (1957) *Envy and Gratitude*, New York, Delta.

KRISTEVA, J. (1982) *Powers of Horror*, New York, Columbia University Press.

LACAN, J. (1977) *Èrits,* London, Tavistock.

LEAB, D. (1976) *From Sambo to Superspade*, New York, Houghton Mifflin.

LÉVI-STRAUSS, C. (1970) *The Raw and the Cooked*, London, Jonathan Cape.

LINDFORS, B. (unpublished) 'The Hottentot Venus and other African attractions'.

LONG, E. (1774) *History of Jamaica*, London, Lowdnes.

MACKENZIE, J. (ed.) (1986) *Imperialism and Popular Culture,* Manchester, Manchester University Press.

MCCLLNTOCK, A. (1995) *Imperial Leather,* London, Routledge.

MERCER, K. (1994) 'Reading racial fetishism', in Mercer, K. (ed.), *Welcome to the Jungle,* London, Routledge.

MERCER, K. AND JULIEN, I. (1994) 'Black masculinity and the politics of race', in Mercer, K. (ed.), *Welcome to the Jungle,* London, Routledge.

MORTON, P. (1991) *Disfigured Images*, New York, Praeger and Greenwood Press.

RICHARDS, T. (1990) *The Commodity Culture of Victorian Britain*, London, Verso.

RIEFENSTAHL, L. (1976) *The Last of the Nuba*, London, Collins.

SAID, E. (1978) *Orientalism*, Harmondsworth, Penguin.

SEGAL, L. (1997) 'Sexualities', Chapter 4 in Woodward, K. (ed.), *Identity and Difference*, London, Sage/The Open University (Book 3 in this series).

STALLYBRASS, P. AND WHITE, A. (1986) *The Politics and Poetics of Transgression*, London, Methuen.

STAPLES, R. (1982) *Black Masculinity: The Black Man's Role in American Society*, San Fransisco, CA, Black Scholar Press.

WALLACE, M. (1979) *Black Macho*, London, Calder.

WALLACE, M. (1993) 'Race, gender and psychoanalysis in forties films', in Diawara, M. (ed.), *Black American Cinema*, New York, Routledge.

READING A: Anne McClintock, 'Soap and commodity spectacle'

In 1899, the year that the Anglo-Boer War broke out in South Africa, an advertisement for Pears' Soap in *McClure's Magazine* [Figure 4.8a] announced:

The first step towards lightening THE WHITE MAN'S BURDEN is through teaching the virtues of cleanliness, PEARS' SOAP is a potent factor in brightening the dark corners of the earth as civilization advances, while amongst the cultured of all nations it holds the highest place – it is the ideal toilet soap.

[…]

The first point about the Pears' advertisement is that it figures imperialism as coming into being through *domesticity*. At the same time, imperial domesticity is a domesticity without women. The commodity fetish, as the central form of the industrial Enlightenment, reveals what liberalism would like to forget: the domestic is political, the political is gendered. What could not be admitted into male rationalist discourse (the economic value of women's domestic labour) is disavowed and projected onto the realm of the 'primitive' and the zone of empire. At the same time, the economic value of colonized cultures is domesticated and projected onto the realm of the 'prehistoric'.

A characteristic feature of the Victorian middle class was its peculiarly intense preoccupation with rigid boundaries. In imperial fiction and commodity kitsch, boundary objects and liminal scenes recur ritualistically. As colonials travelled back and forth across the thresholds of their known world, crisis and boundary confusion were warded off and contained by fetishes, absolution rituals and liminal scenes. Soap and cleaning rituals became central to the demarcation of body boundaries and the policing of social hierarchies. Cleansing and boundary rituals are integral to most cultures; what characterized Victorian cleaning rituals, however, was their peculiarly intense relation to money.

[...]

SOAP AND COMMODITY SPECTACLE

Before the late nineteenth century, clothes and bedding washing was done in most households only once or twice a year in great, communal binges, usually in public at streams or rivers (Davidoff and Hall, 1992). As for body washing, not much had changed since the days when Queen Elizabeth I was distinguished by the frequency with which she washed: 'regularly every month whether we needed it or not'. By the 1890s, however, soap sales had soared, Victorians were consuming 260,000 tons of soap a year, and advertising had emerged as the central cultural form of commodity capitalism (Lindsey and Bamber, 1965).

[…]

Economic competition with the United States and Germany created the need for a more aggressive promotion of British products and led to the first real innovations in advertising. In 1884, the year of the Berlin Conference, the first wrapped soap was sold under a brand name. This small event signified a major transformation in capitalism, as imperial competition gave rise to the creation of monopolies. Henceforth, items formerly indistinguishable from each other (soap sold simply as soap) would be marketed by their corporate signature (Pears, Monkey Brand, etc.). Soap became one of the first commodities to register the historic shift from myriad small businesses to the great imperial monopolies. In the 1870s, hundreds of small soap companies plied the new trade in hygiene, but by the end of the century, the trade was monopolized by ten large companies.

In order to manage the great soap show, an aggressively entrepreneurial breed of advertisers emerged, dedicated to gracing each homely product with a radiant halo of imperial glamour and radical potency. The advertising agent, like the bureaucrat, played a vital role in the imperial expansion of foreign trade. Advertisers billed themselves as 'empire builders' and flattered themselves with 'the responsibility of the historic imperial mission'. Said one: 'Commerce even more than sentiment binds the ocean sundered portions of empire together. Anyone who increases these commercial interests strengthens the whole fabric of the empire' (quoted in Hindley and Hindley, 1972). Soap was credited not only with bringing moral and economic salvation to Britain's 'great unwashed' but also with magically embodying the spiritual ingredient of the imperial mission itself.

In an ad for Pears, for example, a black and implicitly racialized coal sweeper holds in his hands a glowing, occult object. Luminous with its own inner radiance, the simple soap bar glows like a fetish, pulsating magically with spiritual enlightenment and imperial grandeur, promising to warm the hands and hearts of working people across the globe (Dempsey, 1978). Pears,

in particular, became intimately associated with a purified nature magically cleansed of polluting industry (tumbling kittens, faithful dogs, children festooned with flowers) and a purified working class magically cleansed of polluting labour (smiling servants in crisp white aprons, rosy-cheeked match girls and scrubbed scullions) (Bradley, 1991).

Nonetheless, the Victorian obsession with cotton and cleanliness was not simply a mechanical reflex of economic surplus. If imperialism garnered a bounty of cheap cotton and soap oils from coerced colonial labour, the middle class Victorian fascination with clean, white bodies and clean, white clothing stemmed not only from the rampant profiteering of the imperial economy but also from the realms of ritual and fetish.

Soap did not flourish when imperial ebullience was at its peak. It emerged commercially during an era of impending crisis and social calamity, serving to preserve, through fetish ritual, the uncertain boundaries of class, gender and race identity in a social order felt to be threatened by the fetid effluvia of the slums, the belching smoke of industry, social agitation, economic upheaval, imperial competition and anticolonial resistance. Soap offered the promise of spiritual salvation and regeneration through commodity consumption, a regime of domestic hygiene that could restore the threatened potency of the imperial body politic and the race.

THE PEARS' CAMPAIGN

In 1789 Andrew Pears, a farmer's son, left his Cornish village of Mevagissey to open a barbershop in London, following the trend of widespread demographic migration from country to

273

city and the economic turn from land to commerce. In his shop, Pears made and sold the powders, creams and dentifrices used by the rich to ensure the fashionable alabaster purity of their complexions. For the elite, a sun-darkened skin stained by outdoor manual work was the visible stigma not only of a class obliged to work under the elements for a living but also of far-off, benighted races marked by God's disfavour. From the outset, soap took shape as a technology of social purification, inextricably entwined with the semiotics of imperial racism and class denigration.

In 1838 Andrew Pears retired and left his firm in the hands of his grandson, Francis. In due course, Francis's daughter, Mary, married Thomas J. Barratt, who became Francis's partner and took the gamble of fashioning a middle-class market for the transparent soap. Barratt revolutionized Pears by masterminding a series of dazzling advertising campaigns. Inaugurating a new era of advertising, he won himself lasting fame, in the familiar iconography of male birthing, as the 'father of advertising'. Soap thus found its industrial destiny through the mediation of domestic kinship and that peculiarly Victorian preoccupation with patrimony.

Through a series of gimmicks and innovations that placed Pears at the centre of Britain's emerging commodity culture, Barratt showed a perfect understanding of the fetishism that structures all advertising. Importing a quarter of a million French centime pieces into Britain, Barratt had the name Pears stamped on them and put the coins into circulation – a gesture that marvellously linked exchange value with the corporate brand name. The ploy worked famously, arousing much publicity for Pears and such a public fuss that an Act of Parliament was rushed through to declare all foreign coins illegal tender. The boundaries of the national currency closed around the domestic bar of soap.

Georg Lukacs points out that the commodity lies on the threshold of culture and commerce, confusing the supposedly sacrosanct boundaries between aesthetics and economy, money and art. In the mid-1880s, Barratt devised a piece of breathtaking cultural transgression that exemplified Lukacs insight and clinched Pears' fame. Barratt bought Sir John Everett Millais' painting 'Bubbles' (originally entitled 'A Child's World') and inserted into the painting a bar of soap stamped with the totemic word *Pears*. At a stroke, he transformed the artwork of the best-known painter in Britain into a mass produced commodity associated in the public mind with Pears.[1] At the same time, by mass reproducing the painting as a poster ad, Barratt took art from the elite realm of private property to the mass realms of commodity spectacle.[2]

In advertising, the axis of possession is shifted to the axis of spectacle. Advertising's chief contribution to the culture of modernity was the discovery that by manipulating the semiotic space around the commodity, the unconscious as a public space could also be manipulated. Barratt's great innovation was to invest huge sums of money in the creation of a visible aesthetic space around the commodity. The development of poster and print technology made possible the mass reproduction of such a space around the image of a commodity (see Wicke, 1988, p. 70).

In advertising, that which is disavowed by industrial rationality (ambivalence, sensuality, chance, unpredictable causality, multiple time) is projected onto image space as a repository of the forbidden. Advertising draws on subterranean flows of desire and taboo, manipulating the investment of surplus money. Pears' distinction, swiftly emulated by scores of soap companies including Monkey Brand and Sunlight, as well as countless other advertisers, was to invest the aesthetic space around the domestic commodity with the commercial cult of empire.

NOTES

1 Barratt spent £2,200 on Millais' painting and £30,000 on the mass production of millions of individual reproductions of the painting. In the 1880s, Pears was spending between £300,000 and £400,000 on advertising alone.

2 Furious at the pollution of the sacrosanct realm of art with economics, the art world lambasted Millais for trafficking (publicly instead of privately) in the sordid world of trade.

REFERENCES

BRADLEY, L. (1991) 'Trom Eden to Empire: John Everett Millais' Cherry Ripe', *Victorian Studies*, 34(2) (Winter), pp. 179–203.

DAVIDOFF, L. AND HALL, C. (1992) *Family Fortunes: Men and Women of the English Middle Class*, London, Routledge.

DEMPSEY, M. (ed.) (1978) *Bubbles: Early Advertising Art From A. & F. Pears Ltd.*, London, Fontana.

HINDLEY, D. AND HINDLEY, G. (1972) *Advertising in Victorian England, 1837–1901*, London, Wayland.

LINDSEY, D.T.A. AND BAMBER, G.C. (1965) *Soap-making, Past and Present, 1876–1976*, Nottingham, Gerard Brothers Ltd.

WICKE, J. (1988) *Advertising Fiction: Literature, Advertisement and Social Reading*, New York, Columbia University Press.

Source: McClintock, 1995, pp. 32–33 and 210–213.

READING B: Richard Dyer, 'Africa'

An initial problem was that of knowing what Africa was like. There is an emphasis in much of the work Robeson is associated with on being authentic. The tendency is to assume that if you have an actual African doing something, or use actual African languages or dance movements, you will capture the truly African. In the African dream section of *Taboo* (1922), the first professional stage play Robeson was in, there was 'an African dance done by C. Kamba Simargo, a native' (Johnson, 1968 [1930], p. 192); for *Basalik* (1935), 'real' African dancers were employed (Schlosser, 1970, p. 156). The titles for *The Emperor Jones* (1933) tell us that the tom-toms have been 'anthropologically recorded', and several of the films use ethnographic props and footage – *Sanders of the River* (1934, conical huts, kraals, canoes, shields, calabashes and spears, cf. Schlosser, 1970, p. 234), *Song of Freedom* (1936, Devil Dancers of Sierra Leone, cf. ibid., p. 256) and *King Solomon's Mines* (1936). Princess Gaza in *Jericho* (1937) is played by the real-life African princess Kouka of Sudan. Robeson was also widely known to have researched a great deal into African culture; his concerts often included brief lectures demonstrating the similarity between the structures of African folk song and that of other, both Western and Eastern, cultures (see Schlosser, 1970, p. 332). However, this authentication of the African elements in his work is beset with problems. In practice, these are genuine notes inserted into works produced decidedly within American and British discourses on Africa. These moments of song, dance, speech and stage presence are either inflected by the containing discourses as Savage Africa or else remain opaque, folkloric, touristic.

No doubt the ethnographic footage of dances in the British films records complex ritual meanings, but the films give us no idea what these are and so they remain mysterious savagery. Moreover, as is discussed later, Robeson himself is for the most part distinguished from these elements rather than identified with them; they remain 'other'. This authentication enterprise also falls foul of being only empirically authentic – it lacks a concern with the paradigms through which one observes any empirical phenomenon. Not only are the 'real' African elements left undefended from their immediate theatrical or filmic context, they have already been perceived through discourses on Africa that have labelled them primitive, often with a flattering intention.

This is not just a question of white, racist views of Africa. It springs from the problem, as Marion Berghahn (1977) notes, that black American knowledge of Africa also comes largely through white sources. It has to come to terms with the image of Africa in those sources, and very often in picking out for rejection the obvious racism there is a tendency to assume that what is left over is a residue of transparent knowledge about Africa. To put the problem more directly, and with an echo of DuBois' notion of the 'twoness' of the black American – when confronting Africa, the black Westerner has to cope with the fact that she or he is of the West. The problem, and its sometimes bitter ironies, is illustrated in two publicity photos from Robeson films. The first, from the later film *Jericho,* shows Robeson with Wallace Ford and Henry Wilcoxon during the filming in 1937 [Figure 4.20]. It is a classic tourist photo, friends snapped before a famous landmark. Robeson is dressed in Western clothes, and grouped between the two white men; they are even, by chance no doubt, grouped at a break in the row of palm trees behind them. They are not part of the landscape, they are visiting it.

REFERENCES

BERGHAHN, M. (1977) *Images of Africa in Black American Literature*, Totawa, NJ, Rowman & Littlefield.

JOHNSON, J. W. (1968) *Black Manhattan*, New York, Atheneum. First published 1930.

SCHLOSSER, A.I. (1970) 'Paul Robeson, his career in the theatre, in motion pictures, and on the concert stage', unpublished PhD dissertation, New York University.

Source: Dyer, 1986, pp. 89–91.

Richard Dyer

READING C: Sander Gilman, 'The deep structure of stereotypes'

Everyone creates stereotypes. We cannot function in the world without them (see, for example, Levin, 1975). They buffer us against our most urgent fears by extending them, making it possible for us to act as though their source were beyond our control.

The creation of stereotypes is a concomitant of the process by which all human beings become individuals. Its beginnings lie in the earliest stages of our development. The infant's movement from a state of being in which everything is perceived as an extension of the self to a growing sense of a separate identity takes place between the ages of a few weeks and about five months.[1] During that stage, the new sense of 'difference' is directly acquired by the denial of the child's demands on the world. We all begin not only by demanding food, warmth, and comfort, but by assuming that those demands will be met. The world is felt to be a mere extension of the self. It is that part of the self which provides food, warmth, and comfort. As the child comes to distinguish more and more between the world and self, anxiety arises from a perceived loss of control over the world. But very soon the child begins to combat anxieties associated with the failure to control the world by adjusting his mental picture of people and objects so that they can appear 'good' even when their behaviour is perceived as 'bad' (Kohut, 1971).

But even more, the sense of the self is shaped to fit this pattern. The child's sense of self itself splits into a 'good' self, which, as the self mirroring the earlier stage of the complete control of the world, is free from anxiety, and the 'bad' self, which is unable to control the environment and is thus exposed to anxieties. This split is but a single stage in the development of the normal personality. In it lies, however, the root of all stereotypical perceptions. For in the normal course of development the child's understanding of the world becomes seemingly ever more sophisticated. The child is able to distinguish ever finer gradations of 'goodness' and 'badness', so that by the later oedipal stage an illusion of verisimilitude is cast over the inherent (and irrational) distinction between the 'good' and 'bad' world and self, between control and loss of control, between acquiescence and denial.

With the split of both the self and the world into 'good' and 'bad' objects, the 'bad' self is distanced and identified with the mental representation of the 'bad' object. This act of projection saves the self from any confrontation with the contradictions present in the necessary integration of 'bad' and 'good' aspects of the self. The deep structure of our own sense of self and the world is built upon the illusionary image of the world divided into two camps, 'us' and 'them'. 'They' are either 'good' or 'bad'. Yet it is clear that this is a very primitive distinction which, in most individuals, is replaced early in development by the illusion of integration.

Stereotypes are a crude set of mental representations of the world. They are palimpsests on which the initial bipolar representations are still vaguely legible. They perpetuate a needed sense of difference between the 'self' and the 'object', which becomes the 'Other'. Because there is no real line between self and the Other, an imaginary line must be drawn; and so that the illusion of an absolute difference between self and Other is never troubled, this line is as dynamic in its ability to alter itself as is the self. This can be observed in the shifting relationship of antithetical stereotypes that parallel the existence of 'bad' and 'good' representations of self and Other. But the line between 'good' and 'bad' responds to stresses occurring within the psyche. Thus paradigm shifts in our mental representations of the world can and do occur. We can move from fearing to glorifying the Other. We can move from loving to hating. The most negative stereotype always has an overtly positive counterweight. As any image is shifted, all stereotypes shift. Thus stereotypes are inherently protean rather than rigid.

Although this activity seems to take place outside the self, in the world of the object, of the Other, it is in fact only a reflection of an internal process, which draws upon repressed mental representations for its structure. Stereotypes arise when self-integration is threatened. They are therefore part of our way of dealing with the instabilities of our perception of the world. This is not to say that they are good, only that they are necessary. We can and must make the distinction between pathological stereotyping and the stereotyping all of us need to do to preserve our illusion of control over the self and the world. Our Manichean perception of the world as 'good' and 'bad' is triggered by a recurrence of the type of insecurity that induced our initial division of the world into 'good' and 'bad'. For the pathological personality every confrontation sets up this echo. Stereotypes can and often do exist parallel to the ability to create sophisticated rational categories that transcend the crude line of difference present in the stereotype. We retain our ability to distinguish the 'individual' from the stereotyped class into which the object might automatically be placed. The pathological personality does not develop this ability and sees the entire world in terms of the rigid line of difference. The pathological personality's mental representation of the world supports the need for the line of difference, whereas for the non-pathological individual the stereotype is a momentary coping mechanism, one that can be used and then discarded once anxiety is overcome. The former is consistently aggressive toward the real people and objects to which the stereotypical representations correspond; the latter is able to repress the aggression and deal with people as individuals.

NOTES

1 I am indebted to Otto Kernberg's work for this discussion.

REFERENCES

KERNBERG, O. (1980) *Internal World and External Reality: Object Relations Theory Applied*, New York, Jason Aronson.

KERNBERG, O. (1984) *Severe Personality Disorders: Psychotherapeutic Strategies*, New Haven, CT, Yale University Press.

KOHUT, H. (1971) *The Analysis of Self*, New York, International Universities Press.

LEVIN, J. (1975) *The Functions of Prejudice*, New York, Harper & Row.

Source: Gilman, 1985, pp. 16–18.

READING D: Kobena Mercer, 'Reading racial fetishism'

Mapplethorpe first made his name in the world of art photography with his portraits of patrons and protagonists in the post-Warhol New York avant-garde milieu of the 1970s. In turn he [became] something of a star himself, as the discourse of journalists, critics, curators and collectors [wove] a mystique around his persona, creating a public image of the artist as author of 'prints of darkness'. As he [...] extended his repertoire across flowers, bodies and faces, the conservatism of Mapplethorpe's aesthetic [became] all too apparent: a reworking of the old modernist tactic of 'shock the bourgeoisie' (and make them pay), given a new aura by his characteristic signature, the pursuit of perfection in photographic technique. The vaguely transgressive quality of his subject matter – gay S/M ritual, lady bodybuilders, black men – is given heightened allure by his evident mastery of photographic technology.

In as much as the image-making technology of the camera is based on the mechanical reproduction of unilinear perspective, photographs primarily represent a 'look'. I therefore want to talk about Mapplethorpe's *Black Males* not as the product of the personal intentions of the individual behind the lens, but as a cultural artifact that says something about certain ways in which white people 'look' at black people and how, in this way of looking, black male sexuality is perceived as something different, excessive, Other. Certainly this particular work must be set in the context of Mapplethorpe's oeuvre as a whole: through his cool and deadly gaze each found object – 'flowers, S/M, blacks' – is brought under the clinical precision of his master vision, his complete control of photo-technique, and thus aestheticized to the abject status of thinghood. However, once we consider the author of these images as no more than the 'projection, in terms more or less psychological, of our way of handling texts' (Foucault, 1977, p. 127), then what is interesting about work such as *The Black Book* is the way the text facilitates the imaginary projection of certain racial and sexual fantasies about the black male body. Whatever his personal motivations or creative pretensions, Mapplethorpe's camera-eye opens an aperture onto aspects of stereotypes – a fixed way of seeing that freezes the flux of experience – which govern the circulation of images of black men across a range of surfaces from newspapers, television and cinema to advertising, sport and pornography.

Approached as a textual system, both *Black Males* (1983) and *The Black Book* (1986) catalogue a series of perspectives, vantage points and 'takes' on the black male body. The first thing to notice – so obvious it goes without saying – is that all the men are nude. Each of the camera's points of view lead to a unitary vanishing point: an erotic/aesthetic objectification of black male bodies into the idealized form of a homogenous type thoroughly saturated with a totality of sexual predicates. We look through a sequence of individual, personally named, Afro-American men, but what we *see* is only their *sex* as the essential sum total of the meanings signified around blackness and maleness. It is as if, according to Mapplethorpe's line of sight: Black + Male = Erotic/Aesthetic Object. Regardless of the sexual preferences of the spectator, the connotation is that the 'essence' of black male identity lies in the domain of sexuality. Whereas the photographs of gay male S/M rituals invoke a subcultural sexuality that consists of *doing* something, black men are confined and defined in their very *being* as sexual and nothing but sexual, hence hypersexual. In pictures like 'Man in a Polyester Suit,' apart from his hands, it is the penis and the penis alone that identifies the model in the picture as a black man.

This ontological reduction is accomplished through the specific visual codes brought to bear on the construction of pictorial space. Sculpted and shaped through the conventions of the fine art nude, the image of the black male body presents the spectator with a source of erotic pleasure in the act of looking. As a generic code established across fine art traditions in Western art history, the conventional subject of the nude is the (white) female body. Substituting the socially inferior black male subject, Mapplethorpe nevertheless draws on the codes of the genre to frame his way of seeing black male bodies as abstract, beautiful 'things'. The aesthetic, and thus erotic, objectification is totalizing in effect, as all references to a social, historical or political context are ruled out of the frame. This visual codification abstracts and essentializes the black man's body into the realm of a transcendental aesthetic ideal. In this sense, the text reveals more about the desires of the hidden and invisible white male subject behind the camera and what 'he' wants-to-see, than it does about the anonymous black men whose beautiful bodies we see depicted.

Within the dominant tradition of the female nude, patriarchal power relations are symbolized by the binary relation in which, to put it crudely, men assume the active role of the looking subject while women are passive objects to be looked at. Laura Mulvey's (1989 [1975]) contribution to feminist film theory revealed the normative power and privilege of the male gaze in dominant systems of visual representation. The image of the female nude can thus be understood not so much as a representation of (hetero)sexual desire, but as a form of objectification which articulates masculine hegemony and dominance over the very apparatus of representation itself. Paintings abound with self-serving scenarios of phallocentric fantasy in which male artists paint themselves painting naked women, which, like depictions of feminine narcissism, constructs a mirror image of what the male subject wants-to-see. The fetishistic logic of mimetic representation, which makes present for the subject what is absent in the real, can thus be characterized in terms of a masculine fantasy of mastery and control over the 'objects' depicted and represented in the visual field, the fantasy of an omnipotent eye/I who sees but who is never seen.

In Mapplethorpe's case, however, the fact that both subject and object of the gaze are male sets up a tension between the active role of looking and the passive role of being looked at. This *frisson* of (homo)sexual sameness transfers erotic investment in the fantasy of mastery from gender to racial difference. Traces of this metaphorical transfer underline the highly charged libidinal investment of Mapplethorpe's gaze as it bears down on the most visible signifier of racial difference – black skin. In his analysis of the male pinup, Richard Dyer (1982) suggests that when male subjects assume the passive, 'feminized' position of being looked at, the threat or risk to traditional definitions of masculinity is counteracted by the role of certain codes and conventions, such as taut, rigid or straining bodily posture, character types and narrativized plots, all of which aim to stabilize the gender-based dichotomy of seeing/being seen.

Here Mapplethorpe appropriates elements of commonplace racial stereotypes in order to regulate, organize, prop up and *fix* the process of erotic/aesthetic objectification in which the black man's flesh becomes burdened with the task of symbolizing the transgressive fantasies and desires of the white gay male subject. The glossy, shining, fetishized surface of black skin thus serves and services a white male desire to look and to enjoy the fantasy of mastery precisely through the scopic intensity that the pictures solicit.

As Homi Bhabha has suggested, 'an important feature of colonial discourse is its dependence on the concept of "fixity" in the ideological construction of otherness' (Bhabha, 1983, p. 18). Mass-media stereotypes of black men – as criminals, athletes, entertainers – bear witness to the contemporary repetition of such *colonial fantasy*, in that the rigid and limited grid of representations through which black male subjects become publicly visible continues to reproduce certain *idées fixes*, ideological fictions and psychic fixations, about the nature of black sexuality and the 'otherness' it is constructed to embody. As an artist, Mapplethorpe engineers a fantasy of absolute authority over the image of the black male body by appropriating the function of the stereotype to stabilize the erotic objectification of racial otherness and thereby affirm his own identity as the sovereign I/eye empowered with mastery over the abject thinghood of the Other: as if the pictures implied, Eye have the power to turn you, base and worthless creature, into a work of art. Like Medusa's look, each camera angle and photographic shot turns black male flesh to stone, fixed and frozen in space and time: enslaved as an icon in the representational space of the white male imaginary, historically at the centre of colonial fantasy.

There are two important aspects of fetishization at play here. The erasure of any social interference in the spectator's erotic enjoyment of the image not only reifies bodies but effaces the material process involved in the production of the image, thus masking the social relations of racial power entailed by the unequal and potentially exploitative exchange between the well-known, author-named artist and the unknown, interchangeable, black models. In the same way that labor is said to be 'alienated' in commodity fetishism, something similar is put into operation in the way that the proper name of each black model is taken from a person and given to a thing, as the title or caption of the photograph, an art object which is property of the artist, the owner and author of the look. And as items of exchange-value, Mapplethorpe prints fetch exorbitant prices on the international market in art photography.

The fantasmatic emphasis on mastery also underpins the specifically sexual fetishization of the Other that is evident in the visual isolation effect whereby it is only ever *one* black man who appears in the field of vision at any one time. As an imprint of a narcissistic, ego-centred, sexualizing fantasy, this is a crucial component in the process of erotic objectification, not only because it forecloses the possible representation of a collective or contextualized black male body, but because the solo frame is the precondition for a voyeuristic fantasy of unmediated and unilateral control over the other which is the function it performs precisely in gay and straight pornography. Aestheticized as a trap for the gaze, providing pabulum on which the appetite of the imperial eye may feed, each image thus nourishes the racialized and sexualized fantasy of appropriating the Other's body as virgin territory to be penetrated and possessed by an all-powerful desire, 'to probe and explore an alien body'.

Superimposing two ways of seeing – the nude which eroticizes the act of looking, and the stereotype which imposes fixity – we see in Mapplethorpe's gaze a reinscription of the fundamental *ambivalence* of colonial fantasy, oscillating between sexual idealization of the racial other and anxiety in defence of the identity of the white male ego. Stuart Hall (1982) has underlined this splitting in the 'imperial eye' by suggesting that for every threatening image of the black subject as a marauding native, menacing savage or rebellious slave, there is the comforting image of the black as docile servant, amusing clown and happy entertainer. Commenting on this bifurcation in racial representations, Hall describes it as the expression of

> both a nostalgia for an innocence lost forever to the civilized, and the threat of civilization being over-run or undermined by the recurrence of savagery, which is always lurking just below the surface; or by an untutored sexuality threatening to 'break out'.

(Hall, 1982, p. 41)

In Mapplethorpe, we may discern three discrete camera codes through which this fundamental ambivalence is reinscribed through the process of a sexual and racial fantasy which aestheticizes the stereotype into a work of art.

The first of these, which is most self-consciously acknowledged, could be called the *sculptural* code, as it is a subset of the generic fine art nude. [In the photograph of the model, Phillip, pretending to put the shot], the idealized physique of a classical Greek male statue is superimposed on that most commonplace of stereotypes, the black man as sports hero, mythologically endowed with a 'naturally' muscular physique and an essential capacity for strength, grace and machinelike perfection: well hard. As a major public arena, sport is a key site of white male ambivalence, fear and fantasy. The spectacle of black bodies triumphant in rituals of masculine competition reinforces the fixed idea that black men are 'all brawn and no brains', and yet, because the white man is beaten at his own game – football, boxing, cricket, athletics – the Other is idolized to the point of envy. This schism is played out daily in the popular tabloid press. On the front page headlines, black males become highly visible as a threat to white society, as muggers, rapists, terrorists and guerrillas: their bodies become the imago of a savage and unstoppable capacity for destruction and violence. But turn to the back pages, the sports pages, and the black man's body is heroized and lionized; any hint of antagonism is contained by the paternalistic infantilization of Frank Bruno and Daley Thompson to the status of national mascots and adopted pets – they're not Other, they're OK because they're 'our boys'. The national shame of Englands' demise and defeat in Test Cricket at the hands of the West Indies is accompanied by the slavish admiration of Viv Richards's awesome physique – the high-speed West Indian bowler is both a threat and a winner. The ambivalence cuts deep into the recess of the white male imaginary – recall those newsreel images of Hitler's reluctant handshake with Jesse Owens at the 1936 Olympics.

If Mapplethorpe's gaze is momentarily lost in admiration, it reasserts control by also 'feminizing' the black male body into a passive, decorative *objet d'art*. When Phillip is placed on a pedestal he literally becomes putty in the hands of the white male artist – like others in this code, his body becomes raw material, mere plastic matter, to be molded, sculpted and shaped into the aesthetic idealism of inert abstraction [...]. Commenting on the differences between moving and motionless pictures, Christian Metz suggests (1985, p. 85) an association linking photography, silence and death as photographs invoke a residual death effect such that, 'the person who has been photographed is dead ... dead for having been seen'. Under the intense scrutiny of Mapplethorpe's cool, detached gaze it is as if each black model is made to die, if only to reincarnate their alienated essence as idealized, aesthetic objects. We are not invited to imagine what their lives, histories or experiences are like, as they are silenced as subjects in their own right, and in a sense sacrificed on the pedestal of an aesthetic ideal in order to affirm the omnipotence of the master subject, whose gaze has the power of light and death.

In counterpoint there is a supplementary code of *portraiture* which 'humanizes' the hard phallic lines of pure abstraction and focuses on the face – the 'window of the soul' – to introduce an element of realism into the scene. But any connotation of humanist expression is denied by the direct look which does not so much assert the existence of an autonomous subjectivity, but rather, like the remote, aloof, expressions of fashion models in glossy magazines, emphasizes instead maximum distance between the spectator and the unattainable object of desire. Look, but don't touch. The models' direct look to camera does not challenge the gaze of the white male artist, although it plays on the active/passive tension of seeing/being seen, because any potential disruption is contained by the subtextual work of the stereotype. Thus in one portrait the 'primitive' nature of the Negro is invoked by the profile: the face becomes an after-image of a stereotypically 'African' tribal mask, high cheekbones and matted dreadlocks further connote wildness, danger, exotica. In another, the chiseled contours of a shaved head, honed by rivulets of sweat, summon up the criminal mug shot from the forensic files of police photography. This also recalls the anthropometric uses of photography in the colonial scene, measuring the cranium of the colonized so as to show, by the documentary evidence of photography, the inherent 'inferiority' of the Other. This is overlaid with deeper ambivalence in the portrait of Terrel, whose grotesque grimace calls up the happy/sad mask of the nigger minstrel: humanized by racial pathos, the Sambo stereotype haunts the scene, evoking the black man's supposedly childlike dependency on ole Massa, which in turn fixes his social, legal and existential 'emasculation' at the hands of the white master.

Finally, two codes together – of *cropping* and *lighting* – interpenetrate the flesh and mortify it into a racial sex fetish, a juju doll from the dark side of the white man's imaginary. The body-whole is fragmented into microscopic details – chest, arms, torso, buttocks, penis – inviting a scopophilic dissection of the parts that make up the whole. Indeed, like a talisman, each part is invested with the power to evoke the 'mystique' of black male sexuality with more perfection than any empirically unified whole. The camera cuts away, like a knife, allowing the spectator to inspect the 'goods'. In such fetishistic attention to detail, tiny scars and blemishes on the surface of black skin serve only to heighten the technical perfectionism of the photographic print. The cropping and fragmentation of bodies – often decapitated, so to speak – is a salient feature of pornography, and has been seen from certain feminist positions as a form of male violence, a literal inscription of a sadistic impulse in the male gaze, whose pleasure thus consists of cutting up women's bodies into visual bits and pieces. Whether or not this view is tenable, the effect of the technique here is to suggest aggression in the act of looking, but not as racial violence or racism-as-hate; on the contrary, aggression as the frustration of the ego who finds the object of his desires out of reach, inaccessible. The cropping is analogous to striptease in this sense, as the exposure of successive body parts distances the erotogenic object, making it untouchable so as to tantalize the drive to look, which reaches its aim in the denoument by which the woman's sex is unveiled. Except here the unveiling that reduces the woman from angel to whore is substituted by the unconcealing of the black man's private parts, with the penis as the forbidden totem of colonial fantasy.

As each fragment seduces the eye into ever more intense fascination, we glimpse the dilation of a libidinal way of looking that spreads itself across the surface of black skin. Harsh contrasts of shadow and light draw the eye to focus and fix attention on the texture of the black man's skin. According to Bhabha, unlike the sexual fetish *per se*, whose meanings are usually hidden as a hermeneutic secret, skin color functions as '*the most visible of fetishes*' (Bhabha, 1983, p. 30). Whether it is devalorized in the signifying chain of 'negrophobia'

or hypervalorized as a desirable attribute in 'negrophilia', the fetish of skin color in the codes of racial discourse constitutes the most visible element in the articulation of what Stuart Hall (1977) calls 'the ethnic signifier'. The shining surface of black skin serves several functions in its representation: it suggests the physical exertion of powerful bodies, as black boxers always glisten like bronze in the illuminated square of the boxing ring; or, in pornography, it suggests intense sexual activity 'just before' the photograph was taken, a metonymic stimulus to arouse spectatorial participation in the imagined *mise-en-scene*. In Mapplethorpe's pictures the specular brilliance of black skin is bound in a double articulation as a fixing agent for the fetishistic structure of the photographs. There is a subtle slippage between represener and represented, as the shiny, polished, sheen of black skin becomes consubstantial with the luxurious allure of the high-quality photographic print. As Victor Burgin has remarked (1980, p. 100), sexual fetishism dovetails with commodity-fetishism to inflate the economic value of the print in art photography as much as in fashion photography, the 'glossies'. Here, black skin and print surface are bound together to enhance the pleasure of the white spectator as much as the profitability of these art-world commodities exchanged among the artist and his dealers, collectors and curators.

In everyday discourse *fetishism* probably connotes deviant or 'kinky' sexuality, and calls up images of leather and rubberwear as signs of sexual perversity. This is not a fortuitous example, as leather fashion has a sensuous appeal as a kind of 'second skin'. When one considers that such clothes are invariably black, rather than any other color, such fashion-fetishism suggests a desire to simulate or imitate black skin. On the other hand, Freud's theorization of fetishism as a clinical phenomenon of sexual pathology and perversion is problematic in many ways, but the central notion of the fetish as a metaphorical substitute for the absent phallus enables understanding of the psychic structure of disavowal, and the splitting of levels of conscious and unconscious belief, that is relevant to the ambiguous axis upon which negrophilia and negrophobia intertwine.

For Freud (1977 [1927], pp. 351–7), the little boy who is shocked to see the absence of the penis in the little girl or his mother, which he believes has either been lost or castrated, encounters the recognition of sexual or genital difference with an accompanying experience of anxiety which is nevertheless denied or disavowed by the existence of a metaphorical substitute, on which the adult fetishist depends for his access to sexual pleasure. Hence, in terms of a linguistic formula: I *know* (the woman has no penis), *but* (nevertheless, she does, through the fetish).

Such splitting is captured precisely in 'Man in a Polyester Suit', as the central focus on the black penis emerging from the unzipped trouser fly simultaneously affirms and denies that most fixed of racial myths in the white male imaginary, namely the belief that every black man has a monstrously large willy. The scale of the photograph foregrounds the size of the black dick which thus signifies a threat, not the threat of racial difference as such, but the fear that the Other is more sexually potent than his white master. As a phobic object, the big black prick is a 'bad object', a fixed point in the paranoid fantasies of the negrophobe which Fanon found in the pathologies of his white psychiatric patients as much as in the normalized cultural artefacts of his time. Then as now, in front of this picture, 'one is no longer aware of the Negro, but only, of a penis; the Negro is eclipsed. He is turned into a penis. He *is* a penis' (Fanon, 1970, p. 120). The primal fantasy of the big black penis projects the fear of a threat not only to white womanhood, but to civilization itself, as the anxiety of miscegenation, eugenic pollution and racial degeneration is acted out through white male rituals of racial aggression – the historical lynching of black men in the United States routinely involved the literal castration of the Other's strange fruit. The myth of penis size – a 'primal fantasy' in the mythology of white supremacy in the sense that it is shared and collective in nature – has been the target of enlightened liberal demystification as the modern science of sexology repeatedly embarked on the task of measuring empirical pricks to demonstrate its untruth. In post-Civil Rights, post-Black Power America, where liberal orthodoxy provides no available legitimation for such folk myths, Mapplethorpe enacts a disavowal of this ideological 'truth': I *know* (it's not true that all black guys have huge willies) *but* (nevertheless, in my photographs, they do).

REFERENCES

BHABHA, H.K. (1983) 'The other question: the stereotype and colonial discourse', *Screen*, 24(4).

BURGIN, V. (1980) 'Photography, fantasy, fiction', *Screen*, 21(1).

DYER, R. (1982) 'Don't look now – the male pin-up', *Screen*, 23(3/4).

FANON, F. (1970) *Black Skin, White Masks*, London, Paladin.

FOUCAULT, M. (1977) 'What is an author?', in *Language, Counter-Memory, Practice*, Oxford, Basil Blackwell.

FREUD, S. (1977) 'Fetishism', in *On Sexualities*, Pelican Freud Library, Vol. 7, Harmondsworth, Penguin. First published 1927.

HALL, S. (1977) 'Pluralism, race and class in Caribbean society', in *Race and Class in Post-Colonial Society*, New York, UNESCO.

HALL, S. (1982) 'The whites of their eyes: racist ideologies and the media', in Bridges, G. and Brunt, R. (eds), *Silver Linings: Some Strategies for the Eighties*, London, Lawrence & Wishart.

MAPPLETHORPE, R. (1983) *Black Males*, Amsterdam, Gallerie Jurka.

MAPPLETHORPE, R. (1986) *The Black Book*, Munich, Schirmer/Mosel.

METZ, C. (1985) 'Photography and fetish', *October*, 34(Fall).

MULVEY, L. (1989) *Visual and Other Pleasures*, London, Macmillan. First published 1975.

Source: Mercer, 1994, pp. 173–85.

CHAPTER FIVE

EXHIBITING MASCULINITY

Sean Nixon

1 INTRODUCTION

In March 2011, the Italian fashion house Giorgio Armani began a new advertising campaign for its diffusion line of more affordable clothing. The campaign centred on its Armani jeans range and featured the Spanish tennis player Rafael Nadal. The television commercial was shot in high contrast black and white and featured a discordant and atmospheric soundtrack of electronic music. Made up of multiple rapid edits, the commercial presented intense close-ups of the surface of Nadal's body. We see him standing pressed up against a distressed wall wearing only Armani trunks, the lighting highlighting the curve of his back and muscular arms, the gloss of his skin. In another edit in the sequence we see a close-up of his jeans-clad crotch and upper thighs, with water dripping off his glistening torso and hair. In another he bends down to reveal his back, muscular upper body and wet hair.

(Continued)

(Continued)

FIGURE 5.1

The depiction of Rafael Nadal in the Armani Jeans advert, for all its contemporary gloss, reproduced a set of visual codings of masculinity which first appeared in popular culture in Britain in the late 1980s. Writing in the advertising trade magazine *Campaign* in July 1986, the critic George Melly noted the first manifestation of this trend. In a review of a group of adverts (see Figure 5.2) he pondered on the emergence of what he saw as a new use of 'sex' in the process of selling: the use, as he put it, of 'men as passive sex objects' (Melly, 1986, p. 41). Commenting on the television adverts for the jeans manufacturer Levi-Strauss's recently relaunched 501 jeans, Melly noted:

> Jeans have always carried a heavy erotic charge, but the young man who gets up, slips into a pair and then slides into a bath (the water seeps over him in a most suggestive manner) is really pushing it ... there is no question that this method of presenting beefcake is strongly voyeuristic.

(Melly, 1986, p. 41)

Writing from within academic cultural studies in 1988, Frank Mort was also struck by the visual presentation of the male body within the same Levis adverts. He emphasized what he saw as the sexualization of the male body produced through the presentation of the jeans, arguing:

the sexual meanings in play [in the adverts] are less to do with macho images of strength and virility (though these are certainly still present) than with the fetished and narcissistic display – a visual erotica. These are bodies to be looked at (by oneself and other men?) through fashion codes and the culture of style.

(Mort, 1988, p. 201)

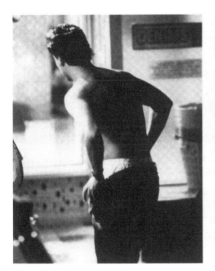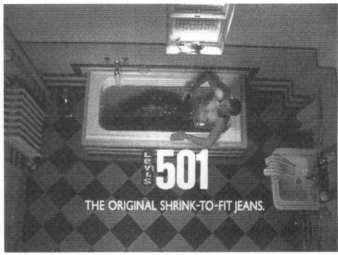

FIGURE 5.2 Television advertisement for Levi 501 jeans, 1985–86, Bartle Bogle Hegarty

By fetishizing, he meant the intense focusing on objects like belt and button-fly as Nick Kamen and James Mardle (the models) undressed in the adverts. By narcissism, he meant the foregrounding of the pleasures associated with the dressing and grooming of the body.

It is these new visual codings of masculinity identified by Melly and Mort and still evident in the Rafael Nadal advert for Armani Jeans which this chapter sets out to explore. There is good reason for such an enquiry. The Levis adverts formed part of a phenomenon. From the mid-1980s there has been a proliferation of images of this sort, and 1986 was a particularly rich year in this process. Along with the broadcasting of the Levis adverts, the advertising agency Tony Hodges and Partners put together a press campaign for Shulton GB's new prestige male fragrance 'Grey Flannel' in August. Appearing in 'style magazines' like *The Face*, the advert featured a three-quarter length, black-and-white photograph of a young man. He was posed alone, looking down and away from the viewers, and he was naked. The image was cropped just above his groin and moodily lit to shadow part of his body and reveal the outline of chest and arm muscles and the curve of his right hip (see Figure 5.3).

MAN IN GREY

FIGURE 5.3 'Man in grey', magazine advert, 1986–87, Tony Hodges & Partners agency

A foregrounding of similar physical characteristics (the developed arm and chest muscles), together with highly groomed hair and skin, also figured in the range of male pin-ups featured on posters, postcards and greetings cards sold by the Athena chain. The best-selling image from 1986 featured a young man cradling a small baby in his muscular arms. Again, reproduced in black and white, the image gave a close-up view of the surface of the male body (see Figure 5.4). The summer of 1986 also saw the launch of a press and poster campaign by Grey Advertising for Beecham's Brylcreem. The campaign featured a range of masculine images, all playing on the 'look' of early 1960s neat and respectable masculinity (itself associated with Brylcreem adverts from this period). The images were subtly updated, however, displaying the highly groomed hair and skin of the models and – in the case of two of the images – their developed arm and upper-body muscles.

This explosion of new imagery had direct connections to changes in consumer markets. By far the biggest slice of it was associated with developments in three men's markets: menswear, grooming products and toiletries, and consumer magazines. In each of these markets, new products were produced (like new ranges of fragrances or new magazines) or the marketing of existing products was reworked (through new packaging or advertising) so as to appeal to what producers and service-providers identified as new groups of male consumers. The emergence of new designs in menswear was particularly significant in this process. It was the innovations in menswear design – for example, broader shouldered suits, more flamboyant coloured ties, shirts

FIGURE 5.4 The image featured on posters, postcards and greetings cards sold by the Athena chain

and knitwear, figure-hugging sportswear lines – which established the key terms for the coding of the 'new man' as a distinctive new version of masculinity. It was through the presentation of these menswear designs in popular representations that the 'new man' was often coded. One important site where this presentation occurred was within menswear shops and I want to come back to these shops later (in section 6). In this chapter, then, I want to reflect on the cultural significance of the 'new man' images which were linked to these men's markets and consider the meaning of these images in relation to established notions of masculinity and masculine culture. In other words, I want to ask what do these images mean? What do they tell us about the changing meaning of masculinity in the 1980s and 1990s? And what are the consequences of these shifts in the way masculinity is being represented for gender relations as a whole?

In setting about this task, I will focus on the images found in the fashion pages of men's 'style' and 'lifestyle' magazines. There are two reasons for privileging these magazines. First, it was within magazine fashion photography that these images initially emerged. Secondly, it was within this form that the images were most extensively elaborated. In developing a reading of these fashion images, I also want to advance a more general argument about the representation process itself, its centrality to the formation of cultural identities (in this case masculinities), and to reflect on the role of spectatorship and looking in this process. The aims of the chapter can be summarized as follows:

- To develop the argument that gender identities are not unitary and fixed, but rather are subject to social and historical variation.

- To analyse the role of systems of representation in shaping the attributes and characteristics of masculinity as they are lived by men.

- To develop the usefulness of Michel Foucault's conceptualization of discourse in analysing visual representations.

- To offer a reading of the significance of the versions of masculinity coded within the 'new man' imagery.

- To explore the debate between Foucauldian and psychoanalytically informed approaches to conceptualizing the impact of these visual representations on the consumers of them.

- To locate historically the forms of looking or spectatorship associated with the 'new man' imagery.

2 CONCEPTUALIZING MASCULINITY

Getting to grips with the 'new man' imagery in ways which focus critically upon its relationship to masculinity and masculine culture requires a more general conceptualization of masculinity. In this section, I want to offer you what I think are some key precepts for this task by drawing upon a large body of literature on masculinity. The starting point for this body of work remains the critique which feminists have advanced over the past forty years. Central to these injunctions has been an analysis of men's power and from this a problematizing of the dominant and exclusive forms of masculinity which were seen to underpin it. What these injunctions have emphasized, then, has been the negative effects of dominant definitions of masculinity on women's relationships with men in both the public and private worlds.

This critique by feminists established the terms on which the writing on masculinity attempted to piece together conceptually a picture of the attributes and characteristics which made up this problematic category of masculinity. The earliest of this work, influenced by the sexual politics of the 1970s, was strongly associated with the men's anti-sexist movement. What emerged from this writing was a particular account of masculinity. In books like *The Sexuality of Men* (Metcalf and Humphries, 1985), the authors described a masculinity characterized by aggression, competitiveness, emotional ineptitude and coldness, and dependent upon an overriding and exclusive emphasis on penetrative sex. In addition, however, for the authors in *The Sexuality of Men*, what also emerged, as men began to reflect critically on masculinity, was a sense of the fears, anxieties and pain expressed by these men in relation to established scripts of masculinity: anxieties about sexual performance, estrangement from emotions, and poor relations with fathers.

A contradictory picture of masculinity was produced in books such as *The Sexuality of Men*. On the one hand, a singular or unitary conception of masculinity was advanced: one that was effectively seen as synonymous with men's dominance over women; while, on the other hand, the burden of masculinity for men was also emphasized.

2.1 Plural masculinities

It is both this unitary conception of masculinity and the confessional emphasis on the burden of masculinity for men which more recent work on masculinity has challenged. The central claim of this work has been an insistence on the plural forms of masculinity against the reductive conception found in works like *The Sexuality of Men*. A concern to speak about masculinities in the plural has become an important starting point for this recent work. What emerges from this work is a conception of masculinities produced as the result of the articulation or interweaving of particular attributes of masculinity with other social variables. There is an emphasis, then, on the way in which the gendering of identity is always already interwoven with other factors. For example, Catherine Hall, in her essay 'Missionary stories: gender and ethnicity in England in the 1830s and 1840s' (1992), makes a strong case for the way a particular kind of ethnicity and 'racial' characteristics – that of white Englishness – was central to the sense of manliness as it was lived by missionary men working in the Caribbean in the period after 1830. In Hall's view, it is impossible to isolate the elements which make up the masculinity of these men without recognizing their dependence upon ethnicity – Englishness – and 'race' – whiteness. Developing a sense of this articulation of masculinity with other social variables is important to the account of the 'new man' which I advance later in this chapter. As you will see, what looms large is the centrality of generation, ethnicity and 'race' to the distinctiveness of the kinds of masculinity that emerged around the figure of the 'new man' in the 1980s.

2.2 Thinking relationally

Insisting upon the differentiation between versions of masculinity does not in itself, however, produce an adequate conceptualization of masculinity. A second key strand of contemporary writing on masculinity is the insistence that particular versions of masculinity are not only constituted in their difference from other versions of masculinity, but are also defined in relation to femininity. This suggests, then, that an adequate understanding of masculinity requires our locating it within the wider field of gender relations as a whole; that is, in relation to the contemporary formations of femininity. An example drawn from Davidoff and Hall's *Family Fortunes* (1987) demonstrates the importance of doing this.

Family Fortunes charts the formation of the English middle class from 1780 to 1850, largely through the personal writings of middle-class men and women. In the book, Davidoff and Hall emphasize not only the way emergent forms of middle-class masculinity in this period were defined against both working-class and aristocratic forms of masculinity, but also that a hardening of gender differences – the attributes and characteristics of men and women – within middle-class culture itself was also central to middle-class men's specific sense of masculinity.

The professionalization of middle-class work that grew apace in the period they cover is important to the formation of middle-class masculinity in Davidoff and Hall's account. Middle-class men's involvement in production, design, building, accountancy and insurance involved quite specific forms of knowledge and skill. The mastery of these procedures – of assessing risk, of accountancy methods, of dealing with capital and investment – represented a set of practices and symbolic forms through which a middle-class manliness was staked out. These competences, as quintessentially manly tasks and skills, were counterposed, not only to the repertoire of skills and competencies associated with aristocratic masculinity (such as the valuing of gambling, sport and sexual prowess) and to the craft skills of artisanal masculinity, but also to the characteristics of middle-class femininity.

Davidoff and Hall also argue that the competences of middle-class manhood were consolidated through a range of formal and informal institutions (such as scientific and professional societies, gatherings at men's clubs). These represented public spaces where the contours of middle-class masculinity were reaffirmed. The chapel was also an important public place where this masculinity was shaped. Practising Christianity, and the rituals associated with communion, forged these men's masculinity as a Christian manhood. As Davidoff and Hall suggest, religious observance shaped and dignified middle-class work through its extension of established Protestant notions of the religious calling and 'doing God's duty in the world' (1987, p. 111). Enterprise and business acumen were worldly solutions to the service of God.

Doing God's work in a broader sense – the work of winning souls for salvation – also fostered what Davidoff and Hall call 'a stress on moral earnestness, the belief in the power of love and a sensitivity to the weak and the helpless' (p. 110). These moral dispositions and emotional languages amounted to a specific repertoire of conduct that set middle-class men apart from, again, aristocratic masculinity. The validation of piety and forms of manly emotion went together with an increasing sobriety of dress among middle-class men. These dress codes confirmed the different cultural space occupied by middle-class and aristocratic men, and set clear boundaries between masculine and feminine appearance among the middle class. The 'gorgeous plumage' of eighteenth-century men's attire fell foul of what J.C. Flugel called the 'great masculine renunciation': in came 'stiff, dark, heavy materials, shapeless nether garments, and narrow black ties ... the ubiquitous trousers and coat' (p. 142).

The creation of the middle-class home in the late eighteenth and early nineteenth centuries formed another determinant of the attributes and characteristics of middle-class manliness. Davidoff and Hall devote a long chapter to the factors that shaped the development of a distinctive middle-class version of the household and 'home': the production of 'my own private fireside'. A central element in its production was the robust demarcation of the public and private worlds. The home became the site of the distinctive 'elementary community of which larger communities and ultimately the nation are constituted' (p. 321), and also a place removed from the world (particularly of work) – separated literally by gates, hedges, walls. The suburban villa stood as the epitome of this new middle-class 'home'; safely distanced from the urban context and its proximity of classes, and offering a flavour of the rustic. It was women, as Davidoff and Hall suggest, who were mainly responsible for creating and servicing the home. And in the demarcation of the public and private, a gendering of the two spheres was increasingly produced: acting in the world through business and social reform, middle-class men staked out key parts of their masculinity in a public sphere that was more and more associated with their masculinity; while the private, domestic realm became the limit of middle-class women's sphere of action. This domestic space, however, as Davidoff and Hall argue, played an important role in middle-class men's masculinity as they moved between the world of the home and the world of public life. These men operated with a powerful investment in domestic harmony as the reward for enterprise as well as the basis of public virtue (p. 18).

The centrality of being able to provide for a household of dependants – in particular a wife – manifested a fierce independence that was important to these middle-class men. This masculine independence was increasingly characterized from the 1830s, as Catherine Hall suggests, by the way it was articulated through a specific English ethnicity. The authority of middle-class men was defined through their power over a range of dependants in the territories of Empire, as well as at home (Hall, 1992).

Always thinking relationally about masculinity – both in terms of the relations between masculinities and in terms of the relations between masculinity and femininity – forces us to consider the power relations operating in and through these relations. Clearly, as contemporary sexual politics has insisted, the field of gender relations is not a powerless universe. It is possible to see in Davidoff and Hall's work that middle-class men's masculinity was not only different from middle-class femininity but was also defined in a position of dominance over it. For some writers, the power relations which mediate gender relations – the relations between masculinity and femininity – point to a recognizable system of patriarchy (Alexander and Taylor, 1994; Walby, 1986). I do not want to explore the concept of patriarchy in this chapter, but I do want to signal a few problems with it as they relate to my arguments about the 'new man'. One central problem concerns the way in which it advances a universal model of the power relations between the genders – one that is weak on the historical specificity of the categories of gender and variations in the relations between them in different periods. In particular, the concept of patriarchy is weak at explaining the relations of power between different masculinities. I think that an adequate account of the field of gender relations, in addition to analysing the relations between masculinity and femininity, also needs to explore the relations of domination and subordination operating between different formations of masculinity. Rather than mobilize the concept of patriarchy, then, I want to suggest that we need to move away from a picture of the field of gender relations as always divided in the same way around the poles of masculine domination and feminine subordination. Rather, a more plural model of power relations is needed – one which grasps the multiple lines of power which position different masculinities and femininities in relation to each other at different times. An important pay-off from this conceptualization is that it allows us to consider dominant, subordinate and oppositional forms of masculinity. This is important because, as John Tosh and Michael Roper (1992) have argued, the field of gender relations has historically included forms of resistance to (as well as collusion with) prevailing notions of gender, on the part of groups of men.

2.3 Invented categories

I want to make a further point about conceptualizing masculinity, which draws this section to a close and leads us into the next one. Underpinning all these arguments about masculinity drawn from recent sociological, historical and cultural analysis is the assertion that masculinity is not a fixed and unitary category. In other words, it is argued that there is no true essence of masculinity guaranteed by God or nature which we can appeal to in analysing men's gender identities. Rather, like all identities, masculinities are, **invented categories** (Weeks, 1991). They are the product of the cultural meanings attached to certain attributes, capacities, dispositions and forms of conduct at given historical moments. Asserting their invented status, however, is not to diminish the force of these categories over us. To argue that masculinities are invented or constructed and therefore lack the guarantee of a foundation (which the idea of rooting masculinity in biology or divinity clearly offers) is not to argue that they are insubstantial. Quite the reverse. Identities are *necessary constructions* or *necessary fictions*. We need them to operate in the world, to locate ourselves in relation to others and to organize a sense of who we are. Emphasizing the invented character of identities, however, does direct us towards the processes through which identities are forged or fictioned. Such an enterprise leads us to the cultural or symbolic work involved in this process. It is my central contention that a large part of the symbolic work through which the meanings historically associated with masculinity are produced takes place within particular cultural languages. In other words, I am emphasizing the constitutive role of representation in the formation of the attributes and characteristics of masculinity through which real historical men come to live out their identities as gendered individuals. Cultural languages or systems of representation, then, are not a reflection of a pre-given masculinity fixed outside of representation. Rather, they actively construct the cultural meanings we give to masculinities. It is to how we might understand the dynamics of these images and the wider system of cultural languages of which they form a part that the next section is devoted. Before I do that, though, let me summarize the key implications of this section for our analysis of the 'new man' imagery.

2.4 Summary

1   I have argued that there is more than one version of masculinity, which means that we have to attend to the specificity of the 'new man' version of masculinity – that is, how the attributes and characteristics associated with it differ from other versions of masculinity which have existed at different periods.

2   I have insisted that relations of power operate both between masculinity and femininity and between different masculinities. This means that we need to consider how the 'new man' version of masculinity fits into the established ranking of masculinities. Does it reinforce dominant scripts of masculinity or does it disturb these dominant scripts?

3 I have argued for the need to locate particular versions of masculinity within the wider field of gender relations. This means being sensitive to the positioning of the 'new man' in relation to femininity. Does the 'new man' version of masculinity reproduce masculine privileges?

3 DISCOURSE AND REPRESENTATION

A persistent theme running through this volume is that forms of representation are not best understood within the terms of what we have called reflective or mimetic theories of representation (see Chapter 1). The key influence here has been post-Saussurian theories of language. You will recall that the central contention of this body of work is its insistence on the active, productive work of language or representation. Language does not simply reflect or passively transmit meanings fixed or established elsewhere – whether in the intention of a speaking or writing individual or in a stable external reality. Rather, what is emphasized is the way in which language is a structured system through which meaning is produced. Pre-eminent in this formulation is Saussure's attention to rules which govern the production of meaning within the structured system which makes up language. These rules – the rules of signification – point to the mechanism through which language generates meaning. It is this necessary submission of meaning production to the rules of signification which is the key to Saussure's conception of language. This general argument about the constitutive role of representation was a major influence on Roland Barthes. As you saw in Chapter 1, Barthes took up Saussure's ambition to extend semiology from written and spoken language to a wider field of cultural languages.

Barthes's work has proved influential on the cultural analysis of visual representations. However, as you saw in Chapters 1 and 3, as we move from Barthes to Foucault we encounter an author who (while he shares the general position of Saussure and Barthes on the constitutive role of representation) breaks in important ways with the semiotic approach to analysing representations. You may already feel comfortable with Foucault's formulations. However, I want to rehearse again briefly the pertinent elements of his arguments as they inform the reading of the 'new man' which I advance in this chapter. Later in the chapter (in section 5.5), I want to return to Foucault's work and open out the way he theorizes the process of subjection or subjectivization to discourse. In doing this, I will be developing a thread in Foucault's work only briefly considered so far in this volume.

3.1 Discourse, power/knowledge and the subject

You will recall from Chapter 1 that Foucault's understanding of discourse shifts attention away from the formal analysis of the universal workings of language proposed by Saussure (and developed by Barthes) towards an analysis of the rules and practices which shape and govern what is sayable and knowable in any given historical moment. In this sense, Foucault uses discourse or discursive formations to refer to groups of statements which provide a way of representing a particular topic, concern or object. These statements might be produced across a number of different texts and appear at more than one institutional site, but are connected by a regularity or underlying unity. In Foucault's later work, this attention to the way discourses make possible certain kinds of representation and knowledge was tied in with a greater attention to the apparatuses and institutions through which discursive formations operated. You will recall that Stuart Hall suggested in Chapter 1 that this new focus in Foucault's work marked his increased interest in exploring the way specific social practices – what individuals did – were regulated by discourse. Central to this focus in Foucault's work was an attention to the way knowledge about certain issues or topics was inextricably linked with the workings of power. Thus, knowledge for Foucault – especially that associated with the growth of the human sciences – was connected with a concern among experts and professionals to regulate and control the habits and actions of the wider population and particular groups of individuals. In Chapter 1, you saw how this concern with regulation worked in positive or productive ways by generating new kinds of knowledge and representations. In addition, you also saw how the body emerged in Foucault's work as the privileged point of articulation of modern regulatory forms of power.

Foucault's conception of discourse also offers a particular account of the place of the subject in relation to discourse. In common with the work of Saussure and Barthes, Foucault problematized traditional notions of the subject which see it as the source and guarantee of meaning in relation to language, representation and knowledge. Rather, as Stuart Hall discusses in his analysis of Velasquez' painting *Las Meninas* in Chapter 1, Foucault emphasized the way the subject was itself produced in discourse. This was a central insistence for Foucault. He argued that there was no possibility of a secret, essential form of subjectivity outside discourse. Rather, discourses themselves were the bearers of various subject-positions: that is, specific positions of agency and identity in relation to particular forms of knowledge and practice.

The consequences of these aspects of Foucault's conception of discourse or discursive formations for our analysis of the 'new man' can be summarized in five points:

1 Foucault's arguments about discursive formations invite us to focus not on one or two privileged images of the 'new man', but to grasp the regularities which linked the different manifestations of the 'new man' imagery together across different sites of representation. Thus, we need to be alert to the way the 'new man' surfaced not just in television adverts, but in shop interiors, magazine spreads, postcards and posters.

2 Foucault's arguments about discursive specificity remind us of the need to be attentive to the specific discursive codes and conventions through which masculinity is signified within magazine publishing, retail design and advertising. These are centrally codes to do with the body, appearance and individual consumption and they will colour the kinds of masculinity it is possible to represent.

3 Foucault's insistence on the operation of power through discursive regimes opens up the possibility of analysing the power relations which function in the construction of these images. Power

will be productive in the constitution of masculinity through specific visual codes, marking out certain visual pleasures and forms of looking. It will also fix the boundaries between the normal and abnormal, the healthy and the sick, the attractive and the unattractive, and so on.

4 Foucault's emphasis on the institutional dimension of discourses directs us towards the way the 'new man' images were rooted within specific institutional practices (within menswear retailing, magazine publishing, advertising) and forces us to be alert to the particular forms of knowledge and expertise which are associated with the representations at each of these sites.

5 Foucault's contention about the discursive production of subjectivity allows us to think of the emergence of the 'new man' as, precisely, a new subject-position opened up within the contemporary visual discourse of fashion, style and individual consumption. It is to a reflection on the novelty of the visual codes associated with the regime of 'new man' representations that I now want to turn.

4 VISUAL CODES OF MASCULINITY

I began this chapter by citing the television adverts for Armani underwear and Levi-Strauss's 501 jeans. As we saw, for both George Melly and Frank Mort, the latter adverts threw up a distinctively new set of codings of masculinity within the domain of popular culture. In introducing the 'new man' imagery through these examples, we got a preliminary sense of the novelty of these codings. What stood out, as Melly and Mort suggested, was a new framing of the surface of men's bodies; one that emphasized not so much the assertive power of a muscular masculine physique as its passive sexualization. In Mort's phrase, these were men's bodies openly inviting a desiring look. In this section, I want to explore in more detail the novelty of the 'new man' codings and the forms of spectatorship associated with them; specifically, the forms of spectatorship staged between the men in the images and the groups of men at whom the images were principally targeted. In doing so I want to focus not on television adverts nor on the images deployed in menswear shops, but rather on the images of the 'new man' found within the fashion pages of 'style' and 'lifestyle' magazines for men.

As a way of organizing my reading of these images, I want to begin by delimiting the scope of what I have to say. One of the significant characteristics of the magazine fashion photography produced over the last decade is the range of new codings of masculinity. In other words, we do not find only one version of the 'new man' represented across these fashion images. This is an important finding in itself. It suggests that we need to think about a range of new codings which share a loose family resemblance. In part because of this range of codings, I want to focus on what I think are three important 'looks' produced across these 'new man' images. These are:

1 The 'street style' version.
2 The 'Italian American' version.
3 The 'conservative Englishness' version.

I want to begin with the 'street style' version. This is because it was principally through these fashion images that a recognizable version of the 'new man' first emerged.

4.1 'Street style'

Let us start with the code of casting (see Figures 5.5 and 5.6). This is a very important code in fashion photography. It relates to the selection of certain physical characteristics in the choice of the model, the connotations of his particular physical 'look'. In Figure 5.4, the model chosen is young, with strong, well-defined features. Together these elements produce a mixture of boyish softness – connoted through the clear skin (and re-connoted by the hat pushed back on his head) – and an assertive masculinity – connoted through the hard edge of his features and the facial tattoo. This combination of 'boyishness' and 'hardness' represents one of a number of contradictory elements of masculinity held together in images associated with 'street style' codings of this sort. This combination of 'soft and hard' is reinforced by the casting of a light-black model. This casting is important and is repeated in Figure 5.5 (in fact, it is the same model, Simon de Montford). In terms of the signification of masculinity, it brings into play two connotations: an equivalence of 'light-black' with sensuality, and of 'black masculinity' with hypermasculinity.

What do I mean by this? This use of black masculinity to signify hypermasculinity has a long history, shaped by a pathologizing of blackness, and has been the site historically of pronounced fantasies about black men's sexuality and physical prowess (Mercer and Julien, 1988; see also Chapter 4 of this volume, section 4.3). These connotations of black masculinity operate as an important trace within the signification of the light-black male; they impart to it the connotations of an assertive masculinity. However, 'light-black' has a partially separate set of connotations. The light-black model makes acceptable or sanctions this otherwise threatening black masculine sensuality. It does this through the indices of skin tone and features. The casting of the light-black model makes possible the playing off of 'soft' and 'hard'.

In the selection of the clothes, Figures 5.4 and 5.5 bring together elements of workwear (the white T-shirt worn under a shirt in Figure 5.4) and strong outerwear (the wool jacket and heavy-duty boots in Figure 5.5). In both figures, the styling of the 'look' is completed with the natty hats worn by the model. This both works to signify the highly stylized nature of the 'look' and draws strongly on the idioms of black street style. This connection to black style is clearly underlined by the title given to Figure 5.5 ('Yard Style Easy Skanking'). The selection and styling of these clothes are typical of the resolutely, stylishly masculine 'look' associated with 'street style' in the magazines. The urban connotations of 'street style' are underlined by the location setting in Figure 5.5: a piece of derelict wasteland within the city.

The posing and model's expressions are the next elements in this coding that I want to consider. In Figure 5.4, the conventions of modelling were knowingly drawn upon in order to attain the perfect pout and that moody stare. The use of these conventions of modelling was often particularly marked in stylings of this sort. Figure 5.5 exemplifies this in that the posing of the model plays

FIGURE 5.5 'Hard are the looks', *The Face*, March 1985

FIGURE 5.6 'Ragamuffin hand me down my walking cane', *Arena*, spring 1987

on the distinctive stylized walk associated with particular forms of black subcultural masculinity (what the title of the whole fashion story calls 'ragamuffin'). The postures and forms of expression mobilized in these figures give a distinctive gloss to what I would call the romantic individuality of male youth. These are street-wise, pretty, hard boys. These romantic masculine identities offered resources for a 'tough', stylish masculinity – men who carried their maleness with a self-contained poise. A certain pre-permissive feel was important in accenting this masculine romanticism. By this I mean that the images draw on masculine codes which predate the shifts in masculinity associated with the late 1960s. This masculine romanticism is signified in Figure 5.5 by the selection of a seamless, glossy, black-and-white reproduction of the image. This alludes to the choice of film stock and lighting of 1940s' and 1950s' star portraits (particularly those associated with the Kobal collection).

Another coded feature of these images is the strongly narcissistic absorption or self-containment of the models. This is most clear in Figure 5.5. Posed alone, the gaze of the model is focused downwards and sideways out of frame, registering self-reflection and a hint of melancholy. Part of this relates to the way the image accents the codes of male romanticism and individualism that register the restrictions on young men in 1980s' 'hard times' culture (reduced life-chances, lack of money, the authoritarian shifts in social life) (Winship, 1986). More significantly, however, the conventions of posing and expression established in the spreads invite the viewer into complicity or identification with the model's narcissistic absorption in his 'look' or self-presentation; complicity with the ways in which he carries his 'looks' and appearance. This is underscored by the manner in which the photograph is cut or cropped and set on the page in Figure 5.5, which produces an intensity in the image: the model is brought close up to the viewer. What is important for my argument is the way this invited complicity between the viewer of the image and the model in relation to his (the model's) narcissism is focused upon men's bodies that are at once highly masculine and openly sensual. Two aspects are crucial here. First, the attention focused upon the model's appearance and the pleasures this establishes (in the quality and styling of the clothes, in his grooming, his 'looks', in the lighting and quality of the paper) are not directed towards an imagined feminine spectator who would mediate the relationship between the male model and the imagined male viewer. In other words, there is no woman in the representation or implicitly addressed by the image at whom these qualities might be addressed. The masculine–masculine look staged by this image is not coded within the norms of heterosexuality; his 'look' is not aimed at attracting an approving feminine look. Secondly, the choice of the model and some of the elements of clothing in the stylings allude to a tradition of representation of masculinity aimed at and taken up by gay men. What I mean here, specifically, is the valorizing of a 'tough' masculinity. In addition, Figure 5.5 draws upon an older tradition of representing male homosexuality associated with the beautiful, but melancholic young man (see Dyer, 1993).

I am not suggesting, however, that Figures 5.5 and 5.6 are gay male codings; or, rather, that they are straightforwardly that. There is a limited displaying of the surface of the body in the fashion spreads, and the choice of models breaks with the tighter generic figures of some more explicitly sexualized gay representations (such as the denim-clad boy or the cop). These images are instead strongly rooted in the stylistic community that they both invoked and simultaneously represented (London 'street style') and this was not strictly defined in terms of sexuality. What is pivotal, however, is the way the styling organizes a masculine–masculine look that draws upon a gay accent without either pathologizing that accent or re-inscribing a binary coding of gay or straight.

4.2 'Italian American'

In commenting on Figures 5.7, 5.8 and 5.9, I want to draw attention to the role of ethnicity as a key element in the coding of these 'new man' versions of masculinity. By this I mean the way a signification of 'Italian-American-ness' is central to the coding of masculinity in these images. Casting is, again, a central code. It is through the casting of the models that 'Italian-American-ness' is principally signified. To make sure we get this message, Figure 5.9 belongs within a fashion story titled 'Wiseguys, goodfellas and godfathers show off their brand new suits'. A dark white skin tone, strong features and a marked sensuality (the lips, in particular, are pronounced) are prominent among the models chosen. As with the 'street style' images, these physical features signify both sensuality and hardness, or a mixture of both 'soft' and 'hard'. Thus, the sensuality connoted by the dark skin, eyes and full lips intersects with both strong chins and noses and the connotations of the bravado and swagger of an Italian American 'macho'. The casting of these models, then, works to produce a set of connotations of masculinity similar to those signified by the casting of light-black models.

The location setting chosen in Figure 5.8 is also important in the signification of 'Italian-American-ness'. The backdrop of buildings and the general invocation of the public space of the city (New York?) grounds the 'look' of the models in this metropolitan landscape. These are men at home in this sophisticated milieu. Figure 5.7 also emphasizes the male camaraderie of being 'out on the town'. This is given greater resonance by the garments worn by the models (naval attire) and the explicit reference to shore leave given in the copy which accompanies the whole fashion story (the reference is to the 1949 movie, *On The Town*).

The selection and styling of garments, which draw upon naval apparel, helps to produce a strongly masculine 'look' through the codes of dress. The caps, wool jacket and heavy-duty canvas coats are resolutely masculine garments which emphasize – in the case of the coats – a solid masculine frame. This emphasis on a broad-shouldered look is equally clear in Figure 5.9 – through the cut of the suit. The accessories worn by the model in this image – the bracelet and the chunky ring – signify a brash, showy masculinity.

The selection of film stock and lighting is very important in these images. The grey-sepia tones signal a 1940s America and, in a similar way to the glossy black-and-white film stock used in Figure 5.5, connote an era of more fixed and conservative gender identities (and, specifically, masculinities). In addition, the selection of this film stock and the glossy reproduction further emphasize the gloss of skin, eyes and hair, together with the texture of the clothing.

Finally, if we turn to the codes of posture and expression, Figure 5.7 mobilizes a similar code of expression to that deployed in Figure 5.5. Here the model's gaze is focused sideways and away

FIGURE 5.7   'The last detail: on the town navy style in P-coats and caps', *Arena*, summer/autumn 1991

FIGURE 5.8   'The last detail: on the town navy style in P-coats and caps', *Arena*, summer/autumn 1991

FIGURE 5.9 'Wiseguys, goodfellas and godfathers show off their brand new suits', *Arena*, spring 1991

from the imagined spectator and is accompanied by his melancholic expression. Again, this stages a sexually ambivalent masculine–masculine look. In Figure 5.9, the model looks moodily towards the camera, looking through the position of the spectator without engaging it.

4.3 'Conservative Englishness'

The casting of the models was key to producing the 'conservative Englishness look' (see Figures 5.10 and 5.11). The models both have pale white skin, with lighter hair and softer features than the Italian-American-looking models and the light-black model. The styling of the hair, however, is particularly important to the coding of the 'conservative Englishness look'. It is cropped at the sides and back, but left long enough on top to be pushed back. Although slightly dressed with hair oil, the hair on top has been cut so that it can flop forward. This combines the romantic associations of long hair with the connotations of the masculine discipline and civilized neatness of the 'short back and sides'.

The repertoire of clothing worn is also key to signifying 'conservative Englishness'. In Figures 5.10 and 5.11, the models wear a version of classic English menswear in the form of three-piece suits. The garments are made of cotton (the shirts) and a wool-mixture (the suits) – materials which signify quality and tradition. These values are also connoted in Figure 5.12, where we see a desk littered with the paraphernalia of the office: a Filofax, leatherbound cases and fountain pens. The selection of these objects and their styling imprecisely evoke an inter-war England.

FIGURE 5.10 'Stitched up', *GQ*, February/March 1989, photograph by Tim Brett-Webb, © The Condé Nast Publications Ltd/GQ

FIGURE 5.11 'Stitched up', *GQ*, February/March 1989, photograph by Tim Brett-Webb, ©The Condé Nast Publications Ltd/GQ

A sense of tradition, however, is not the only factor at play here in accenting the design codes of classic English menswear. Looming large in Figure 5.10 is the contemporary glossing of these codes of menswear by the addition of the bright tie and sunglasses. These contemporary elements work to signify the entrepreneurial codes of business indicated by the reference to 'sharp practices' in the written copy which accompanies the fashion story. The aggressive masculinity associated with these codes of business is reinforced by the posture and expression of the model in Figure 5.10: his pose and expression signify confident manliness and independence. In Figure 5.11, the posture and expression of the model are less aggressive, more open to the viewer. He openly solicits our look at him.

The version of masculinity coded within Figures 5.10 and 5.11, then, is strongly marked by the interplay between, on the one hand, the assertive masculinity associated with a dominant version of Englishness and entrepreneurial codes of business and, on the other, the romantic connotations of narcissistic young manhood. These spreads code a spectatorial look in which identification with the models (especially in terms of the power of their imagined Englishness) sits alongside the sanctioning of visual pleasures in the cut of clothes, lighting and the 'look' of the models themselves.

FIGURE 5.12 'Stitched up', *GQ*, February/March 1989, photograph by Tim Brett-Webb, © The Condé Nast Publications Ltd/GQ

4.4 Summary

Let me take stock of what my reading of these three 'looks' has produced. I have argued that, across these three 'looks':

1   The casting of the models (especially in the 'street style' and 'Italian American' images) codes an ambivalent masculinity which combines both boyish softness and a harder, assertive masculinity. This sanctions the display of masculine sensuality.

2   The clothes worn by the models are assertively masculine and often emphasize a broad-shouldered and solid body shape.

3   The models display highly masculine forms of posture and expression – notably, connoting masculine independence and assurance – as well as the coding of narcissistic self-absorption.

4   The choice of lighting and film stock emphasizes the surface qualities of skin, hair and eyes and the texture of clothing.

5   The cropping of the images works to produce an intensity in many of the images.

In addition, I suggested that these visual codes work to produce a spectatorial look for the imagined spectator. In my reading of the images, I invoked three aspects of this look. First, I commented upon its gendering and emphasized the way the imagined viewer of the images is assumed to be male. This establishes forms of masculine–masculine looking. Secondly, I reflected on its organization of identification; that is, on the way the images invite an imagined male viewer to invest himself in the 'look' being presented by the model. Thirdly, I referred to its organization of a pleasure in looking at an external object or 'other'. My attention to the gendering of the look was important. It directed us towards the way the visual pleasures coded in the representations are connected to wider gender scripts and sexual identities – in other words, who looks at whom and in what way. The coding of the look across the images as a masculine–masculine one frames the visual pleasures signified in the images. What figures prominently in this respect is the organization of identification in the look. It is clear that the imagined male spectator is literally invited to buy into the 'look' of the model; that is, to identify with his 'look'.

Visual pleasures associated with the display of menswear are also in play in the representations. In this sense, the images walk a fine line between inciting identification with the 'look' displayed and the marking of visual pleasures around the model so that he himself becomes the object of a desiring look. This interplay between identification with and pleasure in the models is strongly incited by the coding of masculine sensuality across the images and by the way some of the images draw on forms of looking which were historically the prerogative of gay men – without pathologizing that look. Emphasizing these visual pleasures and the forms of spectatorship or looking associated with them directs us towards a set of arguments about the impact of these images on their readers or viewers. In the next section, I want to open out some of the terms which have been introduced in this section and consider more explicitly how we might theorize the articulation of these images with the readers of them.

5 SPECTATORSHIP AND SUBJECTIVIZATION

We saw, from the discussion of Foucault's conception of discourse in section 3, that he emphasizes the way discourses are the bearers of various historically specific positions of agency and identity for individuals. It is these subject-positions which provide the conditions for individuals to act or know in relation to particular social practices. This conception of subject-positions was key to my reading of the 'new man'. I suggested that we could see the coding of the 'new man' within popular representations as marking the formation of a new subject-position for men in relation to the practices of fashion, style and individual consumption. What is absent from our discussions so far, however, is some sense of how the subject-positions formally produced within representation come to be inhabited by groups of men. In other words, how do we conceptualize the articulation of the 'new man' images with the masculinity of individual men. Embedded in Foucault's conceptualization of subjectivity – notably in his writings in the 1970s – is a particular understanding of the process by which individuals come to inhabit particular discursive subject-positions. It is this question of **subjectivization** which I want to consider in sections 5 and 6, where I pick up a thread in Foucault's work not yet discussed in this volume.

As we've already seen, Foucault's account of subjectivity is strongly accented towards a delimiting of the formal, discursive production of subject-positions. This is writ large in the concerns of his historical surveys. He is interested in the emergence of modern forms of individuality through the growth of new bodies of knowledge and networks of power. The central mechanism which Foucault posits to understand the process whereby historical individuals are subjected to these discursive positions is the operation of power within discourse. Foucault is most explicit on the workings of this process in an interview in *Power/Knowledge* (1980) and in the essay 'The subject and power' (1982). In 'The subject and power', he talks about the way power subjects individuals through the government of conduct. By this, Foucault means the prescribing and shaping of conduct according to certain norms which set limits on individuals but also make possible certain forms of agency and individuality. In the interview in *Power/Knowledge*, Foucault goes even further in describing the moment of subjectivization or subjection. Power is again the central mechanism. He says:

> power relations can materially penetrate the body in depth without depending on the mediation of the subject's own representations. If power takes hold of the body, this isn't through it having first to be interiorized in people's consciousness.

(Foucault, 1980, p. 186)

Individuals are positioned within particular discourses, then, as an effect of power upon them. This might work, for example, through the intensification of the pleasures of the body, its posture and movements and the solidifying of certain practices. This is a productive relation, with power constituting the fabric of the individual and the individual's conduct.

In these comments, then, Foucault emphasizes the way subjectivization does not require individuals to be interpellated through mechanisms of identification to secure the workings of power/knowledge over them. Bodily attributes and capacities (such as dressing, walking, looking) are acquired through the 'brute outcome' of imitation and doing (Hunter, 1993, p. 128). In other words, specific discourse can work upon you – can subject you – without necessarily winning you over in your head.

Despite the richness of these formulations, however, Foucault's attention to the government of conduct and the workings of power upon the body are not without their problems for our purposes. Most importantly, these formulations are extremely vulnerable to the charge that Foucault over-emphasizes the effectiveness of specific power-plays upon individuals and pays insufficient attention to the ways in which individuals might resist them. Foucault also, more straightforwardly, overlooks the possible failure of specific attempts to regulate or govern conduct. The mechanism or process of subjectivization is, in a certain sense, perfunctory in these conceptualizations. The emphasis in Foucault's work at this point is to see the identities inhabited by historical individuals as simply the mirror image of the subject-positions produced within particular discursive regimes. For me, this aspect of Foucault's approach has been unhelpful. It has led me in two directions: first, towards an alternative account of the articulation of representations with individuals found in the appropriation of psychoanalysis within cultural theory; and, secondly, towards a more useful account of subjectivization found in Foucault's late writings.

5.1 Psychoanalysis and subjectivity

Psychoanalysis has provided a rich source of arguments for cultural critics concerned to understand the impact of systems of representations upon real historical individuals. In this section, I want to focus upon three concepts drawn from psychoanalysis which offer a way of conceptualizing the relationship between the 'new man' images and the spectators or consumers of these images. These are the concepts of identification, scopophilia and narcissism. As I hope you will see, these concepts are particularly suggestive for our purposes in that they foreground the organization of gender identities within representation and play up the acts of looking and spectatorship which shape this process.

Identification is the central of the three concepts and carries precise meanings in Freud's writing. In his essay 'Group psychology and the analysis of the ego' (Freud, 1977 [1921]), for example, he explicitly distinguishes between two kinds of relationship which individuals enter into with the external world of objects around them. On the one hand, he says, there is a relationship with the object which involves the focusing of libidinal investments (the sexual drives) upon, usually, another person. On the other hand, there is identification which involves some projection based on a similarity between the individual and an external person and, from that, the moulding of the ego after that person. Freud summarizes this distinction as a distinction between two kinds of desire: a desire to *have* the other person (which he calls **object cathexis**) and a desire to be the other person (**identification**) (p. 135).

What is striking about Freud's comments on these processes is the possessive or proprietorial dimension of object cathexis and the destructive, assimilating tendency in identification. These possessive and aggressive undercurrents of object cathexis and identification emerge very clearly in Freud's account of the **Oedipus Complex**. The Oedipus Complex represented a defining moment in the development of the child for Freud; it was the moment at which gender identity and sexuality (or sexual object choice) were fixed. It is, in addition, a moment which also reveals the importance of two other concepts which, as you will see, are important for the psychoanalytic understanding of identification. These are the concepts of scopophilia and narcissism.

In 'Three essays on the theory of sexuality' (1984 [1905]), Freud claimed that a pleasure in looking was a component part of human sexuality (you may recall the discussion of scopophilia in Chapter 4, section 4.3). This pleasure in looking or **scopophilia** could be channelled along different routes for Freud. One of these was a fascination with the human form. Freud labelled this fascination **narcissism** and it provided him with the mechanism of identification. Centrally, for Freud, the narcissistic pull of identification was largely unconscious, secured beyond the individual's conscious awareness.

Identification, for Freud, organized not only the narcissistic components of the scopophilic drive; it also involved a process of splitting, and we can use Freud's account of the Oedipal drama, which has already been briefly introduced in Chapter 4, section 1.2, to illustrate this. The developmental moment of the Oedipus crisis and its successful dissolution involved – for Freud – a 'boy' child taking up a masculine identification with the father and in the process displacing earlier aggressive fantasies towards the father. It also entailed the stabilizing of a heterosexual object choice. This masculine identification, however, precluded the 'boy' from taking up a feminine identification with the mother, while the stabilizing of heterosexual object choice precluded other kinds of object choice. In the Oedipal scenario, then, Freud posits the formation of sexual difference and sexual identity in a moment of splitting – between the identification that is made (in the case of the 'boy', masculine) and the identification that is refused (feminine). The identification that is refused, Freud argues, has to be actively negated or repressed, and continues to haunt the individual. In this psychoanalytical sense, then, a fixed sexual identity and sexual difference are always unstable and never completely achieved. The subject remains divided, with a precarious sense of coherence (Rose, 1986).

Freud's conceptualization of the process of splitting in the moment of identification forms a central component of the French theorist and psychoanalyst Jacques Lacan's theorizing of identification and the early moments of subject formation. In what is, in large degree, a rigorous reworking of Freud's writings on narcissism, Lacan (in 'The mirror phase as formative of the function of the I', 1968) defines the infant's first sense of itself (its first self-identification) as coming through its imaginary positioning by its own mirror image: that is, by looking at its own reflection, or being literally reflected in its mother's eyes. Lacan argues that the infant misrecognizes itself as its mirror image. Lacan describes this as a moment of primary narcissistic identification, and it is for him the basis and prototype of all future identifications.

5.2 Spectatorship

What is significant in Freud's and Lacan's accounts of identification – including the theorizings on narcissism and scopophilia – is the visual character of the structures of identification they describe. It was within film theory in the 1970s that writers most assertively developed the implications of these aspects of Freud's and Lacan's accounts and laid claim to this lineage of psychoanalysis as offering a privileged way into the analysis of cinematic representations. This work – most notably developed in the journal *Screen* – is instructive for my account of the impact of representations upon individuals in a number of ways. Pivotally, it addressed the power of the visual for the consumers of visual culture, and offered a gendered account of the processes of looking and identification. This filled out the psychoanalytic account of the process of subjectivization.

Laura Mulvey's 1975 *Screen* essay, 'Visual pleasure and narrative cinema', illustrated particularly clearly what a psychoanalytic-informed account could deliver regarding the theorizing of the power of representation (reprinted in Mulvey, 1989). The analysis of the look – and the organization of the pleasure in looking – is most interesting in Mulvey's essay. Drawing on Freud in particular, Mulvey detailed the way narrative cinema mobilized both the narcissistic aspects of the scopophilic instinct (ego libido) and its voyeuristic and fetishistic components (object cathexis) – essentially those forms of active scopophilia. For Mulvey, however, the mobilization of these pleasures in looking was far from innocent. She asserted a very specific organization of **spectatorship** in relation to the scopophilic drives. For Mulvey, in her famous conceptualization, the 'pleasure in looking has been split between active/male and passive/female' (1989, p. 19). She distinguished between three kinds of look: the look from camera to event or scene; the look from the spectator to the screen action; and the looks between characters in the film story. For Mulvey, the interplay between these looks was organized to produce the split in looking characteristic of Hollywood cinema. On the one hand, the male characters were positioned as the bearer of the look (the active eye) in the film story, with the feminine coded as visual spectacle (passive object to be looked at). On the other hand, the look of the spectator was aligned with that of the male character. In these formulations, Mulvey suggests that one important element of this gender imbalance in looking is the careful coding and positioning in the storyline of the film of the male figures. For Mulvey, there is a marked displacement of any erotic, 'spectacular' significations in relation to men in narrative film which maintains the power relations between men and women; between the active masculine control of the look and the passive feminine object of the look.

Mulvey's development of Freudian concepts provides a suggestive way of conceptualizing the moment of articulation between individuals and representational forms. It suggests that the positioning of the individual within the subject-positions established by a particular representation is achieved through the organization of scopophilic drives and the channelling of unconscious identifications. This is also a process that can (depending upon representational conventions) reproduce the positions of sexual difference or gender.

Mulvey's arguments are a major influence on Steve Neale in his essay 'Masculinity as spectacle' (Neale, 1983). Neale's essay is useful for my account in this chapter because it takes up

Mulvey's basic argument about the cinematic gaze, but also extends the theorizing of both the representational conventions of masculinity within narrative cinema and of the positioning of the male spectator in relation to these conventions.

READING A⊢

Now read Reading A, 'Masculinity as spectacle', by Steve Neale, which you will find at the end of this chapter. Consider the following questions as you read the extract:

1 What is a central characteristic of the genres of film which Neale focuses on?
2 How do these films undercut the possibility of an erotic look at the male body?
3 What qualities of masculinity do they privilege?

5.3 The spectacle of masculinity

Does Neale's analysis offer any specific pointers to conceptualizing the moment of articulation between a masculine subject in a text (in this case a film) and historical men? Neale's essay focuses on male genres – such as the western – in which masculinity is necessarily the object of considerable visual attention and visual spectacle. Neale argues, however, that the narrative structure and shot organization of these films work to undercut the potential of an erotic look at the male figures (principally for the male spectator in the auditorium). He argues that the films do this through representing sadism or aggression – that is, by in some way wounding or injuring the male body – as a way of circumventing eroticization. In addition, the codings of masculinity in these films privilege the attributes of toughness, hardness and being in control. These are codings which do not allow the display of ambiguities, uncertainties or weaknesses and therefore, for the male spectator, offer a fantasy of control and power. In other words, they foreground the possibility of a narcissistic identification with the protagonists.

Neale's argument corroborates Mulvey's claims that the representational conventions of narrative cinema and its organization of spectatorship reproduce the terms of sexual difference and the power relations between men and women. A number of objections, however, have been raised to this kind of appropriation of Freud by other writers working within this tradition of film theory. In particular, in line with much psychoanalytically informed work, both Mulvey and Neale foreground questions of sexual difference – differences between masculinity and femininity – and play down differences within these categories. The inability to consider differences between masculinities leads to their failure to consider the organization of other forms of sexual desire in the cinema. The long tradition of eroticizing the figure of the cowboy among gay men suggests an immediate problem with this omission. You will recall, from Chapter 4, that Stuart Hall also develops some of these criticisms in his reflection on Robert Mapplethorpe's photographs of black male models. There are some further, more general objections to both Neale's and Mulvey's arguments which I want to raise by way of drawing this section to a close.

5.4 The problem with psychoanalysis and film theory

I began this section by suggesting that the appropriation of a particular tradition of psychoanalysis within cultural theory (and, in particular, film theory) appeared to offer a more dynamic conceptualization of subjectivization than that found in Foucault's work. This was a conceptualization which was not only sensitive to the gendering of identities, but could also account for the way visual representation worked on individuals through its emphasis on the interlocking of deep-rooted psychic processes with the codes and conventions of cinema. The problems begin, I think, when it comes to thinking about how we might apply Neale's or Mulvey's work to analysing the 'new man' images. Looming large here is the problem of moving from an account of spectatorship and the positioning of viewers developed in relation to narrative cinema to an account of these same processes in relation to very different kinds of visual representation: magazine fashion images, television adverts, shop displays. The first difficulty concerns the staging of the spectatorial look. In Mulvey and Neale's work, the look is conceived as a fixed gaze within the environment of the cinema auditorium. The conditions for this staging of the look are clearly not met in relation to the visual representations which concern us here. This immediately forces us to rethink questions of spectatorship – including the way in which the look is gendered at these other sites. Secondly, and more seriously, the account of spectatorship developed in this section rests upon a particular account of identity, drawn from psychoanalysis. This psychoanalytic account of identity is fundamentally at odds with the Foucauldian account which I set out in section 3, with – in my view – its very proper emphasis on the historical character of identities. Let me explain why I think it is extremely difficult to square the differences between a psychoanalytic and a Foucauldian account of identity.

Lacan and Freud are both explicitly concerned with the primary processes that constitute identity; that is, those processes that forge (in Juliet Mitchell's phrase) 'the human in culture' (Mitchell, 1984, p. 237). These processes are, for psychoanalysis, universal – that is, they have a transhistorical status. In addition, they follow a developmental pattern involving a number of phases; they are secured unconsciously and are fixed by the parameters of Oedipal order – the underlying universal structuring of human relations which Freud and Lacan posit.

It is this universal account of the formation of identity, however, that is so problematic in relation to Foucault's deeply historical emphasis. The psychosexual structures of the Oedipal order are given the privileged position in accounting for (almost) all there is to say about the formation of identity. The arguments of Mulvey and Neale do attempt, certainly, to moderate this universal account of identity. In considering the interplay between psychic structures and historically specific forms of representation (Hollywood cinema), they do suggest that these representations can carry real force. However, in describing the articulation of the social/historical with psychic structures, the psychic is privileged as providing the fundamental parameters of identity. In analysis of the look and the gendered positioning of individuals, there is a search for the positions of looking given by particular visual texts in terms of the fundamental tropes of sexual difference – active/passive, masculine/feminine, mother/son, father/daughter. Subjectivization, then, is conceptualized in these accounts as being secured through the reactivation of the fundamental positions of identity which Freud posits – ultimately, always in the terms of the Oedipal order. Historical and social factors which determine identity are – in the end – reduced to the calculus of psychosexual structures. In addition, the emphasis on psychosexual structures produces a reductive account of identity conceived fundamentally in terms of sexual difference. In other words, psychoanalysis privileges the acquisition of gender and sexual identity as the bedrock of identity. Other determinants upon identity (such as class) are effectively sidelined.

While psychoanalysis can give a clear account of the articulation of individuals with fields of representation, and certainly poses some important questions about the unconscious and about desire and the look, this is in the end too ahistorical and totalizing. It pitches 'secondary' processes of identification only at the level of primary processes and sees identity only in terms of sexual difference (Morley, 1980). Where, then, does this leave our account of subjectivization? The attention to the organization of spectatorship as a way of conceptualizing subjectivization does point to important processes. I want to hold on to this concern with spectatorship, but not in its psychoanalytically understood sense. Foucault's late writings both help to re-situate an account of looking and offer considerable conceptual reach in terms of theorizing subjectivization.

5.5 Techniques of the self

In his late work and in interviews published shortly before his death, Foucault made reference to his interest in what he called practices or **techniques of the self**. He maintained that:

> it is not enough to say that the subject is constituted in a symbolic system. It is not just in the play of symbols that the subject is constituted. It is constituted in real practices. There is a technology of the constitution of the self which cuts across symbolic systems while using them.
>
> (interview in Rabinow, 1984, p. 369)

Foucault elaborates further in his essay 'Technologies of the self' (1988). Commenting on four major types of technology (those of production, sign systems, power and the self), he suggests that **technologies of the self:**

> permit individuals to effect by their own means or with the help of others a certain number of operations on their own bodies and souls, thoughts, conduct and way of being, so as to transform themselves in order to attain a certain state of happiness, purity, wisdom, perfection or immortality.
>
> (Foucault, 1988, p. 18)

Technologies or techniques of the self, in other words, are specific techniques or practices through which subject-positions are inhabited by individuals. Foucault, in his brief comments on these techniques, emphasized his interest in forms of writing such as private diaries or other 'narratives of the self'. These represented, for him, characteristically modern forms of 'practices of the self'.

What is so useful about these assertions is the way they get Foucault away from his earlier exclusive emphasis on how historical identities are produced as the effect of discourses. This represents a shift from an attention to the regulating and disciplining of the subject to a more expanded formulation of agency. 'Techniques of the self' are still – it is important to underline – conducted within fields of power/knowledge and within the domains of a discrete number of discourses. They suggest, though, the putting into practice of discursive subject-positions in ways which emphasize the dynamic nature of this process. More than that, they underline again the important attention Foucault gives to the non-ideational elements of subjectivization; that is, the way in which the body and mental capacities are the product of practices and not (necessarily) of forms of self-representation in either consciousness or the unconscious.

Foucault's comments on 'practices of the self' make it possible to conceptualize the articulation of concrete individuals to particular representations as a performance based upon the citing and reiteration of discursive norms; a performance in which the formal positions of subjectivity are inhabited through specific practices or techniques (Butler, 1993). This lays the basis for an account of subjectivization that is historical in nature and circumvents the deployment of the full psychoanalytic connotations of identification in order to theorize in a dynamic way the process of subjectivization.

In thinking about how we might conceptualize the way the formal subjectivities inscribed within the regime of 'new man' representations might have been inhabited by historical men, Foucault's comments, then, direct us towards a specific set of practices or techniques of the self. A number of techniques of care, consumption and leisure seem to me pivotal in this respect. The practices of grooming and dressing and the activity of shopping represent practices through which the attributes and characteristics of masculinity coded in relation to the 'new man' imagery might be operationalized or performed as a historical identity. At the heart of these techniques or practices of the self, I want to suggest, are specific techniques of looking. By this I mean the acquired acts of looking which cite and reiterate the ways of looking formally coded in advertising images, shop display photographs, and magazine fashion photography. It is these codes and techniques of looking on which I want to reflect in the next section.

6 CONSUMPTION AND SPECTATORSHIP

In the previous section, I suggested that psychoanalysis offered a number of suggestive terms – identification, scopophilia, narcissism – through which we could conceptualize the impact of visual representations upon the consumers of them. Looming large in this, as we saw, was the positioning of the consumer in relation to the image through the codes of spectatorship. I also raised some significant reservations about the wider psychoanalytic conception of identity which underpinned the theories of identification, scopophilia and narcissism as they were developed within cultural criticism. I suggested that Foucault's ideas offered an alternative way of approaching the question of consumers' relationship to visual representations through his comments on 'techniques of the self' and their historically varied performances. In emphasizing the usefulness of Foucault, however, I also suggested that I wanted to retain the attention to the coding of spectatorship. A central part of this reassessment of theories of spectatorship is a concern to chart historically the formation of the codes of looking available to contemporary consumers of the 'new man' imagery. In rethinking spectatorship, I want to offer you an account of how we might understand the forms of looking established between the 'new man' images – in magazine spreads, in shop windows, in television advertising – and the groups of men at whom they were principally aimed.

6.1 Sites of representation

In getting to grips with the codes and techniques of looking associated with the 'new man' imagery, we can usefully begin with the role of shop interiors in the staging of these looks. Shop interiors direct us towards both the establishment of codes of looking and the interweaving of techniques of looking with other practices – handling the garments, trying on clothes, interacting with shop staff – which are integral to the activity of shopping. The interior space of shops and their windows thus represent one of the privileged places for the performance of techniques of the self by individual men in relation to the 'new man' imagery.

In order to explore these issues, however, I need to preface them with some more explicit comments concerning the representation of the 'new man' within shops. How is the 'new man' represented at the point of sale? I want to suggest that there are two distinct moments to this encoding: the first is produced through the design codes of menswear and the second through the design and display techniques of retailing.

The design codes of menswear are easiest to deal with. As cultural forms, menswear garments (like all clothes) carry particular cultural meanings. The choices made by designers in terms of the selection and design of garments, choice of fabrics and colours work to signify, most importantly, particular masculine identities through the menswear. Think of how tweed jacket and brogues signify a certain version of English upper-class masculinity. In the case of the 'new man', then, it was innovations in menswear design which shaped a new version of masculinity.

The forging of these new versions of masculinity through the design codes of menswear, however, was also dependent upon other practices of representation to help fix these meanings around the garments. This is where the design and display techniques used in menswear retailing come into play. Through the presentation of the garments on mannequins or display stands in the shop window and around the shop, through the use of display boards with photographs of the clothes being worn by models, and through techniques like lighting and interior decoration, shop design and display attempt to fix a series of cultural values and meanings around the garments – values centrally to do, in this case, with masculinity. It was through these techniques that the 'new man' was signified within menswear shops as a particular version or type of masculinity.

What was so striking about the design and display techniques deployed by menswear retailers up and down the high street in recent years was the way they addressed their target male customers in highly visual terms. The selection of high-quality materials in the fitting out of the shops, the use of lighting and display boards and the placing of mirrors in the shops offered a particular kind of visual spectacle in which the selling of the clothes took part.

One of the best examples of these new trends in menswear retailing is offered by Next for Men. Central to the design of the Next menswear interiors (including the point-of-sale materials and packaging) was the use of space and materials. The frontage of the stores gave the first indication of this: a large window set in a dark matt grey frame beneath the trademark signage 'Next', in lower-case lettering. The window displays – framed by this frontage – were similarly uncluttered. A combination of garments was displayed on abstract mannequins, backed, often, by large display or show cards that gave written accounts of the merchandise range. The display cards – featuring details of the clothes being worn as well as the accompanying copy – played off the themes of space, colour and line in the shop through their layout and lettering. Inside the shops, the lighting, colouring and organization of space were distinctive. Here were the features that formed a coherent design vocabulary: bleached wooden pigeon-holes and dresser units; downlighting spotlights; gently spi-ralling staircases with matt black banisters. The 'edited' collection of clothes were displayed in a range of ways. Around the sides of the shop, slatted wooden units displayed a few folded jumpers next to hangers with three jackets; socks were folded in pigeon-holes or individual shoes perched on bleached wood units. A dresser unit commanded the central space of the shop, standing upon a classic woven carpet. Such features acted as centripetal counterpoints to the displays of clothes that were set against the walls and encouraged customers to circulate around the shop. The design of the shop interiors, then, combined a number of distinctive stylistic borrowings to produce a shop space in which the assertively modern idioms of cruise-line aesthetics sat alongside the warmer English colourings of dark wood and brass detailing (Nixon, 1996).

What is important for my argument in this chapter is that Next's retail design established a set of ways of visually apprehending the shop environment and the clothes within it through the design and display techniques. In other words – if we put this in slightly different terms – the design and display techniques established particular forms of spectatorship for men at the point of sale; forms of spectatorship directed at the 'new man' masculinity represented through the design, selection and presentation of the garments. As a way of getting to grips with these forms of spectatorship, I want to turn to a body of work devoted to the emergence of consumer culture from the mid-nineteenth century. There is a good reason for such an exercise. I want to suggest that the essential characteristics of the forms of spectatorship associated with menswear shops like Next for Men have their origins in this earlier period.

6.2 Just looking

Rachel Bowlby has offered some useful pointers to the emergence of contemporary consumer culture and its visual characteristics in her book *Just Looking* (1985). Drawing upon the writings of a group of naturalist writers (Emile Zola, George Gissing and Theodore Dreisser) and their responses to the expansion of consumer culture around the turn of the century, Bowlby identifies two related tendencies within the new cultures of consumption. On the one hand, she argues that the latter half of the nineteenth century witnessed the rationalization and systematic organization of selling. Citing the development of the department store, she argues they represented 'factories for selling'. Looming large in this was the rationalizing of selling techniques. This ranged from the establishment of fixed pricing to the organization of sales staff and supervisors. On the other hand, Bowlby also noted that selling itself was transformed by a new emphasis on arranging the goods in displays both in the shop window and inside the store. As she puts it: The grand magasins ... appear as places of culture, fantasy, divertissement, which the customer visits more for pleasure than necessity' (Bowlby, 1985, p. 6).

What figured prominently in this organization of consumer pleasure, for Bowlby, was the pleasure of – in her phrase – just looking; that is, taking in the visual spectacle of the displayed goods. Bowlby's emphasis on the visual pleasures staged by the new consumer culture owes much to the work of the German cultural critic Walter Benjamin. In his extensive study of nineteenth-century Paris – generally known as the 'Arcades Project' – written during the inter-war years but first published in English in 1973, Benjamin offered a celebrated account of the spectacular qualities of consumer culture in the nineteenth century.

READING B

Turn now to Reading B entitled 'Technologies of looking: retailing and the visual', which you will find at the end of this chapter. When you are reading this extract, consider the following questions:

1 How did the arcades establish a new style of consumption?

2 What did the allegorical figure of the *flâneur* principally represent for Benjamin?

3 What kind of cultural identities were privileged in the emergent consumer culture?

4 What role did print culture play in shaping the new styles of consumption described by Benjamin?

6.3 Spectatorship, consumption and the 'new man'

Let me underline the key points from Reading B. It argues that Benjamin's commentary on the *flâneur* pointed us towards the staging of specific ways of looking. These were shaped by the new techniques of consumer display concentrated within the new retail and leisure-based districts of the large metropolitan cities like London and Paris, and by the representation of the city and consumption in visual terms within print cultural forms like periodicals. At the heart of this new kind of looking was a new consumer subject who looked. This spectatorial subjectivity was allegorically represented in Benjamin's description of the *flâneur*. In addition, the reading suggested that these ways of looking were dominated by an interrupted series of looks, rather than a fixed gaze. Within these looks, forms of self-visualization by consumers were also important. In other words, they opened up the narcissistic dimensions of spectatorship.

What can we draw out from this argument about the forms of spectatorship coded in relation to the 'new man' imagery within retailing? I have argued that the forms of spectatorship associated with contemporary menswear retailing (such as Next for Men) reproduced ways of looking associated with the emergence of characteristically modern forms of consumption. Contemporary forms of consumer spectatorship, then, belong within this longer historical formation. In addition, reflecting on the work on nineteenth-century developments in consumer culture reveals that the forms of looking staged within and around shops form part of a larger regime of looking; a regime of looking constructed as much within cultural forms associated with this consumption – be that periodicals, consumer guides or catalogues – as at the point of sale. If we think about the contemporary 'new man' images, it is clear that press and television advertising and consumer magazines played an important role in helping to construct this regime of looking. It is in this sense that we can consider the forms of looking which I detailed in section 4 as being part of a series of looks which crossed from the magazines to the spaces of menswear shops.

7 CONCLUSION

I began this chapter by citing images drawn from television advertising and have, in the course of the chapter, considered in some detail a range of images drawn from magazine fashion photography. A central argument of the chapter has been about the need to grasp the way this imagery signified across these sites, as well as across (notably) menswear shops. Michel Foucault's arguments about discursive regimes have been critical in this respect, allowing me to reflect on the 'new man' images as a regime of representation. In addition, they have pointed me towards the regime of looking or spectatorship which was also produced across the various sites at which the imagery signified. This was a regime of looking, then, which linked a series of looks formally staged within shop interiors, television advertising and magazine fashion photography.

In considering the impact of this new regime of representation on the groups of men at whom it was principally targeted, I suggested that spectatorship played an important role. I proposed that we could identify the specific techniques of looking associated with the formal codes of spectatorship produced across the regime of 'new man' imagery, together with the other practices of the self (the multiple activities included in shopping, the routines of grooming and dressing), as the means for operationalizing the 'new man' images as historical identities.

Foucault's work not only informed my insistence on grasping the 'new man' imagery as a regime of representation and my understanding of the process of subjectivization through techniques of the self; it also alerted me to the institutional underpinnings of the new imagery. Implicit in the account I set out in this chapter, then, was an argument about the way developments within the consumer institutions of advertising, menswear retailing and magazine publishing set the terms for the formation of this new regime of representation.

Getting to grips with the cultural significance of the 'new man' imagery, however, has been the overriding concern of this chapter. I argued that the images were distinctive in sanctioning the display of masculine sensuality and, from this, opening up the possibility of an ambivalent masculine sexual identity; one that blurred fixed distinctions between gay- and straight-identified men. In this sense, much of the significance of this imagery related to the way it redrew relations between groups of men through the codes of style and consumer spectatorship. Much harder to read is its significance for relations between men and women. Women were effectively absent from the space of representation which I detailed. To develop a fuller account of the cultural significance of these images, however, we do need to locate them in relation to the wider field of gender relations. In this regard, it is worth noting that the moment of the emergence of the 'new man' in the mid-late 1980s was also the moment when shifts were occurring in popular representations of femininity. One of the most important in relation to representations of young femininity was the emergence of what Janice Winship (1985) termed a 'street-wise' femininity. This drew upon a set of 'street style' dress codes analogous to those I commented on earlier. These dress codes – which mixed feminine items like mini-skirts with thick black tights and Doc Martens boots or shoes, cropped hair and bright lipstick – played around with the conventions of gender and dress. For Winship, these new visual representations of femininity were most strongly developed within young women's magazines like *Just Seventeen* and *Mizz*. In the magazines, these new visual codes were articulated to appropriations of certain feminist arguments and offered young women a more assertive and confident sense of independent femininity.

In order to grasp fully the cultural significance of the opening up of new consumer pleasures for men through the figure of the 'new man', then, we need to locate it in relation to these contemporary shifts in femininity and also in relation to more recent shifts in popular representations of gender and sexual identity. By doing this, it is possible to see the 'new man' as part of this wider realignment of gender and sexual relations which is registered within popular representations since the late 1980s. Two developments are worth mentioning. The first concerns the rise of the 'new lad' in the early 1990s. The 'new lad' emerged most strongly within magazine culture and was actively and self-consciously promoted by the magazine *Loaded*. The 'new lad' aimed to establish a break with the figure of the 'new man' and to close down the space of sexual ambivalence associated with it. In its place, the 'new lad', especially as it was promoted by *Loaded*, articulated a post-permissive heterosexual script of 'cars, girls, sport and booze'. What was euphemistically called 'glamour' was also legitimated in the 'lad mags'. These were sexualized representations of women that echoed earlier forms of sexual scrutiny of women developed in the late 1960s in popular culture. *Loaded* offered a subtley updated discourse on 'birds', 'babes' and 'totty'.

These depictions of 'glamorous' femininity in the 'lad mags' coincided with the appropriation by groups of young women, and in the consumer culture aimed at them of highly feminine and sexualized version of youthful femininity. These developments saw young women increasingly appropriating elements of masculinity, with a hedonistic culture of excessive drinking, swearing and the pursuit of sexual pleasure. Variously described as 'ladettes' or 'babes', this sexual script was represented in the popular media by figures like the TV presenter Denise Van Outen and the glamour model Jodie Marsh. It is also evident in the number of young women who wore T-shirts with phrases like 'Porn Queen' or 'Porn Star' on them and in the legitimation of women attending lap dancing clubs. And it is evident in the scenes on British high streets on Friday and Saturday nights in which 'drinking to excess, getting into fights, throwing up in public places […] wearing very short skirts, high heels and skimpy tops' has become a way of being for groups of young women (McRobbie, 2009, p. 85).

These shifting forms of gender and sexual identity reveal the malleability of the social norms governing the way individuals in British society imagine and live out their identities as young men and women. I have argued in this chapter that representations are intimately bound up with this process. I have argued, specifically in relation to the 'new man', that images do not simply reflect changing masculinities being lived by groups of men, but play an active role in the process of change.

There is a final important point to make about the reading of the 'new man' images which I have advanced. Any assessment of their cultural impact needs to be clear on the limits of what a purely formal textual analysis can deliver. This means giving due regard to the processes of articulation between these images and their consumers in order to understand the way in which the images might have transformed the masculinity of particular groups of men. Getting at this process requires moving away from the moment of representation towards a different moment in the circuit of culture: the moment of consumption.

REFERENCES

ALEXANDER, S. AND TAYLOR, B. (1994) 'In defence of patriarchy', in Alexander, S. (ed.), *Becoming a Woman, and Other Essays in Nineteenth and Twentieth Century Feminist History*, London, Virago.

BENJAMIN, W. (1973) *Charles Baudelaire: A Lyric Poet in the Era of High Capitalism*, London, New Left Books.

BOWLBY, R. (1985) *Just Looking*, Basingstoke, Macmillan.

BUTLER, J. (1993) *Bodies that Matter*, London, Routledge.

DAVIDOFF, L. AND HALL, C. (1987) *Family Fortunes: Men and Women of the English Middle Class 1780–1850*, London, Hutchinson.

DYER, R. (1993) 'Coming out as going in: the image of the homosexual as a sad young man', in *The Matter of Images: essays on representation*, London, Routledge.

FOUCAULT, M. (1980) *Power/Knowledge: Selected Interviews and Other Writings 1972–77* (ed. Gordon, C.), Hemel Hempstead, Harvester Wheatsheaf.

FOUCAULT, M. (1982) 'The subject and power', in Rabinow, R. and Dreyfus, H. (eds), *Michel Foucault: Beyond Structuralism and Hermeneutics*, Hemel Hempstead, Harvester Wheatsheaf.

FOUCAULT, M. (1988) 'Technologies of the self' in Martin, L., Gutman, H. and Hutton, R (eds), *Technologies of the Self: A Seminar with Michel Foucault,* Amherst, MA, University of Massachussetts Press.

FREUD, S. (1977) 'Group psychology and the analysis of the ego', in *Civilization, Society and Religion,* Pelican Freud Library, Vol. 12, Harmondsworth, Penguin. First published 1921.

FREUD, S. (1984) 'Three essays on the theory of sexuality', in Pelican Freud Library, Vol. 8, Harmondsworth, Penguin. First published 1905.

HALL, C. (1992) 'Missionary stories: gender and ethnicity in England in the 1830s and 1840s', in Grossberg, L., Nelson, C. and Triechler, P. (eds), *Cultural Studies*, London, Routledge.

HUNTER, I (1993) 'Subjectivity and government', in *Economy & Society*, 22(1), pp 123–139

LACAN, J. (1968) 'The mirror phase as formative of the function of the I', *New Left Review*, 51, 71–7.

MCROBBIE, A. (2009) *The Aftermath of Feminism: Gender, Culture and Social Change*, London, Sage.

MELLY, G. (1986) 'Why the tables have turned on macho males', *Campaign*, 18 July, pp. 40–1.

MERCER, K. and JULIEN, I. (1988) 'Territories of the body', in Rutherford, J. and Chapman, R. (eds), *Male Order*, London, Lawrence & Wishart.

METCALF, A. AND HUMPHRIES, M. (eds) (1985) *The Sexuality of Men*, London, Pluto Press.

MITCHELL, J. (1984) 'Psychoanalysis: a humanist humanity or a linguistic science?', in *Women: The Longest Revolution*, Harmondsworth, Penguin.

MORLEY, D. (1980) 'Texts, readers, and subjects', in Hall, S., Hobson, D., Lowe, A. and Willis, P. (eds), *Culture, Media, Language*, London, Hutchinson.

MORT, F. (1988) 'Boy's own? Masculinity, style and popular culture', in Rutherford, J. and Chapman, R. (eds), *Male Order*, London, Lawrence & Wishart.

MULVEY, L. (1975) 'Visual pleasure and narrative cinema', *Screen,* 16(3), 6–18.

MULVEY, L. (1989) *The Visual and Other Pleasures*, Basingstoke, Macmillan.

NEALE, S. (1983) 'Masculinity as spectacle', *Screen*, 24(6), 2–16.

NIXON, S. (1996) *Hard Looks: Masculinities, Spectatorship and Contemporary Consumption*, London, UCL Press.

RABINOW, P. (ed.) (1984) *The Foucault Reader*, Harmondsworth, Penguin.

ROSE, J. (1986) *Sexuality in the Field of Vision*, London, Verso.

TOSH, J. and ROPER, M. (eds) (1992) *Manful Assertions*, London, Routledge.

WALBY, S. (1986) *Patriarchy at Work*, Cambridge, Cambridge University Press.

WEEKS, J. (1991) *Against Nature: Essays on Sexuality History and Identity*, London, Rivers Oram Press.

WINSHIP, J. (1985) 'A girl needs to get "street-wise"', *Feminist Review*, 21, 25–46.

WINSHIP, J. (1986) 'Back to the future', *New Socialist*, September, pp. 5–6.

READING A: Steve Neale, 'Masculinity as spectacle'

I want to turn to Mulvey's remarks about the glamorous male movie star below. But first it is worth extending and illustrating her point about the male protagonist and the extent to which his image is dependent upon narcissistic phantasies, phantasies of the 'more perfect, more complete, more powerful ideal ego'.

It is easy enough to find examples of films in which these phantasies are heavily prevalent, in which the male hero is powerful and omnipotent to an extraordinary degree: the Clint Eastwood character in *A Fistful of Dollars*, *For a Few Dollars More* and *The Good, the Bad and the Ugly*, the Tom Mix westerns, Charlton Heston in *El Cid*, the *Mad Max* films, the Steve Reeves epics, *Superman*, *Flash Gordon*, and so on. There is generally, of course, a drama in which that power and omnipotence are tested and qualified (*Superman 2* is a particularly interesting example, as are Howard Hawks's westerns and adventure films), but the Leone trilogy, for example, is marked by the extent to which the hero's powers are rendered almost god-like, hardly qualified at all. Hence, perhaps, the extent to which they are built around ritualized scenes which in many ways are devoid of genuine suspense.

[...]

In discussing these two types of looking [voyeuristic looking and fetishistic looking], both fundamental to the cinema, Mulvey locates them solely in relation to a structure of activity/passivity in which the look is male and active and the object of the look female and passive.

Both are considered as distinct and variant means by which male castration anxieties may be played out and allayed.

Voyeuristic looking is marked by the extent to which there is a distance between spectator and spectacle, a gulf between the seer and the seen. This structure is one which allows the spectator a degree of power over what is seen. It hence tends constantly to involve sado-masochistic phantasies and themes. Here is Mulvey's description:

> voyeurism ... has associations with sadism: pleasure lies in ascertaining guilt (immediately associated with castration), asserting control and subjecting the guilty person through punishment and forgiveness. This sadistic side fits in well with narrative. Sadism demands a story, depends on making something happen, forcing a change in another person, a battle of will and strength, victory and defeat, all occurring in a linear time with a beginning and an end. (Mulvey, 1975)

Mulvey goes on to discuss these characteristics of voyeuristic looking in terms of the *film noir* and of Hitchcock's movies, where the hero is the bearer of the voyeuristic look, engaged in a narrative in which the woman is the object of its sadistic components. However, if we take some of the terms used in her description – 'making something happen', 'forcing a change in another person', 'a battle of will and strength', 'victory and defeat' – they can immediately be applied to 'male' genres, to films concerned largely or solely with the depiction of relations between men, to any film, for example, in which there is a struggle between a hero and a male villain. War films, westerns and gangster movies, for instance, are all marked by 'action', by 'making something happen'. Battles, fights and duels of all kinds are concerned with struggles of 'will and strength', 'victory and defeat', between individual men and/or groups of men. All of which implies that male figures on the screen are subject to voyeuristic looking, both on the part of the spectator and on the part of other male characters.

Paul Willemen's thesis on the films of Anthony Mann is clearly relevant here. The repression of any explicit avowal of eroticism in the act of looking at the male seems structurally linked to a narrative content marked by sado-masochistic phantasies and scenes. Hence both forms of voyeuristic looking, intra- and extra-diegetic, are especially evident in those moments of contest and combat referred to above, in those moments at which a narrative outcome is determined through a fight or gun-battle, at which male struggle becomes pure spectacle. Perhaps the most extreme examples are to be found in Leone's westerns, where the exchange of aggressive looks marking most western gun-duels is taken to the point of fetishistic parody through the use of extreme and repetitive close-ups. At which point the look begins to oscillate between voyeurism and fetishism as the narrative starts to freeze and spectacle takes over. The anxious 'aspects' of the look at the male to which Willemen refers are here both embodied and allayed not just by playing out the sadism inherent in voyeurism through scenes of violence and combat, but also by drawing upon the structures and processes of fetishistic looking, by stopping the narrative in order to recognise the pleasure of display, but displacing it from the male body as such and locating it more generally in the overall components of a highly ritualised scene.

John Ellis has characterised fetishistic looking in the following terms:

> where voyeurism maintains (depends upon) a separation between the seer and the object seen, fetishism tries to abolish the gulf. ... This process implies a different position and attitude of the spectator to the image. It represents the opposite tendency to that of voyeurism. ... Fetishistic looking implies the direct acknowledgement and participation of the object viewed ... with the fetishistic attitude, the look of the character towards the viewer ... is a central feature. ... The voyeuristic look is curious, inquiring, demanding to know. The fetishistic gaze is captivated by what it sees, does not wish to inquire further, to see more, to find out. ... The fetishistic look has much to do with display and the spectacular.

(Ellis, 1982)

Mulvey again centrally discusses this form of looking in relation to the female as object. This second avenue, fetishistic scopophilia, builds up the physical beauty of the object, transforming it into something satisfying in itself (Mulvey, 1975, p. 14). 'Physical beauty' is interpreted solely in terms of the female body. It is specified through the example of the films of Sternberg:

> While Hitchcock goes into the investigative side of voyeurism, Sternberg produces the ultimate fetish, taking it to the point where the powerful look of the male protagonist is broken in favour of the image in direct erotic rapport with the spectator. The beauty of the woman as object and the screen space

coalesce; she is no longer the bearer of guilt but a perfect product, whose body, stylised and fragmented by close-ups, is the content of the film and the direct recipient of the spectator's look.

(ibid.)

If we return to Leone's shoot-outs, we can see that some elements of the fetishistic look as here described are present, others not. We are offered the spectacle of male bodies, but bodies unmarked as objects of erotic display. There is no trace of an acknowledgement or recognition of those bodies as displayed solely for the gaze of the spectator. They are on display, certainly, but there is no cultural or cinematic convention which would allow the male body to be presented in the way that Dietrich so often is in Sternberg's films. We see male bodies stylised and fragmented by close-ups, but our look is not direct, it is heavily mediated by the looks of the characters involved. And those looks are marked not by desire, but rather by fear, or hatred, or aggression. The shoot-outs are moments of spectacle, points at which the narrative hesitates, comes to a momentary halt, but they are also points at which the drama is finally resolved, a suspense in the culmination of the narrative drive. They thus involve an imbrication of *both* forms of looking, their intertwining designed to minimise and displace the eroticism they each tend to involve, to disavow any explicitly erotic look at the male body.

There are other instances of male combat which seem to function in this way. Aside from the western, one could point to the epic as a genre, to the gladiatorial combat in *Spartacus*, to the fight between Christopher Plummer and Stephen Boyd at the end of *The Fall of the Roman Empire*, to the chariot race in *Ben Hur*. More direct displays of the male body can be found, though they tend either to be fairly brief or else to occupy the screen during credit sequences and the like (in which case the display is mediated by another textual function). Examples of the former would include the extraordinary shot of Gary Cooper lying under the hut towards the end of *Man of the West*, his body momentarily filling the Cinemascope screen. Or some of the images of Lee Marvin in *Point Blank*, his body draped over a railing or framed in a doorway. Examples of the latter would include the credit sequence of *Man of the West* again (an example to which Willemen refers), and *Junior Bonner*.

The presentation of Rock Hudson in Sirk's melodramas is a particularly interesting case. There are constantly moments in these films in which Hudson is presented quite explicitly as the object of an erotic look. The look is usually marked as female. But Hudson's body is *feminised* in those moments, an indication of the strength of those conventions which dictate that only women can function as the objects of an explicitly erotic gaze. Such instances of 'feminisation' tend also to occur in the musical, the only genre in which the male body has been unashamedly put on display in mainstream cinema in any consistent way. (A particularly clear and interesting example would be the presentation of John Travolta in *Saturday Night Fever*.)

It is a refusal to acknowledge or make explicit an eroticism that marks all three of the psychic functions and processes discussed here in relation to images of men: identification, voyeuristic looking and fetishistic looking. It is this that tends above all to differentiate the cinematic representation of images of men and women. Although I have sought to open up a space within Laura Mulvey's arguments and theses, to argue that the elements she considers in relation to images of women can and should also be considered in relation to images of men, I would certainly concur with her basic premise that the spectatorial look in mainstream cinema is implicitly male: it is one of the fundamental reasons why the erotic elements involved in the relations between the spectator and the male image have constantly to be repressed and disavowed. Were this not the case, mainstream cinema would have openly to come to terms with the male homosexuality it so assiduously seeks either to denigrate or deny. As it is, male homosexuality is constantly present as an undercurrent, as a potentially troubling aspect of many films and genres, but one that is dealt with obliquely, symptomatically, and that has to be repressed. While mainstream cinema, in its assumption of a male norm, perspective and look, can constantly take women and the female image as its object of investigation, it has rarely investigated men and the male image in the same kind of way: women are a problem, a source of anxiety, of obsessive enquiry; men are not. Where women are investigated, men are tested. Masculinity, as an ideal, at least, is implicitly known. Femininity is, by contrast, a mystery. This is one of the reasons why the representation of masculinity, both inside and outside the cinema, has been so rarely discussed.

REFERENCES

ELLIS, J. (1982) *Visible Fictions: cinema, television, video*, London, Routledge.

MULVEY, L. (1975) 'Visual pleasure and narrative cinema', *Screen,* 16(3), 6–18.

Source: Neale, 1983, pp. 5–6, 11–16.

Steve Neale

READING B: Sean Nixon, 'Technologies of looking: retailing and the visual'

It was the *flâneur*, the male stroller in the city, who, above all, condensed the quintessentially new in modern life for Benjamin. Significantly, it was through his proximity to the new signs of modern consumption that the modernity of the *flâneur* was shaped. As Benjamin put it:

> he [the *flâneur*] is as much at home among the façades of houses as a citizen is in his four walls. To him the shiny, enamelled signs of businesses are at least as good a wall ornament as an oil painting is to a bourgeois in his salon. The walls are the desks against which he presses his notebooks; news-stands are his libraries and the terraces of cafés are the balconies from which he looks down on his household after his work is done.

(Benjamin, 1973, p. 37)

In particular it was in the arcades that the *flâneur* was at home. They provided the perfect space for strolling and looking. Benjamin quotes from a contemporary illustrated guide to Paris in invoking the arcades:

> The arcades [...] are glass-covered, marble-panelled passageways through entire complexes of houses whose proprietors have combined for such speculations. Both sides of these passageways, which are lighted from above, are lined with the most elegant shops, so that such an arcade is a city, even a world, in miniature.

(Benjamin, 1973, pp. 36–7)

This is a gushing advertisement for the arcades. Nevertheless, it testifies to both their spectacular qualities and gives us a clue to their importance in establishing the basis for a new style of consumption. Underlying the development of the arcades were new production technologies and materials: advances in plate-glass manufacture, iron-working techniques, gas lighting, bitumen and later electricity. These made possible features such as the smooth street surfaces for promenading and the display windows and interiors of the arcades. These technologies also underpinned the development of the department store and consumer spectacles like the Grandeville or world exhibitions in Paris and the Great Exhibition of 1851 in London.

Benjamin saw in these retail spectacles [the arcades, the department stores, the World Exhibitions] a new staging of the commodity, and in the *flâneur* an allegorical representation of the new relationship between the display of commodities and consumers. The way Benjamin conceptualised this new commodity culture is significant for my account. Centrally, Benjamin's description of the *flâneur* suggested the construction of a new spectatorial consumer subjectivity in relation (initially) to the arcades and their window displays of deluxe goods and expensive trifles. In other words, it suggests the formation of a distinct way of looking at 'beautiful and expensive things' (Benjamin, 1973, p. 55). In addition, Benjamin emphasised the way this consumer subjectivity not only established a series of looks at the displays of goods and the detail of the shop interiors, but also invited the consumer to look at themselves amidst this spectacle – often literally, through catching sight of their reflection in a mirror or shop window, *a* self-monitoring look was implicit, then, in these ways of looking. The self-consciousness of the *flâneur* in Benjamin's account underlined this.

Benjamin's account of the *flâneur* also hints at other determinants on the spectatorial consumer subjectivity. Together with the display techniques used in the arcades, the immediate context of the city – and in particular the crowds which filled a city like Paris – shaped specific ways of looking in Benjamin's account. What was produced were a series of interrupted looks or glances. Baudelaire's description of the *flâneur* captured this way of looking well:

> For the perfect *flâneur*, for the passionate spectator, it is an immense joy to set up house in the heart of the multitude, amid the ebb and flow of movement, in the midst of the fugitive and the infinite. To be away from home and yet to feel oneself everywhere at home; to see the world, to be a centre of the world, and yet to remain hidden to the world. The spectator is a prince who everywhere rejoices in his incognito.
>
> (Frisby, 1985, p. 17)

Modern life for the *flâneur* – the life of the arcades and the crowds of Paris – is here visually apprehended through such 'transitory, fugitive elements, whose metamorphoses are so rapid' (Frisby, 1985, p. 18).

Baudelaire's sonnet, 'To a Passer-by', which Benjamin comments on, further underlines the formation of new ways of looking conditioned by the urban environment. In the sonnet, the male narrator catches sight of, and is fascinated by, a woman who passes by in the crowd. In the moment of his desire being aroused, however, the woman is already lost again in the crowd. For Benjamin, this representation of masculine desire in the city is significant. It is, he suggests, a representation 'not so much of love at first sight, as love at last sight'. In other words, the desire experienced by the narrator in seeing the woman is the product of the fleeting quality of his look and the transitory nature of the encounter. It is a representation of the frisson of the passing stranger.

II

Benjamin's commentary on the *flâneur* points us towards the formation of specific ways of looking that were shaped by the new techniques of consumer display and the increasingly differentiated space of the wider city context (such as the distinctions between industrial districts and largely retail and leisure-based areas) (Green, 1990, pp. 23–42), The sonnet, 'To a Passer-by', also alerts us to a further dimension of these ways of looking. That is, the way in which these ways of looking were implicated in a set of gendered power relations of looking.

Janet Wolff and Griselda Pollock, as Elizabeth Wilson has shown, have emphasised in quite similar terms the dominance of specifically masculine pleasures in looking associated with modern city space and its consumer display. Wolff goes so far as to suggest that:

> the possibility of unmolested strolling and observation first seen by Baudelaire, and then analysed by Walter Benjamin were entirely the experiences of men.
>
> (Wolff, quoted in Wilson, 1992, p. 99)

Pollock cites the career of the painter Berthe Morisot and her focus on domestic scenes and interiors, to make the same point. Thus for Pollock:

the gaze of the *flâneur* articulates and produces a masculine sexuality which in the modern sexual economy enjoys the freedom to look, appraise and possess.

(Pollock, quoted in Wilson, 1992, p. 101)

This was a look, importantly, in which women shoppers were as much the object of masculine visual enquiry as the shop displays. Quite deliberate slippages were often made, in fact, in consumerist commentaries between decorative consumer trifles and women's appearances. Rachel Bowlby quotes an emphatic representation of these relations of looking. The illustration from *La Vie de Londres* (1890), titled, 'Shopping dans Regent Street', put it succinctly: "'Shopping is checking out the stores – for ladies; for gentlemen, it's checking out the lady shoppers! *Shop qui peut*'" (Bowlby, 1985, pp. 80–1).

This latter commentary, however, also hints at a more complex picture of the gender ascribed to forms of consumer spectatorship in the nineteenth century than the totalising conceptualisation advocated by Pollock and Wolff. Elizabeth Wilson, in her essay, 'The invisible *flâneur*', takes to task Wolff and Pollock for underestimating the ability of groups of women to actively participate in the new consumer subjectivity and its associated forms of spectatorship. Noting the growth of white-collar occupations for women towards the end of the nineteenth century, Wilson argues that this constituency of women were explicitly courted by commercial entrepreneurs and also participated in the pleasures of 'just looking' associated with consumption. As she says:

the number of eating establishments grew rapidly, with railway station buffets, refreshment rooms at exhibitions, ladies-only dining rooms, and the opening of West End establishments such as the Criterion (1874), which specifically catered for women. At the end of the century Lyons, the ABC tearooms, Fullers tearooms ... the rest rooms and refreshment rooms in department stores had all transformed the middle- and lower-middle class woman's experience of public life. (Wilson, 1992, p. 101)

Nicholas Green also argues that certain groups of women were visible as promenaders and active shopping *voyeurs* around the emergent sites of consumption. An important constituent in this respect were what he calls 'fashionable women' (Green, 1990, p. 41); namely, wealthy women often involved in fashion or part of the new breed of society hostesses. These women had the necessary economic power to consume and were able to negotiate, Green suggests, the uninvited looks of men in the pursuit of the visual and material pleasures of consumption. These women had a privileged and respectable place in the fashionable boulevards of Paris, quite different from the other femininities which also moved across the urban topography. These were 'immoral' women like street prostitutes, lorettes and courtesans, themselves part of the modern phantasmagoria of the city and part of another arena of masculine consumption.

Green's and Wilson's accounts suggest that women of all classes were a much more significant presence within the modern city and around its new sites of consumption than either Wolff or Pollock suggest, and, more than that, were able to enjoy the pleasures of shopping spectacle – albeit within more tightly controlled boundaries than leisured men. It is also important to reassert – in contradistinction to Pollock – that these ways of looking were shaped by the predominance of an interrupted or broken series of looks (including those which involved forms of self-visualisation) rather than by a fixed gaze. What remains clear from these accounts, however, is the specific link which was forged in the formative periods of consumer culture between certain public masculine identities (and the *flâneur* is, of course, exemplary) and the new modes of spectatorial consumer subjectivity.

III

The modes of leisurely looking – at the spectacle of displayed goods and the visual delights of other shoppers – through which the spectatorial subjectivity of the *flâneur* was produced, were determined by more, though, than the spatial configuration of shop display and the built form of the city. My argument is that these ways of looking formed part of a larger 'technology of looking' associated with consumption and leisure. The forms of representation associated with a new style of journalism linked to the expansion of the popular press and popular periodicals, and subsequently (and critically) the circulation of photographic images through these same forms, were the other key components of this technology of looking. Benjamin, again, provides some pointers to these processes and their cultural significance.

A whole popular literature devoted to representing the culture of the metropolis and the new delights of consumption was associated with the development of modern forms of consumption. Benjamin singled out the genre of popular publications called 'physiologies', pocket-sized volumes which detailed Paris and the figures who populated the new districts. These were immensely popular publications, with, as Benjamin details, seventy-six new physiologies appearing in 1841. In addition, other styles of brochure and pamphlet appeared that detailed salon culture and were often tied in with the expansion of art dealing and the trade in contemporary pictures and other *objects de luxe*. What is important for my argument is that these publications represented the city and the new forms of consumption in highly visual terms. In Benjamin's memorable phrase, 'the leisurely quality of these descriptions [of Paris life in the physiologies] fits the style of the *flâneur* who goes botanizing on the asphalt' (Benjamin, 1973, p. 36). I think this can be put more firmly. The spectatorial subjectivity of the *flâneur* had conditions of existence in the visual apprehension of the city represented in these literatures; *the flâneur's* ways of looking were shaped by the organisation of particular looks or ways of seeing within popular publications. The widespread circulation of photographic images of the city and consumer goods which followed the introduction of half-tone plates in the 1880s extended this process through another representational form. Half-tone plates made possible the cheap reproduction of photographic images in newspapers, periodicals, in books and advertisements (Tagg, 1988, pp. 55–6). In practical terms, this massively extended what John Tagg calls the 'democracy of the image', undercutting the previous luxury status of the photograph and turning it into an everyday, throw-away object.

Culturally, this photography set the terms for new forms of perception. For Benjamin, at the heart of this process were techniques like the close-up and juxtaposition. The practices of photography associated with the new 'democracy of the image', then, visually represented modern life in new and distinctive ways. As such, they formed an important part of the 'technology of looking' that structured the experience of consumption in the period around the turn of the century. This was a technology of looking whose precepts went back, as we have seen, as early perhaps as the 1770s and which linked an intertextual set of looks from the interiors of retail environments and the surrounding streets to the written and pictorial representations of city life and consumption in paperbacks, magazines and newspapers. The spectatorial consumer subjectivity associated with the characteristically modern forms of consumption was produced across these constructions of ways of looking or seeing.

REFERENCES

BENJAMIN, W. (1973) *Charles Baudelaire: A Lyric Poet in the Era of High Capitalism*, London, New Left Books.

BOWLBY, R. (1985) *Just Looking: Consumer Culture in Dreiser, Gissing and Zola*, Basingstoke, Macmillan.

FRISBY (1985) *Fragments of Modernity*, London, Polity Press.

GREEN, N. (1990) *The Spectacle of Nature: Landscape and Bourgeois Culture in Nineteenth Century France*, Manchester, Manchester University Press.

TAGG, J. (1988) *The Burden of Representation: Essays on Photographies and Histories*, London, Macmillan.

WILSON, E. (1992) 'The invisible *flâneur*', *New Left Review*, Jan./Feb., 90–110.

Source: Nixon, 1996, pp. 63–9.

CHAPTER SIX

GENRE AND GENDER: THE CASE OF SOAP OPERA

Christine Gledhill with Vicky Ball

1 INTRODUCTION

Earlier chapters in this book have examined a wide range of representations and identities which circulate through different signifying practices: images of cultural differences constructed in the museum; images of the Other, as portrayed in the media; alternative masculinities emerging in the 'new man' of shop window displays and fashion photography. As cultural constructions, such representations address us in the practices of everyday life even while calling on our subjective sense of self and our fantasies: how we relate to those who are in some way 'different', how to be a certain kind of man. What these chapters stress is that all social practices – whether reading magazines, visiting museums, shopping for clothes – take place within representation and are saturated with meanings and values which contribute to our sense of who we are – our culturally constructed identities.

This chapter continues with these concerns, but narrows the focus to that signifying practice which we might think of as specializing in the production of cultural representations: the mass production of *fiction*, of stories – novels, films, radio and television dramas and serials. While many of the issues raised in this chapter are relevant across the range of popular culture, we will focus on the specific example of television *soap opera* to explore how popular fictions participate in the production and circulation of cultural meanings, especially in relation to gender. 'Soap opera' is a particular type or *genre* of popular fiction first devised for female audiences in the 1930s by American radio broadcasters, which has since spread to television around the world.

In section 2, we look at the pervasiveness of soap opera and the role of narrative fiction in popular culture. In section 3, we will consider the impact of gender on mass cultural forms, while section 4 introduces concepts from *genre theory* in order to explore how soap opera works as a signifying practice. The impact of gender on the form of soap opera as a type of programme which seeks to address a female audience is discussed in section 5, where we will encounter feminist debates about *representation* and the *construction of female subject-positions*. But soap opera's extraordinary shift in recent years from the female-dominated daytime to the family primetime schedule – when, research suggests, household viewing choices are more likely to be in the control of men – raises more general questions (dealt with particularly in section 6) about the *gendering of popular genres* and the way in which the soap opera form participates in changing definitions of masculinity and femininity.

This chapter, then, will be asking you to give as much time as you can to watching soap operas aired on television this week, to looking at the way soap operas are presented in television magazines and listings, noting any references to soap opera that may turn up in newscasts, newspapers and magazines.

The key questions to be explored are:

- How does soap opera as an example of mass-produced popular entertainment contribute to the production and circulation of gendered identities?
- How does the nature of soap opera as a *genre* affect the cultural struggle over representations, meanings and identities?
- In what way can it be said that soap opera is a feminine genre?
- What do changes in the content and style of soap operas suggest about gender struggles and changing definitions of masculinity and femininity?

2 REPRESENTATIONS AND MEDIA FICTIONS

2.1 Fiction and everyday life

The term *fiction* suggests a separation from real life. In common-sense terms, sitting down with a novel, going to the cinema, or watching a TV drama is to enter an imaginary world which offers a qualitatively different experience from the activities of everyday life and from those media forms which claim to deal with the real world – such as the news or photojournalism. And in some senses, which this chapter will deal with, this is true. Stories are by definition only stories: they are not real life. This often leads to the dismissal of popular fictions as 'only' or 'harmless' entertainment, or worse, time-wasting money-spinners made by the profit-driven entertainment industries. But granted that popular fictions *are* entertainment and *do* have to be profitable, are they for these reasons either irrelevant to *lived experience* or without *significance*? Just consider for a moment some statistics offered by Robert Allen about perhaps the most notorious example of fictional consumption, soap opera:

Since the early 1930s nearly 100,000 hours of daytime dramatic serials – soap operas – have been broadcast on radio and television in the United States. These hours represent the unfolding of nearly

200 different fictive worlds, many of them over the course of decades. Within 9 years after the debut of the first network radio soap opera in 1932, the soap opera form constituted 90 per cent of all sponsored network radio programming broadcast during the daylight hours. With but a brief hiatus in the mid-1940s, *Guiding Light* has been heard and, since 1952, seen continuously, 260 days each year, making it the longest story ever told. (Allen, 1985, p. 3)

Such statistics demonstrate the *pervasiveness* of soap opera as *a fact of life*. The twice-, thrice-weekly and often daily broadcasting of soap opera serials offers a fictional experience which audiences encounter as part of a routine in which fiction and everyday life intertwine – to such a degree in fact that major events in soap opera characters' lives become national news, as happened in spring 2010 with the *Coronation Street* storyline involving Joe McIntyre, who died in a boating accident while attempting to fake his own death as part of an insurance scam. This narrative drew upon the real-life case of John Darwin, who was imprisoned in 2008 for attempting to fake his own death via a canoeing accident.

ACTIVITY 1

Over the next week keep a media consumption diary and note the different kinds of fiction you (and perhaps other members of your family) encounter:

1 How much of what you read/listen to/view is fiction of one kind or another?

2 On average how many hours a day or week do you each spend in a fictional world?

3 List the different kinds of fiction you encounter, e.g. serials, soap operas, novels, romances, TV dramas, feature films, etc.

4 Does one kind of fiction predominate in your experience over another?

5 What is your immediate reaction to these observations?

Robert Allen's soap opera statistics establish the *centrality of fiction to everyday life* and perhaps your own experience recorded in your media consumption diary will back this up. Ien Ang, in a study of the American soap *Dallas* and its female audience, argues that 'only through the imagination, which is always subjective, is "objective reality" assimilated: a life without imagination does not exist' (Ang, 1985, p. 83). The calculated 'staging' of Joe McIntyre's scam in *Coronation Street* and the news media is worth considering in the light of this claim. In this case, the playing out of the storyline on *Coronation Street* between February and June 2010 focused upon Joe's bungled plan which not only led to his death but also implicated his innocent wife, Gail McIntyre, in his plans. Consequently, connections were made in the press between this national event of the imagination and the case of John Darwin, particularly how *Coronation Street* imaginatively apportioned guilt, by staging Joe's accidental death and rewarding Gail's innocence by letting her go free from prison.

Clearly, in this instance, the fictional imagination of what it is like to experience debt, deception, to conceal a crime, and to face imprisonment in the instance of Gail (similarly to Anne Darwin), became an integral part of public debate about marriage, fraud, and the law. This is not to say anything about what *Coronation Street* contributed to the debate, or about its contradictory representations of women and, by implication, feminism. The point here is that there is a circulation between the events we learn about from one media form – the news – into another – soap opera – and back again. Public debates about debt, marital deception, the law, become material – signifiers and signs – for the construction of an imaginary world which works over the social and gender contradictions of such events and returns them to public discourse.

2.2 Fiction as entertainment

What this chapter is concerned with, then, are the processes involved in this interchange between fiction and the social world it references. We will need to take account of the specific *signifying practices* involved in producing fictions; in particular *how the social world enters fictional discourse* and what happens to it once there; how particular genres *address different audiences* and *invite participation*; the gendered *representations* and *meanings* they construct and – an important and often neglected factor – *pleasure*. It is important that we do not lose sight of this last consideration, difficult though it is to find concepts to analyse such an intangible thing. Box 6.1 will help to illustrate the problem of analysing pleasure.

FIGURE 6.1 *Coronation Street*: Gail McIntyre (Helen Worth) and Deirdre Barlow (Anne Kirkbride) head to head

BOX 6.1

In an episode of *Coronation Street* shown on Friday 13 August 2010, a mixture of melodrama and high farce was employed to expose Lewis as a conman to the street's inhabitants. Lianne Battersby and Peter Barlow (the manager and owners of the bookmakers) are in a race against time to prove that Lewis is a cad who has stolen £4,000 from them before he leaves for Greece with long-time character Audrey Roberts.

Pleasure in the text, then, arises not only from Lewis being exposed as a fraud, a fact which has largely been revealed to the audience in previous episodes but, indeed, *how* he has seduced two of the soap's favourite and long-suffering female characters (the married Deidre Barlow, who works in the betting shop, as well as Audrey Roberts) in order to get away with his fraudulent plans.

True to the use of melodrama in British soap opera, tension is heightened by a series of close-ups of Deirdre Barlow's face and clenched fist as her own affair with Lewis is exposed in front of her husband (Ken Barlow) and son-in-law (Peter Barlow) as they trawl through CCTV footage in the bookmakers. Deirdre's humiliation is then heightened when her moral transgression is shown to a shocked Audrey and friends at her farewell party (at which Lewis has failed to show up).

However, melodrama quickly turns to farce and slapstick as the encounter between Deirdre Barlow and Audrey Roberts reignites an ongoing feud between the two families and Audrey's daughter Gail throws a lemon meringue pie in Deirdre's face, before attempting to throttle her.

While everything else that has been going on in this episode has been comically and melodramatically predictable, much of its pleasure in fact lies in the fulfilment of our expectations, such as the middle-class outsider being confirmed as a duplicitous bounder and the tension between the two families boiling over. Scenes of Deirdre's and Audrey's public humiliation are quickly replaced by scenes of their personal grief, whereby camera and dialogue return to more intimate scenes of domestic realism between Deirdre and Ken, and then Audrey, as they each attempt to deal with their betrayal.

While it might be suggested that this scene circulates outdated gender ideologies regarding the loneliness and naïvety of older women, if we restrict ourselves to these themes we might ignore the pleasurable feelings with which we may respond to its cocktail of farce and melodrama. Moreover, we have to remember that the continuous serial form of soap opera requires that the ending of one episode is the beginning of the next, so that the meaning of events is never easily pinned down. We bring knowledge of previous storylines and representations to our reading of the text at any one particular moment, including our familiarity with Deirdre and Audrey as two of the *Street*'s strong female characters. Similarly, our perceptions can shift and change in light of the way storylines and characters develop in future episodes.

If you remember this episode, you may well want to argue with me about some of the meanings and emotional affects I am attributing to it. But this, for the moment, is not the point. We need to take care in using the concept of representation that we do not use it in a limiting way to refer only to the representation of discourses, figures and events of the social world, and neglect the purpose of fiction in producing the pleasures of drama, comedy, melodrama, as well as the pleasures of recognizing situations we know from lived experience.

Alongside the naming of certain ideological values and stereotypes, I have in these comments made a number of references to features which are to do with the *form* of the programmes:

1 their nature as a particular broadcast *genre*, the soap opera;

2 the *narrative structure* both of this particular episode and of soap opera as a continuous serial;

3 the *organization of shots* – through *visual composition* and *editing structures*;

4 *character types*;

5 *modes* of expression such as melodrama, comedy and realism; and our reception of audio-visual dramatized fiction as *aesthetic and affective experiences*, in which the pacing and ordering of plots, visual organization, pitch of the voice, and the dramatically charged encounters between protagonists register on our senses and our emotions.

My argument is that if we want to know how fictions gain hold of our imaginations so that they effectively become a central part of our 'real' lives on a day-to-day basis, we have to pay attention to these properties of aesthetic form and emotional affect. For these effects produce or imply meanings which we may well find at odds with the ostensible 'messages' we might arrive at through counting stereotypes, themes or plot outcomes.

This means that our study of soap opera will be concerned with questions of representation at the level of story *form*, including different kinds of story type or *genre*, questions of *narrative organization* (the way the story unfolds), and *modes of expression*, such as realism and melodrama, all factors which bear on the pleasure-producing, representational and signifying work of fictional forms and the subject-positions they create.

2.3 But is it good for you?

As a central feature of any society, *fiction* has been an object of public discussion almost since its production began. In our school experiences we have all undergone some kind of training, however rudimentary, in the analysis of stories and characters in classes on 'English Literature', and we all encounter at some level critical discourse about books, films, TV programmes. Indeed, there is a whole industry – educational, journalistic, academic – devoted to the critical assessment and evaluation of dramas, novels, films and television programmes. We do not, then, start out innocently to explore the question of how to understand the phenomenon of soap opera.

ACTIVITY 2

Pause for a moment to take stock of your own starting point by registering your immediate reaction to the idea of taking soap opera as a subject for academic study!

If your reaction is a decided negative, don't be surprised. Nor should those of you who registered a positive response be surprised if in some way you find yourself qualifying your pleasure: 'I like watching soap operas, but …'. Charlotte Brunsdon, a feminist cultural analyst, speaks of how soap opera is popularly used as a measure of 'the truly awful'. However, what I want to emphasize here is that the *practice of critical assessment* is itself a type of cultural production: it defines those works of fiction (novels, plays, films, paintings) which are considered touchstones of a society's culture against which the rest are ranked. This, however, is not a neutral process: it is a way of policing the boundaries of official culture in order to ensure which cultural meanings and possibilities are privileged within a society – witness, for example, political arguments in the mid-1990s about the place of Shakespeare and the English 'classics' in the national curriculum.

3 MASS CULTURE AND GENDERED CULTURE

In this section we take up a number of issues concerning the place of popular narrative in mass culture.

3.1 Women's culture and men's culture

An apparently anomalous feature of mass culture, often noted by feminists, is the provision of a cultural space designated explicitly as 'women's' – the woman's page in daily newspapers, women's magazines, the woman's film, *Woman's Hour*, etc., while a corresponding category for men hardly exists. Although the start of a *Men's Hour* on BBC Radio 5 in the UK in July 2010 might mark a turning point to this cultural tradition, it remains a fact that there is no 'man's page' in the daily newspapers, nor 'man's film' among Hollywood genres. Feminists argue this is because in western society the norm of what counts as human is provided by the masculine and only women's culture needs to be marked as specifically gendered – much in the same way that 'man' is said to stand for men *and* women, or 'his' incorporates 'hers', etc. The gendering of culture therefore is not straightforwardly visible. The central, established values claim universal status and are taken to be gender-free.

Gender only becomes an issue if women as a specific category are in question, when they become discussible as a deviation from the norm. Feminists, from the mid 1970s, for instance, have had to fight a gender-blind academic and critical establishment to get forms such as romance fiction or soap opera on to the agenda as worthy of serious study. Given soap opera's historical association with the female audience, its relegation to the domain of 'the truly awful' suggests a gendered standard that aligns core cultural values with the masculine, which then needs protection from the feminizing deviations of mass culture. We can observe this unconscious gendering of cultural value at work even in feminist and Marxist analysis. For example, feminist film journalist, Molly Haskell described the Hollywood woman's film as 'emotional porn for frustrated housewives' (Haskell, 1974); Marxist critic David Margolies attacked Mills and Boon romances for encouraging their female readers to 'sink into feeling' (Margolies, 1982–83); Marxist analyst Michele Mattelart consigns Latin American soap operas to 'the oppressive order of the heart' (Mattelart, 1985). This identification of *feeling* with female cultural forms is perhaps one reason why men have historically disliked acknowledging their place in the soap opera audience. In the wake of the sexual politics of the 1960s and 1970s, for example, the shifting relationship between public and private spheres and assertions by feminists that the personal is political within the contemporary context has not been matched by a re-evaluation of the hierarchy of gendered cultural values. The increasing tendency of both fictional and factual television texts to foreground values attached to the feminine in western cultures – including the personal and emotional 'life politics' of its characters and participants – has been seen to mark a series of inferior shifts in television and the softening up of 'serious', 'quality' genres, particularly of documentary and current affairs (Moseley, 2001). In this way, contemporary accounts of television serve to reinforce gendered cultural values in the way in which they extend rather than disrupt metaphors and qualities that align television as the 'bad cultural object' of mass culture with 'the feminine' (Brunsdon, 1990; Joyrich, 1996; Modleski, 1982; Petro, 1986).

The questions posed for this book, then, are not only *how is gender constructed in representation, but how does gender impact on the cultural forms that do the constructing and on the way they are perceived in our culture? How, in particular, does the space designated 'woman's' differ from the masculine norm?*

3.2 Images of women vs real women

Early feminist approaches to the media were concerned with the role of the dominant media images of women in maintaining established beliefs about the nature of the feminine and the masculine and the proper roles to be played by women and men, wives and husbands, mothers and fathers. They attacked such images for not representing women as they really are or really could or should be – for being **stereotypes**, rather than positive images, psychologically rounded characters, or real women. In other words, the critique pitted one form of representation against another in terms of their presumed realism: the *stereotype*, because obviously constructed, was assumed to be 'false', while the **psychologically rounded character** was assumed to guarantee truth to human nature. The problem with this analysis is not the rejection of media distortions, but the supposed remedy. What is required, according to this view, is simply a readjustment of the lens, a refocusing of the programme maker's perspective, in order to produce accurate reflections.

But is it as simple as this? The 'mimetic' assumptions which underlie this view were challenged by Stuart Hall in Chapter 1: we encounter very practical problems in appealing to 'reality' as a means of assessing the constructive work of representations. For the category 'women' does not refer to a homogeneous social grouping in which all women will recognize themselves. For a start, gender intersects with other social identities during the practice of daily life – worker, student, tax-payer, etc. And being 'a woman' will be experienced differently according to one's age, class, ethnicity, sexual orientation, and so on.

In opposition to the mimetic approach, the 'constructionist' view of representation outlined by Stuart Hall implies that even the terms 'man' and 'woman' – whether word or image – which touch on what appears most personal to us – our sex and gender – are in fact cultural signifiers which construct rather than reflect gender definitions, meanings and identities. However 'natural' their reference may seem, these terms are not simply a means of symbolic representation of pre-given male and female 'essences'. The psychologically rounded character, so often appealed to as a kind of gold standard in human representation, is as much a work of construction as the stereotype; it is produced by the discourses of popular psychology, sociology, medicine, education, and so on, which, as Sean Nixon suggests in Chapter 5, contribute in their own turn dominant notions of what constitutes feminine and masculine identity. Thus stereotypes and psychologically rounded characters are different kinds of mechanisms by which the protagonists of fiction 'articulate with reality'; the 'stereotype' functioning as a shorthand reference to specific cultural perceptions (as discussed by Stuart Hall in Chapter 4), the 'psychologically rounded character' constructing a more complex illusion from the popular currency of sociological or psychological ideas. Their *cultural significance*, however, cannot be measured in any direct comparison with the real world, but, as we shall see in the following sections, depends on how they are called on within the particular genres or narrative forms which use them, as well as on the circumstances of their production and reception, and on the social context of their audiences.

3.3 Entertainment as a capitalist industry

The higher value placed on the 'character' over the 'stereotype' stems in part from the function which the latter play in the mass-produced formulae of the entertainment and consumer industries. This perception returns us to the question of power. For example, in her investigation of the female audience for *Dallas*, Ien Ang found, among those declaring a dislike of the programme, both a rejection of the profit motive at work in the production of the serial and an implicit sense of the power imbalance between the money makers and the mass audience:

> It really makes me more and more angry. The aim is simply to rake in money, loads of money and people try to do that by means of all these things – sex, beautiful people, wealth and you always have people who fall for it. To get high viewing figures.

> (quoted in Ang, 1985, p. 91)

Many of the *Dallas* haters make an explicit equation between the 'commercial' aims and traditional gender roles validated in the programme. The problem with this critique, however, is that the brunt of the criticism falls on the 'people who fall for it'. The audience so represented never includes the critic, but consists of 'those others, out there'. In other words, 'I' and the 'you' whom I address are not among 'those' people. Nor does this critique acknowledge that money is a necessity for any cultural work whether mass or minority (starving in a garret for the sake of art may be very high-minded but not very practical!). Typically, within what Ien Ang terms 'the ideology of mass culture', it is 'money' *and* the 'mass audience' which are attacked rather than the power relations in play between the media and their audiences.

3.4 Dominant ideology, hegemony and cultural negotiation

What emerges in these perceptions of media manipulation is the question of the link between social and cultural domination. This was initially approached through the early Marxist concept of *ideology*. According to Marx, those groups who own the means of production thereby control the means of producing and circulating a society's ideas. Through their ownership of publishing houses, newspapers and latterly the electronic media, the dominant classes subject the masses to ideologies which make the social relations of domination and oppression appear natural and so mystify the 'real' conditions of existence. The return to Marx in the 1960s and 1970s, after a period in which it appeared that the traditional working class had been 'bought off' by the growing affluence and consumer culture of the 1950s, put the issue of the link between the mass media and dominant ideology at the centre of the agenda of those struggling for social change. For feminists, as for Marxists, the media have figured as a major instrument of **ideological domination**.

The problem with this notion of ideological domination by the media is that it makes it difficult to conceptualize a position from which to resist or challenge it, except through the values or ideas of the dominant elite, which necessarily exclude the mystified masses. A way of moving beyond this impasse was offered in the thinking of the Italian Marxist, Antonio Gramsci, discussed in Chapter 4, which permitted a decisive reformulation of the concept of ideology, displacing the notion of domination by that of **hegemony**. According to Gramsci, since power in a bourgeois democracy is as much a matter of persuasion and consent as of force, it is never secured once and for all. Any dominant group has to a greater or lesser degree to acknowledge the existence of those whom it dominates by winning the consent of competing or marginalized groups in society. Unlike the fixed grip over society implied by 'domination', 'hegemony' is won in the to-and-fro of **negotiation** between competing social, political and ideological forces through which power is contested, shifted or reformed. *Representation* is a key site in such struggle, since the power of definition is a major source of hegemony. In Chapter 4, for example, Stuart Hall points to the way the slogan 'Black is Beautiful' contributed to decisive changes in the meanings of ethnicity and hence the possibilities for changing race-relations in America and the UK. Thus, in the process of negotiating hegemony, ideologies may shift their ground, the central consensus may be changed, and 'the real' reconstructed.

The concepts of hegemony and negotiation enable us to rethink the real and representation in a way which avoids the model of a fixed reality or fixed sets of codes for representing it. And they enable us to conceptualize the production of definitions and identities by the media industries in a way that acknowledges both the unequal power relations involved in the struggle and at the same time the space for negotiation and resistance from subordinated groups. Thus the 'real' is, as it were, an ongoing production, in constant process of transformation, and subject to struggle and contest through equally dynamic processes of signification. Within this framework, ideologies are not simply imposed by governments, business interests or the media as their agents – although this possibility always remains an institutional option through mechanisms of direct control such as censorship. Rather, media forms and representations constitute major sites for conflict and negotiation, a central goal of which is the definition of what is to be taken as 'real', and the struggle to name and win support for certain kinds of cultural value and identity over others. 'Realism', then, is a crucial value claimed by different parties to the contest.

3.5 The gendering of cultural forms: high culture vs mass culture

If we now return to the question of the gendering of cultural forms, what becomes clear is that ranking what counts as culturally significant is 'gendered', and thus the privileging of certain cultural forms or characteristics must also be seen as part of a struggle within patriarchal culture to define 'reality'. We can schematize this struggle like this:

TABLE 6.1

Mass culture/entertainment	High culture/art
Popular genre conventions	Realism
Romanticized stereotypes	Rounded psychological characterization
Glamour	Severity
Emotions	Thought
Expressive performance	Underplaying, understatement
Talk about feelings	Taciturnity, decisive action
Fantasy	Real problems
Escapism	Coming to terms
Private domesticity	The public world
Pleasure	Difficulty
Soap opera	The western
Femininity	**Masculinity**

Such cultural oppositions proliferate and no doubt you could extend the list. I want to draw this section to a close by highlighting two aspects of Table 6.1. First, from the perspective of high culture, all mass entertainment is inferior, and is associated with qualities that are inherently feminizing, while the cultural gold standard of realism is drawn into an alignment with values characterized as masculine. This is not to say that female cultural producers or characters do not operate within high culture; only that when they do, they tend to function on masculinized territory and must abandon or suppress those features characterized as feminizing. Secondly, within a model of hegemonic struggle, Table 6.1 represents not a set of rigidly fixed oppositions but values that exist in tension, in constantly shifting relation to each other. For example, the table may suggest to you why it is that, of all the popular genres, the western has most easily crossed over into the camp of the culturally respectable and worthy (for example, Clint Eastwood's long sought-after Oscar for *Unforgiven*), while soap opera is still popularly the butt of journalistic humour.

Finally, I want to glance at a term you may have expected to find in the table and which it would not be surprising to find among your 'gut responses' to soap opera in Activity 1, namely *melodramatic*. The term 'melodramatic' is often applied to soap opera to describe its emphasis on the heightened drama of family relationships and personal feelings, as opposed to the focus on public action in 'male' genres. But melodrama's long and complicated history demonstrates perfectly the shifting intersections between realism and gender in struggles for cultural definition and control. In the nineteenth century, melodrama constituted a pervasive mode of dramatic and fictional production, with broad class and gender appeal. Cape and sword melodramas, nautical melodramas, frontier melodramas, and so on, were action genres and certainly not aimed at women alone. Nor were such melodramas perceived as antithetical to realism. Rather they were conceived as viewing reality in moral and emotional terms and were judged in terms of their authenticity and labour-intensive technical realization on stage. However, in the twentieth century, melodramatic forms, such as the so-called 'women's picture' or 'weepies' which Hollywood produced in the 1930s, 1940s and 1950s, and the emotionally intense TV drama series and serials, such as soap opera, have become identified as feminine *genres*.

This alerts us to the fact that, like the codes for representing reality, the gendering of genres is not fixed once and for all. Rather, shifts in the gendering of genres may well indicate struggles over defining what counts as masculine and feminine in the construction of social reality. This is important for our investigation of the cultural work of soap opera. Since the late 1970s, for instance, soap operas have hit primetime television, and appears, like nineteenth-century melodrama, to be making appeals to broader and cross-gendered audiences – for example, *Dallas* (USA) or *EastEnders* (UK). Moreover, many 'action'-based serials, conventionally understood as 'male' genres, are incorporating elements of soap opera – such as *The Bill* (UK) and *The Sopranos* (USA). *Do such shifts imply changes in the forms of 'male' and 'female' genres? Or changes in what counts as 'masculine' and 'feminine' themes and characteristics? Or both?* Whatever conclusion we come to, it behoves us not to take the gendering of *genres* as fixed, but to explore what each genre contributes to changing definitions of the masculine and feminine within and around popular fictions since the late 1990s.

The next section turns to genre theory for concepts which can both clarify the signifying work of popular fictional forms and the way they may participate in the contest and negotiation for hegemony within representation.

4 GENRE, REPRESENTATION AND SOAP OPERA

In this section I want to turn to the question of soap opera as a signifying practice. In other words, *how does soap opera produce its meanings?* What are the institutional, discursive and formal mechanisms which enable soap opera and other popular fictional TV programmes to function as sites for the negotiation of meanings and identities, sites of cultural struggle over representation, sites for the construction of the real, and for the production of popular pleasures? Finally, how is gender caught up in this textual work?

4.1 The genre system

To answer these questions we need concepts which can deal with the work of soap opera as a mass-produced form of entertainment; concepts that can handle the work of its conventions and stereotypes in relation to the social world of the audience, without presuming either a fixed reality or a fixed set of codes for representing that reality. And we need a model of the discursive work of soap opera which can address questions of power and hegemony and the processes of cultural negotiation taking place in popular culture.

As one of a range of popular fictional types or genres, soap opera belongs to the overarching *genre system* which governs the division of mass-produced print and audio-visual fictions into distinct kinds: romantic novels, detective stories, westerns, thrillers, sitcoms, as well as soap operas. I shall, therefore, be turning to **genre theory** – especially as it has been applied to film and television fiction – for a number of concepts which together offer a productive approach to the work of soap opera within the context of the media industries. For it is within the working of the genre system that economic and production mechanisms, particular textual forms, and audiences or readers interconnect and struggles for hegemony take place.

4.1.1 The genre product

First, what does the term 'genre' imply about the product to which it is applied? A particular genre category refers to the way the individual fictions which belong to it can be grouped together in terms of similar plots, stereotypes, settings, themes, style, emotional affects, and so on. Just naming these different popular genres – the detective story, soap opera, etc. – will probably invoke for you certain expectations about the kind of stories and affects they offer, even if you rarely read or watch them. Indeed, such categories function as important guides to our viewing choices and practices.

These expectations mean that we already know roughly what *kind* of story we will be watching by, for example, tuning into television programmes such as *CSI* or *Ugly Betty*, or going to the cinema to see *Avatar* or *In Bruges*. Such expectations arise from our familiarity with the *conventions* of each genre – the police series, the sitcom, science fiction or comedy. These conventions represent a body of rules or codes, signifiers and signs, and the potential combinations of, and relations between, signs which together constitute the genre.

ACTIVITY 3

Pause for a moment to note down anything you know about soap opera as a genre, whether or not you are a fan. Use the following headings:

1 format and medium
2 subject matter
3 setting and locations
4 narrative pattern
5 character types
6 plots

Among other things, you have probably listed some of the following:

Format and medium	Radio or television continuous serial (i.e. not series or serialization, see section 5.1.5 below), broadcast once or more per week, usually in 30-minute slots.
Subject matter	Ups and downs of family or community life and personal relationships.
Setting and locations	Home interiors and public places where lots of people can meet, e.g. pubs, launderettes, corner shops, offices, street corners, hospitals, sometimes the workplace.
Narrative pattern	Multiple and interweaving storylines; we probably don't remember or never saw the beginning; no end in sight.
Character types	Multiple and diverse characters across the social spectrum; many female roles, including older women, widows and divorcees.
Plots	Fallings out between family and community members; jealousies, infidelities, dirty dealings, hidden secrets and their exposure, social problems, e.g. illegitimacy, abortion; sometimes work problems, e.g. redundancy.

These are the conventions which define soap opera as a genre. They are shared by the makers and audiences of a genre product and *to a degree* have to be followed if we are to recognize to which genre a particular film or television programme belongs. The fact that you are probably familiar with the conventions I have listed for soap opera even though you may not watch them, indicates the way popular genres circulate as part of widespread public cultural knowledge.

ACTIVITY 4

As a further test of the pervasiveness of genre knowledge, you could pay special attention to an evening's television advertisements or go through one or two weekend newspaper supplements to find how many references to popular genres you can pick up.

4.1.2 Genre and mass-produced fiction

One aspect of the genre product, then, is that it is recognizable by its *similarity* to other products of its kind. It is this that leads to the frequent complaint of predictability. Given an initial clue, we can fill in the rest. Within the ideology of mass culture this use of 'convention' is often associated with industrial mass production as a source of plot formulae, stereotypes and cliches. In this respect, *convention* takes on an inherently conservative connotation, its main function being to reinforce normative meanings and values. Genre theory was developed as a means of countering this deterministic conception by seeking to understand the productive work of convention in the context of three interconnected but distinct 'moments' or 'stages' in the cultural work of the media industries:

1　**Production and distribution:** financiers, studios, TV companies, producers and controllers, censors, script-writers, directors, stars, festivals and awards, advertising and publicity, trade press, etc.

2　**The product or text:** genres and programme formats, conventions, narrative structures, styles, iconography, performances, stars, etc.

3　**Reception:** going to the cinema, the TV schedule, 'girls' night out', the family audience, the kitchen TV, the gaze at the cinema screen, the glance at the TV screen, pin-ups, reviews and reviewers, etc.

The approach from the perspective of 'media domination' argues that it is the iron control of stage 1 – production – over the processes going on in stages 2 and 3 which produces formulaic conventions and stereotypes as part of a cultural assembly line and as a means of maintaining dominant ideologies. However, the variety of procedures and practices involved in the production and consumption of genre fiction undertaken at each stage suggests the complexity of the relations between production, product and reception or 'consumption' and thus the difficulty of imposing economic, ideological and cultural control, even at the level of production.

The alternative approach, developed by genre theory, is useful because it enables us to define the relationship between these three stages, not as the imposition of 'media domination' but rather as a struggle over which meanings, which definitions of reality, will win the consent of the audience and thus establish themselves as the privileged reading of an episode (hegemony). Hegemony is established *and* contested in the interaction and negotiation between: (1) industrial production, (2) the semiotic work of the text, and (3) audience reception. Moreover, each stage contains within itself potential tensions and contradictions between the different economic, professional, aesthetic and personal practices and cultural traditions involved.

4.2 Genre as standardization and differentiation

First, let us examine the genre system at the level of production, focusing on the *repeatability* of genre conventions as a key to the *mass production* of fictions. The economic rationale for genre production is, perhaps, most vividly illustrated by the Hollywood studio system. As is frequently asserted, filmmaking is a hugely costly affair requiring capital investment both in plant – studio buildings, technological hardware, laboratories, cinemas – and in individual productions. Economies of scale require **standardization of production** and the emergence of popular genres – which began with the growth of nineteenth-century mass fiction and syndicated theatrical entertainments – served this need. The elaborate sets, costume designs, and props of one genre film can be re-utilized with a modicum of alteration in the next production; writers familiar with the conventions of plotting and dialogue appropriate to a particular genre can move from script to script in assembly-line fashion; bit-part actors and stars can be groomed to produce the gestural mannerisms, style of delivery and overall 'image' appropriate to the protagonists of a particular genre; studio technicians, cameramen (rarely women), editors and directors become increasingly efficient in the design, lighting and cinematography required to produce the particular visual world and mode of narration of the given genre. *Genre becomes a means of standardizing production.*

ACTIVITY 5

Stop at this point and note down:

1 how investment in a soap opera might contribute to economies of scale, standardization and efficiency, and
2 what special problems the soap opera format might present for this need for standardization.

In looking at soap opera from this perspective you may have noted that the form offers production companies the advantage of extended use of sets and properties over time. This made it economically worthwhile, for example, for Granada to build a permanent set for *Coronation Street*, and *EastEnders* to be granted a permanent back-lot by the BBC as well as a dedicated studio for interior shots. The longevity of soap opera, however, plays havoc with continuity of personnel and story-line. For example, changes of writers can produce terrible mistakes out of ignorance of past relationships or events, to the point that *Coronation Street* employs a serial historian in order to avoid embarrassing slips! This demonstrates an important tension between the pressures for economy at the production stage through standardization and the 'rules' which govern a fictional world, which once brought into being, take on a certain life of their own, not least in the memories of listeners and viewers who ring studios to tell producers when they get things wrong.

This example also shows that genre not only standardizes the production process, it serves *to stabilize an audience*. What we buy with our cinema ticket, television licence or cable subscription is the promise of a certain type of experience – entry to a fictional world as a means of being entertained. This, however, is a state of being, the conditions for which are notoriously difficult to predict or control! By offering familiar tried-and-tested worlds with familiar appeals and pleasures, genres serve not only to standardize production but to predict markets and stabilize audiences. For the film studio or television company, genres become a means of reaching an audience and hopefully of developing a bond with that audience – inducing a kind of 'brand loyalty'.

ACTIVITY 6

Pause for a moment and note down what aspects of soap opera might contribute to 'brand loyalty'.

Genre production, however, is not just about standardization – about fixing conventions and audiences. If all soap operas were exactly like one another, they would soon lose their audiences because they would become too predictable and repetitive. So genre production is equally about **differentiation** – managing product differentiation to maximize, and appeal to, different audiences and to keep tabs on changing audiences. This manifests itself in two ways: the production of a *variety of genres* for different audiences, and *variation within genres* between one example and the next. Thus, for example, one western will in some respects be much like another, but it will differ in well-known ways from a gangster film or a family melodrama. Similarly, the soap opera is defined partly in its difference from the police series, for example. Equally, a new western will differ from past westerns, and a new soap opera will try to open up different territory from its rivals – for instance, several British soap operas have attempted to vary their mode of address in an attempt to appeal to youth markets. Channel 4's teen soap opera *Hollyoaks*, about a group of students in Chester, has been successfully running since 1995 and, more recently, the BBC have launched their own youth-oriented soap opera, *The Cut*, as well as the teenage spin-off from *EastEnders*, *E20*. However, it is not only at the level of representation via the inclusion of a large cast of younger characters that these texts differentiate themselves from 'older' soaps; but through broadcasting on the internet, which is an important factor when addressing a younger generation of viewers in the twenty-first-century digital age.

Such differentiation is vital, ensuring both the pleasure of recognition, along with the frisson of the new. For while we may stick to our favourite brands of soap or washing powder, we do not, on the whole, want to see the same film or television programme over and over again. On the other hand, we may have a particular liking for some genres over others and experience pleasure in revisiting that 'world' again and again. Thus the genre system offers the possibility of variety, enabling film studios and TV companies to offer choice and acknowledge differences among audiences, while retaining the advantage of standardized production procedures with its attendant rewards. For audiences, then, the question that brings us back to our favourite genre is less *what* is going to happen, which as detractors point out we can probably predict, but *how*. The popular audience, far from being the *passive consumers* constructed within the ideology of mass culture, are required to be *expert readers* in order to appreciate the twists and innovations within the familiar which are the pleasures of the genre system.

4.3 The genre product as text

I want now to consider more precisely the work of the genre text as a semiotic site for the production and negotiation of representations, meanings and identities.

What does it mean to define a popular genre as a 'signifying practice'? In Chapter 1 of this book (p. 22), Stuart Hall introduced the work of Claude Lévi-Strauss, the French anthropologist, who:

> studied the customs, rituals, totemic objects, designs, myths and folk-tales of so-called 'primitive' peoples ..., not by analysing how these things were produced and used ..., but in terms of what they were trying to 'say', what messages about the culture they communicated. He analysed their meaning, not by interpreting their content, but by looking at the underlying rules and codes through which such objects or practices produced meaning ...

I have suggested that any given genre provides just such a system of underlying rules and codes by which films or TV programmes are produced and understood. At its most basic level, the genre system orchestrates signifiers which determine the attributes of different fictional worlds: for example, *settings* (e.g. the American West, an East End community); *locations* (e.g. a saloon bar, a launderette); *character types* (e.g. the outlaw, the landlady of a pub); *iconography* (e.g. a smoking Winchester 73, a row of terraced rooftops), *plots* (e.g. a new sheriff arrives to establish law and order by driving out corrupt business interests, a young woman finds out that her sister is her mother). At first sight, generic codes consist of rules of inclusion and exclusion governing what can and cannot appear or happen within particular generic worlds. We would, for instance, be startled, if not downright confused, to see the three flying ducks, which are perfectly acceptable on the Ogdens' living-room wall in *Coronation Street*, adorning the Deadwood saloon; or, conversely, a Winchester 73 hung over the washing machines in the *EastEnders*' launderette! These settings, character types and images become *signs* for a particular kind of fictional world.

However, it is unwise to assert too confidently that particular attributes *cannot* appear or happen in a particular genre, because sooner or later you will be proved wrong. The rules or codes establish limits but they are not eternally fixed. In the early days of analysis of soap opera, it was said, first, that you would never see inside a factory in a soap opera and, later, when Mike Baldwin opened up his clothing factory in *Coronation Street*, that you'd never have a strike in a soap opera. Within a year the Baldwin factory was closed down while the female workforce came out on strike. This is because the semiotic principles of signification determine that generic signs produce meanings through relationships of similarity and *difference*. Of course, repetition and similarity are necessary to establish familiarity with the codes which bind signifier to signified, but meaning is produced only in the difference between signs. For example, the code that matches the iconography of a white hat and horse/black hat and horse with the upright westerner and the outlaw plays on a binary colour coding to mark the difference, and it is that which produces the meaning of the character types. But there are several different combinations that can be made with even these few elements. Switch hats and character types and the new combination produces new meanings through the difference – about, for instance, the 'moral complex' of the law, or the ambivalent position of the outsider. In other words, rather than inert counters with already assigned, fixed and predictable meanings – white hat and horse means upright westerner, black hat and horse means outlaw – generic conventions *produce* meanings through a process of constantly shifting combination and differentiation.

4.3.1 Genres and binary differences

This has led some critics to analyse genres in terms of a shifting series of binary differences or oppositions. For example, Jim Kitzes (1969) explores the western in terms of a series of structuring differences or 'antimonies' which he traces back to the core opposition: wilderness versus civilization. Together, these represent a 'philosophical dialectic, an ambiguous cluster of meanings and attitudes that provide the traditional/thematic structure of the genre'. Within this flexible set of shifting antinomies the opposition masculinity/femininity constitutes one of the ideological tensions played out. Typically, in the western, masculinity is identified with the wilderness/ the individual/freedom and femininity with civilization/community/restriction, but this poses the problem of how to include the gunslinging westerner in the genre's representation of social order which concludes the film. The main point I want to make here, however, is that any given genre film produces its meanings from a shifting pattern of visual, thematic and ideological differences and that gender is a key signifying difference in this orchestration.

ACTIVITY 7

Stop now to consider what you have so far noted as the conventions of soap opera. How far can these be grouped in a series of oppositions or binary differences?

Christine Geraghty (1991) suggests that the opposition 'men/women' is a core organizing difference. How far can you group the differences you have so far noted around this opposition?

Drawing up such lists of oppositions can illuminate what is at stake in the conflicts orchestrated by a particular genre. However, the point of the exercise is not to fix signifiers in permanent opposition, but to uncover a pattern, the terms of which can be shifted to produce a different meaning. It is the shifting of ideological and cultural values across the terms of the oppositions that enables us to pursue the processes of and struggles over meaning.

4.3.2 Genre boundaries

So far I have argued that it is not possible to fix the meaning of particular generic signifiers. Neither is it possible to define genres through a fixed set of attributes unique to themselves. So, for example, guns are key to both the western and the gangster film, and weddings are important to both romantic comedies and soap operas. What defines the genre is not the specific convention itself but its placing in a particular relationship with other elements – a relationship which generates different meanings and narrative possibilities according to the genre: for example, the gun wielded against the wilderness in the western, or against society in the gangster film; the wedding as a concluding integration of warring parties in the romantic comedy or the wedding as the start of marriage problems in soap opera.

Given such overlaps, the boundaries between genres are not fixed either: rather, we find a sliding of conventions from one genre to another according to changes in production and audiences.

This sliding of conventions is a prime source of generic evolution. So, for example, when soap opera left the daytime women's television audience for primetime, with the appearance of *Dallas*, echoes of the western evoked by the Southfork ranch, its landscape and its menfolk extended soap opera's domestic terrain as part of an attempt to produce a more inclusive gendered address for the evening audience. This has led to arguments as to whether, given these western elements, strong male roles, and business intrigues, it is correct to identify *Dallas* as a soap opera. But this effort to fix genre boundaries ignores the dynamic and interdependent processes of signification and media production, where new meanings and generic innovation are produced by breaking rules, pushing at boundaries and redefining difference. The point is less whether *Dallas* is a soap opera or not, but rather what meanings are produced when signifiers from different genres intersect, and in this case when differently gendered genres are involved. As we shall see in section 6, the sliding of meaning, as signifiers shift across the boundaries that demarcate one genre from another, produces negotiations around gender difference which are highly significant for our study of the media and representation.

ACTIVITY 8

Pause here and consider examples of recent popular fictional series on television (like *The Sopranos*, *Doctor Who* and *Supernatural*) which are not classified as soap opera.

1 To which genre would you say these belong?
2 Have they shifted in any significant way from the genre to which they belong?
3 Why might we want either to distinguish them from or relate them to soap operas?
4 What does thinking of these series as soap opera bring to light about the way they work?

The problems that you may have encountered in identifying the genres to which these programmes belong suggests that the definition of genre as a system of inclusion and exclusion with which I started has to be modified.

To sum up so far: despite a grounding in repetition and similarity, difference is key to the work of genre. Our knowledge of any generic system can only be provisional. Genre is a system or framework of conventions, expectations and possibilities, or, to put it in the semiotic terms introduced in Chapter 1, the *genre* conventions function as the deep-structure or *langue*, while individual programmes, which realize these underlying rules, function as *paroles*. Moreover, as the French literary structuralist Tzvetan Todorov argues (1976), each new manifestation of a genre work changes the possibilities of future works, extending the genre's horizon of expectations and changing what can and cannot be said within the framework of a particular generic world. Steve Neale (1981) insists that generic production, like any system for producing meaning, must be considered not as a fixed and static body of conventions but as a *process*.

FIGURE 6.2   Doctor Who: male action series or soap opera?

4.4 Signification and reference

To this point we have considered the work of genre convention as internal to the genre system. Now I want to turn to the question of the relation between the production of genre fictions and social reference, which is central to our consideration of genre's work of cultural negotiation. In Chapter 1, Stuart Hall, describing the three basic elements in the production of meaning – signifier, signified (a mental concept) and the referent – stressed the arbitrary relation between signifier and signified, which produces a sign that refers to, represents, but does not reflect the real world. However, the signs and signifiers of the genre code take signs from our social and cultural world not simply to represent that world but to produce another, fictional, one. In this case we are considering highly specialized signs, produced within and for the genre system. But what exactly is the relation between the signifiers of the generic world and the social? How does genre production engage in reference to the social world while in the process of constructing a fictional one?

4.4.1 Cultural verisimilitude, generic verisimilitude and realism

Steve Neale, in his article on genre (1981), makes two useful distinctions which are helpful in understanding the work of the referent in genre films. First, he distinguishes between *verisimilitude* and *realism*. These terms refer in significantly different ways to the work of the referent. *Realism* is today the more familiar term through which we judge whether a fiction constructs a world we recognize as like our own; but, as we have seen, realism is a highly problematic category. Steve Neale, therefore, revives a concept from literary history, to underline the fact that, in fiction, 'reality' is always constructed. *Verisimilitude*, he argues, refers not to what may or may not *actually be* the case, but rather to what the dominant culture *believes* to be the case, to what is generally accepted as credible, suitable, proper. Neale then distinguishes between **cultural verisimilitude** and **generic verisimilitude**. In order to be recognized as a film belonging to a particular genre – a western, a musical, a horror film – it must comply with the rules of that genre: in other words, genre conventions produce a second-order verisimilitude – what ought to happen in a western or soap opera – by which the credibility or truth of the fictional world we associate with a particular genre is guaranteed. Whereas generic verisimilitude allows for considerable play with fantasy *inside* the bounds of generic credibility (e.g. singing about your problems in the musical; the power of garlic in gothic horror movies), cultural verisimilitude refers us to the norms, mores and common sense of the social world *outside* the fiction.

Different genres produce different relationships between generic and cultural verisimilitude. For example, the generic verisimilitude of the gangster film in the 1930s drew heavily on cultural verisimilitude – what audiences then knew about actual bootlegging and gang warfare in the streets, if not from firsthand experience, then from other cultural sources such as the press – whereas the horror film has greater licence to transgress cultural verisimilitude in the construction of a generic world full of supernatural or impossible beings and events.

ACTIVITY 9

Think about recent episodes of a soap opera you have seen and note the way the form establishes its generic verisimilitude – the norms and common sense of its fictional reality. Then consider how soap opera relates to cultural verisimilitude.

We can now return to the distinction between *verisimilitude* and *realism*. Although these two concepts cannot, in practice, be cleanly separated, the distinction is useful because it suggests how and why *realism* is always a matter of contest. For the demand for realism won't go away, however problematic the notion. And while the concept of verisimilitude refers to normative perceptions of reality – what is generally accepted to be so – the demand for a 'new' realism from oppositional or emerging groups opens up the contest over the definition of the real and forces changes in the codes of verisimilitude. For conventions of cultural verisimilitude get in the way of pressures for social change – newly emerging social groups or practices demand changes in the conventions of representation. Thus *realism* becomes a polemic in an assault on *cultural verisimilitude*: it demands representation of what has not been seen before, what has been unthinkable because unrepresentable. But the new signifiers of the real in their turn solidify into the established codes of cultural verisimilitude and become open to further challenge. The Women's Movement saw this happen in the 1970s, when the dress codes and body language which signified 'women's liberation' circulated into the pages of fashion magazines and advertising – for example, the frequently attacked Virginia Slims adverts which tried to identify liberation with smoking. However, what this demonstrates is that 'cultural verisimilitude' is not monolithic, but fractured by the different signifying practices and discourses through which different social groups stake out their identities and claims on the real.

ACTIVITY 10

Turn back to your notes on the generic and cultural verisimilitude of soap opera and consider whether and how it has been pressured to engage with social change, either by taking on board new kinds of social issues or incorporating characters from previously marginalized groups. Can you identify specifically gendered narrative, thematic or ideological tensions at work in this process?

4.5 Media production and struggles for hegemony

The tension between *realism* and *cultural* and *generic verisimilitude* enables us to link the industrial production of genre fiction to the conceptions of hegemony and cultural struggle introduced in section 3, suggesting how and why the media industries participate in contests over the construction of the real.

We have seen that both the competition for markets and the semiotic conditions of genre production entail a search for difference, for innovation. A genre such as soap opera – a daily 'story of everyday life', itself incorporated into the daily routines of listeners and viewers – is heavily invested in *cultural verisimilitude*. Since, as I have argued, the conventions of cultural verisimilitude are constantly mutating under pressure from shifting cultural discourses and newly emerging social groups, soap operas are driven to engage in some way with social change, if they are not to fall by the wayside as 'old fashioned'. The need to maintain the recognition of existing audiences and attract newly emerging ones, together with the constant need for new story material and the need for an edge over competitors, makes topicality, being up-to-date and controversy all vital factors in the form's continuance. Christine Geraghty comments on the changing British soap opera scene in the 1980s:

A number of factors ... in the early 1980s provided the impetus for change. The launching of a new national channel on British television, Channel 4, gave an opportunity to Phil Redmond who had been experimenting with a different audience for soaps, particularly in the successful school serial, *Grange Hill*. Redmond had a track record of using social issues to generate a greater sense of realism and such an approach tied in with the new channel's overt commitment to appeal to groups not represented on the other three channels. Channel 4 made a long-term commitment to *Brookside*, which enabled it to survive a rocky start and set up a challenge to its staider rivals. At the other end of the spectrum, the US primetime soaps were demonstrating that it was possible to get away with a greater degree of explicitness on sexual issues and a speedier and more dramatic approach to plotting. *EastEnders* took on the *Brookside* commitment to realism through the dramatization of social issues and combined it with US-style paciness. In their various ways, the new serials were thus looking to be marked as different from existing soaps and issues around sexuality, race and class gave them material which would both stand out as different but could be dealt with through the narrative and aesthetic experience already established by soaps. If there were groups in society who were not represented in soaps in the late 1970s, it is also true that soaps with their rapid consumption of material and their continual demand for storylines were particularly receptive to new material.

(Geraghty, 1991, p. 134)

These multiple pressures towards innovation and renewal mean that popular genres not only engage with social change but become key sites for the emerging articulation of and contest over change. So the discourses and imagery of new social movements – for example, the women's, gay, or black liberation movements – which circulate into public consciousness through campaign groups, parliamentary and social policy debates, new and popular journalism, and other media representations, provide popular genres with material for new storylines and the pleasures of dramatic enactment. It is important, though, not to let this suggest a linear model of representation – social change followed by its representation in the media. Rather, what we seek to locate is the circulation of images, representations, and discourses from one area of social practice to another.

How, exactly, does this process take place within the production process? Christine Geraghty's reference to Phil Redmond's role in the development of *Grange Hill* and *Brookside* reminds us of the variety of vested and conflicting interests caught up in the process of media production. Company executives, advertisers, producers, writers, directors and actors, also have different professional and personal stakes in the process of generic innovation and social change.

While such struggles can be viewed on the ground as conflicts between business executives and creative personnel, or between men and women, the acts and decisions of these 'agents' of conflict take place within the movement of cultural discourses discussed by Stuart Hall in Chapter 1 of this book. Feminist academics writing about the hugely popular *Sex and the City* (HBO, 1998–2004) suggest that the series needs to be understood and informed by discourses of post-feminism circulating in culture during this period. *Sex and the City*, similarly to other post-feminist texts, such as *The L Word* and *Desperate Housewives*, is ambivalent in the way it 'works over the terrain of gender in ways which both assume and ignore feminist ideas' (Brunsdon and Spigel, 2009, p. 1).

So, on the one hand, *Sex and the City*'s finale saw each of the four single women conform to the normative path of feminine destiny: by becoming married (in the instance of Carrie, Miranda and Charlotte) or positioned within a loving heterosexual relationship (in the instance of Samantha). On the other hand, the text has been celebrated for its fresh and explicit representations of women's sexuality in television drama (Arthurs, 2003). The text's representation of the dating and sex lives of single women in a post-feminist culture was inspired by Candace Bushnell's *New York Observer* column and book – also titled *Sex and the City* – which, in turn, influenced the show's creator Darren Star to create a comedy about sex from a female perspective that had previously been uncharted territory for television (Sohn, 2002, p. 14). Dissatisfied with the way networks tended to handle adult sexuality – in a wink-wink, nudge-nudge style, euphemistic and adolescent – Star wanted to create an adult comedy that could handle mature female sexuality in a direct and honest way (Sohn, 2002, p. 14).

Given HBO's reputation as the purveyor of quality and sophisticated television drama, the search for new and contemporary ideas meant that the innovation of comedy programming focusing on issues of female sexuality seemed like an attractive idea. However, a consideration of the production context of *Sex and the City* provides a case in point to explore some of the negotiations that took place in bringing representations of female sexuality in this post-feminist and ostensibly liberated context of the late 1990s and 2000s to the television screen.

For instance, the themes and concerns of the text were not only seen as being too risqué for network television (ABC, for example, was reported as being unsure if it could even call the text 'Sex and the City'), but the opportunity to represent the harsh realities of the dating scene that Bushnell's publications aptly captured had to be negotiated in a bid to safeguard the financial interests of the subscription channel, HBO. The executive producer of *Sex and the City*, Michael Patrick King, states, for instance:

> [Candace's] book was brilliant. And very, very sharp like broken glass, laser smart, about who those kind of tragic women were in that time. In order to be in your living room every week, and with this cast, we saw that 'it has to be softer. And emotional. And "real-er". And they have to be clowns."'

(King, as reported in Jermyn, 2009, p. 17)

The generic blending of comedy and drama proved to be a winning formula that addressed sexual taboos such as female masturbation, lesbianism and female sexual satisfaction. However, as Jane Arthurs points out, the extent to which *Sex and the City* transgresses codes of respectability that have historically governed notions of female identity within patriarchal culture are recuperated by the text, given the protagonists' middle-class status and 'bourgeois bohemian lifestyles' and, indeed, their address to a similar demographic of pay-per-view cable television (Arthurs, 2003, p. 92). It would be interesting, for instance, to see if the same level of indecorum and sexual unruliness could be granted to a group of working-class female characters; those most policed in terms of their unruly behaviour (Skeggs, 1997). As it is, the middle-class foursome's transgression of bourgeois codes of sexual decorum and thus their challenge to patriarchal structures are recuperated via their sleek control of the commodified body that makes the text's ideological positioning compatible with capitalism (Skeggs, 1997).

If, for the executives at HBO, the migration of a women-centred and explicit sexual discourse into television drama seemed like a commercially good prospect, for the writers it was an assault on the cultural verisimilitude of television drama in the name of the reality of changing gender roles in society. But the attempt to adapt to changing codes of recognition (women are, in fact, entitled to fulfilling sexual lives outside marriage and long-term relationships; they do try to juggle the demands of paid work and personal relationships) had an inevitable impact on the codes of generic recognition, on what until then had been the norm for television drama. The production of a drama about women's sexual lives and friendships had to draw on a different set of generic codes, aesthetic modes

FIGURE 6.3 Female friendship: trading tales and experiences in *Sex and the City* © Home Box Office, Inc.

and archetypes – for example, the woman's film, soap opera, the sitcom, the independent or liberated woman – through which to express its different themes and issues. It is this hybrid identity of *Sex and the City*, similarly to other post-feminist texts, such as *Ally McBeal* and *Nurse Jackie*, wherein different aesthetic codes are drawn on to express the contradictory emotions the characters are feeling at different points in the narrative which are able to better respond to and reveal the complexity and contradictions in female experience and subjectivity within the contemporary period (Arthurs, 2003, pp. 130–1).

Moreover, female friendship could be convincingly constructed only by drawing on the subcultural codes of women's social discourse and culture. Within a soap opera, these codes are taken for granted as part of its cultural as well as generic verisimilitude. Within other forms of drama and media texts, however, they have a range of consequences for both genre and ideology. Historically, for instance, representations of women in both film and television have primarily been characterized as rivals for male attention rather than as friends and allies (Hollinger, 2002). In the search for credibility with the American female, middle-class, professional audiences which *Sex and the City* sought, this meant drawing on discourses about the importance of women's talk, consciousness-raising, support and 'sisterhood' put into public circulation by the Women's Movement. Yet discourses associated with the women's movement are integrated with aspects of the more traditionally feminine in Sex and the City. This is signified in Figure 6.3 by the way in which the women's talk about sexual taboos and female experience is framed by the pink and girly hues of the mise en scene; the composition of the group shot that suggests caring and sharing female subjectivities and the reinforcement of the feminine in relation to consumerism, exemplified in the image by each character's penchant for couture, cocktails, glamour and luxury. The plotting of *Sex and the City*, then, is made out of a series of negotiations around definitions of gender roles and sexuality, heterosexual relations and female friendships, as well as postfeminism.

4.6 Summary

To sum up so far: popular genres represent patterns of repetition and difference, in which difference is crucial to the continuing industrial and semiotic existence of the genre. Far from endless mechanical repetition, the media industries are constantly on the look-out for a new angle, making genre categories remarkably flexible. Genres produce fictional worlds which function according to a structuring set of rules or conventions, thereby ensuring recognition through their conformity to generic verisimilitude. However, they also draw on events and discourses in the social world both as a source of topical story material and as a means of commanding the recognition of audiences through conformity to cultural verisimilitude. The conventions of cultural verisimilitude are under constant pressure for change as social practices and mores change and newly emerging social groups (and potential audiences) put pressure on representation. This highlights the need to consider the changing historical circumstances of fictional production and consumption. These changing circumstances determine that genres cannot exist by mere repetition and recycling past models, but have to engage with difference and change, in a process of negotiation and contest over representation, meaning and pleasure.

In the next section we will shift from the broad question of how the internal signifying processes of popular genres intersect with social discourses circulating outside the text in order to focus on the intersection of a particular genre – soap opera – with discourses of gender.

5 GENRES FOR WOMEN: THE CASE OF SOAP OPERA

5.1 Genre, soap opera and gender

In what sense can soap opera be said to be a feminine form? It is, after all – feminists argue – produced within male-dominated, multinational media conglomerates and within discursive practices which construct the masculine as the norm. This provokes questions such as:

- What are the generic conventions which contribute to creating soap opera as a world gendered as feminine?
- How do soap operas attempt to construct a gendered cultural verisimilitude?
- How far and in what ways do these conventions construct feminine subject-positions?
- How do soap operas address their increasingly cross-gendered audiences?

First, I want to examine certain of soap opera's conventions for their impact on the representation of gender. Secondly, I will introduce some key concepts used by feminists to analyse how soap opera addresses the female audience or constructs positions of viewing which imply a female (or feminized) spectator.

5.1.1 The invention of soap opera

I will begin by considering the origins of soap opera as an example of how two mass media – American commercial radio and advertising industries – combined in the 1930s to produce a form aimed as a fictionalized product pitch to the daytime female audience of homebound housewives. According to Robert Allen, soap opera was devised as a more effective alternative to the radio magazine/advice column format because of the greater power of serial fiction to capture audiences for the advertising message – which might be given direct from sponsor to audience as part of the credits or embedded in the fiction.

If the motive for the production of mass media forms aimed at a female market lay in the need of advertisers to attract women as consumers, the problem remained how to reach this audience. In the 1930s, the radio and advertising industries turned to previous formats through which women's cultural concerns have circulated – material often produced by women or out of traditions associated with female writing. For example, the idea of using the serial format came from women's magazines, according to Frank Hummert, who, with his wife, Anne, was a major pioneer of soap opera on American radio (Buckman, 1984).

5.1.2 Women's culture

In what sense, then, can these forms be thought to belong to women's culture? First, the term *women's culture* requires some caution. This book has insisted that the language of culture is not neutral but carries social values. If the 'masculine' functions as a cultural norm, mainstream media will privilege a masculinist perspective which must impact on those forms developed for the female market: the woman's page, the woman's film, soap opera. The notion of 'women's culture', then, is not intended to suggest some pure feminine space where women speak freely to each other outside social constraint. Nor, as I have already suggested, can the category 'women' be taken unproblematically, since, as this book contends, gendered and sexual identities are social constructs to which representation contributes. 'Women's culture', then, refers to those spaces on the margins of the dominant culture where women's different positioning in society is acknowledged and allowed a degree of expression. This space may narrow or broaden at different points in history, but here I am using 'culture' in its widest sense to refer to how women live their daily lives in the home and in the workplace – either in women's jobs or in competition with men; to the social forms and discourses through which women interact with each other – mother and toddler groups, townswomen's guilds, women's campaign groups, health groups, and so on; as well as to the women-addressed forms of cultural expression which women use among others – the domestic novel, novelettes, magazine serials, romances, diaries, confessions, letter pages, advice columns, fashion pages, and so on.

In turning to women's cultural forms, then, programme makers sought to attract women to soap opera listening as a prelude to product purchase by constructing a fictional world which they (1) would recognize as relating to them, (2) would find pleasurable, and (3) could access while doing housework or caring for children.

ACTIVITY 11

To begin with, take a few moments to note down your thoughts about:

1　how soap opera differs from other genres,

2　how it might be thought to appeal especially to women, and

3　any problems you perceive with this idea.

5.1.3 Soap opera as women's genre

Probably the feature of soap opera that most strongly suggested a women's cultural form is its *subject matter*: family and community, relationships and personal life – all social arenas in which women exercise a socially mandated expertise and special concern. But we can say little about the meanings produced by this subject matter without considering the impact on it of the textual conventions and discursive strategies of soap opera as a generic form. To what extent do such conventions and discursive strategies have implications for gender representation? As an immediate consequence of soap opera's domestic and community subject matter, for example, we find a greater number of female protagonists than is usual in other types of TV fiction. The construction of soap opera's fictional world out of the extended family, as in older soap operas such as *Dallas and Dynasty*, or a neighbourhood community, as in *Coronation Street*, *Neighbours*, *EastEnders* and *Emmerdale*, entails a variety of female figures representing a cross-section of social or family types. This is reinforced by soap opera's serial format, which needs a multiplicity of characters to fuel the continuous generation of storylines, providing many and diverse entry points for identification and recognition – or, importantly as we shall see below, rejection.

ACTIVITY 12

What is the impact of a greater number of female characters on the kind of fictional world produced by soap opera and on the kinds of narrative action and outcome that can take place in it?

5.1.4 Soap opera's binary oppositions

As we have seen (section 4.3.1), one way of approaching such questions is to explore the structure of *oppositions* and *differences* which characterize soap opera's fictional world. In the course of her analysis of the representation of women in soap opera, for example, Christine Geraghty suggests a series of oppositions that produce a world constructed between the poles of gendered difference:

women   men
personal   public
home   work
talk   action
community   individualism

(Geraghty, 1991)

As soap opera's wide range of female figures work out their life patterns in this world, this structure of oppositions provides considerable scope both for narrative complications and for shifting negotiations and struggles around gender. However, in tracing the shifting play of such oppositions within the world of soap opera, the impact of the peculiarities of its narrative format is crucial. Key here is its defining feature, *continuous serialization* – the source, in Robert Allen's words, of 'the longest story ever told'.

5.1.5 Serial form and gender representation

We can perceive more clearly how the continuous serial works if we compare it to the series and the serial. The *serial* refers to a fiction which is divided into a sequence of parts, so that a strong sense of linear progression is maintained across episodes as the plot unfolds from beginning, through a middle, to the end – for example, the thirteen-part drama serial *The Wire*, or the serialization of a classic novel. The *series* – for example, *Law and Order* or the BBC's recent *Sherlock Holmes* – bases its sense of continuity on the stability of its central characters, to whom different stories happen each week. In this respect, there is a strong sense of beginning, middle and end constructed within each episode. The *continuous serial*, on the other hand, promises a 'never-ending story'.

One of the many interesting features of this type of narrative is its running of several storylines simultaneously. This is not a matter of sub-plots as adjuncts to a central action, but the intertwining of different characters' lives. This clearly helps to keep the serial going, so that as one storyline runs out, another is coming to the boil. Secondly, the endlessness of soap opera contravenes the 'classic' structure of the majority of popular fictions based on the beginning/middle/end formula. The pleasure of such a structure is regularly described in terms of an abstract three-part movement: equilibrium, disruption, equilibrium restored.

Steve Neale (1990) has argued that different genres can be distinguished by the different ways they disrupt and restore equilibrium, and the different relationship they produce between initial and closing stable states. For example, western and gangster films work towards driving out a corrupt old order and establishing a new one, while romantic comedy aims to integrate disrupting elements into a reformed order, and family melodrama reinstates the old order after what

Neale terms 'an in-house rearrangement': despite the evident impossible contradictions and pain of family relations, a new family is established at the drama's end, though significantly often a non-biological family. These differences of narrative resolution produce not only formal or psychological pleasures, but also forms of ideological movement and negotiation in their different organizations of social order.

So what can we say about the impact of continuous serialization on soap opera's shifting structure of gendered oppositions and the negotiations around femininity and masculinity this entails?

ACTIVITY 13

Take a few minutes to consider:

1 the consequences for the narrative and ideological form of soap opera of never being able to end, and

2 what this might mean for the form's construction of its female characters' stories.

Since no end is in sight and we have probably long forgotten the beginning, soap opera has been called the narrative of the 'extended middle'. Christine Geraghty has argued that the form is 'based on the premise of continuous disruption' (1991, p. 15). Compared to the model of the self-contained narrative as a movement from equilibrium through disequilibrium to equilibrium restored, often signalled by a heterosexual kiss or the expulsion of a disruptive woman, 'the premise of continuous disruption' is ideologically significant, for any attempt to *conclude* a storyline must, sooner rather than later, shift into reverse gear. While death is a possibility in soap opera, it cannot be overused without bringing the fiction to an end! As for weddings, Terry Lovell comments:

Bill Podmore, the current producer of ... [*Coronation Street*] ... has remarked in connection with Rita's marriage to Len Fairclough, that marriage easily diminishes a character, and it was no surprise to find, eighteen short months later, that Len and Rita's marriage was under threat, and Rita had left home. However such a 'disturbance' will be resolved, whether by Rita (temporarily) returning to Len or, alternatively, to the marriage market for a lover or husband, the acknowledgement of the difficulty of maintaining the norms of romantic love and marriage still stands, and is reaffirmed again and again in the serial. In this particular case indeed it is difficult to know what constitutes order and what disturbance. In a sense, the conventions of the genre are such that the normal order of things in *Coronation Street* is precisely that of broken marriages, temporary liaisons, availability for 'lasting' romantic love which in fact never lasts. This order, the reverse of the patriarchal norm, is in a sense interrupted by the marriages and 'happy family' interludes, rather than vice versa. The breakdown of Rita and Len's marriage, if it occurs, will be a resolution of the problem which Podmore has created in marrying them in the first place.

(Lovell, 1981, p. 50)

FIGURE 6.4 *Coronation Street:* Len and Rita Fairclough's wedding (Peter Admson and Barbara Knox) – a utopian interlude in the *Street*'s norm of broken marriage

Thus the combination of subject matter, multiple storylines and never-resolving narrative impacts on the *type* of female protagonist who inhabits soap opera. Narrative disruption disposes of husbands and lovers and longevity of narrative leads to an unusual number of older, widowed, divorced and independent female figures. Such figures play an important role in the negotiations around gender that come increasingly to the centre of soap opera as it gives greater space to male characters, an issue to which we will return below.

5.2 Soap opera's address to the female audience

So far we have considered the impact of soap opera's generic conventions on its construction of gender representations which we might assume make it a pleasurable form for female viewers. I now want to turn to the way these conventions are deployed as a means of speaking to – addressing – the social audience of women listeners and viewers. The concept of **address** is important in considering how a genre might be said to be gendered. As the history of the invention of soap opera indicates, writers, programme makers and advertisers produce their products *for* someone. Who they imagine you are affects the way the product is constructed, the way it speaks to you, or solicits your attention – just as our sense of who the doctor, or boss, or naughty child is affects the way we speak to them. The way we address someone incorporates a position for that person within the construction of our statement or question (subject-position). For example, the familiar joke, 'Have you stopped beating your wife?', plays on the power of address to position the addressee – in this case as wife-beater. Cross-examination in the law courts develops this feature of language to a fine art. In the 1970s the feminist slogan, 'Who does this ad think you are?', pasted across street advertisements, sought to expose the hidden power of address to position women as subordinate.

In this respect, it is noteworthy that the serial fiction format was developed as a more effective way of 'hooking' women listeners and viewers than the advice programme.

ACTIVITY 14

Pause for a moment to consider why the continuous serial might prove more effective than a daily advice programme as a listening hook for female audiences.

The advice format, as with many advertisements, incorporates almost by definition, an address from a position of authority to one who is in some way lacking, in need of advice, information, exhortation. How is authority represented in western culture? Much advice to women is given by male experts. But even if proffered by women, advice-giving will generally be authorized by the voice, personage, dress, and language of white, middle-class officialdom. One of the advantages of audio-visual fiction for the advertiser is that the source and mode of address is indirect. It generally appears 'unauthored'. For example, soap operas are announced as if they are already in progress: 'now, over to *Coronation Street*, where ...'; they simply 'appear' on our screens, cued in by their signature tunes and opening credits which *invite us* into a fictional world materialized for us by maps, aerial shots, closer location shots, and perhaps close-ups of the chief players. So we need to consider the different positions constructed for an audience by the different forms of address – advice and invitation. Secondly, to invite women to become involved in a fictional world as women requires positions of identification within the fictional world attuned to a female perspective. One advantage of the serialization of everyday life within the domestic context over the advice format was that it appears to address women on a more equal footing. As we shall see, the degree to which this is simply a question of disguising the male source of address is a matter of debate among feminist analysts.

ACTIVITY 15

Before moving on, you might find it useful to watch ten minutes or so of a soap opera with the following questions in mind:

1 How is this fiction speaking to me?
2 Who does it assume I am?

(Continued)

(Continued)

3 What does it assume my interests are?

4 What does it assume about my interest in these characters?

5 Does my gender count in my responses to what I am watching?

6 Do I feel that I am being asked to take a 'male' or 'female' point of view on the events and characters?

7 Am I being involved in this fiction in a different way from watching, say, a crime or detective series, like *CSI* or *Dexter*?

5.2.1 Talk vs action

To begin answering such questions, a good place to start is with what perhaps is a defining feature of soap opera: its predilection for *talk*. This is not simply a matter of the dependency of radio on dialogue – for dialogue clearly can be used to signify action, as in radio thrillers or science fiction. Moreover, the shift to television has not detracted from this. Try fast-forwarding an episode of *EastEnders* and it becomes clear that its characteristic camera set-up is a 'close-up two shot', producing a drama of talking heads in intimate exchanges or altercation. However, while antipathetic to the criteria of plot development and narrative progression associated with high cultural aesthetics, talk offers a different mode of *social action*: conversation, gossip, dissection of personal and moral issues, and, at crisis points, rows. Talk, in these forms, however, is culturally defined as feminine, involving the exercise of skills and methods of understanding developed by women in the particular socio-historical circumstances in which they live. It is, therefore, a key to establishing *a feminine cultural verisimilitude*, as opposed to the investment of masculine-oriented genres in action. In this respect, soap opera's talk is a major factor in its negotiation of gender, a point that we will return to in concluding this section.

5.2.2 Soap opera's serial world

We started thinking about the way soap opera addresses its audience by considering what kind of viewer is presupposed by *continuous serialization*. What kind of invitation is made by the regular listening or viewing slot at particular times during the week or even on a daily basis? Clearly we are being invited to form a habit, often termed by hostile critics as an 'addiction' which is considered to work in the interests of advertisers, shareholders and dominant ideology. But the more interesting question is, exactly what is it we are addicted to? And what is the meaning of this habit to female audiences? Christine Geraghty has identified as a major effect of serialization its production of a sense of 'unchronicled growth' – the sense that while we are not watching or listening, the lives of the characters in the fictional world are continuing in parallel with ours. Combined with a focus on 'everyday, ordinary life', this sense of unchronicled growth enables the soap opera to function as a 'neighbouring' world – its characters exist, quite literally for the Australian soap of that name, as 'neighbours'.

Is there a gendered dimension in this address to us as a neighbour, soliciting our interest and concern for the daily goings-on in the street, the close, the neighbourhood, the community? Traditionally – if less so in a period of high unemployment – it is women who have formed and held together neighbourhood and community networks of social intercourse: in the shops and supermarkets, play groups and nurseries, launderettes, health clinics and schools. Moreover, the housewife has depended on the neighbourhood for social contact outside the home. The female soap opera viewer, then, is invited to become involved in another community, a fictional one indeed, but one which parallels her own with characters who share many recognizable problems and dilemmas: who, moreover, experience the same passage of time as the listener or viewer, who age with her, go through many of the same 'stages' and crises of life, experience a similar pattern of achievements, frustrations, reversals and disappointments.

Lastly, serialization addresses in a more literal sense the material conditions under which women in the domestic context can listen or view television. Regularity enables the episodes to be built into a domestic routine, often with a considerable degree of planning and timetabling. Fragmentation of the multiple narratives that intertwine to create the soap opera world accommodate the fragmented, semi-distracted state in which many women combine media listening or viewing with other domestic tasks. Continuousness, overlap of segments within and between episodes, and repeated recounting of events between different characters, all help to combat the fragmented viewing situation and the missed episode. It is possible to drop in and out of the soap opera world without losing the narrative thread.

5.3 Textual address and the construction of subjects

I hope by now to have established some of the ways in which soap opera can be said to speak to female audiences by incorporating in its method of storytelling some of the forms usually associated with women's culture. But what does this say about the **subject-position** which soap opera constructs for its viewer? What of the potential power relations implied in the operation of address and the evident inequality between producers and receivers of mass media entertainments? What happens to the audience once they accept the invitation to enter soap opera's serial world? Does soap opera's female address simply reposition its audience in subordination or can we argue that for women to be offered a female position at all in popular fiction is potentially empowering?

I want now to introduce three different ways in which feminist analysts have conceived the text–audience relations of soap opera, which ask in particular how soap opera's conventions of narration and address construct a female subject-position and with what ideological effects.

5.3.1 The ideal spectator

The first approach I want to look at is offered by Tania Modleski, author of an influential analysis of American soap opera, 'The search for tomorrow in today's soap operas' (1982). Her starting point is an argument developed within film theory which concerns the structure of looking in the cinema which has already been touched on in Chapter 5 by Sean Nixon. Because classic Hollywood narrative offers so central a place in its narrative for the glamourized image of woman as object of the male hero's search or investigation, his reward or his downfall, feminist film theorists have argued that the organization of camera and narrative in mainstream cinema is predicated on a masculine spectator. Laura Mulvey (1989 [1975]), quoted by Sean Nixon in Chapter 5, analysed the cinematic spectacle in terms of a relay of looks *at* the woman – the spectator looks with the camera which looks at the hero who looks at the woman – and, drawing on psychoanalytic theory, argues that the narrative and visual form of Hollywood films has been developed according to the Oedipal fantasies and anxieties of the male unconscious. The gaze in the cinema, Mulvey and others have argued, is constructed as a masculinized gaze; in other words, the subject-position offered by cinema's mode of address is masculine. To gaze at, and take pleasure in, the female image is to occupy a male position, one that is set up for us not only in the visual control the male hero has in the organization of the image, which leaves him free to move in and out of frame while the female is frequently trapped at its centre, but also in the narrative agency given to the hero, who drives the plot, makes things happen, and generally gains control of the woman. This argument has had an enormous impact on thinking about the relation between fictional production, gender, and sexual identity.

- What, then, does the argument mean for the female cinema audience?
- What does it mean for those filmic genres (e.g. the woman's film, romantic comedy) that attempt to address that audience directly?
- Can this theory of the masculinized gaze be transferred to television?

Such questions focus attention on a potential disjuncture between patriarchal text and female audience and a crucial distinction between the **ideal spectator** or *subject-position created by the text*, which can be found through textual analysis, and the **social audience** at a given point in time. It is important to note that in this debate the 'spectator in the text', the spectator for whom the text is made, which the text needs in order for its constructed meanings and pleasures to be fully realized, is different from the common-sense use of the term 'spectator' as a synonym for the individual viewer or audience member. For this reason, you will find that critical theories which deal with these questions tend to use the term 'spectator' to refer to the textual spectator or subject-position, which is distinguished from the 'social audience' who buy tickets to see films, watch TV or download programmes for home viewing. As we will see, however, it is often difficult to keep these two meanings of 'spectator' apart.

It is against the background of these debates in feminist film theory that Tania Modleski first posed the question of the kind of spectator which soap opera constructs in its attempt to address female audiences. She begins by noting that unlike the ninety-minute feature film, soap opera does not centre on an individual hero, nor, through his gaze, on the spectacle of the glamourized woman who is his inspiration or downfall. In fact, as Robert Allen points out, soap opera has difficulty in centring at all. Rather, the narrative structuring of soap opera involves fragmentation, interruption, false endings, reversals and new beginnings. The question Modleski explores is what kind of spectator position does this fragmented, constantly interrupted storyline offer to us?

READING A⏋

After giving this question some thought, go on to read the extract from Modleski's article, provided as Reading A at the end of this chapter.

How does Modleski's 'ideal spectator' for soap opera differ from Mulvey's 'ideal spectator' for the Hollywood movie?

According to Modleski, we find in fact two quite different 'spectators' constructed by the two different forms: in the classic Hollywood movie, the filmic spectator is constructed as the voyeuristic male, taking control of events and the female image; in soap opera, the spectator is constructed as the idealized mother, passively responsive to events and endlessly identifying with the needs of a range of conflicting characters. These positions, which the viewer is invited to occupy, irrespective of her or his actual sex, in the process of following the story, are clearly gendered according to dominant conceptions of male and female identity. And Modleski's analysis of the spectatorial position as ideal mother suggests the power of textual address to reinforce the social construction of female identity in so far as the female viewer occupies this subject-position which confirms passivity and long-suffering as the woman's lot.

However, this method of analysis poses some very important questions:

- Does a fiction construct only one, fixed position for the spectator, so that our choice is either to occupy that position or switch channels?
- Is the viewer – the social audience member – in total thrall to the subject-position constructed in the text?
- Can the viewer find – or construct – *other* positions within the text, which coincide more closely with her own particular social experience and outlook, and which may be at variance with dominant gender ideologies?

5.3.2 Female reading competence

You will probably have noticed that, in analysing the spectator of soap opera, Modleski moves between, on the one hand, a strictly textual construction based on its narrative organization and, on the other, a construction based on women's social experience. Thus her interpretation of soap opera's textual spectator as 'ideal mother' is derived from her own knowledge of the social conditions of motherhood, and arises in part because she wants to produce a model of the spectator which, unlike Mulvey's, *could be* occupied by soap opera's female audience. It is, though, only by reference to the social experience and practices of mothering that Modleski is able to bring this gendered perspective to bear on the narrative structure of soap opera.

Nevertheless, Tania Modleski's model of soap opera's address is of an unconscious operation which calls *all* women into a subject-position they are socially and psychologically conditioned to occupy. The match Modleski assumes between the ideological position of the passively for-bearing mother who suffers on behalf of all her troublesome children and the woman in the audience leaves little space for the viewer to resist or otherwise engage with soap opera. There is, however, a more dynamic way of approaching the relation of text and audience through the idea of **reading competence**, a semiotic concept referring to the learned interpretative frameworks and reading skills employed by different social groups or 'readerships' to decode signs and representations.

From this perspective, our capacity to use codes in order to communicate is embedded in the *specific interpretative frameworks and social practices of given groups* and constitutes a form of 'competence' which accounts for *differences in cultural usage*. 'Competence' here does not mean efficiency or correctness, but refers to the common-sense knowledge and perspectives shared by a particular readership. Within the specific cultural competencies exercised by given social groups, the signs of verbal or visual language will take on meanings that may be opaque to those outside. Take, for example, the costume, hair and make-up of landlady Liz McDonald in *Coronation Street*. What exactly these elements of stylization signify will depend on the 'competence' of any given reader to decode them. For the costume designers, hair and make-up artists who constructed this working-class character, these signs could mean: 'this is the sort of thing people like Liz would look like and wear' – a touch of authenticity, an easy cliché, per-haps a patronizing smile. But what do those signifiers mean to the viewers? According to class and cultural frameworks, Liz's stylization could evoke fond recognition or a sign of bad taste. Things become even more complicated if we think of those elements of style worn by a London art student, or by a lecturer in Kent. I leave it to you to think about what these elements of

FIGURE 6.5 Mobile signifiers: Liz McDonald's stylization © ITV

style signify in these situations! But my point is that the cultural meaning of elements of dress, hairstyle and make-up is radically transformed by social context and the reading competence shared by the owner and his or her milieux.

A further point to make is that some *readings* of Liz's stylization have more cultural prestige and social power than others. Some people, through class, ethnic or gender position, education, professional experience, have access to more cultural competences than others. The art student who wears their hair akin to Liz McDonald as a badge is dipping into the cultural competence of one group in order to make another statement within the competence of her or his own and different group. This has led the French cultural sociologist, Pierre Bourdieu, to develop the notion of *cultural capital* in an analogy with financial capital as a source of social division. Just as access to financial capital gives a person economic security and status, so – Bourdieu argued – we use cultural capital to give us knowledge, 'know-how' about the world, practical competences which underpin our status and position, and help us to differentiate ourselves from those who are less well 'culturally endowed' (Bourdieu, 1984). A while back, *Coronation Street*, in an episode that must have been made with cultural studies lecturers in mind, made a humorous drama out of this theory in an argument about stone-cladding at The Rover's Return. Curly, defending his 'puce' shirt as a 'keep off' message to the world, declares to the mystified Jack that 'in the empire of signs', his and Vera's stone-cladding similarly says something about them, although it would take a 'trained semiotician' to tell them what. Jack is dumbfounded and Curly can get no further, but the situation is saved when ex-grammar school boy, Ken Barlow, walks in and bluffs his way through an explanation by putting two and two together!

5.3.3 Cultural competence and the implied reader of the text

Soap opera's address to the socially mandated concerns of women – the family, the domestic arena, personal relationships as they work out both in the family and at work – has led Charlotte Brunsdon (1982) to discuss the gendering of this particular genre in terms of **female cultural competence**. Soap operas utilize, and need to be read according to, the cultural codes and reading competences employed by women. This is not to suggest that they cannot be understood by males; rather that soap operas employ a range of knowledges, perspectives and nuances that emerge out of female cultural experience and can be fully activated only within this framework.

READING B

Now turn to Reading B at the end of this chapter. In what ways is the notion of the feminine 'implied reader' used by Charlotte Brunsdon different from Modleski's 'ideal spectator'?

The first important difference to note is that whereas the ideal spectator is a *textual construction* into which viewers fit or not, with the implied reader the text has to employ the codes which belong to the cultural competence of an actual *particular readership*. Although we are still analysing codes activated by and through the programme, we are being asked to look for a frame of reading reference *outside* the text, the one used by a particular *social audience*. The second difference is the dynamic relation this implies between audience and programme text. Whereas the textual spectator calls us into and fixes us in a subject-position for which we are already conditioned by unconscious and social structures, the implication of a social reader invites readers to deploy the cultural competence derived from their lived experience in their engagement with the text. As has been suggested, the discursive strategies of soap opera narration – talk, gossip, chewing over events, deciding what is likely to or should happen – are all part of the repertoire of female cultural competence. Moreover, as Charlotte Brunsdon notes, the fragmentation of the soap opera text requires considerable extra-textual work to keep track of events. In other words, pleasure comes not from the text alone, but from the extension of the text into the thinking, communicating activity and skills of the viewer.

5.3.4 The social audience

Thus we are passed from *textual spectator*, through the *implied reader*, into the practices of the historically situated *social audience*. Feminist readings of the work of soap opera, such as those made by Tania Modleski and Charlotte Brunsdon, emerge from the serious attention devoted by the Women's Movement to the practices, competences and meanings involved in women's engagement in domestic and community life and in personal and family relationships. It is this cultural knowledge that enables Brunsdon to interpret the dramatic dynamic of a ringing telephone in *Crossroads* for an implied female reader. But it is one thing to know that the textual spectator or the implied reader is gendered. It is another to know what the activity of viewing or reading con-tributes to, or draws from, the gendering of audience identity. The next logical step is to investigate that audience itself.

Ien Ang's work on *Dallas* threw an illuminating spotlight on the audience for soap opera, dem-onstrating the power of both the mental frameworks and social conditions within which viewing takes place to shape reception. Her analysis of letters written to her by *Dallas* fans showed how, as they described their pleasurable responses to the programme, they also, as it were, viewed their own viewing from within the critical perspectives of the ideology of mass culture:

> In fact it's a flight from reality. I myself am a realistic person and I know that reality is different. Sometimes too I really enjoy having a good old cry with them. And why not? In this way my other bottled-up emotions find an outlet.
>
> (quoted in Ang, 1985, p. 105)

Ien Ang, in this study and elsewhere, has insisted on viewing as a social practice which differs according to media form and social context. Going to the cinema, switching on the television, bringing home a DVD are different social practices which have their own specific meanings even before the encounter with a particular film, TV programme or DVD takes place. In fact, several commentators have noted the difficulty of defining or capturing the television 'text' which, as the phrase 'wall-to-wall *Dallas*' suggests, exists as part of the living-room furniture and has to compete for the viewer's attention along with other household and familial activities. The fact that the television is on does not mean that it is being watched and certainly not that it is being given undivided attention. This poses the following sort of questions:

- How, then, do women watch TV?
- What is a woman saying to her family when she leaves the kitchen, sits down in front of the television, and is deaf to requests for the whereabouts of clean socks, the salt or the TV guide?
- What is the difference between a woman watching *Emmerdale* or *Coronation Street* with the whole family, with a daughter, with friends, alone, with a husband or boyfriend?
- How do gender, class, age, ethnicity in general affect the patterns and conditions of viewing?
- What are the knock-on effects of such variable conditions for the meanings produced during that viewing?

An ethnographic study conducted by Ellen Seiter, Hans Borchers, Gabriele Kreutzner and Eva-Maria Warth with a group of female viewers of soap opera in Oregon, USA, looked at the impact of the social context of viewing on the relations of particular audiences to their favourite soaps. The study was based on a series of interview/discussions in all-women groups of friends and neighbours. It found that the sociality of television viewing encouraged these viewers to exercise the female competences implied in soap opera's narrative structure as a means of engaging with but also extending the text as part of their own social interaction. In some cases, friends plugged into the telephone system in order to 'talk about everything as it's happening'. In this respect the researchers suggest:

> soap opera texts are the products not of individual and isolated readings but of collective constructions – collaborative readings, as it were, of small social groups such as families, friends, and neighbours, or people sharing an apartment.

(Seiter et al., 1989, p. 233)

Their preliminary interpretation of their findings takes us further into the distinction between the textual spectator and social audience, identifying a process of negotiation with or even resistance to the viewing position of 'ideal mother', which Modleski argues is constructed by soap opera's narrative structure. Against her view that the female viewer is unconsciously conditioned to occupy this position as 'an egoless receptacle for the suffering of others', the research group argues:

> Modleski offers no possibility for *conscious* resistance to the soap opera text; the spectator position is conceived of in terms of a perfectly 'successful' gender socialization entirely in keeping with a middle-class (and white) feminine ideal. ... While this position was partially taken

up by some of our middle-class, college-educated informants, it was consciously resisted and vehemently rejected by most of the women we interviewed, especially by working-class women. The relationship between the viewer and character more typically involved hostility – in the case of some of the presumably sympathetic characters – as well as fond admiration – for the supposedly despised villainesses ...

(1989, p.233)

6 CONCLUSION

The last section outlined some of the main features through which soap opera was developed as a woman's form seeking to address a female audience. In the process we have seen how certain strategies – for example, daily serialization – produced unlooked-for consequences for the representation of women, most notably the need to extend the woman's story beyond marriage. Another unlooked-for consequence has been the longevity of soaps and circulation into a culture beyond that initially envisaged – first, from women at home to American college students and eventually into the primetime audience. We now need to pick up some of the themes concerning the nature of genre identity and the increasing evolution of genres across gender boundaries which were raised in section 4 in order to answer our initial question: how does soap opera function as a site of contest of gendered meanings and representations?

6.1 Soap opera: a women's form no more?

It used to be relatively safe to identify soap opera as a women's form, since its daytime or early evening scheduling was more likely to net women listeners and viewers than men. But the gradual development of evening soaps for mixed audiences – from *Dallas* and *Dynasty* in the USA to *EastEnders*, *Brookside* and *Coronation Street* in the 1980s in the UK – have meant that soap opera is no longer exclusively associated with women. This development of a mixed address of evening soap opera may appear somewhat ironic given that it is shifts to women employment trends in the latter half of the twentieth century that have made relatively affluent female viewers more attractive for programmers and schedulers of evening schedules to target (Brunsdon, 2000). However the development of evening soap operas to attract not only women but also men, teenagers as well as a more diverse range of audience demographics at the level of ethnicity and sexuality, can be contextualized in relation to the more general feminization of evening schedules. This feminization consists of a 'daytime-ization' of evening schedules (Medhurst, 1999, p. 26), one in which, as Moseley has argued, 'consists of the spaces and discourses conventionally gendered as "feminine" – the personal, the private, the everyday – have been opened up to men in the programming of the [8–9] slot, especially around care of the self through grooming, shopping and cookery' (Moseley, 2001, p. 32). As Moseley's account suggests, such shifts to broadcasting can be perceived less as a move on the part of television to address female viewers explicitly, but rather as an attempt by broadcasters and schedulers to draw on feminine forms of programming to appeal to a wider number of audience segments in the increasingly commercial and competitive broadcasting climate of recent years (Ball, 2012).

For instance, with deregulation and the increase in the range of channels and services from the late 1980s, including the rise of niche broadcasters, the competition from new media technologies such as the internet and gaming consoles, and shifts to multiple TV households, broadcasters have had to find innovative ways of trying to hold on to a sizeable share of the diminishing audience. Amid these considerable shifts to broadcasting cultures in the late 1990s, for instance, Mal Young, the Head of BBC Drama Series, in 1999 claimed that in a time of massive change for television, it is only soap opera which cuts across social boundaries (Young, 1999) via its multi-character and multi-storyline conventions.

These contexts mean that it is necessary to ask: how do evening soap operas attempt to appeal to different audience segments, such as men, teenagers, and black, Asian, gay or lesbian viewers? How do these developments impact upon the conventions and pleasures of the genre? Two changes in particular have struck commentators regarding the shifting address of evening soap operas: first, the increasing centrality of male characters; and, secondly, the increasing incorporation into soap opera of features from male-oriented genres. Thus one of the earliest textual examples that embodied this shift, *Dallas*, incorporates elements of the western in its representation of the Southfork ranch, while British soap operas such as *EastEnders*, *Coronation Street* and *Emmerdale* have drawn on elements of the crime drama for stories involving male characters – for example, Phil Mitchell in *EastEnders* or Richard Hillman in *Coronation Street* – that have resulted in fast action sequences and goal-driven plotting to a degree uncharacteristic of traditional soap opera. British soap operas too have borrowed from masculine forms such as the single play and factual forms of programming by becoming concerned with greater degrees of realism and the dramatization of social issues (Geraghty, 1991, p. 134): from unemployment in the early years of *Brookside* to AIDS and mental health in *EastEnders*.

However, just as soap operas have become 'de-feminized' (Root, 1986, p. 72), it is equally significant that the strategies and conventions of soap opera have been increasingly deployed by what are traditionally thought of as male genres, such as police or law series – for example, *Hill Street Blues*, *The Bill* and *Ally McBeal*. We might even be led to conclude of male-oriented series like *The Sopranos* or *Supernatural* that we have male soap opera! Is this breaking down and intersection of genre boundaries evidence of the reassertion of male cultural dominance – the so-called feminist backlash? Or perhaps a sign of gender negotiation and contest taking place through the interaction of differently gendered genre conventions? In particular, we need to consider how the traditional investment of 'male' genres in action and the public sphere negotiates with the conventions of soap opera, which foreground the realm of the personal and feelings, and which deploy talk – gossip – as its major narrational strategy. What, then, is going on when, in the constant shifting of genre boundaries, men's genres and women's genres interact?

6.2 Dissolving genre boundaries and gendered negotiations

The increasing number of soap operas, their shift into the mainstream, and influence on male-oriented forms, suggest that soap opera has generated a far more extensive potential than its early progenitors ever envisaged, becoming itself a cultural resource to other genres. The question is, what kind of resource? First, as a form aimed at women, soap opera developed in the margins of popular culture as a space for the cultural representation of an undervalued area of experience – personal and emotional life. This fact frequently leads to the confusion of soap opera with melodrama. But such an equation fails to take account of the central role of talk in soap opera, which cuts across melodrama's projection of emotion into expressive action and spectacle. In fact, drawing on melodrama's history, I have argued elsewhere (Gledhill, 1994) that it is the so-called male genres of action and adventure – genres in which monosyllabic heroes and villains project their antagonisms into violent conflict rather than intimate discussion – which are more properly termed 'melodramatic'. Women's genres, such as women's fiction and soap opera, draw on a tradition of domestic realism in which a set of highly articulate discursive forms – talk, the confessional heart-to-heart, gossip – work through psychic and social contradictions which melodrama must externalize through expressive action. Far from representing an 'excess' of emotion which displaces action, talk in soap opera *is* its action, while action in masculine genres more often than not represents unexpressed and often unexpressible male emotion, which needs a melodramatic climax to break out.

In this context, then, we can consider what negotiations are set going by the entry of more central male characters and actions into the soap operatic world. If this world makes greater space for female characters and the female perspective, then power over speech features as a major weapon in the struggles of female characters with their menfolk. Whereas in the majority of genres narrative events are controlled by male characters, in traditional soap operas the greater number of female protagonists exercising authority in the practices of domestic, personal and community life circumscribes and delimits the male characters. This, Christine Geraghty argues, has framed the spectator position within a female perspective, offering a viewpoint which would otherwise be unheard or heard only to be marginalized or mocked. The space given to this female point of view, from which male discourses are perceived and judged, is threatened, she argues, by the increasing number of male characters and actions in contemporary soap operas.

However, as we have seen, of all the genres, soap opera is perhaps the most difficult to fix into particular meanings and effects. Cutting across the impact of male dominance in any given episode are the consequences of the still equal if not greater number of roles for female characters, of narrative inconclusiveness and reversal, of the role of audiences in extending the fiction beyond the bounds of the text, and the primacy, both textual and extra-textual, in this process of the feminine competence of talk. So, for example, in 2010 a big public event or a high drama action, such as the killing of Archie Mitchell or the death of Bradley Branning, were relayed through the discussions and gossip taking place between the serial's characters, discussions in

FIGURE 6.6   Male bonding in *Sons of Anarchy* © Twentieth Century Fox

which, in the case of Archie's death, the general public was invited to join. Or we find, as in the example from *EastEnders*, the diagnostic techniques of soap opera leading the most traditionally masculine of characters, such as Phil Mitchell or Max Branning, into unexpected confessional and introspective moments. As has already been suggested, this breakthrough to articulacy and intimacy for male protagonists is now penetrating action series such as *24*, *Prison Break* or *Sons of Anarchy* so that episodes are as likely to consist of exchanges in the men's washroom as of crime and fighting.

This is not to suggest that talk as a culturally feminized activity is more ideologically acceptable than 'masculine' action, but rather that the submission of one to the other in the increasing inter-mingling of genres produces intersections of gendered modes and values which offer the potential for negotiations around gender definition and sexual identities. Male protagonists enter the confessional sphere of soap opera, but equally, female protagonists imbue action with the values of the personal and domestic in, for example, traditionally masculinized genres such as the police series (e.g. *Trial and Retribution*) or action movies (e.g. *Kill Bill* or *The Girl with the Dragon Tattoo*). The question of what ideological work is performed by the tensions and contradictions between such intersecting gendered discourses depends on how they are viewed by different audiences operating within different reading frameworks.

If we look further afield for a moment and consider the way in which soap opera conventions have been utilized in recent forms of factual programming, namely reality and lifestyle television, we can begin to explore the tensions and contradictions between such intersecting gendered discourses in other areas of television at this time. As I have already indicated in section 3.1, the mixing of gendered values and the focus in reality television programmes on the personal, the private, the emotional and the everyday has been seen (largely by male critics) as marking the 'dumbing down' of evening television in this period. Accounts by those such as Corner (2006), for instance, suggest that the public service ethos to inform, educate and entertain has been reversed so that it is the pleasure principal that is privileged in reality formats through their address to the consumer over the citizen. However, for academics such as Bondebjerg (1996), Moseley (2001) and Brunsdon (Brunsdon et al., 2001), the hybridization of these texts, and the foregrounding of the personal in the public forum of television, can be understood less as a sign of the decline, but rather a democratization of public service discourse; indeed, it is to recognize the increasing emphasis placed upon the personal as political in contemporary social life. In this context, with the waning of more traditional ways of living, television's focus upon the actions and reactions of everyday people imbues great significance as a way of negotiating everyday choices regarding how to be and how to behave in a secular society. It is from this perspective that we can situate Rachel Moseley's claim that:

> Rather than a simple shift from citizen to consumer, then, what [lifestyle] shows represent is a complex conjunction of the two, in which the personal and the private are figured as significant spaces in which citizens can, on a small, local scale, learn to make changes, make a difference, improve the personal for the national good. (Moseley, 2001, p. 34)

While discussions of factual television's 'borrowing' of soap opera conventions have focused on what feminine values have 'done' to masculine forms of programming, it is significant to explore the way in which the intersection of gendered discourses in factual programming make public the gendered politics of the private sphere and women's experiences therein. The reality television programme *Wife Swap* has attracted some (positive) critical discussion in this respect because of the way in which it utilizes the oft-denigrated game-doc format (associated with *Big Brother* and *I'm a Celebrity ... Get Me Out of Here*) to work over the terrain of traditional soap opera: the politics, tensions and contradictions of the personal sphere and the experiences of women in the domestic context of the home. *Wife Swap*, then, shows two wives/mothers swap families for a two-week period in order to learn from alternative approaches to domesticity, parenting and marriage.

⊣READING C

Now turn to Reading C at the end of this chapter. From Holmes and Jermyn's account, can you suggest ways in which female participants in *Wife Swap* are represented similarly to and differently from female characters in soap opera? In what ways does the text reinforce or disrupt existing ideologies of femininity and masculinity, motherhood and fatherhood?

In contrast to accounts which perceive the incorporation of feminine values in forms of factual programming as reducing their cultural significance, Holmes and Jermyn's account of *Wife Swap* suggests that reality television formats have the capacity of extending our knowledge of the dynamics and politics that structure the private sphere. In this respect, programmes such as *Wife Swap*, similarly to soap opera, problematize and disrupt ideologies of femininity with regard to motherhood even as they simultaneously reposition women in relation to classed and gendered positions of caretaker of home and family.

Finally, and returning to soap opera, I want to offer one last summarizing example from *Brookside* and the Mandy Jordash appeal to suggest how, as cultural media analysts, we might approach the intersection of the shifting conventions of soap opera – at their different levels of production, text, reception – with the social circulation of gender discourses. The staging of the appeal over several episodes drew on representations and discourses circulating in society belonging to, or representing, women's action groups, extremists, family violence, lesbians, which interwove with the generic conventions of soap opera and of the trial melodrama, producing through its formal and ideological organization the possibility of contradictory readings for different audience members. The courtroom has long served as a prime site for dramatizing the intersection of public with private life and, moreover, facilitates the stronger male roles favoured by *Brookside*. The public spaces appear to be dominated by male protagonists: in the courtroom itself by male judge and barristers, in the street outside by Sinbad, Mandy's new partner, railing against the women's protest group whose violence has caused the court's doors to be locked. Mandy and her female counsel speak only in the privacy of the anteroom behind the court. Moreover, the women's protest group shouting slogans outside the court are put down as disruptive intruders and lesbians by Sinbad and Mandy's neighbourhood women friends.

But in fact public and private, talk and action, domestic realism and melodrama, intersect to produce tensions that suggest an ideological cross-over between spheres and genders for those in the audience with sympathies to respond. Sinbad is a soap opera protagonist and acts not for the public interest but, on the contrary, claims that the case on trial – one highly charged for feminist politics – is a purely personal, family matter. On the other hand, the formal enactment of the courtroom melodrama brings the personal tragedy witnessed behind the scenes in a private sisterly space between Mandy and her female counsel into full public glare, providing evidence of the opposite contention, that the personal is in fact political. For as the circumstances surrounding Mandy and Beth's life with an abusive husband and father are argued in verbal interchange between male barristers, intercut with close-ups of the silent face of Mandy Jordash, framed behind the railings of courtroom furniture – a woman without a voice in a drama fought out between male protagonists – the pathos of her situation, caught between forces not of her making, becomes a potent symbol of women's oppression. For those among the female audience who find a certain resonance in the idea of disposing of an abusive husband and feel the parallels with the similar real-life case of Sara Thornton or other such cases, the possibility is offered of extending a gendered solidarity with Mandy of the kind represented by the women protesters outside the court but ostensibly put down as extremism. It is, then, as if there is a kind of contest going on between characters, generic and aesthetic forms, ideologies and potential readers as to the ownership of the trial and appeal, and whose interests it is to represent.

FIGURE 6.7 *Brookside*: Beth and Mandy Jordash (Anna Friel and Sandra Maitland) in the dock, July–August 1995

FIGURE 6.8 Sara Thornton, on her release from prison, 29 July 1995

Included in such a contest, of course, will be polemical critiques of the programme's mobilization of stereotypes of the woman protester or lesbian, or personal identifications with the situation of a fictional protagonist that leads to the opening of a helpline after broadcasting. Indeed, part of the cultural work of soap opera is precisely this extension of debate into the public arena beyond the fiction. But as cultural media analysts we must avoid both fixing meanings and deciding the ideological effects of representations on the evidence of the textual product alone. Rather, primed with an awareness of the semiotic and social possibilities of a film or television programme, what we can do is establish conditions and possibilities of gendered (or other) readings and open up the negotiations of the text in order to understand the state of the contest.

REFERENCES

ALLEN, R. (1985) *Speaking of Soap Opera*, Chapel Hill, NC, University of North Carolina Press.

ANG, I. (1985) *Watching Dallas: Soap Opera and the Melodramatic Imagination*, New York, Methuen.

ARTHURS, J. (2003) '*Sex and the City* and consumer culture: remediating postfeminist drama', *Feminist Media Studies*, 3(1).

BALL, V. (2012) 'The feminization of British television and the re-traditionalization of gender: the case of the British female ensemble drama', *Feminist Media Studies*, 12(3).

BONDEBJERG, I. (1996) 'Public discourse/private fascination: hybridisation in "True-Life-Story" genres', *Media Culture and Society*, 18.

BOURDIEU, P. (1984) *Distinction* (tr. R. Nice), London, Routledge.

BRUNSDON, C. (1982) '*Crossroads*: notes on soap opera', *Screen*, 22(4), Spring.

BRUNSDON, C. (1990) 'Aesthetics and Audiences', in Mellencamp, P. (ed.) *Logics of Television*, Bloomington and London, University of Indiana and the British Film Institute

BRUNSDON, C. (2000) 'Not having it all: women and film in the 1990s', in Murphy, R. (ed.), *British Film of the 90s*, London, British Film Institute.

BRUNSDON, C., JOHNSON, C., MOSELEY, R. AND WHEATLEY, H. (2001) 'Factual entertainment on British television: the Midlands TV Research Group's 8–9 Project', *European Journal of Cultural Studies*, 4(1).

BRUNSDON, C. AND SPIGEL, L. (2009) *Feminist Television Criticism: A Reader* (2nd edition), Maidenhead, Open University Press.

BUCKMAN, P. (1984) *All for Love: A Study in Soap Opera*, London, Secker & Warburg.

CORNER, J. (2006) 'A fiction (un)like any other?', *Critical Studies in Television*, 1(1).

GERAGHTY, C. (1991) *Women and Soap Opera: A Study of Prime Time Soaps*, Cambridge, Polity Press.

GLEDHILL, C. (1994) 'Speculations on the relationship between melodrama and soap opera', in Browne, N. (ed.), *American Television: Economies, Sexualities, Forms*, New York, Harwood Academic Publishers.

HASKELL, M. (1974) *From Reverence to Rape*, Harmondsworth, Penguin.

HOLLINGER, K. (2002) 'From female friends to literary ladies: the contemporary woman's film', in Neale, S. (ed.) *Genre and* Contemporary *Hollywood,* London: BFI.

HOLMES, S. AND JERMYN, D. (2008) 'Ask the fastidious woman from Surbiton to hand-wash the underpants of the ageing Oldham skinhead… why not *Wife Swap*?', in Austin, T. and de Jong, W. (eds), *Rethinking Documentary*, Maidenhead, Open University Press.

JOYRICH, L. (1996) *Re-Viewing Reception: Television, Gender and Postmodern Culture*, Indiana, Indiana University Press.

JERMYN, D. (2009) *Sex and the City*, Detroit, MI, Wayne State University.

KITZES, J. (1969) *Horizons West*, London, Thames & Hudson/British Film Institute.

LOVELL, T. (1981) '*Coronation Street* and ideology', in Dyer, R. et al. (eds), *Coronation Street*, Television Monograph 13, London, British Film Institute.

MARGOLIES, D. (1982–83) 'Mills and Boon: guilt without sex', *Red Letters*, No. 14.

MATTELART, M. (1985) 'From soap to serial', in *Women, Media and Crisis*, London, Comedia.

MEDHURST, A. (1999) 'Day for night', *Sight and Sound*, 9(6).

MODLESKI, T. (1982) 'The search for tomorrow in today's soap operas', in *Loving with a Vengeance*, New York, Methuen.

MOSELEY, R (2001) 'Real lads do cook – but some things are still hard to talk about. The gendering of 8-9', *European Journal of Cultural Studies*, 4(1), pp 32–9.

MULVEY, L. (1989) 'Visual pleasure and narrative cinema', in *Visual and Other Pleasures*, Basingstoke, Macmillan. First published 1975.

NEALE, S. (1981) *Genre*, London, British Film Institute.

NEALE, S. (1990) 'Questions of genre', *Screen*, 31(l).

PETRO, P. (1986) 'Mass culture and the feminine: the 'place' of television in film studies', *Cinema Journal*, 25(3): 5–21.

ROOT, J. (1986) *Open the Box*, London, Comedia.

SEITER, E., BORCHERS, H., KREUTZNER, G. AND WARTH, E.-M. (1989) '"Don't treat us like we're so stupid and naïve": toward an ethnography of soap opera viewers', in Seiter, E. et al. (eds), *Remote Control: Television, Audiences and Cultural Power*, London, Routledge.

SKEGGS, B. (1997) *Formations of Class and Gender*, London, Sage.

SOHN, A. (2002) *Sex and the City: Kiss and Tell*, London, Channel 4 Books.

TODOROV, T. (1976) 'The origin of genres', *New Literary History*, 8(1) (Autumn).

YOUNG, M. (1999) 'Days of our lives: the one where he talks about soaps', Huw Wheldon Lecture, Royal Television Society, Cambridge.

READING A: Tania Modleski, 'The search for tomorrow in today's soap operas'

[T]he classic (male) narrative film is, as Laura Mulvey points out, structured 'around a main controlling figure with whom the spectator can identify' (Mulvey, 1977, p. 420). Soap operas continually insist on the insignificance of the individual life. A viewer might at one moment be asked to identify with a woman finally reunited with her lover, only to have that identification broken in a moment of intensity and attention focused on the sufferings of the woman's rival.

If, as Mulvey claims, the identification of the spectator with 'a main male protagonist' results in the spectator's becoming 'the representative of power' (p. 420), the multiple identification which occurs in soap opera results in the spectator's being divested of power. For the spectator is never permitted to identify with a character completing an entire action. Instead of giving us one 'powerful ideal ego ... who can make things happen and control events better than the subject/spectator can' (p. 420), soap operas present us with numerous limited egos, each in conflict with the others, and continually thwarted in its attempts to control events because of inadequate knowledge of other peoples' plans, motivations, and schemes. Sometimes, indeed, the spectator, frustrated by the sense of powerlessness induced by soap operas, will, like an interfering mother, try to control events directly:

Thousands and thousands of letters [from soap fans to actors] give advice, warn the heroine of impending doom, caution the innocent to beware of the nasties ('Can't you see that your brother-in-law is up to no good?'), inform one character of another's doings, or reprimand a character for unseemly behavior.

(Edmondson and Rounds, 1976, p. 193)

Presumably, this intervention is ineffectual, and feminine powerlessness is reinforced on yet another level.

The subject/spectator of soap operas, it could be said, is constituted as a sort of ideal mother: a person who possesses greater wisdom than all her children, whose sympathy is large enough to encompass the conflicting claims of her family (she identifies with them all), and who has no demands or claims of her own (she identifies with no one character exclusively). [...]

It is important to recognize that soap operas serve to affirm the primacy of the family not by presenting an ideal family, but by portraying a family in a constant turmoil and appealing to the spectator to be understanding and tolerant of the many evils which go on within that family. The spectator/mother, identifying with each character in turn, is made to see 'the larger picture' and extend her sympathy to both the sinner and the victim. She is thus in a position to forgive all. As a rule, only those issues which can be tolerated and ultimately pardoned are introduced on soap operas. The list includes careers for women, abortions, premarital and extramarital sex, alcoholism, divorce, mental and even physical cruelty. An issue like homosexuality, which could explode the family structure rather than temporarily disrupt it, is simply ignored. Soap operas, contrary to many people's conception of them, are not conservative but liberal, and the mother is the liberal *par excellence*. By constantly presenting her with the many-sidedness of any question, by never reaching a permanent conclusion, soap operas undermine her capacity to form unambiguous judgments.

REFERENCES

EDMONDSON, M. AND ROUNDS, D. (1976) *From Mary Noble to Mary Hartman: The Complete Soap Opera Book*, New York, Stein and Day.

MULVEY, L. (1977) 'Visual pleasure and narrative cinema', in Kay, K. and Peary, G. (eds), *Women and the Cinema*, New York, E. P. Dutton.

Source: Modleski, 1982, pp. 91–3.

READING B: Charlotte Brunsdon, 'Crossroads: notes on soap opera'

I will consider the [...] question of the type of cultural competence that *Crossroads* as soap-opera narrative(s) demands of its social reader.

Just as a Godard film requires the possession of certain forms of cultural capital on the part of its audience to 'make sense' – an extra-textual familiarity with certain artistic, linguistic, political and cinematic discourses – so too does *Crossroads*/soap opera. The particular competences demanded by soap opera fall into three categories:

1 Generic knowledge – familiarity with the conventions of soap opera as a genre. For example, expecting discontinuous and cliff-hanging narrative structures.

2 Serial-specific knowledge – knowledge of past narratives and of characters (in particular, who belongs to who).

3 Cultural knowledge of the socially acceptable codes and conventions for the conduct of personal life.

I will only comment on the third category here. The argument is that the narrative strategies and concerns of *Crossroads* call on the traditionally feminine competencies associated with the responsibility for 'managing' the sphere of personal life. It is the culturally constructed skills of femininity – sensitivity, perception, intuition and the necessary privileging of the concerns of personal life – which are both called on and practised in the genre. The fact that these skills and competencies, this type of cultural capital, is ideologically constructed as natural, does not mean, as many feminists have shown, that they are the *natural* attributes of femininity. However, under present cultural and political arrangements, it is more likely that female viewers will possess this repertoire of both sexual and maternal femininities which is called on to fill out the range of narrative possibilities when, for example, the phone rings. That is, when Jill is talking to her mother about her marriage (17 January 1979), and the phone rings, the viewer needs to know not only that it is likely to be Stan (her nearly ex-husband) calling about custody of their daughter Sarah-Jane (serial-specific knowledge) and that we're unlikely to hear the content of the phone-call in that segment (generic knowledge), but also that the mother's 'right' to her children is no longer automatically assumed. These knowledges only have narrative resonance in relation to discourses of maternal femininity which are elaborated elsewhere, already in circulation and brought to the programme by – the viewer. In the enigma that is then posed – will Jill or Stan get Sarah-Jane? – questions are also raised about who, generally and particularly, *should* get custody. The question of what *should* happen is rarely posed 'openly' – in this instance it was quite clear that 'right' lay with Jill. But it is precisely the terms of the question, the way in which it relates to other already circulating discourses, if you like, the degree of its closure, which form the site of the construction of moral consensus, a construction which 'demands', seeks to implicate, a skilled viewer.

I am thus arguing that *Crossroads* textually implies a feminine viewer to the extent that its textual discontinuities require a viewer competent within the ideological and moral frameworks, the rules of romance, marriage and family life, to make sense of it.

Against critics who complain of the redundancy of soap opera, I would suggest that the radical discontinuities of the text require extensive, albeit interrupted, engagement on the part of the audience, before it becomes pleasurable. This is not to designate *Crossroads* 'progressive' but to suggest that the skills and discourses mobilized by its despised popularity have partly been overlooked because of their legitimation as natural (feminine).

Source: Brunsdon, 1982, pp. 36–7.

READING C: Su Holmes and Deborah Jermyn, 'Why not *Wife Swap?*'

If there is an ideological 'metanarrative' at work across *Wife Swap*, it is to loosely endorse a position of compromise between the two family set-ups. Extremes are revealed to be flawed, one-sided and suspicious, and following an ideological struggle (in which each family – in Gramscian terms – must engage in 'negotiations with opposing groups, classes and values' (Turner, 1996, p. 178)), the middle ground of the battlefield is often preferred. The episode featuring Deirdre and Margaret illustrates this well. Margaret, 'a stay at home mum for more than 20 years' from Wolverhampton with eight children, swaps places in Leeds with 'self-made businesswoman' Deirdre, who has one child (3-year-old Frankie) and who runs her own multi-million travel business.

[…]

In part through its very careful editing, the programme facilitates a movement between distance from, identification with, the individuals involved in the swap. Indeed, Piper argues that the programme deliberately sets up types (regarding class and gender) only to subsequently take pleasure in problematizing and undermining them (2004, pp. 277, 299). This is facilitated by the way the format sets up a number of perspectives on, and subject positions for, the participants, ranging across the more detached voice-over, the musical soundtrack, to the more 'intimate' confessionals to camera. […] By the end, quite predictably it could be said given the series' emphasis on reaching concession and self-discovery, Margaret is seen tentatively seeking other kinds of fulfilment in part-time work outside the home, having 'managed' Deirdre's business in her absence and Deirdre has committed herself to working less hours in order to spend more time with her son.

Yet along the road to this change of heart and despite their very different lifestyles, both women nevertheless powerfully voice their dissatisfaction with the lot of traditional motherhood. […] As we see Margaret growing in confidence in the workplace, she exposes the lack of recognition that accompanies the work of motherhood, despite her championing of the role. She observes sadly, 'You really are somebody here, whereas at home, I've always felt a bit forgotten.'

[…]

From her initial perspective as career woman, Deirdre too exposes the alienation motherhood holds for her. In a strikingly frank moment, Deirdre admits, 'I play with Frankie infrequently, because if I'm brutally honest, I find it boring … I don't really know what to do with [children].' […]

Deirdre clearly undergoes a process of self-discovery in the course of the programme and subsequently embraces aspects of Margaret's parenting style […]. But if this is the perspective taken by Deirdre by the end of the swap, it is worth noting the long heritage of debate as to whether narrative 'closure' recuperates, or invalidates, the ideological perspectives which have preceded it (Maltby, 1995, p. 337). Indeed, the moment when Deirdre describes playing with her only child as 'boring' remains remarkable for the manner in which it features a young, accomplished and highly articulate mother on television blankly debunking the myths of motherhood. Not only does it question that such skills are innately present in women, but it also questions whether the role is innately rewarding, a position that is interrogated too – albeit in a different manner – by Margaret's simultaneous 'journey'. Furthermore, it is important to recognize that even though women are typically more central (as the series title suggests), it is not merely the wives/mothers who are under scrutiny. Deirdre, as part of her own journey of self-discovery, continually comments on, questions and interrogates Phil's role in his family, for example ('Why don't you eat food here?'… 'Do you feel you could spend more time with [the children]'?) and a recurrent, highly politicized strand of the programme is its rendering of a challenge to the traditionally socially acceptable vision of the distant/preoccupied breadwinner father, or 'the stranger in our home'. […]

REFERENCES

MALTY, R. (1995) *Hollywood Cinema*, London, Blackwell.

PIPER, H. (2004) 'Reality TV, *Wife Swap* and the drama of Banality', *Screen*, 45(4).

TURNER, G. (1996) *British Cultural Studies: An Introduction*, London, Routledge.

Source: Holmes and Jermyn, 2008, pp. 239–41.

INDEX

Page references to non-textual matter such as Figures or Photographs will be in *italics*

Index